Analyzing Business Requirements	See Chapter:
Analyze factors that influence organizational policy requirements.	2
Analyze the existing and planned business models.	2
Analyze the existing and planned business security model.	2, 8
Analyze the existing and planned administrative model.	2, 11

Analyzing Existing and Planned Resources	See Chapter:
Analyze existing server roles.	3
Analyze existing and planned network resources.	3
Analyze existing directory- and name-resolution configurations.	3
Analyze the impact of Exchange 2000 Server on the existing and planned network.	3
Analyze the existing messaging system architecture and potential changes to this architecture.	3,4
Analyze existing messaging client configurations.	3,4

Designing an Exchange 2000 Server Messaging Solution	See Chapter:
Design an Exchange 2000 Server routing group topology.	4, 9
Design an Exchange 2000 Server administrative model.	4,10
Design an Exchange 2000 Server realtime collaboration solution that uses Chat Service, and/or Instant Messaging.	14
Plan public folder usage and implementation.	13
Design an Exchange 2000 Server security plan.	8
Secure the Exchange 2000 Server infrastructure against external attacks.	8
Secure the Exchange 2000 Server infrastructure against internal attacks.	8
Design an authentication and encryption strategy.	8
Plan for coexistence of Exchange 2000 Server with other messaging systems.	6
Plan for coexistence with foreign mail systems, such as Notes, cc:Mail, GroupWise, MS Mail, PROFS, TAO, and SNADS.	6
Plan for coexistence with Exchange Server 5.5.	7,10
Design interorganizational connectivity and synchronization.	10
Designate and design servers.	3,10
Plan traffic flow.	3,10
Design server hardware and disk configurations to achieve fault tolerance and increased performance and to provide for a backup strategy, based on server role.	3, 15
Design an upgrade or migration strategy.	7
Design ADC connection agreements.	6,10
Plan a migration that uses ADMT.	7
Design connection agreements to support container synchronization.	6,10
Decide direction of synchronization.	6,10
Design a strategy for mail access. Messaging clients include MAPI, IMAP4, POP3, and HTTP mail.	5

Designing for Fault Tolerance and Data Recovery	See Chapter:
Design a backup solution.	15
Design a recovery solution.	15
Design fault-tolerance solutions.	15

Deploying an Exchange 2000 Server Messaging Solution	See Chapter:
Deploy routing groups and foreign connectors.	9,10
Deploy administrative groups.	11,12
Plan deployments of messaging clients, such as MAPI, IMAP4, POP3, and HTTP mail.	5
Deploy an Exchange 2000 Server messaging solution in a cluster.	16
Diagnose and resolve coexistence problems.	17
Resolve email delivery problems.	17
Resolve problems with foreign connections.	17
Resolve address synchronization problems.	17
Resolve problems with address and name resolution	17
Diagnose and resolve other deployment problems.	17
Resolve failed deployments that require a rollback to Exchange Server 5.5.	17
Resolve permissions problems.	17
Resolve problems with sending and receiving email.	17
Resolve security problems.	8,17
Resolve DNS name-resolution problems.	17
Resolve problems involving resource limitations.	17

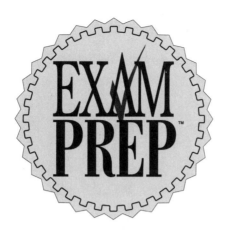

MCSE™
Exchange
2000 Design

Michael Shannon

Dennis Suhanovs

MCSE™ Exchange 2000 Design Exam Prep

Copyright © 2001 The Coriolis Group, LLC. All rights reserved.

Limits of Liability and Disclaimer of Warranty

Trademarks

The Coriolis Group, LLC
14455 N. Hayden Road, Suite 220
Scottsdale, Arizona 85260

(480)483-0192
FAX (480)483-0193
www.coriolis.com

Library of Congress Cataloging-in-Publication Data
Shannon, Michael.
    MCSE Exchange 2000 design / Michael Shannon And Dennis Suhanovs
       p.   cm. -- (Exam prep)
    Includes index.
    ISBN 1-57610-026-1
    1. Electronic data processing personnel--Certification.   2. Microsoft
software--Examinations--Study guides.   3. Microsoft Exchange Server
(Computer file)   I. Title.   II. Series.
    QA76.3 .S464   2001
005.7'13769--dc21
                                                    2001028318

President and CEO
Roland Elgey

Publisher
Steve Sayre

Associate Publisher
Katherine R. Hartlove

Acquisitions Editor
Sharon Linsenbach

Director of Marketing
Susan Hughes

Project Editors
Don Eamon
Stephanie Palenque

Technical Reviewer
Luis Allegretti

Production Coordinator
Thomas Riker

Cover Designer
Laura Wellander

Layout Designer
April Nielsen

CD-ROM Developer
Chris Nusbaum

Printed in the United States of America
10   9   8   7   6   5   4   3   2   1

The Coriolis Group, LLC • 14455 North Hayden Road, Suite 220 • Scottsdale, Arizona 85260

A Note from Coriolis

Our goal has always been to provide you with the best study tools on the planet to help you achieve your certification in record time. Time is so valuable these days that none of us can afford to waste a second of it, especially when it comes to exam preparation.

Over the past few years, we've created an extensive line of *Exam Cram* and *Exam Prep* study guides, practice exams, and interactive training. To help you study even better, we have now created an e-learning and certification destination called **ExamCram.com**. (You can access the site at **www.examcram.com**.) Now, with every study product you purchase from us, you'll be connected to a large community of people like yourself who are actively studying for their certifications, developing their careers, seeking advice, and sharing their insights and stories.

We believe that the future is all about collaborative learning. Our **ExamCram.com** destination is our approach to creating a highly interactive, easily accessible collaborative environment, where you can take practice exams and discuss your experiences with others, sign up for features like "Questions of the Day," plan your certifications using our interactive planners, create your own personal study pages, and keep up with all of the latest study tips and techniques.

We hope that whatever study products you purchase from us—*Exam Cram* or *Exam Prep* study guides, *Personal Trainers*, *Personal Test Centers*, or one of our interactive Web courses—will make your studying fun and productive. Our commitment is to build the kind of learning tools that will allow you to study the way you want to, whenever you want to.

Visit ExamCram.com now to enhance your study program.

Help us continue to provide the very best certification study materials possible. Write us or email us at **learn@examcram.com** and let us know how our study products have helped you study. Tell us about new features that you'd like us to add. Send us a story about how we've helped you. We're listening!

Good luck with your certification exam and your career. Thank you for allowing us to help you achieve your goals.

ExamCram.com Connects You to the Ultimate Study Center!

Look for these other products from The Coriolis Group:

MCSE Exchange 2000 Administration Exam Cram
by David Watts and Will Willis

MCSE Exchange 2000 Design Exam Cram
by William R. Baldwin

MCSE ISA Server 2000 Exam Cram
by Diana Bartley and Gregory Smith

MCSE SQL 2000 Database Design Exam Cram
by Richard McMahon and Sean Chase

MCSE Supporting and Maintaining NT Server 4 Exam Cram
by J. Peter Bruzzese and Christian Wolf

MCSE Exchange 2000 Administration Exam Cram Personal Trainer
by David Watts and Will Willis

MCSE Exchange 2000 Design Exam Cram Personal Trainer
by William Baldwin

MCSE Windows 2000 Core Four Exam Cram Pack
CIP Author Team

MCSE Windows 2000 Directory Services Exam Cram
by Will Willis, David V. Watts, and J. Peter Bruzzese

To my beautiful wife, Samie Shannon, for all of her loving help and support.
—Michael Shannon

To my mom Tania, dad Dimitry, brother Sergey, and the Iannacies—for enormous support when I needed it the most. To Daria, who made my life worth the while. To my friends and family who were of great support and utmost importance through the time and distance. My heartfelt gratitude goes to all of you.
—Yours forever,
Dennis Suhanovs

About the Authors

Michael J. Shannon (BA, MCSE+I, CIW) is President of Plus Ultra Group, Inc., a technology consulting firm. He also serves as a Senior Technical Specialist for ICL/KnowledgePool, Inc. a global e-training company. In addition, he is the Senior Product Designer with InvestorsHelper.com. Michael has consulted and trained students all over the United States in a wide range of technologies. His strongest areas of expertise include all versions of Windows, Active Directory Services, Exchange 2000 Server, and various Macromedia products. An accomplished author, Michael has written several books and articles on Windows 2000 and CompTIA certification. When Michael is not working, he is spending time with his wife, Samie, and is playing with his band, Tripping With Grace.

Dennis Suhanovs is an MCSE+I, CCNA, CCDA, CNA, and MSS on track toward CCNP and other industry certifications, having 17 straight passes and no failures on exams since 1997 from his first certification. Primarily specializing in Microsoft technologies, Dennis has a broad technology experience, has been involved in IT since 1996. His mainstream involvement spans Windows NT/Windows2000; Proxy/ISA and SQL, Exchange 5.5, and 2000 deployment, development and administration; most aspects of networking; database and application programming; Web site design; scripting in various environments; other technologies. In 1998 he was officially confirmed to be the youngest MCSE of his country of origin.

During the daytime, Dennis is a Systems Engineer (Windows NT/2000 and BackOffice technologies) with a multinational corporation in downtown Toronto. After hours and on the weekends, he is building own consulting business ITproConsult.com by helping organizations take advantage of the Information Technology, setting up networks, designing Web sites, programming databases and collaborative solutions. Dennis joined Coriolis as a freelancer in 2000 and was a technical reviewer for two Cisco and Microsoft books prior to co-authoring this title.

On a rare, idle day, Dennis is studying and constantly refreshing his skills. Among other interests he is consumed with motor racing, being a Formula 1 fan for a decade now. He is an active trader and follows the markets on a daily basis. Mr. Suhanovs can be reached at **dennis@suhanovs.com**.

Acknowledgments

I would like to thank my beautiful wife, Samie Shannon, for all of her loving help and support. A special thank you goes out to my friend and agent James Conrad at Accusource Consulting for making this book possible for me. Finally, I want to thank project editors Don Eamon and Stephanie Palenque, and production coordinator Thomas Riker, at Coriolis for their hours of dedicated assistance and encouragement."

—*Michael Shannon*

This book is so much more than just a result of consistent performance and persistence of a single person – it is a grand total of efforts of many people. First, I would like to thank our main co-author, Michael J. Shannon, and entire Coriolis Team, from Acquisitions to Production, who made this possible. I would further like to extend heartfelt gratitude to my parents Tania and Dimitry and their families for bringing me up, for supporting and understanding me in times of challenges and hardship; to Sandra, Ben and Iannaci family for their kindness and much appreciated home-like atmosphere—without you it just would not happen; to Daria Razeva and her family for keeping me on the hook and so immensely motivated for a good one-third of our lives, for showing me a fine line between promise and an illusion; to all my friends in Europe, North America, and around the world, past or present, gone or remaining—you all rule (and I just do not have enough space to fit all your names here!); to the folks at RSDC and Soft-Tronik Riga for assisting me years ago in getting on the track to what is turning out to be a solid and very promising Information Technology career; to all my colleagues in Toronto for making it fun; to all my former teachers and mentors in Riga School 40, Ontario's DeVry, and Sheridan for developing my abilities and ultimately contributing to the project years ahead of time. To all of you who were involved and cared: This is my way of saying "Thank you kindly."

—*Dennis Suhanovs*

Contents at a Glance

Table of Contents

Chapter 3
Analyzing Resources for Exchange 2000 Server 71

Chapter 5
Planning Deployments of Messaging Clients 125

Chapter 8
Designing an Exchange 2000 Server Security Plan 211

Chapter 12
Deploying Exchange 2000 Administrative Groups 325

Chapter 13
Planning Public Folder Usage and Implementation 351

Chapter 15
Designing for Fault Tolerance and Data Recovery 419

Exam Insights

Welcome to *MCSE Exchange 2000 Design Exam Prep!* This comprehensive study guide aims to help you get ready to take—and pass—Microsoft certification Exam 70-225, titled "Designing and Deploying a Messaging Infrastructure with Microsoft Exchange 2000 Server." This Exam Insights section discusses exam preparation resources, the testing situation, Microsoft's certification programs in general, and how this book can help you prepare for Microsoft's Exchange 2000 certification exams.

Exam Prep study guides help you understand and appreciate the subjects and materials you need to pass Microsoft certification exams. We've worked from Microsoft's curriculum objectives to ensure that all key topics are clearly explained. Our aim is to bring together as much information as possible about Microsoft certification exams.

Nevertheless, to completely prepare yourself for any Microsoft test, we recommend that you begin by taking the Self-Assessment included in this book immediately following this Exam Insights section. This tool will help you evaluate your knowledge base against the requirements for an MCSE under both ideal and real circumstances.

Based on what you learn from that exercise, you might decide to begin your studies with some classroom training or some background reading. You might decide to read The Coriolis Group's *Exam Prep* book that you have in hand first, or you might decide to start with another study approach. You may also want to refer to one of a number of study guides available from Microsoft or third-party vendors. We also recommend that you supplement your study program with visits to **ExamCram.com** to receive additional practice questions, get advice, and track the Windows 2000 MCSE program or just get certified on Exchange 2000.

We also strongly recommend that you install, configure, and fool around with the software that you'll be tested on, because nothing beats hands-on experience and familiarity when it comes to understanding the questions you're likely to encounter on a certification test. Book learning is essential, but hands-on experience is the best teacher of all!

How to Prepare for an Exam

Preparing for any 070-200 series test (including "Designing and Deploying a Messaging Infrastructure with Exchange 2000 Server") requires that you obtain and study materials designed to provide comprehensive information about the product and its capabilities that will appear on the specific exam for which you are preparing. The following list of materials will help you study and prepare:

➤ The Exchange 2000 Server product CD-ROM includes comprehensive online documentation and related materials; it should be a primary resource when you are preparing for the test.

➤ The exam preparation materials, practice tests, and self-assessment exams on the Microsoft Training & Services page at **www.microsoft.com/ trainingandservices/default.asp?PageID=mcp**. The Testing Innovations link offers samples of the new question types found on the Windows 2000 MCSE exams. Find the materials, download them, and use them!

➤ The exam preparation advice, practice tests, questions of the day, and discussion groups on the ExamCram.com e-learning and certification destination Web site (**www.examcram.com**).

In addition, you'll probably find any or all of the following materials useful in your quest for Exchange Design expertise:

➤ *Microsoft training kits*—Microsoft Press offers a training kit that specifically targets Exam 70-225. For more information, visit:**http://mspress. microsoft.com/findabook/list/series_ak.htm**. This training kit contains information that you will find useful in preparing for the test.

➤ *Microsoft TechNet CD*—This monthly CD-based publication delivers numerous electronic titles that include coverage of Exchange Design and related topics on the Technical Information (TechNet) CD. Its offerings include product facts, technical notes, tools and utilities, and information on how to access the Seminars Online training materials for Exchange Design. A subscription to TechNet costs $299 USD per year, but it is well worth the price. Visit **www.microsoft.com/technet/** and check out the information under the "TechNet Subscription" menu entry for more details. Part of this database is available online at **http://support.microsoft.com.**

➤ *Study guides*—Several publishers—including The Coriolis Group—offer Windows 2000 titles. The Coriolis Group series includes the following:

➤ *The Exam Cram series*—These books give you information about the material you need to know to pass the tests.

➤ *The Exam Prep series*—These books provide a greater level of detail than the *Exam Cram* books and are designed to teach you everything you need to know from an exam perspective. Each book comes with a CD that contains interactive practice exams in a variety of testing formats.

Together, the two series make a perfect pair.

➤ *Multimedia*—These Coriolis Group materials are designed to support learners of all types—whether you learn best by reading or doing:

> ➤ *The Exam Cram Personal Trainer*—Offers a unique, personalized self-paced training course based on the exam.

> ➤ *The Exam Cram Personal Test Center*—Features multiple test options that simulate the actual exam, including Fixed-Length, Random, Review, and Test All. Explanations of correct and incorrect answers reinforce concepts learned.

➤ *Classroom training*—CTECs, online partners, and third-party training companies (like Wave Technologies, Learning Tree, Data-Tech, and others) all offer classroom training on Exchange 2000. These companies aim to help you prepare to pass the Exchange 2000 test. Although such training runs upwards of $350 per day in class, most of the individuals lucky enough to partake (including humble authors) find them to be quite worthwhile.

➤ *Other publications*—There's no shortage of materials available about Exchange Design. The complete resource section in the back of the book should give you an idea of where we think you should look for further discussion.

➤ *Other online resources*—Online product documentation at **www.microsoft.com/exchange** is a bottomless resource of technical information and whitepapers on Exchange 2000.

By far, this set of required and recommended materials represents a nonpareil collection of sources and resources for Directory Services Design and related topics. We anticipate that you'll find that this book belongs in this company.

Taking a Certification Exam

Once you've prepared for your exam, you need to register with a testing center. Each computer-based MCP exam costs $100 US, and if you don't pass, you may retest for an additional $100 for each additional try. In the United States and Canada, tests are administered by Prometric (formerly Sylvan Prometric), and by Virtual University Enterprises (VUE). Here's how you can contact them:

➤ *Prometric*—You can sign up for a test through the company's Web site at **www.prometric.com**. Within the United States and Canada, you can register by phone at 800-755-3926. If you live outside this region, check the company's Web site for the appropriate phone number.

➤ *Virtual University Enterprises*—You can sign up for a test or get the phone numbers for local testing centers through the Web page at **www.vue.com/ms/**.

To sign up for a test, you must possess a valid credit card, or contact either company for mailing instructions to send them a check (in the U.S.). Only when payment is verified, or a check has cleared, can you actually register for a test.

To schedule an exam, call the number or visit either of the Web pages at least one day in advance. To cancel or reschedule an exam, you must call before 7 P.M. pacific standard time the day before the scheduled test time (or you may be charged, even if you don't appear to take the test). When you want to schedule a test, have the following information ready:

➤ Your name, organization, and mailing address.

➤ Your Microsoft Test ID. (Inside the United States, this means your Social Security number; citizens of other nations should call ahead to find out what type of identification number is required to register for a test.)

➤ The name and number of the exam you wish to take.

➤ A method of payment. (As we've already mentioned, a credit card is the most convenient method, but alternate means can be arranged in advance, if necessary.)

Once you sign up for a test, you'll be informed as to when and where the test is scheduled. Try to arrive at least 15 minutes early.

The Exam Situation

When you arrive at the testing center where you scheduled your exam, you'll need to sign in with an exam coordinator. He or she will ask you to show two forms of identification, one of which must be a photo ID. After you've signed in and your time slot arrives, you'll be asked to deposit any books, bags, or other items you brought with you. Then, you'll be escorted into a closed room.

All exams are completely closed book. In fact, you will not be permitted to take anything with you into the testing area, but you will be furnished with a blank sheet of paper and a pen or, in some cases, an erasable plastic sheet and an erasable pen. Before the exam, you should memorize as much of the important material as you can, so you can write that information on the blank sheet as soon as you are seated in front of the computer. You can refer to this piece of paper anytime you like during the test, but you'll have to surrender the sheet when you leave the room.

You will have some time to compose yourself, to record this information, and to take a sample orientation exam before you begin the real thing. We suggest you take the orientation test before taking your first exam, but because they're all more or less identical in layout, behavior, and controls, you probably won't need to do this more than once.

Typically, the room will be furnished with anywhere from one to half a dozen computers, and each workstation will be separated from the others by dividers designed to keep you from seeing what's happening on someone else's computer. Most test rooms feature a wall with a large picture window. This permits the exam coordinator to monitor the room, to prevent exam-takers from talking to one another, and to observe anything out of the ordinary that might go on. The exam coordinator will have preloaded the appropriate Microsoft certification exam—for this book, that's Exam 70-225—and you'll be permitted to start as soon as you're seated in front of the computer.

All Microsoft certification exams allow a certain maximum amount of time in which to complete your work (this time is indicated on the exam by an on-screen counter/clock, so you can check the time remaining whenever you like). All Microsoft certification exams are computer generated. In addition to multiple choice, you'll encounter select and place (drag and drop), create a tree (categorization and prioritization), drag and connect, and build list and reorder (list prioritization) on most exams. Although this may sound quite simple, the questions are constructed not only to check your mastery of basic facts and figures about Exchange Design, but they also require you to evaluate one or more sets of circumstances or requirements. Often, you'll be asked to give more than one answer to a question. Likewise, you might be asked to select the best or most effective solution to a problem from a range of choices, all of which technically are correct. Taking the exam is quite an adventure, and it involves real thinking. This book shows you what to expect and how to deal with the potential problems, puzzles, and predicaments.

When you complete a Microsoft certification exam, the software will tell you whether you've passed or failed. If you need to retake an exam, you'll have to schedule a new test with Prometric or VUE and pay another $100.

Note: *The first time you fail a test, you can retake the test the next day. However, if you fail a second time, you must wait 14 days before retaking that test. The 14-day waiting period remains in effect for all retakes after the second failure.*

In the next section, you'll learn more about how Microsoft test questions look and how they must be answered.

Exam Layout and Design: New Case Study Format

The format of Microsoft's Windows 2000 exams is different from that of its previous exams. For the design exams (70-219, 70-220, 70-221, 70-227, 70-225, and others), each exam consists entirely of a series of case studies, and the questions can be of six types. For the Core Four exams (70-210, 70-215, 70-216, 70-217), the same six types of questions can appear, but you are not likely to encounter complex multiquestion case studies.

For design exams, each case study or "testlet" presents a detailed problem that you must read and analyze. Figure 1 shows an example of what a case study looks like. You must select the different tabs in the case study to view the entire case.

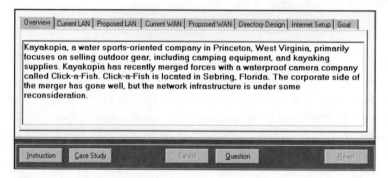

Figure 1   This is how case studies appear.

Following each case study is a set of questions related to the case study; these questions can be one of six types (which are discussed next). Careful attention to details provided in the case study is the key to success. Be prepared to toggle frequently between the case study and the questions as you work. Some of the case studies also include diagrams, which are called *exhibits*, that you'll need to examine closely to understand how to answer the questions.

After you complete a case study, you can review all the questions and your answers. However, once you move on to the next case study, you may not be able to return to the previous case study and make any changes.

The six types of question formats are:

➤ Multiple choice, single answer

➤ Multiple choice, multiple answers

➤ Build list and reorder (list prioritization)

➤ Create a tree

➤ Drag and connect

➤ Select and place (drag and drop)

*Note: Exam formats may vary by test center location. Although most design exams consist entirely of a series of case studies or testlets, a test-taker may occasionally encounter a strictly multiple-choice test. You may want to call the test center or visit **ExamCram.com** to see if you can find out which type of test you'll encounter.*

Multiple-Choice Question Format

Some exam questions require you to select a single answer, whereas others ask you to select multiple correct answers. The following example of a multiple-choice question requires you to select a single correct answer. Following the question is a brief summary of each potential answer and why it is either right or wrong.

Question 1

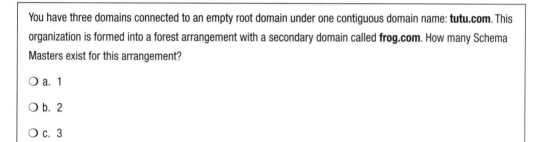

You have three domains connected to an empty root domain under one contiguous domain name: **tutu.com**. This organization is formed into a forest arrangement with a secondary domain called **frog.com**. How many Schema Masters exist for this arrangement?

◯ a. 1

◯ b. 2

◯ c. 3

◯ d. 4

The correct answer is a, because only one Schema Master is necessary for a forest arrangement. The other answers (b, c, d) are misleading because they try to make you believe that Schema Masters might be in each domain, or perhaps that you should have one for each contiguous namespaced domain.

This sample question format corresponds closely to the Microsoft certification exam format—the only difference on the exam is that questions are not followed by answer keys. To select an answer, you would position the cursor over the radio button next to the answer. Then, click the mouse button to select the answer.

Let's examine a question where one or more answers are possible. This type of question provides checkboxes rather than radio buttons for marking all appropriate selections.

Question 2

> How can you seize FSMO roles? [Check all correct answers]
>
> ❑ a. The ntdsutil.exe utility
>
> ❑ b. The Replication Monitor
>
> ❑ c. The secedit.exe utility
>
> ❑ d. Active Directory Domains and FSMOs

Answers a and b are correct. You can seize roles from a server that is still running through the Replication Monitor or, in the case of a server failure, you can seize roles with the ntdsutil.exe utility. The secedit utility is used to force group policies into play; therefore, answer c is incorrect. Active Directory Domains and Trusts are a combination of truth and fiction; therefore, answer d is incorrect.

For this particular question, two answers are required. Microsoft sometimes gives partial credit for partially correct answers. For Question 2, you have to check the boxes next to items a and b to obtain credit for a correct answer. Notice that picking the right answers also means knowing why the other answers are wrong!

Build-List-and-Reorder Question Format

Questions in the build-list-and-reorder format present two lists of items—one on the left and one on the right. To answer the question, you must move items from the list on the right to the list on the left. The final list must then be reordered into a specific order.

These questions can best be characterized as "From the following list of choices, pick the choices that answer the question. Arrange the list in a certain order." To give you practice with this type of question, some questions of this type are included in this study guide. Here's an example of how they appear in this book; for a sample of how they appear on the test, see Figure 2.

Question 3

From the following list of famous people, pick those that have been elected President of the United States.
Arrange the list in the order that they served.

Thomas Jefferson

Ben Franklin

Abe Lincoln

George Washington

Andrew Jackson

Paul Revere

The correct answer is:

George Washington

Thomas Jefferson

Andrew Jackson

Abe Lincoln

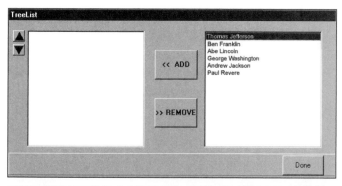

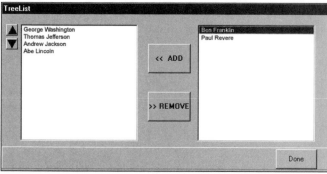

Figure 2   This is how build-list-and-reorder questions appear.

On an actual exam, the entire list of famous people would initially appear in the list on the right. You would move the four correct answers to the list on the left, and then reorder the list on the left. Notice that the answer to the question did not include all items from the initial list. However, this may not always be the case.

To move an item from the right list to the left list, first select the item by clicking on it, and then click on the Add button (left arrow). Once you move an item from one list to the other, you can move the item back by first selecting the item and then clicking on the appropriate button (either the Add button or the Remove button). Once items have been moved to the left list, you can reorder an item by selecting the item and clicking on the up or down button.

Create-a-Tree Question Format

Questions in the create-a-tree format also present two lists—one on the left side of the screen and one on the right side of the screen. The list on the right consists of individual items, and the list on the left consists of nodes in a tree. To answer the question, you must move items from the list on the right to the appropriate node in the tree.

These questions can best be characterized as simply a matching exercise. Items from the list on the right are placed under the appropriate category in the list on the left. Here's an example of how they appear in this book; for a sample of how they appear on the test, see Figure 3.

Question 4

The calendar year is divided into four seasons:

Winter

Spring

Summer

Fall

Identify the season when each of the following holidays occurs:

Christmas

Fourth of July

Labor Day

Flag Day

Memorial Day

Washington's Birthday

Thanksgiving

Easter

The correct answer is:

Winter

Christmas

Washington's Birthday

Spring

Flag Day

Memorial Day

Easter

Summer

Fourth of July

Labor Day

Fall

Thanksgiving

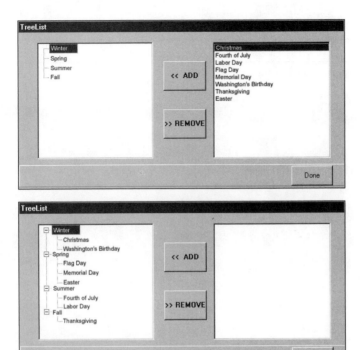

Figure 3   This is how create-a-tree questions appear.

In this case, all the items in the list were used. However, this may not always be the case.

To move an item from the right list to its appropriate location in the tree, you must first select the appropriate tree node by clicking on it. Then, you select the item to be moved and click on the Add button. If one or more items have been added to a tree node, the node will be displayed with a "+" icon to the left of the node name. You can click on this icon to expand the node and view the item(s) that have been added. If any item has been added to the wrong tree node, you can remove it by selecting it and clicking on the Remove button.

Drag-and-Connect Question Format

Questions in the drag-and-connect format present a group of objects and a list of "connections." To answer the question, you must move the appropriate connections between the objects.

This type of question is best described using graphics. Here's an example.

Question 5

The following objects represent the different states of water:

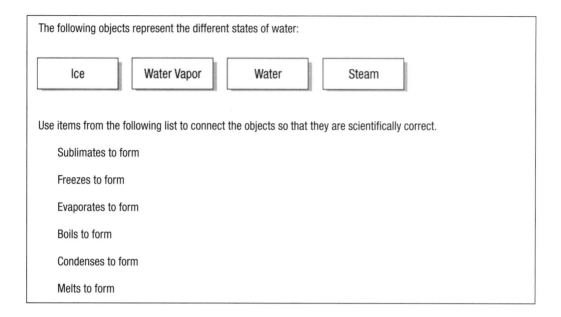

Use items from the following list to connect the objects so that they are scientifically correct.

Sublimates to form

Freezes to form

Evaporates to form

Boils to form

Condenses to form

Melts to form

The correct answer is:

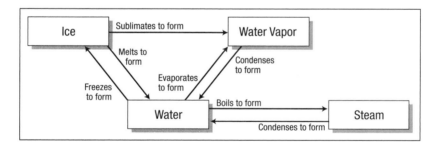

For this type of question, it's not necessary to use every object, and each connection can be used multiple times.

Select-and-Place Question Format

Questions in the select-and-place (drag-and-drop) format present a diagram with blank boxes, and a list of labels that need to be dragged to correctly fill in the blank boxes. To answer the question, you must move the labels to their appropriate positions on the diagram.

This type of question is best described using graphics. Here's an example.

Question 6

Place the items in their proper order, by number, on the following flowchart. Some items may be used more than once, and some items may not be used at all.

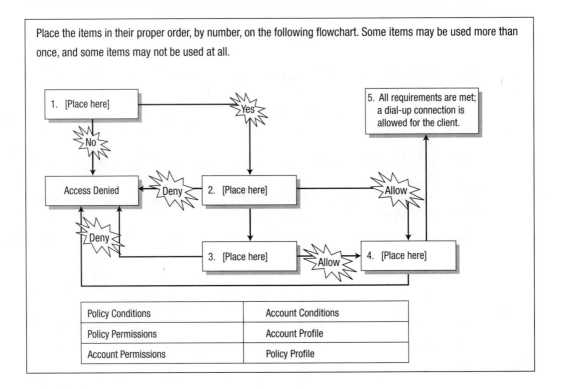

Policy Conditions	Account Conditions
Policy Permissions	Account Profile
Account Permissions	Policy Profile

The correct answer is:

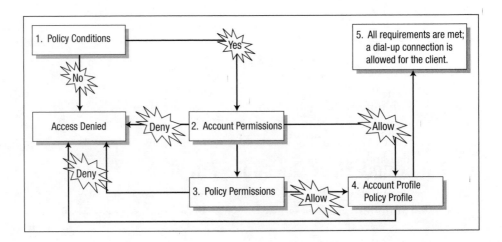

Microsoft's Testing Formats

Currently, Microsoft uses four different testing formats:

➤ Case study

➤ Fixed length

➤ Adaptive

➤ Short form

As we mentioned earlier, the case study approach is used with Microsoft's design exams, such as the one covered by this study guide. These exams consist of a set of case studies that you must analyze to enable you to answer questions related to the case studies. Such exams include one or more case studies (tabbed topic areas), each of which is followed by 4 to 10 questions. The question types for design exams and for Core Four Windows 2000 exams are multiple choice, build list and reorder, create a tree, drag and connect, and select and place. Depending on the test topic, some exams are totally case-based, whereas others are not.

Other Microsoft exams employ advanced testing capabilities that might not be immediately apparent. Although the questions that appear are primarily multiple choice, the logic that drives them is more complex than older Microsoft tests, which use a fixed sequence of questions, called a *fixed-length test*. Some questions employ a sophisticated user interface, which Microsoft calls a *simulation*, to test your knowledge of the software and systems under consideration in a more or less "live" environment that behaves just like the original. The Testing Innovations link at **www.microsoft.com/trainingandservices/default.asp?PageID=mcp** includes a downloadable practice simulation.

For some exams, Microsoft has turned to a well-known technique, called *adaptive testing*, to establish a test-taker's level of knowledge and product competence. Adaptive exams look the same as fixed-length exams, but they discover the level of difficulty at which an individual test-taker can correctly answer questions. Test-takers with differing levels of knowledge or ability therefore see different sets of questions; individuals with high levels of knowledge or ability are presented with a smaller set of more difficult questions, whereas individuals with lower levels of knowledge are presented with a larger set of easier questions. Two individuals may answer the same percentage of questions correctly, but the test-taker with a higher knowledge or ability level will score higher because his or her questions are worth more.

Also, the lower-level test-taker will probably answer more questions than his or her more-knowledgeable colleague. This explains why adaptive tests use ranges of values to define the number of questions and the amount of time it takes to complete the test.

Adaptive tests work by evaluating the test-taker's most recent answer. A correct answer leads to a more difficult question (and the test software's estimate of the test-taker's knowledge and ability level is raised). An incorrect answer leads to a less difficult question (and the test software's estimate of the test-taker's knowledge and ability level is lowered). This process continues until the test targets the test-taker's true ability level. The exam ends when the test-taker's level of accuracy meets a statistically acceptable value (in other words, when his or her performance demonstrates an acceptable level of knowledge and ability), or when the maximum number of items has been presented (in which case, the test-taker is almost certain to fail).

Microsoft also introduced a short-form test for its most popular tests. This test delivers 25 to 30 questions to its takers, giving them exactly 60 minutes to complete the exam. This type of exam is similar to a fixed-length test, in that it allows readers to jump ahead or return to earlier questions, and to cycle through the questions until the test is done. Microsoft does not use adaptive logic in this test, but claims that statistical analysis of the question pool is such that the 25 to 30 questions delivered during a short-form exam conclusively measure a test-taker's knowledge of the subject matter in much the same way as an adaptive test. You can think of the short-form test as a kind of "greatest hits exam" (that is, the most important questions are covered) version of an adaptive exam on the same topic.

Note: Several test-takers have reported that some of the Microsoft exams can appear as a combination of adaptive and fixed-length questions.

Microsoft tests can come in any one of these forms. Whatever you encounter, you must take the test in whichever form it appears; you can't choose one form over another. If anything, it pays more to prepare thoroughly for an adaptive exam than for a fixed-length or a short-form exam: The penalties for answering incorrectly are built into the test itself on an adaptive exam, whereas the layout remains the same for a fixed-length or short-form test, no matter how many questions you answer incorrectly.

Tip: The biggest difference between an adaptive test and a fixed-length or short-form test is that on a fixed-length or short-form test, you can revisit questions after you've read them over one or more times. On an adaptive test, you must answer the question when it's presented and will have no opportunities to revisit that question thereafter.

Strategies for Different Testing Formats

Before you choose a test-taking strategy, you must know if your test is case study based, fixed length, short form, or adaptive. When you begin your exam, you'll know right away if the test is based on case studies. The interface will consist of a tabbed Window that allows you to easily navigate through the sections of the case.

If you are taking a test that is not based on case studies, the software will tell you that the test is adaptive, if in fact the version you're taking is an adaptive test. If your introductory materials fail to mention this, you're probably taking a fixed-length test (50 to 70 questions). If the total number of questions involved is 25 to 30, you're taking a short-form test. Some tests announce themselves by indicating that they will start with a set of adaptive questions, followed by fixed-length questions.

Tip: You'll be able to tell for sure if you are taking an adaptive, fixed-length, or short-form test by the first question. If it includes a checkbox that lets you mark the question for later review, you're taking a fixed-length or short-form test. If the total number of questions is 25 to 30, it's a short-form test; if more than 30, it's a fixed-length test. Adaptive test questions can be visited (and answered) only once, and they include no such checkbox.

The Case Study Exam Strategy

Most test-takers find that the case study type of test used for the design exams (70-219, 70-220, 70-221 and 70-225) is the most difficult to master. When it comes to studying for a case study test, your best bet is to approach each case study as a standalone test. The biggest challenge you'll encounter is that you'll feel that you won't have enough time to get through all of the cases that are presented.

Tip: Each case provides a lot of material that you'll need to read and study before you can effectively answer the questions that follow. The trick to taking a case study exam is to first scan the case study to get the highlights. Make sure you read the overview section of the case so that you understand the context of the problem at hand. Then, quickly move on and scan the questions.

As you are scanning the questions, make mental notes to yourself so that you'll remember which sections of the case study you should focus on. Some case studies may provide a fair amount of extra information that you don't really need to answer the questions. The goal with this scanning approach is to avoid having to study and analyze material that is not completely relevant.

When studying a case, carefully read the tabbed information. It is important to answer each and every question. You will be able to toggle back and forth from case to questions, and from question to question within a case testlet. However, once you leave the case and move on, you may not be able to return to it. You may want to take notes while reading useful information so you can refer to them when you tackle the test questions. It's hard to go wrong with this strategy when taking any kind of Microsoft certification test.

The Fixed-Length and Short-Form Exam Strategy

A well-known principle when taking fixed-length or short-form exams is to first read over the entire exam from start to finish while answering only those questions you feel absolutely sure of. On subsequent passes, you can dive into more complex questions more deeply, knowing how many such questions you have left.

Fortunately, the Microsoft exam software for fixed-length and short-form tests makes the multiple-visit approach easy to implement. At the top-left corner of each question is a checkbox that permits you to mark that question for a later visit.

Note: Marking questions makes review easier, but you can return to any question by clicking the Forward or Back button repeatedly.

As you read each question, if you answer only those you're sure of and mark for review those that you're not sure of, you can keep working through a decreasing list of questions as you answer the trickier ones in order.

Tip: There's at least one potential benefit to reading the exam over completely before answering the trickier questions: Sometimes, information supplied in later questions sheds more light on earlier questions. At other times, information you read in later questions might jog your memory about Exchange Design facts, figures, or behavior that helps you answer earlier questions. Either way, you'll come out ahead if you defer those questions about which you're not absolutely sure.

Here are some question-handling strategies that apply to fixed-length and short-form tests. Use them if you have the chance:

➤ When returning to a question after your initial read-through, read every word again—otherwise, your mind can fall quickly into a rut. Sometimes, revisiting a question after turning your attention elsewhere lets you see something you missed, but the strong tendency is to see what you've seen before. Try to avoid that tendency at all costs.

➤ If you return to a question more than twice, try to articulate to yourself what you don't understand about the question, why answers don't appear to make sense, or what appears to be missing. If you chew on the subject awhile, your subconscious might provide the details you lack, or you might notice a "trick" that points to the right answer.

As you work your way through the exam, another counter that Microsoft provides will come in handy—the number of questions completed and questions outstanding. For fixed-length and short-form tests, it's wise to budget your time by making sure that you've completed one-quarter of the questions one-quarter of the way through the exam period, and three-quarters of the questions three-quarters of the way through.

If you're not finished when only five minutes remain, use that time to guess your way through any remaining questions. Remember, guessing is potentially more valuable than not answering, because blank answers are always wrong, but a guess may turn out to be right. If you don't have a clue about any of the remaining questions, pick answers at random, or choose all a's, b's, and so on. The important thing is to submit an exam for scoring that has an answer for every question.

Tip: At the very end of your exam period, you're better off guessing than leaving questions unanswered.

The Adaptive Exam Strategy

If there's one principle that applies to taking an adaptive test, it could be summed up as "Get it right the first time." You cannot elect to skip a question and move on to the next one when taking an adaptive test, because the testing software uses your answer to the current question to select whatever question it plans to present next. Nor can you return to a question once you've moved on, because the software gives you only one chance to answer the question. You can, however, take notes, because sometimes information supplied in earlier questions will shed more light on later questions.

Also, when you answer a question correctly, you are presented with a more difficult question next, to help the software gauge your level of skill and ability. When you answer a question incorrectly, you are presented with a less difficult question, and the software lowers its current estimate of your skill and ability. This continues until the program settles into a reasonably accurate estimate of what you know and can do, and takes you on average through somewhere between 15 and 30 questions as you complete the test.

The good news is that if you know your stuff, you'll probably finish most adaptive tests in 30 minutes or so. The bad news is that you must really, really know your stuff to do your best on an adaptive test. That's because some questions are so convoluted, complex, or hard to follow that you're bound to miss one or two, at a minimum, even if you do know your stuff. So the more you know, the better you'll do on an adaptive test, even accounting for the occasionally weird or unfathomable questions that appear on these exams. You are unlikely to have adaptive formats on design exams.

Tip: Because you can't always tell in advance if a test is fixed length, short form, or adaptive, you will be best served by preparing for the exam as if it were adaptive. That way, you should be prepared to pass no matter what kind of test you take. But if you do take a fixed-length or short-form test, remember the tips from the preceding section. They should help you improve on what you could do on an adaptive test.

If you encounter a question on an adaptive test that you can't answer, you must guess an answer immediately. Because of how the software works, you may suffer for your guess on the next question if you guess right, because you'll get a more difficult question next!

Question-Handling Strategies

Based on exams we have taken, some interesting trends have become apparent. For those questions that take only a single answer, usually two or three of the answers will be obviously incorrect, and two of the answers will be plausible—of course, only one can be correct. Unless the answer leaps out at you (if it does, reread the question to look for a trick; sometimes those are the ones you're most likely to get wrong), begin the process of answering by eliminating those answers that are most obviously wrong.

Almost always, at least one answer out of the possible choices for a question can be eliminated immediately because it matches one of these conditions:

➤ The answer does not apply to the situation.

➤ The answer describes a nonexistent issue, an invalid option, or an imaginary state.

After you eliminate all answers that are obviously wrong, you can apply your retained knowledge to eliminate further answers. Look for items that sound correct but refer to actions, commands, or features that are not present or not available in the situation that the question describes.

If you're still faced with a blind guess among two or more potentially correct answers, reread the question. Try to picture how each of the possible remaining answers would alter the situation. Be especially sensitive to terminology; sometimes the choice of words ("remove" instead of "disable") can make the difference between a right answer and a wrong one.

Only when you've exhausted your ability to eliminate answers, but remain unclear about which of the remaining possibilities is correct, should you guess at an answer. An unanswered question offers you no points, but guessing gives you at least some chance of getting a question right; just don't be too hasty when making a blind guess.

Note: If you're taking a fixed-length or a short-form test, you can wait until the last round of reviewing marked questions (just as you're about to run out of time, or out of unanswered questions) before you start making guesses. You will have the same option within each case study testlet (but once you leave a testlet, you may not be allowed to return to it). If you're taking an adaptive test, you'll have to guess to move on to the next question if you can't figure out an answer some other way. Either way, guessing should be your technique of last resort!

Numerous questions assume that the default behavior of a particular utility is in effect. If you know the defaults and understand what they mean, this knowledge will help you cut through many Gordian knots.

Mastering the Inner Game

In the final analysis, knowledge breeds confidence, and confidence breeds success. If you study the materials in this book carefully and review all the practice questions at the end of each chapter, you should become aware of those areas where additional learning and study are required.

After you've worked your way through the book, take the practice exam in the back of the book and the practice exams on the CD-ROM. Taking tests will provide a reality check and help you identify areas to study further. Make sure you follow up and review materials related to the questions you miss on the practice exams before scheduling a real exam. Only when you've covered that ground and feel comfortable with the whole scope of the practice exams should you set an exam appointment. Only if you score 85 percent or better should you proceed to the real thing (otherwise, obtain some additional practice tests so you can keep trying until you hit this magic number).

Tip: If you take a practice exam and don't score at least 85 percent correct, you'll want to practice further. Microsoft provides links to practice exam providers and also offers self-assessment exams at **www.microsoft.com/trainingandservices/**). You should also check out **ExamCram.com** for downloadable practice questions.

Armed with the information in this book and with the determination to augment your knowledge, you should be able to pass the certification exam. However, you need to work at it, or you'll spend the exam fee more than once before you finally pass. If you prepare seriously, you should do well. We are confident that you can do it!

The next section covers the exam requirements for the various Microsoft certifications.

The Microsoft Certified Professional (MCP) Program

The MCP Program currently includes the following separate tracks, each of which boasts its own special acronym (as a certification candidate, you need to have a high tolerance for alphabet soup of all kinds):

> ➤ *MCP (Microsoft Certified Professional)*—This is the least prestigious of all the certification tracks from Microsoft. Passing one of the major Microsoft exams qualifies an individual for the MCP credential. Individuals can demonstrate proficiency with additional Microsoft products by passing additional certification exams.

> ➤ *MCP+SB (Microsoft Certified Professional + Site Building)*—This certification program is designed for individuals who are planning, building, managing, and

maintaining Web sites. Individuals with the MCP+SB credential will have demonstrated the ability to develop Web sites that include multimedia and searchable content and Web sites that connect to and communicate with a back-end database. It requires one MCP exam, plus two of these three exams: "70-055: Designing and Implementing Web Sites with Microsoft FrontPage 98," "70-057: Designing and Implementing Commerce Solutions with Microsoft Site Server 3.0, Commerce Edition," and "70-152: Designing and Implementing Web Solutions with Microsoft Visual InterDev 6.0." Microsoft will retire Exam 70-055 on June 30, 2001 and the MCP+SB certification on June 30, 2002.

➤ *MCSE (Microsoft Certified Systems Engineer)*—Anyone who has a current MCSE is warranted to possess a high level of networking expertise with Microsoft operating systems and products. This credential is designed to prepare individuals to plan, implement, maintain, and support information systems, networks, and internetworks built around Microsoft Windows 2000 and its BackOffice family of products.

To obtain an MCSE, an individual must pass four core operating system exams, one core option exam, and two elective exams. The operating system exams require individuals to prove their competence with desktop and server operating systems and networking/internetworking components.

For Windows NT 4 MCSEs, the Accelerated exam, "70-240: Microsoft Windows 2000 Accelerated Exam for MCPs Certified on Microsoft Windows NT 4.0," is an option. This free exam covers all of the material tested in the Core Four exams. The hitch in this plan is that you can take the test only once. If you fail, you must take all four core exams to recertify. The Core Four exams are: "70-210: Installing, Configuring and Administering Microsoft Windows 2000 Professional," "70-215: Installing, Configuring and Administering Microsoft Windows 2000 Server," "70-216: Implementing and Administering a Microsoft Windows 2000 Network Infrastructure," and "70-217: Implementing and Administering a Microsoft Windows 2000 Directory Services Infrastructure."

To fulfill the fifth core exam requirement, you can choose from four design exams: "70-219: Designing a Microsoft Windows 2000 Directory Services Infrastructure," "70-220: Designing Security for a Microsoft Windows 2000 Network," "70-221: Designing a Microsoft Windows 2000 Network Infrastructure," or "70-226: Designing Highly Available Web Solutions with Microsoft Windows 2000 Server Technologies." You are also required to take two elective exams. An elective exam can fall in any number of subject or product areas, primarily BackOffice Server 2000 components. The three design exams that you don't select as your fifth core exam also qualify as electives. If you are on your way to becoming an MCSE and have already taken some exams, visit **www.microsoft.com/trainingandservices/** for information about how to complete your MCSE certification.

Individuals who want to remain certified MCSEs after 12/31/2001 must "upgrade" their certifications on or before 12/31/2001. For more detailed information than is included here, visit **www.microsoft.com/trainingandservices/**.

New MCSE candidates must pass seven tests to meet the MCSE requirements. It's not uncommon for the entire process to take a year or so, and many individuals find that they must take a test more than once to pass. The primary goal of *Exam Prep* and *Exam Cram* test preparation books is to make it possible, given proper study and preparation, to pass all Microsoft certification tests on the first try. Table 1 shows the required and elective exams for the Windows 2000 MCSE certification.

➤ *MCSD (Microsoft Certified Solution Developer)*—The MCSD credential reflects the skills required to create multitier, distributed, and COM-based solutions, in addition to desktop and Internet applications, using new technologies. To obtain an MCSD, an individual must demonstrate the ability to analyze and interpret user requirements; select and integrate products, platforms, tools, and technologies; design and implement code, and customize applications; and perform necessary software tests and quality assurance operations.

To become an MCSD, you must pass a total of four exams: three core exams and one elective exam. Each candidate must choose one of these three desktop application exams—"70-016: Designing and Implementing Desktop Applications with Microsoft Visual C++ 6.0," "70-156: Designing and Implementing Desktop Applications with Microsoft Visual FoxPro 6.0," or "70-176: Designing and Implementing Desktop Applications with Microsoft Visual Basic 6.0"— *plus* one of these three distributed application exams—"70-015: Designing and Implementing Distributed Applications with Microsoft Visual C++ 6.0," "70-155: Designing and Implementing Distributed Applications with Microsoft Visual FoxPro 6.0," or "70-175: Designing and Implementing Distributed Applications with Microsoft Visual Basic 6.0." The third core exam is "70-100: Analyzing Requirements and Defining Solution Architectures." Elective exams cover specific Microsoft applications and languages, including Visual Basic, C++, the Microsoft Foundation Classes, Access, SQL Server, Excel, and more.

➤ *MCDBA (Microsoft Certified Database Administrator)*—The MCDBA credential reflects the skills required to implement and administer Microsoft SQL Server databases. To obtain an MCDBA, an individual must demonstrate the ability to derive physical database designs, develop logical data models, create physical

Table 1   MCSE Windows 2000 Requirements

Core

If you have not passed these 3 Windows NT 4 exams	
Exam 70-067	Implementing and Supporting Microsoft Windows NT Server 4.0
Exam 70-068	Implementing and Supporting Microsoft Windows NT Server 4.0 in the Enterprise
Exam 70-073	Microsoft Windows NT Workstation 4.0
then you must take these 4 exams	
Exam 70-210	Installing, Configuring, and Administering Microsoft Windows 2000 Professional
Exam 70-215	Installing, Configuring, and Administering Microsoft Windows 2000 Server
Exam 70-216	Implementing and Administering a Microsoft Windows 2000 Network Infrastructure
Exam 70-217	Implementing and Administering a Microsoft Windows 2000 Directory Services Infrastructure
If you have already passed exams 70-067, 70-068, and 70-073, you may take this exam	
Exam 70-240	Microsoft Windows 2000 Accelerated Exam for MCPs Certified on Microsoft Windows NT 4.0

5th Core Option

Choose 1 from this group	
Exam 70-219	Designing a Microsoft Windows 2000 Directory Services Infrastructure
Exam 70-220	Designing Security for a Microsoft Windows 2000 Network
Exam 70-221	Designing a Microsoft Windows 2000 Network Infrastructure
Exam 70-226	Designing Highly Available Web Solutions with Microsoft Windows 2000 Server Technologies

Elective*

Choose 2 from this group	
Exam 70-019	Designing and Implementing Data Warehouse with Microsoft SQL Server 7.0
Exam 70-056	Implementing and Supporting Web Sites Using Microsoft Site Server 3.0
Exam 70-080	Implementing and Supporting Microsoft Internet Explorer 5.0 by Using the Internet Explorer Administration Kit
Exam 70-085	Implementing and Supporting Microsoft SNA Server 4.0
Exam 70-086	Implementing and Supporting Microsoft Systems Management Server 2.0
Exam 70-222	Migrating from Microsoft Windows NT 4.0 to Microsoft Windows 2000
Exam 70-223	Installing, Configuring, and Administering Microsoft Clustering Services by Using Microsoft Windows 2000 Advanced Server
Exam 70-224	Installing, Configuring, and Administering Microsoft Exchange 2000 Server
▶ **Exam 70-225**	Designing and Deploying a Messaging Infrastructure with Microsoft Exchange 2000 Server
Exam 70-227	Installing, Configuring, and Administering Microsoft Internet Security and Acceleration (ISA) Server 2000 Enterprise Edition
Exam 70-228	Installing, Configuring, and Administering Microsoft SQL Server 2000 Enterprise Edition
Exam 70-229	Designing and Implementing Databases with Microsoft SQL Server 2000 Enterprise Edition
Exam 70-244	Supporting and Maintaining a Microsoft Windows NT Server 4.0 Network

This is not a complete listing—you can still be tested on some earlier versions of these products. However, we have included mainly the most recent versions so that you may test on these versions and thus be certified longer. We have not included any tests that are scheduled to be retired.

★ 5th Core Option exams may also be used as electives, but can only be counted once toward a certification. You cannot receive credit for an exam as both a core and an elective in the same track.

databases, create data services by using Transact-SQL, manage and maintain databases, configure and manage security, monitor and optimize databases, and install and configure Microsoft SQL Server.

To become an MCDBA, you must pass a total of three core exams and one elective exam. The required core exams are "70-028: Administering Microsoft SQL Server 7.0" or "70-228: Installing, Configuring, and Administering Microsoft SQL Server 2000 Enterprise Edition," "70-029: Designing and Implementing Databases with Microsoft SQL Server 7.0" or "70-229: Designing and Implementing Databases with Microsoft SQL Server 2000 Enterprise Edition", and "70-215: Installing, Configuring and Administering Microsoft Windows 2000 Server" or "70-240: Microsoft Windows 2000 Accelerated Exam for MCPs Certified on Microsoft Windows NT."

The elective exams that you can choose from cover specific uses of SQL Server and include "70-015: Designing and Implementing Distributed Applications with Microsoft Visual C++ 6.0," "70-019: Designing and Implementing Data Warehouses with Microsoft SQL Server 7.0," "70-155: Designing and Implementing Distributed Applications with Microsoft Visual FoxPro 6.0," "70-175: Designing and Implementing Distributed Applications with Microsoft Visual Basic 6.0," and two exams that relate to Windows 2000: "70-216: Implementing and Administering a Microsoft Windows 2000 Network Infrastructure," and "70-087: Implementing and Supporting Microsoft Internet Information Server 4.0."

If you have taken the three core Windows NT 4 exams on your path to becoming an MCSE, you qualify for the Accelerated exam (it replaces the Network Infrastructure exam requirement). The Accelerated exam covers the objectives of all four of the Windows 2000 core exams. In addition to taking the Accelerated exam, you must take only the two SQL exams—Administering and Database Design.

➤ *MCT (Microsoft Certified Trainer)*—Microsoft Certified Trainers are deemed able to deliver elements of the official Microsoft curriculum, based on technical knowledge and instructional ability. Thus, it is necessary for an individual seeking MCT credentials (which are granted on a course-by-course basis) to pass the related certification exam for a course and complete the official Microsoft training in the subject area, and to demonstrate an ability to teach.

This teaching skill criterion may be satisfied by proving that one has already attained training certification from Novell, Banyan, Lotus, the Santa Cruz Operation, or Cisco, or by taking a Microsoft-sanctioned workshop on instruction. Microsoft makes it clear that MCTs are important cogs in the Microsoft training channels. Instructors must be MCTs before Microsoft will allow them to teach in any of its official training channels, including Microsoft's affiliated

Certified Technical Education Centers (CTECs) and its online training partner network. MCT candidates must also possess a current MCSE.

Microsoft has announced that the MCP+I and MCSE+I credentials will not be continued when the MCSE exams for Windows 2000 are in full swing because the skill set for the Internet portion of the program has been included in the new MCSE program. Therefore, details on these tracks are not provided here; go to **www.microsoft.com/trainingandservices/** if you need more information.

Once a Microsoft product becomes obsolete, MCPs typically have to recertify on current versions. (If individuals do not recertify, their certifications become invalid.) Because technology keeps changing and new products continually supplant old ones, this should come as no surprise. This explains why Microsoft has announced that MCSEs have 12 months past the scheduled retirement date for the Windows NT 4 exams to recertify on Windows 2000 topics. (Note that this means taking at least two exams, if not more.)

The best place to keep tabs on the MCP Program and its related certifications is on the Web. The URL for the MCP program is **www.microsoft.com/mcp/**. But Microsoft's Web site changes often, so if this URL doesn't work, try using the Search tool on Microsoft's site with either "MCP" or the quoted phrase "Microsoft Certified Professional Program" as a search string. This will help you find the latest and most accurate information about Microsoft's certification programs.

Tracking MCP Status

As soon as you pass any Microsoft exam (except Networking Essentials), you'll attain Microsoft Certified Professional (MCP) status. Microsoft also generates transcripts that indicate which exams you have passed. You can view a copy of your transcript at any time by going to the MCP secured site and selecting Transcript Tool. This tool will allow you to print a copy of your current transcript and confirm your certification status.

Once you pass the necessary set of exams, you'll be certified. Official certification normally takes anywhere from six to eight weeks, so don't expect to get your credentials overnight. When the package for a qualified certification arrives, it includes a Welcome Kit that contains a number of elements (see Microsoft's Web site for other benefits of specific certifications):

➤ A certificate suitable for framing, along with a wallet card and a lapel pin.

➤ A license to use the MCP logo, thereby allowing you to use the logo in advertisements, promotions, and documents, and on letterhead, business cards, and so on. Along with the license comes an MCP logo sheet, which includes camera-ready artwork. (Note: Before using any of the artwork, individuals must sign and return a licensing agreement that indicates they'll abide by its terms and conditions.)

➤ A subscription to *Microsoft Certified Professional Magazine*, which provides ongoing data about testing and certification activities, requirements, and changes to the program.

Many people believe that the benefits of MCP certification go well beyond the perks that Microsoft provides to newly anointed members of this elite group. We're starting to see more job listings that request or require applicants to have an MCP, MCSE, and so on, and many individuals who complete the program can qualify for increases in pay and/or responsibility. As an official recognition of hard work and broad knowledge, one of the MCP credentials is a badge of honor in many IT organizations.

About the Book

Career opportunities abound for well-prepared Exchange 2000 designers and administrators. This book is designed as your doorway into Exchange Design. If you are new to Exchange or team management administration, this is your ticket to an exciting future. Others who have prior experience with Exchange will find that the book adds depth and breadth to that experience. Also, the book provides the knowledge you need to prepare for Microsoft's certification exam 70-225 "Designing and Deploying a Messaging Infrastructure with Microsoft Exchange 2000." The exam is one of the available electives, and it is an important step in becoming a Microsoft Certified Systems Engineer.

Because Active Directory is to an integral part of Windows 2000 Server, it is marvelously scalable and fits into both large and small organizations. It provides the cornerstone on which to build a Exchange 2000. The success of Windows 2000 Server is reflected in the huge number of software vendors and developers who develop in this environment, or who have switched from other environments to Windows 2000 Server. Many are in the planning stages for switching towards Windows 2000 Server and Active Directory Design will play a major role in that move. Exchange 2000 is the de facto standard messaging and collaboration system that gained a lot of attention in its previous incarnation, and with Windows2000 and Active Directory Exchange saga continues.

When you complete this book, you will be at the threshold of a Exchange Designer career that can be very fulfilling and challenging. This is a rapidly advancing field that offers ample opportunity for personal growth and for making a contribution to your business or organization. The book is intended to provide you with knowledge that you can apply right away and a sound basis for understanding the changes that you will encounter in the future. It also is intended to give you the hands-on skills you need to be a valued professional in your organization.

The book is filled with real-world projects that cover every aspect of designing Exchange 2000 solution. The projects are designed to make what you learn come alive through actually performing the tasks. Also, every chapter includes a range of practice questions to help prepare you for the Microsoft certification exam. All of these features are offered to reinforce your learning, so you'll feel confident in the knowledge you have gained from each chapter.

Features

To aid you in fully understanding Exchange 2000 Design concepts, there are many features in this book designed to improve its value:

➤ *Chapter objectives*—Each chapter in this book begins with a detailed list of the topics to be mastered within that chapter. This list provides you with a quick reference to the contents of that chapter, as well as a useful study aid.

➤ *Illustrations and tables*—Numerous illustrations of screenshots and components aid you in the visualization of common setup steps, theories, and concepts. In addition, many tables provide details and comparisons of both practical and theoretical information.

➤ *Notes, tips, and warnings*—Notes present additional helpful material related to the subject being described. Tips from the author's experience provide extra information about how to attack a problem, how to set up an Exchange 2000 for a particular need, or what to do in certain real-world situations. Warnings are included to help you anticipate potential mistakes or problems so you can prevent them from happening.

➤ *Chapter summaries*—Each chapter's text is followed by a summary of the concepts it has introduced. These summaries provide a helpful way to recap and revisit the ideas covered in each chapter.

➤ *Review questions*—End-of-chapter assessment begins with a set of review questions that reinforce the ideas introduced in each chapter. These questions not only ensure that you have mastered the concepts, but are written to help prepare you for the Microsoft certification examination. Answers to these questions are found in Appendix A.

➤ *Real-world projects*—Although it is important to understand the theory behind Exchange 2000, nothing can improve upon real-world experience. To this end, along with theoretical explanations, each chapter provides numerous hands-on projects aimed at providing you with real-world implementation experience.

➤ *Sample tests*—Use the sample test and answer key in Chapters 18 and 19 to test yourself. Then, move on to the interactive practice exams found on the CD-ROM. The testing engine offers two formats to choose from.

Where Should You Start?

This book is intended to be read in sequence, from beginning to end. Each chapter builds upon those that precede it, to provide a solid understanding of Exchange Design. After completing the chapters, you may find it useful to go back through the book and use the review questions and projects to prepare for the Microsoft certification test for "Designing and Deploying a Messaging Infrastructure with Microsoft Exchange 2000 Server (exam 70-225)". Readers are also encouraged to investigate the many pointers to online and printed sources of additional information that are cited throughout this book.

Please share your feedback on the book with us, especially if you have ideas about how we can improve it for future readers. We'll consider everything you say carefully, and we'll respond to all suggestions. Send your questions or comments to us at **learn@examcram.com**. Please remember to include the title of the book in your message; otherwise, we'll be forced to guess which book you're writing about. And we don't like to guess—we want to *know*! Also, be sure to check out the Web pages at **www.examcram.com**, where you'll find information updates, commentary, and certification information. Thanks, and enjoy the book!

Self-Assessment

The reason we included a Self-Assessment in this *Exam Prep* book is to help you evaluate your readiness to tackle MCSE certification. It should also help you understand what you need to know to master the topic of this book—namely, Exam 70-225, "Designing and Deploying a Messaging Infrastructure with Exchange 2000 Server." But before you tackle this Self-Assessment, let's talk about concerns you may face when pursuing an MCSE for Windows 2000, and what an ideal MCSE candidate might look like.

MCSEs in the Real World

In the next section, we describe an ideal MCSE candidate, knowing full well that only a few real candidates will meet this ideal. In fact, our description of that ideal candidate might seem downright scary, especially with the changes that have been made to the program to support Windows 2000. But take heart: Although the requirements to obtain an MCSE may seem formidable, they are by no means impossible to meet. However, be keenly aware that it does take time, involves some expense, and requires real effort to get through the process.

Increasing numbers of people are attaining Microsoft certifications, so the goal is within reach. You can get all the real-world motivation you need from knowing that many others have gone before, so you will be able to follow in their footsteps. If you're willing to tackle the process seriously and do what it takes to obtain the necessary experience and knowledge, you can take—and pass—all the certification tests involved in obtaining an MCSE. In fact, we've designed *Exam Preps*, the companion *Exam Crams*, *Exam Cram Personal Trainers*, and *Exam Cram Personal Test Centers* to make it as easy on you as possible to prepare for these exams. We've also greatly expanded our Web site, **www.examcram.com**, to provide a host of resources to help you prepare for the complexities of Windows 2000.

Besides MCSE, other Microsoft certifications include:

➤ MCSD, which is aimed at software developers and requires one specific exam, two more exams on client and distributed topics, plus a fourth elective exam drawn from a different, but limited, pool of options.

➤ Other Microsoft certifications, whose requirements range from one test (MCP) to several tests (MCP+SB, MCDBA).

The Ideal Windows 2000 MCSE Candidate

Just to give you some idea of what an ideal MCSE candidate is like, here are some relevant statistics about the background and experience such an individual might have. Don't worry if you don't meet these qualifications, or don't come that close—this is a far from ideal world, and where you fall short is simply where you'll have more work to do.

➤ Academic or professional training in network theory, concepts, and operations. This includes everything from networking media and transmission techniques through network operating systems, services, and applications.

➤ Three-plus years of professional networking experience, including experience with Ethernet, token ring, modems, and other networking media. This must include installation, configuration, upgrade, and troubleshooting experience.

Note: The Windows 2000 MCSE program is much more rigorous than the previous NT MCSE program; therefore, you'll really need some hands-on experience. Some of the exams require you to solve real-world case studies and network design issues, so the more hands-on experience you have, the better.

➤ Two-plus years in a networked environment that includes hands-on experience with Windows 2000 Server, Windows 2000 Professional, Windows NT Server, Windows NT Workstation, and Windows 95 or Windows 98. A solid understanding of each system's architecture, installation, configuration, maintenance, and troubleshooting is also essential.

➤ Knowledge of the various methods for installing Windows 2000, including manual and unattended installations.

➤ A thorough understanding of key networking protocols, addressing, and name resolution, including TCP/IP, IPX/SPX, and NetBEUI.

➤ A thorough understanding of NetBIOS naming, browsing, and file and print services.

➤ Familiarity with key Windows 2000-based TCP/IP-based services, including HTTP (Web servers), DHCP, WINS, DNS, plus familiarity with one or more of the following: Internet Information Server (IIS), Index Server, and Proxy Server.

➤ An understanding of how to implement security for key network data in a Windows 2000 environment.

➤ A good working understanding of Active Directory. The more you work with Windows 2000, the more you'll realize that this new operating system is quite different than Windows NT. New technologies like Active Directory have really changed the way that Windows is configured and used. We recommend that you find out as much as you can about Active Directory and acquire as much experience using this technology as possible. The time you take learning about Active Directory will be time very well spent!

Fundamentally, this boils down to a bachelor's degree in computer science, plus three years' experience working in a position involving network design, installation, configuration, and maintenance. We believe that well under half of all certification candidates meet these requirements, and that, in fact, most meet less than half of these requirements—at least, when they begin the certification process. But because all the people who already have been certified have survived this ordeal, you can survive it too—especially if you heed what our Self-Assessment can tell you about what you already know and what you need to learn.

Put Yourself to the Test

The following series of questions and observations is designed to help you figure out how much work you must do to pursue Microsoft certification and what kinds of resources you may consult on your quest. Be absolutely honest in your answers, or you'll end up wasting money on exams you're not yet ready to take. There are no right or wrong answers, only steps along the path to certification. Only you can decide where you really belong in the broad spectrum of aspiring candidates.

Two things should be clear from the outset, however:

➤ Even a modest background in computer science will be helpful.

➤ Hands-on experience with Microsoft products and technologies is an essential ingredient to certification success.

Educational Background

1. Have you ever taken any computer-related classes? [Yes or No]

   If Yes, proceed to question 2; if No, proceed to question 4.

2. Have you taken any classes on computer operating systems? [Yes or No]

   If Yes, you will probably be able to handle Microsoft's architecture and system component discussions. If you're rusty, brush up on basic operating system concepts, especially virtual memory, multitasking regimes, user mode versus kernel mode operation, and general computer security topics.

   If No, consider some basic reading in this area. We strongly recommend a good general operating systems book, such as *Operating System Concepts, 5th Edition*, by Abraham Silberschatz and Peter Baer Galvin (John Wiley & Sons, 1998, ISBN 0-471-36414-2). If this title doesn't appeal to you, check out reviews for other, similar titles at your favorite online bookstore.

3. Have you taken any Messaging Systems or technologies classes? [Yes or No]

If Yes, you will probably be able to handle Microsoft's networking terminology, concepts, and technologies (brace yourself for frequent departures from normal usage). If you're rusty, brush up on basic networking concepts and terminology, especially networking media, transmission types, the OSI Reference Model, and networking technologies such as Ethernet, token ring, FDDI, and WAN links.

If No, you might want to read one or two books in this topic area. The two best books that we know of are *Computer Networks, 3rd Edition*, by Andrew S. Tanenbaum (Prentice-Hall, 1996, ISBN 0-13-349945-6) and *Computer Networks and Internets, 2nd Edition*, by Douglas E. Comer and Ralph E. Droms (Prentice-Hall, 1998, ISBN 0-130-83617-6).

Skip to the next section, "Hands-on Experience."

4. Have you done any reading on operating systems or networks? [Yes or No]

If Yes, review the requirements stated in the first paragraphs after questions 2 and 3. If you meet those requirements, move on to the next section. If No, consult the recommended reading for both topics. A strong background will help you prepare for the Microsoft exams better than just about anything else.

Hands-on Experience

The most important key to success on all of the Microsoft tests is hands-on experience, especially with Windows 2000 Server and Professional, plus the many add-on services and BackOffice components around which so many of the Microsoft certification exams revolve. If we leave you with only one realization after taking this Self-Assessment, it should be that there's no substitute for time spent installing, configuring, and using the various Microsoft products upon which you'll be tested repeatedly and in depth.

5. Have you installed, configured, and worked with:

➤ Windows 2000 Server? [Yes or No]

If Yes, make sure you understand basic concepts as covered in Exam 70-215. You should also study the TCP/IP interfaces, utilities, and services for Exam 70-216, plus implementing security features for Exam 70-220.

Tip: You can download objectives, practice exams, and other data about Microsoft exams from the Training and Certification page at **www.microsoft.com/trainingandservices/default.asp?PageID=mcp**. Use the "Exams" link to obtain specific exam information.

If you haven't worked with Windows 2000 Server, you must obtain one or two machines and a copy of Windows 2000 Server. Then, learn the operating system and whatever other software components on which you'll also be tested.

In fact, we recommend that you obtain two computers, each with a network interface, and set up a two-node network on which to practice. With decent Windows 2000-capable computers selling for about $500 to $600 apiece these days, this shouldn't be too much of a financial hardship. You may have to scrounge to come up with the necessary software, but if you scour the Microsoft Web site you can usually find low-cost options to obtain evaluation copies of most of the software that you'll need.

➤ Windows 2000 Professional? [Yes or No]

If Yes, make sure you understand the concepts covered in Exam 70-210.

If No, you will want to obtain a copy of Windows 2000 Professional and learn how to install, configure, and maintain it. You can use *MCSE Windows 2000 Professional Exam Cram* to guide your activities and studies, or work straight from Microsoft's test objectives if you prefer.

Tip: For any and all of these Microsoft exams, the Resource Kits for the topics involved are a good study resource. You can purchase softcover Resource Kits from Microsoft Press (search for them at **http://mspress.microsoft.com/**), but they also appear on the TechNet CDs (**www.microsoft.com/technet**). Along with *Exam Crams* and *Exam Preps*, we believe that Resource Kits are among the best tools you can use to prepare for Microsoft exams.

6. For any specific Microsoft product that is not itself an operating system (for example, SQL Server), have you installed, configured, used, and upgraded this software? [Yes or No]

If the answer is Yes, skip to the next section. If it's No, you must get some experience. Read on for suggestions on how to do this.

Experience is a must with any Microsoft product exam, be it something as simple as FrontPage 2000 or as challenging as SQL Server 2000. For trial copies of other software, search Microsoft's Web site using the name of the product as your search term. Also, search for bundles like "BackOffice" or "Small Business Server."

Tip: If you have the funds, or your employer will pay your way, consider taking a class at a Certified Training and Education Center (CTEC) or at an Authorized Academic Training Partner (AATP). In addition to classroom exposure to the topic of your choice, you get a copy of the software that is the focus of your course, along with a trial version of whatever operating system it needs, with the training materials for that class.

Before you even think about taking any Microsoft exam, make sure you've spent enough time with the related software to understand how it may be installed and configured, how to maintain such an installation, and how to troubleshoot that software when things go wrong. This will help you in the exam, and in real life!

Testing Your Exam-Readiness

Whether you attend a formal class on a specific topic to get ready for an exam or use written materials to study on your own, some preparation for the Microsoft certification exams is essential. At $100 a try, pass or fail, you want to do everything you can to pass on your first try. That's where studying comes in.

We have included a practice exam in this book, so if you don't score that well on the test, you can study more and then tackle the test again. We also have exams that you can take online through the **ExamCram.com** Web site at **www.examcram. com**. If you still don't hit a score of at least 80 percent after these tests, you'll want to investigate the other practice test resources we mention in this section. Please do not attempt a real test until you are comfortable with these practice tests and score at least 80 percent or higher.

For any given subject, consider taking a class if you've tackled self-study materials, taken the test, and failed anyway. The opportunity to interact with an instructor and fellow students can make all the difference in the world, if you can afford that privilege. For information about Microsoft classes, visit the Training and Certification page at **www.microsoft.com/education/partners/ctec.asp** for Microsoft Certified Education Centers or **www.microsoft.com/aatp/default.htm** for Microsoft Authorized Training Providers.

If you can't afford to take a class, visit the Training and Certification page anyway, because it also includes pointers to free practice exams and to Microsoft Certified Professional Approved Study Guides and other self-study tools. And even if you can't afford to spend much at all, you should still invest in some low-cost practice exams from commercial vendors.

7. Have you taken a practice exam on your chosen test subject? [Yes or No]

   If Yes, and you scored 70 percent or better, you're probably ready to tackle the real thing. If your score isn't above that threshold, keep at it until you break that barrier.

   If No, obtain all the free and low-budget practice tests you can find and get to work. Keep at it until you can break the passing threshold comfortably.

Tip: When it comes to assessing your test readiness, there is no better way than to take a good-quality practice exam and pass with a score of 80 percent or higher. When we're preparing ourselves, we shoot for 80-plus percent, just to leave room for the "weirdness factor" that most of the time shows up on Microsoft exams.

Assessing Readiness for Exam 70-225

In addition to the general exam-readiness information in the previous section, there are several things you can do to prepare for the Designing and Deploying a Messaging Infrastructure with Exchange 2000 Server exam. As you're getting ready for Exam 70-225, visit the Exam Cram Windows 2000 Resource Center at **www.examcram.com/studyresource/w2kresource/**. Another valuable resource is the Exam Cram Insider newsletter. Sign up at **www.examcram.com** or send a blank email message to **subscribe-ec@mars.coriolis.com**. We also suggest that you join an active MCSE mailing list. Sunbelt Software manages one of the better lists. Sign up at **www.sunbelt-software.com** (look for the Subscribe button).

You can also cruise the Web looking for "braindumps" (recollections of test topics and experiences recorded by others) to help you anticipate topics you're likely to encounter on the test. The MCSE mailing list is a good place to ask where the useful braindumps are.

Tip: You can't be sure that a braindump's author can provide correct answers. Therefore, use the questions to guide your studies, but don't rely on the answers in a braindump to lead you to the truth. Double-check everything you find in any braindump.

Microsoft exam mavens also recommend checking the Microsoft Knowledge Base (available on its own CD as part of the TechNet collection, or on the Microsoft Web site at **http://support.microsoft.com/support/**) for "meaningful technical support issues" that relate to your exam's topics. Although we're not sure exactly what the quoted phrase means, we have also noticed some overlap between technical support questions on particular products and troubleshooting questions on the exams for those products.

Onward, through the Fog!

Once you've assessed your readiness, undertaken the right background studies, obtained the hands-on experience that will help you understand the products and technologies at work, and reviewed the many sources of information to help you prepare for a test, you'll be ready to take a round of practice tests. When your scores come back positive enough to get you through the exam, you're ready to go after the real thing. If you follow our assessment regime, you'll not only know what you need to study, but when you're ready to make a test date at Prometric or VUE. Good luck!

Overview of Exchange 2000 Server

After completing this chapter, you will be able to:

✓ Understand the different versions of Exchange 2000 Server and their overall purpose

✓ Familiarize yourself with the relationship between Exchange 2000 and Active Directory services

✓ Recognize the enhancements to reliability and scalability introduced in Exchange 2000

✓ Describe the key components and tools of Exchange 2000 Administration

✓ Identify the main security enhancements from Windows 2000

✓ Evaluate the enhanced messaging and collaboration features of Exchange 2000

In this first chapter you will gain the necessary knowledge to lay the groundwork for the design and deployment of Microsoft Exchange 2000 Server. This overview of Exchange 2000 features will provide a solid foundation for the concepts to follow. You can return to this chapter as a reference for the overall features and capabilities of this powerful product. Exchange 2000 Server was specifically designed to address the messaging and collaboration requirements for organizations of all sorts and sizes, from small businesses to large distributed enterprises. Exchange 2000 offers an extremely reliable, scalable, and manageable messaging and collaboration design, which is effortlessly integrated with the Windows 2000 operating system and Active Directory.

Exchange 2000 is made available in three different versions. The base product, Exchange 2000 Server, provides the features and functionality that a small to medium organization needs for messaging and collaboration. The next edition is Exchange 2000 Enterprise Server, which provides the dependability and scalability requirements of the most demanding enterprise customers for messaging and collaboration through its unlimited data store and active/active clustering solutions. Finally, Exchange 2000 Conferencing Server allows workers to arrange, manage, and take part in data, voice, and videoconferencing sessions across the intranet as well as the Internet.

Exchange and Windows 2000 Active Directory Integration

Tight integration between Windows 2000 and Active Directory services (ADS) helps to lower the total cost of ownership (TCO) and administrative overhead of the messaging and collaboration design. Microsoft no longer ships a separate directory service with Exchange, but rather incorporates the Windows 2000 Active Directory. By integrating with Active Directory, Exchange 2000 can offer increased reliability and scalability of the overall messaging infrastructure, lower cost of ownership, and a single point of administration with a high degree of security through the use of the operating system's Access Control Lists (ACLs). Another central advantage of Active Directory integration is that all resource access is managed through exactly the same tools that control the access to the rest of your network resources. This results in a reduced learning curve for administrators and can eventually lower the cost of your system administration. In addition, support for protocols has been transferred from Exchange Services to the Internet Information Services (IIS).

Active Directory provides a single place to store the information you need to manage your entire network and messaging design. This information can include the following:

➤ Email and mailbox information

➤ Databases

➤ Connections

➤ Configuration information

➤ Files and folders

➤ Peripheral devices

➤ Web access

➤ Other objects and services

Benefits of Active Directory

Integration with Active Directory also provides increased system performance and manageability while making directory management easier. Some of the benefits of Active Directory include the following:

➤ *Better directory access*—Directory information can be quickly accessed with the Lightweight Directory Access Protocol (LDAP), which is the native access protocol for directory information.

➤ *Centralized object management*—Administrators can control all of the user data in a unified set of utilities. The Microsoft Management Console (MMC) can be used for the administration of all Exchange 2000 and Windows 2000 directory objects.

➤ *Easier security management*—Windows 2000 discretionary access control lists (DACLs) are utilized in the Exchange 2000 Information Store. This allows for a single set of security groups to be applied to the data stored in Exchange 2000 along with Windows 2000 file shares.

➤ *A single distribution list*—You can eliminate the need to create a matching set of distribution lists for each group or department because security groups can be automatically used as distribution lists.

The Active Directory also provides a high degree of topological flexibility by employing drag-and-drop functionality to simplify the administration of dynamic organizations. Exchange 2000 uses a distributed design so that individual Exchange components such as directory services and databases can reside on separate servers. Exchange can also take advantage of the extensibility of the Active Directory schema, which is a description of object classes and attributes that objects possess. This flexible, yet often complex, topology allows larger enterprises to accommodate millions of users. For example, administrators can deploy a system in which users connect to front-end servers and subsequently gain access to messages and data sitting on separate back-end servers. This provides further reliability because system failures can be isolated. Because the Active Directory forest defines the borders of your Exchange 2000 organization, it is feasible to host many different namespaces in the same Active Directory forest and Exchange organization. However, it is not possible to have a single Exchange organization span multiple untrusted Active Directory domains.

Object Unification

A large merger of more than a few Active Directory objects with Exchange objects has lowered the odds of duplicating required management tasks that used to be necessary in the previous versions of Exchange. A number of objects exist that preserve configuration settings for both network access and messaging properties. For example, the user object combines mailboxes and users, the group object combines distribution lists and groups, and the contact object combines custom recipients and contacts.

Active Directory Connector

The main purpose of the Active Directory Connector (ADC) in Exchange 2000 is to replicate and synchronize the Windows 2000 Active Directory with an Exchange Server 5.5 directory. The ADC lets you propagate the Active Directory from directory information already held in Exchange 5.5. This allows existing Exchange 5.5 customers to get a jump on their Windows Active Directory deployment. This is an essential tool for enterprises migrating from Exchange 5.5 to Exchange 2000, as it happened before with the MS Mail Connector when migrating MS Mail to Exchange Server. This also allows administrators to manage Exchange 5.5 directory information through the Windows 2000 Active Directory. Because Active Directory is able to hold all user account details, security data, and messaging information, a separate directory for Exchange 2000 is no longer necessary. Active Directory also provides Exchange 2000 with global address lists, address book views, and offline address books.

Exchange 2000 and Windows 2000 each contain the ADC (both were developed from the same code base). The version of ADC that comes with Windows 2000 replicates information about directory objects between the Exchange directory and Active Directory Service, whereas the Exchange 2000 version is enhanced to replicate information related to domain controllers and replication topology as well as to support mixed Exchange sites. The ADC is installed through the ADC Installation Wizard and runs as a service. After being successfully installed, the connector is configured along with all of the other components through the MMC. Some of the other tasks that the ADC performs are as follows:

➤ Maintaining object reliability and consistency through replication.

➤ Facilitating upgrade and migration from Windows NT to Windows 2000.

➤ Using LDAP application programming interfaces (APIs) to replicate between two directories.

➤ Performing a bulk import/export from Active Directory using the LDAP Data Interchange Format (LDIF).

➤ Incorporating object-matching mechanisms for connecting objects between directories.

➤ Allowing administrators to achieve granular control over the replication schedule, authentication, and the replication schema. Replicating makes changes only between the two directories, where possible.

➤ Hosting multiple connections on a single Active Directory server and managing them through connection agreements.

Replication is the act of updating objects in a common directory namespace to one or more directories. Therefore, the replication of Exchange 5.5 objects and attributes to Active Directory makes the objects and attributes available to Exchange 2000. In contrast, *synchronization* is the process of copying objects from one directory to another with distinct namespaces. The ADC synchronizes changes from Active Directory to the Exchange directory, from the Exchange directory to Active Directory, or both ways, depending on the configuration settings. The ADC synchronizes two discrete types of directory objects:

➤ *Recipients*—These are made up of mailboxes, distribution lists, and custom recipients.

➤ *Configuration information*—This information includes connectors, monitors, protocols, topology, and other configuration properties.

Distributed Services

One of the powerful new features of Exchange Enterprise Edition is a distributed service known as *distributed configuration*. The distributed configuration architecture allows Exchange 2000 to place subsystems, such as directory, protocols, and information store, on different server machines, thereby accommodating millions of users. Normally, Exchange 2000 will be installed on a number of servers throughout your organization. If your enterprise is located in several physical locations, you can make use of features such as routing groups (discussed in the following section, under "Fault Tolerant Routing") and strategically placed connector servers to reduce single points of failure and add to the general availability of the system.

Public folder stores can be distributed to multiple servers in the organization over a wide geographical area. This serves to improve response time for users and applications as well as to provide a backup of public folder data for an additional protection against data loss in case of a hardware failure or other emergency. In addition, because Exchange 2000 is now integrated with Active Directory, it no longer needs to have the directory services hosted on every server computer. This can be of particular benefit to companies (such as Internet service providers, or ISPs) who need large, scalable platforms to meet their clients' messaging and collaboration needs. For example, a string of front-end servers could be earmarked for handling incoming client connections while back-end servers can manage the databases. This is exactly how Microsoft manages its MSN Hotmail mail service on the Web. Other features, such as authentication and security, can also be assigned to IP-addressable front-end servers to improve network performance, reliability, and scalability. This feature, where an IP address is assigned to two or more objects in the network, is known as Virtual Internet Protocol (VIP).

Enhancements to Reliability and Scalability

Many of the features of Exchange 2000 have the advantage of addressing both reliability and scalability goals. Exchange 2000 takes a quantum leap in development by allowing you to divide the Information Store into manageable storage chunks, each of virtually unlimited size. These Exchange 2000 databases are now universally referred to as *stores*. Exchange 2000 continues the tradition of previous Exchange versions by providing transaction logging with realtime rollback recovery. To provide greater scalability, many functions have been separated. Virtual servers, storage groups, and the ability to create multiple public folder trees enhance scalability. Depending on the requirements of the server load, certain processes can operate together on a single server or be moved to multiple servers. For example, protocols have been removed from the Information Store Service so that they can be run on separate servers. A front-end/back-end server model can also be established, if necessary, to provide a unified namespace in one server, the front-end, but support many thousands of users on the back-end. Alternatively, several front-end servers can feed messages to a single back-end server. Further reliability can be achieved by using multinode clustering. This active/active clustering model provides fault tolerance if a server goes down and makes sure the adverse effect on the user is minimal. We now continue with a survey of several features that enhance the scalability and reliability of Exchange 2000.

Storage Groups and the Information Store

A major new feature of Exchange 2000 Enterprise Edition that supports both scalability and reliability is that of storage groups with multiple databases. A *storage group* is simply a logical grouping of databases that share a single transaction log set as well as a central area of administration, backup, and restore. You can set up multiple stores on a single server to afford greater flexibility and better recovery mechanisms for larger sites. In addition, by optimizing through the use of transaction log files for multiple stores, storage groups offer an added degree of effectiveness. An example of this is shown in Figure 1.1.

A storage group can comprise up to six stores, and it runs within a lone instance of the database engine under the store.exe process. Exchange supports up to 90 separate databases per server (a single server can actually host 15 storage groups, each containing 6 databases) and can be mounted or dismounted separately. This feature allows the administrator to recover one without affecting the others in any way as well as to make a store inoperable or unavailable for offline maintenance. Users cannot access a dismounted store, and dismounted stores will not take up any system resources.

In Exchange 2000, you can actually create two different types of stores: the *mailbox store*, which holds user data, and the *public store*, which contains the public folder data. Each store has a related store file that holds native streaming Internet content as well. As mentioned previously, each storage group implements its own set of transaction log files. Therefore, if there are six stores in a storage group, all the transactions for all six stores will be recorded in one set of transaction log files. As the administrator, you will have the judgment to decide on the log file location for each of the storage groups. You can back up and restore an entire storage group so only one copy of the system transaction log needs to be written to tape. You can even do this while other stores in the group are in operation. However, if you

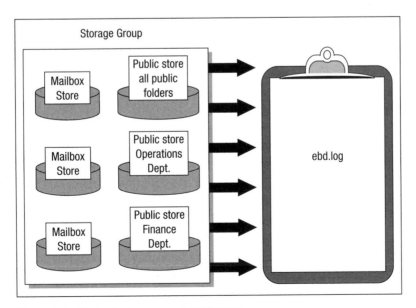

Figure 1.1   The basic storage group architecture.

decide to configure multiple storage groups, we recommend that you place the log files on separate hard disks. All logs are 5MB in size, and Exchange 2000 allocates 10MB of RAM for each mounted store.

Exchange 5.5 had, in essence, one single storage group, meaning that only one database could be backed up at a time. If a database became too large to back up (or restore) in an appropriate manner, mailboxes would have to be moved to another server. Exchange 2000's storage groups allow for a single, logical database to be divided across multiple physical databases, thereby improving system accessibility and reliability. By implementing the storage group concept to create multiple smaller stores, your organization can maintain more users per server. Each storage group can, in turn, be backed up concurrently to an independent storage device. You may also choose to host multiple businesses on a single server, each with its own storage group. This would allow for any business group to totally isolate its information from the other groups. This is particularly handy for such businesses as ISPs or large conglomerates. In this way, particular business mailboxes can be given individual support. For example, you can place mission-critical mailboxes on a dedicated store, or you can implement circular logging for specific storage groups that have a data store that generates a lot of transactions that do not need to be recovered. Literally hundreds of possibilities exist, depending on myriad organizational factors.

Exchange Server has historically presented organizations with a single-instance, transaction-based messaging and collaboration database solution that provides superb levels of performance and dependability. When Exchange 5.5 was introduced, this feature was further improved by getting rid of the previous size limit of 16GB on the message store. Exchange 5.5 made allowances for message stores of up to 16TB (*terabytes*, or trillion bytes). Despite these improvements, the store limitations are still the chief limiting issues experienced in most implementations of Exchange 5.5 today. The Exchange store has traditionally had a practical boundary of 50 to 60GB for reasons of backup and recovery. This allows for a maximum 1,500 to 2,000 users per server using a single store. Although mechanisms for backup and restore historically were provided in the Exchange system, recovery was an offline and frequently time-consuming escapade. In addition, individual mailboxes or public folders could not be specifically recovered because the data was stored in two separate databases.

Exchange 2000's revolutionary new Information Store architecture provides organizations with the prospect for extremely large databases as well as an ability to construct multiple smaller physical databases on a single server. By deploying smaller physical stores, you will give a huge boost to the overall system dependability while allowing for faster backups and recoveries. Logically, if you spread out the user population across multiple data stores, when there is a system crash, the affected number of users will obviously be much smaller. For example, if the hard drive that contains one of your stores fails, only that store is affected, so stores contained on other drives can continue to service their email users. Accordingly, more users will be able to use the system for longer periods of time, thus providing greater availability of the system.

In addition, by offering multiple private information stores and public folder databases grouped into storage groups, Exchange 2000 Server gives your organization the potential to scale the number of users beyond your present limitations. By deploying seven to eight private stores per server, your business could combine many more users onto fewer pieces of hardware and still maintain your existing service level agreements (SLAs). Although the entire Exchange Service can still be administered as a solitary data store, as an administrator or systems analyst, you may opt to host multiple 100GB-plus databases for a large enterprise or even partition a single logical database among several smaller databases. Exchange can be distributed among several servers using load-balancing techniques combined with Windows 2000 clustering technologies.

Active/Active Clustering Technology

Another way that Microsoft Exchange 2000 Server delivers enhanced scalability and reliability for your messaging infrastructure is by supporting two-way and four-way active/active clustering. Two-way clustering technology is offered in Windows 2000 Advanced Server, and four-way clustering is accessible only in Windows 2000 Datacenter Server. A *cluster* is formally made up of two physical computers (or nodes) connected to one another and a shared storage device. Active/active clustering can also be described by a scenario in which both members of the cluster are online and accepting user requests for various services. A visual representation of this is seen in Figure 1.2. This capacity for implementing multiple servers at all times can significantly reduce system costs. In addition, reliability will be greater than before because no dedicated servers are necessary to help recover from system failures.

Exchange Server 5.5 employed active/passive clustering, in which only one component of a cluster provides service to users at any given time. This type of clustering ran on one clustered server but could not be restarted automatically on the other server if there was a system failure. In active/passive scenarios, dedicated failover servers are required, and thus hardware is used less efficiently than with active–active technologies. With active/active clustering, two servers work in concert to vigorously process messaging requests. When a stoppage occurs, it triggers a rollover to recovery mode. This active/active clustering support also allows you to allocate storage groups to be on cluster nodes so that they will fail-over to other servers if necessary. Exchange 2000 can operate simultaneously on several servers and process requests at the same time. In addition, the Exchange servers in the cluster do not have to be configured the same way or even be the same size, which increases the amount of options available to system administrators. Server clusters can also be

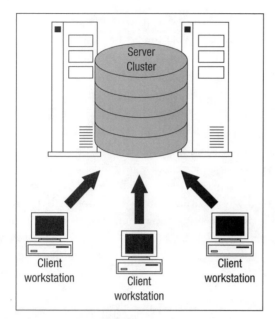

Figure 1.2 A basic clustering scenario.

combined with front-end load-balanced clustered servers to add to their scalability and reliability. A graphical illustration of this concept is seen in Figure 1.3.

Virtual Servers

Exchange 2000 employs a system that runs one or more virtual servers on one of the computer nodes in the cluster. A *virtual server* can be defined as a server that resides on a physical server yet appears to the user as a separate server. Multiple virtual servers can be located on one physical server, each having the capability to run its own applications with individualized access to input devices and peripherals. Clients will then connect to the virtual servers in the same manner that they would connect to a standalone server. The cluster service monitors and manages the virtual servers in the cluster. In case of a failure, the cluster service will restart or move the virtual servers on the failed computer to a working node. For a planned outage, you can simply manually transfer the virtual servers to other computers. Either way, the user will notice only a short disruption in service while the virtual server is in transition. A model of virtual servers is shown in Figure 1.4.

In Exchange 2000, each virtual server will have its own independent configuration information such as domain name, Internet Protocol (IP) address, port number, and authentication configuration. The virtual server will appear to the user as an autonomous stand-alone individual Web site. As an independent host, each virtual server can maintain diverse security levels as well as connect to different networks. For example, you could set up one virtual server to deliver messages only between

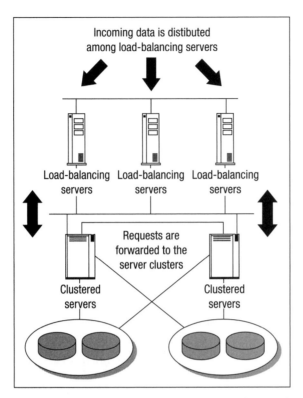

Figure 1.3 Example of a combination load-balancing and cluster server solution.

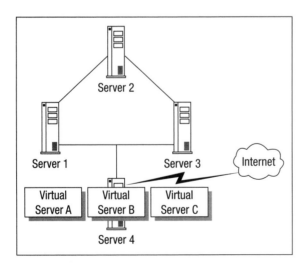

Figure 1.4 Illustration of how several virtual servers can be placed on one physical server.

the Exchange 2000 computers within an organization while configuring another virtual server to connect externally to the Internet. This feature will enable you to set a higher level of security for incoming messages from the Internet or extranet. For example, you may wish to place a restriction on a virtual server to block anonymous access or perhaps perform reverse Domain Name System (DNS) lookups. By default, in Exchange 2000, only one virtual server per protocol exists on each server. The Exchange System Manager is the tool you would use to configure this feature.

Exchange 2000 Public Folders

Since the inauguration of Microsoft Exchange, the principle behind public folders has always been to afford a shared storage area. Quite a few changes, however, have been made to the design of public folders in Exchange 2000. You can now have a large number of folder trees in Exchange. This saves you from having to store all the public folders in one directory tree. You can now send messages through the mail entries stored in Active Directory instead of having to post them directly to the public folder, because Exchange 2000 public folders are now integrated with the Exchange 2000 Information Store and the Windows 2000 Active Directory. Also, a Web browser can be used to easily gain access to public folders with a Uniform Resource Locator (URL). The MMC has a component snap-in exclusively for public folder administration and management. You will also have more administrative control with the ability to secure folder items using the Exchange Installable File System (ExIFS).

The Exchange Installable File System

The ExIFS lets you share public folders and mailboxes, making them available as traditional folders and files through such regular Microsoft Win32 processes as Internet Explorer and the Command prompt. The ExIFS makes this possible by allowing normal network client redirectors to these items. The benefits are that you can map a drive letter or execute a NET USE command to your own mailbox or any public folder. With this functionality, such standard programs as Windows Explorer and Microsoft Office 2000 can read and write information right to the native content store. By default, public folder referrals would allow you to access any folder in the organization between routing groups.

Full-Text Indexing

Another useful new feature for public folders is the ability to perform full-text indexing. A *full-text index* is a list of words that have been acknowledged in each document held in an Exchange 2000 Information Store. For example, this indexing feature allows you to use the Microsoft Outlook Advanced Find feature (or custom application) to rapidly search the Web storage system to find messages and/or documents that have a particular word either in a message body, message subject, or within an attached document. You may also seek out other message properties by using well-established search techniques.

The types of attachments that can be searched through full-text indexing include the following:

➤ Microsoft Word (.doc)

➤ Microsoft Excel (.xls)

➤ Microsoft PowerPoint (.ppt)

➤ Hypertext Markup Language, or HTML (.htm, .html, .asp)

➤ Text files (.txt)

➤ Embedded Multipurpose Internet Mail Extension, or MIME (.eml)

In Exchange 5.5, you could utilize Site Server to create an index of public folder content that users can search. Before planning your Exchange 2000 indexing policy, therefore, you should determine if you are already using Site Server to index your public folders. Exchange 2000 Server creates its own index of public folder and mailbox content. You can enable indexing for any database so that content can be selectively indexed. If you are using Site Server, you must set indexing schedules and properties in the databases in Exchange 2000 so that indexes continue to be created.

The Exchange 2000 full-text search is word based, not character based; therefore, a search for the text "data" will return only documents that contain "data" as a word. The word "database" will not be recognized as a match. Also, you cannot index the properties of documents or binary attachments with the full-text indexing feature. When you make a query for a particular word, any message that has the word in the body or within an attachment will be returned as a result. You can then evaluate each message to see if it is the message or attachment that you want. Note that if you search for a particular word, and this word is found in the message body and in the attachment of another message, the return set will recognize only the messages, *not the specific attachment within the message.*

Full-text indexing is enabled on the computer running Exchange 2000 Server as opposed to the client for the sake of backward compatibility. Therefore, any Messaging Application Programming Interface (MAPI) client can use it when performing a search of server documents. Only MAPI and Internet Message Access Protocol 4 (IMAP4) clients can benefit from full-text indexing. However, if full-text indexing is not configured, MAPI clients will use the sluggish, character-based search of the message to perform searches, just as they always have. Also, attachment searches are supported only when full-text indexing is enabled. Both the Information Store Service and Microsoft Search Service must be running for the index to be created, updated, or deleted. The Search Service constructs the original index used to recognize and log the searchable text by processing the full store, one directory at a time. By forming the index in advance, Exchange 2000 can swiftly return the request to the user.

Internet Information Services Integration

Another feature that improves the scalability and reliability of Exchange 2000 is the fact that protocols have been moved out of the Information Store Service and run within the IIS process. The logical conclusion, of course, is that IIS is now mandatory for Exchange 2000 to function. By integrating protocols into IIS, you can now host protocols on different servers, or multiple servers, off of the server that the Information Store Service runs. Systems architects can build large, scalable, public email systems by spreading components over multiple servers. This component partitioning also improves the reliability of Exchange 2000 organizations of any size by isolating the system failures of one server. A protocol failure would no longer have to affect the Information Store Service or the Active Directory Service.

Exchange 2000 supports the following protocols used by IIS:

➤ Internet Message Access Protocol (IMAP)

➤ Hypertext Transfer Protocol-Distributed Authoring and Versioning (HTTP-DAV or Web-DAV)

➤ Network News Transfer Protocol (NNTP)

➤ Post Office Protocol 3 (POP3)

➤ Simple Mail Transfer Protocol (SMTP)

Fault-Tolerant Routing

The final reliability and scalability feature of Exchange 2000 that you explore here is improved, fault-tolerant routing. SMTP has been implemented as the default transport protocol for routing all message traffic between servers, both within a site and between sites. The robust routing of email messages is one of the best attributes of Exchange Server. Exchange 2000 has appreciably enhanced the messaging and routing algorithms to offer fault-tolerant delivery of messages and to eliminate "message bounce" even if servers have crashed or network service has been interrupted.

Routing Groups

Exchange 2000 effectively uses routing groups, which are best described as collections of well-connected servers running over stable and dependable links. Routing groups are comparable to sites in the previous iterations of Exchange. With

Exchange 2000, the message routing procedure starts with the Exchange Server receiving a message from a host through either a gateway or a connector. The connectors that ship with Exchange 2000 that can be used to connect routing groups are:

➤ X.400 connector

➤ SMTP connector

➤ The routing group connector

The Exchange 2000 Server searches for the recipient in Active Directory and then routes the message to that recipient using SMTP as the primary messaging protocol. This assures superior interoperability between Exchange 2000, other messaging systems, and the Internet. *SMTP* is defined in IETF RFC 821 and is the default transport protocol in Exchange 2000 for routing messages between servers. Exchange still continues, however, to support the X.400 specification that it offered in its previous version. In addition, the use of SMTP removes the need for a high bandwidth connection between servers within a routing group, which was imperative in earlier versions of Exchange.

Link State Tables

Exchange 2000 uses a link state table to determine the shortest path between two routing groups for a given message routing and selection process. A link state table is the database of information on each Exchange 2000 server that stores the status of a server and the link state information propagated by the link state algorithm, as well as the costs of the connections between servers to determine the most efficient route for a message. The table provides an effective method for routing messages and avoiding the bounce effect of a failed link. The link state table is stored on each server running Exchange 2000 and contains the status of each connector in the Exchange 2000 organization. If an Exchange 2000 server cannot find a route for a message after making reference to a link state table, it will not attempt to deliver the message. Note that with added flexibility comes added overhead in planning and routing group management. A graphic example of this concept is shown in Figure 1.5. You explore the design and deployment issues of routing groups in much greater detail in Chapter 9.

Administration and Management of Exchange 2000

A potentially complex collaboration and messaging solution such as Exchange should be as easy as possible to administer. Exchange 2000 offers a wide array of integrated components for diagnostics, directory management, and remote management, as well as a system that is relatively simple to set up and configure. To be able to meet the rapidly changing macro needs of your organization as well as the micro needs of your user, you need to have a firm grasp of a rich and powerful set of tools.

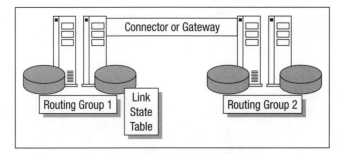

Figure 1.5 A logical message routing group scenario.

Microsoft Management Console

With the MMC, you now have single-seat administration of all messaging and collaboration resources, as well as file and print resources from one easy-to-use management interface. The MMC, which was first released with Windows NT4 Option Pack (which included IIS 5), is a common, extensible interface for application and system management. It has been extended and enhanced in the Windows 2000 operating system. MMC provides a common environment for snap-ins that define the actual management activities. MMC *snap-ins* are Component Object Model (COM) objects that are representative of single units of behavior and are implemented as standalone components or in combination to create more complex tools. Exchange 2000 makes available a collection of snap-ins to the MMC for administering all of your messaging and collaborative resources. This choice of several consoles gives administrators the opportunity to use only the objects they need, as opposed to using the whole Exchange 2000 product. Because other Microsoft products also use the management console, the interface for administration is conveniently combined across all server applications.

In addition, Exchange 2000 has a rich and flexible policy structure that lets you very quickly change settings across a large number of servers or users. Policies are actually a new concept to Exchange 2000. A *policy* is defined as a collection of settings applied to one or more configuration objects. Similar to a template for a word processor or Web-authoring tool, a policy simplifies control and administration by providing a one-stop location to configure a huge number of objects. With policy-based administration, administrators can quickly define policies across hundreds of objects (such as user mailboxes, public folders, servers, and so on) and can change configurations quickly in a single operation. The administrator will use the System Manager tool to employ two different types of policies. Server-side policies are applied to servers, public stores, and mailbox stores, whereas client-side recipient policies apply to mail-enabled objects such as users, groups, contacts, and public folders.

Monitoring Infrastructure

The monitoring infrastructure and user interface for system monitoring in Exchange 2000 is built on the Windows Management Instrumentation (WMI) architecture. The administrator can get a concise and filterable look at all of the servers and connectors in the organizational design and access logs, performance data, disk data, and the status of services. Exchange also uses another set of COM objects in the form of an all-inclusive programming interface to build the business logic for workflow and other customized management applications. This interface is an extension of the Collaboration Data Objects (CDO) interface that enables third party and custom-built applications to carry out a wide selection of mailbox and public folder management tasks as well as extending the MMC snap-ins for custom management components. CDO can be used for rapid application deployment of components to perform the following tasks:

➤ Workflow applications with business logic

➤ Active Directory access

➤ Messaging and contact management

➤ System management

➤ Calendaring tasks

Administrative Groups

Exchange 2000 incorporates a straightforward technique for separating tasks known as *administrative groups*. An administrative group is a group of Exchange 2000 Active Directory objects that are assembled together for permission management purposes. The administrative topology of your organization will be defined by a collection of administrative groups. Your administrative groups can contain a number of routing groups, public folder trees, policies, conferencing services, chats, monitors, servers, and networks. If your company has two discrete groups of systems administrators who manage two separate groups of Exchange servers, for example, you may choose to create two administrative groups—one for each set of servers. You would then include the correct Windows 2000 users and/or groups to the security settings on the two administrative groups to set up your permissions. In a mixed-mode environment, Exchange 2000 will have one administrative group for each Exchange 5.5 site. Although it is possible to create more than one routing group within each administrative group, all of the routing group members must belong to the same administrative group as the routing group.

In Exchange 2000, the site concept is separated into three distinct administrative entities: the administrative group, the routing group, and system policies. These three components function autonomously to provide greater administrative flexibility. The following three areas now work together to fully define the site concept:

➤ A collective administrative entity within an X.500-type directory (Active Directory)

➤ Well-connected Exchange servers running single-hop routing processes between them

➤ An administrative unit to which policies can be applied

Administrative Tools and Components

Microsoft Exchange 2000 provides integrated diagnostics, remote management, and flexible directory support. Exchange is actually very easy to install, configure, and administer. The management and administrative tools and features supported by Exchange 2000 include the following:

➤ *Administrative wizards*—Administrative wizards are graphical utilities that walk you through the process of configuring protocols such as SMTP or NNTP on a per site, per server, or per mailbox basis.

➤ *Deleted item recovery*—The deleted item recovery feature lets you flag objects in the Deleted folder to be deleted from the user's view for a specified period of time.

➤ *Microsoft Systems Management Server (SMS) integration*—SMS integration allows the rapid and well-organized deployment of Exchange and Outlook clients to user desktops.

➤ *Windows 2000 Server Management tool integration*—This integration facet includes incorporation with the Performance Monitor and event log, thereby making it possible for administrators to use the same tools for the network operating system as for the messaging and collaboration server.

➤ *Microsoft Cluster Server*—Cluster services provide higher availability and easier management of data and applications so that users can continue working even when a server goes down.

➤ *Link Monitor*—The Link Monitor tool monitors the links between sites, the intranet, and the X.400 design.

➤ *Message Tracker*—This tracking component grants the ability to follow the path of messages based on certain criteria. This can be done anywhere in a local area network (LAN), a wide area network (WAN), or on the Internet or X.400 network.

➤ *Microsoft Exchange Move Server Wizard*—This wizard allows you to change the structure of your site or organization. Also, rather than waiting until the upgrade to Exchange 2000, you may decide to merge Exchange 5.5 organizations, because there is presently no method for merging two Exchange 2000 organizations.

> *Multiple organization hosting*—This feature allows the separation of the Exchange 2000 directory into multiple virtual containers so that each can include the members of an individual business unit.

> *Server Monitor*—The Server Monitor tool provides the capability to monitor server statistics and take a predetermined action in the event of a problem.

Exchange 2000 Security Enhancements

The Windows 2000 operating system offers many options for defending your Exchange 2000 organization from a wide variety of potential attacks. The Windows 2000 Server enhancements that relate to securing Windows 2000 Server and Exchange 2000 Server include the following:

> Access Control Lists

> Active Directory Service

> Auditing

> Certificate Services

> Encrypting File System

> Internet Protocol Security

> Kerberos

> Security Configuration tool set

> Transmission Control Protocol/Internet Protocol (TCP/IP) filtering

Access Control Lists

Exchange 2000 introduces the native use of the Windows 2000 operating system Access Control Lists. Windows 2000 ACLs can be configured for individual messages and components of messages, not just for access to an entire folder of data. This gives you new degrees of security for workflow and tracking applications. You can use Windows 2000 security descriptors to define the permissions for all messaging and collaboration resources because the Exchange resources and network resources (including public folders) are fully integrated into the Windows 2000 security model. As an administrator, you need learn only a single permissions scheme when managing both the Windows 2000 and Exchange 2000 servers. This single set of security groups will then affect both Windows 2000 or Exchange 2000 resources and objects. Exchange 2000 Server offers network administrators and systems designers much greater power over security by allowing permissions to be set at the object and field levels.

Active Directory Service

The Windows 2000 Server Active Directory Service replaces the Security Accounts Manager (SAM) database implemented in Microsoft Windows NT 4. In effect, a security identifier (SID) links Active Directory objects used in the Windows 2000 and Exchange 2000 servers. Exchange 2000 Server authenticates users in a front-end/back-end server environment by incorporating one of two techniques. When using front-end/back-end servers, the front-end functionality is determined by the authentication method you are using. Windows 2000 DACLs are used in the Exchange 2000 Information Store. This allows for a single set of security groups to be applied to the data stored in Exchange 2000 along with Windows 2000 file shares.

Auditing

Auditing is the security mechanism in Windows 2000 Server that monitors a variety of security-related actions. This type of event monitoring is crucial in identifying intruders and in detecting malicious attempts to compromise data on your systems. A failed logon attempt is a prime example of an event that you may decide to audit. Also, Windows 2000 Server produces a security log that provides a method for viewing the specific reported security events. In addition, the Windows 2000 auditing feature will produce an audit trail to help you stay on top of all security administration events that take place on your system. If someone were to modify the auditing policy so that failed logon attempts were no longer audited, the audit trail would expose this event.

You can also specify that an audit entry be logged whenever certain files are accessed. The corresponding entry would show you the action executed or attempted and the user who did it, as well as the date and time of the action, or who tried to do something that isn't permitted. You can view the security log in Event Viewer. By examining the security log on a regular basis, you can make a preemptive strike at certain attacks, such as password attacks, before they happen. The security log can help you after an intrusion to figure out how the hacker penetrated your system and what they accomplished during the exposure.

Note: Security auditing is not enabled by default. You need to use the Group Policy snap-in to the MMC to set in motion these kinds of required audits. By auditing such Exchange objects as stores and individual servers, you can monitor changes to your Exchange configuration through the event logs. You can audit variances in an Exchange object's permissions, ownership, or configuration. You may also decide to initiate an audit to determine whether a particular object is written to, read, or even deleted.

Certificate Services

Exchange 2000 uses the Windows 2000 Server Certificate Services to generate a certification authority (CA). This authority, in turn, will receive certificate requests, verify information in the request, and identify the requester. The CA also issues and revokes certificates as well as publishes a certificate revocation list. Certificate Services also supplies special services for issuing and managing certificates used in software security systems that incorporate public key technologies. Windows 2000 Server Certificate Services is required in order to use the Key Management Service (KMS) in Exchange 2000.

The KMS is an optional Microsoft Exchange 2000 Server component that is placed on a specified server in an administrative group. The KMS offers centralized management and archiving of private keys. In addition, it administers and maintains each user's private encryption key in a secure encrypted database. These keys are then used for encrypting email messages and digitally signing messages.

Encrypting File System

The Encrypting File System (EFS) is a component of Windows 2000 that lets users encrypt data directly on volumes that use the Windows NT file system (NTFS). The EFS transparently encrypts and decrypts files stored on a hard disk. This feature is especially useful for mobile users who need to encrypt files or folders that contain, for example, personal email, so that if the portable computer is misplaced or stolen, the information cannot be compromised. The Windows 2000 interface for setting EFS is shown in Figure 1.6. The EFS uses certificates based on the X.509 standard for its security specification. If no CA is available, the EFS will automatically generate its own self-signed certificates for users and default recovery agents. When users encrypt a file or folder for the first time, a recovery policy will be put into service involuntarily. This way, users who lose their file encryption certificates and private keys will have access to a recovery agent to decrypt their files.

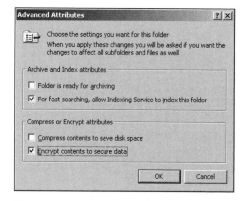

Figure 1.6   Dialog box used to set EFS security on a file or folder.

Internet Protocol Security

Internet Protocol Security (IPSec) is actually a security design framework consisting of open standards that guarantee secure, private communications over IP networks. IPSec employs various cryptographic security services developed by the Internet Engineering Task Force (IETF) IPSec working group to accomplish this goal. Although Certificate Services and KMSs provide security on the application layer, IPSec offers security at the IP transport layer (layer 3). IPSec also supplies a shield for protocol stack components that transmit traffic at the IP layer, such as TCP, User Datagram Protocol (UDP), and Internet Control Message Protocol (ICMP), among others. IPSec is built upon an end-to-end security model. This means that only the hosts that need to know about the traffic being secured are the ones doing the sending and receiving. Each component deals with security at its respective end, always assuming that the communication is not secure.

Kerberos

Kerberos, the primary security protocol used in the Windows 2000 operating system, is tightly integrated into the administrative and security model. Kerberos version 5 offers secure communication between Windows 2000 Server domains and client computers, The Kerberos V5 authentication scheme issues tickets for accessing the many network services. These tickets contain an encrypted password and data to affirm the identity of the user to the requested service. With the exception of manually entering a password, the total authentication procedure is invisible to the user.

An essential aspect of Kerberos V5 is the Key Distribution Center (KDC). The KDC is a service that runs on each Active Directory domain controller and stores all of the client passwords and vital account information. Using this integrated Kerberos authentication, the password is encrypted and therefore cannot be determined by the front-end server as it forwards the authentication request to the back-end server. You will need to use Internet Explorer 5 client software running on Windows 2000 for this functionality in your Exchange 2000 architecture. Internet Explorer clients that are pre-version 5 use the NTLM protocol authentication and cannot take advantage of the front-end/back-end architecture.

Security Configuration Tool Set

The Security Configuration tool set is a combination of two components: the Security Configuration and Analysis tool and the Security Templates tool. You can use these to examine and construct your Exchange organization security policies. The Security Configuration and Analysis tool employs a database architecture that allows you to use personal databases, to import and export security templates, and to merge multiple security templates into one combined security template to perform analysis and configuration. This database is a computer-specific data store, and is the first step in your organizational security management and analysis. You can then add new security templates to the database incrementally and build a more complex security template, depending on your corporate needs.

TCP/IP Filtering

Windows 2000 Server offers you a TCP/IP filtering feature that allows you to spell out precisely which types of incoming IP traffic you want accepted on each IP interface. If routing and remote access or other TCP/IP services are not configured to filter, you can use Windows 2000 TCP/IP filtering to isolate the Internet and intranet traffic servers. An illustration of a possible IP filtering scenario can be seen in Figure 1.7. This feature is disabled by default, so you need to enable TCP/IP filtering for all adapters by using a single checkbox in the interface.

Enhanced Messaging and Collaboration Features

Another of the great benefits of the complete integration of Exchange 2000 and the Windows 2000 Active Directory is the change to the platform, which increases the reliability, scalability, ease of administration, and the performance of the product for enhanced messaging and collaboration. Exchange 2000 offers an assortment of tools and features that support collaboration. Microsoft has increased the performance of Internet messaging and lowered the TCO for messaging and collaboration functions by consolidating users onto fewer servers, thereby reducing the cost of hardware and ongoing operations. Network and messaging administrative tasks are unified to keep the costs of learning and management low. The Internet support provided in Exchange Server allows for better communication with customers and offers new opportunities to more closely manage the vendor supply chain.

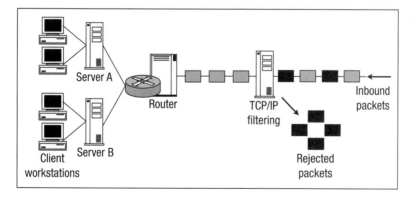

Figure 1.7   An example of a TCP/IP filtering architecture.

Exchange Server has long had built-in support for all of the commonly used Internet standards. In Exchange 2000, this capability is taken to a higher level by providing high-performance Internet messaging. A major new feature of Exchange Server is the support for native Internet content storage. Any Internet traffic coming in from individual email messages is stored directly as MIME content in the Exchange 2000 Server store. Translation to another format is not performed, unless it is absolutely required for delivery to a non-Internet client. This enhances and speeds up performance of Internet mail, especially in the delivery of mail to Internet clients. All of these enhancements are due to the aforementioned tight integration with Microsoft Internet Information Services. This integration can provide the highest levels of performance on protocols such as SMTP and IMAP.

Outlook Web Access, the Exchange Web client, has seen remarkable enhancements in Exchange 2000. Web Access offers Web browser access to all types of users for the following services, among many others:

➤ Email

➤ User and group scheduling

➤ Contacts

The Exchange Web client also offers browser access to collaborative information that is stored in Web Store folders. We take a look at this new feature in the following section.

Web Storage System

The Web Store is a platform that provides a single storage repository for organizing many types of information within one Exchange 2000 infrastructure. The Exchange 2000 Web Store merges the functionality of a file system with the technology of the Web to access and manage information via a single, URL-addressable, locality. The Web Store, which is part of Exchange Server, is a new technology that bolsters the opportunities for collaboration, business applications, and Web applications for your business. A chief element of the Web Store is the Exchange file system. The file system allows clients such as Microsoft Office to read and write documents or even store streaming audio and video. Another aspect of the Web Storage System is the native content store. This component stores data from non-MAPI clients in native MIME format. Another advantage is that Exchange folders and mailbox objects can now be accessed using simple URL addresses based on the folder name alone.

Next to the significance of Active Directory integration, the Web Storage System is likely the most visible enhancement of Exchange 2000. It is a big part of the Microsoft goal of unifying document storage in a Web-oriented concept. In essence, the Web Store is your "one-stop shop for document storage and collaboration" because users are now given the ability to use the Exchange Information Store as the single location for:

➤ Collecting and managing documents

➤ Managing messages and tasks

➤ Full-text searching and indexing of information

➤ Managing documents and versioning through Web-DAV

Additionally, the Web Storage System provides an advanced store for holding and managing email and other documents. It also gives you a platform for both Web and workflow applications, and supports Dynamic Hypertext Markup Language (DHTML) and Extensible Markup Language (XML) standard interfaces to link Exchange into your e-commerce and Internet infrastructures. Primarily through the seamless integration with applications such as Microsoft Office 2000, the Web Storage System collaboration and applications features will greatly increase knowledge worker productivity as well as create new opportunities for teamwork within an organization. The Web Store can be accessed using an email client such as Outlook, a browser, Office applications, or FrontPage Web sites, or even a wireless or handheld device for anytime-anywhere communications.

Microsoft Outlook Web Access

If you want a secure environment to access Exchange 2000 data using an Internet browser, such as Microsoft Internet Explorer, then Outlook Web Access is just for you. Provided you have the proper permissions, you can see and work with any public folder, mailbox, global address list, or calendar from a Unix, Macintosh, or Microsoft Windows-based computer connected to the server. Exchange 2000 includes this fresh Outlook Web Access technology for increased client and server performance and scalability.

Although the Outlook Web Access feature is designed to work best with Internet Explorer 5 (IE5), it does support earlier versions of Internet Explorer as well as some other browsers. Outlook Web Access uses DHTML and XML to offer these browsers full functionality for collaboration programs. IE5 users do benefit from an interface that is closer in design to the full version of Microsoft Outlook. IE5 users can also drag and drop messages between folders and use a folder tree to manage new folders. Additionally, IE5 provides rich-text editing features to add text formatting when creating a message. If you regularly send or receive messages containing embedded items (appointments, contacts, and so on), even better support is provided for Microsoft ActiveX objects. Also, you can now view and read messages in public folders that contain contact and calendar information. Another added bonus with Web Outlook Access is direct support for such multimedia messages as audio and video clips to be imported into a message and sent. Also, you can take advantage of named URLs to reference items.

Outlook Web Access, however, does have limitations. It wasn't intended to fulfill the advanced email and collaboration needs that are met by other Outlook products. In other words, Outlook Web Access *is not* a replacement for the full-featured Outlook Messaging Client for the 16-bit Windows operating system (or for Macintosh). For example, offline access is not provided; therefore, a user must connect to an Exchange server to view information. Outlook Web Access also does not support Microsoft Exchange Server digital encryption/signatures and S/MIME specifications. Additionally, Outlook Web Access does not contain replied and forwarded flags in list views, message flags and inbox rules, three-pane view, message searches, and integration with WordMail and Microsoft Office. Outlook Web Access does not offer views of discontinuous days side-by-side, appointment list, or details with "free" and "busy"; does not track acceptance of meeting attendees, all-day or multiple-day events, task lists, and task management; and does not export to devices such as Timex Data Link watches. Finally, Outlook Web Access does not provide support for Outlook 97 forms, nor does it synchronize local offline folders with server folders. This is quite a list of limitations, so be sure that you take all of these factors into consideration when you are evaluating Exchange 2000 component solutions for your messaging and collaborating architecture.

Web-DAV

Web-DAV is a set of HTTP extensions that allow Web browsers to communicate with Web servers. IE5 clients use this extended version of HTTP to incorporate all sorts of content to the Web into a more collaborative medium. You can use Web-DAV to cooperate with others on word processing documents, spreadsheets, or image files. You can potentially author almost anything that can be stored in a file by using the Web-DAV technology.

Web-DAV offers a diversity of outstanding attributes, such as overwrite protection, which is the key to its collaboration support concept. With file locking features, Web-DAV lets Web users manipulate and edit shared documents without the fear of overwriting another person's work, regardless of which software program or Internet service is being used. This concept is quite familiar to application developers who are used to open source development and version control systems such as Concurrent Version System (CVS). In addition, you can handle Internet files and directories more easily with the namespace management features of Web-DAV. This is similar to the way word processing files and directories are managed on a personal computer. The Properties feature of Web-DAV employs a well-organized method for storing and retrieving what is known as metadata. *Metadata* is information about a Web document, such as the author's name, copyright, publication date, and search keywords. Many Internet search engines commonly use metadata to find and retrieve relevant documents.

Get More Information on Web-DAV:

Web-DAV is defined in Request for Comments (RFC) 2518. You can find out more information on Web-DAV at **www.webdav.org**.

Realtime Collaboration

Realtime collaboration takes communication to a whole new level. This set of features provides new access from both Web browsers and telephony-based or handheld devices to provide for a total video, voice, and data conferencing solution. For anytime-anywhere communication, Exchange 2000 offers you enhanced access from the Web browser using the Outlook Web Access product. In addition, with the Exchange 2000 Conferencing Server, you get voice, data, and full video-conferencing along with instant messaging for a complete unified messaging platform. Exchange 2000 makes available IP-based multicast technology that is perfect for enterprise usage because it allows more simultaneous participants than practically any other solution.

Exchange Conferencing Server makes virtual meetings simple while reducing travel and improving remote office communications. Also, the unified messaging platform simplifies access to email and voice mail from any device. Microsoft Exchange 2000 Server also includes the following:

➤ *Chat*—Enhanced services for chat, a time-honored and widely used tool of the Internet, offer a low-overhead way to achieve realtime communication among the members of a group.

➤ *Presence Information*—The Presence Information technology lets you see if another computer user is currently logged on to a network, corporate LAN, or the Internet.

➤ *Instant Messaging*—Instant messaging (IM) increases the speed of collaboration, letting you (or your customer service representatives) and your customers use instantaneous messaging technology to greatly improve communication.

Instant Messaging Services

IM is built on secure standards-based architecture that is well suited for enterprise deployments and business-to-business communication across the Internet. The IM service is simply the ability to send an immediately posted, text-based message that obliges an immediate response from the receiver. The Presence Information mechanisms allow you to see when other people are online, out of the office, or not receiving calls. For example, suppose the members of your virtual Exchange deployment team are collaborating with each other to produce a single migration

plan for your large multinational corporation, and everyone urgently needs information delivered by IM. Or suppose that your cyber friends simply want to chat in
a live discussion without the overhead of sending cumbersome email messages. The
main dissimilarity between IM and email is that instant messages are not kept in
the Exchange 2000 Information Store. After the message disappears from the
interface, it is forever discarded.

The IM service is an extension of the MSN Messenger product. The client software for instant messaging in Exchange 2000 is called the MSN Messenger Service
instant messaging client. You can have IM start automatically as soon as you log on,
and you can even keep it open in the corner of your screen throughout the day.
While online, a status notification is sent to the IM server, which, in turn, passes
that information on to other members of the group (your "buddies" who are using
the Presence Information features of IM). This also allows a user logging on to the
network to rapidly get an idea of who else is online and track each team member's
communication status (Online, Busy, Be Right Back, Away, On The Phone, Out To
Lunch, or even Appear Offline). Microsoft has also recently released a new MSN
Explorer, which incorporates all of these technologies into an integrated Explorer
interface. Figure 1.8 gives you a glimpse of Microsoft's new MSN Explorer, which
offers many of these new features.

MSN Explorer

Microsoft's MSN Explorer is an all-in-one application that combines many new technologies into an Explorer
Web browser interface. It functions with your existing Internet connection. Get more information and download the tool from **explorermsn.com/jome.htm**.

Exchange Data Conferencing Services

The Exchange 2000 Data Conferencing Services give you the ability to host
virtual meetings and conferences with all the multimedia features available on the
client. This chat service is based on Internet Relay Chat (IRC) and has a scalability
up to 20,000 users on a single server. These components include the use of audio,
video, shared whiteboard, direct file transfer, and chat services. Of all the features
you've looked at in this chapter, this is by far the most sophisticated in terms of
functionality, deployment, and design. There are quite a few server-side conference
management and session coordination components that need to click on all
cylinders to make this possible. The Exchange 2000 Server performs as a full T.120
data conferencing server and is capable of supporting IP multicast audio and video
streams. The client, in turn, uses this T.120 data conferencing standard protocol,
which is integrated into such products as Microsoft NetMeeting. This allows the
client to communicate with the Conferencing Server, join conferences, and
interoperate with other T.120-based products and services.

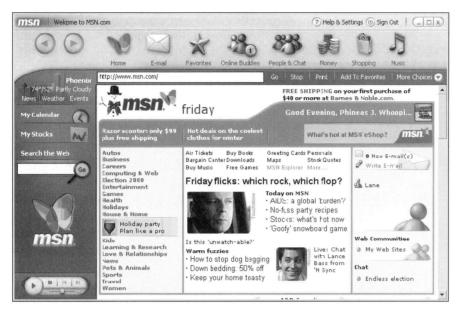

Figure 1.8   MSN Explorer, including Instant Messenger Chat and Media Player audio/video tools.

By integrating Outlook 2000 into your corporate solution, you can schedule online meetings and reserve resources, share applications, swap information through a shared clipboard, collaborate on a shared whiteboard, transfer files, and use a powerful text-based chat feature. By using the collaborative whiteboard tool, you can analyze, produce, and update object-oriented graphic information. You employ simple click-and-drag mouse techniques to control the content. You can also implement a remote pointer or highlighting tool to place focus on certain elements in the shared pages. The shared clipboard feature lets you exchange content with other participants in a conference with familiar cut, copy, and paste techniques. The File Transfer feature is fully compliant with the T.127 standard and enables you to send a file in the background to any conference participant. To do this, you simply drag a file into the main window and it is automatically sent to the conference attendees. They can then accept or decline the file. You can share a Windows-based application running your machine with other conference participants, who can, in turn, examine this same information and see the actions simultaneously while you work within the program. You may choose to collaborate with other conference participants, who can then alternate the roles of editor or director of the shared application. The beauty of all this is that only the person sharing the program has to have the application installed on his or her computer. Conference participants can use text-based chat to converse if there is no support for audio. Also, a "whisper" element allows for detached, private conversations with select individuals during a group chat session.

IP Multicast is the extension to IP that allows for proficient group communication in Exchange 2000. IP Multicast came from a need for a scalable, yet low-overhead answer to the issues related to realtime communications over a network. The IP Multicast conferencing model has the following characteristics:

➤ Routers make multicast infrastructure particulars transparent to the users.

➤ Members of a conference can be added or removed without large-scale coordination.

➤ The transport protocol for IP Multicast is Realtime Transport Protocol (RTP). This protocol offers a standard multimedia header providing timestamp, sequence numbering, and payload format information.

➤ No knowledge of the other users' addresses in a group is necessary for multicast communications. The data is sent to a single IP Multicast address ranging from 224.0.0.0 to 239.255.255.255.

➤ Users make their interest in a particular IP Multicast address known through a router that is configured to handle multicast communication.

Chapter Summary

This chapter presented a grand tour of the many powerful features and messaging and collaboration capabilities of Exchange 2000. The remainder of this book not only prepares you for the Microsoft 70-225 exam, but, more important, it helps you to conquer the challenges that your business or organization will be facing in your Exchange deployment. As an information technology (IT) professional or business manager, you will find Exchange 2000 to be a powerful solution for the messaging and collaboration needs of the present and future. The business challenges are clear. The challenging pace of change for businesses has increased almost exponentially. Looking across a wide selection of industries, you will find that operations costs are rising while talented people are becoming increasingly more difficult to find and hire. The emergence of a "Web lifestyle" is changing many aspects of e-commerce and communication. Along with this phenomenon, people within an organization need tools to help them manage information more clearly, easily, and efficiently. In our global society and multinational economic explosion, more and more companies must do business on a 24-hour timetable as they face nontraditional competitors. Many companies have turned to outsourcing as a way to lower costs and increase functionality. At the same time, they are seeing increased sophistication among their customer and partner bases, and they need to manage the supply chain more effectively.

Exchange 2000 provides many key benefits to help confront and overcome these challenges to your particular business. As we have seen already, many of the features of Exchange 2000 can help reduce costs, meet the technological advances of the future, and drive new products to market more quickly and efficiently. This chapter has presented an overview of some new opportunities for collaboration—within your company, between your company and your vendors, and between your company and your customers. With Exchange 2000, you can streamline business processes in a very secure way through integration with Windows 2000 Active Directory. You can increase customer communication, customer service, and customer retention. Overall, Exchange 2000 lets you embrace innovation while you increase the productivity of the workers at your organization. With Exchange 2000, the business Internet begins here. It is now time to begin your journey into the design and deployment of Exchange 2000 Server.

Review Questions

1. Microsoft Exchange 2000 Server has three different versions. Which of the following products belong to the Exchange 2000 family? [Check all correct answers]
   a. Exchange 2000 Server
   b. Exchange 2000 Datacenter Server
   c. Exchange 2000 Enterprise Server
   d. Exchange 2000 Conferencing Server
   e. Exchange 2000 Instant Messaging Server

2. Which version of Exchange 2000 is best suited for data, voice, and videoconferencing solutions across both the intranet and the Internet?
   a. Exchange 2000 Server
   b. Exchange 2000 Datacenter Server
   c. Exchange 2000 Enterprise Server
   d. Exchange 2000 Conferencing Server
   e. Exchange 2000 Instant Messaging Server

3. By integrating with Windows 2000, Exchange offers a high degree of security through the use of which of the following?
   a. MAPI driver architecture
   b. X.400 compatibility
   c. Access Control Lists (ACL)
   d. Collaboration Data Objects (CDO)

4. What would you use to manage your Exchange Server 5.5 from Exchange 2000?

   a. Active Directory Communicator

   b. Active Directory Installation Wizard

   c. Microsoft Management Console

   d. Active Directory Connector

5. Which text file format allows you to perform a bulk import/export from Active Directory?

   a. LDAP

   b. LDIF

   c. MIME

   d. SLIP

6. Which of the following statements is false concerning the multiple database capabilities of Exchange 2000 Server?

   a. Exchange 2000 provides a method for the message store to be placed into separate databases.

   b. Components for backup and restore are provided in the system.

   c. Individual mailboxes and public folders cannot be specifically recovered.

   d. The entire Exchange service can still be administered as a single data store.

   e. Exchange can be distributed among several servers by using clustering technology.

7. Which of the following are advantages of storage groups?

   a. A single server can host 15 storage groups of 6 databases each for a total of 90.

   b. Administrators can recover one storage group without affecting the others in any way.

   c. Exchange 2000 storage groups offer support for simultaneous backups.

   d. Administrators can back up an entire storage group so that only one copy of the system transaction log needs to be written to tape.

   e. a, b, and d

   f. a, b, c, and d

8. Two servers work together side by side to actively process messaging requests until a failure occurs that triggers the rollover recovery mode. What is this feature of Exchange 2000 called?

    a. Active/passive clustering

    b. Passive/passive clustering

    c. Passive/active clustering

    d. Active/active clustering

9. The monitoring infrastructure and user interface for system monitoring in Exchange 2000 is built on which one of the following architectures?

    a. Windows Management Instrumentation

    b. Microsoft Management Instrumentation

    c. Windows Management Console

    d. Performance Monitor Interface

10. In Exchange 2000, users have the ability to use the Exchange Information Web Store as the single location for managing documents and versioning through which specification?

    a. TAPI

    b. Web-DAV

    c. OWA

    d. Storage groups

11. Which of the following file extensions represent document types that can be searched through the Exchange 2000 full-text indexing feature? [Check all correct answers]

    a. .xls

    b. .asp

    c. .bin

    d. .txt

    e. .eml

    f. .pdf

    g. a, d, and f only

    h. All the above

12. Which database component does Exchange 2000 use to establish the costs of the connections between two routing groups to determine the most efficient route for a message?

    a. SMTP log

    b. ADC connector

    c. Gateway

    d. Link state table

    e. IMAP

13. You have been tasked with leading the security design team for your Exchange 2000 migration. Your organization needs a security design framework that includes open standards that assure secure, private communications over IP networks employing cryptographic security services at the IP transport layer (layer 3) of the TCP/IP protocol stack. Which one of the following solutions would you choose?

    a. KCC

    b. Certificate services

    c. IPSec

    d. TCP/IP filtering

    e. MS-CHAP

14. You are looking for an advanced store that provides a platform for Web and workflow applications and that supports DHTML and XML standard interfaces to link Exchange into your e-commerce and Internet infrastructure. Which of the following would provide these solutions?

    a. Administrative store

    b. IP Multicast

    c. Information Store

    d. Web–DAV

    e. Web Storage System

15. The Exchange 2000 Data Conferencing Services gives you the ability to host virtual meetings and conferences with all the multimedia features available on the client. The Exchange 2000 Server performs as a full data conferencing server and is capable of supporting IP multicast audio and video streams. The client also uses the same data conferencing standard protocol, which is integrated into products such as Microsoft NetMeeting. Which protocol is used as the Exchange 2000 client and server?

    a. T.127

    b. X.400

    c. S/MIME

    d. T.120

    e. X.500

Real-World Project

Project 1.1

You have been tasked with analyzing the future messaging and collaboration requirements at your medium-sized multimedia development firm. Your organization of fewer than 400 employees is presently using Exchange 5.5 for its messaging needs and is not planning to have substantial personnel growth for the next two years. However, you are evaluating whether the new features of Exchange 2000 will justify a migration from the older Exchange implementation. Because the responsibility for selling this possible migration plan to upper management will be the sole responsibility of you and your team, you want to make certain that you understand all of your options.

Review this chapter and other available resources and list in a spreadsheet all of the new features and components of Exchange 2000 that you can identify. Save this spreadsheet in a properly named folder so you can access it for use in future projects in the remaining chapters of this book.

CHAPTER TWO

Analyzing Organizational Requirements for Exchange 2000 Server

After completing this chapter, you will be able to:

✓ Understand the importance of the four-phase model used with the Microsoft Solutions Framework Infrastructure Deployment Process

✓ Determine your organizational model

✓ Analyze the existing and planned business model of a company

In Chapter 1, you evaluated some of the new enhancements of Exchange 2000 Server. Now you can begin to develop a comprehensive implementation plan for Microsoft Exchange 2000 Server. A main concern should be to devise an overall strategy of design and integration based on an organizational and business model. You should first assess the integration challenges that are indicative of your type of organization and attempt to predict, as well as possible, the effects of such factors as corporate politics, organizational structure, geographic location, and the overall business environment.

Because the capabilities of Exchange 2000 go far beyond simple messaging, recognition of the factors that influence organizational policy is extremely important. A wide range of events or factors can characterize business environments and organizational policy. You need to consider the reality or possibility of dynamic events such as the formation of strategic alliances, corporate reengineering or downsizing, buyouts, planned mergers and/or acquisitions, and corporate takeovers. The factors may include any economic factors, as well as the existing and planned human resources model. Other possibilities, such as governmental legislation and regulation, can also affect the business model. Continuous pressures from competitors and the demands of customers will also drastically affect the business model of an organization. As an information technology (IT) professional, you also need to appraise the existing and planned business models as they relate to the distribution of users, individual user mail needs and desires, and the collaboration habits and future plans of individuals and teams within the organization.

As the economy becomes more globally oriented and technologically advanced, you may encounter additional demands from the increasingly diverse and complex offering of products and services, shorter production cycles, and complex cultural issues. Executives and managers operate under these pressures on a daily basis, and the IT specialist must also appreciate these and other factors, because he or she needs to analyze the way in which demands relate to the deployment of an Exchange 2000 messaging and collaboration solution.

You have already reviewed some of the most important new features of Exchange 2000 in Chapter 1. Now you can begin to put together the puzzle based on organizational and business factors. You should realize that, from the perspective of enterprise management, your organization may need to incorporate as much as a five-year plan for porting the infrastructure, procedures, and processes of a monolithic, single-vendor environment to a new Windows 2000 domain using the Exchange 2000-based client-server architecture. One of the first tools to look at to help build a deployment plan is the Microsoft Solutions Framework (MSF).

Microsoft Solutions Framework

Many organizations have historically deployed Exchange 5.5 to provide solutions for their messaging needs. Many of these same organizations, however, are seeing the uses of messaging evolve dramatically, changing the way in which they conduct corporate communications. They still need a system that will not only operate with the same or fewer human resources, but also cost less to sustain and manage. Messaging systems are at the heart of this revolution, and they are now being used in many different ways, with new collaboration technologies that seem to emerge on an almost weekly basis. Dealing with the changing requirements of business-critical processes means that messaging and collaboration systems need to be enhanced in functionality and capacity. This prerequisite, in combination with the ongoing need to reduce total cost of ownership, means that you need to design a messaging solution that includes the new capabilities of Exchange 2000 that can best help your particular organization.

Microsoft has taken great strides to systematically gather information from customers, partners, IT organizations, product managers, and consultants to generate data for detailed analysis. These statistics are organized into practical models and distributed as the Microsoft Solutions Framework. MSF is one of three Enterprise Services frameworks that are focused at separate, but integral, phases in the life cycle of developing first-rate information technology systems on the enterprise. Through specialization, each framework model can deliver practical and thorough data on the people, procedures, and expertise required for the success of each phase. MSF delivers support for the several phases of a project life cycle. This information comes in the form of deployment guides, white papers, case studies, and supplementary courseware in the following areas:

➤ Enterprise architecture

➤ Rapid application development

➤ Component planning

➤ Infrastructure deployment

When preparing for any large deployment project, you can easily become besieged by details. It's best to divide the project into phases to help keep the team organized and make it easier to gauge development. Taking this phased approach to an Exchange 2000 rollout drastically reduces risk and increases the chances for success by making sure that crucial tasks are done in a logical order. Each phase of your deployment project should have understandable goals that permit you to advance to the next phase of the project once the present phase is finished and reviewed. The following list presents a brief overview of the four-phase model used with the MSF Infrastructure Deployment Process (see Figure 2.1):

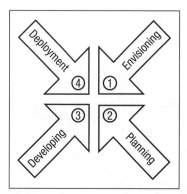

Figure 2.1   The four-phase MSF Infrastructure Deployment Process.

➤ *Phase 1: Envisioning*—The Envisioning phase, also called the Scope phase, is a "big picture" of the business decision to migrate to Exchange 2000. This overview can cover issues such as goal setting, plan execution, project justification and risk assessment, creation of the project team, and executive sponsorship. You will need this to create a vision to help overcome executive and user resistance to change. Spending the right amount of time early on to lay out the scope of the mission will help you to communicate what will actually be necessary from all parties involved to reach your goals. This Statement of Work document is usually delivered in several parts, including, for example:

    ➤ A problem statement, which details your organization's needs for change

    ➤ A vision statement, which itemizes the perceived results and benefits

    ➤ A scope document, which covers issues such as customer service; impact on IT personnel and on the sales, marketing, and operations departments; effect on executives; impact on the budget; and other issues specific to your organization in general

➤ *Phase 2: Planning*—The Planning phase entails the precise explanation of the boundaries of the overall vision and what is to be included in the particular Exchange 2000 project. From a design point of view, you generate comprehensive provisions for deployment in the shape of a functional specification. In addition, you establish a detailed Master Project Plan and Master Project Schedule to help you complete the project on time and within budget. Planning issues can include building the business case, specifying timing of the deployment, dealing with budgetary constraints, winning the cooperation and excitement of users, preparing service level agreements (SLAs) that you plan to offer, and determining the final results you hope to achieve. This planning or implementation phase can best be compared to preparing the business plan that you would submit to a venture capital group.

➤ *Phase 3: Developing*—In the Developing phase, you build the final system by implementing the design and planning information compiled in Phase 2. You finalize and tune systems in pilot projects, and create deployment plans. It involves coordinating the processes for installing and configuring Exchange 2000 Server, including testing of scenarios and custom applications. It is in this phase that you begin to nurture those relationships with departments and managerial/supervisory staff to assess needs and perceptions. You will need to take inventory of systems, hardware, and software to effectively deploy the Exchange 2000 product and related services. You should create processes for open communication with users during this phase to overcome conflict or apprehension. After you have gathered all of the information you can during the Planning and Developing stages, the proof of concept subphase will entail the actual testing of all the organizational and physical facets of the migration and deployment development plan. The process should include proving viability for coexistence, assimilation, and deployment in a situation that closely resembles the final outcome. The final step in the Developing phase is to launch a pilot program that outlines and implements the entire scheme on a particular subset group of users.

➤ *Phase 4: Deployment*—You take the project from the pilot stages of the last phase to full production status in the Deployment phase. You will produce an exhaustive schedule for the product rollout as well as generate the logistics plan for the deployment to users' desktops. After the deployment of Exchange 2000, you will generate an assessment of the implementation process, including any changes necessary for future development and challenges encountered that can be prevented in the next deployment, as well as concerns for application development and new technologies available in Exchange 2000.

Two additional frameworks are the Microsoft Readiness Framework (MRF) and the Microsoft Operations Framework (MOF). MRF represents the "prepare" phase within the IT life cycle. MOF offers established practice, direction, and real-world solutions that enable you to assure the solid performance of your customers and partners for technological ideas on the Exchange platform.

MRF facilitates IT groups and business associates in the recognition and growth of organizational preparedness needed to implement these up-to-the-minute technologies into their business situation. MRF provides an ordered methodology to consistently and proficiently evaluate the organizational readiness needed to successfully plan, construct, and administer information technology solutions on the Microsoft design. You will also use MRF to assure that your organization has the means to take on the level of change necessary for full-scale deployment and migration of a messaging and collaboration initiative. The framework provides several kits that will help your organization meet the requirements of capacity planning, organizational fitness, and individual and organizational evaluations, as well as suggestions for how you can utilize available learning plans and training materials to develop and maintain the organization's IT potential.

MOF provides the complete technical expertise necessary to accomplish mission-critical system reliability, availability, and manageability on Microsoft's products and technologies. This assistance is delivered via white papers, various support tools and preparation guides, best practices, and documented case studies. A graphic of how all of these components work together is shown in Figure 2.2.

Microsoft Solutions Framework

You can find much more comprehensive information on these frameworks at **www.microsoft.com/msf**.

Determining the Organizational Model

Now that you understand the purpose of the Microsoft Solutions Framework, and if you have downloaded the free documents from the Microsoft MSF Web site, you can begin the process of determining the scope of your organization and planning for an Exchange 2000 Server solution. Your next major goal is to identify your company with a particular "type" and look at some of the characteristics and requirements of each organizational type. This is an important exercise because the specifications and acronyms used for categorizing organizational types are used broadly in all forms of industry documentation.

Global Headquarters

A *global headquarters* (GHQ) is simply an office that represents the central core of any global organization. It may be the only location for the organization, or there may be connections over a public or private network from this headquarters to

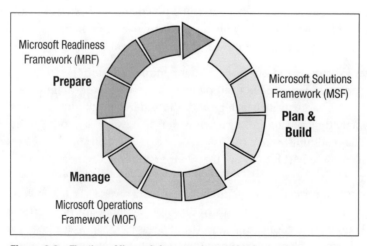

Figure 2.2   The three Microsoft frameworks working in concert.

other branch offices. A GHQ may simply be a large holding company. A GHQ will most likely deploy multiple Exchange servers to accommodate mailboxes, public folders, and connectors (i.e., site connectors, Internet mail connectors, or other messaging systems connectors). We explore connector design in greater detail later in Chapter 10.

A GHQ is an excellent candidate for server consolidation. If you decide to combine the mailbox servers alone, you can reduce the number of servers by more than half. The logical first goal for deploying Exchange in your headquarters site would be to determine how you want your services consolidated. For example, you may decide to merge and replicate multiple public folder servers, each hosting parts of the public folder hierarchy to ensure redundancy. You can then add mailboxes into separate databases on these servers. If you have Internet connectors or Exchange site connectors, you can upgrade these servers and then add mailboxes to them— again using separate databases for the mailboxes. An example of GHQ is shown in Figure 2.3.

Large International Conglomerate

A *large international conglomerate* (LIC) is made up of an organization that is spread over a large geographic area and is often a combination of several smaller but independently recognizable companies. Each business is individually administered and has its own arrangement of regional offices and branch offices located internationally. An LIC typically has a total combined number of employees in excess of 20,000. Each constituent organization is network connected to its own branch office by various wide area network (WAN) links, (Integrated Services Digital Network [ISDN], dial-on-demand, X.25 to T1 with T3, or asynchronous transfer mode [ATM] links) that link the corporate headquarters. Examples of LICs include Fujitsu, Boeing, and Merrill Lynch.

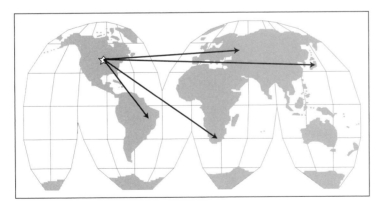

Figure 2.3   A global headquarters.

Large Multinational Organization

A *large multinational organization* (LMO) consists of a central organization with a considerable global presence. This type of organization may have a large corporate headquarters with international regional offices and national branch offices. An LMO has a more centralized administrative structure than an LIC, but the larger branch offices usually have their own dedicated IT departments. The regional and branch offices are joined to the headquarters by a network of various WAN links, from asynchronous dial-up to T1 or possibly T3 links, and usually have a workforce of more than 10,000. Examples of LMOs include Microsoft and Compaq.

Large National Organization

A *large national organization* (LNO) consists of a central headquarters with a network of branch offices throughout a country but without any significant overseas presence. The company consists of a headquarters with a network of small, medium, and large branch offices, with possibly a couple of larger regional offices. With a workforce of 5,000 or more, the various components of the company are connected via various types of WAN links, from asynchronous dial-up to a T1. An example of LNO is shown in Figure 2.4.

Medium National Organization

A *medium national organization* (MNO) is comparable to the makeup of the LNO and has a regional to national range of operations. The MNO typically has a system of small to medium branch offices. Administrative management can be somewhat centralized to heavily centralized, and the branch offices are generally not large enough to have a dedicated IT workforce. Characteristically, with 1,000 employees or more, the different parts of the organization are connected through WAN links, just as in an LNO. Good examples of MNOs include local governments, municipalities, and large universities.

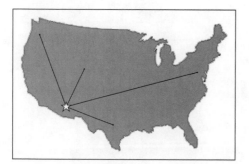

Figure 2.4   A large national organization.

Smaller National Organization

A *smaller national organization* (SNO) is a company that resides in a single country or region with small to medium branch offices that have no local IT support department. A headquarters will usually be in command of the administrative aspects in support of the branch offices. Employees, numbering from 500 up, are typically connected with dial-on-demand or dial-up, although WAN links of up to 64Kbps leased lines are becoming more common as their prices fall.

Small Autonomous Organization

A *small autonomous organization* (SAO) resides in a single locality and has no branch offices. The administrative management is totally centralized or often outsourced to another vendor. The workforce is generally made up of 50 or more employees. Apart from the number of employees, the SAO is the same as the single location organization (SLO), described next. Network connectivity for a SAO is usually some level of ISDN dial-up to a T1 connection on a WAN, depending on the size of the organization. SAOs with fewer than 50 people in the workforce may want to follow Microsoft's recommendation and consider putting Exchange 2000 into operation as part of a Small Business Server (SBS) solution.

Small Business Server

For more information on implementing Exchange 2000 as part of Small Business Server, go to **www.microsoft.com/observer/**.

Single Location Organization

The *single location organization* (SLO) is like the SAO in that all company resources and employees are located in one geographic location. The organization itself can be almost any size, from 50 employees on up, but usually the SLO is smaller than the SAO. Staffing numbers will affect the number of Exchange servers needed. The WAN links are likely going to be to the Internet for Simple Mail Transfer Protocol (SMTP) mail, client access, and possibly newsgroups. Examples of SAOs and SLOs include call centers and Internet start-up companies.

Branch Offices

The following various types of branch offices relate to the preceding organization definitions. A branch office can vary from a group of people set up in a garage to the regional headquarters of a multinational corporation.

Regional Branch Office

Regional branch offices (RBOs) are normally the national headquarters of an LMO or the center of operations of a subsidiary of an LIC. RBOs may use localized versions of Exchange 2000 Server and client software, and they generally have a high level of self-sufficiency, taking charge of their own administration and maintenance. Personnel at RBOs usually vary from 50 to 1,000 workers. RBOs frequently include leased-line connections to the GHQ as well as to the other RBOs of up to T3 or ATM speed. An RBO may also have its own network of branch offices, deploying WAN links of 64 Kbps or higher. An RBO will often perform as a hub within its own region by means of a backbone link to the GHQ as well as to the other RBOs.

If the other branch offices do not have their own local Exchange servers, then a particular RBO should be treated like a large branch office (described next). You would deploy multiple servers at a RBO because it is going to host not only the mailboxes for local users, but also the connectors for down-level offices. These connector servers, however, may be so overwhelmed with messaging traffic to the other offices that you may not want to include the load of the local mailboxes on the server. For performance reasons, you may consider consolidating the mailboxes and even the local public folder replicas and leaving the connector servers with their existing configuration.

Large Branch Office

A *large branch office* (LBO) more often than not will consist of about 20 to 50 people in the workforce using a multiple Windows NT or Windows 2000 server design. An LBO does not normally have any branches under it because this would technically qualify it as an RBO. An LBO can actually be thought of as an RBO without down-level offices. It is directly linked to the GHQ or to an RBO, and on the whole offers services just for its own users. An LBO will probably deploy a separate Exchange 2000 Server for messaging and collaboration. It is probable, however, that this same Exchange Server will also be providing file and print or other network services. Sometimes an LBO will have a small local administrative or IT support department.

In an LBO, you would probably use several mailbox servers, perhaps a public folder server, and generally one connector server. If you plan to deploy redundant connectors, then you need two connector servers. Server consolidation strategies in this office will most likely consist of mailbox server consolidation, which may later include all or some of the other services being combined. The LBO may or may not be its own Exchange site, and is typically connected to either the RBOs or to a GHQ on a WAN utilizing ISDN, an Asymmetric Digital Subscriber Line (ADSL), or a leased-line up to a T1 link.

Medium Branch Office

A *medium branch office* (MBO) has no down-level connections, similar to an LBO, and is often linked to either the GHQ or an RBO. The number of users in the MBO is generally considerably smaller than that in an LBO. The MBO characteristically comprises 5 to 20 people, implementing one or two servers. The servers will be multipurpose in the roles they carry out, one of which will be the Exchange 2000 Server function. Connections to the GHQ or an RBO are usually by way of an asynchronous dial-up, ISDN, or ADSL. MBOs rarely have the luxury of a T1 connection.

Your Exchange design in an MBO is normally one or more servers. If you already have two servers in your office, you may want to consider consolidating them into a single server that could also serve as the Windows 2000 domain controller for the office. You will clearly not be able to consolidate the single server office unless you put other services onto the Exchange 2000 Server.

Small Branch Office

The single server in a *small branch office* (SBO) performs multiple roles and, depending on the WAN connectivity, may not even include Exchange 2000 Server. An SBO is one step down from an MBO, and because it generally has a staff of only two to five people, the SBO will not usually represent a considerable piece of the Exchange 2000 design. Although no consolidation issues and few services are offered locally, considerations relate to possible hurdles for client access through the asynchronous dial-up or possible ISDN link to the GHQ or to an RBO.

Special Situation Scenarios

Unique situations can occur in your organization that will place you in the category of a special situation scenario. The following scenarios may be relevant to any of the aforementioned types of companies. Your organization can actually fall into more than one special category; for example, an organization can be telecommuter friendly and security sensitive.

Collaborating Organizations

Collaborating organizations (COs) come about when two or more main company types work jointly on the same venture (see Figure 2.5). You may be trying to coordinate two mail systems with a CO, so compatibility issues may quickly arise. From an administrative standpoint, the companies are totally separate and autonomous; therefore, a concern is that if both of the companies are using Exchange 2000 Server, there will be at least two Active Directory forests.

A *peer-to-peer network* (PPN) is also a smaller variation of a CO. With a PPN, a number of smaller organizations work collectively without any controlling company. This situation is frequently found between SLOs, although the organizational size and type can be any of the main types mentioned previously.

Figure 2.5 Collaborating organizations work jointly on the same venture.

Planning Expansion Organizations

Organizations that are planning for sudden growth due to a company takeover or merger in the near term are referred to as planning expansion (PE) types. If the merging companies are on an equal footing, you may actually find yourself in the *multiple headquarters* (MH) scenario discussed in the following paragraph. If the companies are not equal partners, you will probably end up with a GHQ and a new LBO or RBO. In a PE organization, the chief messaging concerns are coexistence and upgrading or migration. If both entities are running Exchange 2000 on Windows 2000, then this particular setting will involve extraordinary awareness of the processes involved with integrating the Active Directories of the two companies. Considerations also include whether you should proceed as two distinctive operations, with separate directory spaces and Exchange implementations, or if instead you should merge the directories as well as administrative duties.

Multiple Headquarters

An MH scenario is the direct result of a successful merger of two or more organizations of equal size that results in the formation of separate components within the new organization. Each entity may have a main headquarters campus with its own corporate identity, operating procedures, and staff for IT support. They may also have diverse, and even incompatible, messaging systems, and may be running Windows 2000 with Exchange in two separate forests.

Security-Sensitive Organizations

An example of a *security-sensitive* (SS) company would be a military research-and-development (R&D) firm or an organization such as a biotech or pharmaceutical company that is involved in expensive R&D. SS organizations need to employ techniques such as digital signing of transmissions to protect the data they send over the network. Other precautions may include the encryption of message contents and verification of the identity of a sender.

Telecommuter Friendly Organizations

The *telecommuter friendly* (TF) organization has a considerable portion of its workforce accessing content over a Remote Access Service (RAS) or dial-up networking system from their homes or other remote locations. This type of company is not restricted by size and structure but is normally an SS company. It will most likely encompass supporting an asynchronous or ISDN RAS, or direct

RAS connections over ADSL with Point-to-Point Tunneling Protocol or layer 2 Tunneling Protocol using Internet Protocol Security (IPSec) encryption. TF businesses may also consider deploying Microsoft Outlook Web Access, Post Office Protocol 3 (POP3), Internet Message Access Protocol 4 (IMAP4), and Network News Transfer Protocol (NNTP) access for their clients.

Analyzing the Existing and Planned Business Model

One of the first questions you need to ask when developing a comprehensive profile of your organization or business model is "What is our organizational structure?" In the previous sections, you should have determined the general type of organization with which you are dealing. In this section, we continue to build our profile of the business as it relates to Exchange 2000. You can use tools that Microsoft offers to make this analysis or you can simply document your answers to these questions and build your own report. Either way, the issues remain the same.

The IT business model of a company is the logical configuration of IT management in the company. The three general categories of business models are centralized, decentralized, and outsourced.

A *centralized business model* typically has a single point of management or administration in control of all of the business units. In a centralized IT business model, the systems administrator requires administrative privileges so that he or she has full access to all the files and resources on the network. The systems administrators of the branch offices, who report to the main systems administrator, should also have access, but it should be limited. The groups and policies should be designed after analyzing the IT business model and the user's interaction within the company. Plus Ultra Group, Inc. has a centralized IT business model, with a chief systems administrator at its head office who is responsible for the entire organization.

In contrast, the *decentralized business model* employs separate managers for the different business units of the organization. For example, there may be systems administrators for marketing, finance, human resources, and development. Therefore, its structure will have to be designed so that each systems administrator has full access to the resources of their own unit, but limited access to the resources of the other units.

The *outsourced IT business model* relies on an outside group for IT management. Systems administrators who are not employees of the company will design and maintain the network. In such a model, external systems administrators will also design the Exchange 2000 structure. In an outsourced IT business model, the structure must be planned so that users are able to access the necessary network resources, but only external systems administrators can manage the network.

A company such as Plus Ultra Group is involved in the IT-intensive business of software development, in which the day-to-day business is completely IT-dependent. This company, therefore, requires proficient data exchange between different sites, and the implementation of an efficient Exchange/Active Directory Services (ADS) design. If your company is involved in a non–IT-related business, such as manufacturing sporting goods, in which IT may be used only for specific purposes such as accounting and transaction processing, your company may not require such an efficient Exchange/ADS design.

The next logical step in this process is to identify the different business units that make up your company. Is your organization structured according to differing products or services? Perhaps your company is partitioned based on geographic location or by department. You need to define the business units of your company. Which of these business units share resources and, when they do, what kind of resources do they share? Next, you want to determine which group of individuals provides the present infrastructure for sharing resources—in other words, how does your organization make decisions related to information technology? Are there any elements within your organization that depend heavily on outsourcing or contracting and are likely to turn out a considerable amount of email traffic? Isolate any other relationships in the organization that may also result in message flows.

Understanding the Current Implementation

By asking a few of the right questions and building a team of people who can provide the answers to these questions, you will be much more successful in truly understanding the existing business model of your organization. After all, your Exchange implementation will most likely be defined by the organization, not vice versa. A major factor in answering these questions and getting a finger on the pulse of the organization will be to define the teams and team members who will be instrumental on this rollout.

Some possible roles that participating individuals can assume in your deployment include:

➤ Administrator for the real-time collaboration/chat tools

➤ Browser integration administrator

➤ Database server administrator

➤ Deployment administrator

➤ Desktop administrator

➤ Developer

➤ End-user training team

➤ Enterprise administrator

➤ Help Desk coordinator

➤ Infrastructure administrator

➤ Internet administrator

➤ Intranet administrator

➤ Logistics manager

➤ Messaging administrator

➤ Network administrator

➤ Operations manager

➤ Project manager

➤ Quality assurance team

➤ Site administrator

➤ Technical design architect

➤ Technical support manager

You have now developed a big picture of your organization for your deployment as well as isolated some of the key individuals and teams to help accomplish the vision and planning. You should have a general idea of the organizational layout of your company and the core knowledge workers to assemble your data. This input will be used to completely define the existing and planned business model so you can better determine how Exchange 2000 with ADS integration will fit into your overall business design. You must analyze every detail of the business to obtain a detailed understanding of the requirements and processes of the organization.

First, you must consider the core competency of your company while preparing for an Exchange 2000 deployment. The core competency of a company is that area of business in which the company specializes—in other words, the main ingredient that gives your company a potential edge over other competing organizations. For example, the core competency of Plus Ultra Group is to provide solutions for Microsoft technologies, which involves the development of software.

Before designing the Exchange 2000 ADS structure for your company, reflect on the strengths and weaknesses of your organization. You should design your system so that it enhances the strengths of your company and diminishes any weaknesses. Plus Ultra Group concentrates its business on delivering bug-free software solutions; however, it is inefficient in the management of network resources. Therefore, this issue must be addressed before the deployment of Exchange 2000 goes forward.

The Business Infrastructure

Thus far, you have identified the core competency of your organization as well as observed the strengths and weaknesses inherent in the business design. You have analyzed the logical configuration of IT management in the company and chosen among the three general categories of business models: centralized, decentralized, and outsourced. You also realize that there are many economic considerations that will need to be made. For the effective implementation of Exchange 2000 as a new technology, you now need to further analyze the current business infrastructure of your organization.

The business infrastructure elements can be categorized as follows:

➤ Organizational structure

➤ Current and future geographical scope

➤ Information flow

Organizational Structure

We have already covered in great detail the techniques for discovering the organization type of your company as well as the characteristics and requirements of each organizational type. Examining the organizational structure includes analyzing partnerships, joint ventures, and subsidiaries of an organization, as well as their relationships with the parent organization. For example, an analysis of the relationship between Plus Ultra Group and its partners will help to determine whether to create a single- or a multiple-forest environment and site placement for the Exchange 2000 design.

Geographical Scope

The next element of the analysis of the business infrastructure is to define the current geographical scope or geographical presence of an organization. For example, the current geographical scope of Plus Ultra Group includes the headquarters in Phoenix, a sales office in Austin, and the upcoming branch offices in Las Vegas and Albuquerque. Your analysis of the geographical scope of an organization provides an insight into the number of Active Directory forests and domains you need to create. It also assists you in planning your Exchange database and administrative solutions. The future geographical scope refers to the expansion plans of an organization, including new offices and future acquisitions and mergers. For example, Plus Ultra Group plans to set up two new offices in Las Vegas and Albuquerque. In addition, Plus Ultra Group is in the process of negotiating a merger with Carefree Studios to acquire its multimedia design services. This will also affect the overall business design. Analyzing the future geographical scope of the business allows you to plan now for the modifications you will need to make to the Exchange 2000 structure in the future.

Information Flow

An analysis of the flow of information within your organization is useful in determining the design of Exchange 2000. The flow of electronic mail that already exists among workgroups or business units of an organization usually follows measurable communication patterns. The *80-20 rule* can be applied to get a general feel for this flow. This rule states that 80 percent of communication stays within an individual's workgroup, and the remaining 20 percent flows outside of the unit or workgroup.

Make a preliminary measurement of the present architecture that includes the most significant aspects and the probable changes to your existing messaging implementation, keeping the 80-20 rule in mind. This assessment will allow you to prioritize the deployment of the particular components of Exchange 2000. By collecting data about your current implementation, you will be providing yourself and other team members with important knowledge of the changes that will need to be made for the Exchange upgrade. One of the first discoveries to make to help you understand how the messaging system can take advantage of the new capabilities in Exchange 2000 is to determine what applications have already been deployed within the messaging infrastructure. You also need to be assured that the legacy applications will run under Exchange 2000. Where are the servers located, and what responsibilities do those servers presently carry out in the design? Another key ingredient of this assessment is finding out from each business unit all of the known trouble spots and issues with the current messaging implementation that need to be resolved. Next, make a comprehensive list of all of the business-related tasks that the present solutions help to perform and how messaging will connect to the strategic corporate objectives. What business role should the messaging infrastructure facilitate in the future, and are the current growth and troubleshooting processes adequate? Also, how is the current enterprise administered, and who is managing it?

Determining Strategic Business Objectives

Every organization needs to set specific goals to be successful and/or profitable. To accomplish these directives, your organization will need to pursue a detailed business strategy. The four main factors that influence the business strategy of an organization are:

➤ Organizational priorities

➤ Growth strategy

➤ Risk assessment

➤ Total cost of ownership

Organizational Priorities

You need to consider the priorities of your organization to arrive at an effective business strategy. The core competencies of your organization, as mentioned earlier, are a key component of these priorities. Priorities, however, may not always be the same as the core competencies of an organization. Priorities can also include the future vision for the organization, such as providing better customer service or increasing employee satisfaction. Once you have determined the existing priorities and requirements, you can use Exchange 2000 to find new ways to meet and possibly even improve these organizational goals. For example, email has revolutionized the approach that organizations take toward communication and is presently considered a vital component by most organizations. Therefore, a company's organizational priorities will define their corporate standards for email usage. Organizational requirements and priorities may often include issues such as the legal ramifications of email retention and proper email use.

Growth Strategy

Next, you need to consider the potential for growth in your organization when determining its business strategy. The growth strategy of an organization involves isolating the future trends of your business sector and how your company will react to these trends. For example, Plus Ultra Group has a growth strategy that involves providing effective e-commerce solutions to customers in Mexico and South America in response to global technological trends. In addition, Plus Ultra Group plans to add a new business unit to expand its business into in-house manufacturing of CD-ROMs (compact disc–read only memory) and DVDs (digital versatile discs). This unit will need to be incorporated into the business design for an effective Exchange 2000 structure. Some of the important growth-planning questions that you should gather include:

➤ Is the company currently involved in mergers or acquisitions?

➤ Will the current base of users remain constant or will it increase or decrease?

➤ Will growth be at a single location or dispersed across the organization?

➤ Will the company add any new locations within the next year?

➤ Is the company planning to deploy new technologies, such as instant messaging (IM), online conferencing, chat services, or unified messaging?

Risk Assessment

A key aspect of creating your overall vision of Exchange 2000 is risk assessment. After reviewing the many advantages and technological features of Exchange for your enterprise, you will need to step away from the hype and assess the possible problem areas that may surface during your deployment project. You must then go a step further and develop a process to alleviate the challenges and diminish the negative effect they might have on your rollout. Risk management will be a constant throughout the lifetime of the deployment and will need the cooperation of all of the parties involved. Identifying and addressing the potential risks early in the process will keep the project on track and on schedule. Risk management will always be a high-profile action to guarantee the success of your project. A particular risk should be retired, however, after it's determined that it no longer impacts the success of the project.

A five-step risk-assessment plan that you can use on your Exchange 2000 project is shown in Figure 2.6. The steps are as follows:

1. *Identify risks*—This enables your team to become cognizant of a potential risk and deal with it before it can cause damage to the Exchange 2000 deployment.

2. *Analyze risks*—This involves not only analyzing risks but also processing them into usable data that the team can use for solid decision-making. Each risk is analyzed closely to determine its probability of occurrence and the realistic impact on the overall project. This data can then be used to create a plan to alleviate the problem.

3. *Mitigate risks*—Your team must create a plan to turn the information that is collected into concrete solutions and actions. This will involve developing methods to address the risks, prioritizing the risk actions, and devising an alert point for the team that indicates the mitigation plan must be executed. You may want to consider creating a table at the beginning of the project to assess risks to help you to mitigate the particular risk. You can predict the probability of the issue surfacing and the impact that the risk may have on the project with this table. The table will be continually updated throughout the life of the project as risks are added, deleted, and retired as necessary. The mitigation may be a full-blown plan or simply a set of steps to complete to reduce or get rid of the risk to the deployment.

4. *Monitor risks*—This process entails tracking the most crucial risks and allowing your team to monitor them when steps for resolution are taken.

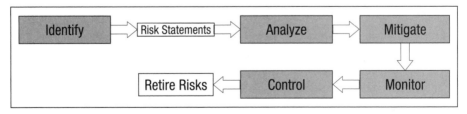

Figure 2.6   The risk-assessment model.

5. *Control risks*—This step involves transitioning the risk management procedure into the day-to-day activities of the Exchange 2000 project. If your team was successful in properly carrying out the previous steps, then risk control involves simply monitoring for alerts and trigger points.

Total Cost of Ownership (TCO)

Another factor that influences business strategies is the TCO. The TCO of an organization refers to the cost of hardware, software, administration, and maintenance. You need to implement systems in your organization in a way that will reduce the maintenance and administrative overhead costs. Exchange 2000 saves time and money by providing an excellent server consolidation platform and lowering the TCO of your messaging system. The only way you can analyze the true value of your Exchange 2000 implementation (and provide justification for a bonus or salary increase) is by comparing snapshots of your pre- and post-migration environments. All organizations worldwide share the common objective of working toward increased profitability. This can be achieved in part by improving productivity and reducing costs. You must consider the economics of the business while planning the Exchange 2000 solution. For example, you should plan for as few domains as possible to reduce the cost of implementation, because each domain requires at least two domain controllers for fault tolerance. In addition, the number of domains in your organization determines the number of licenses that must be purchased.

Economic factors also affect your decisions relating to connectivity among sites. For example, you may decide to have a fast WAN link among sites if cost is not a constraint. Conversely, you may decide in favor of a low-cost solution such as a dial-up link among sites if you are subject to budgetary issues. In addition, a larger number of domains will require administration of multiple trust relationships, which leads to an increase in the cost of administration. Another way to achieve these cost objectives and improve existing systems is to implement new technologies. As technology becomes increasingly complex, the cost of managing technology increases. Adding diverse technologies to your network would require hiring specialists to support each of them, affecting the structure and size of—as well as the load on—the IT management team.

Assessing the company's business needs is a key strategy for gaining approval to deploy Exchange 2000. Companies do not perform upgrades just so they can use the latest version of a product. There must be a business justification for investing in the new technology. Will the tools provide reliability, scalability, and improved collaboration for the enterprise? Every organization will have a unique evaluation process for implementation, based in some degree upon specific business strategies and return on investment predictions. The areas in which companies will expect the most enhancement, or the most rapid implementation of Exchange 2000, rely highly on assessing the currently implemented architecture—how it is being used, whether it meets the business needs—and identifying the most urgent functionality initiatives required from the messaging infrastructure. Although all of the business factors mentioned in this section vary in priority, depending on the customer's specific issues, these areas will likely be the predominant dynamics in the deployment of Exchange 2000 across your organization.

Assessing Your Business Needs

For more information on what MSF is and how it can help assess your business needs, see the MSF Datasheet: **www.microsoft.com/trainingandservices/content/downloads/datasheets/MSFDatasheet.doc**

Analyzing the Existing and Planned Administrative Model

You must consider the following broad categories of Exchange administration when designing the administrative model:

➤ Information technology management

➤ User administration

➤ Exchange system policy

➤ Server management

➤ Public folder management

Note that these functions are not necessarily mutually exclusive (e.g., it is possible for someone to administer both users and servers). Also, each of the broad categories can be further broken down into smaller areas of authority.

Information Technology Management

The IT management of an organization is responsible for supporting various systems. You can divide the IT management of an organization into three areas of responsibility, based on different aspects of the network they support:

➤ Data center management

➤ Network management

➤ Desktop management

Data Center Management

Data center management refers to the group of administrators who are responsible for managing back-office servers and server-based applications. Data center management is responsible for managing security, monitoring resource availability, and implementing disaster recovery. Data center management is also responsible for providing the best possible service to the groups of users. For example, managing the Exchange 2000 Server is the responsibility of data center management.

Network Management

The primary areas of responsibility of network management are the performance, availability, and security of the network. Network management ensures that the data traffic passes through the network in a timely and secure manner. The challenges faced by network management include ensuring network availability and dealing with potential failures on the network. An analysis of your current technical environment is essential while planning for Exchange 2000. Analyzing the technical environment includes an inventory of the existing systems, the available network connectivity, hardware, and bandwidth, as well as security considerations. Analyzing the technical environment helps you to determine the additional requirements and amendments for your current environment, and helps you plan for the expansion of your network.

For example, an analysis of the existing bandwidth and connectivity in your network will help you determine which locations are well connected and where you would need to introduce better connectivity. You need to evaluate the size, geographical scope, and site structure of your organization's network before implementing Exchange 2000. You should also examine the existing WAN and local area network (LAN) topology, a list of physical locations, and the bandwidth available between locations. In addition, you also need to examine the role of objects—domains, organizational groups, storage groups, users, and so on—within your network. An analysis of Internet connectivity, Domain Name System (DNS) authority, messaging paths, routers, switches, and connectivity strategies for remote users is also required.

Exchange 2000 supports a more granular administrative method than did Exchange 5.5. Under Exchange 5.5, giving someone the ability to manage a site gave that person the authority to manage all of the servers as well as the messaging connectors for that site. Exchange 2000 separates server management from the management of connector objects through the use of administrative groups and routing groups; therefore, it is possible to delegate these tasks to different administrators. However, because Exchange no longer maintains its own directory, coordinating Exchange administration with Active Directory administration is a must. Integrating Exchange 2000 with ADS allows you to develop group policies so you can provide a uniform desktop configuration to enhance desktop productivity. You can assign the policies that are valid across a specific site, domain, or organizational unit (OU). Assigning group policies simplifies such tasks as updating operating systems, installing applications, and updating user profiles. In addition, assigning group policies reduces the administration so that management resources can be redirected toward other activities.

Desktop Management

Desktop management is responsible for controlling and managing desktop computers and Exchange client applications (such as Outlook) as well as the operating systems they run. In addition, desktop management is responsible for educating users about machine maintenance, software, and new Exchange 2000 technologies.

For example, your organization might have a variety of desktop computers with different operating systems—ranging from Apple Macintosh to Windows 98/2000 client operating systems—and different corresponding applications. Supporting such diversity might require a management group of individuals who are competent in the various technologies you need to support. It may be necessary to consider migrating to a Windows 2000 Professional platform throughout your organization to provide the best long-term solution. This adds to the cost of an Exchange deployment.

Desktop productivity often suffers because of unfamiliarity or lack of training. This will lead to additional downtime and other problems, such as users modifying the configurations and installing unsupported software packages. This adds to the management cost of the organization. To prevent these problems and reduce costs, you need to control the computer configurations of individuals and groups of users. Exchange uses ADS to provide you with management services necessary to monitor and control the desktop and application configurations, thereby increasing user efficiency and reducing administration and costs.

User Administration

The messaging and collaboration requirements of users will define the features needed to allow them to carry out work responsibilities in a more competent and useful way. You and your deployment team must effectively communicate with users and the managers of these users to collect this critical information. You may wish to classify users as heavy, medium, or light, based on their dependence on and requirements of the network. You also need to evaluate the comfort level and knowledge base of the users in your organization, which will most likely vary by department. This information will assist you in determining the Exchange resources and components required at each location. The accurate collection of this information may at first appear to be an overwhelming task, but you do not have to talk to every individual email user. Conduct your review by asking departmental managers or supervisors to query their employees during planned meetings or by inputting the information through a Web-based form. The more in tune you are with your users' requirements, the more content they will be with the new system.

User requirements aren't usually described in technical terms, so the project team's responsibility may be to translate the user requirements and needs into technical terminology. The Exchange solution decision can then be evaluated to ensure that user needs are met. After you are aware of existing requirements, you can use

Table 2.1 **Examples of solutions for user requirements.**

Requirement	Exchange Solution
Users need to interactively collaborate with other users.	Establish Instant Messenger services.
Users need to publish and manage HTML documents that are stored in public folders.	Use Microsoft FrontPage or Microsoft Word. Implement Exchange 2000, the Web Storage System, and the Exchange Installable File System (ExIFS).
Users need to quickly locate messages and documents stored in public folders.	Enable full-text indexing in mailbox stores and public folder stores.

Exchange 2000 to find new ways to maintain or possibly even improve user productivity. Table 2.1 shows some examples of user requirements and their Exchange technical solutions.

User-related administrative requirements will also affect the configuration and management structure for Exchange 2000 in several ways. This can include the ability to separate user accounts into smaller databases for faster backup and restore operations and definition of users who manage only the routing topology. In addition, the use of policies can be effective for managing mailboxes.

Exchange System Policy

Policies allow administrators to define properties on a large number of objects by defining properties on a single policy object. You can set server, public store, and mailbox store policies as well as recipient policies. The most important principle behind policies is to allow administrators the ability to define settings and parameters for the Exchange 2000 organization on a grand scale. Yet, policies are also flexible enough to accommodate any size organization. Administrators with the ability to modify Exchange system policy will be responsible for logging management, message tracking, database maintenance, mailbox and database limiting, and indexing, among other tasks. System policies will have a significant impact on the operation and maintenance of the Exchange servers, so this person must be knowledgeable in almost all aspects of Exchange.

In previous versions of Exchange, settings affected either a single server or all of the servers within a site. This feature prevented the user from applying settings for all of the sites at the same time. It was also impossible to choose a particular number of servers within the site. Exchange 2000 policies overcome these limitations. When a parameter needs to be modified, the administrator can simply make the change on the policy, thereby affecting all servers, mailbox stores, or public folder stores to which the policy is applied. Administrators can be given permissions to classify policies completely independent of the permissions that they would need to administer servers in administrative groups. After a policy is defined, an administrator who has permissions on the servers within a specific administrative group can apply it. Mailbox administration in Exchange 5.5 was a separate task from user account management. Now that mailboxes are simply an attribute of a Windows 2000 user account, mailbox administration is tightly linked to Active Directory account administration. This type of administration may also include managing recipient policies and global address lists.

One issue that often surfaces when managing mailboxes under Exchange 2000 is whether the administrators of Exchange should also have the ability to create user accounts. You must make this determination on the basis of your individual organization's design. One benefit for giving the administrator this capability, however, is that the Exchange administrators will not necessarily have to coordinate with the Active Directory administrators for fundamental maintenance tasks. If user account security is an issue for your organization, you can decide not to grant your Exchange administrators full control over user accounts. The administrators must at least have the ability to change the private and public information properties for the user accounts. To be able to administer all the mailboxes required, it may be necessary to delegate authority for multiple organizational units. Based on these facts, Exchange administrators should play a vital role in the initial Active Directory design.

You will also need qualified personnel (who understand address spaces and connectors) to manage the recipient policies and address lists. This can be more than one person, if necessary. Address lists allow users to effortlessly view a list of available recipients, which greatly simplifies the process of sending messages. Address lists can also afford a certain degree of security by allowing filtering of the available addresses in the mail client. Recipient policies permit the administrator to rapidly alter the addressing data for a certain group of individuals. An administrator who understands the needs of the users and the security requirements of the organization should manage these. This level of understanding becomes especially crucial in cases of company mergers, acquisitions, or dissolutions.

A second user-related administrative feature that can positively affect the configuration and management structure for Exchange 2000 is the capability to separate mailbox stores, public folders, and transaction logs into smaller databases for faster backup and restore operations. Storage groups with multiple databases are one of the new concepts in Exchange 2000. A *storage group* is a logical assemblage of databases that share a single transaction log set as well as a central area of administration, backup, and restore. Exchange 5.5 has, in effect, one single storage group, meaning that only one database can be backed up at a time. With Exchange 2000, each storage group can be backed up concurrently to an independent device. The advantage of storage groups to organizations is threefold:

➤ Each group can completely segregate its data from that of other groups.

➤ Databases can be independently backed up and restored.

➤ Administrators can allocate a different storage policy to each group as well as assign separate databases to specific individuals or groups.

Because Exchange 2000 uses the concept of storage groups, it's possible to make separate people responsible for different sets of databases, which can be critical if your Exchange server hosts mailboxes from several companies.

A third feature to help with user administration is to define a group of users who manage only the routing topology of Exchange 2000. In Exchange 5.5, separating the concept of message routing from the boundary of the Exchange site is difficult. The concept of *routing groups* has been implemented to make this possible in Exchange 2000. The group of people responsible for message routing should have knowledge of the different types of connectors and their uses, as well as the underlying physical structure of the network. This will allow them to choose the most efficient messaging paths for the organization. In large organizations, messaging paths and available routes can become complex. By giving someone permission to manage a routing group, an administrator can control messaging connectivity for that group of servers. Note that routing groups are available only in native mode Exchange organizations.

Server Management

Exchange 2000 server management can include, among other tasks, managing permissions, backing up and restoring the server, managing system policies, managing protocols, and administering storage groups and databases. With the introduction of the administration-groups concept, applying a standard level of permissions across several servers is very simple, and permissions can be set in a more granular way if needed. By grouping servers into administration groups, you can easily grant certain individuals the right to manage a group of servers. Because Exchange server management engenders so many facets, it may be useful in large enterprises to delegate permissions over smaller components of the administration groups.

Maintenance of the Exchange databases is probably the most essential piece of server management. These databases must be backed up regularly to help prevent irrecoverable data loss. Although your company may be using an automated backup system, your administrators will still need to guarantee that the backups are taking place. You will want to be sure that you have put into place a policy for testing the backups and for performing trial restores.

Protocol management is another important concern. The administrator will have the authority to control message sizes and protocol availability (i.e., restricting who is permitted to access Exchange through a Web browser), as well as to view and flush message queues.

Public Folder Management

Public folder trees can grow to become quite large and contain a lot of information, creating a challenge in administering hierarchies. You should therefore delegate an individual to manage public folders and folder replication. This person should be able to create public folders, map them to database stores, and configure replication to guarantee full-time accessibility. When there are many trees to manage, you may decide to have different individuals administer each public folder tree.

Exchange 2000 supports multiple public folder trees, also referred to as top-level hierarchies, for flexible administrative power over public folders. For example, to collaborate with external users, you could create a separate public folder tree and segregate that content from the default public folder tree. Or, you may decide to produce public folders at a remote site strictly for the users at that location to access pertinent information. Therefore, depending on the circumstances of your organization, the use of multiple public folders may influence your general public folder strategy.

A default public folder tree is created on every public folder server when Exchange 2000 is installed, and its associated hierarchy is always replicated. This default tree is accessible to all Messaging Application Programming Interface (MAPI), IMAP4, NNTP, and HTTP clients. Additional public folder trees, however, have an effect only on the servers on which they are configured. A set of supplementary folders can be located on a single server or on a subset of servers, and the hierarchy for these additional public folders does not have to be replicated to every server. These additional folder trees are available only to NNTP and Web clients, and not to clients such as Microsoft Outlook 2000 unless viewed on a Web page hosted in Outlook 2000.

Chapter Summary

This chapter emphasized that your main responsibility as an Exchange solutions provider should be to develop an overall strategy of design and integration based on existing and planned organizational and business models. You will evaluate the integration challenges that are indicative of your type of organization and attempt to predict the effects of such factors as corporate politics, organizational structure, geographic location, and the overall business environment. You will need to take into consideration the reality or possibility of such events as strategic alliances, corporate reengineering, buyouts, planned mergers and/or acquisitions, and governmental legislation and regulation. The continuous pressures from competitors for public or private dollars as well as the demands of clients will also drastically affect the business model of your organization.

You will very likely combine an understanding of your particular organizational type with the systematically generated analysis tools from Microsoft known as the Microsoft Solutions Framework, discussed in this chapter. After you investigate these free documents from the Microsoft MSF Web site, then you can begin the process of determining the vision for your Exchange 2000 solution. The organization with whom you are working may be a large global headquarters or a small branch office, or anything in between, or exceptional situations might arise in your organization that place you in the category of a special-case scenario. These special categories may involve collaborating organizations, planned expansion, multiple headquarters, or security sensitivity, among others. Your organization may actually fall into more than one special category; for example, it may be telecommuter friendly as well as security sensitive.

This chapter also visited the concept of the logical configuration of IT management known as the IT business model. The three general types of business models are centralized, decentralized, and outsourced. The IT management of an organization may be accountable for sustaining many systems. Therefore, you may decide to partition the IT management of an organization into three general areas of responsibility: data center management, network management, and desktop management. Within this infrastructure you will need to find or define key roles for individuals in your deployment. These roles may include such jobs as collaboration tools administrator, end-user training, team leader, or Enterprise administrator.

Exchange 2000 provides a more granular administrative technique than did Exchange 5.5. Exchange 2000 separates server management from the management of connector objects through the powerful use of administration groups and routing groups, making it feasible to delegate these tasks to different administrators. In addition, the use of Exchange system policies can help administrators control the properties of many objects by simply affecting one system policy object.

The next chapter takes this foundation of information about the organization and uses a team of qualified individuals to analyze the existing server roles. Roles will include mailbox server, public folder server, and bridgehead server. It also examines existing and planned network resources, including hardware, available bandwidth, network topology, and firewall configuration. The next chapter addresses methods for evaluating the existing directory and name resolution configurations.

Review Questions

1. The capabilities of Exchange 2000 exceed those of simple messaging. The new messaging and collaboration features of Exchange will impact the entire organization. Which of the following factors, therefore, can have an influence on your organizational deployment of an Exchange solution? [Check all correct answers]

   a. A planned merger or acquisition

   b. The existing human resources structure

   c. The existing and planned business models

   d. The messaging habits of individual users and groups

   e. a and d only

   f. All of the above

2. Microsoft has systematically gathered data from customers, partners, IT organizations, product managers, and consultants to generate detailed analyses, and has organized this data into practical models. This information is distributed as which of the following?

   a. Microsoft Management Console

   b. Microsoft Solutions Framework

   c. Microsoft Systems Framework

   d. Microsoft Business Framework

   e. Microsoft Preparedness Framework

3. You have compiled all of the information you can from the planning and development stages of the MSF model for your Exchange 2000 rollout. Which of the following choices best represents the phase that will involve the proof of concept and pilot testing of all the organizational and physical aspects of the migration and deployment development plan?

   a. Assessment phase

   b. Development phase

   c. Planning phase

   d. Scope phase

2

4. Before starting your Exchange 2000 migration you want to get a general overview by analyzing issues such as goal setting, execution of the plan, project justification, risk assessment, project team creation, and executive sponsorship. What phase of the Microsoft Solutions Framework Infrastructure Deployment Process would give you this "big picture" look at the entire process?

   a. Assessment phase

   b. Development phase

   c. Planning phase

   d. Scope phase

5. Your company is made up of a central organization with a significant world-wide presence. Your office is located at the large corporate headquarters, but you often travel to several international regional offices and national branch offices. You are the administrator of a centralized administrative structure, although the larger branch offices have their own dedicated IT departments to which you provide corporate direction. The company has a workforce numbering more than 10,000, and the regional and branch offices are joined to your headquarters by a network of T1 links.

Based on the information provided, which one of the following organizational types best describes your company?

   a. Global headquarters

   b. Large international conglomerate

   c. Large multinational organization

   d. Large national organization

6. You are the network administrator of a graphic design company with a workforce of fewer than 50 people. You are contemplating following a Microsoft recommendation to deploy Exchange 2000 as part of a Small Business Server (SBS) solution. Your company resides in a single location and has no branch offices. You are going to handle most of the administration, but you are also considering outsourcing certain services to another vendor. Your network connectivity is an ISDN dial-up to a T1 connection on a wide area network.

Based on the information provided, which one of the following organizational types best describes your company?

   a. Smaller national organization

   b. Small autonomous organization

   c. Single location organization

   d. Small regional organization

7. Which one of the following organizational types characteristically comprises 5 to 20 people implementing one or two servers that are linked to the global headquarters?

   a. Regional branch office

   b. Large branch office

   c. Medium branch office

   d. Small branch office

8. Unique situations can occur in your organization that will place you in a special case scenario category. Which one of the following special scenarios represents a company whose chief messaging concern will be coexistence and migration issues caused by an impending merger?

   a. Collaborating organization

   b. Planning expansion

   c. Security sensitive

   d. Merger friendly

9. The IT business model of a company is the logical configuration of IT management in the organization. Business models comprise three general categories. Which one of the following is *not* one of the general categories?

   a. Distributed

   b. Centralized

   c. Decentralized

   d. Outsourced

10. Which type of IT business model relies on systems administrators who are not employees of the company to design and maintain the network?

    a. Distributed

    b. Centralized

    c. Decentralized

    d. Outsourced

11. Which element of the business infrastructure defines the current physical presence of an organization as it refers to its future expansion plans, including new offices and future acquisitions and mergers?

    a. Information flow

    b. Geographical scope

    c. Organizational structure

    d. Routing group infrastructure

12. The flow of existing electronic mail business units of an organization usually follows quantifiable communication patterns. A large percentage of communication stays within an individual's workgroup and the remaining smaller percentage flows outside of the unit or workgroup. A rule can be applied to get a general feel for this flow. By what name is this rule commonly known?

    a. Murphy's rule

    b. The silver rule

    c. The 80–20 rule

    d. The rule of data flow

13. Identifying and addressing the potential hazards to an Exchange solution early in the process will help keep the project on path and on schedule. What is this high-profile strategic business objective called?

    a. Organizational priorities

    b. Growth strategy

    c. Risk assessment

    d. Total cost of ownership

14. Which of the following terms best describes the method that administrators can use to define properties for the server, public store, and mailbox store on a large number of objects by defining properties on a single object?

    a. Delegation of authority

    b. Organizational modeling

    c. Total cost of ownership

    d. System policies

15. Choose from the following items the component that allows users to readily view a list of available recipients as well as affords administrators a certain degree of security by allowing filtering techniques in the mail client?

    a. Public folders

    b. Address lists

    c. Organizational unit

    d. Filtering folder

Real-World Projects

Project 2.1

Determine the organizational model of your company or organization by using the information detailed in this chapter as a guideline. (If you do not have an organization at your disposal, then survey a friend or associate about his or her organization.)

Project 2.2

You are a systems administrator who has been tasked as the team lead for your organization's Scope/Envisioning phase of an Exchange deployment. Using your company or another company as an example, conduct the following information-gathering survey to obtain data for the solution:

➤ What email features do you use most often?

➤ Would you like to replace any components of the system?

➤ Would you like to add any features to your system?

➤ On a scale of 1 to 5, where 1 is unreliable and 5 is very reliable, how would you rank your current email system?

➤ Does your department use email to communicate to clients or partners outside your organization?

➤ Please describe the importance of electronic mail to your organization's business.

➤ Are there plans to expand the use of electronic messaging as a transport between applications?

➤ Identify mission-critical applications.

➤ Identify the types of the applications.

➤ Is your company or department involved in telecommuting? If yes, please describe the scenario.

➤ What percentage of your office-based employees will access electronic mail from remote locations?

➤ What proportions of potential mail users currently have access to email?

➤ Identify and analyze potential risks (refer to the chapter information on risk assessment) and quantify the potential impact of the risks.

CHAPTER THREE

Analyzing Resources for Exchange 2000 Server

After completing this chapter, you will be able to:

✓ Understand Exchange 2000 system prerequisites and recommendations

✓ Identify the many different server types

✓ Plan for the deployment of Windows 2000 servers

✓ Analyze processor resource configuration

✓ Analyze memory resource configuration

✓ Analyze network resource configuration

✓ Analyze disk resource configuration

Eventually, the planning process of an Exchange 2000 deployment will get to a more practical and physical level. This chapter looks carefully at the types of servers you can introduce into your design. Because these actions can introduce cost factors that will have a direct effect on the bottom line, you will want to be sure that you are making the right decisions. Once you make your server decisions, you will want to make sure that you are prepared to efficiently configure server resources, such as the processor, memory, network, and disk subsystems, to get the best performance environment possible. Before delving into these concepts, we briefly revisit the Exchange 2000 system prerequisites.

System Recommendations and Prerequisites

Before planning an upgrade or migration in your Exchange environment, realize that Exchange 2000 has several dependencies and infrastructure requirements that must be met. Map out the hardware that you plan to set up, or even redeploy, with care. These servers must be on the Hardware Compatibility List (HCL) and be supported by Windows 2000. A large portion of this chapter is dedicated to assuring that the configurations of the central processing unit (CPU), memory, and disk are sufficient for the role each server is to perform in Exchange 2000. Prior to the installation of Exchange 2000, your Windows 2000 domain must run Domain Name System (DNS) and Active Directory services as well. Each system that will be running Exchange 2000 will need the Network News Transfer Protocol (NNTP) and Simple Mail Transfer Protocol (SMTP) services installed. In addition, the Active Directory schema must be extended for Exchange 2000 by using the ForestPrep utility. Each domain, as well, must be primed using the DomainPrep tool. Before upgrading, your existing Exchange server must be running Exchange Server 5.5 with Service Pack 3 (SP3) on Windows 2000 Server.

Tip: *Hardware compatibility list*—You can get the Windows 2000 Hardware Compatibility List by navigating to **www.microsoft.com/hcl/default.asp**, clicking on the HCL plain text link, and downloading the file named win2000hcl.txt.

Hardware Considerations

The minimum hardware recommendations for an Exchange 2000 server deployment exceed the minimum hardware requirements. A minimum of a single Pentium II 400MHz dual processor with 256MB of RAM and 4GB of hard disk space are recommended for Exchange 2000. The minimum requirements are:

➤ Intel Pentium or compatible 133MHz or higher processor

➤ 128MB RAM (supported minimum), 256MB RAM (recommended minimum)

➤ 500MB available disk space for the drive on which Exchange is installed

➤ 200MB available disk space on the system drive

➤ CD-ROM drive

➤ Video graphics array (VGA) or better monitor

The costs of hardware are constantly falling, so be prepared to get the latest and the most that your money can buy. If you are deploying dedicated servers, single processor servers with 20 to 50GB of disk storage and 256MB of RAM will suffice; however, a high-speed, dual- or quad-processor server with larger storage and more RAM may give you "more bang for your buck" as well as accommodate future organizational growth. Another aspect to server planning should include isolating the newer, beefier machines in your organization as candidates for running all of the Exchange 2000 components. Consider using the more obsolete machines as dedicated servers. You need to determine which servers will have higher loads than others. This chapter provides information to help you when buying hardware for your servers. Obviously, you will want to deploy the more demanding services on the high-performance hardware and vice versa.

When choosing your hardware configuration, consider the role that each server will play, including the load that it must support. You should be able to make these determinations in the Envisioning and Planning phases. For example, assume that you already have a dedicated Exchange 5.5 mailbox server deployed for optimal disk performance. The private information store is residing on a separate RAID 5 (Re-dundant Array of Inexpensive Disks 5) drive array, and the transaction log files are stored on a RAID 1 mirror. In Exchange 2000, you will be deploying a comparable mailbox server, but with several mailbox stores. Consider that on Exchange 2000, there will be more databases and more transactional logs than there were in Exchange 5.5. If, for example, Exchange 2000 is installed in a Domain Controller, you have to be wary of the system disk I/O performance because of the Active Directory data-base. Therefore, the best performance would come from placing each mailbox store on a separate RAID 5 drive array. Every set of transaction log files, on the other hand, needs to be stored on a separate RAID 1 drive for each storage group.

If your existing servers are not particularly high-performance, you could deploy that server for other services, bring in a new server with Exchange 2000, and let your existing servers continue to support your email users. Once the new server is operating smoothly, you can make it your primary mail server. This is known as the "leapfrog" method. Then, again, you can shift mailboxes from a server running any version of Exchange to another adequately configured system. You must look at each server closely to establish that it meets the system requirements for Windows 2000 and Exchange 2000. If your existing systems do not meet the requirements for Windows 2000 and Exchange 2000, you need to upgrade your hardware before deploying Exchange 2000. You should also examine page files. Typical configuration questions would include:

➤ How many CPUs are installed and what is the speed of each CPU?

➤ What is the system bus speed?

➤ How much RAM is installed?

➤ Where are the page files located and how large are they?

➤ Are the transaction logs on a volume separate from the databases?

➤ What type of RAID array is deployed?

➤ What type of disk controller is used, and how much memory does the controller have?

➤ How many spindles are present?

➤ In which format is each disk partition?

Software Considerations

A number of special software considerations should be addressed for preparing the operating system for Exchange 2000. As previously discussed, Exchange 2000 is closely incorporated with the Active Directory Service (ADS). Many services that were previously in Exchange are now part of the Windows 2000 Server operating system. You may need to remove and reinstall new versions of any software that interacts with Active Directory. The operating system software requirements for Exchange 2000 Server are the following:

➤ Windows 2000 Server or Windows 2000 Advanced Server or Windows 2000 Datacenter Server

➤ Active Directory Service

➤ DNS service

➤ Windows 2000 Service Pack 1

➤ Internet Information Services (IIS) with SMTP and NNTP support

---

Tip: If you are planning to reuse existing hardware currently running an earlier version of Exchange on Microsoft Windows NT Server 3.51 or NT Server 4.0, upgrade to Windows 2000 Server before you upgrade Exchange.

Some relevant questions are:

➤ What third-party software is installed?

➤ Does the software support Windows 2000 and Exchange 2000?

➤ Can the software be upgraded to Exchange 2000?

➤ Does the software require removal and reinstall after Active Directory is installed?

Exchange 2000 Dedicated Server Types

3

Exchange 2000 Server includes more than a small number of assorted components that can all be run on the same server computer. When you choose to install all the Exchange services on a single machine during installation, you are configuring what is technically known as an "all-in-one" server. This setup will probably be the best choice for small organizations with nominal messaging and collaborating requirements. Because user demands in these circumstances will not lead to a heavy load on server resources, reliability and performance will not be factors when deploying an all-in-one server.

If you work for a larger organization that must offer high-volume chat services to users on the Internet, however, using dedicated servers is an excellent solution. Exchange 2000 servers can be configured as dedicated servers to offer more specialized tasks, thereby achieving optimum performance. This action can also reduce system complexity while improving the interoperability, stability, and reliability of the system configuration. For example, you might choose to isolate mailbox services onto a dedicated mailbox server to ensure that mailbox services will not be adversely affected when other servers in your organization have increased demand for hardware resources.

Another example is one in which you are running Exchange, Structured Query Language (SQL) server, and a custom monitoring application on the same computer. If the custom monitoring component needs a service pack that has not yet been tested for compatibility with Exchange 2000, you may encounter problems that cause instability.

A third example is to configure an Exchange 2000 Server to handle only data and videoconferencing through the Exchange Conferencing Services while configuring another server strictly to provide users with messaging services. Depending on hardware and potential user demand, demanding services such as conferencing can be delegated to higher-performance hardware, and lower-performance hardware can be used for less-demanding services.

Keep in mind that if you decide to have a server for every major Exchange 2000 service, it can be quite an expensive implementation. If you have budgetary restrictions or if hardware is a precious commodity, you may want to consider starting with one server and adding more later when it is financially feasible. You can then begin delegating services onto the new servers and enjoying the resulting performance gains. Although a single server is the still the most cost-effective and easy-to-manage option, you should be knowledgeable of the many different types of dedicated Exchange 2000 servers that are available to your growing organization. The following sections review these server types and their prospective resource requirements and recommendations.

Mailbox Servers

You can provide greater durability for users and fewer disruptions from other services by using dedicated mailbox servers. If your organization is preparing to support many users while simultaneously providing other services such as conferencing, you should employ a dedicated server that provides only mailbox services and no other components. This will also allow you to accommodate the largest possible number of users because resources are dedicated to mailbox services. Because Exchange 2000 also permits multiple mailbox stores to coexist on a single server, you can isolate individual user mailboxes by designating storage groups. You can autonomously start and stop each mailbox store as well as restore a single mailbox store without affecting other users.

As you analyze the existing server configuration, examine the sizes of the mailbox and public folder stores, and consider the following questions:

➤ Are there multiple companies within your Exchange organization?

➤ If there is a limit in the mailbox storage, what is that limit?

➤ What is the retention policy for deleted items?

➤ How many server mailboxes are governed by customer service-level agreements?

➤ Does your organization need mailboxes for certain situations or individuals in your organization?

➤ Who is responsible for creating distribution lists and what is the policy?

➤ Are automated tools used to create distribution lists?

➤ Which protocols are enabled for mail?

If large mailbox stores exist, splitting them into several smaller ones should be considered. In the past, service level agreements (SLAs) have often required the deployment of multiple servers to ensure recovery within the time constraints of these agreements. Using multiple storage groups and databases will allow you to consolidate several servers into a large server with multiple mailbox stores and databases. At Plus Ultra Group, for example, a single large server is used to accommodate more than 1,000 users, each having a mailbox limit of 30MB. Because Exchange 2000 can have mailbox stores on the same server, Plus Ultra Group could later have a large number of mailboxes distributed over several databases. This would result in a reduction in user downtime if a database were being restored after a failure. If your organization falls into a similar category (over 1,000 users), your dedicated mailbox server should have two to four processors and at least 1GB of RAM. The operating system and Exchange binary files would reside on the C: drive and need a recommended 18.2GB in the form of two 18.2GB RAID 1 volumes. The database uses four 18.2GB drives in a RAID 5 configuration to provide about 54GB of storage. This scenario would also require two log disks, each 18.2GB in size, represented by two 18.2GB RAID 1 volumes. The network bandwidth should be 100MB or higher. A smaller organization of fewer than 1,000 users could settle for a dual processor server with 512MB of memory and only one disk for the logs.

The initial release of Exchange 2000 Server allowed deployment of a two-node cluster to provide high availability. Plus Ultra Group may later decide to implement a two-node cluster solution in which one node would serve the main office users and the other node would serve their retail stores. As mentioned previously, one or more mailboxes can exist within a storage group, with each storage group having one set of transaction log files. Plus Ultra Group could implement two storage groups, one on each node of the server cluster. For even better performance, they may decide to place each database on a separate volume and locate each volume on a different controller. To provide fault tolerance and disaster recovery, Plus Ultra Group could further increase performance by placing the transaction log files on a volume separate from the corresponding databases.

Internet Mail Servers

You may be an administrator for an Internet service provider (ISP) and decide to deploy Exchange 2000 as a dedicated Internet mail server to provide for email and newsgroup services. This functionality is an excellent choice because large numbers of Outlook Express and third-party mail clients can contact dedicated Internet mail servers to claim mail and newsgroup messages. You may also be located in a large organization and need to provide these services on an enterprise-wide basis. A dedicated Internet mail server is deployed as part of the standard Exchange Messaging and Collaboration installation option and will use virtual servers to provide Internet Message Access Protocol 4 (IMAP4), NNTP, and Post Office Protocol 3 (POP3) services. The hardware requirements depend on the number of users and level of mail access. You can use the guidelines provided in this chapter for other dedicated servers to create a baseline for resource allocation.

Public Folder Servers

A public folder server is a dedicated server used to hold public folders and to provide public folder data to clients. Public folder servers will use any one of several protocols including Messaging Application Programming Interface (MAPI), Hypertext Transfer Protocol (HTTP), HTTP–Distributed Authoring and

Versioning (HTTP-DAV), or IMAP4. If you must supply public folder access to a large group of users in an organization such as Plus Ultra Group, installing an Exchange 2000 Server to run only messaging and public folders is a great method for isolating traffic to the server. Plus Ultra Group uses one of the new features of Exchange 2000, anonymous public folder access, to permit access to their public folders from the Internet. Using a dedicated public folder server for Internet access of public folders can help you protect your organization's network. Public folder servers are different from mailbox servers in that connectivity to them is not as critical because users are not constantly connected.

Plus Ultra Group is an organization of more than 1,000 users with a large Exchange server dedicated to public folders that is equipped with the recommended two to four processors and at least 1GB of memory. The operating system and Exchange binary files would use about 18.2GB in the form of two 18.2GB RAID 1 volumes. The database uses four 18.2GB drives in a RAID 5 configuration to provide about 54GB of storage. Unlike the mailbox servers, the public folder servers use one storage group. This scenario also holds for one log disk that is 18.2GB in size represented by two 18.2GB RAID 1 volumes. The network bandwidth is 100MB. A smaller organization of fewer than 1,000 users could settle for a dual processor server with 512MB of memory. It's also possible to install public folder servers in a cluster system similar to the mailbox solution mentioned previously.

Connector Servers

A connector server is a dedicated Exchange server set aside to run a connector for Lotus Notes, for example. You might dedicate a specific server to run a connector if that specific connector is connected to foreign systems and creates a huge demand on your design. You could then configure another server to run other connectors, if necessary. Connector servers are dedicated to routing messages, and they do not host mailboxes or public folders. A connector server may connect routing groups, run a Novell GroupWise connector, or connect to the Internet. Depending on the circumstances, connectors can be installed autonomously or in different permutations on dedicated servers. For example, Plus Ultra Group needs a connector to a foreign Lotus Notes system for a dedicated mail server at the enterprise level. Rolling out a dedicated connector server rather than using a high-demand server is probably a better option for this company. Windows 2000 supports the following connectors:

➤ SMTP connector

➤ X.400 connector

➤ Lotus Notes connector

➤ Lotus cc:Mail connector

➤ GroupWise connector

➤ Microsoft Mail connector

Your need for Exchange 5.5 connectors will influence whether you upgrade all of your servers to Exchange 2000 or leave some Exchange 5.5 servers in place to manage those connectors. Therefore you need to determine if you have any Exchange 5.5 connectors installed and, if so, which ones. You need to locate the documentation for each type of connector you have. If you cannot locate this information, then you need to document the connector's configuration.

To lower the cost of implementation and maintenance, a standardized hardware platform should be configured for your connector servers. The cost of hardware will be lower for a connector server, given the relatively smaller load, and the servers don't have to be configured for optimum performance. The dedicated connector server needs two to four processors with a memory configuration of at least 256MB RAM. The operating system and Exchange binary files will reside on an approximate 9GB volume (2×9GB RAID 1), as will the data storage disk and the log disk. The network interface bandwidth should be a minimum of 100MB.

Front-End Servers

The front-end server interrelates directly with clients and has the primary function of passing requests from these clients to back-end servers using IMAP, POP3, or HTTP, which hold the mailbox and public folder stores. By using front-end servers to access their mailboxes, users ultimately reduce the resource load on the mailbox servers and public folder servers. Plus Ultra Group uses front-end servers on the perimeter of their network to service a sales force, as well as on the internal network to service their retail outlets. Because the front-end servers do not host databases, they are configured in a fashion similar to connector servers, except that they usually contain more RAM (for example, 512MB).

Data and Videoconferencing Servers

The data- and videoconferencing server is dedicated to running data and videoconferences on Exchange 2000 Conferencing Server and is probably the most demanding of all dedicated Exchange servers. Data conferencing servers are dedicated to administering and participating in conferences as well as isolating the data and videoconferencing services to the single server. Conferencing services can potentially require massive hardware resources, with videoconferencing being the most hardware-consuming component. This means that data and videoconferencing servers are poor candidates for legacy hardware because the situation can rapidly deteriorate as the number of users increases. IP multicast videoconferencing consumes a lot of the Exchange Server's CPU and memory resources. Therefore, you should dedicate a great deal of time to planning the hardware and network design before attempting to provide videoconferencing services to a large group of users. Don't even think about running videoconferencing services on an Exchange 2000 Server that is also running other Exchange components and is also providing your corporate mail services!

On a typical server hardware system composed of a Pentium II/Pentium III 400MHz computer with 128MB of RAM, videoconferencing will soon consume half of the available resources as a number of users begin to join in the conference session. Therefore, the suggested hardware for a conferencing server is two to four Pentium II/Pentium III 450MHz processors with 1GB of RAM for a large organization such as Plus Ultra Group. Again, conferencing servers do not host mailboxes as a rule, and the subsystems are configured similar to the connector server, with the exception of considerably more RAM.

Instant Messaging Servers

A dedicated instant messaging (IM) server type is devoted to running the Instant Messaging service in an IM domain. An IM domain is a connection of IM users, a home server, and an IM router. You can have a configuration in which IM home servers host users and IM routers route requests. Each home server has the ability to handle a number of simultaneous connections. Plus Ultra Group needs to provide instant messaging to a larger group of users; therefore, they will consider installing multiple home servers. The IM router serves the function of routing traffic to the home servers, and can be extremely critical in providing protection for the internal network. IM servers do not host databases, so the subsystems are configured in a fashion similar to the connector server, except that they need more RAM.

Chat Servers

A chat server is often referred to as a realtime collaboration server and is dedicated to running the chat service. For the most part, the chat service offered by Exchange 2000 Server does not require a great deal of server resources. Therefore, it is uncommon for this to be run as a dedicated service. However, in the unlikely event that your organization plans to offer chat services to a high volume of users, you may want to implement a dedicated chat server. For example, online training companies on the Web provide mentoring services through chat. A company such as this may be one of the exceptions to the rule because chat would be a part of the core business model. For most organizations, this service will likely be installed with another service or on servers that correspond to similar network access. For organizations such as ISPs, chat services as well as Internet mail can be deployed on Exchange Server with Internet connectivity. Like other services that require connections to the Internet, dedicated chat servers can be exposed to the Internet while providing protection for your internal network.

Bridgehead Servers

In earlier versions of Exchange, systems that have one or more connectors linking two Exchange sites or connecting Exchange to the Internet are referred to as *bridgehead servers*. These servers are in charge of sending mail and public folder information as well as replicating the Exchange directory between sites. In

Exchange 2000, bridgehead servers still exist, but the directory information is now replicated by using the Windows 2000 global catalog. You should create a spreadsheet containing information about each existing bridgehead server connector. Questions to consider include:

➤ Are Transmission Control Protocol (TCP) transport stacks being used?

➤ What type of connector is installed?

➤ Do you have documentation for the connector configuration?

➤ What is the site or server destination for this connector?

➤ What is the cost for this connector?

➤ Are there any downstream sites below this connector?

➤ How often does this connector send mail?

➤ Is Exchange directory replication configured?

➤ What is the Exchange directory replication schedule for each site?

➤ Are there message limits on the connector?

Server Planning Issues

Having reviewed the several different dedicated roles that can be assigned to an Exchange 2000 Server, let us look at some planning components that are required, regardless of an Exchange 2000 server's purpose. Planning your servers involves forming a strong picture of the function of each server as well as its hardware and software requirements. For example, if you need some of the advanced security features that Exchange 2000 provides, you need to decide which server computer in your organization will be chosen to manage the security keys. What follows is a discussion of the necessary components, regardless of the server role.

Security

All Exchange 2000 servers within a site must be able to authenticate each other. This is a fundamental of Windows 2000 security for Exchange because all server services within a site must run under the same security framework. Microsoft Exchange 2000 Server uses the Windows 2000 security services to provide the following functions:

➤ Authenticate user logon requests

➤ Authenticate servers with each other

➤ Govern access to objects and the actions that users can take with these objects

➤ Determine the auditing of events

Site Administration

The core network must maintain permanent, relatively high bandwidth connections between the Exchange 2000 servers in a site. The bandwidth must be able to accommodate the amount of data being transferred. These permanent connections can consist of local area networks (LANs), leased lines, and some form of wide area network (WAN) links. Periodic connections, such as dial-up modem connections, are not available at all times and often involve a remote location that you contact only a few times during a day. It's much easier to administer servers that are grouped within a single site because many of the Exchange 2000 Server administrative features are automatically configured within a site. Therefore, you should place as many servers as you can in each site. Also consider the organizational factors discussed in Chapter 2 when planning your Exchange 2000 sites. It's a good idea to assemble people who work together on the same servers and sites to improve system performance, trim down network traffic, and decrease resource usage. For example, Plus Ultra Group has members of the marketing group located on two servers at the same site so that they do not have to replicate public folder information between two sites.

Directory Replication

Within a site, Exchange 2000 replication is a multi-master and event-driven process in which all Microsoft servers automatically exchange their directory information with each other. When creating your site boundaries, keep in mind the way in which directory replication affects cost and performance. Also be aware of latency issues when you are executing potentially precarious tasks because it may take some time for your changes to replicate. A good example of this phenomenon is when you set permissions on a domain controller only to find that it takes time for the changes to replicate to other computers in the same domain and site. It's feasible that Exchange services can request permission-related data from domain controllers without receiving the most up-to-date replication information. Site-to-site replication depends on scheduling, so if you replicate every eight hours, modifications may take up to eight hours to replicate to all of the other sites.

With public folder replication, the system burden will generally be in direct proportion to the rate of recurrence of the changes to the public folder; if your public folders are constantly changing, considerably more resources will be consumed than in a more static public folder scenario. Replication is determined by two factors—available bandwidth and user activity. If access to public folders is not a corporate priority, you could conserve bandwidth by deciding not to replicate public folders to any remote servers. Sites at which public folders are highly used, however, should contain a replica of all the folders. You should examine each site's public folder replicas and keep the amount of replication activity to a minimum. Cautiously place your public folder servers within a site to prevent unnecessary replication.

Affinity Versus Replication

Public folder affinity lets users from one Exchange site access public folders on another Exchange site. If most of your users reside at one large central site, you might store all of the public folders for the company on a dedicated public folder server. If remote sites need limited access to the public folders, you could use affinity to allow access to the folders at the central site. Public folder replication is similar to public folder affinity, except that the participating sites actually house the folders rather than connecting to a remote site.

3

According to Microsoft, you should answer the following questions concerning public folder replication before you deploy Exchange 2000:

➤ Is public folder replication being used?

➤ When is replication occurring?

➤ Which folders are being replicated and to which sites?

➤ Is affinity sufficient for public folder access?

➤ Does your Exchange site contain unnecessary folders from remote sites?

Getting User Feedback

Without a doubt, the most vital server planning issue is to predict what your users' behavior will be. Chapter 2 analyzed a team of individuals and some potential roles in your organization. An excellent strategy would be to interview these key individuals and other power users to collect feedback with regard to the ways they will be using messaging and collaboration tools. After identifying needs and future goals, attempt to relate these needs directly to specific functions and features of Microsoft Exchange 2000 Server. This data will be very useful for determining how you can group users as well as how to place dedicated servers within the organization. This exercise will also assist you in measuring your hardware, software, and training needs. Remember that in the grand scheme of things, most users will be using Exchange 2000 primarily to send and receive email, access public folders, read newsgroups, schedule appointments, and access personal folders and other resources.

Processor Configuration

You will want to be prepared for the necessity to routinely measure the Exchange 2000 Server's responsiveness to service requests. You will want to assure that the service is performing up to speed and you are able to receive warnings of processing impediments and latency issues. Performance tuning in Exchange 2000 involves making performance decisions based on monitoring practices, setting registry keys, and rearranging certain components. The rest of this chapter provides some configuration guidelines for the processor, memory, network, and disk resource components of Exchange 2000 servers.

Processor Usage

If you are planning to upgrade an existing Exchange 5.5 Server to Exchange 2000, one of the first performance actions you should take is to first monitor the total processor usage before starting the upgrade. If the usage of the server is going to be similar after the upgrade, look for CPU usage running at about 30 percent or less to signal ample processing for Exchange 2000. You should strongly think about either upgrading the processor or even migrating the Exchange 5.5 Server if the processor is being pushed beyond 25 or 30 percent. If the processor is already being throttled with Exchange 5.5, Exchange 2000 will definitely be too much of a load. Microsoft recommends a 500MHz Intel Pentium II Xenon processor for Exchange 2000. Generally speaking, the processor should be the best you can find and contain a 2MB level 2 cache.

Mailbox and Public Folder Servers

Mailbox and public folder servers can accommodate a large number of active users, so the processing requirements will depend upon the number of users and their operating habits. In general, you should be able to handle up to 500 users on a single processor and up to 1,000 users with a dual processor configuration. After you go over 1,000 users, you should consider using four processors. The most significant issue for determining the number of mailboxes is usually the storage limits and the service levels for the maximum time needed to back up and restore on the server. Based on this maximum time, you can determine the maximum database size and the number of mailboxes. Service levels and maximum response time requirements are also important factors to consider for how your organization uses public folder servers. The raw processor capacity is not really the key issue.

Connector Server Capacity

Because Plus Ultra Group is a large Exchange 2000 organization, it is deploying a routing infrastructure built around a hub-and-spoke configuration with several hubs. The spokes are defined as routing groups and employ routing group connectors running on dedicated connector servers. The routing group connector servers on the spoke, in turn, interact with the routing group connector servers in the hub. The hub routing group connector server can also manage connections to the Internet and other messaging systems. Connector servers commonly need high processor performance to deal with the processing and message translation. Plus Ultra Group has decided to follow the Microsoft recommendations and use two processors for the spoke routing group connector servers and four processors for the hub routing group connector servers.

Anytime-Anywhere Technologies

Data and videoconferencing servers will also need a high level of processor performance to accommodate the CPU needs for conferences. The recommended CPU configuration for less than 500 simultaneous users is a single processor. Once you get above 500 users, you should move to a dual or quad processor configuration. Instant messaging home servers also have a high CPU performance requirement to handle processing and to sustain the Presence Information services. The recommended CPU configuration for IM servers is a single processor for up to 5,000 IM users. You should move to a multiprocessing scenario when you get above 5,000 users.

Chat servers, however, require a high degree of CPU performance to be able to handle processing and the maintenance of user status. A dual processor configuration is recommended for up to 10,000 chat users, and four processors will be necessary once you get above the 10,000-user threshold.

Memory Configuration

Any Exchange 2000 Server that holds a large mailbox store will also need to have an abundant amount of RAM. Because the Exchange Installable File System (ExIFS) conveys Exchange data as a file share, the amount of data that Windows 2000 caches is dramatically increased. Mailbox and public folder servers place a high demand for processing power and memory on a server. For a mailbox server with fewer than 500 users, a memory configuration of 256MB RAM is recommended. You should double the RAM to 512MB for up to 1,000 users and then move up to 1GB RAM for 1,000 to 2,500 users. If your mailbox server scales to handle more than 2,500 mailboxes, you should configure your server with 2GB RAM.

When you configure memory on your connector servers, the amount of memory depends on which of the many protocols it will accommodate as well as the load for each protocol. The recommended memory configuration for connector servers is technically based on the number of processors in the connector server. If your server is a dual processor machine, 256MB RAM is recommended. If the connector server is configured with a quad processor, at least 512MB RAM is advisable. If the computer is selected merely as a protocol front-end server, then the memory is configured per back-end mailbox. A RAM of 256MB will be sufficient when supporting up to 3,000 back-end mailboxes. For a front-end server serving 3,000 to 5,000 back-end mailboxes, you should double the RAM to 512MB.

The memory configuration for servers dedicated to anytime-anywhere communications will vary, depending on the number of users. The recommended memory configuration for data and videoconferencing servers depends on the number of simultaneous users connected to the dedicated data and videoconferencing server. If there are 500 or fewer simultaneous users, 256MB RAM is sufficient. For a dedicated server serving 500 to 1,000 simultaneous users, 512MB is a good, solid amount of RAM. The dedicated IM server needs 256MB RAM for up to 5,000 users and 512MB RAM for 5,000 to 10,000 users. The suggested memory design for dedicated chat servers is 256MB for fewer than 10,000 users and 512MB for up to 20,000 users.

To improve data access, Windows 2000 Active Directory uses the Directory Service Access (DS Access) component to cache the result of queries to Active Directory in shared memory, which ultimately forces storage requirements on the swap file. In your organization, the global catalog server will very likely be a significant resource that several programs will need to access. Exchange 2000 Server components as well as Outlook users make widespread use of the global catalog. Therefore, you should generally not configure Exchange 2000 Servers as domain controllers or global catalog servers. However, Plus Ultra Group has found it to be cost effective to configure the Exchange Server as a global catalog server at certain retail branch offices where there is a small number of users. If there are only a couple of global catalog servers in one of your physical locations, monitoring the workload is important. Each Exchange 2000 server has a DS Access cache that can be used to help reduce the burden on the global catalog because the cache allows Exchange services to cache directory lookups without having to query the global catalog.

Up to 4MB of directory entries are cached by default for a time period of five minutes. You should add 64MB to the paging file for the DS Access cache. You can monitor the effectiveness of this cache by using the Windows 2000 Server System Monitor tool. You will want to make sure that you strike a fine balance between performance and data access when tuning a caching component. By increasing the amount of time that entries will exist within the cache, you can further reduce network traffic. However, the cache can become stale if entries linger there for too long. You should consider the whole networking environment, methodically test, and completely document your actions before making permanent changes.

Warning: Use a registry editor to edit the Registry only when you have no graphical alternative, because registry editors sidestep the normal safeguards built into administrative tools. These protections avoid the configuration of conflicting settings or settings that could degrade performance or damage the system. Direct editing of the registry can have grave and unforeseen consequences that may prevent the system from starting and even require a reinstallation of Exchange 2000 or Windows 2000. It's best, when possible, to use the applications in the Control Panel or the Microsoft Management Console (MMC). Remember that you edit the registry at your own risk! Always make a backup because not all techniques work as expected in all systems due to configuration issues. Test this in a lab system first.

The parameters that can affect the best size and performance of the DS Access cache are the number of users, the maximum number of entries, the maximum cache size (memory), and the cache expiration time. We next look at adjusting the CacheTTL and MaxMemory keys that provide you with low-level control of the cache.

CacheTTL

The CacheTTL setting can improve performance, but it will also result in increased memory consumption because the entries in the cache are retained longer. To set up the CacheTTL, take these steps:

1. Choose Start|Run and type "regedt32.exe" or "regedit.exe". Then click on OK.

2. In the registry editor, navigate to HKEY_LOCAL_MACHINE\Systems\CurrentControlSet\Services\MSExchangeDSAccess\Instance0.

3. If the Instance0 subkey does not exist, you will need to create it.

4. Select (or create) the CacheTTL entry.

5. To set the time to live setting, assign data type REG_DWORD and value 0x600.

6. In Rededt32.exe, click on the entry, then click on Edit, and then select the correct item. If you are using Regedit.exe, right-click on the entry, click on Modify, and then select the correct item.

7. Close the registry editor.

The maximum number of entries (MaxEntries) and maximum cache size (MaxMemory) are two ways that you can control the size of the DS Access cache. You will probably go through some trial and error before you determine the proper configuration of the cache size by using either registry key. Microsoft recommends that you configure the cache size using the MaxMemory registry key rather than the MaxEntries key because there is a higher degree of control over the memory usage of the server. Based on this recommendation, we now look at the process for adjusting the MaxMemory registry setting.

MaxMemory

First decide what user actions this server will support before modifying this entry. Then figure out the number of entries that correspond to each of these user actions. For example, if several user actions (or protocols) are supported on this server, the maximum number of entries that correspond to a particular user action should serve as the determining factor for this key. You will set the registry value to the product of the number of actions multiplied by the number of entries per action, plus the number of client actions you plan to cache at any given moment. To set the maximum cache size, follow these steps:

1. Choose Start|Run and type "regedt32.exe" or "regedit.exe". Then click on OK.

2. In the registry editor, navigate to HKEY_LOCAL_MACHINE\Systems\CurrentControlSet\Service\MSExchangeDSAccess\Instance0.

3. If the Instance0 subkey does not exist, you need to create it.

4. Select (or create) the MaxMemory entry.

5. To set the maximum cache size in memory, use the data type REG_DWORD and assign a value in kilobytes. The default value is 4,096.

6. Close the registry editor.

Network Configuration

The first thing to consider about your network configuration is the size of the network. An Exchange 2000 Server organization could simply be a single LAN that links a few hosts for purposes of sharing files and printers, or it may be a larger heterogeneous internetwork of LANs that connect systems throughout an organization. Your Exchange 2000 design may traverse a metropolitan area network (MAN) that connects LAN segments of a campus or a city. It may be a company such as Plus Ultra Group, which represents a WAN that is connecting systems in a global organization. In one of these larger networks, for example, you may need multiple sites that will necessitate issues such as directory replication over WAN links between the sites. A smaller organization with a small network, in contrast, might have just one site, so it might not require such issues as data replication over WAN links.

The second important factor to consider is configuring servers with the appropriate network bandwidth. *Network bandwidth* is defined here as the network traffic patterns of moving data on a network link that interconnects a site. In most situations, this calls for 100Mbps network interface cards (NICs) and dedicated links from server to network hub. Your Exchange 2000 servers will often house two network cards, each one connected to a different network hub. *Network traffic patterns* are the conventional trends over a certain time period as data flows through a link. You should be able to conclude whether the total available bandwidth is sufficient to maintain the bursts of traffic that occur during heavy network usage through network traffic monitoring, by measuring the network bandwidth utilization and total packets per second.

The network topology has a huge influence on your Exchange 2000 design. Just because your network is running at 100MB does not necessarily mean that you have all the bandwidth you need for Exchange 2000. What you are also looking for here is the network available bandwidth. Both the network bandwidth and available bandwidth are significant concerns as you plan your organizational deployment of Microsoft Exchange 2000 Server. *Net available bandwidth* (NAB) is the effectual bandwidth that exists after other components consume bandwidth. The NAB on a network link between two servers is the critical factor that influences whether servers can be located within the same site. You might need to increase bandwidth in heavy traffic areas or move servers into different sites. When configuring links between sites, be cognizant of the NAB so that you can choose the most suitable site link, properly configure directory and public folder replication schedules, and ascertain the link costs. You should recognize the strengths and weaknesses of your network to make certain that your design meets or exceeds the best performance requirements for your Exchange 2000 solution.

A third key factor is deciding which network transports and protocols to use to support remote clients. One such protocol is Remote Access Service (RAS). RAS uses the Point-to-Point Protocol (PPP), which allows any client using TCP/IP, Internet Packet eXchange (IPX), or Network BIOS (basic input/output system) Extended User Interface (NetBEUI) to dial in using a standard telephone line, a modem, or a modem pool. Understanding your network transports is significant in properly configuring your site links. You will need to install and configure the network software and hardware required to support the connection before you can select your transport stack. For instance, you would need to install and configure the TCP/IP network software for Windows 2000 Server before configuring a X.400 transport stack and an X.400 connector to talk to another X.400 system over TCP/IP.

Large organizations such as Plus Ultra Group use automated client/server backup technologies. During the backup and restore processes, the servers function as clients to the backup server. Therefore, they use dedicated NICs and hubs exclusively for the backup traffic in order to provide superb performance for the backup server and the users. In contrast, the usual design for connector servers and realtime collaboration servers is to use a single NIC running at 100Mbps. The servers will often be configured with an added NIC, however, that is dedicated for an Internet connection.

Disk Configuration and Storage

Obviously, several factors work together to directly influence the performance of an Exchange 2000 Server. The number of CPUs and their speeds, the amount of RAM, and the network topology and bandwidth are key factors. The disk hardware and configuration options that you select for your Exchange 2000 Server can also affect performance significantly. The hard disk speed (defined as the random access input/outputs, or I/Os, per second) and the I/O subsystem speed are key issues. When you are purchasing disk drives, go with speed first then look at the number of random read/writes that the drive can carry out in a second. In addition, you should monitor for I/O bottlenecks. Through a process of trial and error you must establish a balance between I/O and RAM. This is crucial because if your server doesn't have enough RAM, the system may begin to swap memory on the hard disk, resulting in a burden on the I/O subsystem.

Disk I/O is a vital piece of the total performance pie when configuring an Exchange 2000 Server. You should closely examine the preferred disk aspects of each type of server. This examination should include the following factors:

➤ Where the data is placed

➤ RAID technology configuration

➤ Exchange 2000 paging file settings

➤ Disk controller cache settings

As previously discussed, you can optimize disk performance by putting the public and private store logs on a separate physical hard disk. It is preferable that you use the File Allocation Table (FAT) file system as opposed to the Windows NT file system (NTFS) to avoid the overhead associated with security processing. The remaining drives should be in a striped configuration to significantly improve the random I/O capacity of the drives. Be sure to implement a caching disk controller to boost overall drive speed. Exchange should be installed on a drive with plenty of available disk space because, in times of heavy mail usage, you will need enough disk space to hold the queued SMTP messages. The Exchange 2000 Server Optimizer is a tool that can help you configure your server. During the optimization process, the Optimizer considers the total number of servers, the total number of users, and the total number of users per server. It also analyzes the disk partitions and, if needed, will advise you to move the database log files to another disk. Another invaluable tool is LoadSim, the Exchange Client Simulator. This simulator is helpful for correctly replicating the load on the server based on a varying number of users.

When using Exchange 2000 on the Internet environment, data is saved in Multipurpose Internet Mail Extension (MIME) format in streaming database files. This enables high-performance access from Internet clients. This is also the method used when multimedia content is saved in the Web Storage System. You should prepare for extra disk space capacity because the MIME format calls for more disk space than native or Rich Text Format (RTF) data. If you are implementing content indexing of big public folder stores, plan to set aside up to 30-percent extra disk space because this feature can result in large indexes and high storage space needs. Place the indexes on separate volumes to achieve better performance gains. You should always take into account the future growth of your organization and other potential issues when you size your servers and volumes. If, for example, your system runs into a substantial increase in transactions due to virus attacks or message loops, further disk space will become necessary. In addition, the volume that contains transaction log files should be able to hold up to three times the ordinary number of daily transaction log files. Certain applications, as well, may need to save a copy of a database.

Disk Configuration for Mailbox and Public Folder Servers

Mailbox and public folder servers can be considered the same when it comes to analyzing disk I/O characteristics. Each store consists of an embedded database (EDB) file for standard messages and a synchronous transfer mode (STM) file for native Internet content. Mailbox and public folder stores exist within a storage group, and each storage group shares one set of transaction log files. As discussed previously, you can have more than one storage group on a server if you desire. You should put databases and transaction logs on separate volumes for better reliability and manageability. By putting the transaction log files on a dedicated volume, you will improve performance because the log files are sequential and therefore the disk heads are in the best position to write the next transaction. If possible, each database volume should comprise a number of physical disks. For superlative performance, put all of the databases in different directories on a single volume made up of several disks for load balancing. Finally, place the volumes on separate disk controllers and data buses for superior performance.

When transaction log files are sequentially accessed, mailbox and public folder stores implement a random form of disk read and write operations. The recommended storage technology is either a RAID 5 or RAID 0+1 (mirrored stripe sets) configuration. The advantage of RAID 0+1 is its fast read and writes. The disadvantages are that you have to restore the whole volume if any other disk fails during a rebuild, and you must enable the write-back cache to offer sufficient data protection and write performance. The advantage of RAID 5 is that it can be less expensive than RAID 0+1. RAID 5, however, has the distinct disadvantage of being slow for read and write, it takes longer than a RAID 0+1 to rebuild, and you must restore the entire volume if another disk fails during a rebuild. Even though RAID 5 is often chosen for its lower cost, RAID 5 arrays are not always the best option because they can significantly diminish performance. Because the cost of a 9GB drive is almost the same as an 18GB drive, RAID 0+1 may be the better performance and cost option. In addition, Microsoft does not suggest RAID 5 arrays for drives that are larger than 18GB. RAID 0+1 provides the best performance and adequate dependability for the transaction logs on mailbox and public folder servers.

Controller-based RAID implementations are recommended because they provide better performance and leave the processor to do other duties. You should implement redundant RAID controllers in active/active mode and have one or more standby disks per disk enclosure. The dependence of normal business activities on server applications such as email is becoming more critical. For this reason as well as many others, Exchange 2000 supports active/active cluster architecture. Clustered server environments are becoming increasingly common and are no longer just for data warehousing purposes. It is also useful to put each storage group on its own volume so that a drive loss will result in only a single storage group going offline. To maximize RAID performance, caches should be on disk controllers and not the disk drives because database corruption can occur because they are not protected. Also, all cache memory should be write-back cache because of how write-intensive Exchange 2000 can be. You configure the cache settings on the controllers themselves, and some of the higher-end controllers can actually make adjustments to boost the read-ahead cache, if necessary. Another performance enhancement would be to apply multiple paging files on several physical disks. You should use the same amount of megabytes for the Initial Size and Maximum Size settings to reduce the paging file fragmentation. Realize that Exchange 2000 Server can really throttle the Windows 2000 cache manager because its design is to make full use of server memory.

Disk Configuration for Connector Servers

Typically, a connector server will run only a single type of connector. However, you can run a number of connectors on the same server if the traffic volume is low. Connectors that run as Windows 2000 services can read and write to their corresponding directories. The message transfer agent will use a separate directory for internal queues. At Plus Ultra Group, the connector server runs two X.400 connections and a huge Exchange 2000 and Lotus Notes population. The dedicated Exchange 2000 connector server has high traffic volumes on all connectors. The SMTP service is used for all of the Exchange 2000 server-to-server traffic. In addition, the directories are placed on different disk controllers, different data buses, and separate volumes for the utmost in performance.

RAID 1 technology is preferred for the connector and other directories for ample reliability and read performance. RAID 5 is a bit of overkill because use of the mailbox store is marginal. Because Plus Ultra Group servers have high rates of mail traffic, they have deployed a controller-based RAID 0+1 array for the connector disks. Controller-based RAID provides better performance than software RAID and allows the processor to concentrate on other processes. As explained previously, the use of controller-based caches can offer performance gains. A connector server has a great deal more write operations than read operations. As a matter of fact, almost all connector disk operations are write-only. Therefore, you will want to divide the cache memory to apportion more memory for a write cache than for a read cache.

Disk Configuration for Data and Videoconferencing Servers

Dedicated Exchange 2000 conferencing servers do not have huge prerequisites for disk space. Conferencing services need only to recognize the conferencing calendar mailbox, which saves all conferences scheduled on the Windows 2000 site, and the resource mailboxes, which hold the calendar for the resource and all data in the meeting request, such as attached documents. You can simply follow the same guidelines to configure your mailbox server when setting up a dedicated data and videoconferencing server. If your Exchange mailbox server is also running conferencing services, consider placing the conference resources and calendar mailbox in a separate mailbox store to reduce the downtime necessary to restore conferences or move them to another store.

Disk Configuration for Instant Messaging Servers

IM servers, like conferencing servers, also store very little information in an Exchange database. Assuming a maximum URL size of 256 bytes, a user item would need 540 bytes of storage, and a user monitoring another user's status would need 875 bytes of disk space. Subsequently, a client logged on to an IM home server needs approximately 875 bytes as a storage requirement. For example, Plus Ultra Group has 10,000 users with an average of 20 users being monitored by each user. The total byte usage would be ($[540 + (875 \times 20) + 875] \times 10{,}000$) for a total of 183.5MB of needed disk space for storage. This is actually a relatively low storage requirement compared with other services. Microsoft suggests that an IM server's disk configuration be similar to that of a mailbox server because, like a mailbox store, it implements a nonsequential disk access pattern.

Relocating the Logs and STM Files

No matter what hardware platform your organization is using, a considerable performance gain can be made from separating the log files from the STM files. The log files write sequentially from the database to the hard disk, whereas the STM files randomly carry out input/output. In addition, separating these files will help you to analyze the I/O load from specific user actions by isolating different functions. For the systems with multiple hard drives, Plus Ultra Group has determined the ideal configuration to be one physical drive (spindle) for binaries, one spindle for the system swap file, and a single spindle dedicated to each storage group. Another performance enhancement is to separate the striped sets containing as many spindles as possible for each EDB and STM file. At the very least, you should follow this example and separate random and sequential I/O so that the logs are on spindles separate from the databases. You will also want to use RAID 1 or RAID 5 in your production environment to provide protection for your critical data.

Chapter Summary

This chapter became much more specific about deployment planning than previous chapters by looking at particular server types and their associated resource requirements. When choosing your hardware configuration, consider the role that each server will play and the load that it will be supporting. If you are deploying dedicated servers, such as a mailbox server, a single-processor server with 20 to 50GB of disk storage and 256MB RAM would meet the minimum requirements. Alternatively, a high-speed, dual or quad processor server with larger storage and RAM will give you more bang for the buck and leave room for future growth.

In a typical configuration involving existing servers, you should consider several key items. You need to determine, for example, how many CPUs are installed as well as the speed of each CPU. You also must find out how much RAM is installed and the page file configuration information. You need to know if the transaction logs are on a volume separate from the databases, and what type of RAID array is deployed, if any. You must determine what type of disk controller is being used and how much memory each controller has. Finally, you must verify the number of spindles and what formatting the disk partitions have.

Because many Exchange servers run third-party software and services for backup, monitoring, virus checking, and faxing/paging, you should be aware of potential challenges. All software installed on the server should be checked for full compliance with Exchange 2000. This chapter looked at many options for running dedicated services on a per server basis. The different server types that were addressed are:

➤ Mailbox servers

➤ Internet mail servers

➤ Public folder servers

➤ Connector servers

➤ Front-end servers

➤ Data and videoconferencing servers

➤ Instant messaging servers

➤ Chat servers

➤ Bridgehead servers

Planning your servers involves forming a strong picture of the function of each server as well as its hardware and software requirements. Security is a vital software requirement for an Exchange 2000 server. The Exchange 2000 Server relies on Windows 2000 security services to authenticate user logon requests, connect servers with one another, and control access to objects and the actions that users can take with these objects, as well as to establish the auditing of events. Another consideration concerns site management. It is much easier to administer servers that are grouped within a single site because many of the Exchange 2000 Server administrative features are automatically configured this way. You should place as many servers as you can in each site. When creating site boundaries, be cognizant of the manner in which directory replication affects cost and performance. Also, look out for latency issues when you are performing certain activities, such as changing user properties, because it may take some time for your changes to replicate.

The most vital server planning issue is to forecast the behavior of your users. It's a good idea to have open dialogues with key individuals in your organization to get feedback concerning the manner in which they will be using messaging and collaboration services. Afterwards, compare these needs directly to the specific functions and features of Microsoft Exchange 2000 Server. Remember that most users will be using Exchange 2000 to send and receive email, access public folders, read newsgroups, schedule appointments, and access personal folders and other resources.

This chapter also presented some valuable configuration strategies for the processor, memory, network, and disk resource components of both general and dedicated Exchange 2000 servers. The first Exchange 2000 Server resource that we looked at was processor usage. Remember that if server usage is going to be comparable after an upgrade, look for the CPU utilization levels to run at about 30 percent or less. This represents an ample processing threshold for Exchange 2000. Microsoft proposes using a 500MHz Intel Pentium II Xenon processor for Exchange 2000. The processor should be the best you can find and contain a 2MB level 2 cache.

This chapter also looked at processor specifics for certain dedicated server types as well as memory configuration for these scenarios. Mailbox and public folder servers have high processor and memory requirements. For a mailbox server with fewer than 500 users, a memory configuration of 256MB RAM is recommended. Double the RAM to 512MB for up to 1,000 users and then go to 1GB RAM for 1,000 to 2,500 users. If your mailbox server scales to handle more than 2,500 mailboxes, you should configure your server with 2GB RAM. The chapter also showed how to optimize the DS Access component to improve data access by caching the result of queries to Active Directory in shared memory, and looked at the registry modification to the CacheTTL and MaxMemory keys that provide low-level control of the cache.

The first thing to consider about your network configuration is the size of the network. The second important factor to consider is configuring servers with the appropriate network bandwidth. A third key factor is deciding which network transports and protocols to use to support remote clients. Although the usual design for connector servers and realtime collaboration servers is to use a single network interface card running at 100Mbps, some organizations will use dedicated network interface cards and hubs exclusively for the backup traffic in order to provide superb performance for the backup server and the users.

In regard to the disk subsystem, the hard disk speed and the I/O subsystem speed are the key issues. When purchasing disk drives, go with speed first then look at the number of random read/writes the drive can carry out in a second. You can optimize disk performance by putting the public and private store logs on a separate physical hard disk. Finally, this chapter offered a variety of disk subsystem configuration recommendations for differing types of dedicated servers.

Review Questions

1. Which statements are true regarding the prerequisites that must be in place prior to the installation of Exchange 2000? [Check all correct answers]

   a. Your Windows 2000 domain must run DNS.

   b. Your Windows 2000 domain must run Active Directory.

   c. Each system that will be running Exchange 2000 will need the SMTP services installed.

   d. The Active Directory schema must be extended for Exchange 2000 using the ForestPrep utility.

   e. Each domain must be prepared using the DomainPrep tool.

   f. a, b, and e only.

   g. All of the above.

2. Which of the following are correct minimum hardware Microsoft recommendations for Exchange 2000 Server deployment? [Check all correct answers]

   a. CD-ROM drive

   b. 64MB RAM

   c. Intel Pentium or compatible 133MHz or higher processor

   d. 200MB available disk space for the drive on which Exchange 2000 is installed

   e. All of the above

3. Your existing server is not a high performance server; therefore, you deploy that server for other services and bring in a new server with Exchange 2000 while your existing server continues to support your email users. Once the new server is operating smoothly, you make it your primary mail server. What is the name for this method of deployment of Exchange 2000 Server?

   a. Leapfrog method

   b. Bait and switch method

   c. Balance method

   d. Gateway method

4. A number of special software considerations should be addressed for preparing the operating system for Exchange 2000. Which one of the following is NOT an operating system software requirement for Exchange 2000?

   a. Active Directory

   b. DNS service

   c. Conferencing services

   d. Internet Information Services (IIS)

3

5. You have decided to install all of the Exchange 2000 services on a single machine during installation. This installation is likely the best choice for your small organization, which has nominal messaging and collaborating requirements. You are configuring what is technically known as which of the following?

   a. All-in-one-server

   b. Advanced server

   c. Standalone server

   d. Data center server

6. You have a dedicated mailbox server in your organization of more than 1,000 users. What is the recommended hardware scenario for your dedicated mailbox server?

   a. A single-processor server with at least 1GB of memory

   b. A dual-processor server with 512MB of memory

   c. A dual-processor server with 256MB of memory

   d. Two to four processors in the server with 1GB of memory

7. You are located in a large organization and need to deploy a dedicated Internet mail server as part of the standard Exchange Messaging and Collaboration installation option. You will be using virtual servers to provide services on an enterprise-wide basis. Which of the following are services that you can provide? [Check all correct answers]

   a. IMAP4

   b. NNTP

   c. POP3

   d. SLIP

8. Dedicated public folder servers are used to hold public folders and to provide public folder data to clients. Public folder servers will use which of the following protocols? [Check all correct answers]

   a. MAPI

   b. HTTP

   c. HTTP-DAV

   d. IMAP4

   e. All of the above

9. A connector server is a dedicated Exchange server set aside to run a connector. Which one of the following is *not* a connector that Exchange 2000 Server supports?

   a. SMTP connector

   b. X.400 connector

   c. Lotus Notes connector

   d. AppleTalk connector

   e. GroupWise connector

   f. Microsoft Mail connector

10. In previous versions of Exchange, systems that have one or more connectors linking two Exchange sites or connecting Exchange to the Internet are referred to as which kind of servers?

    a. Bridged

    b. Gated

    c. Bridgehead

    d. Routed

11. You are upgrading to Exchange 2000 on a server that is going to have similar usage after the upgrade. You want to make sure that you have ample processing for Exchange 2000 to prevent having to upgrade the processor or migrate the Exchange 5.5 server to another system. You need the processor utilization to be below what percentage, on average?

    a. 70 percent

    b. 50 percent

    c. 30 percent

    d. 10 percent

12. Mailbox and public folder servers need a lot of processing power and memory on the server. Your dedicated mailbox server handles more than 2,500 mailboxes. At the least, how much RAM will you want, to assure that your system has installed?

    a. 2GB

    b. 1GB

    c. 512MB

    d. 256MB

13. What network software for Windows 2000 Server would you need to install before configuring an X.400 transport stack and an X.400 connector on Exchange 2000 Server?

    a. NetBEUI

    b. IPX/SPX

    c. NWLink

    d. TCP/IP

14. Which of the following statements is false concerning the comparison between RAID 5 and RAID 0+1?

    a. With RAID 0+1, you must restore the whole volume if any other disk fails during a rebuild.

    b. RAID 5 can be less expensive than RAID 0+1.

    c. RAID 0+1 is slower than RAID 5 for read and write.

    d. Microsoft does not suggest RAID 5 arrays for drives that are larger than 18GB.

15. In Exchange 2000, log files write sequentially from the database to the hard disk, in contrast to another important file type that randomly carries out I/O. Separating these files can help realize performance gains as well as help you analyze the I/O load from specific user actions by isolating different functions, regardless of the hardware platform your organization is using. What file types should be separated from the log files for better performance?

    a. EXC

    b. SVN

    c. STM

    d. TTL

    e. None of the above

Real-World Projects

You are the senior systems architect for the Exchange 2000 project for Plus Ultra Group. You are into the server planning stage of your rollout.

Project 3.1

Use your company (or interview a friend who works in IT for a large company) to complete the following survey to begin building your server planning strategy. Answer the assessment questions as fully as possible. You can also use Table 3.1 as a guideline when deploying Exchange 2000 in a real-world environment.

Table 3.1   Guidelines for deploying Exchange 2000.

Component	Response
How many servers are presently running Exchange?	
How many users are on each server?	
What is the size of the private information store on each server?	
What is the size of the public information store on each server?	
What services do these servers provide? (Circle correct answers.)	Calendaring
	Messaging
	Internet gateway
	Other
What are the current mailbox size limits?	
What domain suffix do you use for SMTP addresses (where the user's SMTP address is of the form **uid@domain-suffix**)?	
How much bandwidth is available on your Internet connection?	
What are your average daily messaging statistics for internal and SMTP mail?	Average number of inbound messages:
	Average number of outbound messages:
	Average inbound message size in KB:
	Average outbound message size in KB:
What are your current processes to backup and restore data held in the email message store?	
What backup devices or software do you currently use?	
How long do you keep your backup data?	
What method of backup do you use for your message store (full, incremental, or other)?	
What type of disaster recovery do you use in your email environment?	
Do you have off-site backups of your data?	
Do you have a plan to recover from a physical disaster? If yes, are you testing it on an ongoing basis?	
What is the number of processors and speed in each Exchange Server?	
How much RAM is installed on each Exchange Server?	
What are the free hard-drive space for each server?	
Are you using clustering? If so, list the hardware in use.	
What is the operating system and service pack installed on each Exchange-based server?	
How many Exchange 4 and 5.x sites exist in your organization?	

Project 3.2

Plus Ultra Group has main retail offices in three different cities: Phoenix, London, and Tokyo. They have decided to deploy three large Exchange 2000 mailbox servers in each of the three main offices. The Phoenix server has the largest number of users (4,500). Each Exchange 2000 Server is for the office and the retail stores that connect directly to it via a WAN link. This solution helps to reduce the downtime when the server fails, but doesn't eliminate downtime. You are tasked with finding a solution to provide high availability. What would you propose?

Solution: The best way to provide high availability in this scenario would be to create a cluster solution. Plus Ultra Group's situation is perfect for a two-node cluster solution. With the initial release of Exchange 2000, a two-node cluster is possible. For Plus Ultra Group, one node would serve the main office users, and the other node would serve the retail stores.

Project 3.3

More than one mailbox can exist within a storage group on an Exchange 2000 Server. Plus Ultra Group has opted to use two storage groups, one on each node of the server cluster. Each storage group has one set of transaction log files. Where would you place the databases to get maximum performance? Where would you locate each volume? Where would you put the transaction log files to provide fault tolerance and disaster recovery?

Solution: For maximum performance, place each database on a separate volume. Moreover, locate each volume on a different controller and data bus. To provide fault tolerance and disaster recovery, place the transaction log files on a volume separate from the corresponding databases. Placing the transaction log files on a separate and dedicated volume increases the performance.

CHAPTER FOUR

Analyzing the Existing Messaging System Architecture

After completing this chapter, you will be able to:

✓ Analyze the existing messaging system architecture

✓ Plan for the possible changes to the messaging system architecture

✓ Analyze existing mail routing

✓ Analyze the existing server configuration

✓ Analyze existing messaging client configurations

Y ou almost certainly have resolved that your organization needs to replace the current mail system with a more robust, cost-effective, and efficient messaging and collaboration solution. Before moving from the server planning phase, you should take full advantage of the benefits, as well as reduce the risks, of your Exchange 2000 deployment by forming a solid understanding of the existing messaging environment. You should pay particular attention to four critical areas that exist for any messaging and collaboration system within an organization. If you focus on these areas and establish your present design, you will be better able to provide basic messaging functions before adding the more advanced features available in Exchange 2000 discussed in later chapters. This information will also be valuable when providing solutions for future customers or employers.

The four main areas can best be categorized as:

➤ Existing messaging system

➤ Existing mail routing

➤ Existing server configuration

➤ Existing client configuration

Analyzing the Existing Messaging System

An Exchange 5.5 site is designed based on administrative and network connectivity requirements. All servers within an Exchange 5.5 site talk directly to each other, and this communication can extend over multiple geographic locations as long as there is adequate network bandwidth. If you do not already have a comprehensive diagram of the current structure of your existing Exchange organization, you should create one as early as possible in the planning process. This diagram will assist you greatly in the design of the new Exchange 2000 organization as well as provide you with an excellent tool for troubleshooting the organization at a later time.

Consider using Microsoft Visio 2000 to assess your current organizational infrastructure. Visio 2000 can directly access your Exchange 5.x (or Windows 2000) infrastructure and construct an illustration of it. This map can then serve as a starting point for any modifications you may decide to make before the deployment. Navigate your browser to **http://www.microsoft.com/office/visio** for more information. In addition, Microsoft Exchange Server Topology Diagramming Tool (EMap.exe) reads an Exchange directory with ActiveX Data Objects and automatically generates a Visio diagram of your site topology. You can download this tool from the Exchange Web site at: **http://www.microsoft.com/ TechNet/exchange/tools/topology.asp**.

To further supplement the construction of these diagrams, you must also determine whether multiple Exchange organizations already exist in your organization.

Presupposing the existence of multiple organizations, you should decide whether it would be beneficial to combine them into a single organization or an Active Directory forest. The decision to separate or combine multiple organizations depends on whether the organizations were created because of a merger or acquisition and how these different organizations directories are connected together. In Exchange 2000, the organization will no longer use an independent directory that resides on every Exchange 5.5 server. Rather, the directory will be integrated with Active Directory and bound by the Windows 2000 forest in which it resides. You should also use all the documentation related to the current installation. These documents reveal when the deployment was done, how it was done, all issues that surfaced during the process, as well as other general information. Reading this material will give you the big picture of how the existing email system was deployed.

To successfully begin the analysis of the first component—the existing messaging system—you should divide the messaging system organization for further investigation as follows:

1. Catalog your existing Exchange 5.5 site design (if applicable).

2. Map out the backbone architecture.

3. Scrutinize your all-important Internet connectivity design.

A good understanding of these three areas will help you establish your existing messaging design. The fundamental transport and routing component of a messaging system is critical to successful communications. This core engine is essential to the operation of an efficient and reliable enterprise messaging system, especially if users are distributed around the country or the world. By using Simple Mail Transfer Protocol (SMTP) as the native communications protocol between servers running Microsoft Exchange 2000 Server, some of the deployment issues with earlier transport implementations disappear. For example, companies with a distributed user base normally design their Exchange site model around the availability of network bandwidth rather than around the desired administration model. Because Exchange 2000 no longer uses remote procedure call (RPC) for message transfer, you can now devise a more flexible routing scheme. In addition, Exchange 2000 is organized into administration groups and routing groups rather than sites. This gives you more flexibility in both administration and routing.

Administrative groups and routing groups will also substitute for your existing Exchange 5.5 sites. Administrative groups are sets of Exchange 2000 servers that share a common administrative design. Plus Ultra Group, for instance, has an organization with 100 Exchange servers. If the same team of administrators handles 10 of those servers, you could place those 10 servers in an administrative group. A routing group, in contrast, is a group of Exchange 2000 servers that are linked to each other by a high-speed connection. Servers in a routing group use SMTP to communicate directly with each other. Your existing Exchange 5.5 implementation most likely has a different SMTP address for each site. In Exchange 2000, the default scenario is one recipient policy with one SMTP address that represents all of the users in an entire organization, although you could have several recipient policies so that different SMTP addresses could apply to different users. The important property is that Exchange 2000 allows you to configure one SMTP domain for all users.

You should divide your existing Exchange organization into pieces and examine it carefully, taking into consideration these new administrative and routing group models. Exchange 2000 Setup will prompt you to indicate the administrative group to which the server will belong at installation. Keep in mind, however, that once a server is installed in an administrative group, it cannot be moved. This is just one reason why it is so important for you to establish an administrative group before you install Exchange 2000.

Separate Exchange Organizations

Let us look first at a scenario in which you have decided that your multiple Exchange organizations will remain as detached organizations. This presents two immediate issues that must be addressed. First, how will you set them up in Windows 2000? Second, what features will you lose? Setting up multiple Exchange organizations necessitates synchronization because recipients in other forests will not be security principals in the local forest. The other recipients will have to be retained as contacts—the Active Directory equivalent of Exchange 5.5 custom recipients. You can use Active Directory Connector (ADC) as well as several other tools to synchronize between forests. When you choose to synchronize by creating connection agreements between forests, you specify that the connection agreement is an "inter-organization agreement." In the connection agreement configuration, you can also indicate which users were created as contacts. Now for the second issue of what will be lost. What you will lose with multiple forests is comparable to what you lost having multiple Exchange 5.5 organizations. You lost access to public folders, access to calendar free and busy information, and access to other users' appointment books. Another restriction, when compared with Exchange 5.5, is that you can't assign permissions to Active Directory contacts. Active Directory contacts are not security principals (users). This differs from Exchange 5.5, which offered its own security model.

Exchange 2000 in Its Own Forest

Your present Exchange 5.5 may be employed in resource domains that trust separate Windows NT 4.0 account domains. Likewise, Exchange 2000 can be implemented in its own Windows 2000 resource forest that trusts account domains in other Windows 2000 forests. The key to this concept is that users will log on to their home forest and use security credentials from that forest to log on to Exchange. To make this possible, the user's account must first have permissions to the

Exchange 2000 mailbox. Also, a down-level trust is necessary from the domain containing the Exchange servers to every domain in every forest that contains users with Exchange mailboxes. This setup is demonstrated in Figure 4.1.

If your Exchange 5.5 servers are presently located in one or more resource domains, you can implement this design by following these simple steps:

1. Upgrade your Windows NT 4 resource domain to a Windows 2000 domain in a new forest of its own. If you have more than one resource domain, you can upgrade the rest of them and join the forest, or you could migrate the servers across forests.

2. Install ADC and configure a connection agreement that enables you to create users in the new forest. The ADC will create disabled "mailbox-enabled" user accounts by default. The main Windows NT account from the Exchange 5.5 directory will be added to the mailbox security descriptor attribute.

3. Upgrade the Exchange servers, or install new Exchange 2000 servers and move the mailboxes. As soon as a user's mailbox is on an Exchange 2000 server, the user will be able to log on using his or her existing credentials from Windows NT 4 or 2000.

This approach is very useful because all of the users will be in a single Exchange organization, and any other method would involve assigning mailbox permissions to the user's existing security credentials. Another advantage to this method is that the visibility of public folders, free and busy information, and appointment books is practically guaranteed. It will also be incorporated with a completely functional security model. A disadvantage of this method, however, is that you will have another forest to manage along with another set of accounts. ADC can create this

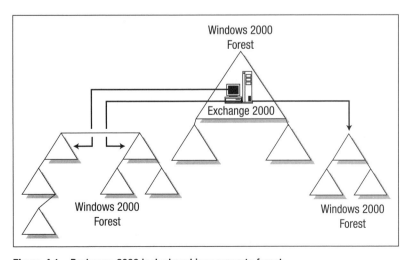

Figure 4.1 Exchange 2000 is deployed in a separate forest.

environment easily if you begin with an Exchange 5.5 organization. After you are running Exchange 2000 throughout your organization, you will need to take measures to synchronize the disabled user accounts with users' primary accounts in the forests to which they log on.

Multiple Exchange 5.5 Organizations

To combine two or more Exchange 5.5 organizations, you could use the Move Server Wizard. Rather than waiting until you upgrade to Exchange 2000, you should merge the organizations while still on Exchange 5.5. You can migrate user accounts and servers between forests, but you cannot migrate Exchange databases. You can use the Exchange 5.5 Move Server Wizard to migrate Exchange 5.5 servers into a mixed-mode Exchange 2000 organization only if the server you are moving exists in a site with Exchange 5.5 only, and at least one Exchange 5.5 server is already running in the target site. Assuming that you have an existing Exchange 5.5 site, you will want to answer the following questions as a supplement to your architectural design diagram:

➤ How would you describe your enterprise-wide messaging system architecture? (Use the messaging system topology diagram that illustrates your basic architecture.)

➤ What messaging systems/versions does your enterprise use?

➤ What is the approximate number of users supported by these systems?

➤ What kind of messaging gateways/connectors does your enterprise use? (Use any information on the traffic that goes through these gateways.)

➤ Does a central messaging/networking management and administration team exist? If not, how is the messaging enterprise managed?

Analyzing Existing Mail Routing

Before discussing the existing mail routing architecture, you need to review some Exchange 5.5 routing basics. The Message Transfer Agents (MTAs) for Exchange 5.5 and earlier versions are built upon the X.400 standard for addressing and carrying e-mail messages. The X.400 specification supports several transport methods, including Ethernet, TCP/IP (Transmission Control Protocol/ Internet Protocol), X.25, and dial-up. If you are working with an existing pre-Exchange 2000 environment, your servers are probably grouped with full-time, reliable connections into Exchange sites. All the servers in a site transport messages to each other directly by employing remote procedure call (RPC) functionality. To connect sites to each other, you may be using the RPC-based Site Connector, an X.400 Connector, or, in some circumstances, the Internet Mail Connector, which is based on SMTP. Sites are governed according to the existing network bandwidth or administrative borders. When a client system that is running an earlier version of Exchange sends a message, one of the following procedures takes place in the message routing process:

➤ Exchange decides whether the destination address is on the same server as the source address. If it is, the Web Storage System puts the message in the proper mailbox. The MTA is not drawn in unless Exchange 5.5 Service Pack 1 or later is installed and message journaling is configured.

➤ If the destination address is on another server on the site, the MTA transfers the message straight to the destination server's MTA by using RPC communications.

➤ If the destination address is on another server at a remote site, the MTA routes the message to the remote site through a connector. Either the address will be the address on an adjacent site (and can be reached by a connector), or it will be outside the organization and can be reached by a connector on this site (or on another site).

Tip: *Message journaling*—Message journaling is configured on a database to create a copy of every message received by users on that database and to send the copy to a folder for archival purposes.

Exchange Routing Groups

An Exchange routing group identifies a set of Exchange 2000 servers that converse directly with each other. Your existing sites have built-in restrictions that routing groups do not have. For example, routing groups can be fashioned and removed as needed, and server membership can be changed on the fly as well. With Exchange 2000 routing groups, your entire organizational routing architecture will be easily modified without having to reinstall. The Exchange 2000 routing network will take maximum advantage of any fundamental network infrastructure change, such as upgrading a network link. The Exchange organization must be operating in native mode, however, and all routing groups must be an element of the same administrative group.

While analyzing your existing architecture, it is also important to remember that SMTP is the only transport protocol used by Exchange 2000 servers in the same routing group. As a matter of fact, once you have an Exchange 2000-only environment, RPC connectivity is not even offered as an option. RPC *is* used, however, between Exchange 2000 and earlier versions of Exchange when an Exchange 2000 server is joined to an existing Exchange 5.5 site. Exchange servers must belong to the same Windows 2000 forest as well as have direct and permanent SMTP connectivity to each other to be members of a routing group. All servers within a routing group will always need to be able to contact the routing group master. If the basic network performance between the servers in the routing group suffers due to recurrent reliability issues, or if low-bandwidth connections are necessary between servers, a routing group might need to be divided.

Tip: *Routing connectors*—All enterprise-messaging systems require a way of passing routing data between each other. In Exchange 2000, when a connector is placed between two routing groups, a cost is associated with the link. A cost represents route preference when multiple routes are available; the lower the cost, the more preferable the route.

Your earlier version of Exchange may use a routing calculation server that composes the available routes and costs from the directory and forms a Gateway Address Resolution Table (GWART). This table is designed to circulate the routing topology for the organization to all of the other servers in the Exchange site. However, if a network link (or bridgehead server) is unavailable, you have no mechanism to get this information to the rest of the Exchange organization. Exchange 2000 will resolve these types of issues with changes to directory and messaging architecture. Although you will be able to create any number of routing groups, you should limit the number of groups to less than 1,000 for administrative reasons. More routing groups will not drastically influence the performance of the messaging infrastructure, although it will result in larger link state databases with potentially more status data to replicate. In an Exchange organization with 200 routing groups, 250 connectors, and 500 servers, for example, you should plan for about 32 kilobytes of memory on each server for the link state database. As a general rule, each object in the link state database will call for approximately 32 bytes of memory.

To meet its requirement in the past, Plus Ultra Group had to deploy very wide Exchange sites that spanned low-bandwidth networks. As the Exchange site forced the messaging and directory replication model to use RPCs over low-bandwidth links, additional challenges occurred. The decision was made to create a new matching backbone architecture based on Exchange 2000 servers. With this architecture, all of the locations will steadily migrate to the new backbone, which is using the advanced routing capabilities in Exchange 2000. The plan also includes migrating all the users from an independent department to the central Exchange organization in due time. At the start of the deployment of the backbone, administrative groups will match routing groups one-to-one. When the entire migration to Exchange 2000 is complete, Plus Ultra Group will switch to Exchange 2000 native mode, in which the administration of routing groups and administrative groups will be more flexible and will respond to the different needs of the company.

Exchange 2000 Message Transfer Agents

A version of the MTA still exists in Exchange 2000, even though the resident transport has been changed to SMTP. The MTAs in Exchange 5.5 and Exchange 2000 do not differ much. If an Exchange 2000 server exists in an Exchange 5.5 site, for example, the single-hop-based nature of an Exchange 5.5 site doesn't change. All servers that run earlier versions of Exchange will still be able to communicate with the MTA using RPC. If two or more Exchange 2000 servers are in an Exchange 5.5 site, the Exchange 2000 servers route messages to one another by using SMTP rather than the MTA process. Therefore, Plus Ultra Group can eventually take advantage of the advanced queuing and routing mechanisms that exist in Exchange 2000. Plus Ultra Group used earlier Exchange 5.5 systems to connect to their existing Lotus Notes host system. They also plan to migrate existing users of cc:Mail, Lotus Notes, and GroupWise to either Exchange 5.5 or directly to Exchange 2000 servers.

Routing Group Connectors

Once you define the routing group boundaries, the groups will need to be connected to one another using a connector. The routing group connector is the ideal connector for this purpose because it uses SMTP and gathers its routing and next-hop information from the link state database. It can also be configured with one or more existing bridgehead servers on either end of the connector. This provides redundancy should one of the bridgehead servers fail. Exchange 2000 has the ability to choose another bridgehead server from within the routing group to pass on the message. Several scenarios may come up for connecting routing groups. If you have an intermittent connection (or no direct connectivity) between routing groups, you may deploy an X.400 or an SMTP connector to enable messaging. Such connectors are appropriate where asynchronous dial-up through a modem is the only method of connectivity between locations. Unlike earlier versions of Exchange, Exchange 2000 does not include a Dynamic Remote Access Service (RAS) Connector. Instead, Windows 2000 supplies a more efficient routing connector for an on-demand connection, which utilizes the routing and remote access mechanisms included in Windows 2000. SMTP connectors are also used to connect servers that perform different tasks.

If you have areas of your network that are X.25-based, the X.400 connector is the only way for you to join routing groups. To connect two routing groups with the X.400 connector, you construct X.400 connectors in both routing groups to create a two-way connection. To provide load balancing, the Exchange designers at Plus Ultra Group configured multiple connectors between the two routing groups. They decided on this option because implementing multiple connectors offered the best results. Small text messages are transferred over fast SMTP, and larger messages go over X.400. It is fine to employ parallel connectors between routing groups because they utilize link state data to compute the best route. In addition, if the network link goes down, the messages will not bounce back and forth between the connectors because both connectors depend on the same physical link.

Internet Mail

Internet mail makes up a significant percentage of message flow within an organization. You must document Internet message traffic before you upgrade to Exchange 2000. In earlier versions of Exchange, configuration information for outbound message content was stored on each Internet Mail Service. In Exchange 2000, content configuration is managed individually for each organization. Using the software previously mentioned, you should create a diagram that shows inbound and outbound message traffic to and from the Internet. Include information about firewalls and virus scanning. In addition, you should provide answers to the following questions:

➤ Does the Internet Mail Service send SMTP mail to any internal systems? If so, what is the name of the system and the configuration information? (This includes, for example, IP address, Domain Name System (DNS) name, and so on; the business purpose; and the contact information.)

➤ Are you implementing virus-scanning software on inbound and outbound messages? If so, document the antivirus software vendor and how the software is configured, as well as how often the virus patterns are updated.

➤ Is the Internet Mail Service configured for rerouting? If so, document the rerouting configuration.

➤ Does a firewall exist between the Internet and the Internet Mail Service server? If so, does the server allow them to traverse the firewall or does it queue the messages?

➤ Does your firewall apply any messaging size restrictions?

➤ Does your firewall have special rules that apply to email (for example, domain restrictions, antiviral, masquerade, and so on)?

➤ Which individual is responsible for maintaining the external mail exchanger (MX) records for your organization? Which MX records are registered?

➤ Are the MX records configured in a load-balancing design?

Finding solid answers to these questions and scenarios will help you to plan for upgrading to Exchange 2000 and securing mail swapped over the Internet. Also, remember that configuration information that previously existed for each Internet Mail Service is not updated when you upgrade to Exchange 2000. It also now applies to the entire organization. You must migrate all of your Internet Mail Service configuration information to the Exchange System Manager before you add any SMTP connectors from Exchange 2000 servers to the Internet.

Analyzing the Existing Server Configuration

Your existing Exchange 5.5 site topology will not restrict Exchange 2000 in any way; therefore, you can deploy servers in any order and with whatever design you choose. You can also effortlessly adapt the topology to fit shifting conditions. The key planning issue will be the effect of Active Directory integration. A good example of this integration would be making sure that the global catalog servers are properly placed within your design. You should already have a general idea of what you might be able to consolidate, so now look at what you might want to do in your organization.

To take the best advantage of server consolidation, your organization will have a great number of mailboxes hosted on numerous Exchange servers in a central data center. Your company will also probably contain multiple Exchange sites, each with dedicated, remotely managed connector servers and mailbox servers. Within a site, servers are usually categorized by their function (including mailbox servers, connector servers, and Outlook Web Access servers). In a small organization, however, connectors and mailboxes are most likely kept on the same server.

Dedicated mailbox and public folder servers contain only mailboxes and public folders, respectively. Although, theoretically, an unlimited number of mailboxes can exist on an Exchange 5.5 server, the number of users is actually restricted by several factors. These governing issues include the amount of random access memory (RAM), processor speed, and the time it takes to recover from a significant system failure. When you analyze the existing server configuration, you should examine the sizes of the mailbox and public folder stores. Consider the following questions as well:

➤ Which protocols are enabled for mail?

➤ Does your Exchange organization have more than one company? If so, is it necessary to recover them separately?

➤ What is the default storage limit on mailboxes?

➤ What is the policy for retaining deleted items?

➤ Who is responsible for creating distribution lists?

➤ What is the strategy for distribution lists?

➤ Do you implement automated tools when creating distribution lists?

➤ How many mailboxes on a server are associated with customer service level agreements (SLAs)?

➤ Is there a need to offer VIP mailboxes?

If large mailbox stores exist, you may want to consider dividing them into several smaller ones. Your present SLAs may require the deployment of multiple servers to ensure recovery within the time limitations of the agreement. In Exchange 2000, multiple storage groups and databases allow you to combine these servers into one larger server with multiple mailbox stores and databases. Each Exchange organization is unique, and these numbers are obviously relative. on one extreme, your organization may have only two servers (one for mailboxes and one for an Internet connection), but you sense that they should be consolidated. At the other extreme, Plus Ultra Group has 16 mailbox servers, but for compelling reasons, they have decided that they do not want to consolidate them. This is completely up to each organization to determine.

Coexistence Issues

Most organizations, including your own, quite likely will be migrating from an earlier version of Exchange. During the migration process, the Exchange 5.5 and Exchange 2000 designs will be coexisting in a mixed environment. You must have at least one computer running Exchange 5.5 Service Pack 3 on the site before you can successfully install the Exchange 2000 Server on the existing Exchange 5.5 site. When the Exchange 2000 Server is installed on an Exchange 5.5 site, one administrative group and one routing group are created in Active Directory. Both of these groups will inherit the name of the original site.

In most situations, you have an existing Exchange 5.5 server that is designated as a Routing Calculation server. It produces a GWART to be used by the Exchange 5.5 servers to spread the connector information. The Exchange 2000 routing group master can generate the GWART in Active Directory if there are no Exchange 5.5 servers in an administrative group or site. The Site Replication Service (SRS) replicates the GWART to the Exchange 5.5 directory in neighboring sites. All Exchange 2000 group and connector information is stored in Active Directory and is replicated to the entire organization. Exchange 5.5 uses the GWART to notify the Exchange 5.5 servers that they can route messages to Exchange 2000 servers and connectors on the same site, and vice versa. The Exchange 2000 servers, however, do not use a GWART for routing.

Exchange 2000 servers on an Exchange 5.5 site converse with each other via the SMTP protocol. Exchange 2000 servers, however, transfer messages to Exchange 5.5 servers using RPC. This occurs especially if an organization uses earlier connectors that have not been updated to run on Exchange 2000.

Bridgehead Servers

In earlier versions of Exchange, servers that have one or more connectors linking two Exchange sites (or connecting Exchange to the Internet) are called *bridgehead servers*. Within a mixed Exchange site, you can upgrade your bridgehead server to Exchange 2000 even if you are connecting together Exchange 5.5 sites. After your hub or multiple bridgehead servers are upgraded to Exchange 2000, they begin to communicate by using SMTP. This increases throughput and provides resilience to slow network connections.

Bridgehead servers are in charge of distributing mail and public folder information between sites, as well as replicating the Exchange directory between sites. In Exchange 2000 designs, bridgehead servers can still exist, but the directory information is now replicated by using the global catalog. Part of your message system architecture analysis will be to create a table with information about each bridgehead server connector. Some key questions concerning bridgehead servers are:

➤ What type of connector is installed? Document the configuration of the connector.

➤ What is the site or server destination for this connector? What is the cost for this connector?

➤ What type of link (bandwidth) uses the connector?

➤ Are any sites downstream to this connector?

➤ How often does this connector send mail?

➤ Is another route defined for this server?

➤ Is Exchange directory replication configured?

➤ What is the Exchange directory replication schedule for each site?

➤ Does the connector have message limits? If so, document the message restrictions.

➤ Are TCP or TP4 transport stacks being used?

Topology Considerations

Exchange 2000 presents improvements over the Exchange 5.5 Site Connector if one of the source bridgehead servers is out of commission. Exchange connectors do not automatically attempt to use that server until it comes back up again. If several connectors have the same cost, each server chooses a random connector and uses it for a certain period of time. With multiple servers, this mechanism produces round-robin activity. The superfluous cost tables that were maintained in the previous versions of Exchange are eliminated as well. When a client must use an alternate server to access the content of public folders, Exchange 2000 implements routing groups to compute the nearest available server. It makes this determination by using a cost property configured on the routing group connector. This cost is then stored in a single cost database that is shared with e-mail routing calculations.

In Exchange 5.5, site affinities are not transitive. If you set up an affinity between site 1 and site 2 and between site 2 and site 3 as well, for example, you do not automatically get affinity between site 1 and site 3. This is the nontransitive nature of Exchange 5.5. In Exchange 2000, due to the replication schema of Windows 2000 Active Directory, affinities are transitive. Because RPC is the resident transfer mechanism for Exchange 5.5, you must deploy more routing groups in Exchange 5.5 sites compared to Exchange 2000. Also, unlike Exchange 5.5, where intrasite and intersite RPC communications are encrypted, SMTP communications in Exchange 2000 are not encrypted. Upgrading an Exchange

5.5 hub, in a hub-and-spoke design, also appreciably boosts hub performance and reliability because Exchange 2000 and the use of SMTP improve performance. Link state routing is most valuable in architectures with multiple routing groups using multiple paths. In a traditional hub-and-spoke design, you do not have the same degree of improvement as you do in a mesh network or multiple connections network. By adding routing groups, you increase the size of the link state table and increase potential link state status messages. This can increase the amount of link state message traffic. Exchange will no longer include a Dynamic RAS Connector either. Exchange 2000 will instead use the on-demand capabilities of Windows 2000. This is accomplished primarily through the blend of the routing group connector and the routing and remote access demand-dial interface.

Analyzing the Existing Client Configuration

One of the first steps you should take to analyze your client configuration is to carry out a user census. To properly plan for addressing the data needs of users, you need an accurate representation of the individuals who will eventually be using the Exchange 2000 Server. Cluster your Exchange users based on organization or network location and assemble them together with their data. Next, scrutinize each group to see the type of information they produce and exchange, their public folder usage, and their storage and performance requirements. All messages coming into your organization or moving within it between systems should be categorized. By grouping users that are apt to send messages to one other, you can reduce the traffic and maintain server performance. This information will be invaluable later when analyzing performance, load balancing, and budgetary issues, and as you settle on which users will have mailboxes on a particular server. One technique is to observe the organizational chart of the company or a survey of each local area network (LAN) segment. Add the names of the groups to your layout along with an approximation of the number of people in each group. Do your best to place users into groups that offer a degree of flexibility when planning your servers later. Finally, think about dividing your larger groups so that all groups are sized as equally as possible.

Analyzing Message Traffic

You can also size up your Exchange Server by the amount of message traffic it will be managing. A good first step is to derive an average server load number based on any existing records for your current mail system. To approximate the number of messages that each person receives in a day, you need to count the number of recipients for each message that the user sends. Do your best to find an average for each group, even though disparities among users in a group always do exist. You can bring this data together in several ways. If your current system allows you to retain all sent mail, you could survey some users in each group to get a handle on how many messages are sent each day. Another loose approximation can be garnered by simply asking users who have been out of the office for more than a day or two to check how many new messages they received while they were gone. This technique can also be used to find out how much mail is being saved by your organization's users.

The next logical move is to use your network diagram, and to sketch or add notes that describe each group's typical traffic pattern. Determine whether mail is usually sent within the group, to other specific groups, or to other specific sites and gateways. The key here is to identify trends in messaging traffic. Besides doing a sample survey of sent mail or in-boxes, you could invest in some network reporting software to facilitate the analysis of mail transfer. Users' mail needs will be dissimilar, depending on whether they partake in many mailing lists, distribution lists, or newsgroups. Making server choices based simply on the number of users is unrealistic. You need to classify the users with some sort of benchmark. To make it easier to estimate the load and performance processes, Microsoft defines three user types based on real-world usage data on current mail systems, as shown in Table 4.1.

Analyzing Storage Needs

You can also assess the Exchange Server capacity needs through the message store. The message storage can affect the performance of Exchange just as message volume can. Therefore, you should have a grasp on the storage habits of each of the different groups. In Exchange 2000, personal mail folders can be stored on the server in the Information Store (IS), in personal folders on each workstation, or in both. Public folders sharing information among users, in contrast, are always stored in the IS.

The IS uses single-instance storage architecture to trim down disk usage. If a particular user sends one message to 20 recipients on a server, for example, each recipient's mailbox simply receives a pointer to the single shared copy of the message. Administrative disk quotas can also be employed to help limit disk usage on the server by further controlling the quantity of private mail. This is a vast improvement over MS Mail. Exchange 2000 also offers policies that give you the ability to control private mail storage in the IS. You can help to reduce the storage needs on a server by managing the sizes of the sent and received messages.

Table 4.1   Microsoft-defined basic user types.

Parameters	Light	Medium	Heavy
Maximum inbox size (in messages)	25	125	> 250
Other old mail processing (times per day)	5	15	20
Total sends per day (average)	8	20	40
Total receipts per day (average)	20	60	120

Tip: Keep in mind that the Exchange 2000 Server backup will archive only those messages stored in the server Information Store. If users store mail in personal folders on their client workstations, that data will not be administratively backed up.

Client Applications

Your organization may not be able to deploy new client software at the same time that you roll out Exchange 2000. Backward compatibility with your previous versions of Exchange is then critical. If your organization is presently using Outlook 97 or Outlook 98 client software with an earlier version of Exchange, you will be compatible with Exchange 2000. At present, however, Outlook 2000 is the only client that can directly contact the global catalog in Exchange 2000 that provides the global address list to users. Exchange 2000 will relay address list information to allow previous versions of Exchange access to the global address list data. During your survey of the existing messaging infrastructure, make sure that you document all of the anticipated changes to client computer access. This information-gathering process should include whatever messaging client software has been deployed (Exchange, Outlook 97, Outlook 98, Outlook 2000, Outlook Express, or Outlook Web Access). You also should note the version of operating system being used on each machine. You need to know which version of each client is deployed, if there is a plan in place to upgrade to Outlook 2000, and when this deployment is scheduled to occur.

You also need to identify which Web browser is installed as well as the versioning. In addition, catalog all applications that are dependant on your existing email system and prioritize these programs by their importance to the functions of your organization. Besides the previous issues, you should scrutinize existing Outlook Web Access scenarios to see how they were used. You need to determine how many user logons occur each day as well as how many messages are being read and sent per day. Also, you need to determine the average session time for users. Gathering this usage data will help you immensely in determining the client load on Exchange and the extent to which Outlook Web Access will be used. You may also want to plan on upgrading any Exchange clients or Web browsers that are heavily used.

Chapter Summary

This chapter laid some groundwork in preparation for the next two chapters, which explore planning the deployments of messaging clients in Exchange 2000 and planning for coexistence of Exchange 2000 Server with other messaging systems. The overall analysis of the existing messaging system architecture isolated four main areas of investigation: the existing messaging system, mail routing, server configuration, and client configuration. You must understand all of these areas in relation to the messaging architecture currently in place, if applicable. The Web provides more information about Microsoft Visio 2000 and the Microsoft Exchange Server Topology Diagramming Tool to assist you in creating invaluable diagrams of your existing Exchange site topology.

Your topology diagram will help to map out your multiple organizations. Several major decisions must be made to determine whether it is advantageous to merge multiple organizations into a single organization or an Active Directory forest. This determination depends on whether the organizations were created because of an acquisition or merger, and how the different directories are linked together. Remember that in Exchange 2000; the organization no longer makes use of an autonomous directory residing on each Exchange 5.5 server. The directory is instead incorporated with Active Directory and bound by the Windows 2000 forest in which it resides. You may decide to continue with separate Exchange organizations, you may keep Exchange 2000 in its own forest, or you may retain multiple Exchange 5.5 organizations.

It is best to merge the multiple organizations while still on Exchange 5.5 rather than waiting until you upgrade to Exchange 2000 because there is no way to merge two Exchange 2000 organizations. You can migrate user accounts and servers between forests, but you cannot migrate Exchange databases.

The excellent questions presented in this chapter help with the analysis of your messaging system architecture. Make sure that you include the answers to these questions with the diagram you create in Visio 2000 (or other similar application).

Review Questions

1. While analyzing your existing architecture, you realize that SMTP is the only transport protocol used by Exchange 2000 servers in the same routing group. To be included in a routing group, Exchange servers must obey which of the following rules? [Check all correct answers]

   a. The servers must belong to the same Windows 2000 forest.

   b. The servers must have permanent and direct SMTP connectivity to one another.

   c. All servers within a routing group should always be able to contact the routing group master.

   d. All of the above.

   e. None of the above.

2. You need to assess your current organizational infrastructure and construct an illustration of it. This diagram can then serve as a starting point for any modifications you may decide to make before the deployment. Which of the following tools can you use to accomplish this task? [Check all correct answers]

   a. Microsoft Paint

   b. Excel 2000

   c. Visio 2000

   d. Exchange Server Topology Diagramming Tool

   e. FrontPage 2000

3. The native communications protocol used between servers running Microsoft Exchange 2000 Server eliminates some of the deployment issues of earlier transport implementations. What is this protocol?

   a. RPC

   b. POP3

   c. SMTP

   d. SNMP

4. Which one of the following terms represents a set of Exchange 2000 servers that share a common organizational design and will substitute for your existing Exchange 5.5 sites?

   a. Policy groups

   b. Administrative groups

   c. Managerial groups

   d. Plus Ultra groups

5. You must establish an administrative group before you install Exchange 2000 because after a server is installed in an administrative group, it cannot be moved. True or false?

6. Your organization has decided to have your multiple Exchange organizations remain as separate organizations. This presents immediate issues that must be addressed. Which of the following represent accurate statements regarding multiple Exchange 2000 organizations? [Check all correct answers]

   a. You cannot use the Active Directory connector to synchronize between forests.

   b. Setting up multiple Exchange organizations will require synchronization because recipients in other forests will not be security principals in the local forest.

   c. The other recipients cannot be retained as contacts.

   d. You will lose access to public folders, access to calendar free and busy information, and also access to other users' appointment books.

7. You have decided to merge two or more Exchange 5.5 organizations while still on Exchange 5.5 because you cannot merge two Exchange 2000 organizations. Which tool will you employ?

a. Amalgamation Tool

b. Migration Tool

c. Merge Server Wizard

d. Move Server Wizard

8. You are considering performing a future Exchange migration between forests. Which one of the following statements is false in this scenario?

a. You can migrate user accounts between forests.

b. You can migrate servers between forests.

c. You can migrate Exchange databases between forests.

d. You can migrate Exchange 5.5 servers into a mixed-mode Exchange 2000 organization only.

9. The message transfer agents for Exchange 5.5 and earlier versions are built upon which standard for addressing and carrying email messages?

a. X.500

b. X.400

c. X.25

d. SMTP

10. What is the component configured on an Exchange 5.5 database that is used to create a copy of every message received by users on that database and to send the copy to a folder for archival purposes?

a. Message transferring

b. Message journaling

c. Message realigning

d. Message archiving

11. All enterprise-messaging systems need a way to pass routing data to one another. In Exchange 2000, when a connector is placed between two routing groups, a certain mechanism represents the route preference when multiple routes are available. What is the term for this mechanism?

a. Rate

b. Price

c. Charge

d. Cost

4

12. Earlier versions of Exchange may use a routing calculation server that composes the available routes and costs from the directory and forms a table designed to circulate the routing topology for the organization to all of the other servers in the Exchange site. What is this table called?

    a. Gateway Address Resolution Table

    b. Gateway Attendance Resolution Table

    c. Gateway Address Restoration Table

    d. Gateway Access Resolution Table

13. In Exchange 2000, Internet mail content configuration will be managed individually for each organization. In earlier versions of Exchange, which of the following components stored this outbound message content configuration information?

    a. Simple Mail Transfer Service

    b. Exchange Mail System

    c. Internet Mail Service

    d. Internet Message System

14. To make it easier to estimate the load and performance processes, Microsoft defines three basic user types based on real-world usage data on current mail systems. Which one of these categories best describes a scenario in which the maximum in-box has about 125 messages, the average total sends per day is 25, and the average total receipts per day is 60?

    a. Light

    b. Average

    c. Medium

    d. Heavy

15. In Exchange 2000, personal mail folders can be stored on the server in the Information Store and in personal folders on each workstation, in personal folders that reside in a server share, or both. Public folders sharing information among users, in contrast, are always stored where?

    a. Group Policy Object (GPO)

    b. Public folder repository (PFR)

    c. Information Store (IS)

    d. Personal folders (PST)

Real-World Projects

You are the team leader for one of the Exchange 2000 deployment teams at a large insurance company. Your team has been tasked with analyzing the existing message system architecture.

Project 4.1

The development team is behind schedule and your team has been asked to help them evaluate the current client application scenario in the organization. You need to create a detailed Application Inventory Document to present to the developers. Using your company (or an associate's organization or the imaginary Plus Ultra Group), create this Application Inventory Document based on data that you deem most valuable. Examples would include all client applications used, versioning, necessary upgrades, custom applications, and so on.

4

Project 4.2

You need to create a report that will help the entire deployment team get a handle on the present messaging situation so they can successfully upgrade Exchange 5.5 sites to Exchange 2000 routing groups and administrative groups. This information will also help you plan how Exchange sites will integrate with future Exchange 2000 organizations

Create a detailed report that first determines what the site addressing is for each existing Exchange 5.5 site in your organization (or an associate's organization or the imaginary Plus Ultra Group). Next, find out what default SMTP format is being used for addressing the existing user mailboxes. Third, document the default mailbox display names and aliases. A final issue to address is what recipient containers are being used to generate the offline address book.

CHAPTER FIVE

Planning Deployments of Messaging Clients

After completing this chapter, you will be able to:

✓ Analyze the deployment of MAPI clients

✓ Examine the use of IMAP4 clients

✓ Investigate the application of POP3 clients

✓ Analyze the operation of HTTP mail clients

✓ Understand Outlook 2000

✓ Implement Outlook Web Access

✓ Explore client issues relating to Windows 2000 policies

This chapter continues the planning for Exchange 2000 Server by considering the different types of clients that your users will use with Exchange 2000. This chapter assists you in assessing the needs of your users as well as making the best determination of which of the existing mail clients will work best in your environment. Exchange Server has always relied on a client/server model; therefore, your users will need to use a mail client for such Exchange 2000 services as email and contacts. This chapter also focuses heavily on the advantages of Outlook 2000 as an Exchange 2000 client program. Although Outlook 2000 is the ideal client for Exchange 2000 Server, several other client applications have varying levels of functionality with Exchange as well. Email clients available on the market, such as Eudora and Netscape, can access and retrieve messages from an Exchange 2000 Server. As a matter of fact, any mail clients that are fully SMTP/POP3 (Simple Mail Transfer Protocol/Post Office Protocol 3) and IMAP4 (Internet Message Access Protocol 4) compliant can access mail stored in the Exchange 2000 Information Store. Most Exchange functions, however, call for an IMAP4-compliant client. This chapter explores several different client formats, such as MAPI (Messaging Application Programming Interface), IMAP4, and POP3, and also looks at the function of the Internet HTTP (Hypertext Transfer Protocol) mail clients. Additionally, this chapter overviews the Outlook Web Access service, which presents an Outlook-type appearance to browser-based users. Finally, this chapter explores how Windows 2000 policies can work within the framework of Exchange 2000 to manage client configurations.

After you fully deploy Exchange 2000 into your organization, your clients will access the directory on Windows 2000 global catalog servers. With Exchange Server 5.5 and earlier versions, the clients accessed the directory on the mailbox server because there was no real integration between the Exchange directory and the Windows NT directory. Microsoft Outlook 2000 and Outlook 98 Service Pack 2 have the distinct advantage of being able to directly access the global catalog servers. Earlier clients will still direct their requests to their mailbox server, which then redirects the clients to a global catalog server. This redirection capacity is a critical element of how Exchange 2000 supports earlier client applications. Although Exchange 2000 has this built-in support for earlier clients, your organization's Exchange administrators need to be aware of several issues. Most important, these Exchange administrators must be on the Active Directory planning team. Exchange 2000 is the first enterprise-wide application that must have Active Directory; therefore, it is probable that the Exchange administrators will greatly affect the deployment of Active Directory. This chapter addresses many of the client-side issues that are critical to a successful integration of Exchange 2000 with existing systems.

Exchange 2000 Compatibilities

Although this chapter looks at a select group of protocols and formats, for testing purposes you should be aware of all of the following protocols, components, and formats that Exchange 2000 implements.

The following list shows the network protocols:

➤ Hypertext Transfer Protocol (HTTP)

➤ Web Distributed Authoring and Versioning (Web-DAV)

➤ Simple Mail Transfer Protocol (SMTP)

➤ Network News Transfer Protocol (NNTP)

➤ Internet Message Access Protocol version 4 (IMAP4)

➤ Post Office Protocol version 3 (POP3)

➤ Lightweight Directory Access Protocol (LDAP)

The following list shows the API components:

➤ ActiveX data objects (ADO)

➤ Active Directory Service Interfaces (ADSI)

➤ Collaboration Data Objects (CDO)

➤ Object linking and embedding Database (OLE DB)

➤ Messaging Application Programming Interface (MAPI)

This list shows the network formats:

➤ Request for Comments 822 (RFC 822)

➤ Multipurpose Internet Mail Extension (MIME)

➤ Hypertext Markup Language (HTML)

➤ Extensible Markup Language (XML)

Analyzing MAPI Clients

MAPI is a structure built into Exchange 2000 that allows different email applications to work together to distribute mail. Applications can share mail messages if both are MAPI enabled. Extended MAPI version 1 is an industry-wide standard for writing messages and email, and for workflow applications. MAPI comprises a set of common application programming interfaces and a dynamic-link library (DLL) component. The interfaces are used to generate and access varied messaging programs and systems. The DLL stores the MAPI subsystem, which controls the communication between front-end messaging applications and back-end messaging systems and also offers a common user interface for recurrent tasks. The MAPI subsystem works as a kind of main clearinghouse to merge the diverse messaging systems and screen clients from their functional and versioning differences.

Exchange 2000 and many other common messaging programs use MAPI interfaces to function with different messaging applications and messaging systems. This gives Exchange a constant setting for development and application, and offers autonomy for both. Client applications will perform messaging tasks as either their primary or secondary duty. For example, applications that send and receive email conduct messaging as their chief focus. In contrast, nonmessaging client applications perform messaging as a secondary element. Client applications are generally placed into one of following three categories:

➤ Messaging aware

➤ Messaging enabled

➤ Messaging-based workgroup

Messaging-Aware Applications

A messaging-aware application does not need the components of a messaging system; however, it includes messaging options as an added feature. Microsoft Word 2000, for example, is an application that includes a Send To command from its File menu to allow documents to be sent to mail recipients. This feature is considered as messaging aware.

Messaging-Enabled Applications

A messaging-enabled application needs the functionality of a messaging system and characteristically runs on a network or an online service. Microsoft Outlook is a good example of a messaging-enabled application.

Messaging-Based Workgroup Applications

The messaging-based workgroup applications are more sophisticated client applications than the others. A workgroup application needs full access to a broad range of messaging system services. These functions can include message storage, addressing, and transport services. Messaging-based workgroup applications are intended to function on a network in which users do not manage the network communication of the application. Workflow automation programs and bulletin board services are examples of these applications.

Client applications can also operate without a user interface in an automated scenario. Even though MAPI provides a set of common dialog boxes and a standard user interface, client applications do not necessarily have to present a user interface. All of the processing can be handled within the application, if preferred. Inventory management software designed to route a particular type of data to recipients on a regular basis is an example of an automated client application.

Earlier MAPI clients, such as the Microsoft Exchange client and Outlook 97/98, made MAPI directory service requests to an Exchange server. Examples of these requests would be resolving text into user names at the To box of messages or presenting objects from the global address list. In Exchange 2000 Server, a proxy forwards any MAPI directory service requests to a local global catalog server on the network. This helps to provide compatibility with any existing MAPI client base. Because Active Directory supports a number of protocols, including LDAP and MAPI directory service, an Outlook directory request is applicable even when it is made directly to a global catalog server. The global catalog server will return the result to the Exchange 2000 Server, which in turn returns it to the requesting MAPI client. This process is transparent to the client and it takes no additional time to complete.

Note: MAPI clients cannot access front-end servers and simultaneously use back-end servers.

Investigating POP3 Clients

POP3 is an Internet protocol that allows its clients to download email from a server. This works quite well for computers that cannot keep up an uninterrupted connection to a server. POP3 functionality is integrated into the Exchange 2000 Information Store, in a fashion similar to MAPI, to allow POP3 fast, easy access to data while still offering the security of Exchange and Windows 2000. One of the key issues that you will have to decide is whether you want to allow existing POP3 clients to access Exchange 2000 Server as a POP server or to have them implement Outlook 2000. This decision will revolve around such issues as the user environment, the users' need for a POP3 account, or the gains you will experience using IMAP4 with Outlook 2000. We will look at the advantages of Outlook 2000 in the section "Outlook 2000."

The POP3 protocol was intended first and foremost for offline users to read messages from the server, as well as to access the email server through a dial-up connection. POP3 lets a user connect to Exchange 2000 Server and download all of the mail messages from the inbox to the client. Users can function within a mode in which their mail can be left in the server inbox, but there is no access to other mail folders on the server. When a POP3 client transmits a message, the Internet Mail Service routes the message, depending on the recipient's address, to the computer running Exchange (or to other SMTP hosts). Both POP3 and IMAP4 are Internet messaging protocols that allow clients to access their mail; however, these protocols differ in some respects. One disparity concerns the place where the client actually works with the messages. For example, POP3 provides access to a user's inbox only and doesn't support access to public folders. Also, POP3 allows the user simply to download email from an inbox on a server to the client computer and then manage the messages there. POP3 doesn't allow users to manipulate messages on the server. It is possible, however, for a POP3 client to leave email in the server inbox although they cannot access other folders on the server. IMAP4, in contrast, lets the client access and manipulate mail on the server itself. The next section, "Examining the Use of IMAP4 Clients," looks more closely at IMAP4 and its capabilities to access public and private folders.

In Exchange 2000, the Active Directory Service (ADS) manages the POP3 user mailboxes and holds all messaging directory data. Earlier versions of Exchange use their own database to store directory information as well as manage recipients through the Exchange administrator tool. Because a separate directory for Exchange 2000 will not be needed, all of the future mailbox administration will be synchronized in Directory Service Manager. Once you install Exchange System Manager on a Windows 2000 computer, a group of component extensions is added to the normal Active Directory console. With this added functionality, an Exchange mailbox can be created automatically when a new user account is defined in the Active Directory Users and Computers tool. Keep in mind that only users with Windows 2000 accounts will be able to have a mailbox and send or receive mail. If the account is mail enabled but not mailbox enabled, users will be allowed only to send mail. Clients that are also mailbox enabled can receive mail and configure further settings and properties.

Tip: By implementing a unified namespace, you can provide easier administration of multiple POP3 servers. You can configure clients to connect using the same POP3 server and then use load-balancing software or hardware to distribute the load at random to any of the multiple POP3 servers. If you decide to move a user's mailbox from one server to another, the client will not need to reconfigure the name of the server. Also, as the number of users in your organization grows, you can simply add more computers to the front-end collection of servers without having to reconfigure the clients.

Advantages of POP3

Some advantages of deploying a POP3 client include:

➤ POP3 provides essential functionality while requiring minimal configuration.

➤ POP3 is a fast protocol standard that is used extensively on the global Internet.

➤ POP3 diminishes user downtime when utilization is active, except when you are synchronizing mail that was received or sent.

➤ Most mail-enabled firewall solutions permit the POP3 protocol to pass through by default.

➤ POP3 provides an offline system for your organization to read and send messages.

Disadvantages of POP3

Some potential disadvantages of deploying a POP3 client include the following:

➤ POP3 does not provide the ability to manage folders on the mail server except for the deletion of messages.

➤ Upgrades and service packs must be distributed to every workstation.

➤ Sent messages are not preserved on the mail server, but instead are held in the local message store.

➤ POP3 does not provide access to any folder on the mail server except the inbox.

➤ Although it is possible to configure messages, POP3 messages are normally not centrally stored. In a transaction-based scenario or for legal or accounting purposes, this is characteristically unacceptable.

➤ POP3 clients typically do not support collaboration software or integration of portal functionality (the exception being feature-rich clients such as Outlook 2000).

Examining the Use of IMAP4 Clients

IMAP is an Internet messaging protocol that allows a client to access mail on a server instead of downloading it to the user's computer. IMAP is meant to be deployed in a scenario in which users log on to the server from an array of different workstations. In such situations, downloading mail to a specific computer is obviously not practical. IMAP version 4 (IMAP4) is employed extensively in educational institutions or large research facilities where users may connect to the mail server from different departments or labs throughout a campus. Once they are connected, the users can then access their mailboxes as though their mail was stored locally. IMAP4 enables user interaction from a variety of terminals with information stored in Exchange 2000 Server. In addition, IMAP4 enables users to access and manipulate messages stored within private and public folders. Users with an IMAP4 client can access mail in their Exchange mailboxes without downloading the entire mailbox to a specific computer. They can access multiple mailboxes to retrieve specific messages or parts of a message, such as an attachment. IMAP4 clients also have the ability to search a mailbox and flag messages that have been read.

To send outbound messages from Exchange 2000 Server, an IMAP4 email client such as Outlook 2000 will use the Internet Mail Service or any other SMTP host, depending on the recipient's address. IMAP4 does not provide mail transport; SMTP provides this functionality. IMAP4 and POP3 are two protocols used by Exchange 2000 for accessing electronic mail. Although Exchange 2000 Server supports both protocols, your organization will have to incorporate an IMAP4-compliant client to receive all of the benefits of Exchange 2000. Using only a POP3 client will allow users to access Exchange 2000 Server email, but not the contacts, calendar, notes, or journal folders.

You can configure your Exchange 2000 IMAP4 server to grant or deny access to individual computers, groups of computers, or domains, as well as grant or deny access to a single computer based on an IP address. You can grant or refuse access to a group of computers, based on their subnet address and subnet mask. You can also control access to an entire domain by specifying the domain name. In addition, you could also configure the server to override IMAP4 access on a per-user basis.

Advantages of IMAP4

The advantages of deploying an IMAP4 client include the following:

➤ IMAP4 allows the user to read messages based on the folder infrastructure on the mail server.

➤ IMAP4 allows management of mail-based folders and messages.

➤ IMAP4 provides offline capability by either maintaining a copy of the mail server folder structure or by allowing the user to copy messages to a local message store on the workstation, depending on the messaging client (Outlook Express or Netscape Messenger).

➤ IMAP4 allows access to the public folders.

➤ IMAP4 further minimizes user downtime during active usage, except when synchronizing received or sent mail.

➤ IMAP4 allows only message headers to be downloaded initially, to reduce synchronization time.

Disadvantages of IMAP4

Some of the possible disadvantages of deploying an IMAP4 client solution include:

➤ IMAP4 does not allow for an intuitive interface for nonmessage-based folders, such as calendar information, contacts, and so on.

➤ Depending on the client, sent messages are not stored on the mail server.

➤ Except for such rich clients as Outlook 2000, clients typically do not support collaboration software or integration of portal functionality.

➤ Upgrades and service packs must be distributed to every workstation.

Analyzing HTTP Mail Clients

HTTP provides a method to connect to the Internet. An HTTP client, such as Microsoft Internet Explorer, is a Web browser that uses the HTTP specification to access information on an Internet Information Services (IIS) server. The Outlook Web Access feature also allows Exchange 2000 to integrate with an IIS server and get connected to the Internet. This provides the capability for users to access email and public folders in the Web Storage System using an ordinary Web browser. The three main HTTP functions used by the Web Storage System are **GET**, **PUT**, and **POST**. The **GET** function retrieves a document. The **PUT** function "puts" an item in a folder. The **POST** function submits an item to a folder.

Exchange 2000 Server employs the HTTP protocol for the Distributed Authoring and Versioning (DAV) component, which allows a client to perform file-system–type actions on a remote server. Exchange 2000 supports an extension to HTTP 1.1 called Distributed Authoring and Versioning (Web-DAV). Web-DAV, which is an Internet standard defined in RFC 2518, allows clients to perform file-system operations on a remote server and provides the capability for simple publishing. Exchange implementation also includes replication, notifications, and versioning, and provides the necessary functions for simple publishing. DAV extends HTTP by standardizing a universal set of functions implemented by most client/server protocols. The protocol defines techniques for manipulating resources such as email, directory administration, and newsgroups. In addition, users can use Exchange as a central repository for mail by accessing the Exchange Information Store through HTTP. Also, Microsoft Office 2000 programs can open and save documents as well as browse public and private folders within the Exchange store.

The Web-DAV protocol provides access to an extensible collection of related properties. Web-DAV defines commands that are used to copy, move, delete, search, lock, and unlock resources as well as to create new folders. These capabilities make Web-DAV an excellent tool for creating interoperable, shared applications. Web-DAV provides several great features in Exchange 2000 (such as concurrency control). Long-duration exclusive and shared write-locking features prevent two or more authors from writing to the same file without first being forced to merge the changes. Web-DAV locks are independent of any individual network connection that would affect the duration of the lock. This feature is useful because it provides robust Internet-scale collaboration capabilities, whereas network links might be randomly disconnected. Additionally, XML properties can be set, deleted, and retrieved using the Web-DAV protocol, and Web-DAV supports copy and move

5

operations. Collections (such as file system directories) also can be produced and listed by using Web-DAV.

Implementing Outlook Web Access

Outlook Web Access is the feature that allows HTML Web page access to authorized mailbox and public folder stores when users read mail from a browser. This component delivers an Outlook-style graphical interface to browser-based users with varying functionality, depending on the choice of browser. Outlook Web Access is optimized to perform with Microsoft Internet Explorer 5. Internet Explorer can run slowly on systems with limited hardware resources. If you have clients that lack the processing power needed to run Internet Explorer 5.X, consider using Internet Explorer 4 Service Pack 2 or Netscape Navigator 4. The version of Outlook Web Access that comes with Exchange 2000 works on an Exchange 2000 server with IIS 5. Outlook Web Access is also intended to capitalize on server-based scalability features such as the use of front-end protocol servers. Outlook Web Access can be valuable if you need to retrieve and manipulate data stored on Exchange 2000 using Internet browsers on platforms such as Unix, Macintosh, or versions of Windows other than Windows 2000 Server.

To circumvent costly telephone charges, users can access the Internet locally and connect to their Exchange accounts with their browser while on business or personal trips. In addition, Outlook Web Access can provide Web-based public access to Exchange 2000 Server public folders and the address book. Users can log on to their personal accounts to read private email, launch messages, generate contacts, and schedule appointments. By utilizing the features of Outlook Web Access, your organization can develop and organize information as well as optimize corporate communication.

Advantages of Outlook Web Access

The advantages of deploying Outlook Web Access include:

➤ Outlook Web Access presents an Outlook-style experience for users with browser-based clients. Client hardware requirements are smaller because Outlook Web Access needs only a browser.

➤ Outlook Web Access allows Exchange 2000 as well as Outlook 2000 to be implemented on a wide range of hardware and operating systems.

➤ Outlook Web Access does not need a lot of configuration.

➤ Outlook Web Access has an intuitive interface for access to specialized folders, such as those that store appointments on calendars or store contact information. It also provides URL access to the private message store.

➤ Outlook Web Access uses a centralized set of upgrades and service packs.

Disadvantages of Outlook Web Access

Outlook Web Access does have some possible disadvantages for your organization, including:

➤ Outlook Web Access does not directly support the spell check feature.

➤ The component possesses no real offline capacity.

➤ User experience can be inconsistent, depending on the browser being used.

➤ Outlook Web Access does not provide the same full-feature set as Outlook 2000.

Outlook 2000

You should strongly consider employing Outlook 2000 throughout your organization to capitalize on the many great features that Exchange 2000 offers. Generally speaking, you can consider Outlook 2000 a direct substitute for the Microsoft Exchange client on your workstations. There will be no interruption of performance because your users will continue to work with email messages in Outlook 2000 as they did with the Exchange client. Your users will still be able to share messages with people on the Exchange client with no problem. The only difference will be new features and a new look. Additionally, the Exchange client can still open folders and email messages produced by the advanced features of Outlook 2000 (the folders and messages may look a little different in the Exchange client than they do in Outlook 2000, however). Outlook 2000 is the standard Microsoft Exchange client that is included with Microsoft Office 2000. It is a full MAPI client that performs well in a well-connected network such as a local area network (LAN). Outlook 2000 takes full advantage of all of the features of Exchange by providing access to the public and private information stores as well as such other functions as calendar data, contacts, tasks, and notes.

Exchange 2000 Server needs Windows 2000 as the server operating system, but your organization may be implementing multiple sites using varied server platforms. For example, the headquarters of Plus Ultra Group runs Windows 2000 Server and Outlook 2000 as a client for Exchange 2000, but a recently acquired company uses Unix with a POP3 messaging system. Microsoft Outlook 2000 is a better choice of email clients for accessing mailboxes on Exchange 2000 Server. Table 5.1 clearly shows that Outlook 2000 is the only application that supports every feature available through Exchange 2000 Server.

Table 5.1   Clients and their supported Exchange 2000 features.

Client Application	Contacts	Calendar	Email	Journal	Notes	Tasks
Outlook 2000	Yes	Yes	Yes	Yes	Yes	Yes
Outlook Express	Yes	No	Yes	No	No	No
Outlook Web Access	Yes	Yes	Yes	No	No	No
Netscape Communicator 4.X	No	No	Yes	No	No	No

Outlook 2000 is also a commanding collaboration tool that empowers users with the ability to communicate with other users as they systematize and share information on their workstations. Outlook 2000 is a full-featured email client and personal information manager (PIM) that provides unparalleled integration. A major benefit of Outlook 2000 is that it integrates so effortlessly with Office 2000, Internet Explorer version 5 (IE5), and the Internet. Outlook 2000 offers a number of productivity enhancing features, including the new Outlook Bar, efficient email message administration, easy menus and commands, and improved communication over the Internet.

The Outlook Bar

A helpful feature of Outlook 2000 is the new Outlook Bar. This component enables you to get speedy access to all of your necessary data from within Outlook 2000, including Web pages, files, and folders. You can create a handy shortcut on the Outlook Bar so that your most vital information is simply a click away. Outlook 2000 is HTML based; therefore, you can click on a Web page shortcut and open a Web page directly in the Outlook 2000 window instead of running a separate browser application.

Email Message Administration

Outlook 2000 provides several functions to assist you in managing email messages. You can generate folders, format messages, and apply different views and filters to sort and scan junk email. Outlook 2000 has improved the Rules Wizard to allow users to easily establish rules for such functions as forwarding or flagging certain incoming or outgoing messages.

Easy Menus and Commands

Outlook 2000 has simplified the menus and dialog boxes so navigation is much easier. The Options dialog box, for example, now has only one row of tabs. Outlook 2000's menus are automatically personalized to display the commands your users access most frequently and to remove commands they rarely use, such as all Office 2000 applications. An Actions menu that holds commands specific to the user's particular view has also been added.

Improved Communication over the Internet

Your personal or team calendars can be uploaded to a Web page or sent in email messages that are viewable by any browser. Contact information can also be effortlessly shared across the Internet with vCard technology. Support for iCalendar technology group scheduling and HTML mail also makes it feasible for your organization to set up online meetings, share scheduling, and send and/or receive content-rich email messages. The Contact Manager utility offers the capability to map client locations, make phone calls, schedule meetings, and send email messages. Outlook Today is the central place to see your daily appointments, organize your task list, and review your inbox. Messages and email can be generated in HTML, rich text format (RTF), or simple text format. You can even switch between formats dynamically in the middle of writing a message.

The vCard and iCalendar Technologies

vCard technology automates trading personal information that would normally be found on a conventional business card. vCard is used in such programs as Internet mail, voice mail, Web browsers, telephony applications, call centers, videoconferencing, personal information managers (PIMs), personal data assistants [PDAs], pagers, faxes, and smart cards. vCard information goes well outside the realm of transferring simple text; it can include such objects as pictures, corporate logos, live Web addresses, and more. The Internet Engineering Task Force (IETF) has recently released the specification for vCard version 3. The RFCs for this technology are RFC 2425: MIME Content-Type for Directory Information; and RFC 2426: vCard MIME Directory Profile.

The iCalendar specification defines a format for exchanging, calendaring, and scheduling information by a simple, automated, and reliable method. It grabs information about events and "to-do" items that are usually used by PIMs and group schedulers. Applications that use Calendar can exchange vital information about events, so you can schedule meetings with anyone who has an iCalendar-aware program. The Internet Engineering Steering Group (IESG) has accepted the specification for iCalendar as a proposed standard. The three RFCs for this technology are RFC 2445: Internet Calendaring and Scheduling Core Object Specification (iCalendar); RFC 2446: iCalendar Transport-Independent Interoperability Protocol (iTIP)—Scheduling Events, BusyTime, To-Dos and Journal Entries; and RFC 2447: iCalendar Message-Based Interoperability Protocol (iMIP).

More Advantages of Outlook 2000

Among the many advantages of using Outlook 2000 in your organization are the following:

➤ Outlook 2000 offers a large feature set, including spell check, search, and rules.

➤ It supports multimedia messaging services.

➤ Outlook 2000 is fully integrated with Office 2000 with a customized user interface.

➤ Outlook 2000 does not depend upon network links for processing because the majority of the processing takes place on the local workstation.

➤ Outlook 2000 provides access to notes, journals, and sticky notes; has the capability to manage folders; and features user-friendly interfaces for a variety of functions such as calendars or contacts.

➤ Outlook 2000 delivers an excellent offline solution for reading and sending messages as well as folder and message management.

➤ Outlook 2000 supports Secure Multipurpose Internet Mail Extensions (S/MIME) encryption and signing and is easily configured in a secure environment that uses digital signatures and certificates of authority.

➤ Outlook 2000 provides support for POP3 and IMAP4 protocols as well as such directory access protocols as LDAP.

➤ Outlook 2000 takes advantage of the Windows 95/98/NT and Windows 2000 operating systems.

➤ The address book in Outlook 2000 is integrated with directory searching.

Disadvantages of Outlook 2000

Some possible disadvantages in deploying Outlook 2000 include:

➤ Outlook 2000 runs only on Windows 95/98/NT or Windows 2000 operating systems.

➤ Outlook 2000 requires installation and drive space on the local computer.

➤ Outlook 2000 is bandwidth intensive from a protocol standpoint in the sense that it requires custom ports and open firewalls.

➤ You must buy either multiple copies of Outlook 2000 or end-user licenses, you must manage licenses when user status changes, and you must either configure each client or provide installation instructions.

➤ Outlook 2000 users will need extensive training time due to all of the features available to them.

Outlook Express

Outlook Express is a Web-integrated email and news feature that is complete and easy to use. It is free, and comes bundled with Internet Explorer. Although it is a viable alternative for accessing Exchange 2000 Server, you should avoid using it in your organization. Outlook Express offers very limited functionality, as shown in Table 5.1. It supports only the email and contact features available on Exchange 2000 Server. Furthermore, Outlook Express does not let users access several other capabilities, including tasks and calendar. Before you decide on an email client to implement with Exchange 2000 Server, you need to carefully appraise which clients can support Exchange 2000 features, based on your organizational needs. For example, Plus Ultra Group does not need Exchange 2000's journal, notes, or tasks features; however, the users must have access to the inbox for email, contacts, and calendar functionality. Outlook Express is not suitable for this environment, yet Outlook 2000 and Outlook Web Access are excellent solutions.

Nevertheless, Outlook Express has journeyed far since introducing the three-pane view, HTML mail, and stationery features. Outlook Express also has the capability to receive mail from multiple accounts in a single inbox. Microsoft's latest version, Outlook Express 5, builds upon the features of Outlook Express and even offers Hotmail support. The new capabilities of Outlook Express 5 include:

➤ Support for Hotmail lets users integrate Outlook Express with their Hotmail accounts in a single graphical interface.

➤ Identity Management features allow the creation of multiple user profiles so they can share the client but still maintain control of their own mailbox and contents.

➤ Improved connection management features allow Outlook Express to track Internet connections and automatically redial if a connection drops.

➤ Outlook Express 5 provides features that help improve users' ability to sort and filter incoming email, thus helping to regulate the flow of mail.

➤ Outlook Express 5 enables users to share contacts and effortlessly access address book information through the Outlook Express window.

➤ Outlook Express 5 enables users to create multiple customized signatures that can be easily added to messages.

➤ The new Start Page makes it easier for users to get focused from the beginning of a session.

➤ The Online/Offline Synchronization feature simplifies managing emails or newsgroup messages while offline.

➤ Outlook Express 5 offers a set of stationery options designed to improve the presentation of messages.

Upgrading from the Microsoft Exchange Client to Outlook 2000

The upgrade process from the Microsoft Exchange client to Outlook 2000 client is actually quite easy. You just need to install Outlook 2000. Outlook 2000 automatically uses the email file you have been using with the Microsoft Exchange client, thus removing the need to import your email file into Outlook 2000.

Note: *The .pst file is upgraded to the version that is used with Outlook 2000.*

This section explores how some Microsoft Exchange client features function within Outlook 2000. For example, many features in Exchange 2000 Server are offered as add-ins in Outlook 2000, and most of the Microsoft Exchange client add-ins will function in Outlook 2000 without further modifications. Outlook

2000 custom forms, however, are not at all compatible with Microsoft Exchange clients. As a result, an Exchange client does not recognize the Outlook 2000 custom forms. Therefore, when Exchange client users open an Outlook 2000 form, they will see only the customary message form properties. Furthermore, an Exchange client user will not even be able to open a form if the Outlook form is totally customized. If a Microsoft Exchange client user opens a folder, for example, Exchange will display only the views that have been saved in Microsoft Exchange format. Outlook 2000 supports all the custom view features of Microsoft Exchange, however, including several of the new features.

Based on this information, the upgrading strategy will usually entail only some groundwork and distribution/licensing issues. Outlook 2000 is quite compatible with Exchange clients and earlier versions of Outlook, and it also can share files with other Microsoft email and calendar applications. Before you begin the upgrade process, however, you must decide whether your organization is going to implement the Corporate/Workgroup configuration or the Internet Mail Only support configuration option. Decide also whether you want to incorporate the Schedule+ calendar system or the Outlook 2000 Calendar. Of course, you will need to decide which Web browser your company will use as well as which security settings you need for your users. Also you must be sure that you clean up your existing email folders in preparation for the upgrade process. You should delete any unnecessary email messages or personal folders as well. Finally, it is vitally important that you create a backup copy of your existing email folders to prevent the permanent loss of data during the upgrade process.

Exploring Policies

Exchange 2000 Server introduces the advanced use of policies, which are a collection of configuration settings that can be applied to one or more Exchange objects. These policies are subsequently used to set and manipulate different facets of the Exchange 2000 system behavior across a set of servers. A policy can be used as a solution to contain the configuration settings for an entire Exchange 2000 Server design. As an administrator, you can define a policy that controls the configuration settings across literally hundreds of servers or objects. You can fashion policies that designate the configuration of mailbox size limits, for example, as well as the retention of deleted items. You could apply one policy to most of the servers and then give a different policy selectively to other servers. Plus Ultra Group has designated special policies for servers accessed by the top executives of the company, for instance. Policies can also be used in administrative groups separate from the servers to which they apply. This allows you to use policies to administer some server settings and delegate other administrators with server management duties.

Two general types of policies are available in Exchange 2000—system policies and recipient policies. Both system and recipient policies are intended to apply configuration settings to objects in Windows 2000 domain containers and are optimized to affect millions of objects across distributed Windows 2000 domains.

System Policies

System policies are applied to Exchange 2000 configuration objects that are characteristically referred to as "server-side" objects. These objects can consist of, for example, stored databases or the servers themselves. Exchange 2000 supports three different classes of system policies:

➤ Mailbox store policies

➤ Public folder store policies

➤ Server policies

Recipient Policies

Recipient policies are generally applied to mail-enabled objects to generate email addresses. They can apply to literally thousands of users, multiple groups, and multiple contacts in Active Directory. The main recipient policy supported in Exchange 2000 is the email address generation policy. Recipient policies employ a "background-apply" technique for producing the configuration changes. For example, as the administrator, you create a policy, you then define the settings the policy should implement, and then you link the policy with one or more objects using the potent LDAP query engine. The policy is then applied at a later time using the schedule determined by the Recipient Update Service.

Recipient Update Service

The Recipient Update Service is an Exchange 2000 service that updates the recipient objects within a domain with explicit sorts of information. This service can update recipient objects with address list membership and email addresses at intervals scheduled by the administrator, for example. Each domain with objects that have Exchange settings must have a server with the Recipient Update Service installed. This component allows proxy requests defined in the recipient policies to be generated for each user. You will need to determine where you want this service to reside. You will most likely decide to create a separate domain controller dedicated to this task to reduce the load on large networks. During a migration, you may need to run Recipient Update Service every hour. If your design is steady, and user changes happen only once a day, you could schedule your Recipient Update Service to run shortly after the updates apply to Active Directory.

Multiple Addresses

In Exchange 5.5, your user proxy addresses were created on the Site Addressing tab in the Exchange Administrator program. In Exchange 2000, however, you config-ure user email proxy addresses using the recipient policies component of Exchange System Manager. Recipient policies are much more flexible than site addressing because you can formulate multiple addresses of a given type. You can also use filter rules to determine to which recipients the policies apply. For example, the merger of two companies originally formed Plus Ultra Group. Therefore, for a time, the company used recipient policies to offer all of the users with an SMTP address that reflected the merged company name as well as different SMTP addresses that represented the previous company. You can use recipient policies to allocate several SMTP addresses to users so that every instance of a user's email address is repre-sented. For instance, if a user's name changes, you can use recipient policies to represent all iterations of the user. By assigning multiple SMTP addresses in this way, you can remove the need to have alias files on other systems. Recipient policies, therefore, affect the configuration of objects that are classically considered as user-side objects, such as users, mailboxes, groups, and contacts.

Tip: After you have defined and implemented policies, modifying the configuration across all servers requires only a simple editing of the policy and subsequently applying the changes one time in the Exchange 2000 administrative console.

Recipient Management

Exchange 2000 Server has been retooled to more accurately mirror the manner in which most customers use Exchange in their actual network environments. Ex-change 2000 allows you to use an administrative model to organize the Exchange 2000 Server topology so that it is more accurately mapped to your business re-quirements. Recipient management is a process of influencing object attributes and properties within the Active Directory. Once an Active Directory user object becomes mail-enabled, specific Exchange 2000 attributes, such as the mailbox server and email address, are propagated to this particular object. In Exchange 5.5, changing a user's phone number required connecting to an Exchange server and changing the attributes of a mailbox object in its directory. With Exchange 2000, changing a user's phone number simply necessitates connecting to a domain controller and modifying the attributes of a user object in Active Directory. If your organization has existing Exchange 5.5 servers, you must understand how previous Exchange objects will change in Exchange 2000. Table 5.2 explains how some Exchange 5.5 components are now represented in Exchange 2000.

Table 5.2   Exchange 2000 terminology comparisons.

Exchange 5.5 Component	Exchange 2000 Equivalent
Mailbox	Active Directory mailbox-enabled user
Custom recipient	Active Directory mail-enabled contact or user
Distribution list	Active Directory mail-enabled group
Public folder	Active Directory public folder

Chapter Summary

This chapter provided solid groundwork for preparing not only to test but also to deploy client technologies in your Exchange 2000 design. Exchange 2000 Server is quite dependent upon a client/server model; thus your users will need the best mail client to contact Exchange 2000 services such as email and contacts. Even though Outlook 2000 is the most powerful and fully compliant client for Exchange 2000 Server, several other client programs deliver various levels of compatibility with Exchange 2000. Clients such as Netscape Communicator 4.X can access and retrieve messages from an Exchange 2000 Server. In fact, any SMTP/POP3- and IMAP4-compliant mail client can access mail stored in the Exchange Information Store. For the majority of Exchange functions, however, an IMAP4 compliant client is needed.

Extended MAPI version 1 is an industry-wide specification for writing messages, email, and workflow applications. Even more important, Exchange 2000 uses MAPI interfaces to work with other messaging applications and systems. This MAPI functionality provides Exchange with an ongoing environment for application development. The three major categories of MAPI clients are messaging-aware, messaging-enabled, and messaging-based workgroup applications. POP3 functionality is built in to the Exchange 2000 Information Store in a fashion similar to MAPI to allow POP3 quick access to data while still offering the security of Exchange and Windows 2000. You will have to determine if you want to allow existing POP3 clients to access Exchange 2000 Server as a POP server or instead have them implement Outlook 2000. For newer deployments, the disadvantages of POP3 most likely outweigh the few advantages. Some organizations will have no choice other than to run Exchange 2000 as a POP3 server during the interim, however. IMAP4 and POP3 are two protocols that are employed by Exchange 2000 for accessing email. Although Exchange 2000 Server offers both protocols, your organization should use an IMAP4-compliant client to garner all of the benefits of Exchange 2000. Using only a POP3 client will allow users to access Exchange 2000 Server email, but not the contacts, calendar, notes, or journal folders. The advantages to IMAP4 override the few disadvantages for most organizations.

This chapter also explored the advantages of support for the HTTP protocol for the Web Distributed Authoring and Versioning (Web-DAV) component. Web-DAV

5

is a tool that permits a client to conduct file-system-type behavior on a remote server. The Exchange 2000 implementation of Web-DAV also includes replication, notifications, and versioning, and it also provides what is needed for simple publishing. One of the benefits of Outlook Web Access is that it can be used to circumvent costly telephone charges. You can access the Internet locally and connect to Exchange accounts with a browser while on a business or personal trip.

This chapter emphasized that Outlook 2000 is the best choice for most deployments of Exchange 2000, citing its numerous advantages. Although Outlook Express is a free alternative with some nice features, it is not recommended as a corporate client solution over Outlook 2000.

This chapter ended the discussion of planning the deployments of messaging clients with some recommendations for migrating from Microsoft Exchange Client to Outlook 2000. The policies to look forward to under Exchange 2000 and Windows 2000 Active Directory are system policies and recipient policies. The next chapter builds on this knowledge to show you how to migrate from other client solutions, such as Lotus Notes and GroupWise, as well as to continue planning for coexistence with Exchange 5.5.

Review Questions

1. Which one of the following represents a format that is *not* supported by Exchange 2000?

    a. Request for Comments 804 (RFC 804)

    b. Multipurpose Internet Mail Extensions (MIME)

    c. HTML

    d. Extensible Markup Language (XML)

2. Which of the following protocols is an industry-wide standard for writing messages and email and for workflow applications?

    a. MIME

    b. Extended MAPI version 1

    c. HTTP

    d. IMAP4

3. Which of the following components is the Exchange 2000 equivalent of the Exchange 5.5 distribution list?

    a. Active Directory public folder

    b. Active Directory mail-enabled contact or user

    c. Active Directory mail-enabled group

    d. Active Directory Group Policy

4. Which one of the following is an Exchange 2000 service that renews the recipient objects with address list membership and email addresses at intervals scheduled by the domain administrator?

   a. Recipient Renewal Service

   b. Recipient Update Service

   c. Recipient Object Updater

   d. Recipient Revision Service

5. Which of the following are the general types of policies that are implemented in Exchange 2000? [Check all correct answers]

   a. Mail-enabled policies

   b. System policies

   c. Recipient policies

   d. Outlook 2000 policies

6. In the context of MAPI compatibility, client applications are generally placed into one of three categories. Which of the following represent these categories? [Check all correct answers]

   a. Messaging-compatible applications

   b. Messaging-aware applications

   c. Messaging-collaborating applications

   d. Messaging-enabled applications

   e. Messaging-based workgroup applications

   f. Messaging-alert applications

7. You have installed the System Manager tool on a Windows 2000 computer. As a result, a set of component extensions was added to the normal Active Directory console. With this added functionality, you can create an Exchange mailbox automatically when a new user account is defined in the Active Directory Users and Computers component. Which of the following statements is true in this scenario?

   a. Only users with Windows 2000 accounts will be able to have a mailbox and send or receive mail.

   b. If the account is mailbox enabled, users will be allowed to send mail only.

   c. Clients that are mailbox enabled cannot receive mail or configure further settings and properties.

   d. None of the above statements is true.

8. Despite the advantages that were introduced with POP3, there are some disadvantages associated with the protocol. Which of the following statements does *not* accurately represent a disadvantage of POP3 functionality?

   a. POP3 does not provide the ability to manage folders on the mail server except for the deletion of messages.

   b. Sent messages are not preserved on the mail server, but instead are held in the local message store.

   c. POP3 does not provide access to any folder and cannot be centrally stored.

   d. POP3 clients typically do not support collaboration software or integration of portal functionality (the exception being such feature-rich clients as Outlook 2000).

9. Although Exchange 2000 Server supports several protocols, your organization must enjoy all of the benefits of Exchange 2000 including access to Exchange 2000 Server email, contacts, calendar, notes, and journal folders. Which protocol option should your organization choose?

   a. POP3

   b. Web-DAV

   c. IMAP4

   d. IMAX

10. Which one of the following features allows Exchange 2000 to integrate with an IIS server and get connected to the Internet in order to provide the capability for users to access email and public folders in the Web Storage System using a standard browser?

    a. IMAP4

    b. Web-DAV

    c. Outlook Express

    d. Outlook Web Access

11. You need a tool to create interoperable, shared applications in Exchange 2000. Which one of the following protocols gives you further access to an extensible collection of related properties and commands that can be used to copy, move, delete, search, lock, and unlock resources, as well as to create new folders?

    a. Outlook Web Access

    b. XML

    c. Web-DAV

    d. DHTML

12. Which one of the following statements is true concerning Outlook Web Access?

    a. Outlook Web Access fully supports the spell check feature.

    b. Outlook Web Access has support for offline functionality.

    c. Outlook Web Access can access specialized folders that store appointments on calendars as well as contact information.

    d. Outlook Web Access provides the same full-feature set as Outlook 2000.

13. To which of the following technologies does Outlook 2000 conform? [Check all correct answers]

    a. Personal information manager (PIM)

    b. Microsoft Office 2000

    c. Internet Explorer 5

    d. The Internet

14. Which of the following technologies automates the trading of personal information that would normally be found on a conventional business card?

    a. vCard

    b. iCard

    c. bCard

    d. pimCard

15. Your small company is considering using the free Outlook Express tool that is built in to Windows 2000 Professional within the Exchange 2000 design. Which of the following features will Outlook Express support? [Check all correct answers]

    a. Contacts available on Exchange 2000 Server

    b. Tasks available on Exchange 2000 Server

    c. Calendars available on Exchange 2000 Server

    d. Email available on Exchange 2000 Server

Real-World Projects

You are the senior systems architect for the Exchange 2000 project for the Plus Ultra Group. You are into the server planning stage of your rollout.

Project 5.1

The following table compares the available functionality of each client for Exchange 2000. Use this table to quickly determine which client option provides the functionality that your organization requires. Make a list of the features that your organization needs and which tools you should use.

Function	Outlook 2000	IMAP4/POP3	Outlook Web Access
Calendar scheduling	Yes	No (Outlook supports publishing free/busy information to a URL)	Yes
Free/busy	Yes	No (Outlook supports publishing free/busy information to a URL)	Yes
Contact management	Yes	Local only—client dependent	Yes
PIM	Yes	Client dependent	Partial (tasks, but not notes or journals)
Integration with Office 2000	Yes	Client dependent	Limited, based on choice of browser
Offline capability	Yes	Client or protocol dependent	No (very minimal with IE5 offline capability)
Rich-text support	Yes	Client dependent	Yes
Spell check	Yes	Client dependent	No
Inbox rules	Yes	No	Through Office 2000 only
Notes	Yes	POP3: No; IMAP4: read only	No
Journals	Yes	POP3: No; IMAP4: read only	No
Public folder access	Yes	POP3: No; IMAP4: read only	Yes
Server folder management	Yes	POP3: No; IMAP4: Yes	Yes
S/MIME encryption/signing	Yes	Client dependent	Client dependent
Integrated with Microsoft Office	Yes	No	No
Supports non-Microsoft operating systems	No	Client dependent	Yes
Integrated address book	Yes	Partially through LDAP	Yes
Integrated Directory Search	Yes	Partially through LDAP	Yes
Supports URL Access	Yes	No	Yes
Supports Collaboration	Yes	No	Yes
Minimal workstation requirements	No	Client dependent	Yes

Project 5.2

The IETF has recently released the specification for vCard version 3. You have been tasked with exploring and reporting on the viability of this technology for your company. Using the Web, locate the RFCs for this vCard (RFC 2425 and RFC 2426) and write a brief report on its features and capabilities.

Project 5.3

Your management was impressed with your report on the vCard technology. They now want more information concerning the iCalendar standard. Your boss read an article about this technology while on a cross-country flight. The three RFCs concerning this specification are RFC 2445: Internet Calendaring and Scheduling Core Object Specification (iCalendar); RFC 2446: iCalendar Transport-Independent Interoperability Protocol (iTIP)—Scheduling Events, BusyTime, To-Dos and Journal Entries; and RFC 2447: iCalendar Message-Based Interoperability Protocol (iMIP). Using the Web, locate the RFCs for this new iCalendar specification and write a brief report on its features and capabilities.

CHAPTER SIX

Planning for Coexistence of Exchange 2000 Server with Other Messaging Systems

After completing this chapter, you will be able to:

✓ Examine key coexistence issues

✓ Map out strategies for coexistence with MS Mail

✓ Plan for coexistence with Lotus cc:Mail

✓ Arrange for coexistence with Lotus Notes

✓ Prepare for coexistence with Novell GroupWise

✓ Examine coexistence issues with PROFS and SNADS

O rganizations often already have a messaging system in place when they decide to deploy Exchange 2000 Server. Some organizations have a business requirement that calls for exchanging messages and sharing directory information between diverse messaging systems. To make deploying Exchange 2000 Server in your organization easier, Exchange Server 2000 includes a suite of tools that supports coexistence with another mail system while you migrate to Exchange as well as long-term messaging connectivity with other mail systems. Before linking your Exchange 2000 environment to another system, you need to prepare a strategic plan. This chapter discusses planning steps to follow for using connectors to other email systems and provides a deeper look at the Active Directory directory service and the vital role it plays in Exchange 2000.

Before connecting to another email system, you need to identify each mail system in your organization and the connectors that you use to connect these systems together. Exchange 2000 provides connectors to the following systems:

➤ Microsoft Mail

➤ Lotus cc:Mail

➤ Lotus Notes

➤ Novell GroupWise

➤ SNADS (provided in Exchange 5.5)

➤ PROFS (provided in Exchange 5.5)

This chapter explores the planning issues for coexistence between Exchange 2000 and these messaging systems.

Tip: Exchange 2000 also provides the SMTP Connector, the X.400 Connector, and the Routing Group Connector. The SMTP Connector can be used to connect to the Internet or other Internet mail systems that support SMTP. The X.400 Connector can be used with other organizations that connect through X.400 Connectors. The Routing Group Connector can join other Exchange 2000 routing groups within your Exchange design.

Regardless of the system, you must determine several factors that are universal to the planning process. First of all, you should establish the number of users that are on each non-Exchange system. This will be a very important factor as you continue to plan and configure your connector design. You must recognize how much mail travels through the connectors as well as how many connectors you will need for the system. A large number of users will most likely mean more email traffic.

Second, you need to make a record of the locations of the other systems' email servers. Document the type of connectivity being used to connect to those systems once you locate them. Keep the Exchange connector and the system to which you are connecting close to one another if possible. For example, if you have an Exchange Server in Phoenix, and a Notes community in London, you may decide to install an Exchange Server with a Notes Connector in London.

Third, you should verify some key information. Confirm that the required network connectivity and protocols are available where you need to connect them. Before you add connectors, verify the architecture behind the other systems. If the architecture has not been properly described, then document the architecture of the other email systems.

Next, plan your directory synchronization with the other email systems. When taking into consideration other email system connectivity, examine all of the policies and standards of the system to which you will be connecting. Also, consider the features that email users employ. For example, the public folders in Exchange- and/or Notes-based applications for Lotus Notes are features that users can use on their day-to-day work. Remembering this will help you deploy an integral corporate solution.

Finally, take into consideration the implications of deploying Active Directory. Active Directory uses Lightweight Directory Access Protocol (LDAP) as a protocol for the directory, as opposed to Directory Application Programming Interface (DAPI). Therefore, if you are using Exchange 5.5 and have your own directory synchronization scripts, make sure that these will continue to function in the Exchange 2000 and Active Directory environments.

Coexistence with Exchange 2000 and Microsoft Mail

The Microsoft Mail (MSMail) messaging software is the predecessor to Exchange Server. MSMail is still considered a reliable electronic mail system for small- to medium-sized organizations, even though it is nowhere near as feature rich and scalable as other systems. A fair number of organizations are still deploying MSMail, although larger organizations usually have it in just a few departments. Because of the limitations imposed by MSMail's reliance on the Shared File System (SFS), most organizations will choose to migrate to Exchange 2000 as opposed to coexisting with MSMail. In some circumstances, however, coexistence might play a transitory role or even an open-ended solution. Therefore, we review here some of the most important coexistence issues involved with MSMail and Exchange 2000 Server.

The Existing MSMail Environment

Before you connect to Exchange and synchronize the directories, you should first document, assess, and resolve any existing issues within the MSMail environment.

You may see little worth in documenting the existing MSMail system, particularly because you will soon migrate over to a new one, but by documenting and tidying up the existing MSMail messaging system, you can save substantial time and effort during the coexistence and migration phases. You should document all MSMail hubs, gateway post offices, and Message Transfer Agent (MTA) instances of MSMail so it will be easier to troubleshoot message transfer problems within the MSMail system or between MSMail and Exchange.

Message Transfer Agents

MSMail for PC Networks uses Message Transfer Agents (MTAs) to move mail between Mail for PC Networks post offices. This will be either a DOS-based application that resides on a dedicated computer or a process that runs as a Windows NT service. The MSMail Connector MTA is a more robust and efficient MSMail MTA. Once you have configured the connector, this MTA can take over the job of transporting mail between the MSMail post offices.

Additionally, you should document the MSMail directory synchronization (DirSync) configuration as well. The DirSync portion of Mail is done through a directory synchronization server and directory synchronization requestor. A directory synchronization server sends updates to all of the other post offices. Each MSMail network has only one directory synchronization server. A requestor solely sends updates to the server and receives updates from the server. Each post office in the MSMail network, including the directory synchronization server, has a requestor. DirSync should already be functioning properly within the MSMail environment. Resolve any DirSync issues before attempting Mail/Exchange 2000 coexistence.

You also want to evaluate the current MSMail routing topology to assess if any routing changes are necessary to improve coexistence with Exchange Server. You can establish the routing design by saving routing tables from hub and downstream post offices with the help of the MSMail Administrator program called ADMIN.EXE (from the menu, select External-Admin | Report | Setup | All Postoffices | File). Repair any existing problems with the MSMail post office data, message delivery, or directory systems as well. For best results during coexistence and migration, update and maintain the MSMail environment and routing documentation until all of the MSMail post offices have been migrated to Exchange.

Last, you want to check for existing MSMail database troubles. The MSMail Postoffice Diagnostics Utility (PODIAG.EXE) has a set of components that test out the database and analyze widespread problems. You can obtain the PODIAG utility from the installation software for Microsoft Mail for PC Networks 3.5.

PODIAG is best used in report-only mode. After it identifies a problem, you can either use TechNet to get repair instructions, or contact Microsoft technical support for assistance. Microsoft does not recommend using PODIAG to actually fix database problems due to several known issues. Search the Microsoft Knowledge Base using the keyword (PODIAG) for a list of known problems. If you want to try it on your own, be sure to back up the entire MSMail post office before attempting any repairs. Gathering all of the infrastructure information will help you to configure the Exchange Server's Microsoft Mail Connector.

Exchange Microsoft Mail Connector

The Exchange Microsoft Mail Connector delivers mail between Exchange and MSMail. The Microsoft Mail Connector permits mail to travel between the two systems as long as users know the fully defined address. The connector installs Exchange Microsoft Mail Post Office on the Exchange Server, which can interact with other Microsoft Mail post offices. As shown previously, directory synchronization for MSMail occurs through the Microsoft Mail DirSync protocol of requestor and server post offices. The directory synchronization services and connectors are installed at the same time. The Microsoft Mail Connector directory on the Exchange Server is in the \Exchsrvr\Connect\Msmcon folder. You can configure the Microsoft Mail Connector with Microsoft Management Console (MMC). Configure the connector with a MSMail Connector (PC) MTA service, or PCMTA. (Do not confuse this with Exchange MTA stacks, which Exchange also employs for mail delivery.) Because the MTA service connects a number of MSMail post offices, you must plan ahead for how many MTA services you will need and the number of post offices that are under each MTA service.

The Exchange MTA provides service only to post offices that are defined as direct connections. For indirect post offices, the Exchange MTA deposits mail in the outbound mailbag of the hub post office so a different MTA can handle the mail. To avoid this issue, define post offices as direct connections. You should also construct the Microsoft Exchange Connector Post Office to be a DirSync requestor to receive and send directory updates between MSMail and Exchange. If you configure it instead as a DirSync server, you will end up having to do more work on the MSMail side of the equation. The number of instances of the PCMTA that can run on the same Exchange Server is limited. In most environments, the practical threshold is seven combined instances of the various connectors or DirSync on a system running Windows NT 4 and Microsoft Exchange Server 4.

In addition to restricting the number of PCMTA instances, you should also control the number of Microsoft Mail post offices served by any single PCMTA instance. Consider carefully your hardware and network capacity when you add MSMail post office connections to each PCMTA instance. By monitoring the Microsoft Mail interchange (MSMI) and PCMTA Performance Monitor counters after implementing the MSMail Connector, you can get a better pulse of the limitations of your system and then fine-tune it as required. If an existing network connection is known to be unsteady, check for other physical connection options between the existing MSMail system and Exchange Server to reduce the impact. Take into account the network topology being used. It should be no surprise to find an organization using MS Mail with all or part of the network topology relying on a BNC cabling structure. This would substantially limit the overall network performance. Employ link monitors to identify delays in traffic across the gateway, and implement server monitors to watch the Exchange Server with the gateway installed. Performance Monitor can watch the Exchange Server's queue size for the gateway as well. Use the monitor in Alert view to warn administrators if the queue grows too large. Normally, you will implement the MSMail Connector when the first Exchange Server is introduced into an existing MSMail network. This should provide you with delivery speeds that are equivalent to those on the MSMail network.

Another facet of documenting the current environment is to study the overall routing plan. Consider if there are any issues or problems with the existing MSMail environment that a reconfiguration would resolve. Make sure that the existing routing configuration corresponds well to the network topology. For example, make sure that you find out if any MSMail hubs are located on either side of a slow wide area network (WAN) link. You may want to consider relocating hubs between post offices located across slower links to solve performance problems.

Messaging Client Interoperability

An Exchange 5.5 custom recipient is often a recipient using MSMail. During coexistence, your organization will very likely have a mix of MSMail and Outlook messaging and collaboration clients. One of the most important issues to consider when planning client interoperability is calendaring. The Exchange MSMail Connector provides a Free/Busy Connector that permits existing Microsoft PC Mail 3.x users with Schedule+ 1 and Microsoft Exchange Server users with Schedule+ 7 to see each other's free/busy information for calendaring purposes. Requests for meetings and free/busy information can be synchronized with the Schedule+ Free/Busy Connector. This connector also allows for the transfer of free and busy periods between the two systems. When the MSMail Connector is selected from Setup, the MSMail Connector and the Free/Busy Schedule Connector install by default. Microsoft Mail for PC Networks 3.x clients use Schedule+ 1.

Free/Busy Connector

For more information on how to set up the Free/Busy Connector and its requirements, see Microsoft Knowledge Base article #Q147698: XADM: Configuring the Schedule+ Free/Busy Connector. For more information on interoperability and coexistence issues that can affect users, administrators, and developers, navigate your browser to **www.microsoft.com/office/outlook/interop.htm**.

Keep in mind that Outlook users on Exchange Server can view the free or busy information of Schedule+ 7/95 and Schedule+ 1 users who are also on Exchange Server, but they cannot view the details of those on Microsoft Mail Server. Schedule+ 1 and non-Win32 Schedule+ 7/95 users cannot view Outlook users' free/busy details. Outlook users who have at least Read permission to another user's calendar can see when that user is free or busy. They can also view the details of that user's scheduled appointments and activities in the Meeting Planner. A Free/Busy folder is automatically produced on the first server that is deployed in a site, and, just as with any public folder, it can be replicated to other site servers. As an MSMail administrator, you must run the SCHDIST application on the Microsoft Mail 3.x side to move PC Mail users' free/busy updates into Microsoft Exchange Server and to be given free/busy updates from Microsoft Exchange Server users. If your organization has many users running Schedule+ 7, you should replicate the hidden folder that contains the Schedule+ 7 free and busy times.

To optimize interoperability between Schedule+ 1, Schedule+ 7, and Outlook, you should upgrade all members of a workgroup at the same time. Be sure to upgrade resource accounts after upgrading the users who use those resources. If you upgrade resource accounts to Outlook while the users are running Schedule+, those users will not be able to open the Calendar folders of the resource accounts. As a result, they will not be able to reserve those resources. Once you undertake the actual upgrade to Outlook, you should select the option to continue using Schedule+, instead of Outlook, for scheduling. Your organization will probably decide to migrate users to Outlook in phases for messaging, and then after the messaging migration is completed, everyone will migrate from Schedule+ to Outlook at the same time. Make sure that your users do not delete their Schedule+ files until the entire organization is ready to migrate to Outlook for scheduling. If users do delete their Schedule+ files too early, these files will have to be restored from a backup because Outlook cannot export its calendar data back to Schedule+ files. If no backups are available, you will have to manually reenter the data into Schedule+.

Microsoft Exchange to Microsoft Mail for PC Networks Directory Synchronization

Directory synchronization for MSMail takes place through the MSMail DirSync protocol of requestor and server post offices. The DirSync service populates the mail addresses and enables you to easily select the applicable email address from both systems. The DirSync service can perform the role of a requestor or a server. Your present MSMail design will establish the kind of service that your organization needs. In general, if your organization has more than one MSMail post office, you will have a native MSMail DirSync server that handles all the global address lists. The Exchange Server therefore becomes a DirSync requestor in the native MSMail setup. If your environment is running MSMail Server, it can coexist with the Exchange Server acting as a DirSync server. DirSync, for a computer running Microsoft Exchange Server, can be configured at the same time as the MSMail Connector. Remember that a MSMail environment has only one DirSync server. This configuration is also applicable to a company using Exchange 2000. Plan carefully which post offices will be DirSync requestors and which server will play the role of the DirSync server. In a new environment, make the DirSync server the Exchange Server.

MSMail implements a time point mechanism (T1, T2, and T3) to define its directory synchronization cycle. You can use the Command prompt to manually synchronize on the DirSync server and to force updates if directory synchronization is not working after the T1, T2, and T3 time points, which are as follows:

➤ *T1*—All the requestors send their updates to the DirSync server.

➤ *T2*—All the updates process on the server; T2 indicates when all changes propagate back to the requestors.

➤ *T3*—Requestors receive the new updates from the DirSync server.

The Exchange Connector post office can be defined as a remote MSMail post office as well as a requestor on the current DirSync server. Once configured, directory updates will be sent to the Exchange server when DirSync occurs. Although the MS-DOS DirSync agent (DISPATCH.EXE) still needs to run against the existing Microsoft Mail for PC Networks post offices, it should not be run against the Microsoft Exchange Connector post office. Microsoft Exchange services handle their own sending and receiving of updated directory lists. The directory synchronization services and connector are installed at the same time. The Microsoft Exchange Directory Synchronization Agent (DXA) automatically distributes updated directories to all of the post offices in the messaging scheme. The DXA provides this service whether the directories are on the same local area network (LAN), asynchronously connected, or linked by means of a gateway. The DXA can be a directory synchronization server and/or a requestor. A local DXA service is always installed for every instance of the MSMail Connector. The administrator configures the local DXA service to be a server or a requestor based on the topology. The DXA improves directory synchronization with flexible scheduling techniques, and also improves time zone administration and update scheduling. The

DXA can make a directory synchronization server more robust by reducing the maintenance of address lists, increasing security, and improving efficiency. The following list represents the main comparisons between the Microsoft Mail for PC Networks DirSync and the Exchange Server DirSync:

➤ MS Mail uses templates to record extended information about recipients. For example, it may store recipients' phone numbers or extensions in templates. To include MS Mail template information with other address information exchanged during directory synchronization, map the template information to recipient attributes in Active Directory.

➤ A Mail for PC Networks post office can schedule only one DirSync per day, whereas Exchange Server DirSync can be run as often as hourly. (An administrator can perform a directory synchronization manually, however.)

➤ Exchange Server DXA servers and requestors use the same DirSync protocol as the one used in Mail for PC Networks.

➤ Exchange Server DXA servers and requestors do not auto-create new definitions in a Mail Connector; Exchange Server implements the Update Routing feature instead.

➤ Exchange Server DXA servers and requestors will immediately apply changes.

➤ Exchange Server can have more than one DXA server or requestor, one for each Mail for PC Networks system.

➤ Exchange Server does not use DISPATCH.EXE against the Mail Connector post office; however, it must still be run against the Mail (PC) post offices.

Generally, you should preserve the current MSMail DirSync configuration and set up Microsoft Exchange as a DirSync requestor to export Exchange users into the DirSync stream. New Exchange mailboxes are created in the recipient container of the site by default. However, you can create new containers specifically for MSMail custom recipients. When you define the DirSync requestors on Microsoft Exchange, you can indicate where to store the MSMail usernames. MSMail custom recipients are typically created and tracked in separate recipient containers. When you create custom recipient containers, document which containers will be imported and which will be exported, as well as the originating MSMail post office of the recipients. This will make management and control of replication easier.

Do not permit the MSMail custom recipients to be exported from Exchange when an Exchange server is operating as a requestor to the MSMail DirSync server. Only the originating MSMail post offices hosting these users should be sending user updates or changes to the DirSync server. You should hide them or raise the trust level to 100 to keep them from being exported. Improper adding or removing of recipient containers on the DirSync stream can spawn redundant DirSync transactions and possibly cause the momentary loss of PCMail address information from Global Address Lists (GALs).

You must configure the connectors in the following order:

1. The MSMail Connector, which sends mail between Exchange and MSMail

2. The DirSync requestor or server, which populates the user list with the mail addresses of the other system

3. The Free/Busy Connector, which generates the free/busy schedules that appear in meeting requests

Coexistence with Exchange 2000 and cc:Mail

Although the Lotus cc:Mail messaging product has been available for many years, Lotus has announced plans to discontinue this product line in three phases:

➤ *Phase 1*—Lotus cc:Mail to be withdrawn from the market by October 31, 2000.

➤ *Phase 2*—All Lotus cc:Mail development to cease as of January 31, 2001.

➤ *Phase 3*—Lotus cc:Mail telephone support to cease by October 31, 2001.

The Lotus cc:Mail product comprises a number of components, ranging from front-end clients to back-end databases to gateways and monitoring programs. Compared to Microsoft Exchange 2000 Server, however, cc:Mail has few desirable features. For example, Exchange 2000 Server supports LDAP and Network News Transfer Protocol (NNTP) as well as such other key Internet protocols as Simple Mail Transfer Protocol (SMTP), Post Office Protocol 3 (POP3), Hypertext Transfer Protocol (HTTP), Internet Message Access Protocol (IMAP), and Secure Multipurpose Internet Mail Extensions (S/MIME). Therefore, before deciding about coexisting Lotus cc:Mail with Exchange 2000, you should substantiate this decision by looking at all of the factors. You want to weigh the business requirements along with the technical requirements of your organization to determine if you will need to coexist or migrate. The role of the cc:Mail Connector is to move messages from the Exchange Information Store into the foreign post office of cc:Mail. Lotus cc:Mail does not support a shadow post office; therefore, the router MTA is not necessary. The cc:Mail Connector translates messages and places them directly in the destination cc:Mail post office. In addition, cc:Mail supports only one post office connection, meaning that the connector can communicate with only one cc:Mail post office. As a result, Exchange will funnel messages to one post office, and the onward routing is carried out by cc:Mail. Another limitation of cc:Mail is that it does not support asynchronous or X.25 connections. Also, the cc:Mail post office with which the Exchange Server communicates must be available on the LAN or WAN.

If your organization still resolves to coexist Exchange 2000 with cc:Mail, then you will first need to determine which versions of cc:Mail are currently running. The Lotus cc:Mail product suite has had several iterations throughout its existence. You will also need to determine the method of connectivity between the two mail systems. Before attempting to put into play a coexistence design between Lotus cc:Mail and Exchange 2000, make sure that you that understand both products completely. You may want to consider reviewing the cc:Mail documentation to enhance your understanding of the product. Many knowledge gaps can occur when you are using a product in an isolated environment. Incorporating Windows 2000 into the mix can introduce many new issues as well.

At this early stage, take into consideration what your organization is planning to achieve, such as the following possibilities:

➤ Your company has an existing cc:Mail system, but it must interoperate with an Exchange 2000 Server network. This may be the result of a corporate merger, or perhaps a business partner needs a better level of integration than can be provided by SMTP mail.

➤ You have fewer than 10 post offices in an existing cc:Mail network, and you would like to migrate everything to Exchange 2000 Server.

➤ Your organization has an existing medium or large cc:Mail network, and you would like to coexist temporarily until you eventually migrate everything to Exchange 2000 Server.

Clearly, this list is not complete, but most organizations will fall into one of these three categories. For example, your first order of business will probably be to configure one or more Exchange 2000 connectors for cc:Mail in your Exchange 2000 Server network. You can then work toward full migration within a specified period of time. If your cc:Mail network is large, it might not seem feasible to migrate everyone to Exchange 2000 in a weekend. With proper planning and risk alleviation, however, it could be achieved.

Before installing the Microsoft Exchange Connector for Lotus cc:Mail, you must be aware of a few prerequisites. You must check the database version cc:Mail is using. You must have either Lotus cc:Mail Post Office Database version 6 (DB6) with cc:Mail Import version 5.15 and Export version 5.14, or Lotus cc:Mail Post Office Database version 8 (DB8) with cc:Mail Import version 6, Export version 6, and the Ie.ri file. Generally speaking, DB8 is more robust and stable than DB6. Most cc:Mail administrators normally prefer DB8 because they can do maintenance online without having to shut down the post office. Exchange Server can communicate with both formats.

You can find out the database and post office version numbers you have using the Analyze32.exe utility, or by looking at the files in the \ccdata directory. Analyze(32).exe is primarily a utility inside Lotus to check the integrity of the file structures and to identify a corrupt post office. The major advantage of this tool, compared to Chkstat or Reclaim, among others, is that you do not need a password to run it. All the Lotus cc:Mail utilities support the **/?** help switch.

In addition to the database, you need the name and password of the cc:Mail post office to which you want to connect. Also, you need to determine if the cc:Mail post office you are connecting to has Automatic Directory Exchange (ADE) selected. Determine how the cc:Mail network is configured before you implement the cc:Mail Connector. If all you need to perform is a direct message transfer between the two systems, then just retain the default configuration of cc:Mail. However, your organization will probably need to configure DirSync. This is where many issues can arise. As stated previously, you should review the cc:Mail documentation. Retrieve the documentation and take note of several elements of the existing cc:Mail network. You need to know the number of post offices along with their physical locations, the operating system, the gateways, and basically any other relevant information that you can find. Once you obtain this information, move on to acquire all of the documentation concerning the message routing configuration between all the post offices. Determine the number of router MTAs (by using ROUTER.EXE) and how they connect with each post office. The next, very important, step is to find out which post offices do all of the routing. You should also know how the ADE topology has been configured and establish whether your Exchange users will be visible to all of the cc:Mail post offices and vice versa. Also, look at the address structuring inside the post office.

Be sure to plan where Exchange 2000 Server is going to connect to your cc:Mail environment. One approach would be to link directly into a cc:Mail hub post office. A more conventional method would be to connect Exchange 2000 to a "dummy" post office, similar to a MSMail shadow post office. The dummy post office should be placed on the Exchange 2000 Server itself. Then you would use the cc:Mail Router program (the Windows NT version is preferable) to route between this dummy and the existing cc:Mail system. If you decide to implement a dummy post office, you will need to place it in either a broadcaster or enterprise ADE relationship with the main cc:Mail environment. Many organizations choose a broadcaster relationship because it offers the best solution for most situations. It is generally a poor idea to perform directory synchronization of Exchange 2000 with a cc:Mail subordinate post office because the Exchange users will not be visible outside of the local post office.

After you take care of all these predeployment issues, you are ready to look at some good rules concerning implementation of the cc:Mail Connector. It is, of course, possible to break some of these rules, but be careful to configure your environment thoughtfully. Make your choices cautiously and document completely the connection strategy that you choose.

➤ Each physical Exchange Server can have one cc:Mail Connector.

➤ You can have as many cc:Mail Connectors in the same site as you have servers, if necessary.

➤ You should not have two Exchange servers in the same site connected to a single cc:Mail post office.

➤ You should not configure dual cc:Mail Connectors for fault tolerance unless you are equipped to manually tune the cc:Mail post office routes if a failure occurs.

➤ Only one cc:Mail Connector should have DirSync enabled. The rest of the connectors should be pure messaging connectors.

Note: You can configure Exchange and cc:Mail to forward mail to either a public folder or a bulletin board. However, due to the limitations in the propagation of bulletin board messages, you can configure message forwarding for one direction only (cc:Mail to Exchange, or Exchange to cc:Mail). Configuration of cross-postings between a cc:Mail bulletin board and an Exchange public folder may cause message looping.

Coexistence with Exchange 2000 and Lotus Notes

If your organization has decided to have Lotus Notes coexist with Exchange 2000, then only the Notes application is converted to Exchange 2000. The implementation of the application is restricted by the Notes configuration, which, in turn, confines the features that Exchange can provide. Due to such limitations, you must carefully consider the effect that the application will have on your organization when planning your Exchange deployment.

Exchange Lotus Notes Connector

The Exchange Lotus Notes Connector connects Exchange 2000 with Lotus Notes servers. The connector has such features as built-in messaging, directory synchronization, and meeting request capacities. The Notes Connector provides reliable messaging between Notes and Exchange and supports features such as:

➤ Delivery status

➤ Delivery receipts

➤ Delivery Notification Status, such as a non-delivery report (NDR)

➤ Read receipts

➤ Doc-links, such as Rich Text Format (RTF), Uniform Resource Locator (URL), and object linking and embedding (OLE)

➤ Options

➤ Importance (high, normal, low)

➤ Type (private, confidential)

➤ Formatting

The Lotus Notes Connector also permits synchronization between the Notes address books and Active Directory. You will use MMC to set up the connector for messaging and directory synchronization. The mapping files with default mapping rules for your attributes are located in the \exchsrvr\conndata\dxamex and \exchsrvr\conndata\dxanotes folders. The Notes Connector uses both of these directories during the directory synchronization process.

Table 6.1 lists the directory files and their uses. These files are for directory synchronization and have default values that are adequate in most cases. You may need to edit these files, however, to create custom rules.

Services to Use During Coexistence

An organization incorporates a coexistence phase for two reasons. The first reason is to introduce a transitory coexistence period while the Exchange and Notes migration occurs. The second is to avoid any additional installation of Notes within the organization that might obstruct or draw out the migration process. For the coexistence phase, you will implement the following services:

➤ *Mail connectivity*—Mail connectivity allows for the transport of standard email messages between Notes and Exchange. This should include support for messages and replies, as well as extended email forms such as telephone messages, tasks, and routing slips.

➤ *Directory synchronization*—Directory synchronization is bidirectional synchronization between Active Directory and Notes directories. It provides users with

Table 6.1   Files used by the Notes Connector.

Directory	File Name	Purpose
dxamex	Mapnotes.tbl	Mapping rules: entries going from Notes to Exchange
dxamex	Amap.tbl	Defines Exchange fields to be synchronized
dxanotes	Mapmex.tbl	Mapping rules: entries going from Exchange to Notes
dxanotes	Amap.tbl	Defines Notes fields to be synchronized

precise and total address data in which to identify other users on either system. Directory synchronization will be particularly vital during the migration phase because the addressing information is so volatile during this period.

➤ *Replication of databases*—Replication involves the discussion and document distribution databases, which are widely used Notes applications. Their Exchange and Outlook equivalents are public folders. These services permit Exchange and Notes users to communicate no matter which system they are using.

Coexistence services have delivered quite a few benefits for the Plus Ultra Group. The users who migrated to Exchange were not cut off from users, information, or applications that they had been able to access in Notes. Plus Ultra Group users who had not yet migrated to Exchange could communicate with their colleagues who had. This transparency helped to remove doubts or fears about accomplishing work after they migrated to Outlook or Exchange.

Coexistence Architecture

When planning coexistence, and ultimately migration, you need to consider the domain architecture, user account issues, and options for gateway configuration. The Windows 2000 domain design provides security boundaries, which can mean certain limitations that will affect the design. During directory synchronization between Notes and Exchange, the Lotus Notes recipient will exist in only one Windows 2000 domain. The Lotus Notes contact information should be located in the Windows 2000 domain where the users will eventually migrate. If the users are not placed into the proper domain, delete the contact information and re-create it in the correct domain during the migration process. This process may become more complex if the Lotus Notes entries must match the Windows 2000–enabled user accounts. If most of the users already have Notes and Windows 2000 accounts, it will probably make more sense to map the Lotus Notes account to the Windows 2000 account instead of adding contacts for each Lotus Notes account to Windows 2000, which would double the number of users in Active Directory.

After deciding where to place your gateways, determine if the synchronized Lotus Notes entries will be stored in Active Directory as contacts or user accounts, or be synchronized with existing accounts. When setting up directory synchronization, your options are to create either a disabled Windows 2000 user account, a new Windows 2000 user account, or a Windows 2000 contact. Most Notes users will probably already have a Windows 2000 account; therefore, directory synchronization can be set to create Windows 2000 contacts. The Windows 2000 contact will then eventually be merged to the appropriate user account through the Active Directory Account Cleanup Wizard.

Other aspects to consider when setting up synchronization and gateways are the following: You can convert Notes Doc-links to OLE documents, RTF attachments, or URL shortcuts. Convert Doc-links to URL shortcuts if all of the Lotus Notes servers in the organization are Domino servers and are configured to support Web-enabled applications. If they are not, convert them to RTF attachments, which is the default. Also, by using mapping rules, the connector allows you to map Lotus Notes fields to Active Directory attributes (and vice versa). Be sure to figure out beforehand which fields you want to synchronize. Last, produce the suitable SMTP addresses on the Lotus Notes contacts in Active Directory. This is vital because the SMTP gateway will be moved to Exchange, and Lotus Notes recipients will expect to continue to receive email being sent to their current SMTP addresses. Therefore, you should generate a suitable mapping rule during setup.

Coexisting with Exchange 2000 and GroupWise

This brief overview shows how to coexist with Novell GroupWise 4.x/5.x and Exchange 2000. The GroupWise Connector supports the Free/Busy query functionality of the Exchange Calendar Connector. Microsoft provides new tools and strategies for migrating from Novell GroupWise to Microsoft Exchange 2000 and Exchange 5.5. The Novell GroupWise messaging architecture is very similar to the SFS architecture of MS Mail. Both systems use multiple post offices that move mail between them through the use of MTAs. Exchange 2000 Server includes three tools that help you set up coexistence between Exchange 2000 Server and Novell GroupWise:

➤ Exchange Connector for Novell GroupWise

➤ Exchange Calendar Connector

➤ Windows 2000 Active Directory Account Cleanup Wizard

A Basic GroupWise System

Before we look at the functionality of these tools, let us look at a basic GroupWise system. A basic system will normally comprise a single domain with one post office, a document library, and one or more users. Each GroupWise user has a mailbox in the post office and uses the GroupWise client application to access the mailbox as well as to send and receive mail. The GroupWise agents transport messages between mailboxes in a post office and route messages between post offices in a multiple post office system. In a multiple post office system, the domain organizes post offices into logical groups for addressing and routing purposes. The role of the domain is as the chief administration unit for the GroupWise system. When you add GroupWise information via a NetWare administrator, the information is stored in NetWare Directory Service (NDS) as well as the GroupWise domain database. The information is dispersed to each post office database through the domain database. Users subsequently receive their information from their post office database. Keep in mind that the domain structure adds more overhead, although the GroupWise architecture can accommodate scaling beyond a single post office installation.

The basic GroupWise components are as follows:

➤ The MTA, which routes messages between domains, post offices, and gateways

➤ The Post Office Agent (POA), which delivers messages to users' mailboxes

➤ A domain, which offers a logical grouping for the functions of addressing and routing

Exchange Connector for Novell GroupWise

The Exchange Connector for Novell GroupWise provides support for transferring messages and calendar requests, as well as for directory synchronization. Exchange Connector for Novell GroupWise performs bidirectional interchanges of major message types between Exchange 2000 Server and GroupWise. You deploy Exchange Connector for Novell GroupWise so that the two systems can coexist, either temporarily or for the long term. The messaging system of a department that is not moving to Exchange 2000 Server, for instance, may need a permanent, long-term connection.

The directory synchronization process circulates Exchange 2000 user directory information from Windows 2000 Active Directory to the directory of a GroupWise system. It also propagates information about GroupWise users to Active Directory for Exchange 2000 to use. When synchronization is complete, each system will have an entire copy of the organization so that users on one system can send email to users on the other system. Active Directory uses directory objects to represent Exchange 2000 users on GroupWise that are synchronized with Exchange 2000. Directory synchronization comprises two distinct and sequential procedures:

➤ Importing recipients from GroupWise

➤ Exporting recipients from Active Directory

During the scheduled directory synchronization, this is a bidirectional process. Every time directory synchronization occurs, the Exchange Connector takes information from Active Directory and routes the information, along with a request for a GroupWise directory, to Novell GroupWise through an API gateway. The API gateway enables communications between GroupWise systems and Exchange 2000 Server. GroupWise processes the data from Active Directory and subsequently replies to the directory request by tapping its own directory and then returning the information to the API gateway. Exchange Connector for Novell GroupWise then receives the information from the API gateway and populates Active Directory.

Importing Recipients from GroupWise

To import directory entries, as previously mentioned, Exchange Connector for Novell GroupWise issues a request to the GroupWise directory and places the request into the input queue of the GroupWise API gateway. The API gateway then routes the message to the GroupWise system. Next, after polling the GroupWise directory, the GroupWise system generates a response. GroupWise then sends the response back to the output queue of the API gateway at the chosen polling intervals. When the API gateway receives messages, it processes them from the queue.

Exporting Recipients from Active Directory

To export directory entries from Exchange 2000, Exchange Connector for Novell GroupWise polls Active Directory and generates an export message that contains the necessary transactions to perform a complete reload. Exchange Connector for Novell GroupWise sends the export message to the input queue of the GroupWise API gateway. The API gateway sends the message to the GroupWise system and then deletes the files from the input queue. Finally, the GroupWise system updates the GroupWise directory.

Filtering

GroupWise provides several mechanisms that can be used to filter addresses that you export from Exchange 2000. To filter addresses during an export, you can create containers to hold subsets of Exchange 2000 Server users. You would then select only the suitable containers to export to GroupWise. You could define a special container for imported GroupWise users, for example, which you would not include in an export list. A second technique is to choose whether to export contacts (such as Internet users) whom you may not want to export to GroupWise in your export containers. Third, you can choose whether to export groups. When choosing recipients to import, use the Import Container tab in Exchange Connector for Novell GroupWise, and specify the container to which to import GroupWise recipients. Under Filtering, on the Import Container tab, select which recipients to import from GroupWise. You can specify domains, post offices, and individual recipients to be included or excluded.

Message Delivery

Message delivery has evolved from plain email messages to a plethora of different message types. Novell GroupWise offers support for simple email, posted messages, posted appointments, tasks, notes, and posted tasks. Exchange 2000 Server supports meeting requests, tasks, task requests, and notes as well as posts, journal entries, and email messages. Exchange Connector for Novell GroupWise will provide the needed support for the broadcast and mapping of diverse message types between GroupWise and Exchange. A message that cannot be mapped to a corresponding message type in the target domain will automatically be converted to an email message.

Sending Messages from Exchange 2000 to GroupWise

The following steps explain the process for sending messages from Exchange 2000 to GroupWise:

1. Exchange 2000 concludes that a user is a GroupWise recipient, based on the target address, and subsequently sends the message to Exchange Connector for Novell GroupWise.

2. Exchange Connector for Novell GroupWise translates the message into the suitable API gateway format and sends the message to the GroupWise API gateway, which then converts the message into GroupWise format.

3. The GroupWise API gateway transfers the message to the GroupWise MTA, which then delivers it to the recipient.

Sending Messages from GroupWise to Exchange 2000

The following steps explain the process for sending messages from GroupWise to Exchange 2000:

1. GroupWise recognizes mail sent to Exchange 2000 users as being targeted to foreign users. GroupWise converts the message to API gateway format and sends it on to the GroupWise API gateway.

2. Exchange Connector for Novell GroupWise grabs messages dropped in the API gateway folder and subsequently translates the message from GroupWise API gateway format to Exchange 2000 format.

3. The message is sent to Exchange 2000 for routing purposes.

Exchange Calendar Connector

The Exchange Calendar Connector gives Exchange 2000 and GroupWise users the ability for near real-time access to free/busy calendar data. Exchange Calendar Connector runs on a computer as an Exchange 2000 Server service and extends the calendar interoperability features of Exchange Server. In an Exchange and GroupWise mixed-product environment, the support of queries for free/busy information enhances group scheduling. Exchange 2000 offers native messaging support, however, between the GroupWise and Microsoft Exchange Server environments, thus removing the connector's dependency on SMTP for message delivery between Exchange and GroupWise.

Active Directory Account Cleanup Wizard

The Active Directory Account Cleanup Wizard is a utility that combines GroupWise mailboxes, Active Directory user accounts, and contacts. When the Exchange Server Migration Wizard (see Chapter 7 for more on this wizard) or Exchange Connector for Novell GroupWise imports directory information from your existing messaging system into Exchange 2000, it places the information into Active Directory.

Troubleshooting and Monitoring

In addition to the utilities included with Exchange 2000 Server, you can also use some of the following familiar Windows NT tools to monitor, manage, and troubleshoot Microsoft Exchange Connector for Novell GroupWise.

Control Panel

You can use the Control Panel, Administrative Tools, or Services in Windows 2000 to stop and start Exchange Connector for GroupWise services.

Event Viewer

You can use the Windows 2000 Event Viewer to view message flow, logs, and errors connected to Exchange Connector for Novell GroupWise activity that occurs between the Exchange 2000 Server and GroupWise systems.

Performance Monitor

You can also implement the Windows 2000 Performance Monitor to monitor messages, queues, and the bytes that are transferred between GroupWise and Exchange 2000. Performance Monitor will also show you the number of messages in the output queue, as well as the number of messages sent back due to nondelivery.

Queue Object

You can monitor the stream of mail through Exchange Connector for Novell GroupWise with the Queue object in the Exchange System Manager MMC console. In addition, you can find and delete individual messages if necessary. Check the queues whenever there is a message delivery problem involving the Exchange Connector for Novell GroupWise. A long queue may indicate a problem with the physical connection between servers or a configuration problem with a server or connector. Use the Queue object also to remove corrupted messages that hinder message flow in your system.

Link Monitors

Link monitors view the roundtrip time of "ping" messages (i.e., echo request and reply) that are sent between a computer running Exchange 2000 Server and a GroupWise system. A notification is triggered if the roundtrip exceeds certain selected parameters.

Coexistence with Exchange 2000 and PROFS/SNADS

The Professional Office System (PROFS) or Office Vision connector is not supported in Exchange 2000. The System Network Architecture Distribution System (SNADS) connector is also not supported in Exchange 2000. Directory synchronization is important for moving mail between dissimilar systems. As a result, the Exchange PROFS connector and the Exchange SNADS connector must stay on your Exchange 5.5 connector server. If you presently have a PROFS or SNADS design on Exchange 5.5, you will continue to use the synchronization process established for your environment, even during later migration to Exchange 2000. In a mixed-Exchange environment, connecting to PROFS and SNADS systems enables making PROFS/SNADS addresses for contacts and mailboxes. Because the proxy address generators and templates are located on Exchange 5.5, you will need to replicate these templates to Active Directory using the Active Directory Connector (ADC). The ADC will permit synchronization of these proxies across platforms to the Active Directory. Because SNADS and PROFS connectors are not included with Exchange 2000, you will need to maintain a segment of your Exchange 5.5 infrastructure to serve as connector bridgehead servers to these systems. This will also necessitate directory synchronization between Exchange 5.5 and Active Directory with the ADC.

Microsoft Metadirectory Services

If you have multiple directories from a variety of systems, you might want to think about using Microsoft Metadirectory Services. Metadirectory Services allow you to send and receive updates from a multitude of systems, including the flat files created by PROFS. In addition, Metadirectory Services can synchronize directly with Exchange 5.5 or Active Directory. If you decide to incorporate Active Directory, Metadirectory Services can help bring all of your directories into Active Directory. Metadirectory Services can also synchronize with other email systems.

Microsoft Metadirectory Services

For more information and to obtain Microsoft Metadirectory Services, navigate your browser to **http:// microsoft.com/windows2000/news/bulletins/mmsma.asp**.

Chapter Summary

Although most organizations will want to eventually migrate completely to Exchange 2000 from a variety of systems, Exchange Server 2000 includes a variety of tools that support coexistence with another mail system as long-term messaging connectivity or while you plan your migration to Exchange. Exchange 2000 provides connectors to Microsoft Mail, Lotus cc:Mail, Lotus Notes, and Novell GroupWise.

Whatever your scenario is for system coexistence, you should determine how many users are on every non-Exchange system. You will also need to make a detailed record of the location of the other systems' email servers. Remember to confirm that the required network connectivity and protocols are available where needed and to verify the architecture behind the other systems. Plan your directory synchronization with the other email systems, and then consider the results of deploying Active Directory.

Many organizations are still deploying other systems, although larger organizations usually have them in just a few departments. Environments exist in which coexistence plays a transitory role and, in rare cases, even an open-ended solution. Before you connect through an Exchange connector, you should first document, evaluate, and fix any existing issues within the environment. Although you may see little value in documenting the existing system, particularly because you will soon migrate over to a new one, by documenting and tidying up the existing messaging system, you can save substantial time and effort during the coexistence and migration phases. It is important to also document the existing directory synchronization architecture as well as the use of routing, gateways, and agents.

Every system has a diverse set of idiosyncrasies and particulars that make understanding the non-Exchange system as well as Active Directory vitally important. This is true when deciding to have two systems, such as Novell GroupWise and Exchange 2000, coexist. The importance of understanding all of the available tools and components becomes crucial as you begin the migration-planning phase. We explore this topic in greater detail in Chapter 7.

Review Questions

1. Before connecting to another email system, you must identify each mail system in your organization and the connectors that you use to connect these systems together. Exchange 2000 provides connectors for which of the following systems? [Check all correct answers]

   a. Microsoft Mail

   b. SNADS

   c. Lotus cc:Mail

   d. Lotus Notes

   e. PROFS

   f. Novell GroupWise

   g. SMTP

2. Your organization has multiple directories from a variety of systems. Which service will allow you to send and receive updates from a whole host of systems?

   a. Microsoft Management Console (MMC)

   b. Microsoft Coexistence Connector (MCC)

   c. Microsoft Metadirectory Services (MMS)

   d. Microsoft Multiple Directory Services (MMDS)

3. Regardless of which systems you are coexisting with, several factors must be determined that are universal to the planning process. Which of the following represent important factors? [Check all correct answers]

   a. Establish the number of users that are on each non-Exchange system.

   b. Document the location of the other systems' email servers.

   c. Verify that the required network connectivity and protocols are available where you need to connect them.

   d. Plan your directory synchronization with the other email systems.

   e. Take into consideration the implications of deploying Active Directory.

4. Which one of the following tools could be used specifically to view the roundtrip time of PING messages that are sent between a computer running Exchange 2000 Server and a GroupWise system?

   a. Queue monitors

   b. Link monitors

   c. Control Panel

   d. Event Viewer

5. Most organizations running MSMail will be performing a migration to Exchange 2000 as opposed to coexistence, in part due to the limitations of Mail's reliance on which of the following file systems?

   a. File allocation table (FAT)

   b. Network Filing System (NFS)

   c. Shared File System (SFS)

   d. High Performance File System (HPFS)

6. Which one of the following tools gives Exchange 2000 and GroupWise users the ability for almost real-time access to free/busy information?

   a. Active Directory Connector

   b. Exchange Calendar Connector

   c. Free/Busy Connector

   d. Exchange Queue Connector

7. Which of the following components best describes an MS-DOS-based mail application that resides on a dedicated computer that Microsoft Mail for PC Networks uses to move mail between Mail for PC Networks post offices?

   a. Microsoft Coexistence Connector (MMC)

   b. Asynchronous transfer mode (ATM)

   c. Active Directory Connector (ADC)

   d. Message Transfer Agent (MTA)

6

8. You are implementing the Exchange Connector for Novell GroupWise to provide needed support for the transport and mapping of different message types between GroupWise and Exchange. What will happen if a message cannot be mapped to a corresponding message type in the target domain?

   a. The message will automatically be converted to a task.

   b. The message will be automatically converted to an email message.

   c. The message will automatically be dropped from both systems.

   d. The message will automatically be returned to the sender with an error message.

9. In which folder on the Exchange 2000 Server will you find the Microsoft Mail Connector?

   a. \Exchsrvr\Connect\Msmcon

   b. \Exchsrvr\Connect\Mailcon

   c. \Exchsrvr\Gateway\Msmcon

   d. \Exchsrvr\Gateway\Mailcon

10. Which one of the following is *not* a basic GroupWise component?

    a. Domain

    b. Message Transfer Agent (MTA)

    c. Post Office Agent (POA)

    d. NetWare Directory Service (NDS)

11. Which of the following files resides in the \exchsrvr\conndata\dxamex folder and is responsible for the mapping rules of entries going from Notes to Exchange?

    a. Mapmex.tbl

    b. Dxanotes.tbl

    c. Amap.tbl

    d. Mapnotes.tbl

12. Which one of the following statements is true regarding the comparisons between the Microsoft Mail for PC Networks DirSync and the Exchange Server DirSync?

    a. Exchange Server DXA servers and requestors use a different, more complex DirSync protocol than that used in Mail for PC Networks.

    b. Exchange Server DXA servers and requestors will auto-create new definitions in a Mail Connector.

    c. Exchange Server DXA servers and requestors will immediately apply changes.

    d. Exchange Server can have only one DXA server or requestor.

13. You are carefully considering the business and technical requirements of your organization to determine if you will need to coexist or migrate with Lotus cc:Mail. Which of the following is a true statement that may affect your decision?

    a. cc:Mail does not support a shadow post office; therefore, the router MTA is not necessary.

    b. cc:Mail supports only one post office connection, meaning that the connector can communicate with only one cc:Mail post office.

    c. cc:Mail does not support asynchronous or X.25 connections.

    d. All of the above.

14. You are preparing to install the Microsoft Exchange Connector for Lotus cc:Mail. You check the database version that cc:Mail is using. Which of the following are required and supported versions necessary to install the Exchange Connector for Lotus cc:Mail? [Check the two best answers]

    a. Lotus cc:Mail Post Office Database version 6, with cc:Mail Import version 5.15 and Export version 5.14

    b. Lotus cc:Mail Post Office Database version 6, with cc:Mail Import version 6 and Export version 6

    c. Lotus cc:Mail Post Office Database version 7, with cc:Mail Import version 5.15 and Export version 5.14

    d. Lotus cc:Mail Post Office Database version 8, with cc:Mail Import version 6, Export version 6, and the Ie.ri file.

15. All of the Lotus Notes servers in your organization are Domino servers and are configured to support Web-enabled applications. To which format should you convert the Doc-links?

    a. OLE documents

    b. Rich Text Format (RTF) attachments

    c. URL shortcuts

    d. Windows Metafile (WMF)

Real-World Projects

Project 6.1

During coexistence, your organization will have a combination of MSMail and Outlook messaging and collaboration clients. You are team leader for issues relating to client interoperability through calendaring. You need to permit your existing PC

Mail 3.x users using Schedule+ 1 to see the free/busy information of the new Exchange Server users with Schedule+ 7 for calendaring purposes. For help in doing this, use the Web to locate the Microsoft Knowledge Base article #Q147698 along with documentation from this chapter and the following URL: **http://www.microsoft.com/office/outlook/interop.htm**. Create a brief report that explains which tools you will use to accomplish this task as well as any limitations that your organization will have from allowing your existing PC Mail 3.x users using Schedule+ 1 to see the free/busy information of the new Exchange Server users with Schedule+ 7.

Project 6.2

You are the team leader at Plus Ultra Group for the deployment of the Exchange Connector for Novell. You have been tasked with allowing the GroupWise and Exchange 2000 systems to coexist in the developers' department, which is not moving to Exchange 2000 Server in the foreseeable future. Therefore, your developers need a permanent, long-term connection solution. You are preparing a report for a selected information technology (IT) professional in the development department to explain the import and export process. Using information found in this chapter, explain these processes in a brief report.

Project 6.3

Your team is using the Microsoft Management Console to set up the Lotus Notes Connector for messaging and directory synchronization in your large organization. Due to time constraints, you have been delegated some tasks by the team leader in your department. She is handing over to you all of the duties of mapping Lotus Notes to Exchange. Create a table for your team that shows the directory locations, files, and purposes of the files to facilitate the mapping process.

CHAPTER SEVEN

Designing an Upgrade or Migration Strategy

After completing this chapter, you will be able to:

✓ Examine the current Exchange 5.5 environment to see where Exchange 2000 will provide benefits

✓ Determine whether to upgrade or migrate from Exchange 5.5 to Exchange 2000

✓ Plan and design for the appropriate ADC connection agreements

✓ Prepare for a migration that uses the Active Directory Migration Tool

✓ Design connection agreements

✓ Decommission down-level Exchange servers

✓ Create a strategy for migrating from Lotus Notes to Exchange 2000

✓ Create a strategy for migrating from GroupWise to Exchange 2000

✓ Create a strategy for migrating from cc:Mail to Exchange 2000

✓ Create a strategy for migrating from MSMail to Exchange 2000

Planning a Successful Exchange 2000 Migration Strategy

Migrating from Windows NT and Exchange Server 5.5 to Windows 2000 and Exchange 2000 can be a complex and time-consuming process. By implementing a plan and setting realistic goals, your organization can accomplish the migration phase with a high degree of success. By performing a rapid migration, you will save your company the cost of running two systems and reduce the burden on users, administrators, management, hardware, and network resources. This chapter uses the terms "upgrade" and "migrate" with specific meanings. For Exchange servers, the term "migrate" means to move the resources from a down-level Exchange server to an Exchange 2000 server. The term "upgrade" refers to promoting an Exchange 5.5 Service Pack 3 (SP3) server to Exchange 2000. When referring to "upgrading" an Exchange site, however, it means that the servers in that site begin as down-level Exchange servers and wind up as Exchange 2000 servers.

Examining the Current Exchange 5.5 System

The first six chapters of this book have provided information for you to assess the potential for Exchange 2000 in your organization. Now you need to examine your current Exchange 5.5 system to discover where Exchange 2000 will offer the most payback. Consider examining your organization on three levels, if applicable: the data center, the infrastructure at an Exchange site, and each individual server.

The Data Center Level

The most important reason to appraise your organization at the data center level is that characteristically most Exchange 5.5 servers are located at data centers. If your team can manage to consolidate these servers first, you can more rapidly and readily combine Exchange 5.5 servers down to fewer Exchange 2000 servers without a complete topological or system redesign. For example, if you had four Exchange 5.5 servers in a data center and a single Exchange 5.5 server in each of two remote offices, you should first consider consolidating the four Exchange 5.5 servers before moving to the other two remote servers. By beginning your migration with the large number of users and mailboxes at the data centers, you will save time and have less downtime at the remote offices.

Chapter 2 in this book examined several types of organizations. The three major types of offices for which an Exchange server reduction would be most advantageous are the global headquarters (GHQ), the regional branch office (RBO), and the large branch office (LBO). You could potentially consolidate the servers in medium branch offices (MBOs) in rare circumstances, but small branch offices (SBOs) generally have no local Exchange server. The GHQ is made up of the central organizational offices. Normally, this is where you will find the highest confluence of Exchange 5.5 servers. This is also where most large organizations house their principal information technology (IT) support staff. In a company such as Plus Ultra Group, the GHQ has a number of Exchange 5.5 mailbox servers and public folder servers, combined with connector servers that link to other messaging systems. Plus Ultra Group, for example, could decide to mark any of these Exchange 5.5 servers for consolidation to Exchange 2000.

An RBO might have a moderate regional support staff and will usually serve as the central office for a region. As a result, the RBO will typically host servers and services for the offices of that region. The RBO is linked to the GHQ as well as other kinds of offices. An RBO may host quite a few mailbox and connector servers in addition to public folder servers, depending on how widespread the hierarchy of the organization's public folders is. Your organization may want to consider a consolidation of any of these Exchange 5.5 servers to Exchange 2000.

An LBO may also house a large number of Exchange 5.5 mailbox servers. Therefore, you can reduce the number of Exchange 5.5 servers at your LBO by consolidating on Exchange 2000 servers.

The only consolidation in an MBO would occur when the office has more than one Exchange 5.5 server, or when the Exchange server is centralized, which would leave the MBO without an Exchange server. Make certain plenty of available network bandwidth exists for remote access if you decide to centralize an MBO.

The Site Level

If your Exchange sites extend across multiple locations, you should decide if you are going to reduce the number of locations in a site where Exchange servers reside. If you actually have adequate bandwidth (at least 256 Kbps) for a single site, you could host user connections to remote Exchange servers instead of having a local Exchange server. Before you take this consolidation strategy, make sure that your client response service levels are not compromised.

The Individual Server Level

Once you have finished your analysis at the data center and site levels, you should complete the process at the individual Exchange 5.5 server level. Your goal here is to determine which Exchange 5.5 servers can be upgraded and consolidated, which can be upgraded but not consolidated, and which can be decommissioned after their resources are moved to another server. During this process you would probably notice that some servers are utilized more than others. You may also discover that some of your mailbox servers are already bound to the central processing unit (CPU) due to mailbox rules. Some Exchange servers may presently be hosting applications or connectors, such as PROFS or SNAD, that cannot be upgraded because Exchange 2000 will not offer support. Be sure to classify these legacy systems and evaluate them if they are essential to your organization.

Exchange 2000: Upgrade or Migration?

One of the most important decisions that your organization will have to make regarding Exchange is whether to upgrade your servers or to migrate their resources to Exchange 2000. If your design architecture consists of Exchange 5.5 connector servers (bridgehead servers), you may be able to upgrade the servers. This should be a pretty quick process because the Exchange 5.5 connector servers have such a small information store. Keep in mind that if you have Exchange 5.5 mailbox servers with large information stores, your service level agreements may not allow for email being unavailable for a certain period of time. You may have to migrate the mailboxes to new Exchange 2000 servers instead, to make sure that interruption to email service is minimized.

Because Exchange 2000 does not support all of the connectors that Exchange 5.5 does, you will need to determine which current Exchange 5.5 server connectors can be supported on Exchange 2000. If a particular server has several connectors configured and a particular connector is not supported, you might consider moving the unsupported connector to another Exchange 5.5 server. You could then upgrade the original server to Exchange 2000. Another alternative would be to replace this connector with an alternate that is supported on both systems. For example, many messaging systems now support Simple Mail Transfer Protocol (SMTP); therefore, it might be feasible to continue messaging connectivity without the unsupported connector. This should be tested in a lab environment first, and if the connectivity is sufficient, the other connectors can be removed.

Migration to Exchange 2000 can be accomplished (for all supported resources) on your Exchange 5.5 server through the "move resource" procedure. If your Exchange 5.5 servers are hosting directory replication connectors, however, they will perform a full replication of the entire directory back to the down–level Exchange servers during migration. When upgrading these Exchange servers, the upgrade will generate the Site Replication Service (SRS). The role of the SRS is to replicate the Exchange 2000 configuration information to the down–level Exchange environment. Therefore, if your Exchange servers are hosting directory replication connectors, you should perform an upgrade instead of a migration. Public folders can be migrated to Exchange 2000 without any downtime through the public folder replication process, which permits you to move the public folders and subsequently decommission the old public folder servers at the proper time.

Table 7.1 lists specific recommendations regarding upgrading or migrating the various types of Exchange servers.

Table 7.1   Specific upgrade/migrate recommendations for various Exchange servers.

Type of Server	Upgrade/Migrate	Rationale
Directory replication server	Upgrade	This server provides for automatic generation, configuration, and initiation of the SRS.
Server with supported connectors	Upgrade	The small size of the information store permits a very fast upgrade procedure. The backup server can handle the load during upgrade.
Server with unsupported connectors	Must coexist	These servers cannot be migrated to Exchange 2000 and must stay on down-level versions of Exchange. However, these connectors can be substituted with supported connectors and removed from the server. Then the server will be hosting supported connectors only.
Public folder server	Either	The decision whether to upgrade or migrate depends on the amount of data that would need to be upgraded and if hardware is available for the parallel servers.
Mailbox server	Either	As with public folder servers, the decision whether to upgrade or migrate depends on how much data needs to be upgraded. In many organizations, however, the extra prerequisite of server consolidation makes the decision to migrate mandatory for many servers.
Clustered Exchange server	Must migrate	No upgrade path exists for clustered Exchange 5.5 servers. Because these are primarily mailbox servers (very few connectors can be clustered, and public folders allow replication for redundancy), the mailboxes should be migrated to another server, which can be a clustered Exchange 2000 server.

Timing the Exchange 2000 Server Upgrade or Migration

After you have resolved whether to upgrade a server or migrate, you should settle on which servers you would upgrade first in the organization. This decision obviously depends on your organizational requirements and design. One company may choose not to risk an upgrade of their directory replication bridgehead servers, but rather to install clean mailbox servers. Another company may figure that the directory replication bridgehead servers are going to host the site replication service anyway, and they will choose to upgrade these servers first so they do not have to have other SRS servers. These are both legitimate techniques; once an upgrade/migration decision is made, your organization must also determine the order that is most appropriate.

If you have a part in your organizational upgrade solution, begin the process with a site over which you have direct control. If you are upgrading a site with three or fewer servers, begin with the directory replication server in the site, and then move on through the upgrade. The upgrade process does not have to be performed sequentially, so you can be upgrading one Exchange site and then start another upgrade before the first one is finished. Pick a site with lower usage and then a server with lower usage as your first upgrade candidate. You can then upgrade the bridgehead server in the site first, giving it the SRS.

If one of your servers is constantly running more than 30 percent CPU utilization, consider migrating to a new hardware solution instead of upgrading. When you upgrade the public folder servers, the owner mailboxes in the public folder Access Control Lists (ACLs) must be in the Active Directory prior to the upgrade process. Confirm that all Exchange 5.5 services are in excellent condition before starting the upgrade by stopping and restarting the Exchange 5.5 services. Generally speaking, established sites on legacy hardware will most likely need to have the servers replaced during the upgrade process, and remote sites should be upgraded as rapidly as possible.

Hindrances to a Smooth Upgrade or Migration

One of the biggest barriers to a smooth migration to Exchange 2000 is being in a scenario in which your organization has too many NT domains. As you know, Exchange Server 5.5 relies on NT for security and user authentication. You may have existing Exchange servers in a master account domain in a small- to medium-sized design, or you may be in a larger corporate environment, such as Plus Ultra Group, and have implemented a separate resource domain just to house the Exchange servers. Resource domains are an excellent solution for separating Exchange servers from other applications for protection from administrative users. In Windows 2000 architectures, however, child domains will substitute for resource domains and will remove the need for separate resource domains that form administrative and security boundaries.

Vast improvements in operating systems, symmetric multiprocessing, clustering technologies, CPU speed, and disk controllers have allowed for greater mailbox capacity within the last few years. Information store partitioning into multiple databases and the emergence of active/active clustering technologies also combine to allow Exchange 2000 to support more mailboxes. As a result, organizations will often have more servers to contend with in their migration plans. Because Exchange 2000 servers will be communicating with SMTP, you will be better able to support low-bandwidth connections across low-latency links. Exchange 2000 supports routing groups and administrative groups instead of sites. Routing groups offer a universal set of policies for message routing throughout the organization. Because routing groups define how Exchange routes messages, you will use routing groups to develop the sites that presently hold connector servers or serve as routing hubs. Therefore, you will have to create a different site structure that implements fewer routing groups to reduce administrative and routing complexity.

Another hindrance to your migration process will be too many users with administrative permissions, or "too many cooks in the kitchen." Rights, permissions, and server management can get knotty when you have multiple account domains in a distributed environment. This situation will not be conducive to a smooth migration, so you may want to consider trimming back the number of individuals who have administrative rights during the process. Exchange 2000 is closely tied with Windows 2000 and throws out the older permissions in favor of Windows 2000 ACLs. This will give you an opportunity to take a fresh approach toward system security that is based on one set of privileges. In your migration plan, include an assessment of privileges before you allocate or delegate authority privileges.

Unfortunately, many Exchange 2000 administrators have assumed that optimal replication means recurrent and excessive replication without considering if the organization actually needed such current data and public folder replication. The larger the organization, the greater the number of likely replication partners. It is important to get a handle on replication early in the process. Exchange 2000 uses Windows 2000 Active Directory instead of a separate directory store. You will need to make sure that replication is functioning well because Windows 2000 replicates much more data than Exchange 5.5 typically requires. You should realize that although every Exchange 5.5 server takes part in the directory replication process, only domain controllers replicate Active Directory information; thus, Exchange 2000 has fewer replication partners. You will most likely be replicating data between Exchange 2000 servers and Exchange 5.5 servers during the migration process. Exchange 2000 can exist in a mixed-mode organization working with legacy servers as if they all resided in an Exchange Server 5.5 organization.

Designing for the Appropriate ADC Connection Agreements

Every additional connector that is operating in an Exchange organization increases the level of message routing complications. Make sure you are using exactly the right number as well as the best-selected connectors in your design. Historically, the fixed nature of the Gateway Address Resolution Table (GWART) used by the Exchange Server 5.5 Message Transfer Agent (MTA) has forced many system administrators to bring in multiple X.400 or SMTP connectors. This was done to make sure that messages are delivered if a connector became inoperative due to a system failure. Exchange 2000 still supports X.400 as a protocol and uses the MTA; however, it moves away from using the X.400-based MTA in favor of SMTP. Exchange 2000 also employs a new routing engine based on the SMTP service found on all Windows 2000 servers.

The only method for getting the right Exchange data placed into Active Directory is to implement the Active Directory Connector (ADC). The role of the ADC will be complicated because you are not simply upgrading Exchange, but synchronizing the upgrade with an upgrade/migration to Windows 2000 Server from Windows NT 4 (see Figure 7.1). Regardless of the complexities of your particular corporate

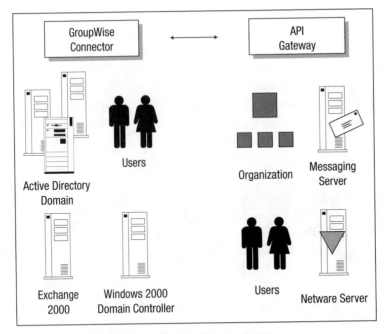

Figure 7.1 An example of a GroupWise Migration design.

environment, you should finish the main tasks to upgrade or migrate to Windows 2000 Server before installing the ADC. The sections that follow present five different scenarios from Microsoft that may help you identify the best ADC connection agreement design for your organization.

Scenario 1

The first scenario is to execute an in-place domain upgrade, and then to run the ADC. An in-place domain upgrade is a relatively clear-cut process in which all of the Windows NT 4 account domains are upgraded to Windows 2000. At the very least, the primary domain controller (PDC) in each applicable domain must be upgraded. All of the domains must be in the same forest. A maximum of one of the upgrades can create a new forest, and the remainder of the upgrades must join their domains to the existing forest either as child domains of an existing domain or as root domains of a new tree. When this is done, you will be able to install and configure the ADC with connection agreements that synchronize Exchange 5.5 mailboxes with Active Directory user accounts. The ADC matches up the security identifier from the primary Windows NT account to the primary security identifier (SID) of an Active Directory user account. Then the ADC populates the existing account in Active Directory with the data from the Exchange 5.5 directory. This can be information such as an email address or a phone number.

Security Identifiers

A security identifier (SID) is a statistically unique number that identifies each user and group. When a new user or group is created, Windows 2000 generates an SID for that account. Windows 2000 uses the identifier to confirm access permissions when a user requests access to an object. The SID is used rather than the user name. Because SIDs do not change during the upgrade from Windows NT to Windows 2000, ADC will match the mailbox to a user account based on the existing SIDs.

Scenario 2

A second scenario that may be viable for your organization is to run the ADC, upgrade later, and then run the Active Directory Cleanup Wizard. You may want to start the upgrade to Exchange 2000 before you migrate to Windows 2000 Server. If so, you could use the ADC to populate Active Directory with the basic required user accounts in Exchange 2000. You can later upgrade the existing Windows NT 4 account domains, and then merge the resulting duplicate account objects during a cleanup phase by using the Active Directory Cleanup Wizard. Before running the ADC, however, a basic Active Directory infrastructure must be in place. You must also designate a target domain, such as the root of the domain forest, for the ADC to create disabled user accounts. When you run the ADC, a disabled user account will be generated in Active Directory for each Exchange 5.5 mailbox. Every disabled user account holds all of the Exchange configuration information. Mailbox permissions are then copied from the security descriptor of the Exchange 5.5 mailbox and applied to the Windows 2000 user account. You are now ready to upgrade user mailboxes to Exchange 2000 by either moving the mailboxes to an Exchange 2000 server or by upgrading the server on which the mailboxes dwell. Users will still be able to access their mail using their Windows NT 4 security credentials. You will upgrade the Windows NT 4 account domains to Windows 2000 at a later time, when these domains will join the forest that Exchange 2000 is using either as child domains of the existing root domain or as root domains of a new tree. At this point, two accounts exist in Active Directory for each Exchange user: the original disabled user account and the fresh upgraded account.

Scenario 3

The third scenario that you may want to explore is to run ADC and then clone it later using the Active Directory Migration Tool (ADMT). This scenario begins just like the second scenario, except that you have no intention of upgrading the Windows NT 4 account domains. Instead you decide to migrate the user accounts at a later point in time. The ADC generates the disabled user account in a fashion similar to that described in scenario 2 so that you can commence the Exchange 2000 deployment. You have a couple of options when migrating the users under this scenario. You can merge the accounts during migration or you can opt to migrate to a different account and merge later by using the Active Directory Cleanup Wizard. With the first technique, you can use the ADMT to merge accounts during migration. If you use the ADMT to migrate accounts into the domain that contains the disabled user accounts created by ADC, it will detect the duplicate accounts and follow whatever conflict-handling behavior has been configured.

The options for conflict handling are as follows:

➤ *Ignore*—This option does nothing.

➤ *Replace*—This option merges the accounts.

➤ *Rename*—This option creates a separate account using a prefix or suffix supplied by the administrator.

When you merge accounts during migration, you must choose the replace option when you run the ADMT.

The second method under this scenario is more complex. With this technique, you migrate to a different account and then merge later. You create duplicate objects, replicate them into the entire Active Directory, and then merge the details in a second process that generates a second round of replication. This technique may also have an effect on the way you implement domains during the upgrade/migration process. In Exchange 5.5, when users and mailboxes are generated at the same time with the Exchange Administrator application, the NT 4 user accounts and Exchange directory names are the same by default. If they are the same, however, you cannot migrate those user accounts directly to the domain that includes the disabled user accounts created by ADC. You have to designate that the disabled user accounts are not to be created in the domain to which you want to migrate the users. Therefore, you should create a child domain under your root domain and use this as a transition domain in which to create the disabled user accounts. This will let you migrate user accounts right into the domain that you choose. Afterward, you can use the Active Directory Cleanup Wizard to delete all the disabled user accounts, and then you can remove the transition domain.

Scenario 4

The fourth scenario involves running the ADMT with the program sIDHistory, and then running the ADC. Running the ADC after fully migrating all of your user accounts is a simple process. Even though you can utilize the ADMT to clone users from one (or more) NT 4 domains into one (or more) Windows 2000 domains, you should attempt to consolidate the user accounts. In this fourth scenario, you configure the ADMT so that the sIDHistory attribute is updated with primary and group SIDs from the source account. Cloned users receive new SIDs, yet they can still access the resources for which their old SIDs have permission. The

ADC identifies sIDHistory and matches the Exchange 5.5 mailbox's primary Windows NT account with the old primary SID that is now stored in sIDHistory.

Scenario 5

The fifth and final scenario is running the ADMT without sIDHistory, re-creating ACLs, and then running the ADC. You may not need to clone users when you migrate to a new Windows 2000 design because security and administrative issues with sIDHistory may make you choose to migrate without copying the users' old SIDs. Without sIDHistory, a recently migrated account cannot access any of the resources to which the old account had access. This is why the migration process needs to comprise steps to reapply the new SID to all of the resources to which the old SID had permissions. You must carry out this step before transferring the user over to the new account so that users will always be able to access resources. For this scenario to work well with the ADC, you need to update the permissions on the Exchange 5.5 mailboxes before you run the ADC. This will make it simple for the ADC to match mailboxes and accounts after you are done. You can update the permissions manually, although this is not practical for a lot of users. The ADMT has an option to recreate ACLs that set permissions on Exchange mailboxes. You can thus use ADMT to recreate ACLs that are associated with migrated accounts.

Decommissioning Down-Level Exchange Servers

No chapter on planning a migration would be complete without a section on removing old Exchange servers from the design. Table 7.2 lists what you need to consider when you are decommissioning servers.

Table 7.2   Considerations for decommissioning down-level servers.

Type of Server	Scenario
Directory replication servers	If these servers are replaced rather than upgraded, they will no longer have the directory replication connector. They should no longer be considered directory replication servers when the Exchange 2000 server with the SRS and directory replication connector are established. If these servers have another resource on them, they should be reclassified for that resource.
Servers with supported connectors	Once the Exchange 2000 connector or connectors have been tested, this connector should be set with a cost of 100 to keep it from being used, although it is still available if needed. If there are no issues with this setting and if no messages are seen when using this connector, this server can be decommissioned. If there are multiple connectors on this server, this step will have to be repeated for each connector, but it can be a parallel process.
Servers with unsupported connectors	These servers cannot be decommissioned and must remain until they are no longer needed.
Public folder servers	After all the public folders hosted by this system have been completely replicated to the Exchange 2000 servers, the replica can be removed from the server. Once all public folder replicas are removed, this server can be decommissioned.

(continued)

Table 7.2 **Considerations for decommissioning down-level servers** *(continued).*

Type of Server	Scenario
Mailbox servers	After all mailboxes have been moved to Exchange 2000 servers, this server can be decommissioned.
Clustered Exchange servers	After all resources hosted by this server have been moved to Exchange 2000 servers, this server can be decommissioned.
The down-level Exchnage First Server	With the exception of the routing calculation, the Exchange First Server resources should be moved to Exchange 2000 servers. The routing calculation service is required as long as there is a down-level Exchange server in the site, but this can be moved to other down-level Exchange servers if necessary.
Other server types	If other server types exist in your environment, and these are required for the Exchange 5.5 servers, they will have to remain until all other Exchange 5.5 servers are decommissioned. If these servers cannot be recreated on Exchange 2000 and are required for your environment, you may not be able to decommission them. If neither of these situations is an issue, you can decommission them at your discretion.

Migrating from Lotus Notes to Exchange 2000

When your organization finally decides to migrate from Lotus Notes to an Exchange 2000 system, it is best to divide the process into five steps:

1. Connect the Exchange client to existing systems by using a connector

2. Create directory and mailbox entries

3. Set up a gateway for connectivity

4. Update the directory

5. Migrate the Notes applications

Basically, three levels of migration exist for Microsoft Exchange Server: coexistence, new mailbox deployment, and full migration. Coexistence, which was covered in Chapter 6, can be used when the migration process is going to cover a long period of time. Coexistence includes configuring your messaging infrastructure to share address directories and transfer mail from Lotus Notes over to Exchange 2000 Server. The new mailbox deployment method entails migrating mailboxes without the existing mail. Only the user account information is moved, and new empty mailboxes are generated. You can create the empty mailboxes before proceeding with the migration of existing mailbox data. The mailboxes can eventually contain more mailboxes, distribution lists, public folders, and custom recipients. A full migration entails migrating mailboxes, messages, attachments, and the scheduling information as well. This saves the user-stored messages, attachments, and scheduling information from Lotus Notes. A full migration can take longer and will need more testing than other techniques, so you will probably carry it out in phases so that you can protect all of the user data during the migration process.

Migration is the technique of transporting the Notes messaging system to Exchange 2000. For example, the Plus Ultra Group migration will involve making copies of existing mailboxes, messages, calendars, and other information, and importing that information into Exchange 2000. The migration process will also entail moving personal archives and personal address book information, and migrating the Lotus Notes distribution lists to Exchange 2000. Plus Ultra Group will use the Migration Wizard components: the source extractor and the migration file importer. The source extractor copies directory information, messages, calendar information, and collaboration data from Lotus Notes and saves the information into a file. The Exchange 2000 Server Migration Wizard is shown in Figure 7.2. The migration file importer imports the created file into Exchange. Although you can run both of these tools in one step, Plus Ultra will be running them each as separate tasks.

Migration Wizard may generate duplicate accounts in Active Directory, but the Active Directory Account Cleanup Wizard can simplify the process of deleting duplicate accounts. This tool may not be necessary during the migration, however, if the coexistence plan was successfully executed and Active Directory was properly set up in the previous phase. The Outlook 2000 Import feature and the Lotus Notes Mail Importer may be needed as well. Plus Ultra Group will use a multiphase approach and move users in different groups separately while constantly testing and improving the migration process. The goal of this approach is to reduce downtime. During the migration process, you can use the Application Converter for Lotus Notes tool to move the Notes databases to Exchange public folders. However, if the application needs complex programming, consider leaving it on the Notes server, especially if the application is Web-enabled. Keeping an application

7

Figure 7.2   The Exchange 2000 Server Migration Wizard's welcome tab.

on Notes may involve some additional planning to allow users to access it from the Internet.

Migration Process

The first step in the migration process is to connect Lotus Notes to Exchange, and to make sure that the email is flowing smoothly between the systems. Also, you need to decide if you will connect your gateways between organizations simultaneously or separately in steps. The benefit of connecting your gateways at the same time is that your users are interrupted only once. Connecting your gateways in stages may take longer, but it has its advantages as well. During the first stage, users will not be affected because Notes connects to Exchange over one gateway, and Exchange has an empty directory. After that connection is made, you will have some time before the next two stages, which require that Notes Named Networks be disconnected from the present Notes environment and reconnected with Exchange 2000.

After the Lotus Notes environment connects to Exchange, you can move the SMTP gateway from Notes to Exchange, if needed. This is to assure a steady backbone for the migrated users as well as to avoid scheduling a downtime after the migration. The Exchange 2000 SMTP connector is also a more dependable gateway than the Notes SMTP MTA. You can improve Internet email for your Notes users by moving the gateway to Exchange in the early phases. After the backbone is unwavering, the migration can proceed. The environment will then be cleaned up after the users migrate. The Lotus Notes servers will be decommissioned and the connectors removed from the Exchange servers.

You should plan carefully for a migration from Notes to Exchange 2000. You need to have a deep understanding of the business role and the technical complexity of the application that you are migrating. If your organization decides to migrate Notes to Exchange, the result will be that the Notes application will be discarded after the migration. All the data, along with the adapted design and logic of the application, will be migrating to Exchange 2000. This offers your organization an opportunity to revamp its application to take advantage of the new capabilities of Exchange 2000. Microsoft offers the Microsoft Application Services for Lotus Notes, a migration toolset consisting of two applications: Microsoft Exchange Application Analyzer for Lotus Notes and Microsoft Exchange Application Converter for Lotus Notes. This can be found at **www.microsoft.com/TechNet/ exchange/tools/services.asp**. These utilities will help you migrate Notes application to Exchange and Outlook. First consider the pecking order of Notes services, which fall into four categories, listed here from easiest to most complex. Additionally, the number of applications that are deployed from a given category usually decreases from the first to the last category in this list.

➤ *Core messaging services*—These are services such as email, address books, and directories. These databases are not considered Notes collaborative applications.

➤ *Standard collaboration databases*—These are components such as discussion and document libraries, which are based on Notes templates.

➤ *Custom applications*—These are internally developed programs that can range from simple to complex applications. This category can also include components that have been customized from Notes templates.

➤ *Complex custom applications*—These are applications designed by solution providers or internal Notes application developers. These may access two or more Notes databases or use workflow as well as other intricate concepts. Complex custom applications are often business-critical.

Lotus Notes Connector

The Lotus Notes Connector offers functionality for bidirectional mail transfer, directory synchronization, and scheduling processes. Exchange 2000 also includes the Lotus Notes Application Connector, which synchronizes Exchange public folders with Lotus Notes databases. These connectors have comprehensive directory synchronization (DirSync) capabilities along with elaborate mapping rules for attributes in other email systems. You should map out the attributes that you will include in the Dirsync from both systems. If applicable, you should define rules for how these attributes will appear in their respective systems.

Plus Ultra Group is using Lotus Notes version 4.6 as its messaging system. To migrate to Exchange 2000, Plus Ultra Group will consider one of two options: a phased migration or one-step migration. If they go with a phased migration, the Notes system will coexist with Exchange 2000, and the users will be migrated according to location or department (see Chapter 6). If they decide upon a one-step migration, all users will be migrated simultaneously with no coexistence required. Plus Ultra Group may find a one-step migration difficult because it would be applied to many distributed users. It would, however, save the administrators from the chore of planning for coexistence and maintaining two environments. The challenge for Plus Ultra Group is that migration will require an adequate support staff to facilitate the users during and after migration. Therefore, in a large distributed organization such as Plus Ultra Group, a phased migration is the preferred option. This migration strategy would be divided into two overlapping phases: coexistence and migration. Each phase has its own tools and techniques.

Suppose that Plus Ultra Group has four Notes Named Networks, each located in one of the four main offices. The three points of access to the Internet are New York, London, and Hong Kong. Plus Ultra Group has two possible solutions for this migration challenge. The first solution would be to keep one gateway placed in

7

one domain, and to repopulate the directory during the migration. The second solution would be to create three Notes-to-Exchange gateways, in each one of the three Windows 2000 domains. The Notes servers in Plus Ultra Group would, in essence, become three separate environments, based on the three continents and the main offices. Each server would connect to the nearby gateway. Sorting out the Lotus Notes design for Plus Ultra Group is relatively easy because the company already has four Notes Named Networks. The second solution is easier for management and migration to Notes because Exchange works with backbone messaging.

Some final considerations should be examined. The Notes directory will be down throughout the transition. Thus, the users in New York, for example, will lose the entries of the users in London and Hong Kong until they retrieve them from Exchange 2000. Similar situations will also occur in the London and Hong Kong locations. It is critical, therefore, that you understand user expectations and policies. In addition, the Notes local address books on the client computers will need to be resynchronized because the directory will be altered. The decision makers of your organization must understand that the Notes-to-Notes traffic will go through Exchange. After all of these issues are resolved, separate the Notes environment to provide a smoother migration.

Migrating from GroupWise to Exchange 2000

Migration from GroupWise to Exchange 2000 is the technique of moving your existing GroupWise messaging system to an Exchange 2000 Server. This involves producing a copy of your existing mailboxes, messages, and other data, and importing that information into Exchange 2000. Plan your strategy carefully to avoid downtime, minimize the consequences on users, and avert loss of critical data. Exchange 2000 supports migration from Novell GroupWise 4.x and 5.x, and offers the Microsoft Exchange Server Migration Wizard to help you in this process. The Migration Wizard lets your organization easily move users, messages, and calendar information from your GroupWise system to Exchange 2000.

The Exchange Server Migration Wizard comprises two primary pieces: the source extractor and the migration file importer. The source extractor component copies directory information, messages, calendar information, and collaboration data from an existing message system. It then stores the data in an Exchange Server Migration Wizard importable format. The migration file importer imports the directory, calendar, and collaboration information to Exchange 2000. You can transport users from a GroupWise system to Exchange in two ways: a single-phase migration and a multiphase migration. Most migrations are performed in multiple phases because this allows you to test the process as well as the new system. It is important that you understand the impact of the migration process on your organization. Table 7.3 represents the expected migration output of four different scenarios.

Table 7.3   The expected migration output scenarios.

Scenario	Migration Technique
Contact and Windows 2000 account	The account is mail-enabled and the contact information is merged with information from the GroupWise system. Contact is deleted.
No contact and Windows 2000 account	The account is mail-enabled and combined with information from the GroupWise system.
Contact and no Windows 2000 account	A new account is generated and mail-enabled. Contact information is merged with the GroupWise system information.
No contact and no Windows 2000 account	A new account is generated and mail-enabled. Contact information is merged with the GroupWise system information.

Single-Phase Migration

In a single-phase migration, you move all of the users on your messaging system to Exchange 2000 at one time. This type of migration is well suited for a small organization. You might consider using the Exchange Server Migration Wizard only once for the entire organization. The Migration Wizard will mine data from your existing system and create a migration file. It will then import the file into Exchange so that users can get to email, calendar information, and public folders from their Exchange 2000 mailboxes by using Outlook or some other client.

Multiphase Migration

Multiphase migration allows you to transport groups of users to Exchange at different times. In the beginning, your present environment will coexist with Exchange 2000 until the migration is complete (see Chapter 6). During a multiphase migration, you need to install the Microsoft Exchange Connector for Novell GroupWise and configure it between both systems for users to communicate with each other during the migration. Multiphase migration should be considered if you cannot move all groups or departments to Exchange 2000 simultaneously. You may want to consider testing the migration first on a group of experienced users in a multiphase migration.

Getting Ready for Migration from GroupWise to Exchange 2000

After you decide on which coexistence method to use, as outlined in Chapter 6, you must consider how to provide messaging connectivity during migration. You also want to focus on keeping the directories updated in both systems. In preparation for migration from GroupWise to Exchange, make certain that each user has proxy access to the GroupWise account you are using to carry out the migration.

Tip: You can assure that your users have proxy access to the GroupWise account by automating the process through the macro included on the Exchange 2000 Server compact disc in the Migrate|Tools|Gwise directory.

You should also trim down the amount of data being migrated by deleting GroupWise mailboxes that are no longer used. Run the Exchange Server Migration Wizard, and select the users that you want to migrate. If contacts have been generated for GroupWise users, map contacts to Active Directory Users. If contacts were not already generated, then use the Exchange Server Migration Wizard to create new users.

One-Step Migration Process

To migrate data from a Novell GroupWise post office in one step, click Start, point to Programs, point to Microsoft Exchange, and then click Migration Wizard. On the Migration page, in the Migration list, select Migrate from Novell GroupWise *X.x*, and then click Next. This Wizard is shown in Figure 7.3.

Next, The Novell GroupWise *X.x* Migration page confirms that you must install the Novell GroupWise *X.x* client and a Novell NetWare client. You must also grant the Novell GroupWise migration user access to all source user IDs. Click Next to continue. The resulting dialog box is shown in Figure 7.4. Then, on the Migration Procedure page, click a migration method, type in a path to store the files for temporary use during the migration, and then click on Next.

On the Migration Destination page, click Migrate to a computer running Exchange Server; from the drop-down lists, enter a specific computer and information store or click Migrate to .pst files, and then click Next.

On the GroupWise Domain page, in the Path text box, type the full uniform naming convention (UNC) path for the GroupWise post office, or click Browse to select the path you want to use, and then click Next.

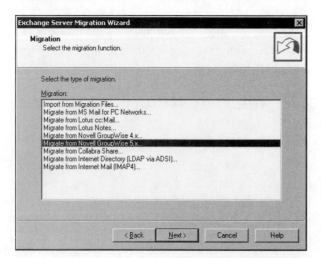

Figure 7.3   Using the Exchange Migration Wizard with GroupWise.

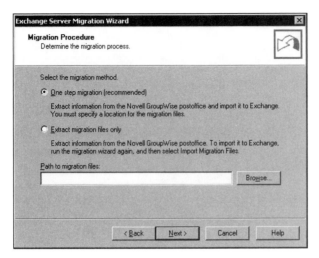

Figure 7.4   The Migration Procedure tab of the wizard, in which you determine the migration process.

7

On the GroupWise Postoffice page, select the Novell GroupWise post office you are migrating from, and then click on Next.

On the Migration Information page, select one or more of the options outlined in Table 7.4, and then click on Next. This dialog box is shown in Figure 7.5.

On the Account Migration page, select the accounts you want to migrate, and then click Next. On the Container For New Windows Accounts page, select the destination directory container for the new mailboxes, and then click Options.

In the Account Creation Options dialog box, select a method to create passwords for new user accounts. If you are using a template to facilitate setting up

Table 7.4   Descriptions of options on the Migration Information page.

Option	Description
Information to create mailboxes	Migrates the user's mailbox data. This information is used to create a mailbox for each migrated user in Exchange 2000. Clearing this checkbox imports messages to existing mailboxes or converts existing custom recipients to mailboxes.
Mail	Migrates email messages.
Phone messages	Migrates phone messages.
All	Migrates all messages.
Dated from	Migrates email messages in the specified date range.
Appointments	Migrates appointments.
Notes	Migrates notes.
Tasks	Migrates tasks.
All	Migrates all calendar data.
Dated from	Migrates calendar data in the specified date range.

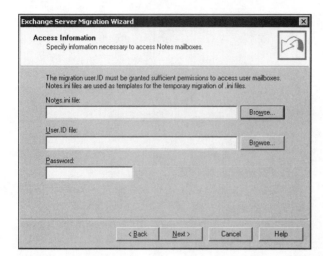

Figure 7.5   Specifying information needed to access LotusNotes mailboxes.

nonpersonal attributes, in the Template "object to be used for nonpersonal attributes" box, click Browse, select the template, and then click OK. When you complete the selection, click on Next. The Exchange System Manager tool is shown in Figure 7.6.

On the Windows Account Creation and Association page, choose Existing Windows Account or New Windows Account, and then click on Next. The Migration Process page displays information about the current migration. Click Finish to continue. After migration is complete, you can review the Application Event Log

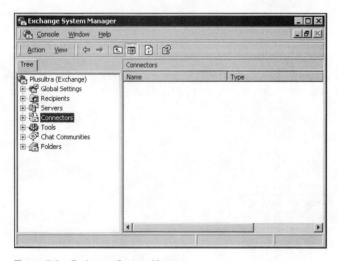

Figure 7.6   Exchange System Manager.

for more information. Additionally, you can view the Migrated User object in Active Directory Users and Computers. Click OK to continue.

Migrating from cc:Mail to Exchange 2000

The best approach to migrating cc:Mail to Exchange 2000 is to install the Exchange 2000 Server Connector for Lotus cc:Mail component when you install Exchange 2000 Server. This way you can access the Lotus cc:Mail property pages from the Exchange System Manager component in the Exchange menu. A visualization of the migration can be seen in Figure 7.7.

Exchange 2000 Server Connector for Lotus cc:Mail

This section covers the Exchange 2000 Server Connector for Lotus cc:Mail location in Exchange System Manager.

Post Office Configuration Tab

From the Properties window, select the Post Office tab, which allows you to designate the following information:

➤ The administrator's mailbox

➤ Which cc:Mail post office to use for communication

➤ The language setting for the post office

➤ Secondary Automatic Directory Exchange (ADE) propagation options

➤ Preservation of forwarding information in messages

➤ Which Windows 2000 account to use to connect to the path

Notice the Allow ADE To Propagate Synchronized Entries checkbox on the Post Office tab, which refers to those entries synched to cc:Mail downstream post offices. This checkbox (which is selected by default) is extremely important and

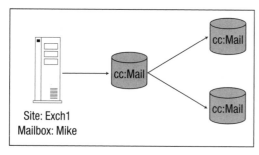

Figure 7.7 The migration process.

worth special mention. When checked, any Exchange 2000 directory entries that are propagated to the cc:Mail post office directory will be repropagated through the cc:Mail ADE to other post offices if the necessary relationships are established between those post offices. This is performing a directory import with the /PROP switch from the Lotus standpoint. If the post office with which you are communicating does not have ADE enabled, or if you wish to stop the Exchange 2000 directory entries from propagating to any other post offices (other than the post office with which you are directly connecting), clear the checkbox. This option will have no effect on propagation for cc:Mail 8 and later because they use a newer version of ADE that re-propagates entries regardless of the setting.

General Configuration Tab

Previously, you would have used the General Configuration tab to set a message size limit on Exchange 2000 Connector for Lotus cc:Mail, but that option is now on the Advanced Configuration Property window. Use the General tab to enter such information as an Administrative note.

Address Space Tab

The Address Space tab is used to define the routes from the Exchange Server network to each of the cc:Mail post offices with which you are communicating. The Address Space tab is a standard Microsoft Exchange Server feature and is present on all connectors.

Exchange 2000 Server Connector for Lotus cc:Mail will automatically create the necessary queue entry on the cc:Mail post office if you want to implement DirSync between Microsoft Exchange and Lotus cc:Mail. If, however, you want to test messaging connectivity before executing DirSync, you must log on to the cc:Mail post office and manually create the queue for Exchange.

Exchange Server as a Gateway

Lotus cc:Mail clients can also use an Exchange 2000 Server as a gateway to other messaging environments such as SMTP and X.400. Exchange Server offers a dependable, robust, and low-cost solution because these components are actually built in. The most important requirement is probably for cc:Mail users to have full inbound and outbound Internet mail. You can do this by simply configuring the Internet Mail Service (IMS) on one of the Exchange servers.

Exchange Server synchronizes its directory with cc:Mail via an automated import and export process. Before configuring DirSync between your two systems, investigate the current setup carefully. Although it is fairly straightforward to configure the

DirSync tabs on the Connector for cc:Mail, you might run into issues if you do not carefully examine the process. By default, Exchange assumes that you want your cc:Mail users to appear on the Global Address List (GAL) in First Name, Last Name format. It also assumes that the Exchange alias is constructed using the first name and one character from the last name.

Import Container Tab

When configuring the connector for DirSync, you have to designate the imported recipients that are to be placed by Exchange. If you are deploying Exchange as a message-switching backbone, generate a separate container to hold these contacts. If you will ultimately need cc:Mail connectivity to migrate all users to Exchange, put the entries in the standard recipients container. The Migration Wizard will automatically place the X.500 proxy on migrated mailboxes so that mail will not go undelivered.

The next item you may need to configure in the import process is import filtering. The default behavior is to import every entry from the cc:Mail post office. You may need however, to import only particular entries or to exclude importing addresses from certain cc:Mail post offices. You configure the import filtering strings similar to the way you configure the Address Space tab.

Export Containers Tab

The Export Containers tab determines which containers you want to export to cc:Mail. You must understand, however, that it is not the GAL that gets exported. A company the size of Plus Ultra Group may have 10 Exchange sites from which they are exporting all of the recipient containers to cc:Mail. If you create another container, or a new site comes online, you will have to reconfigure the Exchange Connector for Lotus cc:Mail to export these as well. If you have a mixture of Exchange mailboxes and cc:Mail contacts in a container, you may also want to export your import container. If you choose to take this route, Exchange will make sure that duplicate addresses are not created.

The DirSync Schedule Tab

The DirSync Schedule tab governs when directory synchronization takes place. You should change the default setting, which is Never. If you choose Always, a full DirSync will occur at 15-minute intervals. This is really overkill for most situations. If you select Complete Hours, DirSync will happen only on the hour of each hour selected. After configuring the synchronization process with DirSync, confirm that all of the Exchange recipients are in the cc:Mail directory. Next, you should verify that the import container is populated with the contacts that correspond to the cc:Mail users.

7

Migrating with Exchange Server Migration Wizard

The Exchange Server Migration Wizard (Mailmig.exe) is an extremely serviceable tool that transfers most of your cc:Mail data over to Exchange 2000. This tool, however, is limited in what it can migrate. If you are running Exchange 5, you can use the Migration Wizard to migrate Database version 6 (DB6) and DB7 post offices. If you are running Exchange 5.5, you can migrate DB6, DB7, and DB8 post offices. The Exchange 2000 Migration Wizard can migrate users right into Active Directory. Users will notice after migration that the contents of their drafts folders are now special mail messages in their inboxes. They may also see a special folder called Clipboard, which cc:Mail uses for internal reasons. This folder can be deleted after the migration is done without consequence. Before relocating information to Exchange, be certain that you understand all the requirements for Exchange 2000. By this time, support staff, help-desk personnel, and end users should all be well trained. Help-desk personnel should also be totally competent with all of the features of the Exchange/Outlook client. Make sure that you alert all your users about the migration by performing the following tasks:

➤ Inform users to rename their cc:Mail personal folders if they are called Calendar, Notes, Journaling, Tasks, or Contacts.

➤ Have users discard unnecessary emails in their Inbox, Messages Log, Trash, and private folders.

➤ List the procedures for Lotus cc:Mail archived files.

➤ Explain how to import Lotus Organizer information.

➤ Point out what information will not be migrated.

➤ Lay out the rules that must be implemented in Lotus cc:Mail.

Note: As an administrator, you could choose to forcibly delete information from Inboxes, Message Logs, Trash, and private folders by using the Chkstat tool. By enforcing a policy on how much data is migrated, you can decrease migration time substantially. You should consider servicing the post offices that you will be transporting with the Analyze, Chkstat (DB6), and Reclaim utilities. This will help to reduce discrepancy or corruption in your post office(s). If there is a grave inconsistency in the post office, the Migration Wizard may stall.

The steps for migration from cc:Mail to Exchange 2000 are as follows:

1. Begin the process by determining if your organization will be migrating to Exchange 2000 Server, or to server-based storage or locally based storage. At the Migration Wizard prompt, you must choose a one-step or two-step migration. The two-step migration usually allows for greater direction over the migration. Use the two-step method if incorporating a new naming standard or if you have cc:Mail user names that are longer than 64 characters. The final

action in this step is to designate a location for the migration data. (This consists of one packing list file and many primary and secondary files.)

2. Specify the post office path, name, and password to migrate from by inserting them into the appropriate fields on the Migration Wizard page, and then click on Next.

3. Choose what you would like to transfer:

   ➤ Information to create mailboxes

   ➤ Personal email messages (all or date range)

   ➤ Bulletin boards

   ➤ Private mailing lists (personal address books, or PABs)

4. Next, select the users to migrate.

5. At this point, the cc:Mail data will be extracted from the post office and placed in a set of migration files.

6. When Step 5 is complete, you should see the files listed in Table 7.5 under the migration directory:

7. At this point, you may decide to modify the primary file for the post office. This is where you can dictate how imported entries are going to appear in the Exchange GAL.

8. If this is a two-step migration, run Exchange Server Migration Wizard for the second time, which will actually perform the import process of the migration. You will then see the options that permit you to choose the organizational unit in which to place the migrated users, as well as other options.

Tip: You can order or download the Exchange Server Migration Wizard from the following Microsoft Web site: **www.microsoft.com/exchange/downloads/migrationwizard.htm**.

Table 7.5   Files appearing in the migration directory.

File Name	Purpose
Post Office Name.PKL	Packing list file. This matches the primary and secondary files with the mailbox name.
Post Office Name.PRI	Directory import file. Specifies how entries are going to appear in the Exchange directory after being imported.
Xxxxxxxx.PRI	Sequentially numbered primary file. This holds the message headers and folder names for migrated messages.
Xxxxxxxx.SEC	Sequentially numbered secondary file. This holds the message bodies relative to the headers defined in the primary file.

Migrating from MSMail to Exchange 2000

Before you connect to Exchange and synchronize directories for migration purposes, you need to document your organization's present MSMail routing topology, DirSync configuration, and the user population of each post office. You must assess if any routing modifications are in order to improve your Exchange coexistence. All your users should clean up their MSMail inboxes down to approximately 20–30MB to facilitate an even migration. Fix any existing issues with MSMail post office data, message delivery, or directory systems. Then you will be ready to configure the Microsoft Exchange Connector post office to be a DirSync requestor so that it can send and receive updates between Mail and Exchange. Remember that if you set it up as a DirSync server, you will have more configuring to perform on the Mail side. DirSync needs to be functioning properly within the Mail environment. Resolve any DirSync issues before trying to migrate Mail users to Exchange 2000. Verify that the latest Microsoft Exchange Server version and service pack are installed.

After you have adequately documented, appraised, and repaired your company's MSMail design, you must develop a plan for implementing the Exchange MSMail Connector. You can also investigate the online Exchange Server books and product documentation for the complete setup information.

Microsoft Exchange Directory Synchronization Agent

The Microsoft Exchange Directory Synchronization Agent (DXA) automatically propagates updated directories to all post offices in your messaging system, regardless of whether they are on the same local area network (LAN), connected asynchronously, or linked by a gateway. The DXA augments directory synchronization with flexible scheduling and a multithreaded design. Because of its multithreaded nature, the DXA can provide a more robust directory synchronization server by reducing the need to manage the address list, increasing security, and providing an efficient environment. The DXA can be a directory synchronization server and/or a requestor.

DirSync for Exchange Server can be configured together with the Microsoft Mail Connector. The Exchange Connector post office can be defined as a remote Microsoft Mail post office and as a requestor on the current DirSync server. Once set up, directory updates will be sent to the Exchange server when DirSync occurs.

Note: The MS-DOS DirSync agent, Dispatch.EXE, still needs to run against the existing Microsoft Mail for PC Networks post offices, but should not be run against the Microsoft Exchange Connector post office. Exchange services will handle their own sending and receiving of updated directory lists.

After configuring, testing, and validating the message transport and directory synchronization configurations, focus on migrating Microsoft Mail data and clients over to Microsoft Exchange Server. Once the coexistence logistics have been finalized and implemented (see Chapter 6), the last step is to start migrating MSMail user mailboxes into the Exchange environment.

Build the Migration Plan

When planning your migration, give serious consideration to which post offices will migrate as well as the order and timeline of the migration. Keep this plan in a project management application such as Microsoft Project, Excel, Access, or Word. Include the following information in this report:

➤ Type of migration (full or partial migration)

➤ The required prerequisites, such as other tasks, migrations, or events that have to be done before the post office migration can occur

➤ The projected date of a post office migration

➤ The actual date of the post office migration

➤ The post offices that are being migrated

➤ The number of users being migrated with a post office

➤ The Exchange Server to which the post office will be migrated

➤ The category of post office: hub, directory synchronization server, gateway, or user post office

➤ The postmigration dependencies, such as other migrations or critical events

The Five Phases of MSMail Migration

You may want to consider dividing the MSMail migration progression into the following five phases:

1. Migrate the hub post offices

2. Migrate the DirSync components

3. Migrate the SMTP gateways to connectors

4. Migrate the user post offices

5. Migrate the clients

Before you initiate the migration process, run a pilot migration of at least one backup Mail post office to a test Exchange Server system. This will allow you to recognize problems that are distinctive to your environment. Issues will surface that you simply failed to anticipate. Document specific processes for migrating a Mail post office to Exchange Server. Move through the migration steps utilizing a backup (or a dummy) post office. Be sure to document any unanticipated consequences and update the original migration plan with the results of your test.

Single-Phase versus Multiphase Migration

A single-phase migration transports all of the users simultaneously, whereas a multiphase migration moves users in groups at different times. If you are in a smaller organization using MSMail, you will most likely implement the single-phase variety. A huge organization, such as Plus Ultra Group, will opt for multiphase migration because it has a more complex and far-reaching design. It's impossible for all their MSMail departments to upgrade at once. Additionally, hardware must be made available in the early phases so that it can be redeployed later. Also, the Exchange Server implementation group at Plus Ultra Group cannot migrate all of the users within an acceptable downtime to employ a single-phase migration.

Chapter Summary

This chapter and Chapter 6 are valuable studies in planning and implementing a coexistence and migration to Exchange 2000 from a variety of perspectives. By employing a strategy and having attainable objectives, you will be able to complete a migration to Exchange 2000 with a high level of success. Performing the migration rapidly, whether you take a single-phase or multiphase approach, could give your organization huge savings in time and resources. This will also help to diminish the load on your users, administrators, and managers, as well as on hardware and network resources.

This chapter considered examining an organization on the data-center level, the infrastructure of an Exchange site, and at each individual server level. The most important reason to evaluate at the data center level is due to the large number of Exchange 5.5 servers in data centers. If your Exchange sites traverse multiple environments, you should determine if you are going to reduce the number of locations in a site where Exchange servers reside. Once you are through analyzing the data center and site levels, determine which Exchange 5.5 servers can be upgraded and consolidated, which can be upgraded but not consolidated, and which ones can be eliminated after their resources are moved to another server.

One of the most important factors that your organization will have to face is whether to upgrade your servers or migrate their resources to Exchange 2000. Table 7.1 in this chapter can assist your organization in making this decision. Some key timing issues as well as common hindrances to a smooth migration must also be considered.

Designing for the appropriate ADC connection agreements is vital as well. Every additional connector that is operational in an Exchange organization only increases the level of message routing complication. The only way to get the proper Exchange 5.5 data placed into Active Directory is to implement the Active Directory Connector (ADC). Five different scenarios for implementing the ADC were presented in this chapter. The first was to execute an in-place domain upgrade, and then to run the ADC. The second one involved running the ADC, upgrading later, and then running the Active Directory Cleanup Wizard. The third scenario was to run the ADC, and then clone later by using Active Directory Migration Tool. This scenario begins just like the second scenario, except that you have no intention of ever upgrading the Windows NT 4 account domains. Scenario 4 entailed running the Active Directory Migration Tool with sIDHistory, and then running the ADC. The fifth method involved running the Active Directory Migration Tool without sIDHistory, re-creating Access Control Lists (ACLs), and then running the ADC. The last aspect of Exchange 5.5 migration dealt with the subject and methodology of decommissioning down-level servers.

This chapter also looked at migration to Exchange 2000 from Lotus Notes, GroupWise, Lotus cc:Mail, and Microsoft MSMail. When migrating from Notes, the process should be partitioned into four steps: connecting the Exchange client to existing systems by using a connector, creating directory and mailbox entries, configuring a gateway for connectivity, and updating the directory. The three basic levels of migration from Notes to Exchange Server are coexistence, new mailbox deployment, and full migration. The tool of choice is the Exchange Server Migration Wizard, which has two main components: the source extractor and the migration file importer. The source extractor copies directory information, messages, calendar information, and collaboration data from Lotus Notes and saves the information into a file. The migration file importer imports the created file into Exchange. Although you can run both of these tools in one step, larger organizations will probably run them as separate tasks.

Another tool investigated in this chapter is the Active Directory Account Cleanup Wizard. The Migration Wizard can create duplicate accounts in Active Directory, and the Cleanup Wizard can simplify the process of deleting these duplicate accounts. The Lotus Notes Connector offers functions for bidirectional mail transfer, directory synchronization, and scheduling processes. Exchange 2000 also includes the Lotus Notes Application Connector, which synchronizes Exchange public folders with Lotus Notes databases. These connectors have comprehensive DirSync capabilities along with elaborate mapping rules for attributes in other email systems.

7

The next system for migration presented in this chapter was GroupWise. Migrating from GroupWise to Exchange 2000 involves moving the existing GroupWise messaging system to Exchange 2000 Server. To do this, you copy the existing mailboxes, messages, and other data, and import that information into Exchange 2000. Exchange 2000 supports migration from Novell GroupWise 4.x and 5.x. This chapter revisited the Migration Wizard to easily move users, messages, and calendar information from the GroupWise system to Exchange 2000.

This chapter also investigated how to migrate from cc:Mail to Exchange 2000. The best approach is to install the Exchange 2000 Server Connector for Lotus cc:Mail component when you install Exchange 2000 Server. The property pages that have similarity regardless of the type of connector being configured were detailed in this chapter. The same kind of consistency is found in the Migration Wizard as well.

The final migration environment discussed in this chapter was a migration from MSMail to Exchange. Good planning and strategy information was presented, as well as the five phases of an MSMail migration: migrating the hub post offices, migrating the DirSync components, migrating the gateways to connectors, migrating the user post offices, and finally migrating the clients.

Review Questions

1. You are the system designer for a large organization with several departments using MSMail environments. Due to the more complex and extensive nature of your design, it is not feasible for all of your MSMail departments to upgrade at once. What type of migration will you choose?

   a. Single-phase migration

   b. Multiphase migration

   c. Two-step migration

   d. Pilot migration

   e. Bidirectional migration

2. You need to examine your current Exchange 5.5 SP3 system to discover where Exchange 2000 will offer the most benefit. You are going to scrutinize your organization on three different levels. Which one of the following is *not* one of these levels?

   a. Exchange site level

   b. Domain level

   c. Individual server levels

   d. Data center level

3. Which one of the following is not one of the steps to migrate MSMail to Exchange 2000?

    a. Migrate the hub post offices

    b. Migrate the Dirsync components

    c. Migrate the DXA controller

    d. Migrate the gateways to connectors

    e. Migrate the user post offices

    f. Migrate the clients

4. What is the name of the component that is generated when upgrading Exchange servers that host directory replication connectors and that serves the role of replicating the Exchange 2000 configuration information to the down-level Exchange environment?

    a. System Redirection Service

    b. Site Replication Service

    c. System Replication Service

    d. Site Reconnection System

5. You have an Exchange 5.5 Server with unsupported connectors that cannot be migrated to Exchange 2000 and must stay on down-level versions of Exchange. What is Microsoft's specific recommendation for upgrading/migrating in this scenario?

    a. They must coexist.

    b. You must migrate.

    c. You must upgrade.

    d. You can either migrate or upgrade.

6. Your organization has decided to perform an in-place domain upgrade, and then to run the ADC. Which of the following statements are true when employing this technique? [Check all correct answers]

    a. At the very least, the PDC in each applicable domain must be upgraded.

    b. All of the domains must be in the same forest.

    c. A maximum of one of the upgrades can create a new forest.

    d. The remainder of the upgrades must join their domains to the existing forest either as child domains of an existing domain or of root domains of a new tree.

7

7. You are using the Active Directory Migration Tool to merge accounts during migration. You are implementing ADMT to migrate accounts into a domain that contains disabled user accounts that were created by the ADC. ADMT detects the duplicate accounts and follows the configured conflict-handling behavior. Which of the following are valid conflict-handling options? [Check all correct answers]

    a. Undo

    b. Ignore

    c. Replace

    d. Rename

    e. Delete

8. You are migrating from Exchange 5.5 to Exchange 2000 by running the Active Directory Migration Tool without sIDHistory, recreating the Access Control Lists (ACLs), and then running the ADC. Which of the following statements is true under this scenario? [Check all correct answers]

    a. For this scenario to work properly with the ADC, it is recommended that you update the permissions on the Exchange 5.5 mailboxes before you run the ADC.

    b. You cannot update the permissions manually under these circumstances.

    c. Without sIDHistory, a recently migrated account cannot access any of the resources to which the old account had access.

    d. All of the above.

9. You are considering a move from Lotus Notes to Exchange 2000. Which one of the following is *not* a basic level of migration for Microsoft Exchange Server?

    a. Coexistence

    b. New mailbox deployment

    c. Partial migration

    d. Full migration

10. The Migration Wizard may generate duplicate accounts in Active Directory. Which tool can you use to simplify the process of deleting duplicate accounts?

    a. Exchange Server Migration Tool

    b. Active Directory Account Cleanup Wizard

    c. Microsoft Exchange Application Converter for Lotus Notes

    d. Exchange 2000 SMTP Connector

    e. Microsoft Exchange Application Analyzer for Lotus Notes

11. Which of the following are tools that Microsoft provides to help you migrate your Notes application to Exchange and Outlook? [Check the two best answers]

    a. Exchange Server Management Tool

    b. Active Directory Reconciliation Wizard

    c. Microsoft Exchange Application Converter for Lotus Notes

    d. Exchange 2000 SMTP Connector

    e. Microsoft Exchange Application Analyzer for Lotus Notes

12. Which one of the following components offers functionality for bidirectional mail transfer, directory synchronization, and scheduling processes between Lotus Notes and Exchange 2000?

    a. Lotus Notes Application Connector

    b. Lotus Notes Connector

    c. Microsoft Application Services for Lotus Notes

    d. Exchange Server Migration Tool

13. The Exchange Server Migration Wizard lets your organization easily move users, messages, and calendar information from your GroupWise system to Exchange 2000. This tool comprises two primary pieces. What are they? [Check the two best answers]

    a. Flux capacitor

    b. Source extractor

    c. Migration file importer

    d. Calendar wizard

    e. Multiphase migration tool

14. In your GroupWise migration, you are selecting a method to create passwords for new user accounts. You will be using a template to facilitate setting up nonpersonal attributes. Which dialog box of the Migration Wizard will you use to perform this task?

    a. The GroupWise Domain dialog box

    b. The Migration Information dialog box

    c. The Account Creation Options dialog box

    d. The Account Migration dialog box

7

15. Lotus cc:Mail clients can use an Exchange 2000 Server as a gateway to which of the following messaging environments? [Check the two best answers]

    a. SLIP

    b. SMTP

    c. X.400

    d. X.300

    e. NetBEUI

Real-World Projects

As the system designer for Plus Ultra Group, Inc., you need to plan for the deployment of Exchange 2000 in your enterprise. The scope of your project will be a limited deployment, consisting primarily of server consolidation within your existing Exchange 5.5 organization. The following projects will provide guidelines for the parts of the infrastructure you will need to review when you build your Exchange 2000 project plan. It will help you through planning your Exchange 2000 Server installation order, both at a site level and a server level.

Project 7.1

Obtain or construct a complete diagram of your current Exchange architecture. This can be your present company or the organization of an associate, or you can choose one of the case studies from **www.Microsoft.com/exchange/productinfo/2000casestudies.htm** as a prototypical organization for an example.

Project 7.2

Obtain or construct a complete diagram of your current Windows 2000 architecture. This can be your present company or the organization of an associate, or you can choose one of the case studies from **www.Microsoft.com/exchange/productinfo/2000casestudies.htm** as a prototypical organization for an example.

Project 7.3

Obtain or construct a complete diagram of your current physical network. This can be your present company or the organization of an associate, or you can choose one of the case studies from **www.Microsoft.com/exchange/productinfo/2000casestudies.htm** as a prototypical organization for an example.

Project 7.4

Determine your office strategies by listing your offices and their types in Table 7.6. Expand the table as necessary for additional offices. Valid office types are Global

Headquarters (GHQ), Regional Branch Office (RBO), Large Branch Office (LBO), Medium Branch Office (MBO), and Small Branch Office (SBO). *Note: SBOs should have no Exchange servers.*

For each office listed in Table 7.6, you will need to determine whether you have any Exchange 2000 plans. These plans include upgrading current servers, installing new servers, and migrating resources (mailboxes, public folders, or connectors, as well as which connectors) to Exchange 2000 servers. List these in Table 7.7.

Project 7.5

Determine your Exchange site strategies. Begin by listing your current Exchange sites in Table 7.8.

After you have listed your sites, determine what plans you have for Exchange 2000 in each site, and explain them in Table 7.9. This may map directly to your office plans from Project 7.4 if each office is its own site.

7

Table 7.6   Office strategies.

Office Name	Office Location	Office Type	Number of Exchange Servers

Table 7.7   Exchange 2000 plans.

Office Name	Explain Exchange 2000 Plans

Table 7.8   Exchange site strategies.

Site Name	Geographic Description	Number and Roles of Exchange Servers

Table 7.9   Exchange plans descriptions.

Site Name	Explain Exchange 2000 Plans

Having outlined your Exchange 2000 plans for each site, you will now build a sequence for these actions. If you have no plans for Exchange 2000 in any specific site, you may leave that site out of Table 7.10.

Project 7.6

Determine Exchange server plans for each server in your organization, determine if it will be upgraded, if it will have its resources migrated to another system, or if it will be left alone, and list in Table 7.11. Remember that some Exchange 5.5 connectors are not available in Exchange 2000 in this process.

From the servers listed for upgrade or migrate in Table 7.11, you need to determine sequencing. List all servers in these classes and their sequence in Table 7.12. Ensure that this sequence aligns with the sequencing in your site-sequencing table (Table 7.10).

Table 7.10   Planned sequence of actions to take.

Step	Site Name
1	
2	
3	
4	

Table 7.11   Plans: Upgrade or migrate?

Server Name	Server Type	Exchange 2000 Plans

Table 7.12   Server sequencing.

Step	Server Name	Exchange 2000 Plans
1		
2		
3		
4		

CHAPTER EIGHT

Designing an Exchange 2000 Server Security Plan

After completing this chapter, you will be able to:

✓ Secure the Exchange 2000 Server infrastructure against internal attacks

✓ Secure the Exchange 2000 Server infrastructure against external attacks

✓ Design an authentication and encryption strategy

Securing the Infrastructure Against Internal Attacks

Exchange 2000 Server supplies security features expressly for securing messages. These features can protect messaging between users, facilitate in discouraging unsolicited email, divide managerial capacities in your company, and provide users with methods of secure communication with Exchange 2000 Server. To enable you to design an Exchange 2000 Server security plan, you need up-to-date documentation on your existing Exchange security design, your present Windows 2000 security design, and on your current network security architecture. You also need to have a firm grasp of the external information that will influence your security design, including legal factors and requirements. Additionally, you need to be aware of the strategies that have yet to be fully implemented in your existing Exchange design. Once you have all of this information, you can carry on with your development. This chapter explores techniques for securing your organization against internal as well as external attacks. It investigates authentication and encryption strategies along with a variety of critical technologies, and wraps it all up with key management services.

Before designing your internal security design for Exchange 2000, you should fully appraise your organizational security needs. The most logical starting point is your present Exchange 5.5 security model. Because Exchange 2000 implements Windows 2000 as its security provider, however, there are key distinctions. Historically, Exchange systems were justifiably driven by security requirements. Therefore, these systems were based on the specific Exchange rights that were granted to segments of the Exchange organization. Exchange 5.5 security models are characteristically motivated by the security requirements on the assorted pieces of the Exchange infrastructure as well as security integration into the Exchange site topology. In Exchange 5.5, you grant permissions to either Exchange mailboxes or Windows accounts, depending on the type of resource you are securing.

As just mentioned, Exchange 2000 depends upon Windows 2000 for applying permissions to the system, so there is only one level of permissions that you need to consider. With Exchange 2000, you configure both the public folder permissions and the connector permissions, for instance, using Windows 2000 accounts or groups.

Organizations typically need a security design that restricts who has access to different parts of the messaging system. You can utilize an amalgamation of permissions, restrictions, and auditing in different areas of the system to make certain that users are not vulnerable through normal usage. You want to be sure that when they try to bend the rules, however, you will know who has been doing what, with whom, and when. A good solution would be to employ journaling on some or all of your mailboxes to guarantee that you have copies of all messaging traffic from certain mailboxes. Journaling makes it much easier to configure permissions, document the permissions that have been granted, and explain the permissions to other administrators or security personnel.

At the Exchange site level, cross-domain trust issues are now a moot point because Exchange 2000 can be installed only in a Windows 2000 environment. If your organization has a Windows NT 4 domain environment that is being replaced by a Windows 2000 environment, you may actually now have even more trust issues than before. The tightest security structure may be one in which you have two-way trusts between all domains that are hosting your Exchange 2000 servers and your Exchange 5.5 servers, and you can then add trusts between your Windows NT 4 account domains and your Exchange 2000 servers as necessary.

Although Exchange 2000 can reduce the complexity in the process of granting permissions in your Exchange system at the object level, it may actually create a more complex scenario when coexisting with Exchange 5.5 and Windows NT 4. As you design your Exchange 2000 security model, you need to be aware of the implications of coexistence. If you are designing your architecture for coexistence between Exchange 5.5 and Exchange 2000, even though you will reduce the complexity of your permissions, you will increase the number of Windows trusts you need to maintain.

When you have gathered data from your Exchange organization and know the added security requirements for your physical organization, you can design your Exchange 2000 security model. Once you have mirrored your current environment as much as possible, you need to expand your design to include other requirements your system will have to satisfy. These may be requirements that were not implemented in your current system because the needs are newer than the current system, because they are requirements that the current system was not capable of, or because the requirements were too complex to implement in the previous version of Exchange.

Exchange 2000 Server comes with a variety of predefined permissions for groups of users that are reserved for administering Exchange and the Windows 2000 Server organizations. Within these groups are assorted levels of administrative permissions that can help you assign appropriate permissions to the users who are responsible for different administrative duties. Exchange 2000 Server installation also provides you with alternative methods to install Exchange 2000 Server to accommodate the typical separation of permissions between network administrators and messaging administrators found in many organizations. You can grant many different types of permissions on a per-user or per-group basis. Table 8.1 shows five predefined user groups with permissions already granted on the Exchange organization.

Table 8.1   Predefined user groups that have already been granted permissions.

Permission	Admins	Authenticated Users	Domain Admins	Enterprise Admins	Exchange Domain Servers
Full control	Yes	No	No	Yes	No
Read	Yes	No	Yes	Yes	Yes
Write	Yes	No	Yes	Yes	No
Create all child objects	Yes	No	Yes	Yes	No
Delete all child objects	Yes	No	No	Yes	No
Administer information store	Yes	No	Yes	Yes	No
Create named properties in the information store	Yes	No	Yes	Yes	No
Create public folder	Yes	No	Yes	Yes	No
Create top-level public folder	Yes	No	Yes	Yes	No
Modify public folder admin Access Control List	Yes	No	Yes	Yes	No
Modify public folder replica list	Yes	No	Yes	Yes	No
View information store status	Yes	No	Yes	Yes	No

Note: Domain Admins (Administrator) is the Domain Admins group for the root domain in the forest. The permissions for Enterprise Admins and Domain Admins are inherited from the parent container.

Delegated Roles

A discussion of internal security would not be complete without a survey of some of the delegation abilities as well as the different roles of the varied users and groups. The Exchange Administration Delegation Wizard can help you delegate control of Exchange configuration objects in Active Directory (AD). By using the Exchange Administration Delegation Wizard, you can dispense the tasks of managing different parts of Exchange 2000 to different users. You will assign these tasks by assigning roles to users.

Exchange Full Administrator

The Exchange Full Administrator role gives the user the ability to completely manage Exchange system information as well as modify permissions. Users assigned the Full Administrator role will have full control of the Exchange organization.

Exchange Administrator

The role of the Exchange Administrator is to fully administer the Exchange system information, but without the ability to modify permissions. This role may be a practical one for support staff employed to administer an Exchange organization without the need to modify permissions.

Exchange View Only Administrator

The Exchange View Only Administrator role grants the user permission to view the Exchange configuration information only, without the ability to change it. This role may also be useful for certain members of your support staff.

Levels of Administration

You can also easily arrange Administrator groups and grant the suitable permissions by generating groups of administrators who possess similar access privileges. Three levels of administration will meet most organizational requirements: enterprise administrators, administrative group administrators, and recipient administrators.

Enterprise Administrators

Windows 2000 Server adds certain groups to the built-in container in Active Directory Users and Computers by default. The built-in local security group named Administrators has all of the necessary permissions to administer the Windows 2000 Server domain. The Domain Admins (Admininstrators) and Enterprise Admins global security groups are members of the Administrators group and thus are given all permissions in the Windows 2000 domain. The Domain Admins and Exchange Admins global security groups are granted rights to administer the Exchange 2000 environment. These rights are inherited from the server's configuration container, which is the parent object. By adding users to the Enterprise Admins group you can assign them administrative privileges for the whole enterprise. By default, members of Enterprise Admins have nearly full control of both Active Directory and Exchange 2000.

Note: Exchange System Manager hides the configuration container. You can view the configuration container by running Adsiedit.exe from Windows 2000 Server Support Tools.

Administrative Group Administrators

You can also create a global security group in Active Directory and assign this security group one of the roles for the specific administrative group through the Exchange Administration Delegation Wizard. These permissions are applicable within the selected administrative group and should be equivalent to those for Enterprise Admins.

Recipient Administrators

Recipient administrators manage all the different facets of the user objects. Recipient administrators must have the ability to generate accounts in Active Directory as well as enable a mailbox in Exchange 2000. You can employ the built-in Windows 2000 Server Account Operators security group as a sole location for recipient administrators. You should apply the Account Operators group Exchange View

Only permissions role with the Delegation Wizard. All user administration permissions must consist of rights to Active Directory as well as to Exchange 2000.

Note: Any user that you wish to administer objects at any level in Exchange 2000 must have at least Read permissions on the Exchange organization container.

Active Directory Connector

The administrator must be given explicit permissions in order to perform tasks such as installing the Active Directory Connector (ADC) and creating connection agreements. Installing the first ADC in a Windows 2000 Server forest entails extending the Active Directory Schema and copying files to the local computer. To fulfill these duties, the administrator has to be a member of the Schema Admins group, Enterprise Admins group, and the Administrators group of the target computer. When the first ADC is installed, the Schema is updated. This removes the requirement for the user to be a member of the Schema Admins group. The user performing the installation, however, must be a member of the Domain Admins group on the local domain, the Administrators group on the target computer, and the ADC service account. This third group is mandatory because you must have a service account when you install the ADC. A separate service account is implemented because the ADC can be used without Exchange 2000 Server being installed. This is so because some of the components necessary for the Active Directory Connector are part of Windows 2000 Server. Exchange 2000 Server has components to prepare Active Directory for installation of the server that involves such tasks as setting permissions for the Local System services to Active Directory. The ADC service account must have the following permissions and credentials:

➤ Member of the Built-in\Administrators group

➤ Member of Enterprise Admins if used only with Windows 2000

➤ Member of Enterprise Admins or Exchange Full Administrator role if used with Exchange 2000 Server

➤ Connection Agreement Credentials

Securing the Infrastructure against External Attacks

Microsoft Exchange Server has traditionally provided an Advanced Security subsystem to allow users to secure their mail messages. The Advanced Security component assures privacy and integrity of content and verifies the authenticity of the sender. Advanced Security features deliver end-to-end message security from the point the sender signs and encrypts the message (even in Exchange Server's

Information Store or in a user's personal folders) until the receiver reads it. Advanced Security is based on the discretionary Key Management Service (KMS). KMS is discussed in more depth later in this chapter, in the "Key Management Service" Section.

Designing an Authentication and Encryption Strategy

Encryption is the arithmetical conversion of data from a decipherable, clear text structure into an unreadable, cipher text form. This conversion usually requires added undisclosed data, called a *key*, which can be obtained only by the sender and recipient. The key permits a message to be encrypted by the sender, and then decrypted only by the intended recipient. Decryption is the opposite of encryption, it converts unreadable, cipher text data back into readable, clear text form. The utilization of cryptography offers privacy as well as a special identity each time a user logs on to a network, accesses voice mail, or uses a user name and password to access resources. This special identification process, called authentication, is a critical aspect of network data security. Because of the proliferation of electronic transactions over networks, documents must be electronically signed, and cryptography offers the ability to create digital signatures. In many situations, digital signatures are as legally binding as written signatures. The four main types of cryptographic ciphers in use today are symmetric, asymmetric, block, and stream.

Symmetric

Ciphers are a method of data encryption in which a single key, known by both sender and recipient, is used to encrypt and decrypt a message. Symmetric cipher is also known as a shared-key cipher. This type of encryption is proficient and effectual, but it is often difficult to share the key between both parties in a secure manner. The sender must exchange the key with the recipient in a secure way.

Asymmetric

The asymmetric cipher is also called a public-key cipher. This is a method of resolving the key management challenges of symmetric key encryption. Asymmetric ciphers use two keys: one key for encryption and another key for decryption. One key is the public key and the other is the private key. You can use either the public key or the private key for encryption, and the opposite key is used for decryption. The public key is placed in a location, such as a folder, that is accessible to other users. The private key, however, is stored in a secure location available only to the owner of the key pair. With an asymmetric cipher, the sender and recipient do not have to agree on a key before the data is sent.

Block

A block cipher also uses shared-key encryption. It breaks a message into fixed-length blocks (usually 64 bits) and applies the shared-key encryption to each individual block. The decryption procedure decrypts each encrypted block with the same shared key and then rebuilds the original message.

Stream

A stream cipher is another symmetric encryption method that processes small bits of plaintext. Stream ciphers are faster than blocks and can be applied to data as it is sent or received. You do not need to know the size of the message, or even to receive the entire message before beginning to decrypt it. This is handy for encrypted conversations over a network as opposed to implementing individually encrypted messages.

Exchange 2000 Server can implement the following encryption algorithms:

➤ CAST-64

➤ CAST-40

➤ DES

➤ 3DES

➤ RC2-128

➤ RC2-64

➤ RC2-40

40-bit versus 128-bit Encryption

Transferring information over a network without encryption is comparable to relaying a confidential message through the mail by postcard. If we extend this logically, 40-bit encryption is like using a plain white envelope; 56-bit encryption is similar to using the special secure envelope that has printing to keep people from seeing through it; and 128-bit encryption, in contrast, is like encasing your information in a one-foot thick titanium safe that is being moved by armored car with a police escort. Many banks require 128-bit encryption for online banking because of the weaknesses and limitations of 40-bit and 56-bit encryption. Microsoft Outlook, for example, ships with a North American version that offers stronger encryption algorithms than the international version. You can use Server Gated Cryptography (SGC) to export 128-bit encryption outside of North America only if it is used for the e-commerce applications or programs listed in the U.S. Cryptography Law Exception List.

Inbound Encryption

One option for your organization is to configure the Exchange 2000 Simple Mail Transfer Protocol (SMTP) and Post Office Protocol 3 (POP3) virtual servers to require inbound encryption when a client is attempting to communicate with the server. Requiring security on your SMTP virtual server can discourage users from sending and receiving unsolicited email. As shown in the section "Secure Sockets Layer" later in this chapter, you can implement the Secure Sockets Layer (SSL) protocol with basic authentication to add another layer of protection to your messaging architecture.

Encrypted Remote Procedure Calls

Although Exchange 2000 Servers use SMTP as the native transport protocol between servers, scenarios arise that use remote procedure calls (RPCs). Therefore, another recommendation is to configure your client to use encrypted RPC. Encrypted RPC helps to ensure that Internet messages between clients and servers are secure and untainted. Exchange 2000 Server uses RPC for communications between the client and the server as well as the built-in RPC security to authenticate client-server and server-server connections. You can employ encrypted RPC to shield your client-server communication when a Messaging Application Programming Interface (MAPI) client with encryption enabled connects to the Exchange 2000 server. Encrypted RPC can also be used if an Exchange 5.5 server connects to another server in the same site or over Site Connector, or if an Exchange 2000 server connects to an Exchange 5.5 server (whether in the same mixed site and routing group or over Site Connector and Routing Group Connector). In addition, you can encrypt the whole client-server communication for secure mailbox access over the Internet.

Encrypted RPC differs from advanced security encryption in that it provides protection for data only while it travels from point to point on the network. Advanced Security encryption protects a message until the recipient decrypts it by using the client application, despite the number of hops to the destination.

Tip: Remember that encrypted RPC can be used to provide increased security for messages sent on internal networks as well as to external places on the Internet.

Encrypted RPC implements a 40-bit encryption algorithm called RC4 to encrypt data while it is on the network. You can configure Outlook to use encrypted RPC so that communication between clients and servers is secure and no users can interfere with the messages while in transit. The necessary steps to configure encrypted RPC are as follows:

1. In Microsoft Outlook 97, select Tools | Services.

2. In the list of information services, click Microsoft Exchange Server, and then click Properties.

3. Click the Advanced tab.

4. Under Encrypt information, select both checkboxes to encrypt all client/server communication.

S/MIME

S/MIME is short for Secure Multipurpose Internet Mail Extensions, which is a newer version of the Multipurpose Internet Mail Extension (MIME) protocol that supports secure encryption for electronic messaging. S/MIME is based on an RSA Data Security, Inc.'s public-key encryption technology (RSA stands for Rivest, Shamir, and Adelman). S/MIME is the de facto standard for secure messaging on the Internet, and many organizations use S/MIME as the foundation of their public key infrastructure (PKI) deployment. This level of security can be configured, for example, in the Change Security Settings dialog box in Outlook 2000, as seen in Figure 8.1.

MIME

An Internet mail message consists of a message header, which contains sender and recipient information, and an optional message body. The original MIME specification allows a message body to also contain data types other than ASCII. You can use MIME to add nontext objects such as graphic images, audio, and Word documents to your messages.

Advanced Security uses S/MIME (and X.509 certificates, which are discussed in the following section, "S/MIME Certificates" later in this chapter), and is an excellent example of a hybrid cryptographic solution that combines the muscle of asymmetric and symmetric ciphers and hashing. *Hashing* is a number that is generated from a string of text. The Internet Engineering Task Force (IETF) standardized S/MIME 3.0 in June 1999. S/MIME is widely integrated into email and messaging

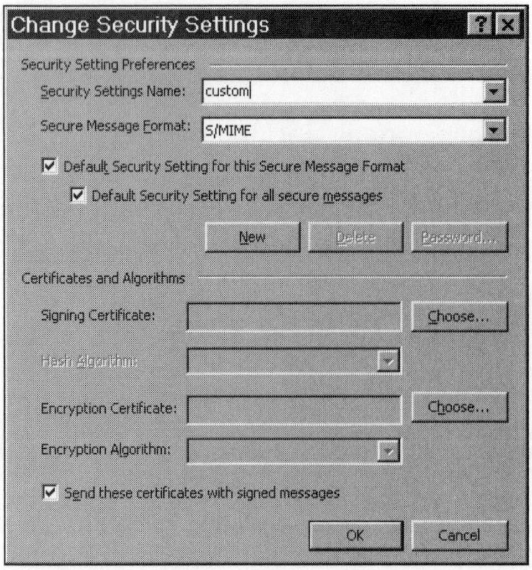

Figure 8.1 The Change Security Settings dialog box in Outlook 2000.

products to allow people to send secure email messages to each other regardless of which email clients they are using. The users in your organization will benefit greatly from the extensive implementation of S/MIME for reasons of privacy, data integrity, and authentication. S/MIME is already moving beyond simple email as vendors implement S/MIME in electronic data interchange software, Internet push products, and online e-commerce services.

S/MIME adds security only to the message body. The header data must continue to be unencrypted so that messages can successfully traverse gateways between the sender and receiver. Because no communication occurs between the sender and the recipient before the message is relayed, the sender may not be aware of the recipient's S/MIME compatibilities. S/MIME clients and non-S/MIME–enabled mail clients can both read clear-signed messages. When you send S/MIME clear-signed messages from Outlook 2000 to Outlook Express 5, the sending 2000 client will use MAPI conventions to lay out the message and then the SMTP gateway will ultimately convert the message over to MIME format. This conversion modifies the plaintext part of the message as well. The result of this behavior is that the receiving client's check of the signature forces it to return an invalid result, as if an intrusion had occurred. This invalidation error occurs less often in Exchange 2000 than it did in Exchange Server 5.5 because the Exchange 2000 streaming database stores native MIME messages. Thus, Exchange 2000 transforms MIME messages to MAPI messages only when absolutely necessary.

Microsoft Outlook and S/MIME

Outlook 2000 is the most recent version of the full-featured Microsoft mail client. Microsoft Outlook Express 5, in contrast, is a thinner Internet-oriented mail client that comes with Internet Explorer 5. Outlook Express 5 can connect to Exchange 2000 or Exchange Server 5.5 by way of POP3 or Internet Message Access Protocol version 4 (IMAP4) protocols. The mail client can also access a directory through Lightweight Directory Access Protocol (LDAP). Outlook 2000 can be installed in Corporate/Workgroup mode, Internet Mail Only mode, or No E-mail mode. Corporate/Workgroup mode is a full MAPI client that offers added support for SMTP and POP, as well as optional support for LDAP. Internet Mail Only mode is an Internet service provider (ISP)-oriented mail client that offers SMTP, IMAP, POP, and LDAP protocol support. To switch between modes in Outlook 2000, go to Tools | Options, click on the Mail Delivery tab, and use the Reconfigure Mail Support button (see Figure 8.2). Outlook 2000 reconfigures the mode at the machine level so that it applies to every user who logs on to the machine. A basic distinction exists between the two modes from the S/MIME point of view. If your organization needs to provide encryption key recovery for its enterprise mail clients, install Outlook 2000 clients in Corporate/Workgroup mode. This will allow you to register clients in Exchange 2000 Advanced Security and allow them

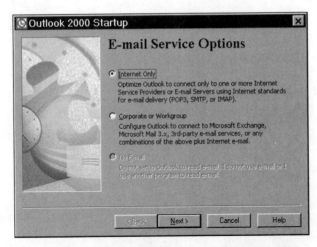

Figure 8.2 E-mail Service Options component in Outlook 2000.

to enjoy the benefits of the S/MIME encryption options for Exchange 2000 and Active Directory.

Extended S/MIME

In Exchange 2000, Microsoft has extended its S/MIME capabilities through the tight integration of Active Directory and the Windows 2000 Certificate Server, along with several KMS components. Before sending an S/MIME message, every client with Advanced Security enabled queries the Active Directory for each recipient's encryption capacities. Advanced Security uses an encryption algorithm and a key length that every recipient can support in order to secure the message. For an Advanced Security–enabled client to send an encrypted message, it must first receive a signed message from the proposed recipient, which comes with the recipient's encryption certificate and public key.

S/MIME adds fresh MIME content types that offer extended features such as data privacy, integrity defenses, and authentication services. S/MIME presents extensions that enable MIME components with the ability to encapsulate such components as digital signatures and encrypted messages. The MIME content-type application indicates that the message carries MIME attachment data and that an application will be needed to process the data before the recipient can view it. The MIME header serves to classify the name of the MIME attachment. Some mail clients need the attachment to recognize the S/MIME content, whereas other, newer mail clients ignore attachment names and rely entirely on the content-type data to spot MIME entities.

S/MIME Certificates

S/MIME defines a format for digital certificates by building upon such open standards as X.509 version 3, which is supported by all of the most recent

Microsoft products. Exchange 2000 also provides support for X.509 version 1 certificates for compatibility with Outlook 97 and Exchange Server 4 and 5. Window 2000 Certificate Server, however, issues only X.509 version 3 certificates, although you can configure the Exchange 2000 KMS to issue either version 1 or version 3 certificates. Outlook 2000 and Outlook Express 5 can receive certificates from a directory or those that are attached to signed mail messages. Outlook 2000 and Outlook Express 5 will weigh different criteria to decide if you can use the certificate's public key for cryptographic S/MIME operations. You must validate a certificate before you can use it.

Viewing S/MIME Certificates

To view the content and format of S/MIME certificates, load the Microsoft Management Console (MMC) Certificates snap-in for your account, open the Personal Certificates container, and then double-click on S/MIME certificate.

You may experience issues when you send a signed message from an Exchange 2000 Advanced Security–enabled user to Netscape Messenger or to Outlook Express 5 users. A certificate that you issue using the KMS does not include the certificate subject's Request for Comments (RFC) 822 name. The subject field instead contains an X.500 Distinguished Name (DN). In addition, the certificate does not have a Subject Alternative Name field. The Windows 2000 Certificate Server must issue S/MIME certificates that set the Subject Alternative Name field to the subject's RFC 822 name to resolve this issue. Internet Explorer 5, Outlook Express 5, Outlook 2000, and Windows 2000 Professional each ship with improved support for certificate validation.

IP Security

IP Security (IPSec) is a structure of open standards for providing private, secure communications over Internet Protocol (IP) networks. This group of protocols was developed by the IETF to provide secure transfer of packets at the IP layer of the Open Systems Interconnection (OSI) model (see Figure 8.3). IPSec is extensively deployed for virtual private networks (VPNs). IPSec supports two encryption modes: transport mode and tunnel mode. Transport mode encrypts only the payload (or the data portion) of each packet and leaves the header unaffected. Tunnel mode provides a more secure encryption of both the header and the data payload. An IPSec-compliant device will decrypt each packet on the recipient side.

Both sending and receiving hosts must share a public key for IPSec to function. The protocol known as Internet Security Association and Key Management Protocol/Oakley (ISAKMP/Oakley) helps the receiver obtain a public key and

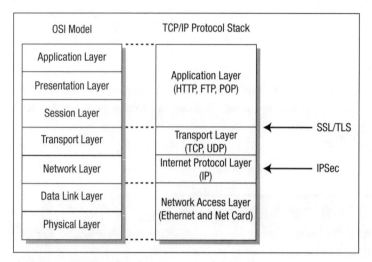

Figure 8.3 IPSec in the OSI Model.

authenticates the sender through digital certificates. IPSec offers security on the IP transport layer, or layer 3, for Transmission Control Protocol (TCP), User Datagram Protocol (UDP), Internet Control Message Protocol (ICMP), and other protocols that transmit at the IP layer. IPSec can send blocks of data, with each block secured by a different key, so that an attacker is prevented from obtaining an entire communication with a single compromised key. The chief benefit of securing data at a lower layer is that IPSec can protect all applications and services that use IP to transport data, such as Exchange 2000, without any modification to the applications or services. IPSec at layer 3 secures messages between Exchange 2000 servers in a way that is transparent to the servers.

IPSec is based on a model in which the only systems that need to know about the secure messages are the sending and receiving computers. Each host deals with security at its own end under the assumption that the communication medium is never secure. Exchange 2000 engages in the following steps to secure its intranet messaging through IPSec (see Figure 8.4):

1. Exchange Server A sends a message to Exchange Server B.

2. The IPSec driver on Server A looks at its stored IP Filter Lists to see whether the packets should be secure.

3. The IPSec driver informs Internet Key Exchange to start the negotiations.

4. The Internet Key Exchange on Server B receives a message requesting a secure negotiation.

5. The two systems set up a security association (SA) and shared master key.

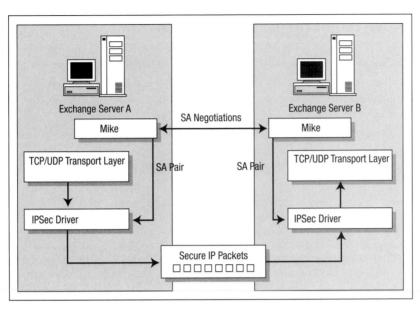

Figure 8.4   The IPSec model.

6. An inbound SA pair and one outbound SA are negotiated.

7. The IPSec driver on Server A uses the outbound SA to sign and encrypt the packets.

8. The IPSec driver passes the packets to the IP layer, which routes the packets to Server B.

9. The network adapter driver on Server B receives the secure IP packets and passes them on to the IPSec driver.

10. The IPSec driver on Server B uses the inbound SA to check the integrity signature and decrypt the packets.

11. The driver passes the decrypted packets up to the TCP/IP driver, which passes them on to the receiving Exchange 2000 Server virtual server.

Note: Any routers or switches in the data path between the communicating computers will forward the secure IP packets to their destination. However, if a firewall, security router, or proxy server exists, it must have IP forwarding enabled, so that IPSec and Internet Key Exchange protocol traffic can pass through a network address translator. The Internet Key Exchange negotiation contains IP addresses in the encrypted messages, which a network address translator cannot change because the integrity hash is broken or because the packets are encrypted.

The New Technology LAN Manager

The New Technology LAN Manager (NTLM) protocol is a challenge/response authentication protocol that was the default for network authentication in Windows NT version 4 and earlier. NTLM (also known as Integrated Windows Authentication) is still supported in Windows 2000, but it is no longer the default protocol. NTLM authentication uses existing credentials provided at logon to access a server, and no additional authentication is necessary. Because passwords are encrypted when they are sent to the server, security is enhanced. Internet Explorer versions 4 or 5 running on Windows both support NTLM, although other browsers do not. Clients using Windows 2000 authentication use Kerberos. Non–Windows 2000 clients use NTLM protocol for authentication.

Note: Integrated Windows Authentication isn't supported in the front-end and back-end configuration.

Msv1_0.dll is the NTLM authentication protocol. This protocol authenticates clients that do not use Kerberos authentication.

Instant Messaging uses NTLM protocol and digest authentication to permit user access to the service. Windows 2000 domain controllers authenticate users and return configuration information to Instant Messaging MMCs. Domain controllers also facilitate Instant Messaging servers in determining whether a resource is local or needs to be relayed to some other network location.

Digest Authentication

MD5 is an algorithm created in 1991 by Ronald Rivest that is used to create digital signatures. It is intended for use with 32-bit machines and is safer than the MD4 algorithm, which has been broken. MD5 is a *one-way hash function*, meaning that it takes a message and converts it into a fixed string of digits, also called a message digest.

The representation of text in the form of a single string of digits is created by using a formula known as a one-way hash function. Encrypting a message digest with a private key creates a digital signature, which is an electronic means of authentication. When using a one-way hash function, one can compare a calculated message digest against the message digest that is decrypted with a public key to verify that the message has not been tampered with. This comparison is called a *hashcheck*.

Secure Sockets Layer

SSL is a protocol developed by Netscape for transmitting private documents via the Internet. SSL works by using a private key to encrypt data that is transferred over the SSL connection. Both Netscape Navigator and Internet Explorer support SSL, and many Web sites use this protocol to obtain confidential user information, such as credit card numbers. By convention, Web pages that require an SSL connection start with "https:" instead of "http:".

The SSL protocol runs above TCP/IP and below such higher-level protocols as HTTP or IMAP. It uses TCP/IP on behalf of the higher-level protocols, and in the process allows an SSL-enabled server to authenticate itself to an SSL-enabled client, allows the client to authenticate itself to the server, and allows both machines to establish an encrypted connection. These capabilities address fundamental concerns about communication over the Internet and other TCP/IP networks.

SSL server authentication allows a user to confirm a server's identity. SSL-enabled client software can use standard techniques of public-key cryptography to check that a server's certificate and public ID are valid and have been issued by a certification authority (CA) listed in the client' list of trusted CAs. This confirmation might be important if the user, for example, is sending a credit card number over the network and wants to check the receiving server's identity. SSL client authentication allows a server to confirm a user's identity. Using the same techniques as those for server authentication, SSL-enabled server software can check that a client's certificate and public ID are valid and have been issued by a CA listed in the server's list of trusted CAs. This confirmation might be important if the server, for example, is a bank sending confidential financial information to a customer and wants to check the recipient's identity.

An encrypted SSL connection requires all information sent between a client and a server to be encrypted by the sending software and decrypted by the receiving software, thus providing a high degree of confidentiality. Confidentiality is important for both parties to any private transaction. In addition, all data sent over an encrypted SSL connection is protected with a mechanism for detecting tampering—that is, for automatically determining whether the data has been altered in transit. The SSL protocol includes two subprotocols: the SSL record protocol and the SSL handshake protocol. The SSL record protocol defines the format used to transmit data. The SSL handshake protocol involves using the SSL record protocol to exchange a series of messages between an SSL-enabled server and an SSL-enabled client when they first establish an SSL connection. This exchange of messages is designed to facilitate the following actions:

➤ Authenticate the server to the client

➤ Allow the client and server to select the cryptographic algorithms, or ciphers, that they both support

➤ Optionally authenticate the client to the server

➤ Use public-key encryption techniques to generate shared secrets

➤ Establish an encrypted SSL connection

Key Management Service

The KMS is a service of Exchange 2000 Server that uses Windows 2000 Certificate Services to provide secure messaging. The KMS uses a variety of cryptographic technologies and methods. With the increasing need to communicate mission-critical data over such public networks as the Internet, it is important to keep data private. Cryptography is a way to protect data, thus keeping data private. However, keeping data private is only a part of cryptography. Several other features of cryptography are discussed in the following sections. The main KMS features are as follows:

➤ Encryption

➤ Hash functions

➤ Ciphers

➤ Algorithms

➤ Certificate Services and the Key Management Service

Certificate Services and the KMS

Exchange 2000 KMS uses Certificate Services to provide security at the application layer of the network messaging system. The KMS generates X.509 version 3 user certificates for digital signature and encryption employed by Exchange 2000 and Outlook 2000. These X.509 version 3 certificates are recognized by all S/MIME clients and provide interoperability for different Internet clients. The Exchange Server KMS secure messaging mechanism has evolved quite a bit. Originally, the KMS generated X.509 version 1 certificates. Advanced Security has always offered a unique key scheme for recovering copies of a lost or deleted encryption key.

Don't confuse key recovery, however, with key escrow. Key escrow is concerned with controlling government access to encrypted user data. Key recovery focuses instead on users' access to their encrypted data and is server-oriented. The KMS database holds replicas of the current and former private encryption keys for all of the Advanced Security-enabled users. This technique for storing keys represents the implementation of a dual-key-pair system, whereby users have one key pair for encryption and a different pair for signing. Advanced Security would not be able to assure digital signature services if it used only one key pair and stored the pair's private key in the KMS database for key recovery purposes. Digital signatures require that users can access only their private signing keys; otherwise, anyone could impersonate a certain user. For these reasons, Exchange 2000 Server stores the signing pair's private key on the client side only. A server-oriented technique will call for greater administrative overhead because administrators must enroll users in Advanced Security, then put a regular KMS database backup scheme in place and recover users' encryption keys whenever necessary.

KMS Deployment Scenarios

The evolution of Exchange 2000 KMS is the first step toward Advanced Security's complete integration into an enterprise PKI. The following sections offer practical design issues concerning the configuration of different KMS scenarios. These scenarios present some issues to consider when planning an infrastructure that supports Exchange 2000 secure messaging.

Intracompany Email Security Scenario 1

Your organization may need only a basic implementation of a messaging environment that uses a PKI infrastructure for S/MIME. Before you begin to deploy the CA design, you should first consider several key issues. You want to determine if you need to install the High Encryption Pack for Windows to support the Microsoft Enhanced Cryptographic Provider. If so, the deployment must include the Outlook High Encryption Pack as well. You should also research other platforms and applications in your organization to determine their level of high encryption compatibility. It may be necessary to update the platforms and applications to the correct versions.

8

High Encryption Pack for Windows 2000

The High Encryption Pack for Windows 2000 is necessary only on the CA servers. However, you may want to consider deploying the High Encryption Pack on Exchange 2000 KMS servers as well as the Outlook clients. This should guarantee a consistent high encryption environment. Consider, for example, SSL connections to Web servers that do not have the High Encryption Pack installed; this would have the effect of essentially downgrading clients with high encryption to normal encryption.

In this PKI infrastructure for S/MIME, you also want to figure out how many CA levels are necessary to support the organizational requirements. The root CA will take substantially more time to deploy than the subsequent CAs. The root CA will usually be installed with a long expiration period, up to four or five years. The public key digital signature length will generally be 2,048 bytes. The root certificate is exported for signing additional CAs, and the computer is taken offline and placed in a secure area. You will also want to bone up on the X.509 specification of the International Telecommunication Union (ITU) relating to the format and naming conventions for the attributes for CAs.

X.509 Specification

You can review the X.509 specification at the following Web site: **www.itu.int/itudoc/itu-t/rec/x/x500up** and click on "x.509".

After you install the High Encryption Pack for Windows 2000 on the appropriate systems, the next step is to install Certificate Services. The CA should be configured as an enterprise root CA supporting the enhanced cryptographic service provider having a public key length of 2,048 bytes. Next, deploy an enterprise subordinate CA to issue certificates to users and computers. Make sure that the enterprise root CA certificate is in the Trusted Root Certification Authority Store of the computer. This is an automatic process enforced through Windows 2000.

Note: Typically, issuing CAs are installed with a shorter public key due to scalability considerations.

The next step is to add the Exchange User, Enrollment Agent (Computer), and Exchange Signature Only templates to the system before installing the Exchange 2000 KMS. The computer account in which the KMS will reside is thus given rights on the issuing CA to manage, enroll, and read.

After you accomplish these tasks, the KMS installation is now a smooth process. Simply select the startup method, which defines how the password for the KMS is maintained, and define for which Exchange 2000 administrative group this KMS is responsible.

Note: You must make sure that the password for the KMS is in a highly secure location to prevent intruders from cracking the system and recovering the keys.

KMS offers extra possibilities for S/MIME to Outlook 98/2000 clients. Through the System Manager utility, you can directly start the enrollment process through the Key Management server. You have the ability to enroll users by selecting them from an address list of users with mailbox resources on servers in a specific administrative group, or by choosing mailbox stores available in a specific administrative group. Certificate enrollment for Outlook Express and Netscape Communicator is performed through the Certificate Web Enrollment tool on the issuing CA. You can also configure Outlook Express by setting the security properties for the Signing and Encryption Certificate via the mail account properties dialog box. Outlook Express can be configured to use a dual-key pair by enrolling the User Certificate and User Signing Certificate. The model for S/MIME and Outlook Web Access clients is illustrated in Figure 8.5.

All of the certificates that are enrolled by Certificate Services, and therefore by the KMS in S/MIME mode, are stored in Windows 2000 Active Directory. Outlook 2000 uses Active Directory as the global address list so that all certificates are accessible automatically to Outlook 2000 clients. If you are using Outlook Express on a Windows 2000 Professional system, then Active Directory already exists as the default entry for directories so that you can automatically look up information in AD.

If you plan to run Outlook Web Access over SSL, you need a Web Server Certificate for Internet Information Services (IIS). This is accomplished by employing the

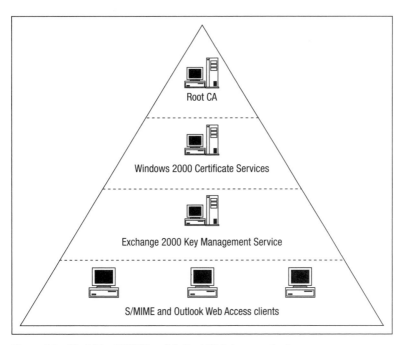

Figure 8.5   Model for S/MIME and Outlook Web Access clients.

Web Server Certificate Wizard on the Web site hosting Outlook Web Access. Then, after the Web Server Certificate has been installed and configured, SSL must be enabled through the Properties page of the Exchange virtual root. To implement client authentication, a user certificate must be enrolled on the client as well. Mapping a user to a certificate in Active Directory is quite simple. Navigate to the Internet Services Manager tool and right-click the name of the server in which IIS is running, and then click Properties. Next, on the Internet Information Service tab, in Master Properties, click Edit. On the Directory Security tab, check Enable The Windows Directory Service Mapper. This allows the exclusive basic and clear-text authentication clients to securely connect to Outlook Web Access by authenticating with their certificate. This is known as *mutual authentication*.

Intracompany Email Security Scenario 2

This second intracompany scenario adds another administrative group to the Exchange organization with an additional Key Management server. A sample environment may consist of one Active Directory domain with one domain controller, the root CA, one issuing CA, and two servers running Exchange 2000 Server and the KMS. The same considerations presented in the first scenario will apply to this scenario. For example, both Key Management servers use the same issuing CA (see Figure 8.6).

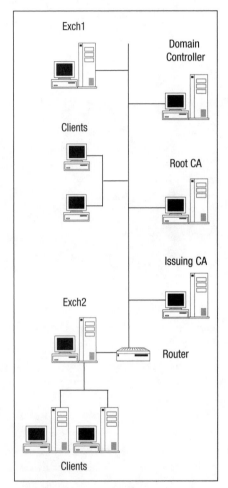

Figure 8.6 A sample of a KMS design.

The KMS offers a lot of flexibility for dealing with issuing CAs. The KMS will actually find any available CA and use the one that is returned. You can force the KMS to use a specific issuing CA by taking the other CAs offline, establishing a connection from the KMS to the specific issuing CA, and bringing the other issuing CAs back online. Consider this technique when planning your design if your organization's deployment environment will involve specific CA mapping. Also, possible fail-over and fail-back issues should be taken into consideration and added to your plan design. In this intracompany email security scenario, the S/MIME email security for the second Exchange administrative group is established with an additional issuing CA and Key Management server. This particular scenario can be implemented for situations in which independent divisions or departments want to have the authority for their PKI.

Note: Although it is not necessary for S/MIME email security, Windows 2000 is configured through policies to allow communication between sites using IPSec only. If similar security requirements exist in your environment, contact the appropriate information technology (IT) staff to make sure that the proper ports and filters are configured according to security policies. Realize as well that encryption may disable additional security features, such as virus checking, which is the primary function of some firewall solutions.

Intercompany Email Security Scenario 3

This third scenario addresses the requirements for allowing two individual companies to communicate using S/MIME (see Figures 8.7 and 8.8). Before implementing the S/MIME design in this scenario, both organizations must have a PKI in place. In addition, both companies must have agreed on and implemented PKI trust relationships. Both companies must also agree on how to manage certificate management issues, such as Certificate Revocation Lists (CRLs). A CRL is the list

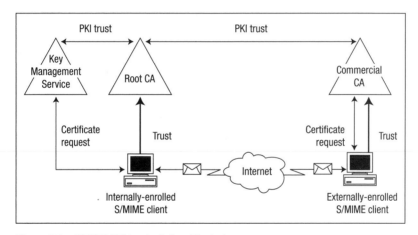

Figure 8.7   S/MIME PKI trust relationship design.

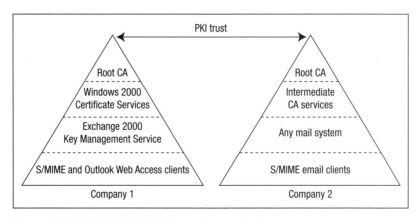

Figure 8.8   Model for PKI Trust between two organizations.

of users whose security tokens have been revoked and therefore should not be authenticated as secure. Define how these CRLs will be managed for the organizations. You need to determine how both companies will access and exchange certificates for S/MIME as well as define the access method to the certificates of the companies. Consider also how the root certificates of the companies are imported.

In an intercompany email security scenario, you need to configure directory replication between both directories in order to synchronize the user objects from one company to import as contacts to the another company. The CRLs of one company are copied to a Web site of the other company for end users to download.

Smart Card Scenario

You can introduce smart cards into the design to test how messaging clients work with certificates generated by a smart card cryptographic service provider. Realize that the available smart cards permit only single key pair encryption. Because the smart card is in itself a provider of cryptographic services, your first consideration will be the issues of implementing smart cards together with Key Management servers. KMS cannot use the cryptographic service provider on the smart card to create the encryption certificate. Also, realize that Outlook uses its own mechanism to generate the signing certificate along with the Key Management server enrollment. Based on these factors, the Key Management server cannot be used for smart card users. It is possible, however, to use smart cards for S/MIME security through the typical enrollment process that comes with Windows 2000 Certificate Services. A certificate can be generated that is usable with both the Windows 2000 logon as well as S/MIME by using the certificate template for a smart card user.

As with the other scenarios, it is necessary to configure the appropriate security options in Outlook 2000 and Outlook Express. Certificates that are enrolled for smart cards using this method will not require any additional preparations for SSL-based security access. When a dual key pair-enrolled Outlook 2000 user sends email to a single key pair-enrolled user, Outlook 2000 does not acknowledge the enrolled certificate for the dual key purposes and accepts the certificate, just not as an encryption certificate. Smart card enrollment typically follows the same methodology as a Key Management server does. Smart card certificates are generated on behalf of a user. The prepared smart card is then sent directly to the user. To enroll certificates for other users, the person who executes the enrollment will need to have an Enroll Request Agent (User) certificate.

Trusted Third-Party Scenario

This scenario involves a trusted third party acting as a directory service for separate organizations that need secure communications (see Figure 8.9). This scenario necessitates each participating company to establish a PKI. By involving a trusted third party, you can streamline many of the PKI processes that would otherwise

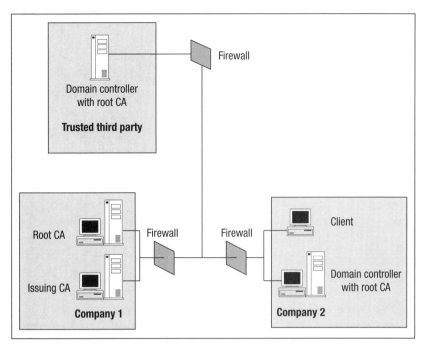

Figure 8.9   Each participating company that participates establishes a public key infrastructure.

need to be organized independently from each organization. This solution could possibly be a goal for every intercompany PKI because it also improves the administrative processes for scalability and flexibility. You can link the KMS with Certificate Server to allow the Exchange 2000 KMS to implement X.509 version 3 certificates. The installation of the expolicy.dll module on each Certificate Server is no longer needed because the policy module that ships with Windows 2000 Certificate Server is totally compatible with Exchange 2000.

The new KMS still offers support for X.509 version 1 certificates to provide compatibility with earlier versions of Outlook. Double-click the Key Manager object, enter the KMS administrator password, go to the Enrollment tab, and select the "I have Outlook 97 or older clients in my organization. Issue Version 1 and Version 3 certificates" checkbox. The KMS will automatically detect the client's capabilities at the moment of user enrollment. Subsequently, the KMS either will create an X.509 version 1 certificate (for Outlook 97 clients), or it will generate an X.509 Version 1 certificate and pass a request to the Certificate Server for an X.509 version 3 certificate (for Outlook 98 or later clients).

KMS Installation and Administration

Prior to installing Exchange 2000 Advanced Security, you will need to install Windows 2000, Active Directory, and Exchange 2000 Server, as well as an operational Windows 2000 CA. The install requirement of a Windows 2000 CA represents a major difference between the Exchange 2000 KMS and earlier versions. You must integrate the CA with Active Directory (Enterprise CA) and install the Machine Enrollment Agent, Exchange User, and Exchange User Signature certificate templates. Certificate templates offer an excellent method to determine which types of certificates a CA can issue. The Machine Enrollment Agent certificate type allows a machine to request a certificate on behalf of other hosts. The Exchange 2000 KMS functions primarily as a registration authority to request S/MIME certificates for Exchange 2000 users.

To install the KMS from the Installation Wizard, expand Microsoft Exchange 2000 in the Component Selection dialog box, expand Microsoft Exchange Messaging and Collaboration, select Microsoft Exchange Key Management Services, and click Install in the left column. You can choose between floppy disk mode and manual KMS-startup mode during the KMS setup, as in earlier versions of Exchange. The installation process generates a new Windows 2000 global group called Exchange KMServers and issues a Machine Enrollment Agent certificate to your Key Management server. The installations also modify the Active Directory Configuration Naming Context to reflect changes in the organization related to Exchange 2000 administrative groups. The KMServers group serves the purpose of administering some KMS-CA–related access control settings and contains the machine account of every KMS server. The Exchange 2000 KMS uses machine credentials to authenticate the KMS to other services when accessing resources. This is an essential difference from Exchange Server 5.5. The Exchange 2000 machine account feature provides better password-quality and password-change-interval security, and it helps to avoid the issues that come with using an administrator's user account as a service account.

Exchange 2000 Administrative Groups

Exchange 2000 administrative groups are logical collections of Exchange 2000 objects used to delegate administration. When you install the KMS on an Exchange 2000 system, the KMS extends the Active Directory schema and adds the Advanced Security container to each administrative group in your Exchange Server organization.

The Advanced Security container can include the Encryption Configuration object and the Key Manager (KM) object. The KM object is available only in administrative groups containing a KM Server. The Encryption Configuration object is available in all the administrative groups, and you can configure different encryption options for each group. After you install the KMS, you will need to give the Exchange KM servers group permission to read and manage the CA object. You can use the MMC-CA snap-in on the CA container's security properties to grant these permissions. The KM Server must have these permissions to revoke certificates for the KMS administrator. The certificate templates are regular Active Directory objects that are associated with a Windows 2000 ACL.

You must add the Exchange KMServers with enroll permission on every template to allow the KMS to enroll for Exchange 2000 certificates. To accomplish this task, simply open the MMC Sites and Services snap-in and select the Show Services Node from the View menu. Double-click the Services container and the Public Key Services container, then select the Certificate Templates container. Right-click the appropriate certificate template from the right pane, select the Security tab, and change the permissions as necessary.

To confirm that you have installed an Enterprise Certificate server, review the properties page of your CA object in the MMC-CA snap-in, or run the command-line Certsrv utility with the **-z** switch to confirm the installation. The CA issues two certificates for every user enrolled in Advanced Security. A fundamental difference exists between the Windows 2000 Enterprise policy module and the Exchange Server 5.5 policy module used to connect the KMS to the CA. Once you install the Exchange Server 5.5 policy module, you cannot issue any other type of certificate. In contrast, the Exchange 2000 KMS version can issue more than just Exchange 2000 certificates. As already established, Windows 2000 publishes Enterprise CAs in Active Directory. Any client that can browse Active Directory can access the location information of your corporate Active Directory-integrated Enterprise CA servers. In Exchange 2000, it is not necessary to point the KMS to a fixed-certificate server, as you had to do in Exchange Server 5.5. The Exchange 2000 KMS will automatically query Active Directory to find another CA if the KMS-CA goes down. This fault-tolerant feature removes the need for complicated KMS-CA rollover processes.

Another notable enhancement to Exchange 2000 KMS is the ability to build multilevel CA hierarchies. You can link a single CA server to multiple KM servers. Windows 2000 also adds enhanced integration capabilities with other CA hierarchies. To improve interoperability, your Windows 2000 CA can be subordinate to a commercial CA, although the KMS-CA must run Microsoft CA software. Such enhancements improve interoperability.

You can implement the MMC Exchange System Manager snap-in or start up Advanced Security as a standalone snap-in to administer the KMS. Remember that you can enroll a single user from the MMC Users and Computers snap-in console. In Exchange 2000, Microsoft removes the password memory feature in the Advanced Security administration interface. This feature temporarily caches the administrator password in system memory so that you do not need to submit the password every time you open a new dialog box in the KMS administration interface. Exchange 2000 includes a set of administrative tasks that you can perform in bulk: enrollment, revocation, recovery, bulk export, and bulk import. Microsoft also adds buttons at the top of the MMC Exchange System Manager snap-in to speed up administrative tasks. You can perform bulk operations at three different levels in Exchange 2000: administrative group, server, or individual user. Exchange 2000 also addresses the performance issues that take place in large Exchange Server 5.5 bulk operations.

The KMS backup process has also been enhanced. The KMS database is now a part of the Windows 2000 Backup Exchange container. This allows online backups. Realize that you must back up the KMS and KMS-CA simultaneously in order to synchronize at the certificate-revocation level. The primary source of KMS troubleshooting information is still the NT Event Viewer's application folder. Exchange 2000 does extend the number of logging entries, however, and logs events such as updating CRLs and enabling Advanced Security for user accounts.

Another important enhancement to Exchange 2000 is the ability to export and import user accounts and their key and certificate histories from one KMS database to another. To facilitate the new export-import technique, Exchange 2000 uses the Exchange KMS Key Export Wizard. This wizard secures the export-import process using the CA's certificate, but you can run this wizard only once. The Exchange KMS Key Export Wizard logs the results of the export and import processes into the filename.explog and filename.implog files.

Note: The Key Export Wizard exports the user's record and also deletes it from the KMS database.

Exchange 2000 KMS still offers support for a multiple-password policy for important KMS operations, meaning that the KMS would require more than one set of administrator's credentials to perform a particular administrative task. In Exchange 2000, you can do the following administrative tasks as well:

➤ Set multiple-password policies to add and delete administrator accounts

➤ Recover and revoke user keys

➤ Change the support for X.509 version 1 or version 3 certificates

➤ Import and export user accounts

Exchange and KMS

Keep in mind that the administrator accounts that you implement on the KMS level will differ from the regular Window 2000 accounts: Exchange 2000 stores the KMS accounts together with the associated password in the KMS database.

Certificate Enrollment and Renewal

The Exchange 2000 KMS administrator commences the Advanced Security enrollment process. The administrator will create and distribute the enrollment tokens that clients use to enroll for S/MIME certificates and keys. Only the KMS-CA, which is loaded with Exchange 2000-specific certificate templates, can generate Advanced Security certificates. When you use a Windows 2000 Enterprise CA, your clients can enroll using a Web-based (**http://servername/certsrv**) or GUI-based (MMC Certificates snap-in) interface. If one of your users receives a certificate from the CA and still cannot send S/MIME-signed messages, check their S/MIME settings in Outlook 2000. Certificate renewal is as vital as enrollment. Almost all Microsoft mail clients will warn users when the users' certificates expire or when the CA or KMS administrator has revoked the certificates. The Outlook 2000 Corporate/Workgroup mode, combined with the Exchange Server KMS, offers the highest level of automation. A dialog box will prompt users to enroll for new certificates, which the CA transparently creates when users accept the prompt. Users of Outlook 2000 Internet Only mode or Outlook Express 5 must rerun the enrollment process to replace expired or revoked certificates.

You do not need to install personal S/MIME certificates or enroll in Advanced Security to read signed messages in Outlook 2000 or Outlook Express 5. Outlook Express 5 users do not even need a personal S/MIME certificate to send encrypted mail. When a client receives a message with a valid signature, the software automatically adds the sender to the Outlook Express Contact List. A Contact List entry contains the sender's account certificate; after you have an account's certificate, you can send encrypted mail to that account. Outlook 2000 requires users to manually add senders to their Contact List or personal address book (PAB), and users must have personal S/MIME certificates to send encrypted messages.

Chapter Summary

This chapter explored the many facets and new improvements involved in designing an Exchange 2000 security plan. Once you have the following sources of information, you can begin planning your security design:

➤ Recent documentation on your existing Exchange security design

➤ The present Windows 2000 security architecture

➤ Your current network security architecture

➤ Knowledge of the external information that will influence your security design, including legal factors and requirements

➤ Strategies that will later be fully implemented in your existing Exchange design

Security processes in Exchange 2000 are different than processes you'll find in Exchange 5.5. Exchange 2000 relies on Windows 2000 for applying permissions to the organization. In addition, only one level of permissions needs to be considered. Both the public folder permissions and the connector permissions, for example, are configured using Windows 2000 accounts or groups. The tightest security structure may be one in which you have two-way trusts between all domains that are hosting your Exchange 2000 servers and your Exchange 5.5 servers. You can then add trusts between your Windows NT 4 account domains and your Exchange 2000 servers as necessary. You need to be aware of the implications of coexistence as you design your Exchange 2000 security model. If you are designing your architecture for coexistence between Exchange 5.5 and Exchange 2000, you will increase the number of Windows trusts that you need to maintain.

Exchange 2000 Server comes with a plethora of predefined permissions for groups of users reserved for administering Exchange 2000 and the Windows 2000 Server infrastructure. Assorted levels of administrative permissions are available within the groups that can assist you in assigning the best permissions to administrative users. The Exchange 2000 Server installation provides you with alternative methods to accommodate the typical separation of permissions between network administrators and messaging administrators found in many organizations. Also, you can assign different roles through the Exchange Administration Delegation Wizard. These include the Exchange Full Administrator, Exchange Administrator, and the Exchange View Only Administrator.

This chapter approached the concept of protection against internal attacks through the concept of permissions applied to the ADC service account. These permissions must include being a member of the Built-in\Administrators group, the Enterprise Admins if used only with Windows 2000, and the Enterprise Admins or Exchange Full Administrator role if used with Exchange 2000 Server.

This chapter illustrated how Exchange 2000 secures itself to external attacks by looking at several aspects of the KMS as well as a variety of scenarios that you may find comparable to your own organization. In Chapter 9, we move from our secure environment into a deeper level of configuration with the design of an Exchange 2000 Server Routing Group Topology.

Review Questions

1. Which mode will you implement in combination with the Exchange Server KMS to provide the highest level of automation for Outlook 2000?

   a. Exchange Mixed mode

   b. Exchange Native mode

   c. Internet Only mode

   d. Corporate/Workgroup mode

2. To protect against internal attacks, permissions should be applied to the Active Directory Connector service account. Which of the following memberships apply? [Check all correct answers]

   a. Built-in\Administrators group

   b. Enterprise Admins if used only with Windows 2000

   c. Enterprise Admins if used with Exchange 2000 Server

   d. Exchange Full Administrator role if used with Exchange 2000 Server

3. Which one of the following administrative tasks can be performed in Exchange 2000? [Check all correct answers]

   a. Set multiple-password policies to add and delete administrator accounts

   b. Recover and revoke user keys

   c. Change the support for X.509 version 1 or version 3 certificates

   d. Import and export user accounts

4. Which of the following represent the files that the Exchange KMS Key Export Wizard uses to log the results of the export and import processes? [Check all correct answers]

   a. filename.explog

   b. filename.implog

   c. export.log

   d. import.log

5. What component is the primary source of the Key Management Services troubleshooting information?

   a. Exchange 2000 Troubleshooter

   b. Windows 2000 Performance tool

   c. NT Event Viewer's application folder

   d. KMS MMC snap-in

6. Which of the following tools can you use to administer the KMS? [Check all correct answers]

   a. Use NT Event Viewer

   b. Implement the MMC Exchange System Manager snap-in

   c. Invoke Advanced Security as a standalone snap-in

   d. Employ Microsoft Systems Management Server (SMS)

8

7. What tool reports the users whose security tokens have been revoked and therefore should not be authenticated as secure?

   a. Certificate Returning Utility

   b. Certificate Trust List

   c. Token Revoking tool

   d. Certificate Revocation List

8. You are planning to run Outlook Web Access over SSL. Which one of the following components will you specifically need to install to achieve this added functionality?

   a. Internet Services Manager

   b. Web Server Certificate for IIS

   c. Mutual Authentication Mapper

   d. Microsoft Systems Management Server (SMS)

9. You want to support the Microsoft Enhanced Cryptographic Provider on your CA server in your Exchange 2000 infrastructure. Which one of the following components will you need?

   a. High Encryption Pack for Windows

   b. Trusted Root Certification Authority Component

   c. Microsoft Systems Management Server (SMS)

   d. Advanced Security Administration tool

10. Exchange 2000 Key Management Service generates X.509 version 3 user certificates for digital signature and encryption employed by Exchange 2000 and Outlook 2000. At which layer of the networking message architecture does Certificate Services provide security?

    a. Transport layer

    b. Network layer

    c. Application layer

    d. Physical layer

11. Which one of the following is *not* a main feature of the Key Management Service?

    a. Encryption

    b. Hash functions

    c. Ciphers

    d. Audits

    e. Certificates

12. Which of the following is an algorithm created in 1991 by professor Ronald Rivest that is used to create digital signatures and is intended for use with 32-bit machines?

    a. IPSec

    b. MD5

    c. SSL

    d. NTLM

13. Which encryption modes are supported by IPSec? [Check the two best answers]

    a. Data payload mode

    b. Transport mode

    c. Tunnel mode.

    d. Cipher mode

14. Which of the following is the de facto standard for secure messaging on the Internet and is the foundation for many public-key infrastructure deployments in organizations?

    a. MD5

    b. IPSec

    c. NTLM

    d. S/MIME

    e. Encrypted RPC

15. Of the four main types of cryptographic ciphers in use today, which one of the following ciphers is also called a public-key cipher and uses two keys: one key for encryption and another key for decryption?

    a. Symmetric

    b. Asymmetric

    c. Block

    d. Stream

Real-World Projects

Project 8.1

You have been hired specifically for the task of heading up the team in charge of designing the security server plan at a medium-sized manufacturing firm. Your team has collected data from your Exchange organization. You have mirrored your current environment as closely as possible, and you will need to expand your design to include other requirements that your system needs to satisfy. Briefly, describe what these requirements may entail so that you can include them in your report to middle management.

Project 8.2

As previously mentioned, many types of permissions exist that can be granted on a per-user or per-group basis. Review table Table 8.1 (in a previous section of this chapter) that shows the five predefined user groups with permissions already granted. The five predefined groups are Administrators, Authenticated Users, Domain Admins, Enterprise Admins, and Exchange Domain Servers. Describe briefly how you would delegate the groups in your organization and for what purpose. Break down the reasoning behind why you might need certain individual permissions.

Project 8.3

You are using the Exchange Administration Delegation Wizard to smooth the progress of the delegation of control of Exchange configuration objects in Active Directory. You decide to dispense the tasks of managing different parts of Exchange 2000 to different users. Describe the three administrative roles you can assign, as well as why you have chosen the certain individuals. Create a memo for your manager to justify your decision.

Project 8.4

There are four main types of cryptographic ciphers in use today: symmetric, asymmetric, block, and stream. Your boss has no idea about forms of cryptography. Put together a memo that briefly defines a cipher and also explains in lay terms the different forms, so that your boss will be better informed.

Project 8.5

The development of the Key Management Service in Exchange 2000 is the first step toward Advanced Security's complete integration into an enterprise Public Key Infrastructure. Because you are the team leader for security deployment in your organization, it's your duty to lay out this integration. Your managers are interested in how this fits into your interorganizational security model. Based on this chapter and other resources found in the appendix of this book, create a probable KMS scenario/solution for your interoffice email design. Be as thorough as possible in your report to management.

CHAPTER NINE

Designing an Exchange 2000 Server Routing Group Topology

After completing this chapter, you will be able to:

✓ Understand the overall Exchange 2000 Server routing group topology

✓ Have a grasp of deployment issues for routing groups

✓ Know when to use multiple routing groups

✓ Understand how to connect multiple routing groups

✓ Use routing groups with multiple folder trees

✓ Implement public folders in Active Directory with your routing topology

Overview of Message Routing in Exchange 2000

When you map out your Exchange 2000 Server routing topology, take into consideration the physical locations that you have, how they are connected, and whether you want to control the message flow. This task will be similar to designing Exchange sites in earlier versions of Exchange as well as designing Windows 2000 Active Directory sites. Your routing topology is central to the entire implementation of Exchange 2000 because it is one of the foundations of your messaging system. Therefore, you must prepare your routing topology with network, bandwidth, and geographical considerations in mind. You need to generate a routing topology that functions with your existing system's environment and network. You must design connectors for communicating with recipients outside of your organization. However, before delving into the particulars of designing the routing group topology, we first review some key concepts here.

The routing process for a message starts at the point when an Exchange 2000 server receives a message, through a connector or gateway, from a user, a different Exchange server, or another external messaging system. The Exchange 2000 server looks up the recipient in the Active Directory and routes the message on to the recipient. Exchange 2000 Server is built upon the Exchange Server 5.5 Message Transfer Agent (MTA), but further implements a full-featured Simple Mail Transfer Protocol (SMTP) transport for all of its native communications. The X.400 protocol supports such extra features as MIME Internet X.400 Enhanced Relay interoperability (see Request for Comments [RFC] 2156). In many scenarios, you will use the X.400 MTA to connect Exchange 2000 servers to other external X.400 systems. SMTP is used instead for native message transport between Exchange 2000 servers.

By using SMTP as the native communication method between Exchange 2000 servers, you can circumvent some of the deployment challenges of earlier implementations. For instance, environments with a distributed user base typically design their Exchange 5.5 site models using available network bandwidth instead of designing them for administrative expediency because all Exchange 5.5 servers within a site use remote procedure calls (RPCs) to communicate with one another. Also, low-bandwidth and high-latency networks are unproductive for the synchronous nature of RPCs. Because Exchange 2000 Server does not use RPC to transfer messages, you can create a more flexible routing topology even when low-bandwidth and high-latency networks are a practical necessity.

Routing Groups

Routing groups are simply collections of Exchange 2000 servers connected over reliable and permanent links. If you have a collection of several Exchange 2000 servers linked by full-time, reliable connections, then you have a routing group. As previously mentioned, Exchange 2000 Server uses SMTP, rather than RPC, as its primary proto-col. With SMTP, it is not as important to have a high-bandwidth connection between servers. In addition, SMTP is more reliable than RPC over restricted bandwidth connections. It is of greater significance for servers in a routing group to have perma-nent, reliable connectivity than to have high bandwidth between them.

Within routing groups, all mail is transferred in a straightforward manner among servers. If you have a single Exchange 2000 server, or if all of your servers are connected over a full-time high-bandwidth link, you will not need to define multiple routing groups. Even if you are not planning to deploy routing groups, however, you will still find the topics in this chapter useful for understanding how Exchange 2000 transfers messages within your organization as well as for planning for future growth of your messaging infrastructure. Some of the chief advantages of separating your Exchange 2000 server into routing groups are to gain control over the mail flow, to troubleshoot message transfer between server groups, and to track messages.

Note: *Exchange 2000 servers in the same routing group have full-time high-bandwidth connectivity. This allows servers in the routing group to correspond directly with each other and permits messages sent between any two servers to be routed directly from source to destination.*

A single group of servers with full-time high-bandwidth connectivity requires no special routing groups. In this case, you might consider generating routing groups between these servers to control the message flow across political or departmental boundaries. You must define the routing groups in the Routing Groups area of the Exchange 2000 System Microsoft Management Console (MMC) snap-in. If you fail to do this, the group will not appear, and instead you will see only the Connec-tions container.

If you are upgrading an existing Exchange 5.x site to Exchange 2000, the Exchange site will automatically convert into a single administrative group and a single routing group. Both of the groups will have the same name as the existing site name. This occurs because Exchange 5.x uses the X.500 protocol for address resolution, and the X.500 distinguished name (DN) refers to the site name. In Exchange 2000 Server, however, the DN refers to the adminis-trative group. Although Exchange 2000 Server can coexist with previous versions of Exchange, you are able to create new routing groups or transport servers between routing groups only if the servers are members of a single administrative group.

Routing Group Naming

When naming your routing group, choose a unique name that relates directly to the server's purpose or locality. Use a name that you will not need to change in order to have room for any broad modifications to the organizational or corporate business model. This is important because routing group names are not easy to change. Your routing group names can have up to 64 characters, with the exclusion of a few characters.

Communication between routing groups is often managed over slower (or intermittent) links. You might need to use a connector to connect two routing groups. You can choose any of three connectors, which are discussed in the section "Connecting Routing Groups" later in this chapter: the Routing Group Connector (recommended), the SMTP Connector, and the X.400 Connector.

Message Routing and Global Catalogs

All message routing information, including data for routing groups and bridgehead servers, is held in the configuration-naming context of the Windows 2000 Active Directory. To make a routing choice, the Exchange Server contacts a local domain controller and subsequently retrieves the information. If a message is sent to a universal group, the SMTP virtual server that is configured to carry out the expansion uses Lightweight Directory Access Protocol (LDAP) to contact a global catalog and thus fill the message header with the group membership information. If the message is heading for a domain local or global group, the expansion server should be in the same domain as that group and should be configured to use only global catalogs from the local domain in which the group resides.

All Exchange servers will attempt to use global catalogs from their local domain and site by default. However, if not enough global catalogs exist in the local domain and site, Exchange extends the scope and requests global catalogs from the local site only. Exchange 2000 prefers to use the global catalogs that are closest; however, if they become unavailable, it will use a global catalog not from the same domain as a domain local or global group. This can result in email not being sent to the membership of the domain local or global group. In this situation, Exchange 2000 may use 10 or more global catalogs from the local domain in the same site as the expansion server. Conversely, no global catalogs from any other domain should exist in that site. If this is the case, however, DS Access should be configured to employ only global catalogs from the same domain as the expansion server and the global or domain local group.

Routing Messages within the Same Server

When an Exchange 2000 server figures out that a recipient is on the same server as the sender, Exchange 2000 delivers the message to the recipient's mailbox in the following manner:

1. The Messaging Application Programming Interface (MAPI) client transmits the message.

2. The message goes to the advanced queuing engine regardless of whether it is local or remote.

3. The advanced queuing engine deposits the message in the "pre-categorizer" queue.

4. The message "categorizer" grabs the message from the pre-categorizer queue and processes the message. The categorizer expands groups when necessary and checks the sender and recipient limits.

5. The message categorizer drops the message in the local delivery queue if the recipient is local.

6. The Web Storage System associates the message with the recipient's mailbox.

Routing Group Topology

In Exchange 5.5 and earlier versions, the Exchange site made up the boundary for both the administrative and routing topologies. With Exchange 2000 Server, the server model is collectively controlled by means of the administrative group. In addition to this change, a routing group now handles single-hop routing. You can place an Exchange 2000 server into an administrative group for management purposes, but it does not have to belong to one of the routing groups listed within the administrative group. A single administrative group can actually contain all of the routing groups within the organization. In addition, you can authorize other administrative groups to administer the day-to-day management of a subset of the larger administrative group.

The site concept in earlier versions of Exchange defined three separate boundaries:

➤ Single-hop routing

➤ Collective administration unit

➤ Namespace hierarchy

To offer a more flexible deployment and administration configuration, in Exchange 2000 Server, all three boundaries are separate:

➤ A routing group defines single-hop routing.

➤ An administrative group defines collective administration.

➤ The namespace hierarchy exists in Active Directory in the form of a domain.

When administrating Exchange 2000 messaging systems, you will regularly work with administrative groups and routing groups. Routing groups are logically located beneath administrative groups. The routing and administration models were tied together in Exchange Server 5.5. In Exchange 2000, however, a relationship exists between routing groups and administrative groups. Within an administrative group, you can configure the servers so that a few of them route messages directly to one another, whereas others forward the messages to a bridgehead server.

As you have probably discovered, the configuration-naming context within Active Directory is responsible for storing all administrative group, routing group, connector, and cost information. Therefore, all routing information is accessible to the whole Exchange 2000 organization because the naming context is entirely replicated among all domain controllers within the Active Directory forest. Although every Exchange Server can automatically become aware of all other servers within the organization, you must still define the connections between servers to allow for flexible routing.

To create ample load balancing and fault tolerance for your organization, you can configure multiple connectors between two routing groups. Exchange 2000 Server offers several ways to route mail outside your organization. You can route mail to the Internet or to other SMTP systems within an organization by using an SMTP Connector, or you can route to an X.400 provider or other X.400 systems by using an X.400 Connector. You can also connect to any of the following non-Exchange systems by using the appropriate connector:

➤ cc:Mail

➤ Lotus Notes

➤ MSMail

An enterprise-messaging system must be fast, scalable, and reliable, so it must depend on a strong underlying transport and routing engine. Exchange 2000 Server is built on the legacy of the Exchange MTA, yet it also uses a full-featured SMTP transport for all native communications. However, not all Windows 2000 native mode organizations will provide for the needs of users because they may also need to connect to foreign systems. Thus, by using SMTP as the native communication method between Exchange servers, you open up a number of new opportunities. In this case, your message system may require a mixed-mode type of Windows 2000 organization, complete with routing groups that are linked together and replicated across the entire Exchange organization.

Routing Group Design Factors

Message traffic analysis should be a major aspect of your ongoing routing group design. It can provide helpful information about which servers most often communicate with each other. You may want to consider placing servers that communicate on a regular basis into the same routing group. When designing routing groups, however, do not base the design exclusively on traffic analysis; also look at the management overhead for the most efficient solution. Other factors that can impact the design of a routing group include the following:

➤ Routing groups are dynamic and they can change at any time.

➤ Servers may be connected over slow, reliable links as part of the same routing group.

➤ The routing group architecture determines the public folder access.

Before rolling out the messaging system, you should reflect on other facets of the new routing transport architecture in Exchange 2000 Server. To be precise, you should consider the answers to the following questions:

➤ Are you capable of creating hundreds of routing groups without negatively affecting the remaining Exchange organization?

➤ Will you implement the same routing group design that you did with your past Exchange sites?

➤ Will your routing group design affect any other workings of Exchange?

➤ Is your SMTP data transfer going to exceed that of the messages sent with Exchange Server 5.5?

➤ If your network is in a state of constant change, is it possible for the link state data to overwhelm your infrastructure with status messages?

➤ What options are available to you for connecting routing groups?

➤ What protocol should you use when having Exchange 2000 servers coexist with Exchange 5.x servers?

Questions such as these should help you realize that you must approach the design and planning differently when deploying Exchange 2000 Server than you did with earlier versions of Exchange. Remember that servers must have permanent connectivity between them if they are placed alone in a solitary routing group. The messages will be delivered without delay in a single hop with no messaging delivery scheduling. Servers in the same routing group communicate directly with each other. The following rules apply to servers within the same routing group:

➤ Servers running Exchange must belong to the identical Active Directory forest.

➤ Servers running Exchange must have permanent and stable direct connectivity to one another.

➤ All servers within a routing group must be able to make contact with the routing group master.

When the server determines that the recipient's mailbox is on a different server within the same routing group, the routing process is slightly more complicated than when messages are routed within the same server. If the message recipient's server runs Exchange 2000, the message is routed through SMTP to the recipient's server. If the message recipient's server is running an earlier version of Exchange, the message is routed to the recipient's servers using RPC protocols. Regardless of the protocol in use, however, message transfer within a routing group is point-to-point. In other words, the originating server communicates directly with the recipient's server. The Web Storage System running on the sender's server routes the message though SMTP to the recipient's server in the same routing group. The recipient's server receives the message and delivers the message to the recipient's mailbox.

When the recipient's mailbox is on a server in a different routing group, the message must be transferred over a routing group connector. The sender's server identifies a route for the message to take and routes the message to the appropriate bridgehead server. That bridgehead server sends the message to the bridgehead server in the recipient's routing group. The receiving bridgehead server routes the message to the recipient's server. This method of routing is also referred to as "store and forward."

Multiple Routing Groups

If you have a single physical location and all of the servers are connected through a reliable, permanent link, you might not need to implement multiple routing groups. You might need multiple routing groups, nonetheless, if your network connectivity is unreliable, if you want to schedule messaging between two locations, if you want to control the message paths in an Exchange organization, or if you want to control public folder referrals.

Using Multiple Routing Groups Bridgehead servers function with special connectors to transfer messages between routing groups. They are similar to the site connectors that transfer messages between sites in previous versions of Exchange. A distinct routing group connector, which identifies a logical channel between routing groups, must be created in both directions. From a topological point of view, routing groups are equivalent to sites in earlier versions of Exchange. By sorting out servers into routing groups, you are able to control email flow, troubleshoot message transfer between groups of servers, and track messages. The Exchange 2000 Server routing and selection process implements a link state table to determine the shortest path between two routing groups from a given message. If a connection fails between two routing groups, Exchange will update the link state table and inform all servers throughout the organization. We revisit the link state mechanism in greater detail in the section "Link State Tables" later in this chapter.

Determining a Route through Multiple Routing Groups

If multiple routing groups exist within an organization, the sending server uses the link state table to determine the best route based on connection cost and status. The message then goes through the appropriate bridgehead servers until it reaches the destination routing group. Each bridgehead server repeats the routing and selection process by referencing the link state table. It then routes the message to the next bridgehead server. This process repeats until the message arrives at the recipient's routing group. Depending on the path a message must take to arrive at the recipient's mailbox, the message might travel through multiple servers and routing groups. If multiple routes have the same cost, the server chooses a random route to provide load balancing.

The route the message takes is as follows:

1. The message is sent from the sending user's server to the bridgehead server in routing group A that connects to the bridgehead server in routing group B.

2. The bridgehead server in routing group B receives the message, and sends the message to routing group C through its bridgehead server connected to routing group C.

3. The bridgehead server in routing group C receives the message and sends it to the recipient's server.

Routing Group Connectors function only within an Exchange organization. If a message must be transferred to a recipient whose mailbox resides on another messaging system or within another Exchange organization, the message must transfer over a connector that connects to that other system. The message might need to travel through one or more routing groups before finding a bridgehead server that hosts a connector to that messaging system. It is not necessary for a routing group in an Exchange organization to host connectors to every other system.

Link State Tables

A *link state table* is defined as a database that stores the up/down status of a server. It also contains the costs of the connections between servers. The link state table replaces the Gateway Address Resolution Table (GWART). The Exchange 2000 link state table delivers an efficient system for routing messages as well as preventing the bouncing and looping (ping-pong) effect if a link has failed. The link state table provides the data for determining the route a message takes between servers and is replicated between all servers in all routing groups. The link state table is housed on each server running Exchange 2000 and contains the status of each connector in the Exchange 2000 infrastructure. If a server running Exchange 2000 cannot locate a route for a particular message after referring to a link state table, it will not even attempt to deliver the message. With this flexibility, however, come additional complexities in planning and properly grouping servers within a routing group.

To formulate a proficient routing group, for example, you must analyze messaging traffic to determine which groups of users communicate with each other most often. Suppose public folder replication traffic has been steadily flowing between the marketing department and the operations department. By placing the servers for those departments within the same routing group, you could create a more efficient environment. In the case of a permanent connection between Exchange 2000 servers, however, such an approach may not be practicable.

As another example, take into consideration a situation in which a company's branch office Exchange 2000 servers are connected to the North American head-quarters by a slower link. A full-mesh topology would not be effective when a slower or a nonpermanent network link is introduced into this physical topology. In this case, servers in the headquarters can be grouped into one routing group, and servers in the branch offices can be placed in a separate routing group. Within each routing group, servers are connected by high-speed, permanent connections, with a slower or intermittent connection between the two groups.

Link State Algorithm

Exchange 2000 figures out the route that messages will take based on a "least cost" basis. Although Exchange 2000 uses routes and costs, it also uses a link propagation protocol, called the link state algorithm (LSA), which determines the actual message routes. Remember that a server running Exchange 2000 also has a diagram of the entire message topology of which it is a member. This map is represented in the link state table and gets updated regularly. Subsequently, this mapping is disseminated among all of the servers so that each can determine the least expensive way to deliver a message as well as whether all of the connectors are functioning properly. The available routes and costs in the organization are available to any Exchange 2000 server.

Only two states exist for any given link in an Exchange 2000 organization: up or down. Exchange 2000 does not propagate connection information, such as whether a link is active or in a retry state. This information is known only on the server involved in the message transfer. The LSA is accountable for propagating the condition of the messaging system in almost real time to all Exchange 2000 servers. This situation has several advantages. Every Exchange 2000 server will make the best routing choices at the time it receives a message by using the most current data from the link state table. Therefore, messages are not sent along a path with a failed link. In addition, the LSA removes the likelihood for message bounce and loops between multiple servers. This is made possible because each Exchange 2000 server knows if other alternate or redundant links are up or down.

Link State Propagation

Link state data is distributed between routing groups through SMTP on port 25, and within the routing group by using Transmission Control Protocol (TCP) port 691. If the connection status changes, the link state table is updated by the following method:

1. The bridgehead server with the new connection status labels the connector as "up" or "down" in the link state table.

2. The bridgehead server updates the routing group master over TCP port 691.

Routing Group Masters

You designate a server to be the routing group master for a routing group. The routing group master maintains the link state information received from different sources. The routing group master collates this data and makes it available to other servers within the routing group by using propagation algorithms. Although the first server added to a routing group is automatically designated the routing group master, you can change this behavior by using the Exchange System Manager utility. If the routing group master fails, you must nominate a new routing group master. The servers running Exchange 2000 in the routing group continue to use the existing link state table, without updates, until the original routing group master comes back online or a new routing group master is designated.

9

Tip: You can view the status of connectors by using System Manager: click Tools, and then click Monitoring and Status.

3. The routing group master updates its link state table and updates all of the other servers running Exchange 2000 in the routing group over TCP port 691.

4. All other bridgehead servers in the routing group update the routing groups to which they are connected over TCP port 25.

5. The bridgehead servers then update their routing group masters over TCP port 691, and so on until all routing groups are updated. Exchange 2000 Server uses an SMTP command rather than a message to transfer link state status.

This link state apparatus offers a flexible way to design routing groups, predominantly by allowing multiple paths between routing groups. In earlier versions of Exchange, most site topologies were hub-and-spoke, with only a single connector between the hub and each spoke. This took into account the possible message bouncing that occurs when sites have multiple routes between them. In contrast, Exchange 2000 uses the link state table, which renders this topology unnecessary because messages do not bounce back and forth. If a connector fails, the message can be rerouted through another routing group, and will bounce back to the original routing group because Exchange determines if the connector is down and propagates that information around the organization.

Connecting Routing Groups

Multiple routing groups may be necessary if network traffic is unreliable due to saturation or other network issues. In addition, you may want to manage the message conduits in your Exchange infrastructure or schedule messaging between two locales. If you have a single physical location and all of the servers are connected through a reliable, permanent link, however, you may not need to put multiple routing groups into operation.

Routing groups are coupled together using connectors. The following three connectors for routing groups are available with Exchange 2000 Server:

➤ Routing Group Connector

➤ SMTP Connector

➤ X.400 Connector

The Routing Group Connector can connect only routing groups, and it provides the simplest and easiest way to connect two routing groups. It is similar in function to the Site Connector in earlier versions of Exchange. However, the Routing Group Connector uses SMTP message transport protocol rather than RPCs to deliver messages. Benefits of the Routing Group Connector include the following:

➤ It is easy to configure.

➤ You can configure it with multiple target bridgehead servers.

➤ You can use it to connect to earlier versions of Exchange that are configured with the Site Connector, which uses RPCs.

You should use SMTP Connectors when the following conditions exist:

➤ The remote server connector is the Internet Mail Service (IMS) from earlier versions of Exchange.

➤ A pull relationship is required between servers in which one side queues messages and the other side pulls them by using the **TRN** or **ETRN** command.

➤ You want to define Transport Layer Security (TLS) or other security parameters.

Other connectors provide connections to external systems in addition to connecting routing groups within the Exchange 2000 organization. When you configure a connector on a server, the connector is included in the routing process for messages destined outside of the routing group. Servers running Exchange 2000 that host routing group connectors are called bridgehead servers. All messages that are delivered through routing groups pass through the bridgehead server that hosts the Routing Group Connector.

Tip: You cannot use connectors designed for third-party email systems to connect routing groups.

Planning Routing Group Boundaries

The necessary prerequisites for grouping Exchange 2000 servers into a routing group are permanent, reliable network connections, and contact to the routing group master.

You would divide Exchange 2000 servers into multiple routing groups for any of the following situations:

➤ Routing group prerequisites are incompatible.

➤ Network connections are unreliable.

➤ The messaging path must be altered from single-hop to multi-hop.

➤ Messages must be queued and sent on a schedule.

➤ Low-bandwidth network connections exist for which X.400 connectivity is more appropriate.

➤ Client connections to public folders exist.

When calculating available bandwidth, first answer the following questions:

➤ Do any groups of users transmit huge messages on a regular basis?

➤ What is the average size of messages that travel across the network?

➤ Which public folders do users use?

As you can see, you can group multiple locations together to form single routing groups, although you need to be aware of the impact this has on client connections to public folders. Routing Group Connectors offer the best feature set and the highest level of flexibility. Each Routing Group Connector uses the concept of source and target bridgehead servers. To get the maximum efficiency from the network, you can configure bridgehead servers so that all connections occur over a single network link. In contrast to the Site Connector in Exchange 5.5, multiple target bridgehead servers specified on a connector are not used in a cost-weighted system. Nor are they used sequentially. When message transfer occurs, a local bridgehead server accesses the list of target servers and selects the one at the top of the list. If the first server is unavailable, then the bridgehead server uses the second server, and so on. Successive messages use this same algorithm.

9

Bridgehead Servers

Each SMTP Connector can specify multiple bridgehead servers within each routing group. All messages from the bridgehead servers to the target routing group are either delivered directly after mail exchange (MX) resolution by the Domain Name System (DNS) or are forwarded to a smart host. You can configure the Routing Group Connector with one or more bridgehead servers on either end of the connector. This allows you to control which servers send and which receive messages between routing groups. An advantage of having multiple servers identified as bridgehead servers for a Routing Group Connector is that if a bridgehead server is not functioning, Exchange can choose another bridgehead server within the routing group to transmit the message.

Messaging Security

Exchange 2000 Server provides SMTP authentication between bridgehead servers. Message encryption between bridgehead servers is disabled by default. If encryption is required, you can implement Internet Protocol Security (IPSec), which is a standard encryption method for TCP/IP network security.

Resolving the Target Server IP Address

Exchange 2000 server performs MX record resolution for SMTP, but, more often than not, it finds the target server by using an A (host) record. This simplifies the arrangement of the Routing Group Connector because an Exchange or DNS administrator does not have to create or manage MX records. The SMTP Connector first tries to find the destination server by using DNS MX records. If an MX record does not exist, the sending server attempts to resolve the destination server's IP address by using the host name resolution process, which includes querying DNS for an A record. If it still does not find the destination server, the bridgehead resolves the IP address by using the network basic input/output system (NetBIOS) name resolution process.

When a bridgehead server that hosts the Routing Group Connector receives a message to transport across the connector, the bridgehead server tries to resolve the target server's IP address by using the typical SMTP resolution process just described. In other words, the bridgehead server first attempts to resolve the target server defined on the Routing Group Connector by using DNS MX records. If no MX records exist for the target server, a DNS query for an A record is performed for the target server. The result is that an A record must exist in DNS for all servers running Exchange. The Windows 2000 DNS service registers A records for all servers running Windows 2000 Server, counting all Exchange 2000 servers. If an A record for the target server is not found, the bridgehead server tries to resolve the

IP address by using the NetBIOS name resolution process. When numerous target servers exist for a Routing Group Connector, Exchange 2000 Server intercepts the request, looks up the bridgehead servers, and returns them to SMTP before SMTP resolves the MX record against a DNS server.

When multiple servers exist for an SMTP Connector, Exchange 2000 intercepts the request, looks up the target servers, and returns them to SMTP before SMTP resolves the MX record against a DNS server. You can optimize the message transport to a greater extent with an SMTP Connector than you can with a Routing Group Connector. SMTP Connector options include authenticating remote domains before sending email, designating specific times when email can send, and setting multiple permissions levels for multiple users on the connector.

Using a Smart Host or DNS Resolution of an MX Record

A smart host is a go-between host that uses DNS to resolve the destination host's IP address and then sends the message to the destination host. The smart host server must be able to process email for the remote address space or routing group that the SMTP Connector needs to reach. The SMTP Connector relays all messages through the smart host, which in turn passes them on to the remote destination by using DNS.

A smart host is accommodating for messages traveling between servers on the Internet—for example, when the remote domain can be reached infrequently or only at certain times. Instead of continually contacting the domain until a connection is made, the server running Exchange needs to transport only to the smart host. The smart host then makes the remote connection. If a smart host is not chosen, a DNS lookup is made on every address to which the SMTP Connector sends email.

Note: *If you use an IP address to identify the smart host, enclose the address in brackets ([ ]) to increase system performance. The SMTP service first checks for a server name, then an IP address. The brackets identify the value as an IP address, so that it bypasses the DNS lookup.*

You can also configure the SMTP Connector to recover queued email from a remote SMTP server at specific time intervals. This means, in essence, that you can configure a remote domain to accept and hold email on behalf of the destination domain. Messages sent to the remote domain are held until the SMTP **ETRN** command is received from an authorized account on your local Exchange 2000 server. You can also use the **ETRN** command to remove email from a queue. You select Request ETRN/TRN when sending messages, then select the times you want the SMTP Connector to contact the remote domain and trigger the delivery of queued email.

9

Rerouting Mail

If a connection fails between routing groups, messages are automatically rerouted. The message reroute process works as follows:

1. The sender's server sends the message to the bridgehead server in routing group B that then connects to routing group A.

2. The bridgehead server in routing group A attempts to open an SMTP connection to the bridgehead server in routing group C. This connection fails.

3. If multiple destination bridgehead servers are specified on the connector in routing group C, the local bridgehead server in routing group A attempts to open a connection between each of those servers until either it finds a connection or no more servers are available.

4. If the link between routing group A and routing group C is still not functioning after three connection attempts, the bridgehead server marks the connection as down and propagates the link state information.

5. The bridgehead server in routing group A calculates an alternative route to routing group C through routing group D.

6. The message is rerouted from routing group A to routing group C through routing group D.

Retries

The operating bridgehead server will continue to attempt the connection until it is restored. You should take into consideration the following factors if you are tracking a message or working on a failed connection:

➤ If all of the routes to the destination routing group stop working, the cost of the connection is then set to infinite. The active bridgehead server checks on the status of the links three times, at 60-second intervals. Next, the active bridgehead server retries according to the schedule set on the Delivery tab of the SMTP virtual server. If the failed connection becomes available again, it designates the connection as being "up" in the link state table.

➤ Exchange 2000 holds messages meant for the failed routing group in the local message queues. Exchange does not send messages through routing groups to a routing group that has no functional connectors. If the expiration time-out specified on the Delivery tab of the SMTP virtual server exceeds 48 hours, then the messages return to the originators as nondelivered.

➤ When Exchange sends a message to a connector (or gateway) for another system, such as MSMail, it considers the message officially delivered when it reaches the connector, and rerouting does not occur, even if the other system connector is unable to deliver the message.

➤ Exchange does not reroute a message routed to a connector with a remote initiated activation schedule unless the activation schedule changes before the message is delivered.

➤ Exchange stores a retry count on each message for each connector that it attempts. When a message fails to connect to the remote system, Exchange increments the retry count and immediately reroutes the message. If Exchange cannot deliver the message after it tries all of the connectors, or it reaches the maximum number of retries, it returns the message with a nondelivery report (NDR).

Recovering a Connection

When a connection fails, the bridgehead server with the failed connector continues to repeat the connection attempt three times at 60-second intervals. It then retries according to the schedule set on the Delivery tab of the SMTP virtual server. Although messages are rerouted, the bridgehead server continues to try to open port 25 on the destination server. After a connection is reestablished, the bridgehead server alerts the local routing group master that the connection is available. The routing group master, in turn, notifies all of the servers in the routing group that the connection is available. Finally, all of the bridgehead servers in the routing group notify the bridgehead servers to which they are linked in neighboring routing groups.

9

Managing Public Folders

Multiple folder trees and public folders also relate to designing an Exchange 2000 Server routing topology. As previously discussed, with Exchange 2000 Server, you can make use of multiple public folder trees to guarantee efficiency, and you are afforded several options to successfully administer these trees. Exchange 2000 Server offers administrative power and flexibility by sustaining multiple public folder trees, also known as top-level hierarchies.

Managing public folders includes determining which public folders to mail-enable, and creating public folder replicas and referrals. The following sections describe the management tasks necessary to optimize your public folder hierarchy. For instance, you can generate a segregated public folder tree to work in concert with external users and keep that content separate from the default public folder tree. You can create an extra tree at a remote location, as well, for users at that site to access information that is pertinent only to them. Each public folder tree stores its data in a single public folder store per server. You can replicate specific folders in the tree to every server in the organization that has a public folder store associated with that public folder tree.

Support Considerations

When planning your routing group architecture, you should consider the following if you want to support multiple public folder trees:

➤ Exchange generates the default public folder tree on every public folder server. It also always replicates its list of folders. Additional public folder trees have an effect only on the servers on which they are configured. As a result, you can create a set of departmental or local folders on only one server or a subset of servers. You do not need not replicate these additional public folders to every public folder server.

➤ You can use additional public folder trees to minimize the overall size of the default public folder tree, which simplifies navigation and reduces the cost of replicating the hierarchy of the default tree.

Client Support

When you install Exchange 2000 Server, it creates the default All Public Folders Tree. This tree is available to all MAPI, IMAP4 (Internet Message Access Protocol 4), NNTP (Network News Transfer Protocol), and HTTP (Hypertext Transfer Protocol) clients. Additional public folder trees are available only to NNTP and Web clients, not to clients such as Outlook 2000 (unless viewed on a Web page hosted in Outlook 2000). You can use non-MAPI-accessible folders for collaboration with browsers and applications (e.g., Microsoft Office 2000) that can use HTTP to access the Web Storage System.

Latency Issues

The record of public folders in the Global Address List (GAL) and Exchange System Manager is controlled by Exchange Server services that are different from the ones that manage public folder replication. As a result, the following situations might occur:

➤ When you administer the same public folder tree on two different servers, you do not see exactly the same list of folders. This means that changes to the public folder hierarchy, such as a new, renamed, or deleted folder, are not yet replicated among all servers.

➤ Public folders appear in the hierarchy with the client, but you cannot see them in the address book. If you cannot view a public folder in the address book, the address list has not yet been regenerated because the folder is mail-enabled (or you might need to restart the client).

➤ The Public Folder Properties dialog box in Exchange System Manager does not show the directory-specific pages. This results when the replication of the public folder hierarchy has occurred faster than the relocation of the newly created directory data, which includes the address information.

Public Folders in Active Directory

You can configure every public folder in a public folder store to materialize as a mail recipient in Active Directory. When planning your routing topology, note that the following conditions can occur after you mail-enable a public folder:

➤ The System Attendant connects to Active Directory and generates an object for the public folder in a container, such as Users. This container is designated on the General tab of the properties configuration of the public folder tree and applies to all public folders in the tree.

➤ A directory entry exists with a name consisting of Folder Name + Global Unique Identifier. Users with access to Active Directory can use the email address properties of the object to send email to the public folder.

➤ Additional tabs are available for the public folder in the Exchange System Manager, and the Active Directory Users and Computers snap-in. These tabs are designated E-mail Addresses, Exchange General, and Exchange Advanced.

➤ You can configure the page to appear in the GAL for such clients as Outlook.

Note: In Exchange Server 5.5, public folders are placed in the directory by default, but they do not display in the GAL. In an Exchange 2000 mixed-mode environment, however, this does not occur. New public folders are mail-enabled and configured as visible in the GAL. If you run Exchange 2000 in native mode, new public folders are not mail-enabled, by default.

9

Public Folder Replicas

When you create a public folder, only one copy of the public folder will exist in the organization. A public folder can exist in an organization either as a single copy or as multiple copies. Multiple copies are known as replicas. Public folder replicas offer redundant data points as well as load balancing for information access. A replica, which is copied from one server to another, is a separate instance of a public folder and its contents. When designing your Exchange 2000 environment, you might need to create additional replicas of system folders to control your network traffic. This can be a contributing factor to designing your routing group topology as well. Table 9.1 describes common system folders that are created on a server when it is installed as the first server in an administrative group.

Connecting to a Public Folder Replica

When a client attempts to access public folder data, the client must be able to connect to a server that contains a replica of the data. The client will try to attach to any replica to give the requested data to the user. To take full advantage of efficiency, the client attempts a connection to servers in the following order:

Table 9.1 Common system folders.

Folder Name	Description
Reforms Registry	Storage for forms saved to the Organization Forms Library.
Events Root	Contains scripts for an Exchange Server 5.5–compatible event service.
Offline Address Book	Stores offline address books for clients to download.
Schedule + Free Busy	Stores schedule information for clients to download.
Schema	Defines properties for objects kept in the public folder store.
StoreEvents	Contains Exchange 2000 event sink code for a specific server.
System Configuration	

1. The default public folder store for the clients. The default public folder store is determined by the configuration of the mailbox store containing the user's mailbox. If the default public folder store is not accessible, the client receives a list of servers that include the replica.

2. A server to which the client has an existing connection.

3. Each server within the same server routing group as the public folder server routing group for the client.

4. Other routing groups. If the client cannot connect, the Web Storage System instructs the client to try to connect to other routing groups in the order of the routing group connection values.

5. Random selection. The servers containing the replicas are pooled together and selected at random as if they were in the same routing group because the connections to routing groups have the same cost.

Public Folder Referrals

Public folder referrals are significant to the design because they allow you to route information and requests to explicit folders. You can allow public folder referrals to servers in another routing group by implementing and configuring a Routing Group Connector between the two routing groups. The Routing Group Connector is in one direction only. It requires the configuration of two instances for bidirectional traffic. You can, however, configure public folder referrals for the routing group going in each direction. Public folder referrals between routing groups are transitive and allow all referrals over the connection when enabled.

Chapter Summary

This chapter presented a broad overview of some of the key factors to consider when designing an Exchange 2000 server routing group topology. When you generate a diagram of your routing group topology, take into account all of your organization's physical locations, the way they are connected, and if you will need to manage the message flow. This process is similar to designing Exchange sites in earlier versions of Exchange as well as designing Windows 2000 Active Directory sites.

The message routing process in Exchange 2000 proceeds as follows. It begins when the Exchange 2000 server gets a message via a connector or gateway from a user, a different Exchange server, or another external messaging system. Because Exchange 2000 Server does not use RPC to transfer messages, you can create a more flexible routing topology even when low-bandwidth and high-latency networks are a practical necessity. Exchange 2000 servers in the same routing group have full-time high-bandwidth connectivity. This permits servers in the routing group to communicate directly with each other, and allows messages sent between any two servers to be routed directly from source to destination. If you are upgrading an existing Exchange 5.x site to Exchange 2000, the Exchange 5.x site will automatically convert into a single administrative group and a single routing group. Both of the groups will have the exact same name as the existing site name because Exchange 5.x uses the X.500 protocol for address resolution, and the X.500 distinguished name (DN) refers to the same site.

This chapter also addressed interaction with Windows 2000 global catalog servers. All Exchange servers will try to use global catalogs from their local domain and site by default. However, if not enough global catalogs exist in the local domain and site, Exchange 2000 will expand the reach and will request global catalogs from the local site only. Exchange 2000 prefers to use the global catalogs that are nearest in proximity; however, if they become unavailable, it will use a global catalog that is not from the same domain as a domain local or global group.

Some important factors for routing group design discussed in this chapter are as follows: Routing groups are dynamic and they can change at any time. Also, servers can be connected over slow, reliable links as part of the same routing group. In addition, the routing group architecture determines the public folder access. The next chapter explores how to design interorganizational connectivity and synchronization processes.

Review Questions

1. You want to allow public folder referrals to servers in another routing group. How can you best accomplish this task?

    a. By implementing and configuring an ADC between the two routing groups

    b. By implementing and configuring circumference logging between the two routing groups

    c. By implementing and configuring consistency logging between the two routing groups

    d. By implementing and configuring a Routing Group Connector between the two routing groups

    e. By implementing and configuring a gateway between the bridgehead servers.

2. Which of the following common system folders is created on a server when it is installed as the first server in an administrative group and contains scripts for an Exchange Server 5.5–compatible event service?

   a. Reforms Registry

   b. Events Root

   c. Schema

   d. StoreEvents

3. When a connection fails, the bridgehead server with the failed connector continues to repeat the connection attempt how many times and at what intervals?

   a. 5 times at 60-second intervals

   b. 3 times at 60-second intervals

   c. 5 times at 45-second intervals

   d. 3 times at 45-second intervals

4. Which of the following factors should you take into consideration when you map out your routing topology?

   a. The physical locations that you have

   b. How the physical locations are connected

   c. Whether you want to control the message flow

   d. All of the above

5. Your organization has only a single group of servers with full-time high-bandwidth connectivity. What type of routing group is required?

   a. Single administrative groups

   b. Bidirectional routing groups

   c. No special routing groups are required

   d. Routing groups between these servers to control the message flow

6. How many characters can a routing group name have?

   a. Up to 256 characters

   b. Up to 240 characters

   c. Up to 218 characters

   d. Up to 64 characters

7. All Exchange servers will attempt to use global catalogs from their local domain and site by default. However, if not enough global catalogs exist in the local domain and site, what will Exchange do?

   a. Exchange will expand the scope and request global catalogs from a remote site.

   b. Exchange will expand the scope and request global catalogs from the local site only.

   c. Exchange will restrict the scope and request global catalogs from the local domain only.

   d. Exchange will not use the global catalogs.

8. When an Exchange 2000 server figures out that a recipient is on the same server as the sender, it delivers the message to the recipient's mailbox. First, the MAPI client transmits the message. Which of the following best reflects the next step, regardless of whether the message is local or remote?

   a. The message "categorizer" grabs the message from the pre-categorizer queue and processes the message.

   b. The message categorizer drops the message in the local delivery queue.

   c. The message goes to the advanced queuing engine.

   d. The Web Storage System associates the message with the recipient's mailbox.

9. The site design in earlier versions of Exchange defined three separate boundaries—single-hop routing, collective administration unit, and namespace hierarchy. Exchange 2000 Server provides a more flexible deployment and administration configuration. Which of the following statements is true concerning this feature? [Check all correct answers]

   a. All three boundaries are separate.

   b. An administrative group defines single-hop routing.

   c. A routing group defines collective administration.

   d. The namespace hierarchy exists in Active Directory in the form of a domain.

9

10. When you have servers within the same routing group, certain rules will apply. Which of the following represents an applicable rule in this scenario? [Check all correct answers]

    a. The servers running Exchange must belong to the identical Active Directory domain.

    b. The servers running Exchange must belong to the identical Active Directory forest.

    c. At least one server running Exchange must have a permanent and stable direct connectivity to the other servers.

    d. At least one server within a routing group needs to be able to make contact with the routing group master.

11. If multiple routing groups exist within an organization, which mechanism does the sending server use to determine the best route based on connection cost and status?

    a. Gateway Address Resolution Table

    b. Linking algorithm

    c. Link state table

    d. Bridgehead server

12. Which type of server would you designate to maintain the link state information received from different sources and make data available to other servers within the routing group using propagation algorithms?

    a. The routing group master

    b. The infrastructure master

    c. The Windows 2000 router

    d. The global catalog server

13. In which of the following conditions should you use SMTP Connectors to connect routing groups? [Check all correct answers]

    a. When the routing group connector is implemented between Windows 2000 forests.

    b. When the remote server connector is the Internet Mail Service from earlier versions of Exchange.

    c. When a pull relationship is required between servers in which one side queues messages and the other side pulls them by using the **TRN** or **ETRN** command.

    d. When you want to define Transport Layer Security (TLS).

14. Which of the following are valid reasons to divide Exchange 2000 servers into multiple routing groups? [Check all correct answers]

    a. Network connections are unreliable.

    b. Messages must be queued and sent on a schedule.

    c. Low-bandwidth network connections exist for which X.400 connectivity is more appropriate.

    d. Client connections to public folders exist.

    e. None of the above.

    f. a and c only.

15. To simplify the arrangement of the Routing Group Connector, which type of record resolution does Exchange 2000 Server perform more often than not?

    a. Mail exchange (MX) record

    b. A (host) record

    c. Name server (NS) record

    d. Start of authority (SOA) record

Real-World Projects

You are the training manager for a large multinational corporation based in the United States. The head of the deployment team has requested that you lead the training initiative for the primary phase of deployment. You will be creating training modules for the information technology (IT) support staff as well as other trainers and key individuals in all departments of your corporation. You will be using Microsoft PowerPoint presentation software or an equivalent.

Project 9.1

You are to train your deployment team on migrating from an Exchange 5.5 environment to Exchange 2000. Create a PowerPoint slide presentation, including text and graphics, to explain the process that occurs when messages are routed within the same Exchange 2000 server.

Project 9.2

The next presentation that you will create in your presentation software is supposed to help the IT staff design the routing group technology. Based on this chapter and supplementary resources, present some other factors that can impact the design of a routing group.

Project 9.3

Because your deployment will involve the upgrade of several servers from Exchange 5.5 to Exchange 2000, you must educate your staff on the important changes in Exchange/Windows 2000. The next presentation you create for key personnel will involve the replacement of the Gateway Address Resolution Table (GWART) with the link state table. Create a PowerPoint presentation that explains all of the key information about the link state table and associated algorithm.

Project 9.4

For this project, you will need to train the IT support staff on the fundamentals of planning the routing group boundaries. By using PowerPoint and its graphics capabilities, explain the necessary prerequisites when grouping Exchange 2000 servers into a routing group as well as the reasons to divide Exchange 2000 servers into multiple routing groups.

CHAPTER TEN

Designing Exchange 2000 Connectivity and Synchronization

After completing this chapter, you will be able to:

✓ Understand Exchange 2000 connectors in greater detail

✓ Know the viable options for connecting to other systems

✓ Configure VPN Access to Exchange 2000 Server

✓ Understand connection agreements

✓ Master replication and synchronization with the ADC

✓ Know the best practices for ADC replication

Chapter 9 explored the concepts and strategies involved with developing an effective routing group topology for an assortment of organizations. This chapter further investigates methods for designing connectivity and synchronization within and between organizations. The first topic of this chapter is a review of the different connector types and their uses. This is followed by a look at the design of connectivity between separate organizations by using a variety of connectors and protocols. The chapter then concludes with a necessary, in-depth view and review of the Active Directory Connector (ADC) and its implementation.

Review of Exchange 2000 Connectors

The form of connectivity required by your Exchange 2000 design will dictate the type of connector(s) that you choose. Chapter 9 revealed that when you connect two routing groups consisting of only Exchange 2000 servers, your best alternative is the Routing Group Connector (RGC). However, if you are connecting an Exchange 2000 Server to a previous Exchange release, if you are connecting to another organization's system, or if you want a higher level of flexibility, you might opt to implement a different connector type. The three major types of connectors used to attach routing groups *within* an organization are:

➤ Routing Group Connector

➤ SMTP Connector

➤ X.400 Connector

The Routing Group Connector Revisited

The Routing Group Connector is the connector of choice for linking groups in Exchange 2000. This connector is the counterpart to the site connector deployed in earlier versions of Exchange. The Routing Group Connector offers the most capable method for connecting two groups of servers because it requires smaller numbers of configuration settings and needs the connection of only two routing groups. The native transport for the Routing Group Connector is the Simple Mail Transfer Protocol (SMTP), and routing and next-hop information is held in the link state table. By design, the Routing Group Connector is unidirectional, so two of them must be generated to appropriately connect two routing groups together. The Exchange System Manager tool will automatically configure the corresponding connector when a Routing Group Connector is generated, if you so choose. A Routing Group Connector can have multiple bridgehead servers. However, if all of the mail in your organization flows through one computer, then a single bridgehead will be ample. You should employ multiple bridgehead servers in situations for which you need fault tolerance or load balancing. By using bridgehead servers, you can decide which servers send and receive messages between the routing groups.

You can even set up all of the servers in a routing group to carry out the role of a bridgehead server.

SMTP Connector

Exchange 2000 still relies on the remote procedure call (RPC) for communication with servers running earlier versions of Exchange. Conversely, the main purpose of SMTP is the task of providing messaging capabilities between an Exchange organization and a non-Exchange system or the Internet. SMTP serves three principal functions in your Exchange 2000 infrastructure:

➤ SMTP replicates data and transfers necessary information.

➤ Servers use SMTP to route messages.

➤ Clients use SMTP to submit messages.

Once you mount Exchange 2000 on a server system, you automatically include a routing engine that possesses amplified capabilities for message queuing with the SMTP service. Exchange further provides advanced address resolution functionality by activating and broadening the basic Windows 2000 message categorizing capability. This offers a finer level of control over the messaging system at every point during the transport process. Subsequently, SMTP connectors will connect one or more bridgehead servers directly to a smart host or to a remote server where the recipient addresses are stored. A smart host is a host that can constantly be reached using SMTP anywhere on the network. It relays messages and usually has a direct link to the destination. The SMTP Connector uses the Domain Name System mail exchanger (DNS MX) record to send messages to multiple servers in the non-Exchange system.

An SMTP Connector performs essentially the same functions as an RGC, although the SMTP connector is more flexible. SMTP Connectors comprise options for selecting definite times for sending specific mail and authenticating remote domains prior to sending mail. In addition, these connectors configure multiple permission levels for different users. When you create an SMTP Connector, you ought to consider that all outgoing messages for remote domains can be routed through a smart host as opposed to sending them directly to the domain. This provides for message routing over more direct links or less expensive connections than through other routing options. When generating an SMTP Connector, remember that when a Messaging Application Programming Interface (MAPI) client sends a message in Rich Text Format (RTF), Exchange 2000 will convert the rich text into an attachment that is sent just like any other attachment. Realize also that only Outlook 97 or later clients can, in fact, generate and receive Exchange rich text over an SMTP Connector. If the SMTP Connector is sending to another Exchange Server, RTF is automatically rendered for any client.

10

The X.400 Connector

An X.400 Connector can be implemented to produce a route between two Exchange routing groups. It can also be used to generate X.400 communications between an Exchange routing group and an X.400 system. An X.400 messaging route establishes the conduit that a message takes on its way to the final destination. One server in each routing group is nominated as the bridgehead server to provide the communications link between the routing groups.

You will need to set up an X.400 transport stack prior to defining an X.400 Connector. The following list describes the transport stacks that you can define:

➤ A TCP/IP X.400 transport stack is used when the core protocol is TCP/IP (Transmission Control Protocol/Internet Protocol). This stack choice would occur, for example, when the X.400 Connector is deployed on the Internet.

➤ The X.25 X.400 transport stack is used when the fundamental protocol is X.25.

➤ The Dynamic Remote Access Service (DRAS) X.400 transport stack is implemented when the underlying protocol is RPC over Remote Access Service (RAS). This is implemented with a dial-up modem.

Connecting to Other Systems

An Exchange 2000 site is a solitary unit of synchronous, high-bandwidth network connectivity. Sites are defined for the most part by the network and messaging topology. Exchange Server can subsist on its own site and be linked through connectors with other sites. The following list describes the suitable connectors to use when linking to other types of systems:

➤ Internet Mail Service (IMS) is used to connect to the Internet or to an SMTP backbone.

➤ The Microsoft Mail Connector will link existing Microsoft Mail 3.x gateways, such as Professional Office System (PROFS), System Network Architecture Distribution System (SNADS), and NetWare MHS.

➤ The X.400 Connector takes advantage of a connection to an existing X.400 backbone. X.400 Connectors support a variety of protocols. TCP/IP Microsoft Exchange Connectors for Lotus cc:Mail are implemented when it is necessary to transfer messages and/or synchronize between Microsoft Exchange Server and Lotus cc:Mail system directories. Also, Transaction Processing version 4/Connectionless Network Protocol (TP4/CLNP) connectivity offers an Open Systems Interconnection (OSI) standard interface across a local area network (LAN). Exchange 2000 Server has a TP4 driver interface that enables it to communicate with other systems using the TP4 during message transport. TP4 is made for a connectionless mode network. The network service access point (NSAP) address used by TP4 is set up through the Windows 2000 Control Panel on that server. The CLNP sends data without using a connection request.

Configuring VPN Access to Exchange 2000 Server

A virtual private network (VPN) allows you to carry information between two hosts over a shared or public internetwork. The VPN will appear to function like that of a Point-to-Point Protocol (PPP) private connection. This emulation is accomplished by wrapping data with a header that includes routing information. To imitate a confidential private connection, the sent packets are encrypted so that, if intercepted on a shared or public network, they will be impossible to decipher without the encryption keys. Therefore, the VPN is the connection link in which the private data is encapsulated and encrypted. Figure 10.1 provides an illustration of the logical view of a VPN.

VPN connections that use PPP connectivity have a number of qualities. First of all, the VPN server authenticates by verifying that the VPN client manufacturing the connection has the appropriate permissions. Second, the VPN offers a scheme for encapsulating private data packets with a header, enabling it to confidentially move over the network. A third property is that of data encryption, which guarantees the confidential transmission of data over a shared or public transit internetwork. The data is encrypted by the sender and subsequently decrypted by the receiver. Both the sender and the receiver must know the common encryption key for the encryption and decryption processes to be successful.

In addition, the VPN provides for address and name server allocation services. When setting up a VPN server, you will generate a virtual interface that serves as an agent for all of your VPN connections. On the client side, a virtual interface is engendered to represent the interface connected to the VPN server. A VPN client is connected to the virtual interface on the VPN server that generates the point-to-point VPN connection.

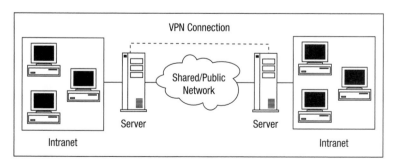

Figure 10.1   A virtual private network.

The process of creating a VPN for remote connections is similar to that of establishing a PPP RAS connection using dial-up networking and demand-dial routing. Therefore, remote connectivity can be enhanced by using the VPN technology. A remote access client and a single-user computer generate a RAS VPN connection that links to a private network. The VPN server gives access to the resources of the attached VPN server. The packets sent from the remote client across the VPN connection start off at the remote access client computer. You can also create a router-to-router VPN connection, in which a router connects two portions of a private network. The VPN server provides a routed network connection to the attached VPN server. As a rule, router-to-router VPN connections do not originate at the routers.

Remote Access over the Internet

A VPN connection using remote access over the Internet is faster and more cost-effective than the typical dial-up scenario. From the client standpoint, instead of having to make a long-distance telephone call to a corporate network access server (NAS), the client can just make contact with a local Internet service provider (ISP) for connectivity. In this approach, the remote-access client starts a VPN connection over the Internet to the company VPN server. The remote-access client can then access the private intranet's resources once the VPN link is generated. When systems are connected over the Internet, a router will forward the packets to another router using the VPN connection. This scenario is illustrated in Figure 10.2.

Managing Virtual Private Networking

VPN security issues—above all, Internet VPN connections—must be conscientiously considered. You should be mindful of where all of the user account data is stored. Make sure you know who has permission to generate VPN connections and how the addresses are dispensed to VPN clients. Be aware of how the VPN server

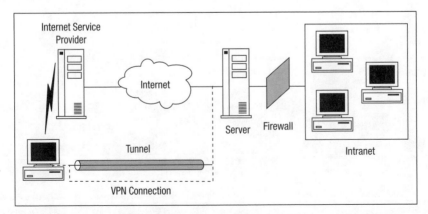

Figure 10.2   Two Exchange organizations linked across the Internet by a VPN connection.

authenticates users attempting to make VPN connections. You also want to be sure that a course of action exists for monitoring and recording the VPN server's virtual activities. Management protocols and tools should be in place to manage these VPN connections. The administration of Windows 2000 remote access VPN connections is accomplished through the Dial-in Properties page on user accounts. To control remote access on a per-user basis, simply enable the Grant Dial-in Permission To User setting on the Dial-in Properties tab of the user accounts that are able to make remote access connections. Next, adjust the properties of the RAS or the Routing RAS (RRAS) for the necessary connection parameters.

Tip: Supporting the administration of separate user accounts on separate servers for the same user while keeping all the accounts simultaneously current is an unworkable task. You will most likely configure a master account database on the domain controller or a RADIUS server. This design will permit a VPN server to send authentication credentials to a central authenticating device. The same user account can be used for dial-in remote access as well as VPN-based remote access.

A VPN server must have a store of available IP addresses so that it can allocate them to the VPN server's virtual interface. The server also needs the addressees for the VPN clients to use throughout the IP Control Protocol negotiation phase of the connection creation process. The IP address allocated to a VPN client is assigned to the virtual interface of the VPN client. These same addresses are obtained through the Dynamic Host Configuration Protocol (DHCP) service by default in Windows 2000. You can also configure a static IP address pool.

10

VPNs and Firewalls

A firewall uses packet-filtering technologies to sort out particular types of data traffic. IP packet filtering offers a method to define precisely what IP traffic you want to cross your firewall. This technology is essential for organizations that link private intranets with public networks such as the Internet. VPN server firewalls can employ one of two approaches. The first approach involves VPN servers that are connected to the Internet, with the firewall between the VPN server and the intranet. In the second scenario, the firewall is attached to the Internet, and the VPN server is between the firewall and the intranet.

Setting up SMTP Virtual Servers

A virtual server uses port 25 to take delivery of SMTP connections and listen in on all of the network interfaces. Your design may implement multiple virtual servers on a single Exchange 2000 Server. Each virtual server can acknowledge an unlimited number of inbound SMTP connections; however, each virtual server must have a separate listening port or different bound IP address configured. Furthermore, you should block SMTP connections on network servers that are directly connected for the sake of network security (especially if Internet connections exist). The quantity of outbound connections that each virtual server turns out is limited only by the server hardware resource capacity. For scenarios in which your Exchange 2000 Server may be performing functions other than simple message routing, you should consider doing the following:

➤ When making outbound connections, consider setting your virtual server to connect with a port number other than 25.

➤ For better security, place a limit on objects such as the number of inbound and outbound connections as well as session time-outs.

➤ Endeavor to keep your server from being overloaded by SMTP connections.

Tip: The default value for a SMTP session time-out is 600 minutes.

Security Issues

Although, the techniques for security were covered in greater detail in Chapter 8, let us investigate a few issues related to setting up SMTP virtual servers. Your organization may have to embark on a strict program of SMTP port security, which can be accomplished in quite a few ways. You can configure your system to necessitate authentication before the message transfer session is established. You may also want to take advantage of Windows 2000 Certificate services for security. Consider generating a secure channel by linking a certificate to the virtual server. You also have at your disposal filtering capabilities that allow you to direct certain computers to connect to the SMTP port.

Be aware that security breaches can be transferred through a virtual server. There-fore, you can inadvertently make your organization vulnerable to users forging or spoofing messages from other users. To prevent this calamity, give the connecting SMTP client the capability to control access to the virtual server. For example, you could configure a virtual server to immobilize message relays unless the incoming message is from a well-known client. The IP address, group IP address, or even the domain name can be the criteria used to determine this. Guarding and monitoring your valued virtual server resources is an extremely prudent policy. Email user security must be one of your overriding concerns when configuring your Ex-change 2000 Server. Due to the relative simplicity of SMTP, intruders may be able to forge messages from other users. One approach to preventing this infringement is to set up a virtual server to do a reverse DNS lookup against the sender of the message. This allows you to confirm if the SMTP client is truly a member of the DNS domain that corresponds to the one in the Mail From field. By using this technique, you can compel the virtual server to reject the message whenever the name does not match. The downside to configuring a reverse lookup is that this task can have a severe impact on message transfer performance, which could essentially result in hindering messages being relayed across multiple hops. Instead, the best solution to the forging problem is to implement a digital certificate infrastructure.

Performance Issues

You must consider the possible performance "hit" before you decide to generate a reverse DNS lookup. Some additional factors exist, however, from a performance standpoint. The following default configurations may be restricted to prevent servers from being inundated:

➤ The SMTP session size is limited to 10,240KB.

➤ The message size is limited to 2,048KB.

➤ The number of messages for each connection is limited to 20.

➤ The number of recipients for each message is limited to 100.

These parameters can evidently be modified to attain the perfect balance among performance, workability, and flexibility. The 2MB message size limit may be unreasonable for your growing organization. You may want to consider increasing this value. In addition, a limit of 100 recipients in the message header may generate additional network traffic, because multiple messages will be generated when the message header has more recipients than the number configured on the virtual server. Consequently, you may want to consider raising this threshold, depending on the size of your organization and the amount of available resources. If you kept the recipient limitation at 100, and a message was addressed to 120 recipients, the routing engine would relay two identical messages. One message would be for the first 100 recipients and the other message would be bound for the remaining 20 recipients.

Tip: A virtual server may transact with a continuous stream of messages between the same servers. In this scenario, you can improve performance by up to 10 percent by not limiting the number of messages in a single connection.

Characteristically, every virtual server will try to transport a message at the moment the message shows up in the queue. If a total communications failure occurs on the network, the virtual servers will, as a rule, queue the message for ensuing retries or even reroute the message. This also happens when a momentary problem crops up with the next-hop server. If a message remains in the queue longer than the set time period on the server, the sender will be told that the message was not delivered. The default time period that a message will remain in the Exchange 2000 queue is 12 hours. After two days, if the message has still been cleared from the queue, a nondelivery report is sent to the sender.

Replication and Synchronization with the ADC

You cannot have a truly comprehensive dialogue of connectivity and synchronization without exploring the ADC in greater detail. Because Active Directory can amass all the details, messaging information, and security data for a user account, a separate directory for Exchange 2000 is no longer a requirement. The ADC holds the responsibility for replicating and synchronizing the Active Directory with an Exchange Server 5.5 directory. This process makes Exchange 5.5 objects and attributes available to Exchange 2000. Active Directory offers Exchange 2000 the global address list and address book views, as well as offline address books.

Replication can be defined as the process of copying data and objects from one Windows 2000 Active Directory namespace to another. Synchronization is the process of copying objects from one directory to another with discrete namespaces. The ADC can coordinate modifications to the directory in one or both directions. It can synchronize from the Exchange directory to the Active Directory, from the Active Directory to the Exchange directory, or both ways, depending on the design settings. The ADC synchronizes recipients, mailboxes, distribution lists, and custom recipients, as well as configuration information, connectors, monitors, protocols, topology, and other information.

The core features of the ADC are described in the following list:

➤ The ADC controls the reliability of data objects through the replication process.

➤ The ADC employs the Lightweight Directory Access Protocol Application Programming Interface (LDAP API) to reproduce data between two directories.

➤ The ADC does not host the active replication components on a foreign system. It hosts only the components on Active Directory.

➤ The ADC can host multiple connections on a single Active Directory server and deal with them via connection agreements.

➤ Whenever possible, the ADC replicates only changes between the two directories.

When running in native mode, Exchange 2000 Server allows for the partitioning of administrative and routing tasks through administrative groups and routing groups. Exchange 2000 can carry this out despite the elemental network infrastructure.

Note: During a migration, administration and routing groups are the same. They will show up as sites in the Exchange 5.5 directory while coexisting with Exchange 5.5. You can redefine routing groups once the Exchange Server 5.5 is no longer in the environment.

When you are performing an installation, the ADC is installed as an additional component for Windows 2000 Server and Exchange 2000 Server. Therefore, you do not need Exchange 2000 to get the Active Directory Connector. The Active Directory Connector Manager console can be used to configure the connection agreements between Active Directory and the Exchange 5.5 destination directory.

The ADC has two editions. One is the ADC for Windows 2000, which ships with Windows 2000 Server, and the second type is the Exchange 2000 enhanced ADC, which ships with Exchange 2000 Server.

The Windows 2000 ADC will replicate directory information, such as distribution lists, from Exchange 5.5 directories to Active Directory and vice versa. The role of the Windows 2000 ADC is to prepare Active Directory for Exchange 2000 during a Windows 2000 deployment but before the installation of Exchange 2000. If you are running earlier versions of Exchange, the ADC will let you upload nearly all of the directory data to Active Directory at one time. This can significantly trim down the time it takes for installations. Designated Windows 2000 users can then synchronize and manage the Exchange 5.5 users.

The Exchange 2000 enhanced ADC version adds functionality that allows you to replicate configuration data (i.e., protocol and connector information). This allows for concrete coexistence between Exchange 5.5 and Exchange 2000 servers. Because the Exchange 2000 ADC adds functionality, you should unquestionably perform the seamless upgrade of the Windows 2000 version to the enhanced Exchange 2000 version. One option would be to roll out the Windows 2000 ADC to rapidly populate your basic Active Directory and then use the Exchange 2000 ADC to migrate from Exchange 5.5 to Exchange 2000.

Site Replication Services

A number of extra components are accessible to you when you install the Exchange 2000 ADC. One of these components is a Site Replication Service (SRS), which aids the coexistence of Exchange 2000 and Exchange 5.5 servers during migration. The SRS is a customized Exchange 5.5 directory that works on the Exchange 2000 Server to assist replication between Exchange 2000 SRS and the residual Exchange 5.5 servers. SRS allows for integration with Exchange 5.x sites that use both RPC and mail-based replication processes. It represents the Exchange 2000 side of the ADC configuration connection agreement. SRS allows the Exchange 2000 system to imitate an Exchange 5.5 system so that Exchange 5.5 is considered a part of the organization. SRS translates information from Active Directory into the Exchange 5.5 directory service and vice versa. It makes further use of the Exchange 5.5 replication engines to connect to Exchange 5.5 servers as well as the ADC inter- and intra-site functionality. Because SRS has total awareness of the corporate topology, it can acclimatize to any change to avert a disruption of service or data loss.

SRS is comparable to the Exchange 5.5 Directory Service except that the MAPI functionality is disabled. With SRS, reconfiguring the connection agreement endpoint every time an Exchange 5.5 Server is upgraded to Exchange 2000 is superfluous. SRS implements Exchange 2000 servers as bridgehead servers for earlier Exchange sites using the usual mail-based replication process.

Recipient Update Service

Another additional component that ships with Exchange 2000 is the Recipient Update Service. This element is a part of the system attendant. It surveys the directory continually to check on which objects are showing up in the MAPI address book on global catalogs. This service also applies recipient policies. During the polling process, it queries for all objects that hold to a set of selected rules or criteria. During installation, Exchange 2000 creates an address list configuration object for the domain. This configuration is transparent so that client systems that are searching for address lists will experience no affect.

Key Reasons to Implement the ADC

One of the key reasons to implement the ADC during an Exchange 2000 migration is to merge the Exchange 5.5 mailbox with a Windows 2000 user account. The consequence of this action is to produce a Windows 2000 "mailbox-enabled" user. Active Directory must have a user object for all existing Exchange 5.5 mailboxes, together with the appropriate Exchange attributes, and this must be done before the first Exchange 2000 corporate installation takes place. The ADC is an indispensable tool in Windows 2000 mixed-mode environments. Your organization will not be able to utilize its own directory synchronization tools because the ADC synchronizes all of the information. This information includes attributes such as legacy-distinguished names; administrators may not even be aware of legacy-distinguished names.

Another reason to deploy the ADC is because Exchange 2000 does not have direct access to the Exchange 5.5 directory. Active Directory needs to have a faultless, synchronized depiction of the information in the Exchange 5.5 directory, and Exchange 2000 Server uses the Windows 2000 Active Directory. A third basis for using the ADC is that it forms a firm bond between the user and an Exchange 5.5 mailbox. This relationship is maintained until your company's last Exchange 5.5 Server has been upgraded or put out to pasture. The ADC is no longer compulsory once the organization consists solely of Exchange 2000 Servers.

In addition to these rationales, the ADC also provides the capability to leverage the Exchange 5.5 user information. You can improve the replication process by having the data automatically copied over to the Active Directory without having to re-input it. The ADC allows you to create a situation in which Active Directory and the Exchange 5.5 directory are centrally administered. Probably the best aspect is that you can uphold your existing Exchange 5.5 environment in a status of coexistence while deploying your Exchange 2000 solution.

Exchange 5.5 server objects can be changed only in the Exchange site that generated them. Active Directory enables any object to be altered on any server that has a full replica of the Windows 2000 site. This feature also goes a long way toward improving the flexibility of the replication process. Active Directory uses a scheme that replicates only the "changed property," as opposed to the entire object. Because changes in the attributes of an object can ensue in two locations concurrently, the time it takes to replicate is minimized. ADC integration also lowers the incidence of replication conflicts.

Exploring Connection Agreements

As shown in previous chapters, you must generate a connection agreement in order to establish a link between existing Exchange sites and the Active Directory. A connection agreement stores data and configuration information. The most common information held by the connection agreement includes the following:

➤ The names of servers to contact for replication

➤ The object classes to replicate

➤ Target containers

➤ The replication schedule

Note: The replication agreement for configuration data is actually created between Active Directory and Site Replication Services as opposed to Active Directory and the Exchange 5.5 Server.

Two varieties of connection agreements exist in the ADC: the user connection agreement and the configuration connection agreement.

User Connection Agreements

The user connection agreement is in charge of replicating recipient objects and data between the Exchange 5.5 directory and Active Directory. These are the only types of user connection agreements that can be created with the ADC. The administrator wholly manages them. A connection agreement determines the following attributes:

➤ The synchronization schedule (default is 8 hours)

➤ The directories to be synchronized

➤ The Windows 2000 and Exchange 5.5 synchronization objects

➤ The one-way or two-way direction of synchronization

➤ The process for removing synchronization objects

Default Synchronization Schedule

The default synchronization schedule can be modified on a per agreement basis. For instance, you could set up several connection agreements for an Exchange 5.5 site and configure one on a twice a week synchronization schedule and another one to synchronize daily. By configuring the connection agreements to alternate schedules, you can better manage data flow on the network.

If you want two-way replication configured so that you can govern all objects from a central management location, simply create a connection agreement to each Exchange site. To prevent incessant circular replication, connection agreements configured to write to the Exchange 5.5 directory can interrelate with objects in only one Exchange site. You will create a one-way connection agreement from Exchange if you need to upload Exchange 5.5 directory data to Active Directory. Because the ADC does not have to write data back into the Exchange 5.5 directory, recipient containers from numerous Exchange sites can be retrieved through one connection agreement. This is helpful in situations for which a distributed security infrastructure exists or if you have several legacy Exchange sites in your organization.

Tip: The destination directory bridgehead server must be running Exchange 5.5 Service Pack 3 (or later) if you are generating a connection agreement to an Exchange site, although the other Exchange servers within the site do not necessarily have to run Exchange 5.5.

The method of synchronization is vastly improved if you synchronize the entire Exchange 5.5 site as opposed to synchronizing individual recipient containers. You can also improve synchronization by selecting the entire Exchange 5.5 site as source and target of the connection agreement on the Exchange Server. In addition, with a two-way connection agreement, you should pick the Active Directory Domain as the source and target on the Active Directory side.

Configuration Connection Agreements

The second type of connection agreement is the configuration connection agreement. This module will replicate Exchange-specific configuration data between Active Directory and the Exchange 5.5 directory. These agreements also support the coexistence between Exchange 2000 and preceding iterations of Exchange and

Windows NT. Exchange 2000 automatically generates configuration connection agreements. The Exchange 2000 ADC generates a read-only configuration connection agreement to move configuration information bidirectionally. This is done despite the connection agreements that already exist for the Windows 2000 ADC. ADC will display these configuration connection agreements along with the bridgehead servers that they use.

During the Exchange 2000 installation into an existing Exchange 5.5 infrastructure, the SRS generates the first configuration connection agreement by default. This connection agreement is called **Config CA_AdministrativeGroupName_ Exchange2000ServerName**.

Before you can observe the configuration connection agreement, the Exchange 2000 Server must be in an Exchange 5.5 organization. You can still see the connection agreement in the Active Directory Connector Manager, although you can only affect a few settings. All Exchange 5.5 sites will show up in the Active Directory as administrative groups after the replication process. Conversely, the Exchange 2000 administration groups will be defined in Exchange 5.5 as sites. The result of this design is that you can administer from either side of the connection agreement. Generally speaking, you will administer other objects, such as mailboxes, from the administrative interface of the Exchange server that holds the object.

If your organization wants to maintain its Exchange 5.5 container structure in the new Active Directory, you need only to complete the following tasks:

1. Generate a single connection agreement for each domain.

2. Consolidate all of the Exchange containers into one organizational unit in Active Directory, managed by the ADC.

3. After replication, use the Active Directory Users and Computers snap-in to move the objects to the correct organizational unit.

4. Create one connection agreement for each Windows 2000 domain.

The Active Directory Connector Manager allows you to change a pair of attributes to adjust the configuration connection agreements. The first is the Boolean value for the **MsExchReplicateNow** attribute. If this is set to "True", the ADC will immediately conduct a replication cycle for the connection agreement. You can also set this value from a remote location. To set this value from the Active Directory Connector Manager, right-click the configuration connection agreement and select Replicate Now. Another Boolean value that you can tweak is **MsExchDoFullReplication**. If "True", the two directories will refresh. In Active Directory Connector Manager, right-click the configuration connection agreement and select Properties, click the Schedule tab, and then choose the checkbox for Replicate The Entire Directory The Next Time The Agreement Is Run.

ADC Object Matching

Exchange 5.5 recipient objects will ultimately translate to native Windows 2000 objects in the Active Directory domain container. The ADC has its own set of rules for matching attributes between the Exchange 5.5 directory and Active Directory. Table 10.1 shows how objects match up with the ADC.

Note: Active Directory objects that are not mail-enabled are not replicated back to the Exchange 5.5 Server.

The matching rules for all connection agreements are stored in the default ADC policy object for the ADC. You can see the rules by right clicking on Active Directory Connector Management in the Active Directory Connector Manager and choosing Properties. Under Properties, you will see an **msExchServerXSchemaMap** field. The number 1 signifies Active Directory-to-Exchange matches, and the number 2 represents Exchange-to-Active Directory matches. Matching can also be accomplished by using the Label Distribution Protocol (LDP) program in binary mode in addition to the Active Directory Connector Manager.

A series of configurable options on the connection object are available for mapping objects. You can mailbox-enable an existing Windows 2000 user account. You can also generate a mail-enabled or mail-disabled contact in the Windows 2000 container. You can even configure it not to create any objects.

LDP Utility

The LDP tool is situated in the \Support\Tools folder on the Windows 2000 Server installation CD. LDP is a graphical tool that allows such LDAP operations as search, modify, add, and delete. You can use LDP to see objects and object metadata in Active Directory. You can also use LDP to observe attributes, but you must realize that the rules format for matching attributes is very specific. You also may not be able to see all of the attributes of an object unless your user account has Administrator permissions. You can also use LDP to modify other configuration connection agreement attributes, although Microsoft does not recommend this.

The ADC may undertake to create an object that already exists in the target directory. When this occurs, a numeric value prefixed with a hyphen (ranging from –1 to –9999) will be appended to the common name of the object. This scheme

Table 10.1   Matches between Active Directory and Exchange 5.5 objects.

Active Directory Object	Exchange Directory Service Object (in the Target Container)
Mailbox-enabled user	Mailbox
Mail-enabled user	Custom recipient
Mail-enabled contact	Custom recipient
Mail-enabled distribution group	Distribution list
Mail-enabled security group	Distribution list

for resolving conflicts applies to objects in either the Exchange directory or the Active Directory. To make sure that an object will be distinctive, the ADC will append the **-n** to the end of the relative distinguished name of the new object.

ADC Replication

To replicate the domain-naming context within a domain, employ synchronous RPC. When replicating data between two different systems, however, the data format and conventions may not match. The Active Directory Schema holds the prescribed definitions of all of the object classes and their attributes. The ADC, therefore, performs the obligatory conversion by resolving the restrictions imposed by the target directory. This method of Schema conversion accommodates several types of data discrepancies between the directories. Schema conversion accounts for the attribute mapping, data format, and presentation, as well as restrictions on the field length.

Best Practices before ADC Deployment

Always install the ADC on a member server in the Windows 2000 domain for the best possible performance. Be ever mindful of the replication schedule because the ADC can be processor intensive—more so than ever if several connection agreements are deployed. Take the proper steps to make certain that the server hardware can handle the added processing load if you are planning to place the ADC on a global catalog server or a domain controller (DC). The connection agreement should be configured between a Windows 2000 global catalog server and the Exchange 5.5 Server if possible. You may also want to consider introducing the ADC in close proximity (on the network) to a global catalog in the same Windows 2000 site.

If you are deploying the ADC in a multiple domain infrastructure, each connection agreement should be a global catalog server. Also, be sure to position all of the global catalog servers for all the domains in the same Windows 2000 site. If this is a large deployment, multiple instances of the ADC can be generated. In such a scenario, you should create the connection agreements so that different sets of objects are replicated by each connection agreement. Usually, you would not want to deploy multiple instances of the ADC for the sake of fault tolerance. However, you can diminish the risk of downtime by having more than one server running the ADC.

Note: *Although the connection agreements are created and run on the ADC server, the source and target folders may actually be on other computers.*

Microsoft suggests using directory replication bridgehead servers to help replicate between Exchange 5.5 servers and Exchange sites. Whenever feasible, you should employ the same servers for ADC connection agreements—servers that should be the last to migrate to Exchange 2000. If your design has multiple domains, position a separate connection agreement at an appropriate DC for each of the other Active Directory domains. Another solution would be to install ADC and suitable connection agreements on a separate server for each domain that you need to replicate with the Exchange 5.5 directory. Make sure that your resolutions are based solidly on load and network capacities. The ADC uses LDAP and RPC to communicate to the Exchange 5.5 directory, so you must have direct IP connectivity. These protocols are often blocked by a firewall. If this occurs in your organization, install the ADC on a server in each domain. Then the replication of Active Directory between domains can take place over SMTP. Place the server with the ADC on the same subnet (if possible) as the Exchange 5.5 Server and Active Directory bridgehead servers.

When the ADC initially runs, it will replicate every object that is *not* in Active Directory. All of those objects will then replicate to every DC and global catalog in the Exchange infrastructure. In a large organization, this may take a while. After you run ForestPrep, DomainPrep, and the ADC installation, allow an adequate amount of time for the replication process to complete the changes throughout the Active Directory infrastructure. The ForestPrep and DomainPrep components are addressed in greater detail in a later section in this chapter. The ADC does not actually complete its work during the migration process. Rather, it is continuously keeping the two directories synchronized. Another best practice would be to install the ADC, SRS, and Recipient Update Service on a dedicated Windows 2000 member server. This configuration will make management easier and improve availability.

Finally, you should recognize the security implications of groups as well as the differences between connection agreement directions. Because Active Directory groups provide for access control and distribution lists, avoid making changes to group membership. This could compromise your system security. Remember that the consequences of two one-way connection agreements may be different from that of one two-way connection agreement. Be extra cautious when making configure modifications at the From Windows and From Exchange tabs on the Active Directory Connector Manager. Make sure that you coordinate and match the correct containers as well as the direction in which the information flows.

Additional ADC Predeployment Issues

Another question you should consider before deployment is whether you want to handle all of the objects from Active Directory. You can use the Active Directory Users and Computers snap-in to supervise Exchange 5.5 mailboxes collectively with Active Directory users. If your organization needs this functionality, you should generate each connection agreement so that both can write an array of attributes into each directory.

This activity will cause a singular network performance hit because each Exchange object in the site is initially re-replicated within the native environment. If you are in a large Exchange infrastructure, these modifications can cause directory and network traffic issues to surface. You could consider alternating the deployment of connection agreements to reduce this burden on your design.

In addition, you need to determine how many Active Directory domains your design entails because Active Directory will not integrate the namespace with the directory replication model. This represents a disparity between earlier versions of Exchange. With Windows 2000, the domain-naming context replication in the domain happens with the use of synchronous RPC. You also need to reflect on how many servers running ADC you will need to replicate the data. Even though an ADC can have connection agreements for numerous Active Directory domains, LDAP is used with perhaps only a few RPC requests for writing to the Exchange directory. Both of these protocols stipulate direct IP connectivity.

Another decision may involve whether to upgrade your master accounts domain before installing the ADC. Each Exchange mailbox matches up with a primary Windows NT account. If the account's domain has been upgraded to Windows 2000 ahead of the rollout of the ADC, then it will be unnecessary to merge objects that exist in Active Directory with objects from the upgraded account domain. If a domain has not been upgraded to Windows 2000, ADC creates new security principals to symbolize the users as mailboxes in the Windows NT 4 domain. The ADC marks the security descriptor so that Windows NT 4 users can still contact their mail. When the Windows NT 4 domain is upgraded, run Active Directory Account Cleanup Wizard to join together the ADC-created objects with the upgraded Windows 2000 user accounts. Mailboxes are inaccessible to those accounts until this cleanup is done.

A concluding concern that may surface involves whether you have defined your container structure in the existing Exchange system. An Exchange 5.5 site defines only the recipients container. Your organization may have engendered other containers for additional types of objects or special containers for different object classes, such as distribution lists and custom recipients. You may need to create multiple connection agreements to the same Exchange site.

Deploying the ADC

You should be aware of some minimum requirements for installing the ADC. If you are installing the ADC on a Windows 2000 member server, the hardware should well exceed these minimum requirements for an Exchange 2000 Server. Some guidelines follow:

➤ Intel Pentium 133MHz or faster processor

➤ 128MB of random access memory (RAM); 256MB recommended

➤ Microsoft Windows 2000 Server operating system

➤ At least 500MB of available disk space for Exchange 2000 on the installation drive

➤ At least 200MB of available disk space on the system drive

➤ A Paging file set to a recommended minimum of twice the amount of system RAM

➤ Video graphics array (VGA)–resolution monitor, or higher

➤ A CD-ROM drive

In addition, the following logistical requirements should be met:

➤ The Windows installation account is logged in to the same domain as the server.

➤ The Windows account used for the ADC installation must not be an Exchange 5.5 service account.

➤ The Windows installation account has access to the global catalog.

➤ The Windows installation account must be a member of the Schema Admins security group.

➤ The Windows installation account must have Domain Administrator rights for each domain to which the ADC will connect (i.e., be a member of the Domain Admins security group) and for the member server on which the ADC is installed.

➤ The ADC service account specified during Setup is a member of the Enterprise Admins or root Domain Admins group. This is necessary to successfully fill in user information in all necessary domains.

➤ Windows 2000 and DNS services should be deployed in agreement with the Windows 2000 documentation.

➤ The ADC-target Exchange 5.5 server has Service Pack 3 installed.

Tip: Place separate servers into dedicated service roles for better manageability and reliability. Services that are located on the same server with ADC, such as SMTP, will present added configuration difficulty.

You should resolve the following issues in Exchange 2000 to properly prepare Active Directory for mixed-mode environment during migration. First, you will need to extend the Active Directory Schema with schema and display specifiers. Next, you will generate groups and then delegate authority and predefined domain-level permissions to explicit Exchange 2000 processes. Finally, you should perform explicit access control list changes to avert existing domain and enterprise administrators from acquiring Exchange 2000 Administrator permissions through inheritance.

ForestPrep and DomainPrep

ForestPrep and DomainPrep get organizations ready for Exchange 2000 Server installation by distinguishing the setup modules that entail high-level network permissions from parts that need Exchange Administrator permissions only. To carry out the tasks mentioned in the previous paragraph in environments that have Active Directory, Exchange 5.5, and Windows domain administrators with disparate permissions, you must use the ForestPrep and DomainPrep tools.

ForestPrep and DomainPrep need not be run, however, if all of the following conditions are met:

➤ All of your Exchange 2000 servers are going to be in a single domain.

➤ All of the Exchange users are in the domain.

➤ The domain contains the DC with the schema master role.

➤ The account used to install Exchange 2000 has Enterprise Admins and Schema Admins permissions.

ForestPrep is run one time per forest. It will accomplish the goals of enlarging the Active Directory Schema, appointing the Exchange 2000 Administrators, generating the Exchange 2000 organization object in the configuration-naming context, and setting up the permissions configuration.

DomainPrep is run once per domain. Its function is to make the public folder proxy container and set permissions within the domain. You do not need to run DomainPrep in a domain until you are ready to install Exchange 2000. DomainPrep must be run in all domains in which you install Exchange 2000 and in all domains that have recipient objects, such as mailboxes or distribution lists.

If you determine that your team needs to run the ForestPrep utility because of your environment, complete the following information-gathering tasks:

➤ Determine if this is a new Exchange 2000 organization or a connection to an existing Exchange 5.5 organization.

➤ Know what account will be the Exchange 2000 Administrator account.

➤ Know the new organization name, if applicable.

➤ Know the existing Exchange 5.5 server name if you are joining an existing Exchange 5.5 organization.

➤ Determine the Exchange 5.5 service account password if you are joining an existing Exchange 5.5 organization.

10

➤ Run ForestPrep in the same domain as the Schema Master.

➤ Run ForestPrep from an account with Windows 2000 Enterprise Admins and Schema Admins permissions.

➤ Run ForestPrep from an account that has at least View-Only Administrative permissions on the Exchange 5.5 site and configuration container if joining an existing Exchange 5.5 organization.

➤ Install Exchange Server 5.5 Service Pack 3 and the ADC that comes with Exchange 2000 prior to running ForestPrep if joining an existing Exchange 5.5 organization, because the ADC that ships with Windows 2000 is inadequate.

ForestPrep will extend the Active Directory Schema to comprise the Exchange-specific information. This affects the total forest and usually takes about half an hour. If the forest is large, it may take noticeably longer to replicate changes to every domain and domain controller. ForestPrep will also prompt for and generate the Exchange organization name and object in Active Directory. It nominates the first full Exchange 2000 Administrator account. This account uses the Exchange Administration Delegation Wizard to delegate Exchange Administrator rights to other new Exchange Administrator accounts. When ForestPrep and DomainPrep are through doing their work, this account will correspond to an organizational-level Exchange Full Administrator. Once added to the local Administrators group, it can install the first occurrence of Exchange 2000. This Exchange Administrator account can also farm out various Exchange 2000 Administration roles to other users or groups using the Delegation Wizard.

DomainPrep is run in every domain in which Exchange 2000 exists and where there are recipients as well. Exchange 2000 and Exchange 5.5 Administrator permissions are not required to run DomainPrep. Run DomainPrep after ForestPrep and replication occurs in each domain where an Exchange 2000 server is to be installed. This normally takes about 20 minutes for a single Windows 2000 site, although it can take longer in some circumstances. Run DomainPrep in each domain where you want to install Exchange 2000 as well as the domain where you ran ForestPrep. DomainPrep can be run from any server in that domain. You must also run it if you want Exchange 2000 mail-enabled users for whom you want to create a Recipient Update Service in domains where Exchange 2000 is not installed.

DomainPrep produces the compulsory global groups for Exchange Administration and Directory Service to Active Directory. The account for this tool must have Domain Admins and local Administrator permissions in each of the domains to which the ADC will affix itself. DomainPrep will create two new domain groups, called Exchange Domain Servers (a global security group) and Exchange Enterprise Servers (a domain local security group).

DomainPrep will enable Exchange Domain Servers to contain the computer accounts of all Exchange 2000 servers in the domain. DomainPrep is required for Recipient Update Service. Exchange Enterprise Servers will also contain the Exchange Domain Servers groups from all the domains running Exchange due to DomainPrep. The tool will generate the public folder proxy container as well as grant the proper permissions for Exchange 2000 Administrators and Exchange Servers on these objects.

After you run ForestPrep and subsequently run DomainPrep in each domain where Exchange is to be installed, Exchange 2000 Setup queries Active Directory for configuration data. This simplifies the deployment of Exchange throughout the forest. ForestPrep will then assign Exchange Full Administrator permissions to a specified account that will have the power to install Exchange throughout the forest. After the first installation of Exchange 2000, you will use this account to run the Exchange Administration Delegation Wizard, which sets up the Exchange-specific roles for administrators throughout the forest.

Remove anomalous (or inconsistent) objects in the Exchange 5.5 directory prior to the first ADC replication for a smooth migration process. An anomalous object is an Exchange 5.5 mailbox whose **mailNickname** attribute does not equate to the **loginID** attribute of the primary Windows security account related to it in the same domain. These mailbox objects are regularly associated with a resource and are administered by several different people over the lifetime of an organization. In an Exchange 2000/Windows 2000 setting, each mailbox can have only one primary Windows user account in the same domain associated with it. In an Exchange 5.5 environment, this one-to-one relationship is not compulsory. In fact, with the Exchange 5.5 mailbox, association with a security principal is not mandatory.

A similar resource mailbox functionality can be accomplished in the Windows 2000/Exchange 2000 situation via the design of disabled security principals. These are security principals that, for reasons of improved security, have no logon rights in Active Directory and are connected to each resource mailbox. If necessary, provide several different Windows security principals to serve as secondary, or alternate, users of that account's mailbox. This can be executed through the Advanced View tab of the Active Directory Users and Computers console.

If at all feasible, your organization should set up two servers capable of sustaining the ADC. Theses servers should be brought online as Windows 2000 member servers in a domain. One server will perform the role of the core system and will execute the daily necessities of the ADC. The other will be a backup server, providing redundant services in the event of a system stoppage. If the primary system becomes unavailable, this backup system will go online to keep up the ADC functionality until the primary system is restored.

ADC Deployment Contingency Plan Preparation

If the ADC experiences a failure, perform the following steps to revert back to an operational state:

1. Disable the connection agreement.

2. If this does not solve the issue, shut down the ADC service.

3. If data is corrupted, remove the organizational unit in which the data was stored, and perform a restore from a tape with a known good state.

4. Finally, use the Windows 2000 LDP tool to edit data in Active Directory.

Chapter Summary

When connecting two routing groups consisting of only Exchange 2000 Servers, your best alternative is the Routing Group Connector, as was shown in Chapter 9. In this chapter, however, you found that if you are connecting Exchange 2000 Server to a past version of Exchange or another organization's system, you might want to implement a different connector type. You may even need a higher level of flexibility in your design. This chapter took a deeper look at the RGC, the SMTP Connector, and the X.400 Connector.

This chapter also looked at configuring VPN access to Exchange 2000 Server as a means to transfer information between two hosts over a shared or public internetwork. The VPN emulates a private PPP connection encapsulating data with a header that includes routing information. To imitate a confidential private connection, the sent packets are encrypted so that they will be impossible to decipher without the encryption keys if captured on a shared or public network. In essence, a VPN is the connection link in which the private data is encapsulated and encrypted.

VPN servers authenticate by verifying that the VPN client generating the connection has the appropriate permissions. Also, a VPN offers a technique for encapsulating private data packets with a header, thus enabling the packet to confidentially move over the network. A third feature is that of data encryption. Finally, a VPN provides for address and name server allocation services. In addition, a VPN connection using remote access over the Internet is by and large faster and more cost effective than the typical dial-up scenario. From the client standpoint, instead of having to make a long distance phone call to a corporate network access server, the client can just make contact with a local ISP for connectivity.

The remainder of this chapter was dedicated to the fact that you cannot have a comprehensive discussion of connectivity and synchronization without exploring the Active Directory Connector in greater detail. Active Directory encompasses all of the details, messaging information, and security data for a user account; therefore, a separate directory for Exchange 2000 is no longer a requirement. The ADC holds the responsibility for replicating and synchronizing the Active Directory with an Exchange Server 5.5 directory. This process makes Exchange 5.5 objects and attributes available to Exchange 2000. Active Directory offers Exchange 2000 the global address list and address book views, as well as offline address books. This chapter provided valuable insight into the best practices for deploying the ADC. The next chapter looks into the intricacies of designing an Exchange 2000 Server administrative model that is built upon the connectivity infrastructure explored in the last ten chapters.

Review Questions

1. Your Active Directory Connector has experienced a failure. Which one of the following four actions would represent a *last* resort to revert back to an operational state?

   a. Shut down the ADC service.

   b. Disable the connection agreement.

   c. If data is corrupted, remove the organizational unit where the data was stored, and perform a restore from a tape with a known good state.

   d. Use the Windows 2000 LDP tool to edit data in Active Directory.

2. SMTP serves three principal functions in your Exchange 2000 infrastructure. Which of the following is *not* one of these primary functions?

   a. SMTP replicates data and transfers necessary information.

   b. SMTP encapsulates private data packets with a header, enabling packets to confidentially move over the network.

   c. Servers will use SMTP to route messages.

   d. Clients will use SMTP to submit messages.

3. The administration of Windows 2000 remote access VPN connections is done through the Dial-in Properties page on user accounts. To manage remote access on a per user basis, which of the following settings would you enable on the Dial-in Properties tab of the user accounts that are able to make remote access connections?

   a. Grant Dial-in Permission To User

   b. Manage Remote Access For User

   c. Enable Dial-in Permission To User

   d. Grant Remote Access For User

10

4. Which one of the following techniques best describes the method to define precisely what IP traffic you want to cross your firewall and is an essential technology for organizations linking private intranets with public networks such as the Internet?

   a. IP security filtering

   b. IP datagram filtering

   c. IP network filtering

   d. IP packet filtering

5. A virtual server uses which port to take delivery of SMTP connections and listen in on all of the network interfaces?

   a. Port 15

   b. Port 20

   c. Port 25

   d. Port 30

6. In your organization, email user security is one of the overriding concerns when configuring your Exchange 2000 Server. Due to the relative simplicity of SMTP, intruders may be able to forge messages from other users. Which one of the following is a relatively simple approach for preventing this type of infringement?

   a. Set up a virtual server to do a reverse DNS lookup against the sender of a message.

   b. Configure your system to necessitate authentication before the message transfer session is established.

   c. Generate a secure channel by linking a certificate to the virtual server.

   d. Use filtering capabilities that allow you to direct certain computers to connect to the SMTP port.

7. Which one of the following statements does *not* represent a default configuration that you may consider restricting in order to prevent servers from being inundated?

   a. The SMTP session size is limited to 10,240KB.

   b. The message size is limited to 2MB.

   c. The number of messages for each connection is limited to 20.

   d. The number of recipients for each message is limited to 200.

8. What is the default time period that a message will remain in the Exchange 2000 queue? (After two days, if the message has still been cleared from the queue, a nondelivery report is sent to the sender.)

   a. 6 hours

   b. 12 hours

   c. 18 hours

   d. 24 hours

9. Which of the following statements represent core features of the Active Directory Connector? [Check all correct answers]

   a. ADC controls the reliability of data objects through the replication process.

   b. ADC makes use of the LDAP API to reproduce data between two directories.

   c. ADC hosts the active replication components on foreign systems.

   d. ADC can host multiple connections on a single Active Directory server and deal with them via connection agreements.

10. Which of the following are versions of the Active Directory Connector? [Check the two best answers]

    a. Windows 2000 Legacy ADC

    b. Routing Group Connector

    c. ADC for Windows 2000

    d. Enhanced ADC for Exchange 2000

    e. ADC SMTP Connector for Exchange

11. Which of the following components is a customized directory that allows for integration with Exchange 5.x sites that use both RPC and mail-based replication processes, assisting replication between Exchange 2000 and the residual Exchange 5.5 servers?

    a. Exchange 2000 Replication Wizard

    b. Recipient Update Service

    c. Exchange 5.5 Directory Service

    d. Site Replication Service

12. Which of the following is information held by the connection agreement? [Check all correct answers]

    a. The names of servers to contact for replication

    b. The object classes to replicate

    c. Target containers

    d. The replication schedule

10

13. Which of the following are varieties of connection agreements found in ADC? [Check all correct answers]

    a. User connection agreement

    b. Replication connection agreement

    c. Configuration connection agreement

    d. Synchronization connection agreement

14. Exchange 5.5 recipient objects will ultimately translate to native Windows 2000 objects in the Active Directory domain container. The ADC has its own set of rules for matching attributes between the Exchange 5.5 directory and Active Directory. Which of the following objects will match up to the Exchange Directory Service distribution list object? [Check all correct answers]

    a. Active Directory object

    b. Mail-enabled distribution group

    c. Mail-enabled security group

    d. Mailbox-enabled user

    e. Mail-enabled contact

15. Which of the following is a graphical tool that allows you to perform LDAP operations and view objects and object metadata in Active Directory?

    a. ADSI

    b. ADP

    c. LDP

    d. ADC

Real-World Project

Project 10.1

You are the team lead for the Exchange 2000 deployment at your medium-sized software company. You must put together a game plan for designing connectivity and synchronization for your organization. Based on the information in this chapter and other available resources, generate a 20-point connectivity and synchronization checklist of issues and tasks that need to be addressed before undertaking this deployment.

CHAPTER ELEVEN

Designing an Exchange 2000 Server Administrative Model

After completing this chapter, you will be able to:

✓ Understand the overall Exchange 2000 Server administrative model

✓ Understand various administrative concepts

✓ Plan your administrative environment

✓ Plan and implement administrative groups

✓ Plan and implement administrative policies

✓ Understand Exchange objects, inheritance, and permissions

In earlier versions of Exchange, Microsoft introduced the X.500-based hierarchical directory to ease navigation of various configuration settings and components when managing and administering Exchange. With Windows 2000, the X.500 directory—Active Directory (AD)—stores all of the enterprise configuration information, including user accounts, domain policies, and most of the Exchange-related settings in our case. Because Exchange 2000 configuration is essentially a part of AD, all AD rules apply when it comes to managing and configuring Exchange Server 2000. If you are familiar with earlier versions of Exchange, you should be very comfortable with AD and Exchange 2000 administration. Nonetheless, the latest reincarnation of Exchange implements an administrative model that is different from that of previous versions. The Exchange 2000 administration model comprises a number of components, and it is very important to understand the concept before you plan and deploy your Exchange organization.

Administrative Model

Microsoft Exchange Server 2000 relies on a very granular administrative approach, contrary to that of Exchange 5.5 and earlier versions, in which you had either an administrative level of access or none at all. The Exchange 2000 administrative model organizes system objects and topology design into manageable groups based on the needs of organization, geography, departmental or political structure, or any other criteria. The administrative model is comprised of administrative groups, routing groups, policies, and permissions. Administrative groups are used to define the organizational/administrative topology of the Exchange organization, whereas routing groups are used to define network and message routing topology. Please refer to Chapter 9 for detailed information on routing groups.

Administrative Groups

With Exchange Server 5.5 and earlier versions, sites were the only way to organize your intraorganizational structure, and this applied to both administration and routing. Servers that were on the same high-bandwidth network were organized in one site, and directory replication and other message traffic was secluded within the boundaries of that site. To delegate administration to organization departments, or based on other parameters, you would have to assign View Only Admin rights to the container and Admin rights to the object within that container that you wanted to delegate, or even implement other sites for those departments and make them a part of your Exchange organization. This design requirement often translated into an excessive administrative burden, and sometimes into additional hardware and intersite directory synchronization traffic, if additional servers and sites were necessary. In a large organization, this was very difficult to implement without mistakes, and next to impossible to manage.

In Exchange 2000, all configuration and objects are based on and included in AD. Administration is no longer server- or site-centric, and, as a result of AD integration, it is much more flexible. By using administrative groups, you can divide your object topology into separate logical manageable entities. You can assign appropriate rights and policies to administrative groups, and all objects within that group inherit assigned permissions. Most commonly, administrative groups are used in large organizations where department-level control is needed, the user base requires more manageable user object groups, and a relatively large number of Exchange servers and Exchange administrators are involved (see Figure 11.1). In other words, an administrative group forms a logical management boundary of Exchange 2000 objects (e.g., users, servers, and services).

By default, administrative groups are not displayed. To enable administrative groups, in Exchange System Manager, right-click on the Organization Root (topmost) container and click on Properties. This will bring up the Organization properties

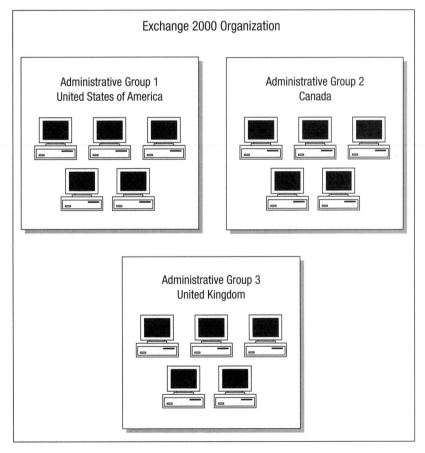

Figure 11.1   Administrative groups.

sheet, where you can choose to display administrative and/or routing groups. When enabled, each administrative group will appear as a parent container that has child containers. The number and types of child containers depend on the services (e.g., chat, conferencing, and so on) your Exchange organization is providing. The generally available child containers are the following:

➤ Chat communities

➤ Conferencing services

➤ Folders (public folder trees)

➤ Routing groups

➤ Servers

➤ System policies

Administrative groups are used to simplify the management of permissions. Consider, for example, the following scenario: An organization is deploying Exchange and has a dozen servers that need to be included in the design. Instead of configuring and assigning permissions to each individual server, the administrator creates an administrative group container, assigns all necessary permissions to it, and then adds objects, which, in this case, could be the 11 other servers or 1,000 users. Child objects will inherit all permissions from their parent container. Should circumstances change, the administrator can implement another administrative group, assign a different set of permissions, and drag-and-drop any objects that need the new set of permissions into the new administrative group. Therefore, to maximize the effectiveness and manageability of the entire administrative group concept, you should define permissions on the top level of the object hierarchy.

Types of Administrative Models

Administrative models can be of three types: centralized administration model, decentralized administration model, and mixed administration model. In most cases, Exchange administrative models mirror the information technology (IT) support team structure within the organization.

Centralized Administration Model

The centralized administration model relies on a very small number of administrative groups (usually just one) with a centralized management in one location, and a large number of routing groups to better manage routing functions (see Figure 11.2). Typically, this represents the majority of deployments for small- and medium-sized businesses, in which one IT support team takes care of all IT needs within the company. This is also applicable to medium to large organizations if high-speed connections exist between headquarters and all regional branch offices. When implementing a centralized model, consider the size of the organization, its business

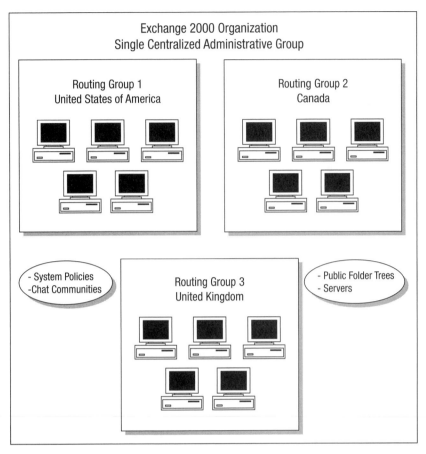

Figure 11.2   Centralized administration model.

requirements, and the connectivity speeds and costs. If a company has only one or very few locations, and only one central IT support team, unless connectivity is an issue, the centralized model would be most effective. In contrast, if a company has regional branches, each with its own solid user base and local IT management team, the decentralized administration model should be considered.

Decentralized Administration Model

The decentralized administration model (see Figure 11.3) is most effective in large organizations, and it has the same effect as sites in Exchange 5.5. Each division or region within the company has complete control over standards, administration, and routing of Exchange 2000 deployment, although the central management team has or may have control over standards as well. Day-to-day administration is the responsibility of the local management teams, and regional administrative groups may logically be further split into groups to map the organization down to city or branch or even departmental level. If your organization still maintains Exchange 5.5

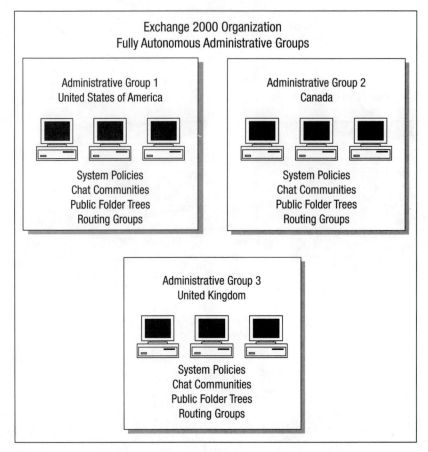

Figure 11.3 Decentralized administration model.

servers, by design or due to transition, Exchange 2000 will automatically assign each Exchange 5.5 site into a separate administrative and routing group.

Mixed Administration Model

Sometimes organizational needs may dictate geographically disperse administrative control over the Exchange 2000 installation, but the political requirements of the company may still necessitate centralized control over certain aspects. For example, Exchange policies or routing groups may have to be controlled centrally to minimize the risk of security breaches and malfunctioning routing configurations, but day-to-day management of servers, databases, and public folders may still be delegated to local administration teams. This type of configuration is implemented with the mixed administration model. In mixed administration, central groups are used to define corporate-wide policies and routing, and regional groups are used to define location-specific tasks.

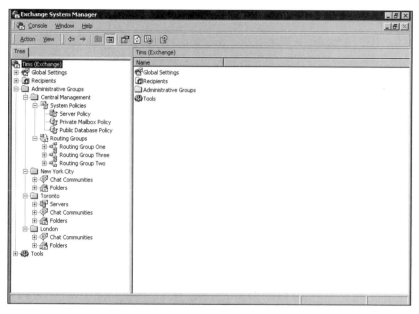

Figure 11.4   Mixed administration model.

Figure 11.4 illustrates the principles of the mixed administrative model by using three administrative groups—Toronto, New York City, and central management. The Toronto group has servers, folders, and chat communities; and the New York City group has only folders and chat communities. This enables the corporate administrator to delegate specific tasks to Toronto and New York office IT personnel. In this case, the Toronto group is well positioned to maintain its own databases of public folders and private mailbox storage, run daily backups and defragmentation, manage its own chat communities and channels, and look after the servers. The New York personnel have the capability of managing chat communities and public folder trees only. The corporate administrator, as a member of the centralized corporate technology team, has control over system policies and routing—and no one else has this control unless the administrator delegates this authority.

Note that you cannot nest administrative groups within administrative groups. The administrative group parent node can contain individual administrative group child nodes, and within those nodes you can create task-specific objects, such as a servers group, chat communities group, routing group, and so on. You cannot, however, create another general administrative group in which you have to create task-specific groups. Another very important point is that when you first install Exchange 2000 Server, it runs in mixed mode (see the section "Mixed Mode" later in this chapter). In mixed mode, administrative groups are treated as Exchange 5.5 sites for compatibility reasons.

Policies

Exchange 2000 introduced policies, a core part of the Exchange administrative model. A policy is a collection of settings, or properties, that you can apply to multiple objects of the same class within your Exchange organization. Polices significantly reduce administrative overhead by eliminating the need to do the same changes to many objects manually. It also significantly improves manageability because in a large organization, manual management of a multitude of objects with dissimilar settings was next to impossible. After initial settings are applied, if there is a need to change a setting, it can easily be done to one policy and reapplied to all pertaining objects, as opposed to the previous method of manually changing one property on many objects. This strategy is consistent with the user policies present in Windows NT and Windows 2000, but instead is Exchange specific.

The two major types of policies are system policies and recipient policies. System policies relate to server objects, public folder databases, and private mailbox databases. They are contained in the System Policies object, which can be specific to an administrative group, or to the organization, depending on your administrative model design. Recipient policies are applicable to address-bearing objects within the Exchange object hierarchy. This can be an individual public folder with an email address, or an email-enabled user object. Recipient policies are found outside the scope of administrative groups, in the Recipients container, Recipient Policies object. Please refer to Figure 11.4 and note where these containers are located in the system hierarchy.

System Policies

System policies are sometimes referred to as server-side policies, primarily because they affect server and back-end database objects rather than users and recipients. These are of the apply-time implementation type, which means policy settings affect system objects when the administrator configures and applies them. Every system object (a server, for example) to which a policy was applied lists it on the property pages, and settings that were affected by this policy become disabled to prevent further administrative changes and configurations that do not conform to the implemented standards.

Several types of system policies exist, and different settings apply to different policy types. Table 11.1 lists the policy types and the settings that apply to them.

Table 11.1   System policy types and settings.

Policy Type	Settings Group	Description
Server policy	General	Policy-specific and general settings, such as policy name
Private store policy	General, database, limits	Policy-specific settings, database settings such as deleted item retention period, storage limits, storage group membership settings, and maintenance settings
Public store policy	General, database, limits, replication	All of the above plus replication settings such as replication interval and message size limits

Recipient Policies

Recipient policies are sometimes referred to as user-side policies because the settings affect users and other email-enabled objects in the hierarchy, such as groups and contacts. These are of the background-apply implementation type. The administrator specifies a policy and all the settings that it should enforce, associates the policy with a set of users or recipients by using the Lightweight Directory Access Protocol (LDAP) query result set, and applies the policy. LDAP is used to look up information in Active Directory. Changes do not become effective until later, when the System Attendant is scheduled to perform routine maintenance of recipients and email addresses. Recipient policies are used primarily to manage recipient addresses and add or modify them if necessary. For instance, you might want to add **@department.company.com** email addresses to your existing **@company.com** ones, or add cc:Mail, Microsoft Mail, Lotus Notes, Simple Mail Transfer Protocol (SMTP), or X.400 addresses to enable your recipients to send and receive messages to and from corresponding mail systems. You can specify and apply multiple SMTP or X.400 addresses using recipient policies.

Policy Conflicts

It is not possible to apply more than one policy to the same object in the hierarchy. If you try to apply a second policy to an object on which a policy is already applied, you will receive a statement that the object on which the apply procedure was attempted is already controlled by another policy. You will then be offered a choice of whether to discard the previous policy and apply the new one, or to leave it as is and cancel the new policy. If you keep the existing policy, you will get an error message stating, "The object *objectname* could not be associated with the policy *policyname* because you refused to remove the object from the control of conflicting policies."

Permissions

Permissions are one of the core components of your administrative model. Microsoft Exchange Server 2000 stores its configuration data in AD, and although security is tightly integrated with AD, Exchange also adds an extended permission set. The Exchange 2000 configuration is organized in a hierarchy of objects of different types. Some of these objects can contain other objects, and these are referred to as container objects; an example is an administrative group folder. Some objects cannot contain other objects, and these are referred to as items, or leaf objects; examples are server objects, policy objects, database objects, and so forth. Administrative groups, or containers, are called parent objects with regard to the objects they contain, which are referred to as child objects. An organization object is another type of container—a root container—that serves as a starting point when referencing or searching for an Exchange organization object. Every object in AD, either a container or a leaf object, has its own a set of rules. Because Exchange

11

2000 directory (configuration) is a part of AD, management of permissions of your Exchange organization is very consistent with that of Windows 2000.

Delegation

Permissions on an object can be assigned either manually or by using a delegation wizard. The delegation process assigns the permissions you specify to all the child objects contained within the folder (container object) on which you run the wizard. Delegation is a very convenient administrative tool because it makes the practice of manual permission management almost obsolete. However, in certain circumstances, you may need to manually set permissions on certain objects, such as on a database that may contain certain confidential information that requires very specific rights. Please refer to Chapter 12 for more information on delegation.

Inheritance

When you apply a certain set of permissions on a container object, by default, permissions flow down the hierarchy within that container, and all child objects (either containers or items) get the same set of permissions. This is referred to as inheritance—and it is very similar to the way NTFS permissions are inherited in the file system. When a set of permissions is said to be inherited, it means a child object received these permissions from a parent container object. That container object might have received these permissions as a result of administrative practice or inheritance from its own parent container. Inheritance is analogous to real-life.

As with policies, when an object inherits permissions from its parent, the security settings of that object become grayed out to prevent further administrative changes that do not comply with the inheritance rule. This can be manually overridden in the properties of that object; on the Security tab at the bottom of the property sheet, you can alter the inheritance property. If you try to remove inheritance, you will see a dialog box asking if inherited permissions should be copied to the object, if the object should restore the permissions that were set manually before the current permissions were inherited, or if you want to abort the requested operation. If you choose to copy inherited permissions, the effective permissions will essentially remain the same, but now you will be able to change permissions as needed. If you decide to restore the permissions that originally had been set on the object before the current permissions were inherited, chances are this object will have a blank Access Control List (ACL), unless permissions were modified manually after installing Exchange.

The ACL concept has been around since the early days of Windows NT 4. Every object in AD has an ACL—a list of all objects (users) that have a specified access to this object. This can be No Access as well, so the fact that a user appears on the ACL does not warrant that this user has any type of control over this object. If access was not explicitly granted, it is implicitly prohibited. To take maximum advantage of the ACL concept, you should put users into groups and define access based on groups. In that way, further permission management has less administrative overhead. During the process of delegation, ACLs that you define in the wizard are copied to all child objects. Because AD concepts are tightly integrated into the Exchange design, it is strongly recommended that you become familiar with Windows 2000 management and administration fundamentals. You should use only the Exchange System Manager MMC (Microsoft Management Console) snap-in to manage your Exchange 2000 permissions and other settings.

Inheritance affects the permissions of newly created objects as well. When you create an object within a container that has a set of permissions defined, this object gets a copy of the permission set that is defined on its parent level. After you create a number of objects within one container, you can easily change the set of permissions on the parent level, and, as a result, all child objects will inherit the same permissions. Inheritance ensures that permissions of newly created objects are consistent with your existing set of permissions. For information stores, public folder trees, and address lists, you can customize the degree of inheritance. Because these objects (especially public folders) often do not adhere to certain permission sets and usually have different levels of access defined, it may make more sense to adjust inheritance to one of the following configuration setting choices based on the three types:

➤ This Object Only

➤ Inherit Only

➤ This Object and Subcontainers

➤ This Object and Children Objects

➤ Subcontainers Only

➤ Children Objects Only

➤ This Object, Subcontainers, and Children Objects

➤ Subcontainers and Children Objects

These custom inheritance properties will govern permission propagation through the hierarchy of the object to which you are assigning permissions. You can define what inheritance strategy you want to use when you define permissions on the object.

Default Group Accounts

When the first Exchange 2000 Server is installed, it creates two default administrative groups—Exchange domain administrators and Exchange enterprise administrators—in Active Directory Users and Computers. You can use these two group accounts to start designing your security or administrative model, as well as to create your own groups, add users to these groups, and assign appropriate permissions to these groups. Any change in group membership will affect user permissions on Exchange objects. That is, if you assigned to group A full control to over routing group 4, if you then add another user to group A, that new user will have full control over routing group 4 as well.

Standard and Extended Permissions

Exchange 2000, as previously discussed, has its object-level security topology tightly integrated with AD. All objects in Exchange 2000 can have standard permissions and extended permissions set on them. Standard permissions come with Windows 2000, and they include the following:

➤ Read

➤ Write

➤ Execute

➤ Delete

➤ Read permissions

➤ Change permissions

➤ Full control

Please note that this permissions list is in no way complete. Some objects in Exchange come with extended permissions, an Exchange object-specific set of predefined actions on the object. The following objects in the Exchange hierarchy have extended permissions:

➤ Public folder trees

➤ Servers

➤ Protocols

➤ Address lists

➤ Databases

➤ Chat channels

Note that these objects have only three chat-specific permissions—user, sysop, and administrator. Please refer to Chapter 14 for more information.

Table 11.2 lists the extended Exchange permissions in alphabetical order and provides descriptions of what functionality this provides. Most, if not all, of these settings are enforced and exercised by Information Store Service.

Table 11.2   Extended Exchange permissions.

Extended Permission	Description
Add Public Folder to Admin Group	Controls addition of public folders to administrative groups.
Administer Information Store	Used by the information store to check if a user has enough authority to perform certain operations on the database.
Create Named Properties in Information Store	Allows or prohibits creating named properties. "Named property" is an information store attribute that can be accessed by its name.
Create Public Folder	Allows or prohibits creating public folders within the public folder tree.
Create Top Public Level Public Folder	Allows or prohibits creating top-level public folders in a specific public folder tree.
Full Store Access	Allows or prohibits full access to the information store.
Mail Enable Public Folder	Allows or prohibits enabling an email address on a public folder. Public folders can participate in Exchange 2000 just as regular recipients do. This is very useful when designing company collaboration and document routing solutions.
Modify Public Folder ACL	Allows or prohibits redefining public folder ACLs (permissions).
Modify Public Folder Admin ACL	Allows or prohibits redefining administrative ACLs.
Modify Public Folder Deleted Item Retention	Allows or prohibits modifying how long items deleted from the public folder shall remain in the information store.
Modify Public Folder Expiration	Allows or prohibits modifying content expiration policy on public folders.
Modify Public Folder Quotas	Allows or prohibits modifying maximum size allowed to a public folder.
Modify Public Folder Replica List	Allows or prohibits creating or altering public folder replication partners. For this permission to work, it has to be granted on both partners where replication is being set up.
Open Mail Send Queue	Allows or prohibits accessing the information store in/out mail queue.
Read All Metabase Properties	Allows or prohibits reading Internet Information Services (IIS) metabase settings. Exchange cannot function without IIS.
Remove Public Folder From Admin Group	Allows or prohibits removing public folders from the public folder tree.
View Information Store Status	Allows or prohibits viewing information store status details.

11

Windows 2000 Active Directory

Windows 2000 Active Directory is a topic in a class of its own, and it deserves a separate publication; however, a few core concepts that you must understand when planning your Exchange 2000 administrative model are presented here.

In addition to the core concepts, such as child objects and parent objects, covered earlier in this chapter when discussing Exchange 2000 policies, is the important concept of the organizational unit (OU). OUs are the smallest entities within AD to which you can delegate authority. They are logical units, or containers, used to organize objects such as users, computers, printers, groups, applications, and file shares, among others. When organized, object collections are managed much easier and in a more consistent manner compared to managing and keeping track of the changes manually. If planned and organized in a consistent, scalable manner, a collection of OUs represents the managerial backbone of your entire enterprise. The OU structure can map to departments within a company, branch offices, regional locations, or any other business criteria; they can also combine several criteria. For instance, suppose your company has five locations across Europe and North America, and each location is a branch with its own departments. As a central information technology specialist, you can create five OUs that map to geographical locations, and then another set of OUs within those regional OUs to map down to the departmental level. This gives you a lot of flexibility when designing your Windows 2000 enterprise administrative model.

For maximum scalability and reduced administration, Microsoft recommends setting up your Exchange administrative groups and AD OUs in a consistent manner, as closely mirrored as possible. Note that you can nest OUs within OUs in AD, but you cannot nest administrative groups in Exchange. So if you want to create a one-to-one copy of AD and the Exchange 2000 organization structure, you have to keep your OUs shallow.

If you are still supporting Exchange 5.5 servers, you can configure up to three connection agreements. Connection agreements are used to replicate AD data into the Exchange 5.5 database. If you create a mail-enabled user in AD that was set up for a connection agreement, the user object will be replicated from AD to Exchange 5.5 as a mailbox recipient.

Administrative Modes

Exchange 2000 was designed to coexist with existing Exchange 5.5 installations, just like Windows 2000 coexists with Windows NT, to accommodate migration over time and make transition as smooth as possible. Just like the Windows 2000 domain controller, Exchange 2000 runs in two modes: native mode (for a pure Exchange 2000 environment) and mixed mode (for backward compatibility with Exchange 5.5). When you first install Exchange 2000 Server, it will function in mixed mode by default until you change it to native mode manually through Exchange System Manager | Organization properties. This is done to ensure that Exchange 2000 will interoperate with existing Exchange 5.5 servers whenever you install a new server. Note that organization transition from mixed mode to native mode is a one-way process and cannot be rolled back.

Native Mode

Native mode, as the name implies, is used when the organization has moved completely to an Exchange 2000 platform and there is no need to maintain Exchange 5.5 sites. An important difference exists between interoperability and simple coexistence when it comes to an Exchange 2000 native mode switchover. Both versions can coexist separately from each other on the same physical network having separate namespaces and Exchange organizations. This coexistence is supported through regular connectors, which makes it possible to exchange email messages between two systems on the SMTP communication level; however, directory information will not be the same as a result of the different namespaces. You should run Exchange 2000 in native mode whenever possible, provided that there is no need for two versions to coexist as part of the same logical organization sharing the same namespace. However, there might be a number of reasons why you would have to support both systems, for instance legacy application migration cycle or third-party connectivity configurations. During this dual-system period you will not be able to switch to native mode without severely affecting functionality of Exchange deployment. Native mode takes maximum advantage of the new Exchange 2000 functionality.

Mixed Mode

When running in mixed mode, as was mentioned earlier in the section "Administrative Groups," Exchange 2000 treats its administrative groups the same as sites in Exchange 5.5. This limits Exchange 2000 functionality dramatically, but this is the only way to provide interoperability between two systems within the same logical organization. As a result, the following restrictions are imposed on a mixed mode deployment:

➤ All members of all routing groups must be members of the same administrative group; for instance, you can move servers from one routing group to another as long as collectively they belong to the same administrative group.

➤ Mailboxes cannot be moved between servers that do not belong to the same administrative group.

➤ You cannot use all of the commands available in Exchange System Manager to manage Exchange 5.5 servers; some of them will not work.

➤ All Exchange 5.5 objects and properties get replicated into AD via Active Directory Connector (ADC) Service Pack 3 (SP3), and you can view them in Exchange System Manager. However, you are presented with read-only properties.

Exchange 5.5 Sites

Before moving on to planning your future Exchange 2000 administrative model, it is important that you understand the existing environment, which in many cases will be Exchange 5.5; in some cases, it will be a different mail system or no system at all. If it is a previous version of Exchange, then you have to be aware of what Exchange sites are and how they function to plan a seamless migration and minimize administrative overhead, because in mixed mode environment administrative groups of Exchange 2000 are treated as sites in Exchange 5.5.

In earlier versions of Exchange, sites were server-centric, and contained at least one server or a grouping of servers that were functioning as routing and administrative units. Most of the changes were done on the site level, and they were replicated to all of the servers that were members of that site. This reduced administrative overhead significantly. Message routing was contained within the site, and a message sent outside the site had to go to a bridgehead server on which connectors to external mail systems were defined. It was recommended that all the servers on a local area network (LAN) be put into the same Exchange 5.5 site because traffic associated with Exchange directory replication that was taking place within the site required a LAN or a permanent high-speed wide area network (WAN) connection (usually defined as at least 64 kilobits per second, or Kbps). In these earlier Exchange versions, you had to have at least one server to create a site. If you had two or more servers and wanted to separate them for security, routing, political, or administrative purposes, you would most likely install them into two or more sites.

Sites could be routed and managed as a unit. This feature maps exactly to the definition of administrative groups in Exchange 2000, although administrative groups allow much more flexibility and granularity in terms of management. Administrative groups do not depend on your physical boxes—they exist only as logical units that contain your administrative duties within a certain AD space, or otherwise restrict administrative authority based on specific duties. This no longer affects routing because you have the ability to put all your routing groups in a separate administrative group. An administrative group in Exchange is much like an OU in AD. You have to consider very carefully how and why the existing site model was implemented before you plan your Exchange 2000 administrative model.

Building Your Administrative Model

Prior to designing your Exchange 2000 administrative model, be sure to identify all the key aspects of the existing Exchange 5.5 (if you are upgrading) or other mail system (if you are migrating). You should carefully consider how many people are administering Exchange, and list their responsibilities. If your previous system design was not working very well, this analysis is critical for you to understand what exactly was not working very well or could have been improved. If everything was working well, you should still carefully plan and analyze the new Exchange 2000 features and see how your design, which already was tested and approved in production, can be further enhanced with administrative groups and delegation.

When planning and implementing Exchange 2000, you should consider several general areas of the Exchange administrative model. You can break down or consolidate the following areas as you see fit for your organization and Exchange management personnel:

➤ User administration

➤ Recipient policies

➤ Server and database management

➤ Routing

➤ Public folders

➤ Collaboration

➤ Address lists

User Administration

In Exchange 5.5, user administration was a process separate from recipient mailbox administration, and the related information was stored in two different directories or databases. Recipients were stored in Exchange X.500 directory and were mapped to a Windows NT user account, and user accounts were stored in the Security Account Management (SAM) database. When you created a domain user in NT 4 domain, you had an option of creating a corresponding mailbox in Exchange 5.5, which would be a completely different object in a different database. Now, with Exchange 2000, the process has changed dramatically. Because the Exchange 2000 directory is AD, on which Windows 2000 domain relies, user accounts are created in the Active Directory Users and Computers MMC snap-in, and on one of the property sheets of the user accounts is an option to email-enable a particular user object. No separate process to create a mailbox exists. This brings up a good point: Who manages mailboxes now? Will it be the Windows 2000 administrator or the Exchange 2000 administrator? The problem is that there are no longer any mailboxes, only AD user object properties and a database that stores actual mailbox contents.

The three standard administrator types in Exchange 2000 are:

➤ View-only administrator

➤ Administrator

➤ Full administrator

View-only administrators cannot make any changes whatsoever. They just have access to view how things are configured on your end. This is useful when the management of Exchange is distributed and autonomous due to the nature of the business, and it

11

might be necessary to allow administrators from other branches to browse through your configuration settings when troubleshooting or doing research.

The standard type of Exchange administrator designated as simply "administrator," is allowed to change configuration settings but not allowed to change permission settings, assign permission to others, or elevate permissions for themselves.

The account used to install Exchange 2000 becomes a full administrator account. This account is in power to do any Exchange-related directory changes, and therefore membership in this elite group should be kept to a minimum, similar to administrative access in your Windows 2000 domain.

Perhaps the hottest question that arises involves who should manage user accounts and who should mail-enable them. Microsoft suggests that a unified team manage both because it will decrease response times, support costs, and minimize chances of a human error. Please refer to the review of the Microsoft Systems Framework (MSF) team and process models in Chapter 2 of this book. Note that it is entirely up to you—and it's technically possible, if you want—to have two teams doing these tasks separately. A unified team is a better solution, however, if you consider that mail-enabled groups and accounts can be needlessly duplicated if different personnel perform these tasks.

Recipient Policies

Recall from the "Policies" section earlier in this chapter that two types of policies exist, one for managing recipients and one for managing servers (systems). Recipient policies allow quick and efficient management of recipient email address namespaces. This attribute is very helpful when merging, acquiring, or simply deploying another coexisting mail system—instead of manually going through all recipients, you create an address policy and assign it to a set of users. During the next maintenance period, System Attendant will add or modify existing addresses to reflect policy changes.

Server and Database Management

Server management involves assigning and managing permissions, protocol configurations, system policies, storage groups, and databases. Administration groups allow a very granular approach when it comes to Exchange 2000 server management—you can take advantage of the delegation and inheritance features that are applicable to or involve containers, which in directory terms are administrative groups. You can organize your servers into administrative groups, and assign appropriate permissions to the group. Inheritance will propagate these permissions by default down to children objects, and if you ever need to change a permission on all of the children objects, you need change it only once, on the parent container. After permissions are configured in an administrative group, if you add a new object (a server, for example), you do not need to reassign permissions on it because new objects inherit these permissions automatically.

Routing

Routing groups are used to complement administrative groups, and they completely substitute for the server-centric sites concept of Exchange 5.5. Depending on the size of your organization, routing can become quite sophisticated—it can contain many routing groups, have multiple routing paths (for redundancy and fault tolerance), and use a variety of mail connectors (SMTP, X.400, Lotus Notes, and so forth). Routing groups are covered in Chapter 9. A messaging team that would manage company-wide email traffic as well as traffic leaving and coming into the company should control routing and global messaging settings.

Public Folders

In Exchange 2000, Outlook is no longer a requirement for accessing public folders. This can be achieved through the WebAccess component (which was present in Exchange 5.5 as well) or through custom-developed Web-based applications. If your Exchange serves as a platform for collaborative solutions, your public folder structure may become complex and planning the folder will require more detailed attention. Public folder planning should be done together with the development team. A public folder team might be needed if your enterprise relies heavily on public folder storage. This team should be empowered to create folders and administer replicas to ensure the highest availability possible.

Collaboration

Chapter 14 explores the realtime collaboration services of Exchange 2000. Depending on their scale and importance, these services will require additional personnel and administrative roles within the Exchange 2000 administrative model. In smaller companies, features such as chat and instant messaging may seem like a waste of company resources, but some companies, such as Internet service providers (ISPs), may rely on these services for their core business. In companies such as ISPs, where the user base requires several servers dedicated to instant messaging needs only, a realtime collaboration administrator is indispensable.

Address Lists

Address lists (which exist in Exchange 5.5 as well) are used to organize all recipients and their contact information into a comprehensive list that can be presented to users upon request from their Exchange client (Outlook 2000). Different views of the list can be generated to facilitate access and/or enforce security (by hiding certain information). These lists are much more flexible in Exchange 2000 than they were in Exchange 5.5.

11

Chapter Summary

This chapter reviewed the conceptual fundamentals of the administrative model, the important functions upon which it is built, and how to plan and implement it. The Exchange 2000 administrative model is comprised of administrative groups, policies, permissions, and routing groups. Administrative and routing groups together substitute for Exchange 5.5 sites and make that concept obsolete.

Administrative groups are logical management units that define the boundaries of authority when assigning permissions or delegating access to someone else and enabling them to execute specific tasks.

Permissions are tightly integrated with Windows 2000 Active Directory, and are of two types—standard Windows 2000 permissions and extended Exchange 2000 permissions. Standard permissions are used to secure basic access to Exchange objects, such as read, write, execute, and delete. Extended Exchange permissions provide control over service-specific and Exchange object-specific functions, such as queuing mail to the information store, adding or removing public folders, managing public folder replicas, and so on.

In addition, permissions come with two features—inheritance and delegation. Once an administrative group is created and permissions are assigned to it, Access Control Lists are propagated down the object hierarchy, and all children objects inherit permissions from their parent administrative group container. This behavior occurs by default and can be overridden on the individual object level if necessary. Delegation is used to automatically assign a person to do specific tasks within specific administrative groups using a wizard-based approach.

The administration mode affects your administrative model. Exchange 2000 supports a compatibility mode with Exchange 5.5 that is called a mixed mode. To take maximum advantage of your Exchange 2000 administrative model, however, you have to migrate completely and turn your Exchange 2000 organization into native mode.

The three major administrative models are centralized, decentralized, and mixed. In the centralized model, a central IT team from a single location manages the administration of Exchange 2000. The centralized model is characterized by a single administrative group and a relatively large number of routing groups. In the decentralized model, disparate parts of the same Exchange organization are managed by local administration teams. This design includes separate administrative and routing groups for each division. The third design is a mixed model design, which combines the strengths of both the centralized and decentralized designs. It allows centrally managed policies and corporate messaging standards, but leaves day-to-day administrative management to the local teams.

Review Questions

1. In Exchange 2000, Outlook is no longer a requirement for accessing public folders. This can be achieved through which one of the following components?

   a. WebAccess

   b. Internet Explorer

   c. Administrative Tools

   d. DCPROMO

2. Which components make up the Windows 2000/Exchange 2000 administrative model? [Check all correct answers]

   a. Administrative groups

   b. Routing groups

   c. Policies

   d. Permissions

3. Which one of the following statements is true about administration in Exchange 2000?

   a. Administration is server-centric.

   b. Administration is site-centric.

   c. All objects are included into Active Directory.

   d. Compared to Exchange 5.5, use of administrative groups is limited.

4. In most cases, Exchange administrative models mirror the information technology support team structure within an organization. Which one of the following is not one of the three types of administrative models?

   a. Centralized administration

   b. Decentralized administration

   c. Mixed administration

   d. Site administration

5. Which one of the following administrative models is most effective in large organizations, and has the same effect as in sites Exchange 5.5?

   a. Centralized administration

   b. Decentralized administration

   c. Mixed administration

   d. Site administration

11

6. Which of the following statements are true concerning administrative groups? [Check all correct answers]

    a. You can nest administrative groups within administrative groups.

    b. An administrative group's parent node can contain individual administrative group child nodes.

    c. You cannot create another general administrative group where you have to create task-specific groups.

    d. In Windows 2000 native mode, administrative groups are treated as Exchange 5.5 sites for compatibility reasons.

7. Several types of system policies exist, and different settings apply to different policy types. However, which one of the following system policy types encompasses the functions of the others while also addressing such settings as replication interval and message size limits?

    a. Server policy

    b. Client policy

    c. Private store policy

    d. Public store policy

8. The Exchange 2000 configuration is organized in a hierarchy of objects of different types. Some objects cannot contain other objects and are referred to as items, or leaf objects. Which of the following are leaf objects? [Check all correct answers]

    a. Server objects

    b. Administrative group objects

    c. Organization objects

    d. Policy objects

    e. Database objects

    f. Parent objects

9. Which one of the following is not a type of inheritance configuration setting?

    a. This Object Only

    b. Parent Object Only

    c. This Object and Subcontainers

    d. This Object and Child Objects

    e. Subcontainers Only

10. When the first Exchange 2000 server is installed, it creates two default administrative groups in Active Directory Users and Computers. Which of the following represent these groups? [Check the two best answers]

    a. Exchange domain servers

    b. Exchange site servers

    c. Exchange enterprise servers

    d. Exchange realm servers

11. Which of the following objects in the Exchange hierarchy has extended permissions?

    a. Public folder trees

    b. Protocols

    c. Address lists

    d. All of the above

    e. None of the above

12. Which of the following is a component of Active Directory that represents a logical container that is used to organize objects such as users, computers, printers, groups, applications, and file sharing, among others?

    a. Administrative group

    b. Global group

    c. Organizational unit

    d. Group policy

    e. Global catalog

11

13. Which administrative mode is implemented when an organization has moved completely to an Exchange 2000 platform and there is no need to maintain Exchange 5.5 sites?

    a. Mixed mode

    b. Native mode

    c. Exchange 2000 Mode

    d. Migration mode

    e. Conversion mode

14. In Exchange 5.5, user administration was a separate process from administering recipient mailboxes. True or false?

    a. True

    b. False

15. Which one of the following is not one of the three standard administrator types in Exchange 2000?

    a. View-only administrator

    b. Administrator

    c. Full administrator

    d. Read-only administrator

Real-World Projects

Project 11.1

Administrative groups are hidden by default. If you are to work with administrative groups, you first have to make them visible.

1. Click on Start | Programs | Microsoft Exchange, and open Exchange System Manager.

2. Right-click on the root container of your Exchange organization and select Properties.

3. On the property sheet that will appear, select the Display Administrative Tools checkbox. This procedure is irreversible once you implement your administrative groups. Administrative groups are now visible in your Exchange directory.

Project 11.2

When you install Exchange 2000 Server, it is put into mixed mode (Exchange 5.5 coexistence mode). If your organization has migrated from Exchange 5.5 completely and the old servers are now decommissioned, or if you do not support interoperability and the same namespace between Exchange 2000 and Exchange 5.5, then you should switch your Exchange 2000 organization into native mode to take maximum advantage of new features and the enhanced administrative model.

1. Click on Start | Programs | Microsoft Exchange, and open Exchange System Manager.

2. Right-click on the root container of your Exchange organization, and select Properties.

3. On the property sheet that will appear, in Operations Mode, click the Change Mode button. Note that this is a one-way process, and after your organization is switched to native mode, you will not be able to install or support Exchange 5.5 servers in the same namespace without reinstalling the entire Exchange 2000 organization back into mixed mode.

Project 11.3

The most challenging side of administrative groups is their planning. Implementing them is just a few clicks away. This project assumes you went through Project 11.1 and made your administrative groups visible.

1. Click on Start | Programs | Microsoft Exchange, and open Exchange System Manager.

2. Right-click on the Administrative Groups container and select New | Administrative Group.

3. Give your new administrative group a name according to your designed structure. On the Details tab you can optionally give this group a description (administrative note).

4. Click OK. Your administrative group is now created, and you can move on to creating service-specific subcontainers.

Project 11.4

After you have set up your administrative group structure, you are ready to move on to the next step, creating child objects within your administrative model.

1. Click on Start | Programs | Microsoft Exchange, and open Exchange System Manager.

2. Browse to the administrative group in which you want to create the system policy.

3. Right-click on the group container, select New | System Policy Container. If this is the first system policy container that you are creating, it will automatically be added to your group. Otherwise, you will get an error message that one already exists.

4. Right-click on the System Policies container that you created, select New | Server Policy. A dialog box will appear prompting you to select property tabs that you want to include in this policy. For Server Policy, only the General tab is available. Check the General checkbox and click OK.

5. In the property sheet that will appear, first type in the name of your policy, and then define all the settings on other tabs in accordance with your administrative model design. When finished, click OK. Your policy is created, and now you have to apply it to select or all server machines in your Exchange 2000 organization.

6. To apply a policy to a certain server, right-click on the policy that you created in your System Policies container, and choose Add Server. You will be presented with the computer browser, where you can select which machines you

11

want to be controlled by this policy. Click OK when done. You will be prompted to choose if you want to apply these changes immediately. Click OK to apply this policy now. If you choose to do that later, you can right-click on the policy and choose Apply.

Project 11.5

Now that all the basic steps are covered, implement the mixed mode administration model comprised of two geographical locations—Toronto and New York City—and a centralized administrative group for system policy and routing group management.

1. Click on Start | Programs | Microsoft Exchange, and open Exchange System Manager.

2. In the Administrative Groups container, create three administrative groups: Toronto, New York City, and Central Management.

3. In Toronto and New York City, create Servers, Chat Communities, and Folders containers as needed. Configure them in accordance with your policies.

4. In the Central Management administrative group, create three subcontainers: System Policies, a Routing Group for New York, and another Routing Group for Toronto. This will give your central team the ability to control system policies and a message routing configuration enterprise-wide without giving access to local administrative teams. You will later delegate New York and Toronto group access to the local administrator teams that will be taking care of day-to-day duties. Delegation is discussed in the Chapter 12.

CHAPTER TWELVE

Deploying Exchange 2000 Administrative Groups

After completing this chapter, you will be able to:

✓ Effectively deploy Exchange 2000 administrative groups

✓ Analyze existing and planned models

✓ Assign administrative roles and permissions

✓ Delegate administrative access through the Administration Delegation Wizard

✓ Understand the access control model

✓ Understand and manage Exchange recipients

✓ Deploy and manage policies and administrative groups

Deploying Administrative Groups

Chapter 11 discussed Exchange administrative model components, planning considerations of your administrative environment, and the significance of administrative groups in your Exchange 2000 design. This chapter puts the finishing touches on these concepts by discussing in finer detail the topics of delegation and the access control model, as well as Exchange policies, recipients, and permissions that apply when implementing the administrative model as opposed to planning it. Two types of groups are reviewed—Exchange administrative groups and Windows 2000 user groups, which in many aspects serve as a base for administrative groups.

Windows 2000 Integration

As the previous chapters showed, Exchange 2000 is tightly integrated with Active Directory (AD) in Windows 2000, and, as a result, many changes regarding administrations and planning are involved. To better deploy your Exchange 2000 infrastructure, you should carefully consider the differences between Exchange 5.5 and Exchange 2000 mail-enabled units (if you are an Exchange 5.5 administrator). You should also know all the nuances of Windows 2000 group types and their role in deploying Exchange 2000.

Overview of Windows 2000 Groups

In Exchange 5.5, administrators had to deal with three major organizational units when managing recipients: Windows NT domain local groups, NT domain global groups, and Exchange distribution lists (DLs). Windows NT Security Accounts Manager (SAM) user accounts and the Exchange 5.5 directory were not integrated, which meant that mailboxes (recipients) were separate items in the Exchange 5.5 directory and had to be associated with Windows NT user accounts before a user could access his or her mailbox. The Exchange 5.5 DL is a collection of individual recipients that make up a mail distribution group. For example, an administrator could create a DL in the Exchange 5.5 directory and include all of the employees' mailboxes as members; then all one had to do to send an email to everyone in the company was to send an email addressed to that DL. Exchange would look it up in the directory, expand it (extract all the addressees that belong to a DL), and send this message to all of the DL members.

The previous Exchange version environment had two Windows NT groups for security (permissions) management and one for mail distribution management. This unwieldy approach is now gone for good with the introduction of AD. Whereas before, DLs played an important role when assigning and managing Exchange permissions on public folders because they were the only Exchange-specific way to group recipients, now both access control and mail distribution rely heavily upon

AD users and groups. This is a very important concept to understand when planning and deploying your administrative groups because you will later have to assign and manage permissions. The whole concept of Exchange administration is eased.

A Windows 2000 AD object is considered mail-enabled if it is configured to accept mail. Both users and groups in AD can be mail-enabled, and DLs no longer exist. Every mail-enabled recipient is now an integral part of AD. Different types of mail-enabled groups can substitute for Exchange 5.5 DLs. The following sections take a look at each one separately. When you create a Windows 2000 user group (either domain local, domain global, or universal), you can specify whether this group is for security group or mail distribution purposes (see Figure 12.1). Universal groups are strongly recommended for mail distribution, but keep in mind that universal groups are not available in the Windows 2000 mixed-mode environment (NT4 compatibility mode). You have to be running your Windows 2000 organization in native mode to take advantage of universal groups.

One of the major planning and deployment advancements offered by Windows 2000 is the fact that one group can be used for both security and mail distribution purposes. For you to be able to assign permissions to a group, the group has to be of the security type, and then if you also want to mail to the same group, you can mail-enable it. Distribution groups cannot be used to control access.

Windows 2000 Groups with Domain Local Scope

The basic functionality of a local group is the same as in Windows NT, and in Windows/Exchange 2000 it can be of either the distribution or security type, or a combination of the functionalities of both if it is a mail-enabled security group. The

12

Figure 12.1   Choosing between mail distribution and security group.

following items apply to local groups and have to be kept in mind when planning and deploying your administrative groups:

➤ When AD is running in native mode, local groups can contain user accounts, local groups from the same domain, global groups, and universal groups from any domain in the AD forest. In mixed mode, universal groups do not exist, and local groups can contain user accounts and global groups regardless of what domain they belong to.

➤ In Windows 2000 native mode, local domain groups can be nested (meaning one local group can contain other local groups). Local groups can be converted to universal groups if they do not nest other local groups.

➤ When defining access, local groups can be set to access resources local to the domain in which they were created; that is, they cannot cross trusts in Windows NT and be used in different domains within one forest in Windows 2000.

➤ Group membership is retrieved on demand when someone is mailing to a local group object. In the global catalog, the group object is listed but membership is not. This applies to Messaging Application Programming Interface (MAPI) clients as well—group membership is not visible in Microsoft Outlook (the de facto client standard for Exchange).

Windows 2000 Groups with Domain Global Scope

Groups with domain global scope are much like global groups in Windows NT. They contain only members local to the domain where global groups are defined, but they can be referenced in Access Control Lists (ACLs) in different domains, can cross trust relationships, and can be used for both security and mail distribution purposes. Global groups in Windows 2000 allow one level of nesting. That means global groups can contain other global groups, but these in turn cannot contain a third level of global groups. The following items apply to global groups:

➤ In native mode, global groups can contain other global groups and user accounts from the same domain. In mixed mode, global groups can contain only user accounts.

➤ Global groups are allowed to contain objects from the domain in which global groups are defined. Global groups have global scope, which means they can be listed on ACLs anywhere in the AD forest.

➤ Global groups can be converted to universal groups if they do not have membership in other global groups.

➤ Global groups are listed in the global catalog, but their membership is not. The same rules apply as they do with local groups when it comes to global catalog listing and membership retrieval.

Windows 2000 Groups with Universal Scope

Windows 2000 introduces a group with a new scope—the universal group. Universal groups can be implemented only in Windows 2000 running native mode (where no Windows NT domain controllers coexist), and they are strongly recommended when implementing Exchange 5.5 DL-like functionality. Two types of universal groups exist—the universal distribution group (UDG) and the universal security group (USG). USGs require a native mode environment, but UDGs exist in both mixed-mode and native-mode environments. In single-domain environments, however, universal groups are unnecessary because they span members across domains, and no need exists to do that when there is only one domain. In such a deployment scenario, global groups are just as good. The following items apply to universal groups:

➤ Universal groups can contain users, global groups, and universal groups from any domain in the Windows 2000 AD forest.

➤ USGs require native mode environment; UDGs are available in both mixed and native mode.

➤ Universal group membership does not need to be retrieved, and membership is available to Outlook users.

➤ Universal groups cannot later be converted to any other group.

➤ Universal groups can be referenced on ACLs anywhere in the AD forest.

UDGs Versus USGs

All Windows 2000 groups can be of either security or distribution type, or combine the functions of both. Universal groups also are divided into two types: UDGs and USGs deserve a separate section due to the purpose of Exchange 5.5 DLs. Exchange 5.5 DLs allowed you to enable your users to send messages to entire departments, or the whole company, or any other grouping of users based on certain criteria. DLs also better defined and managed access to public folders. In Windows 2000 and Exchange 2000, UDGs provide mail distribution functionality, and USGs control access to public folders. As with other groups, you can combine a USG and a UDG to be represented by the same group, but the group has to be defined as a USG and then be mail-enabled.

When planning and deploying your administrative groups, this design of AD can prove to be very efficient because you would most likely have to define your groups once with both security and mail distribution functions in mind. You should understand this before you even install your first Windows 2000 server and run **dcpromo** on it, not just when you are just about to roll out your Exchange 2000 administrative groups. Depending on the approach and business requirements of your organization, you will end up dividing your company resources and user

12

accounts based on certain criteria, such as departmental, geographical, or organizational-hierarchical to closely match your HR charts. In any case, with wise planning, you would define these groups once, and when you reach the point of deploying your Exchange solution and administering it, the underlying infrastructure would already exist. Recall from Chapter 11 that your AD and Exchange designs should be consistent with each other in terms of resource organization and user access.

Planning and Deploying Windows 2000 Groups

When deploying Windows 2000 groups in an Exchange 2000 organization, try to use USGs as much as possible because they provide maximum membership and reference flexibility within the AD forest. If your organization consists of only one domain, universal groups do not give you any advantage over global groups; however, you should always plan ahead based on projected or anticipated company growth and expansion. If you do go with USGs, ensure that the domain in which you define these groups is a native mode Windows 2000 domain. If you want to create one group for various purposes, then a USG is still a better choice because it allows you to define permissions and reference this group on objects' ACLs, and you can still define a Simple Mail Transfer Protocol (SMTP) address for the USG to become mail-enabled.

Reducing Replication Traffic

Global catalog (GC) servers in AD list universal groups with all the particulars about their members, so any change to universal group membership creates replication traffic between GCs. In Windows 2000 AD, replication is supported on the property-based level, which means if you change the telephone number on a user object, the object itself is not replicated, but instead only the property that has been changed is replicated. Still, membership information is a multivalue property, which means this entire property gets replicated. To reduce this traffic, use a hierarchical nest of universal groups. If you change membership in one of the subgroups, only this group's membership property has to be replicated, as opposed to replicating membership information for the entire universal group. All of the members within these subgroups will be visible to Outlook clients because this information is listed in the GCs and is available through the Global Address List (GAL) in Exchange 2000. On the contrary, if you nest global groups within universal groups, member information will not be visible to Outlook clients and will not be available in the GAL because it is not listed with the GC. Therefore, no replication traffic will occur between GCs if the global group membership is modified.

Group Membership Expansion

When you send a message to a group, if the group is a USG or UDG, group membership is taken from the local GC server. In contrast, if it is a domain local group or domain global group, members will be looked up on one of the local domain controllers. This process is referred to as expansion. It usually consumes hardware resources and should be considered when planning your groups.

Public Folder Permissions

When assigning permissions to public folders—either within administrative groups or individually—replicas of public folders that are being copied outside the domain where the replicating public folder exists will create a security risk if you have assigned permissions based on global security groups. Because these kinds of permissions are valid only within the domain in which the global group is defined, replica permissions outside the domain will not be effective, and anyone could gain access to the contents you are replicating. Use universal groups whenever possible. Actually, Exchange 2000 was built and extensively tested around universal groups, and they are recommended for managing your users.

Designated Management Domain

Sometimes, a wise deployment strategy may be to have one Windows/Exchange 2000 domain dedicated to managing users and groups in a mixed-mode environment. USGs are not available in mixed-mode domains, but because USGs are recommended for deploying your users and groups, you may consider deploying one native mode domain for user and group management, and still have mixed-mode domains for Exchange 5.5 interoperability. This strategy allows you to combine backward compatibility and Windows 2000–specific features, but it naturally requires some hardware and software resources as well as additional planning and administrative maintenance.

Limited Universal Group Membership

Your member count in root universal groups should be as low as possible, and the members should be grouped into subgroups that belong to the same parent universal group. As was stated previously, membership information is a single multivalue property of a group object, and this property is replicated among all GC servers when a change is made in a universal group membership configuration. All members of universal groups and subgroups are visible to Outlook clients. You may choose to use global groups as subgroups within universal groups to restrict membership information from being replicated. Because global groups are not replicated between GC servers, global group membership information is not visible to Outlook clients. However you decide to subpartition your groups, whenever possible, you should use a USG as your top-level container.

Consider the following example. Suppose that you have a certain volatile group of users that changes on a weekly or monthly basis (for example, co-op students, business affiliates or partners on a business mission to your company, or contract

12

labor for specific short-term assignments such as data entry). This group of users comprises no more than 100 user accounts. Suppose that you also have another group of user accounts that is rather stable and changes very rarely, and it is 10 times larger than the volatile group. In total, then, you have an estimated 1,100 users in your Windows/Exchange 2000 system. You include all volatile users into 3 different USG subgroups: students, partners, and contractors. The remaining 1,000 permanent users are split into 10 departmental USG subgroups. All of these 13 USG subgroups have membership in the same parent USG group, and whenever a change is made to, for example, the contractors universal subgroup, only that subgroup replicates member information to GC servers, which may be a third of the 100 users as opposed to 1,100 users. In a volatile environment (education facilities, for instance), where information changes frequently and regularly, this subgrouping makes a significant difference. This is especially true in international corporations that may have GC servers in different parts of the world, which may as well be connected by somewhat unreliable and saturated wide area network (WAN) links.

Administrative Group Deployment Considerations

Administrative group planning was the topic of Chapter 11. This section deals more with the issues and considerations that affect your administrative group deployment, primarily the fundamentals of system management—user, group, and delegation considerations.

A recommended approach to implementing administrative groups is first to review your existing enterprise, technical implementation, and business structure. The next step is to evaluate what design flaws existed in previous implementations and what functionality should be implemented with the new version. Then you have to carefully plan your new structure and services based on the analysis and research that was done in the first steps. After planning is complete, run a downsized pilot project to prove your theory, if you have enough hardware, labor, and time resources. In medium-to-large organizations, this pilot project often is a turning point in the designing process and is often a requirement for the theory to be approved. You should set forth criteria that will evaluate the success of your pilot project and theoretical design—a measurement baseline with which to compare your pilot deployment results. Microsoft offers a tool called LoadSim to help you test system responsiveness. You should also pay special attention to your administrative model design during this phase and evaluate how manageable your proposed design is.

Note: We cannot possibly overemphasize the importance of planning. A wise man once said, "If you fail to plan, you plan to fail."

Human and Business Resources Considerations

The following sections discuss the personnel usually involved in the process in Exchange-centric organizations, where Exchange is a mission-critical or business-supporting product. Carefully consider your management and technical support and development hierarchy to effectively deploy administrative groups. In larger organizations, management may not necessarily require access to everything, a fact that is commonly the case in smaller companies.

Technical support personnel would need a lower level of administrative privileges to allow them to perform day-to-day duties in response to Help Desk calls, such as managing mailboxes and modifying their properties or settings as may be considered necessary. The advanced administrative team (systems engineering team) usually has complete control over the administrative group. These personnel are the escalation point of all problems that cannot be solved at the technical support level due to insufficient access, the advanced nature of the problem, or a lack of knowledge. In midsize companies, this group usually is the root of administrative authority and is ultimately responsible for the overall health and robustness of the system. Corporate administrative teams, which are common to large multinational companies, are usually responsible for building and designing decisions that affect the entire company, as well as administrative authority delegation, security, policy, and routing planning, configuration, and management.

Personnel information is important to consider because it is the basis of group design in AD, which in turn will be crucial in the delegation of Exchange 2000 permissions. Such information is important to deploying administrative groups because you delegate access to administrative groups, and also because administrative groups are the building blocks of your administrative hierarchy in Exchange 2000.

12

Management

The management of a company comprises the following personnel:

➤ *Business decision makers*—These are the people at the top who define the guidelines of the project.

➤ *Project managers and program managers*—These managers are the focal point of the entire project. They report to the Director of Information Technology.

➤ *Product manager*—If Exchange 2000 is used as a development platform, this person brainstorms on product functionality and features. Often higher management may define the general functionality guideline or product strategy.

➤ *Information flow and corporate procedures management*—This group of people defines the overall logistics and information distribution and circulation around the company.

Consider placing these people in separate global groups, or, depending on the size of the group, place them in separate universal subgroups and unite these subgroups into a single management mail-enabled USG. Depending on the size of the organization, this group may have to be delegated full administrative rights to the Exchange organization. This delegation will occur in most companies, even though higher-echelon management may never need to exercise these privileges.

System Architects and Designers

The system architects and designers comprise the following personnel:

➤ *Exchange architects*—These are the designers of your Exchange services and organization.

➤ *Deployment and migration planning specialist*—This specialist implements the plan designed by the Exchange architects group.

➤ *Network security and traffic analyst*—This person performs communication analysis that provides Exchange architects with a better understanding of how to properly design the system.

➤ *Consultants*—Larger companies usually bring aboard foreign expertise to enrich their experience base and to provide a third-party evaluation of the proposed architecture.

Exchange architects and implementers are usually the people who are responsible for system design and deployment, and therefore they will have access to everything that has to do with Exchange, including AD. A network analyst may not require access to the Exchange system at all. Consider placing consultants into a separate mail-enabled USG, and architects and implementers into another separate USG. Architects may require View-Only Admin privileges because they usually develop the theory behind the scenes of Exchange deployment. The implementation team will be installing Exchange and deploying administrative groups, so it will have Full Admin privileges on the Organization root level. Members of this team may be further subgrouped into regional deployment teams with Full Admin access only to their own administrative groups and with View Only Admin access to the rest of the organization, so that they can always see configuration information in other parts of the organization when troubleshooting or configuring their administrative groups.

Various Administrative Roles

Various administrators comprise the following personnel, among others:

➤ *Exchange organization administrator*—This person provides advanced support contact, post-deployment support, and maintenance on the highest level.

➤ *Exchange client administrator*—This person provides advanced support contact for client-, connector-, and user access-related issues and strategies.

➤ *Message traffic administrator*—This person handles advanced issues that have to do with email volume, mail queues, response times, and network saturation issues.

➤ *Network administrator*—This is the person who deals with physical medium issues.

Depending on the size of the company, all of the duties in this list may be focused on one person, or you may have an administrative team. Depending on the number of people, you should deploy mail-enabled USGs and delegate appropriate view only or administrator access on the respective administrative groups. The organization administrator has to have at least administrator privileges on the Organization root container.

Other Exchange 2000 Users

Other Exchange 2000 users may include the following:

➤ *Quality assurance (QA)*—This is the testing and bug report team.

➤ *End-user trainers*—These are the personnel tasked with training end-users. They should not require any administrative access to the system other than client software connectivity (i.e., mail-enabled user accounts).

➤ *Technicians or monitors*—These personnel have some sort of administrative access, usually on the lowest level, and often just enough to resolve relatively unsophisticated and straightforward issues on a daily basis.

➤ *Help Desk support*—The Help Desk support staff provide frontline client-base support.

➤ *Security specialist*—This specialist can be application-specific (e.g., Exchange view-only administrator for configuration evaluation purposes), network-specific, or organization-wide.

➤ *End users*—These are the ultimate users of the system.

Apart from the users, who are more than likely to be present in most Exchange 2000 deployments, you may have other specific groups that will need appropriate access privileges to the system, either on the user or administrative level. QA people usually have more privileges than anybody else in this group. Technicians should be able to administer objects within an assigned Exchange administrative group on a daily basis because they deal with issues that escalate from Help Desk support personnel, who are the front line when dealing with user-related problems and should not have any administrative access to the system.

Recipients Deployment Considerations

Earlier in this chapter, the "UDGs versus USGs" section discussed the difference between UDGs and USGs and how they affect your administrative group planning.

This section focuses on individual recipients and their roles in the Exchange 2000 organization. This knowledge is helpful when you plan administrative groups because different types of recipients have different requirements as far as Exchange 2000 design is concerned, so you should plan for appropriate resources to be grouped consistently.

Exchange 2000 took a step from the Exchange 5.5-based X.500 autonomous directory and now is fully based on AD. In AD, you can have several types of recipients, and their functionality maps to that in Exchange 5.5. In Exchange 5.5, you had user mailboxes (actual user logons and private storage on Exchange 5.5 Server), distribution lists (used to organize mail receiving objects in Exchange 5.5 and manage access to public folders), and custom recipients (simply an entry in the X.500 directory that is visible in the GAL). The GAL maps to an email recipient that belongs to the Exchange 5.5 organization and yet the user can have that address conveniently located in the same address book that is used intraorganizationally. The custom recipients designation is best used for consultants who join the company for a period of time and are not an integral part of it. AD objects in Windows 2000 and Exchange 2000 provide the same functionality as Exchange 5.5 directories.

Mailbox

The Exchange 5.5 mailbox is no longer a separate object; it is a private storage space in the information store that is associated with a mailbox-enabled recipient (user) in AD. A user is said to be mailbox-enabled when email delivery information such as an email address is configured in its properties. All objects in AD can further be subdivided into three major categories, as follows:

➤ *Mail-disabled*—An object that is mail-disabled cannot accept mail by design.

➤ *Mail-enabled*—An object that is mail-enabled can accept mail but does not have its own storage to which to send mail. An example of a mail-enabled recipient is a Windows 2000 distribution group or mail-enabled security group.

➤ *Mailbox-enabled*—An object that is mailbox-enabled can receive mail and provide logon and mail retrieval functionality to the end-user. When planning administrative groups, account for the fact that mailbox-enabled recipients require mailbox storage space in the form of a mailbox store within storage groups. You should consider grouping these in the same security and group context in AD and Exchange 2000 to facilitate further delegation and management.

Distribution Lists

Distribution lists are local, global, and universal groups within AD. Recall from earlier in the chapter, in the section "Overview of Windows 2000 Groups" and Figure 12.1 (see page 327), that groups can be created as distribution groups or security groups.

Either group can serve as a distribution list (a distribution group is a distribution list by design, and a security group can be mail-enabled by configuring an email address in its properties). The major difference between the two is the security identifier (SID). Distribution lists do not have SIDs, and therefore they cannot be referenced on ACLs (i.e., they cannot be used to assign permissions). Conversely, security groups do have SIDs and are designed to participate in ACL definitions.

Custom Recipients

Custom recipients in Exchange 2000 are called mail-enabled contacts. They do not have an SID, and therefore cannot be used to log in. They do not have a space allocation in the information store (i.e., no mailbox); all they have is certain configurable contact information that can be specified in their properties.

Permissions Deployment Considerations

Chapter 11 reviewed three Exchange 2000 predefined administrative roles in the context of administrative model planning—view-only administrator, administrator, and full administrator. When the Administration Delegation Wizard process is reviewed later in this chapter, it may prove helpful to understand what kind of permissions are involved in each role, and how the level in the hierarchy where the role is applied affects the effective rights as opposed to assigned rights. As you follow the next few sections, keep in mind that, by default, child objects, on which permissions are applied, inherit permissions down the hierarchy unless you configure them to do otherwise. These child objects can be both leaf objects and container objects.

Exchange View-Only Administrator

The Exchange view-only administrator role is for administrators of different administrative groups who need to know how certain objects are configured in those groups in which they should have no access to changing any configuration information.

The rights at the Organization root level include the following:

➤ Read, List Objects, and List Contents on the MsExchConfigurationContainer and its subcontainers

➤ View Information Store Status on the Organization container and its subcontainers

The rights at the administrative group level include the following:

➤ Read, List Objects, and List Contents on the MsExchConfiguration Container only

12

➤ Read, List Objects, and List Contents on the Organization container only

➤ Read, List Objects, and List Contents on the Administrative Groups container only

➤ Read, List Objects, List Contents, and View Information Store Status on a particular administrative group and its subcontainers

➤ Read, List Objects, and List Contents on the MsExchRecipientPolicies, Address Lists, Addressing, Global Settings, and System Policies containers and subcontainers

Exchange Administrator

An Exchange administrator, as was discussed in Chapter 11, has sufficient administrative authority to fully administer Exchange system configuration information but not access rights.

The rights at the Organization root level include the following:

➤ Grant all but Change Permissions on the MsExchConfigurationContainer and subcontainers

➤ Deny Receive As and Send As on the Organization root container and all subcontainers

The rights at the administrative group level include the following:

➤ Read, List Objects, and List Contents on the MsExchConfiguration Container only

➤ Read, List Objects, and List Contents on the Organization container and subcontainers

➤ Grant all but Change Permissions; deny Send As and Receive As on an administrative group and its subcontainers

➤ Grant all but Change Permissions on the Connections container and subcontainers

➤ Read, List Objects, List Contents, and Write Properties on the Offline Address Lists container and subcontainers

Exchange Full Administrator

Exchange full administrator, as discussed in greater detail in Chapter 11, is capable of fully administering Exchange 2000 deployment, including modifying permissions.

The rights at the Organization root level include the following:

➤ Full Control on the MsExchConfigurationContainer and subcontainers

➤ Grant all but Send As and Receive As on the Organization container and its subcontainers

➤ Read and Change Permissions on Deleted Objects in the Config NC container and subcontainers

The rights at the administrative group level include the following:

➤ Read, List Objects, and List Contents on the MsExchConfigurationContainer only

➤ Read, List Objects, and List Contents on the Organization container and subcontainers

➤ Grant Full Control and deny Send As and Receive As on an administrative group and its subcontainers

➤ Grant Full Control, except Change Permissions, on the Connections container and subcontainers

➤ Read, List Objects, List Contents, and Write Properties on the Offline Address Lists container and subcontainers

As one can infer from the preceding lists, a very simple-looking single-step Administration Delegation Wizard does quite a bit of configuration. Use delegation wizards to delegate administrative privileges in your Exchange 2000 environment. Assigning rights individually on each object in the preceding lists is not recommended because this method is prone to human error. Permission wizards, in contrast, were tested and verified to assign appropriate rights to securely delegate administrative rights. Administration Delegation Wizard is reviewed later in this chapter in the "Administration Delegation Wizard" section. Table 12.1 further details the effects of delegating administration on different levels within your organization.

12

Table 12.1   Effective permissions chart (assigned permissions at the top, effective permissions on the left).

	View-Only Admin (Group)	Admin (Group)	Full Admin (Group)	View-Only Admin (Org)	Admin (Org)	Full Admin (Org)
View-Only Admin (Group)	V	V	V	V	V	V
Admin (Group)		V	V		V	V
Full Admin (Group)			V			V
View-Only Admin (Org)				V	V	V
Admin (Org)					V	V
Full Admin (Org)						V

Exchange 2000 Access Control Model

When deploying your administrative groups, you will have to assign and delegate administrative authority—in fact, that is the very purpose of having administrative groups. The access control model (ACM) in Exchange 2000 is completely redesigned from that in Exchange 5.5, and this time it closely matches the Windows 2000 ACM. Permission management is no longer container-based; it is object-based and even property-based. As a result of this major change, ACM in Exchange 2000 is much more granular and flexible.

When a user logs on to a Windows 2000 machine, the logon process generates an access token. This access token bears the following: a user SID, all groups to which this user belongs, and other vital security information. When the user attempts to access a resource, this token is used to verify user access rights; it also is attached to every process that the user initializes. Each object in Windows 2000 (and Exchange 2000 because the ACMs are the same) has a security descriptor attached to it; this descriptor specifies group and user SIDs that have access to this object, and it also specifies what kind of access each object (user or group) has. This collection of access rights, or security descriptors, is known as a Discretionary Access Control List (DACL), or an ACL.

If there is no ACL on an object, everyone has full control access to it. If an ACL exists but no Access Control Entries (ACEs) are specified, then no one has control over this object (of course, the administrator can always forcibly take over the ownership). ACE entries on an ACL are used to specify the SID of the objects that have access to this object, and what kind of access was granted (or denied). The ACL of the accessed object is verified against the user token every time that user requests access to it, and if the matching SID is found on the ACL, then the specified access rights are given to the user; otherwise, access is denied. In much the same way, Exchange 2000 manages its own objects in AD, and every Exchange object—be it a container or a leaf object (item within a container)—has an ACL defined for it in AD, against which every request is checked.

Item-Level ACE

The granularity in access control in Exchange 2000 allows selectively restricted access to specific objects within a container. For instance, say you were using Administration Delegation Wizard to assign full administrative rights to user Brock for administrative group A. Suppose that you then discovered that there were one or more select few objects that you wanted to prevent Brock from accessing. You can manually override inheritance for this object by copying delegated permissions from the parent Administrative Group container, and then adjusting Brock's permissions so that he can no longer access this object. So now in Exchange 2000, you have the ability to control access on the object-by-object level when you perceive there is such a need. This is called item-level ACE—defining permissions in the ACL of an object that regulates access to that object.

Property-Level ACE

With the introduction of AD, we now have property-level ACEs. A property-level ACE defines access down to the level of properties of an object. For example, you can block access to the email address property of a certain group of user objects within your directory. This effectively prohibits access to that particular information and (during a search targeted to find those objects by email addresses), those blocked objects will not show in the results pane.

Administration Delegation Wizard

Delegation in the Exchange 2000 and Windows 2000 environment can be of two types: Exchange 2000 infrastructure-level delegation and Windows 2000 directory-level delegation. The first of these is performed in the Exchange 2000 System Manager MMC (Microsoft Management Console) snap-in, and is a result of tight product integration between the Windows 2000 delegation and the Exchange environment. The second type of delegation, Windows 2000 directory-based delegation, is done in the Active Directory Users and Computers MMC snap-in, and is somewhat related to Exchange administrative group access delegation as well.

Directory-level delegation is performed on organizational units (OUs) in AD to empower certain users to access, manage, or otherwise make changes to the contents of OUs' hierarchy. This is an important consideration when delegating access to certain user groups at the Exchange infrastructure level. It may be possible that you can delegate a group of people to manage your Exchange organization, and another set of users could have administrative authority delegated to them in AD over this first group of people you just added to manage your Exchange. This may result in someone going into the Active Directory Users and Computers MMC snap-in and modifying the membership of the group you delegated in Exchange by adding a person or two. Now these newly added people could manage your entire Exchange infrastructure because they are members of the group you delegated as an ACE on the Exchange organization ACL. This may prove to be a very useful administrative feature that eases your administrative overhead if properly planned. Without consistency in design between the two structures, however, this becomes a security risk, so make sure that your administrative group rollout has both infrastructure and directory delegation on the agenda.

Exchange 2000 employs an Exchange Administration Delegation Wizard to delegate administrative authority on two levels—the Organization root container and the Administrative Group container. These are the only types of containers you can delegate, so you must deploy your administrative groups consistently with your design and company requirements for distribution of administrative functions.

12

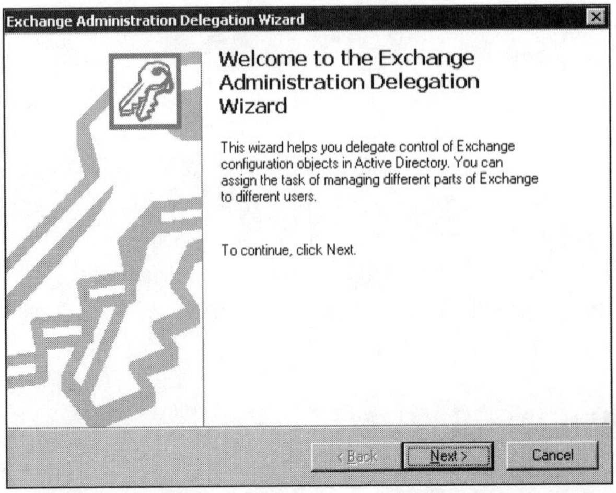

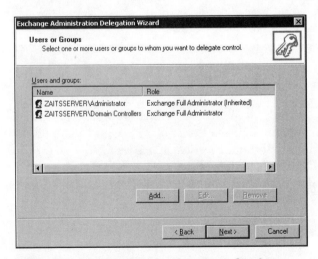

Figure 12.2 The Exchange Administration Delegation Wizard welcome screen.

To access the Exchange Administration Delegation Wizard, right-click on the administrative group to which you want to delegate administration, and select Delegate Control from the pop-up menu. This will bring up the wizard, as shown in Figure 12.2.

The screen that follows the welcome screen, as shown in Figure 12.3, allows you to add security groups to or remove security groups from the list of delegated control. As was discussed earlier in this chapter in the section "Exchange 2000 Access Control Model," only groups and individual accounts with an SID can be added to the ACL (delegated control to an administrative group, in our case).

Figure 12.3 Administration delegation process, Step 2.

Whether you are running your AD domain in mixed mode or native Windows 2000 mode defines whether you can have USG and nested global groups assigned to an ACL. Using these two object types is preferred, although not required. A UDG can exist in a mixed-mode environment, but it does not have a security context (its own SID), and therefore it cannot be defined as an ACE on an ACL. After you are done defining what groups you want to add and to which one of the three administrative roles you are assigning these groups, click Next and you will be presented with a confirmation screen with a summary of the changes that you are about to make (see Figure 12.4). If you click Finish, your changes will be applied to your administrative groups.

Please note that the Administration Delegation Wizard is one of several methods that can be used to delegate control of administrative groups. The Active Directory Service interface (ADSI) exposes the AD object model to programming and opens a world of opportunities to automate most tedious and labor-intensive tasks. It also provides new interfaces for management that are totally up to the administrators and programmers to design, and they can be as flexible or as restrictive as may be required. Other methods at this time are Windows Scripting Host (WSH) VBScripts and JavaScripts, which use the ADSI model, and ASP pages through Web-based administration. Another method is the MMC wizard, which was reviewed previously in this chapter.

Administrative Group Deployment Considerations

You need to account for the following considerations, among others, when deploying your administrative groups:

➤ You may have to group together certain objects that require nonstandard permissions. This is done to facilitate administrative management and reduce

12

Figure 12.4   Administration delegation process, Step 3.

the inheritance override to one group instead of being used in every group. You can use policies to control the behavior of different types of objects; however, you cannot control ACLs with policies.

➤ It is strongly recommended to define your permissions at the top level of your administrative hierarchy, or close to it. In this way you can manage your permissions more effectively.

➤ After you have deployed your administrative groups and delegated access, you can still manually override access permissions on individual objects down the hierarchy tree from where delegation was performed.

➤ You can create only one level of administrative groups; administrative groups cannot be nested inside one another. You can create specific containers within administrative groups that will contain system objects of different types. If you have to delegate different types of access to the same type of objects, you might have to create two administrative groups and delegate them accordingly.

➤ Access delegation can be done at only two levels: the administrative group level or the Organization root level. This is why administrative groups are considered to be a fundamental unit of administration in Exchange 2000.

➤ You can use a property-level ACL to fine-tune object behavior. Consider placing the objects into a separate container within an administrative group; if this isn't feasible, consider deploying another administrative group.

➤ You can move objects between the same types of containers that belong to different administrative groups. For example, if you created chat community A in administrative group London, you can move it from the Chat Communities subcontainer in the London administrative group to the Chat Communities subcontainer in the Toronto administrative group.

➤ You cannot have more than one container of the same type in the same administrative group. For instance, you can have only one routing group subcontainer within an administrative group. All routing group objects should be defined within the routing groups subcontainer of that administrative group. If there is a need to separate some of the routing group objects among different routing group subcontainers, you might have to create another administrative group.

➤ You cannot delete an administrative group while it still has some items remaining within it. You can delete an administrative group, however, if it has only subcontainers defined within it and no leaf objects remain in those subcontainers.

Chapter Summary

Chapter 11 has discussed planning considerations that are involved in administrative model design, and the basic elements of what comprises that administrative model. This chapter continued this subject, with more emphasis on deployment considerations of administrative groups.

This chapter opened with a discussion of Windows 2000 integration and considerations involved in deploying administrative groups. Windows 2000 has three major types of user group scopes—local, global, and universal. The mode in which the domain is running makes a difference because certain functions and features of certain group types may not be available in a mixed-mode environment.

Each of these user groups can participate in one of two modes. Each group can be employed to serve as either a distribution group or a security group. Distribution groups are used only for mail delivery. Security groups have their own SID identifiers and can be listed as ACEs on ACLs of virtually every object in AD or the Windows NT file system (NTFS). Security groups also can be mail-enabled, which would provide the same functionality as distribution groups when configured with an email address.

Universal groups have a special significance in deploying administrative groups because they can nest any types of group and user objects, including universal groups. The umbrella-like structure of universal groups can be implemented to reduce GC server replication traffic when a member property of one of the subgroups changes. Universal groups are the recommended way of implementing mailing lists and managing Exchange users because they provide more flexibility and granularity. Also, the membership of universal groups is visible to Outlook clients.

Universal groups can be of two types—USGs and UDGs. A UDG is designed to serve the same function as a DL in Exchange 5.5. It groups users and other Exchange 2000 recipients and allows for convenient email distribution within the organization, which may include foreign recipients. A UDG can exist in mixed-mode domain environments, but it does not have an SID and therefore it is useless when delegating control. The USG has an SID identifier and can be mail-enabled to provide functionality similar to that of the UDG, but the downside is that the native mode domain is required for the USG to be available.

A fine difference exists between mail-enabled and mailbox-enabled objects in AD. A mail-enabled object is a group object that does not have a mailbox associated with it. It serves the purpose of mail distribution to its members. Mailbox-enabled objects, in contrast, have mailboxes associated with them and can store and access mail correspondence in the Exchange mailbox store.

Finally, this chapter reviewed various aspects and considerations when deploying administrative groups, and examined the delegation process.

12

Review Questions

1. Which of the following are the major organizational units with which administrators had to deal when managing recipients in Exchange 5.5? [Check all correct answers]

   a. NT domain local groups

   b. NT domain global groups

   c. NT organizational groups

   d. Exchange distribution lists (DLs)

2. One of the major planning and deployment advancements that Windows 2000 has to offer is the fact that one group can be used for both security and mail distribution purposes. True or False?

   a. True

   b. False

3. Global groups in Windows 2000 allow how many levels of nesting?

   a. None

   b. One

   c. Two

   d. Four

4. Which of the following statements is false concerning Windows 2000 groups with domain global scope?

   a. Global groups are allowed to contain objects from the domain in which global groups are defined.

   b. Global groups can be converted to universal groups if they do not have membership in other global groups.

   c. Global groups are listed in the global catalog, but the membership is not.

   d. In mixed mode, global groups can contain other global groups and user accounts from the same domain.

5. Which new scope, introduced in Windows 2000, can be implemented only in Windows 2000 running native mode?

   a. Domain global group

   b. Enterprise group

   c. Universal group

   d. Organizational group

6. Two types of universal groups exist in Windows 2000. Which one of these is the valid universal group that can exist in both mixed-mode and native-mode environments?

    a. Universal distribution group (UDG)

    b. Universal security group (USG)

    c. Universal domain group (UDG)

    d. Universal system policy group (USPG)

7. Which of the following statements represent the recommended ways to use universal groups in Windows 2000 and Exchange 2000? [Check the two best answers]

    a. Use universal distribution groups (UDGs) to control access to public folders.

    b. Use universal distribution groups (UDGs) to provide mail distribution functionality.

    c. Use universal security groups (USGs) to provide mail distribution functionality.

    d. Use universal security groups (USGs) to control access to public folders.

8. You are deploying Windows 2000 groups in an Exchange 2000 organization. Which universal group should you try to use as much as possible because it provides maximum membership and reference flexibility within the Active Directory forest?

    a. Universal distribution group (UDG)

    b. Universal security group (USG)

    c. Universal domain group (UDG)

    d. Universal system policy group (USPG)

9. When you send a message to a domain local group or domain global group, the members are looked up on one of the local domain controllers groups. However, when you send a message to a USG or UDG, from where is the group membership information gathered?

    a. Primary domain controller (PDC)

    b. PDC emulator

    c. Universal system policy server

    d. Global catalog server

12

10. Which of the following is a Microsoft tool that is designed to help you test your system responsiveness and measure baselines?

    a. Network monitor

    b. NetDIAG

    c. LoadSim

    d. Dcpromo

11. All objects in Active Directory can further be subdivided into major categories. Which term describes the type of object that can accept mail but does not have its own storage to which to send mail?

    a. Mail-disabled

    b. Mail-enabled

    c. Mailbox-disabled

    d. Mailbox-enabled

12. Which of the following are valid differences between the distribution list and the security group? [Check the two best answers]

    a. Distribution lists do not have SIDs and cannot be referenced on ACLs.

    b. Distribution lists have SIDs and are designed to participate in ACL definitions.

    c. Security groups have SIDs and are designed to participate in ACL definitions.

    d. Security groups do not have SIDs and cannot be referenced on ACLs.

13. Which component is used to assign administrative privileges in your Exchange 2000 environment?

    a. Delegation wizards

    b. Assignment wizards

    c. Dcpromo

    d. LoadSim

    e. Group policy

14. Which feature of Exchange 2000 is completely redesigned from that of Exchange 5.5 to match the object-based and even property-based model of Windows 2000, rendering this feature much more granular and flexible?

    a. Delegation Wizard model (DWM)

    b. Security identifier model (SIM)

    c. Active Directory model (ADM)

    d. Access control model (ACM)

15. The Administration Delegation Wizard is just one of several methods that can be used to delegate control of administrative groups. Which of the following are other methods? [Check all correct answers]

    a. With Windows Scripting Host VBScript, by using the ADSI model

    b. Through the LoadSim tool

    c. By JavaScript, by using the ADSI model

    d. By ASP pages through Web-based administration

Real-World Project

Project 12.1

In the real-world projects in Chapter 11, you created New York, London, and Toronto administrative groups. Now, you are asked to come up with a user group structure for your organization and to decide to add a group to administer the London administrative unit.

1. Click on Start | Programs | Microsoft Exchange | System Manager. The System Manager MMC will now load.

2. Expand the Administrative Groups container and locate your London administrative group.

3. Right-click on London, then click on Delegate Control. The wizard will now appear.

4. On the welcome screen, click on Next.

5. On the following sheet, click Add, and a new dialog box will appear that allows you to choose the new group to which you want to delegate control and one of the three predefined administrative roles.

6. Click on Browse, select your group, and click OK.

7. Choose one of the three predefined administrator types. Click OK. Repeat this process for every group or individual user you want to delegate.

8. Click Next. The confirmation screen will appear with a summary of the changes you are about to make. Click Finish to delegate control to your administrative group.

12

CHAPTER THIRTEEN

Planning Public Folder Usage and Implementation

After completing this chapter, you will be able to:

✓ Describe the benefits of using public folders

✓ Describe the features of public folders in Microsoft Exchange 2000

✓ Design a public folder hierarchy

✓ Create public folders

✓ Secure access to public folders

✓ Manage public folder replication

T he goal of this chapter is to introduce you to the features of public folders that will help you plan and implement public folders in your messaging environment. This chapter examines the public folder hierarchy and replication methodology as well.

Defining Public Folders

A public folder stores messages or information that users in your organization can share. This can include many different types of information, such as custom forms, which provide the basis for such applications as discussion groups, bulletin boards, and so forth. You can create and manage public folders by using one of two tools, either a client such as Microsoft Outlook or the Exchange System Manager. The client will allow you to perform basic configuration tasks, whereas the Exchange System Manager will provide you with more administrative functions.

Public Folder Features

Exchange 2000 provides a number of powerful features for public folders, including the following:

➤ Support for the creation of many top-level folder hierarchies, or *folder trees*

➤ Implementation of the information store in Exchange 2000 and the Active Directory directory service

➤ The ability to secure items in public folders through Exchange Installable File System (ExIFS)

➤ Accessibility from the file system through ExIFS

➤ Accessibility from the Web

➤ Full text indexing

➤ Referrals enabled by default

Public Folder Hierarchies

One new feature of Exchange 2000 is the capability to create multiple folder trees, also known as *hierarchies*, which allow you to store public folders in more than one tree. Public folder hierarchies afford a better level of administrative control as well as innovative approaches to public folder design. Public folder hierarchies are also referred to as top-level hierarchies and public folder trees. An application of hierarchies might be to generate a separate public folder structure so that internal users in your organization can collaborate with external users. In doing so, you can also keep this content separate from the default public folder hierarchy. Each public folder tree holds its data in a single public folder store. Folders in the tree can then be replicated to all of the servers that have a public folder store linked to that public folder tree. Each public folder tree (also known as the default tree) uses a separate database on an Exchange server. Unfortunately, only the initial tree is visible from within Messaging Application Programming Interface (MAPI) clients such as Microsoft Outlook. Other trees can be viewed only from Outlook Web Access (OWA), Windows Explorer, or another application through the ExIFS.

This feature of multiple public folders can affect your organization's strategy for public folder usage and implementation. The default public folder hierarchy is generated on each public folder server, and its hierarchy is always replicated. Other public folder hierarchies, however, have an effect only on the servers where they are configured. You can implement extra public folder hierarchies to minimize the general size of the default public folder hierarchy, to make navigation easier, or to lower the total cost of the default hierarchy replication.

The default public folder store includes the All Public Folders hierarchy. This is listed as Public Folders in System Manager. This public folder store needs to be linked to every mailbox store on a server to make certain that the All Public Folders hierarchy is exhibited in Internet Message Access Protocol (IMAP) and MAPI mail clients.

General-Purpose Hierarchies

General-purpose hierarchies are any other hierarchies that you create. These are available from standard Windows applications in which the folders can be mapped as network drives using Exchnage Installable File System (ExIFS) or Web Distributed Authoring and Versioning (Web-DAV), as well as by Network News Transfer Protocol (NNTP) clients.

You can generate extra public folder hierarchies or trees as file repositories for groups, departments, or projects. Table 13.1 explains which hierarchies are visible to which clients.

13

MAPI client permissions for the top-level hierarchy are the conventional MAPI permissions. Client permissions for the general-purpose hierarchies depend upon the Windows Access Control Lists (ACLs). Windows 2000 mixed mode allows only

Table 13.1   Hierarchy visibility to various clients.

Client	Hierarchy
POP3	None
IMAP	All public folders
MAPI	All public folders
NNTP	Internet newsgroups
Web-DAV browsers	All public folders and other mailboxes and folders
Windows applications	Other mailboxes and folders shared with IFS

one MAPI public folder hierarchy for each organization. You can, however, have multiple general-purpose hierarchies for an organization. In the MAPI public folder hierarchy, folders are mail enabled by default; in general-purpose hierarchies, folders are not mail enabled by default.

Creating Public Folders

To create and manage public folders, you can use both the Exchange System Manager as well as a MAPI client such as Microsoft Outlook 2000. Users as well as managers can create public folders. Much of the creation and management of public folders occurs in the Outlook client because most users work in this client; however, the Exchange System Manager provides more in-depth control for administrators.

When you create a public folder, that folder is placed in the public folder store of your Exchange server, if it has one. A server might not have a public folder store if it was configured to be dedicated to some other specific task, such as a mailbox-only server. A public folder created in the public folder store of one server can then be replicated to the public folder stores of multiple additional servers. In most cases, not all of the public folders exist on one server. Instead, they are distributed across several servers throughout the organization.

As stated previously, an Exchange organization can host multiple public folder trees, with each tree consisting of a separate hierarchy of public folders. The top-level public folders reside at the top of a public folder tree. When a user creates a top-level public folder, it is placed in the public folder store on that user's home server. When a user creates a lower-level public folder, it is placed in the public folder store containing the parent folder in which the new folder is created.

Note: Some administrators prefer to use dedicated public folder servers and dedicated mailbox servers. A dedicated public folder server is one from which the mailbox store has been removed, and a dedicated mailbox server is one in which the public folder store has been removed. Dedicated servers are useful in organizations that have a large amount of users and/or public data, and frequent access to that data consumes a great deal of server resources.

Creating a Public Folder in Outlook

Creating a public folder by using Microsoft Outlook is a simple task. Figure 13.1 shows the main Microsoft Outlook window, with the folder list displayed and the Public Folders item expanded.

To create a public folder, ensure that either the All Public Folders object or the folder in which you want to create the new folder is selected, and choose New Folder from the File menu. You can also right click on the parent folder and choose New Folder. The Create New Folder dialog box opens, as seen in Figure 13.2. Here you will enter the name of the public folder that you want to create, choose

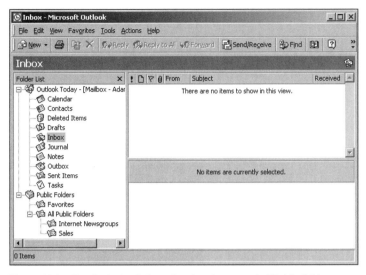

Figure 13.1   The Outlook window, showing the expanded Public folder.

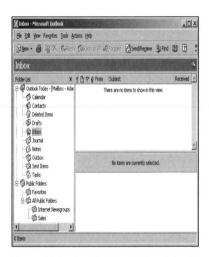

Figure 13.2   Create New Folder dialog box.

the type of items that folder should contain, select the folder in which it should be created, and click OK. You can set the types of messages that can be posted in the new folder, including appointment items, notes, tasks, and mail items. The default is the type of item that can be posted in the parent folder.

Creating a Public Folder by Using Exchange System Manager

To create a public folder by using the Exchange System Manager, expand the Tree | Administrative Groups | First Administrative Group | Folders container as

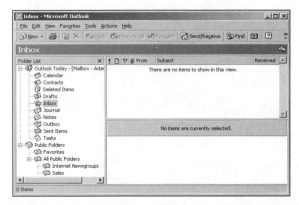

Figure 13.3   Creating a new public folder by using the Exchange System Manager.

shown in Figure 13.3. Then right click Public Folders, select New, and then select Public Folder. Enter the name of the new public folder in the Name text box, and then click OK.

Managing Public Folders

Now that you have created a public folder, you can configure it by using one of two tools: the Outlook client or the Exchange System Manager. Because users can create public folders, ideally they should be allowed to have some managerial responsibilities, which is why part of the management occurs in the client.

When you create a public folder, you automatically become that folder's "owner." You are then responsible for configuring the folder, which includes such tasks as configuring the access permissions, rules, and association of electronic forms. To perform this management, you can simply open the property sheet for a particular public folder in Outlook. You can also create and configure public folders in the Exchange System Manager. Certain tools for managing public folders are available only in this tool. For example, you can create and modify the top-level public folder hierarchies only in the Exchange System Manager. The Outlook option works for users because the user can do most of the managerial duties from within a single application.

Managing Public Folders by Using Outlook

To manage public folders using Outlook, right click on the folder and choose Properties from the pop-up menu. Table 13.2 presents a description of the configuration options available in the Public Folders Properties dialog box. Each of these dialog boxes is explored in greater detail in the following sections.

Table 13.2   Public folder configuration settings.

Tab	Settings
General	Identifies the description of the folder and enables read/unread information that improves client access
Replication	Designates which servers in the organization contain public folder replicas; also indicates the times at which this public folder is replicated to designated servers all through the organization
Limits	Specifies the age, storage limits, and retention length for deleted items
Details	Accepts an administrative description of the public folder
Permissions	Configures the folder, message, directory, and administrator rights on the folder

General Tab

The General tab of a public folder's property sheet, shown in Figure 13.4, allows you to perform the following tasks:

➤ Change the name of a public folder.

➤ Enter an optional description of that folder.

➤ Choose the name of an electronic form that should be used to post new items to the folder. By default, the generic Post form is selected.

➤ Specify that the Exchange client views of the folder be generated automatically. The Exchange client and Outlook process forms in different ways. This option provides compatibility in the Exchange client for folders created in Outlook.

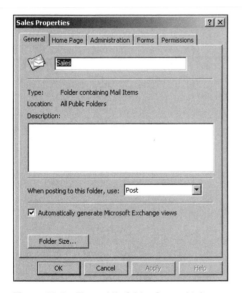

13

Figure 13.4   The public folder General tab.

Administration Tab

The Administration tab, shown in Figure 13.5, sets various options governing a public folder's use. The settings on this tab include the following:

➤ *Initial View On Folder*—This setting determines the initial Outlook view that is used whenever the public folder is opened. The available views are the default Normal threaded view and views grouped by discussion subject, topic, and poster.

➤ *Drag/Drop Posting Is A*—This setting regulates what happens when an item is dragged into a public folder. The two options are Move/Copy and Forward.

➤ *This Folder Is Available To*—This field has two options that specify whether the folder is accessible by anyone who has appropriate permissions or only by the folder owners.

➤ *Folder Assistant*—This button allows you to create rules that apply to messages as they arrive in the folder. Rules include such actions as forwarding the message automatically to a moderator or automatically replying to or rejecting messages based on the posting user or subject.

➤ *Moderated Folder*—This button allows you to set up this folder to be a moderated folder. This is also where you can establish one or more moderators for the folder. Setting up a folder as a moderated folder causes all items posted to the folder to be forwarded to a designated recipient or public folder for review. You must give one or more users permissions to move these items back into the folder once they have been reviewed by them and approved for viewing by others. Keep in mind that users' posts to the folders will not appear immediately in a moderated folder. For this reason, you can configure an automatic

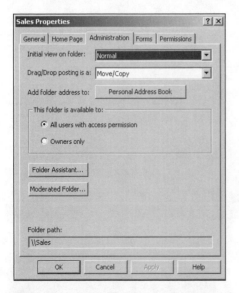

Figure 13.5 The public folder Administration tab.

reply to messages posted to moderated folders, letting users know that the moderator has received their message. You can do so by using the Reply To New Items With area, and configuring either a standard or custom response.

Forms Tab

The Forms tab, shown in Figure 13.6, allows you to specify the forms that can be used when posting to this public folder. The forms specified on this tab appear as the choices in the drop-down list for the When Posting To This Folder, Use option on the General tab. You can also manage any associated form from this tab.

Permissions Tab

The Permissions tab, shown in Figure 13.7, allows you to assign permissions to users on the current public folder. Each user can be assigned one of several roles; each role has a set of permissions associated with it. The available permissions are as follows:

➤ *Create Items*—This permission allows the user to post items in the folder.

➤ *Read Items*—This permission allows the user to open any item in the folder.

➤ *Create Subfolders*—This permission allows the user to create subfolders within the folder.

➤ *Edit Items*—This choice specifies which items in the folder the user can edit. The None option indicates that a user cannot edit items. The Own option indicates that the user can edit only items that he or she created. The All option indicates that a user can edit any item in the folder.

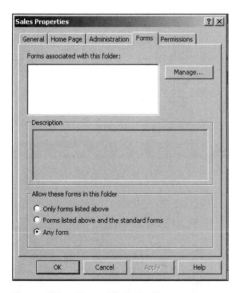

Figure 13.6   The public folder Forms tab.

13

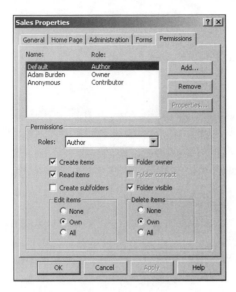

Figure 13.7 The public folder Permissions tab.

➤ *Folder Owner*—This choice grants the user all permissions in the folder, including the ability to assign permissions.

➤ *Folder Contact*—This permission specifies that the user is to receive copies of any status messages regarding the folder, including nondelivery reports.

➤ *Folder Visible*—This choice permits the user to see the folder in the public folder hierarchy.

➤ *Delete Items*—This choice specifies which items in the folder the user can delete. The None option indicates that a user cannot delete items. The Own option indicates that the user can delete only items that he or she created. The All option indicates that a user can delete any item in the folder.

You can modify the permissions associated with any given role. Table 13.3 shows the available roles and the default permissions granted for each role.

Table 13.3   Default permissions for public folder roles.

Role	Create	Read	Edit	Delete	Subfolders	Owner	Contact	Visible
Owner	Yes	Yes	All	All	Yes	Yes	Yes	Yes
Publishing editor	Yes	Yes	All	All	Yes	No	No	Yes
Editor	Yes	Yes	All	All	No	No	No	Yes
Publishing author	Yes	Yes	Own	Own	Yes	No	No	Yes
Author	Yes	Yes	Own	Own	No	No	No	Yes
Nonediting author	Yes	Yes	None	Own	No	No	No	Yes
Reviewer	No	Yes	None	None	No	No	No	Yes
Contributor	Yes	No	None	None	No	No	No	Yes
None	No	No	None	None	No	No	No	Yes

Managing Public Folders by Using Exchange System Manager

The previous section described how to configure public folders using the Outlook client. Now let's take a look at some of the tasks that can be completed by using the Exchange System Manager to manage public folders.

Creating a Public Folder Tree

Creating a new public folder tree is a three-step process:

1. Create a new top-level root folder that contains the new tree structure.

2. Create a new public folder store on the server to hold the contents of the new tree structure.

3. Connect the new top-level folder to the new public folder store.

Creating a New Top-Level Root Folder

The first step in creating a new public folder tree is to create a new top-level root folder. Keep in mind the purpose of this folder tree and why it is being created when choosing a name for it. For example, if you are creating a tree for use only by the marketing department, you might name the new top-level root folder Marketing.

To create a new top-level root folder, first select the Folders container for the administrative group in which you want to create the folder, as shown in Figure 13.8. If you have only one administrative group, or if you have Exchange System

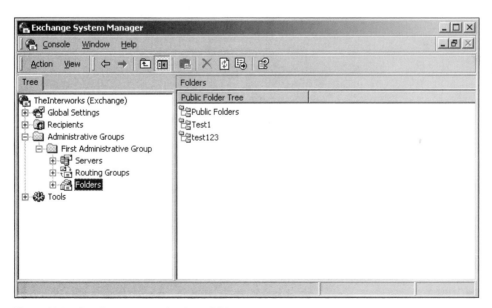

Figure 13.8   Creating a new top-level root folder.

set to not display administrative groups, the Folders container should appear directly under the root node. Each top-level root folder you create exists on the same level as the Public Folder Tree. Top-level root folders have their own database on each Exchange server that contains replicas of any of the folders in the tree's hierarchy.

Right click on the Folders container, and choose New | Public Folder Tree from the menu. This opens the property sheet (Properties window) for the new folder, as seen in Figure 13.9. Enter a name for the new tree in the Name field. The General tab contains a field that shows which public store is associated to the folder tree. Click OK to close the Properties window and create the new public folder tree.

Creating a New Public Folder Store

Public folders reside in the public folder store. Each public folder tree uses its own database in the store. After you have created the new top-level root folder for a tree, you must then create a new public folder store to hold that tree. In the Exchange System Manager, locate the container for the storage group on the server on which you want to create the new tree, as shown in Figure 13.10. You will create the new public folder store in this storage group.

Right click on the Storage Group, and choose New | Public Store from the menu. This opens the property sheet (Properties window) for the new store, as shown in Figure 13.11. Enter a name for the new store in the Name field. Next, click the Browse button to open a dialog box that lets you select a public folder tree to associate with the new store. Select the tree you created previously. After you finish, click OK to close the Properties window. You will be prompted to mount the new store once it has successfully been created. Click on Yes to mount the new store.

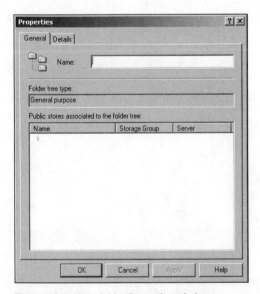

Figure 13.9 New folder Properties window.

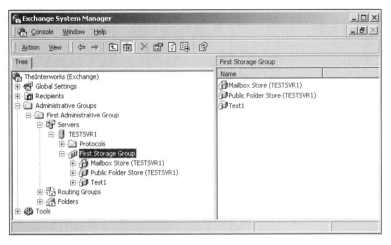

Figure 13.10   Storage group container.

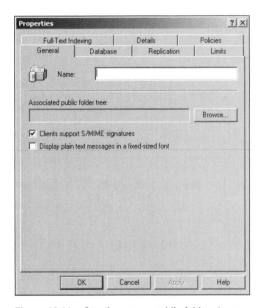

Figure 13.11   Creating a new public folder store.

The Public Folder Store's subcontainers, shown in Figure 13.12, allow you to view useful information, such as which users are logged on and using the public folders, as well as public folder details. These subcontainers are the following:

➤ *Logons*—Shows which users are logged on and using the public folders

➤ *Public Folder Instances*—Allows you to view the folders in the public store, configure the properties of a folder, and replicate a public folder to a specific public store

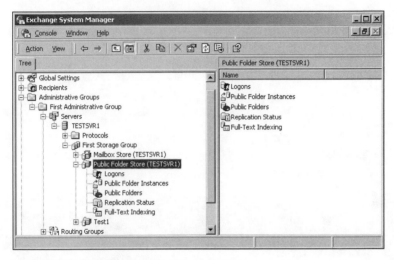

Figure 13.12 Public Folder Store subcontainers.

➤ *Public Folders*—Provides the ability to view such public folder details as the path, the size of the folder, the total number of items in each folder, when it was created, and the last time the folder was accessed

➤ *Replication Status*—Lists each folder, the last received time, the number of replicas, and the replication status

➤ *Full-Text Indexing*—Displays the current state of indexing, provided that indexing is enabled

Connecting to the Public Folder Store

The last step in creating the new public folder tree is to go back to the top-level root folder that you created earlier and connect it with the new public folder store. In the Exchange System Manager, right click on the top-level root folder in the main Folders container and choose Connect To from the menu. This opens the dialog box shown in Figure 13.13, which displays the available public folder stores.

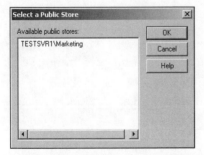

Figure 13.13 Connecting to the public folder store.

You should see the one you just created. Select the store that you just created and click OK. The store is now connected to the public folder tree and is listed on the Public Stores tab of the property sheet for the top-level root folder.

By default, only the Domain and Exchange Administrators groups have permissions to modify the root folder. You may want to set permissions governing which users can make changes to the root level of the tree. To do so, just open the property sheet for the top-level folder and switch to the Security tab. Click the Add button to specify permissions for additional users.

Client Support for Multiple Public Folder Trees

The All Public Folders hierarchy is available to all MAPI, IMAP4, NNTP, and HTTP (Hypertext Transfer Protocol) clients.

When you create additional hierarchies, they are accessible from standard Windows applications in which the folders are mapped as network drives using IFS, Web-DAV, and NNTP clients. Outlook cannot see these hierarchies unless they are viewed on a Web page hosted in Outlook 2000.

Multiple Public Folder Support Considerations

When planning multiple public folder trees, keep in mind the following considerations:

➤ You do not have to configure replication of additional hierarchies to all public folder servers in the organization. Because the All Public Folders hierarchy is created on every public folder server and its list of folders is replicated through-out the organization, additional hierarchies replicate only to servers with which they are configured to replicate.

➤ You might want to use additional public folder trees to make navigation easier for users and to ease the burden of replication. The size of the default public folder tree can be reduced if some of the content is moved to additional hierarchies.

➤ Only one MAPI top-level hierarchy per organization is allowed in mixed mode, but you can have multiple general-purpose top-level hierarchies per organization.

➤ The MAPI top-level hierarchy folders are mail enabled by default. When you create additional hierarchies, they are not mail enabled.

Creating a Public Folder in Exchange System Manager

In the past, Exchange Server could create public folders only when using an Exchange client, such as Microsoft Outlook. However, Exchange 2000 Server lets you create public folders easily by using the Exchange System Manager.

13

First, you will need to decide on which folder tree your new folder will reside. In Exchange System Manager, right click on the public folder tree on which you want to create a new folder and choose New | Public Folder from the menu. This command opens the property sheet (Properties window) for the new public folder, as seen in Figure 13.14. To finish the process of creating a new public folder, simply enter a name in the Name field and click OK. The Exchange System Manager will create the new folder, and users with the appropriate permissions should be able to access it immediately. Optionally, you can also enter a description for the folder. At the bottom of the General tab for a public folder is the option Maintain Per User Read And Unread Information For This Folder. If you select this option, the folder itself will keep track of messages that each individual user of the folder has read and mark them as having been read. However, most clients already keep track of this information, and therefore it is usually not necessary to enable this option.

You can set up a public folder to appear as a mail recipient in Active Directory. Once you have created a new public folder, you can accomplish this by mail-enabling the folder and configuring the public folder's mail-related settings for your organization. To mail-enable a folder, right click the folder in Exchange System Manager and choose All Tasks | Mail Enable from the menu. The command should take effect immediately, although you will get no feedback from Exchange System Manager after executing it. When this occurs, the System Attendant connects to Active Directory and creates an object for the public folder in the Microsoft Exchange Systems Objects container. Users with access to Active Directory can use the mail address properties to send email to the public folder. Once you have mail-enabled a folder, the property sheet for that folder will include several extra

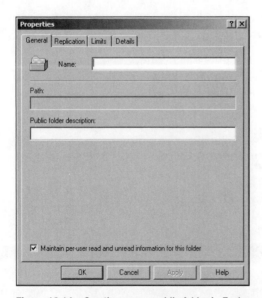

Figure 13.14 Creating a new public folder in Exchange System Manager.

mail-related tabs, including Exchange General, E-Mail Addresses, and Exchange Advanced. These tabs work like the equivalent tabs for other recipients and allow you to perform such functions as setting delivery options and restrictions, changing the display name and alias, and setting custom attributes. These settings are similar to the ones for other types of recipients.

Once you mail-enable a folder, two settings are added to the General tab. The first setting controls whether you want the public folder to be visible in the Global Address List (GAL), so that users can send mail to it. The second setting allows you to configure the way the name is displayed in the address list, whether it is the same name as the folder or a different name.

Note: If you run Exchange Server 2000 in native mode, new public folders are not mail-enabled, by default. In mixed mode, new public folders are mail-enabled and configured to be visible in the GAL.

Managing Public Folders in the Exchange System Manager

Managing public folders is done at two levels in Exchange System Manager—at the public folder store and at the public folder itself. At the public folder store, you specify general default parameters for how that public folder store should handle public folders. At the public folder itself, you specify properties that control the folder, which often override settings made at the store level.

Managing Public Folders at the Public Folder Store Level

When you create a new public folder, you have the option of setting limits for each individual folder, or you can use the default settings from the public folder store. Recognize that a new individual folder inherits default settings from the public folder store.

To configure these properties, you would access the property sheet (Properties window) of the Public Folder Store object. Most of the tabs on this Properties window govern public folder replication, which is discussed in the section "Replicating Public Folders" later in this chapter. The tab of interest here is the Limits tab, as shown in Figure 13.15.

The settings on the Limits tab allow you to configure storage limits for all public folders in the public folder store. The three settings that you can configure for limits are:

➤ Issue warning at (KB)

➤ Prohibit post at (KB)

➤ Maximum item size (KB)

13

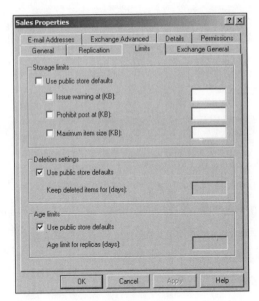

Figure 13.15   The public folder store Limits tab.

As indicated, all of these settings are in kilobytes. You can override these storage limit settings at the folder level for individual folders. Also consider that a limit assigned to an individual folder cannot be higher than the limit assigned to the respective folder tree. Another option in the Storage Limits section is the Warning message interval field. The default is "Run daily at midnight," but you can create a customized schedule by clicking on the Customize button.

The next section of the Properties window contains the Deletion settings. Exchange 2000 Server supports a useful feature called "Deleted-item recovery." When a user deletes a message from a folder, that message is marked as hidden and is actually retained for a certain number of days on the server before being permanently deleted. Within that period, the user can recover the item; however, to do so, the user must be using Microsoft Outlook 8.03 or later. To enable this feature for the public folder store, set the number of days that you want to keep deleted items on the server. The default setting is 0. You can also specify that items not be permanently deleted from the public folder store until at least one backup has occurred.

The final limit that you can set on the Limits tab is Age limits. This is the default number of days for which items are kept in the public folders in the public folder store. The default is no age limit at all.

Note: Public folder age limits work in combination with deleted-item retention time. For example, if you set a 5-day age limit on your public folders and a 1-day deleted-item retention period, then if a user deletes an item on day 4—one day before it would automatically expire—then the deleted-item retention period, which applies only to user-deleted messages, starts at this point. If the item is recovered within the deleted-item retention period, the age limit for the newly recovered item is reset to add 5 more days.

Managing Public Folders at the Folder Level

You can also manage public folders in Exchange System Manager on a folder-by-folder basis by using the folder's property sheet. The General tab allows you to change the description of the folder and the option for maintaining per-user read and unread information. It also allows you to change the way the folder name is displayed in the address list. The Replication tab deals with public folder replication, which is covered in the section "Replicating Public Folders" later in this chapter. The Limits tab, as seen in Figure 13.15, defines messaging limits for the public folder. Any setting made at the public folder level overrides the setting made for the public folder store.

The Storage Limits section has four settings:

➤ Use public store defaults—Allows you to use the default settings that you configured at the public store, as described in the previous section.

➤ Issue warning at (KB)—Indicates the amount of disk space, in kilobytes, that a folder can take up before a warning is issued to the folder's owner.

➤ Prohibit post at (KB)—Indicates that if a folder reaches this size, no new posts will be accepted.

➤ Maximum item size (KB)—Regulates how large each item in the public folder can be. If the item is over the limit, the post will be rejected.

The Deletion settings section defines the number of days that deleted messages are retained in the folder before being permanently removed. You can use the default defined for the public folder store or override that setting for this particular folder.

The Age limits section specifies the maximum number of days that a message remains in this public folder before it expires. If not specified, the default set at the public folder store level applies.

13

Configuring Public Folder Permissions

If you configure public folder permissions by using Outlook, Exchange will automatically configure the corresponding Windows 2000 permissions. You can assign permissions to folders, objects, and attributes. Active Directory is responsible for enforcing security on Exchange 2000 resources.

When implementing security with Exchange 2000, you can apply the same type of permissions for folders and objects and assign them to a Windows 2000 user or security group. Also, permissions can be denied. This allows an administrator to deny access to users who may be members of a larger group that has been granted access. Denied permissions always take precedence over granted permissions.

You can assign permissions to a parent folder and then have those permissions propagate to all folders in the tree below it. You can set these by going to the

Properties window for the tree and then choosing the Security tab. Folders will inherit permissions from parent containers in the hierarchy.

The available permissions for public folders that you can assign at the Organization, Administrative Group, and the Public Folder Tree objects are the following:

➤ *Create Public Folder*—This permission allows a user to create a public folder.

➤ *Create Top Level Public Folder*—This permission specifies who can define top-level folders.

➤ *Modify Public Folder ACL*—This permission specifies who can configure administrative rights.

➤ *Create Named Properties in the Information Store*—This permission specifies who can create named properties.

The available permissions for public folders that you can assign at the Administrative Group object are the following:

➤ *Modify Public Folder Deleted Item Retention, Public Folder Expiry, Public Folder Quotas*—These permissions specify who can change these configuration properties.

➤ *Modify Public Folder Replica List*—This permission is used to define who can configure where the public folder is replicated.

➤ *Administer Information Store*—This permission specifies who can manage the public information store.

➤ *View Information Store Status*—This permission specifies who can view status on the public information store.

Public Folder Categories

Four separate categories of permissions exist in Exchange 2000:

➤ *Folder rights*—Controls who has access to the folder.

➤ *Message rights*—Defines which users can gain access to messages sent to a mail-enabled folder.

➤ *Directory rights*—Allows control of which users can configure the mail-enabled Active Directory object.

➤ *Administrators rights*—Allows assignment of specific administrative rights to certain administrators; helps in delegating administrative tasks to multiple administrators.

Distribution Lists and Security Groups

In Exchange 5.5, you could use distribution lists to apply permissions to public folders. Exchange 2000 now implements the Windows 2000 universal security groups to accomplish this same task. Universal security groups cannot exist, however, unless your Windows 2000 forest has at least one native mode domain present in the infrastructure. This means that you can create at least one native mode domain in a forest inhabited with distribution lists from your existing Exchange 5.5 design. These distribution lists are originally placed in Active Directory as universal distribution groups.

When you run an in-place upgrade, Active Directory Connector (ADC) creates universal distribution groups in a native mode domain. Permissions for public folders with distribution lists will be replaced with universal distribution groups. The first time a member of a universal distribution group tries to access the contents of the folder, Web Storage System will attempt to convert the universal distribution group to a universal security group. If the universal distribution group was created in a mixed-mode domain, however, the upgrade to a universal security group will fail. If the universal distribution group was from a native mode domain, Web Storage System will upgrade it to a universal security group. If you do not want to use universal security groups or change your environment over to native mode, use domain local or global groups for public folder access control. Keep in mind that this technique will demand constant monitoring and administration.

Tip: Your organization may decide to limit the conversion of universal distribution groups to universal security groups by setting the msExchDisableUDGConversion attribute on the organization object. The default value of this attribute is 0, meaning that the Web Storage System will automatically change universal distribution groups to universal security groups. If the attribute's value is 1, Web Storage System will not automatically convert the universal distribution groups. If a request comes from a client, on the other hand, replication and upgrade can still translate universal distribution groups to universal security groups. If the value of this attribute is 2, Web Storage System will not convert a universal distribution group to a universal security group.

13

Replicating Public Folders

Public folder replicas enable an organization to provide redundant information as well as load balancing for accessing data. Active Directory controls the replication of public folder directory objects, and the Exchange store controls the replication of the hierarchies.

The Exchange administrator controls the replication of the contents of the public folders. By default, a public folder exists in only one location throughout the organization. The administrator can replicate the public folder to other public stores in the organization. The multiple copies are called replicas. The contents of public folders are not replicated to other public folder stores in the organization automatically. If you want replication to occur, you must set it up manually, on a per-folder basis. You can configure each public folder individually to have replicas on multiple public folder stores. When you set up replication for a parent folder, its child folders are also replicated, by default, although you can change this for individual child folders.

Public folder replication follows the multimaster replication model, in which every replica of a public folder is considered a master copy, similar to the method used by Active Directory.

When you have decided which folders you want to replicate, you will need to manually create and configure the replicas. This can be accomplished in either of two ways. The first method uses the Replication tab (Figure 13.16) to configure the properties of a public folder. In this method, you will be able to add or remove the public stores that will receive the replica. This is a "push" method of replication. The Replication tab lists any public stores that already contain a replica of the public folder. Click the Add button to open a dialog box that lists the available public stores in your organization that do not have replicas of the folder. Select the store to which you want to replicate the folder and click OK. The public store is then added to the list of stores that contain replicas.

Below the list of public folder stores is a drop-down menu named Public Folder To Replicate. Use this menu to schedule the replication of the public folder to the other public folder stores. Several options are available:

➤ *Never Run*—Essentially turns off replication of the public folder, which is handy if you want to stop the replication temporarily to, for example, troubleshoot a bad connector.

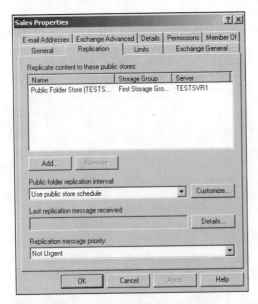

Figure 13.16 Public folder Replication tab.

➤ *Always Run*—Essentially keeps replication going all the time. Because this option would cause excessive traffic, it is generally a poor choice. However, it can be useful when you first configure a new replica and you want it to be created as soon as possible. In this situation, turning on the Always Run option ensures that the content will be replicated quickly. Be sure to set the schedule to something more reasonable afterward, however.

➤ *Run Every 1, 2, or 4 Hours*—Causes replication to occur at the defined interval.

➤ *Use Custom Schedule*—Allows you to define a custom schedule for replication. Click the Customize button to bring up a dialog box with a calendar of hours you can use to set up the replication schedule.

➤ *Use Default Schedule*—Causes the folder to replicate according to the default replication schedule set for the public folder store to which the public folder belongs. This option is the default.

Other options on the Replication tab let you see the last replication message Exchange Server generated regarding the current public folder and set the priority that replication messages concerning this folder should have in your Exchange system.

The second method for configuring the replication of public folders involves accessing the Public Folder Instances object under the Public Information Store in the Exchange System Manager. You can right click on the object and choose All Tasks | Add Replica to send the replica of any public folder to your server, as shown in Figure 13.17. This is a "pull" replication.

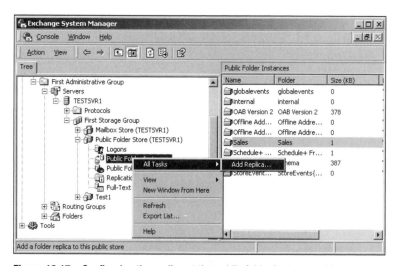

Figure 13.17 Configuring the replica at the public folder instances object.

13

Once you have created replicas of a public folder and configured how replication should behave at the folder level, you can also configure how replication should behave at the public folder store level. To do this, open the property sheet (Properties window) for the Public Folder Store object and switch to the Replication tab, as shown in Figure 13.18.

You can take two actions on this tab. The first is to configure replication defaults that apply to all of the folders in that store. You do this with a drop-down menu like the one used to configure a schedule for an individual folder, as described in the previous section. The value you specify here will apply to all of the folders in the store, unless you specify something other than the Use Default Schedule setting on an individual folder's property sheet. In other words, if you set a schedule for an individual folder, that schedule overrides the setting on this tab.

The second action you can take on the Replication tab for a public folder store's property sheet is to define limits for replication. By default, no limits are defined. If bandwidth between servers is a consideration, you can specify the maximum time, in minutes, that replication is allowed to go on when it occurs. You can also define the maximum size, in kilobytes, of a single replication message.

Public Folder Affinity

If you deploy Exchange 2000 server into an existing Exchange 5.5 site that implements public folder affinity to get to folders in remote sites, Exchange 2000 users as well as Exchange 5.5 users can access the remote folders. Exchange 2000 permits

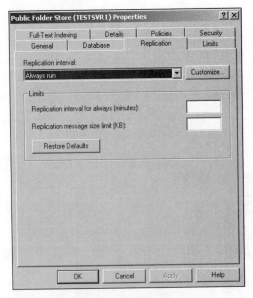

Figure 13.18   Public folder store Replication tab.

public folder referral over an Exchange 5.5 network link by default. In Exchange 2000, public folder affinity is transitive. Therefore, if an affinity exists between site A and site B and an affinity exists between site B and site C as well, an affinity automatically exists between site A and site C. In contrast, public folder affinity is not transitive in Exchange 5.5 and earlier versions.

Each folder tree can be replicated to other Exchange 2000 servers in the organization so that if a server is not available, a client can still use an alternative server to get to the public folder's contents. Exchange affinities use a routing group that is configured to refer the client to another server. This referral allows the client to access content when a specific server is unavailable or known. This feature is enabled by default. Most Exchange 2000 organizations will generally implement routing groups for improved mail flow. If you allow for public folder referrals, however, they will be available to all other servers in the connected routing groups, because public folder affinity is transitive. You can circumvent this functionality by restricting public folder referrals in a connector's properties. You can select or clear the "Do not allow public folder referrals" checkbox on Exchange 5.5 site connectors and Exchange 2000 X.400 and Simple Mail Transfer Protocol (SMTP) connectors. When this option is selected, the connector has an infinite referral cost and will not handle referrals. If connections to two or more routing groups have the same cost, the servers containing replicas are pooled together, and a server is then selected at random.

A client that tries to access a public folder must have the ability to connect to a server that is holding a data replica. The client will try to connect to any replica to give the data to a user. To make this process more efficient, the client will attempt to make a connection to servers in this order:

1. The user will first attempt to reach the default public store for the client. This default is determined by the mailbox store configuration that holds the user's mailbox. If the default is unavailable, the client will then receive a list of servers that contain a replica.

2. Next, the client will attempt to contact a server to which it has an existing connection.

3. Finally, each server in the routing group where the client's public folder server resides will be contacted.

4. If the client cannot connect to any of the servers in the clients' own routing group, the Web Storage System forces the client to attempt a connection to other routing groups. These attempts are made in order of cost, first trying the lowest cost to reach the routing group in which there is a replica.

13

Full Content Indexing

In Exchange 5.5 you could use Site Server to generate a searchable index of public folder contents for users. Exchange 2000 Server will create its own index of public folder and mailbox contents that users can use for searching. You can enable this indexing feature for any database to allow content to be indexed. Check to see, however, if your organization is already using Site Server to index your public folders before planning an indexing policy. If you are using Site Server, you will need to set schedules for indexing as well as the database properties in Exchange 2000 to accommodate the continued creation of full-content indexes.

Administering Public Folders

Another transformation in Exchange 2000 public folder usage and implementation is the administrative model. In earlier versions of Exchange, you could connect to a server and administer the public folders on the server as long as you were an Exchange Full Administrator on the server. As shown in the section "Configuring Public Folder Permissions" earlier in this chapter, administration of public folders in Exchange 2000 depends on permissions set on various objects (top level hierarchies, administrative groups, and public folders themselves). Assorted permissions can be configured for a variety of public folder activities, such as changing age limits, in Exchange 2000. Exchange 2000 is fairly consistent with Exchange 5.5, although the administrative model does not match precisely, which can create some administrative challenges.

Just to review, a public folder tree is a hierarchical grouping of public folders that can exist on one or more Exchange 2000 public folder stores. In Exchange 2000, you can have multiple public folder trees, each tree having its own public folder store. A public folder store can host only one public folder tree.

In Exchange 5.5, the system was restricted to a single public folder tree called Public Folders. Also, the placeholders for all public folders within a public folder tree were represented on all public information stores linked to that public folder tree. Similar to Exchange 5.5, Exchange 2000 provides support for the MAPI public folder tree, but it also supports multiple non-MAPI public folder stores. In addition, ADC populates and synchronizes Active Directory with public folder data from the Exchange 5.5 directory. You can generate connection agreements for recipients to synchronize mailboxes, custom recipients, and distribution lists as well as public folders between a Windows 2000 server and an Exchange 5.5 server.

Note: You can generate connection agreements for public folders only if an Exchange directory container exists in the domain with which you want to make the connection. When you enter the name of the Exchange 5.5 server on the ADC connection agreement Connections tab, the values on the From Windows and the From Exchange tabs will automatically be entered into the Exchange directory container.

Finally, to move public folders to Exchange 2000, you will replicate existing public folders on the old Exchange server to the new Exchange 2000 Server, and then remove the instances from the old Exchange server. Users will then automatically connect to the Exchange 2000 public folder on their next access attempt. When upgrading an existing Exchange 5.5 server to Exchange 2000, all of the existing Exchange sites will correspond directly to Exchange 2000 administrative groups and routing groups.

Chapter Summary

Public folders are a powerful means to provide centralized storage of virtually any type of document or message and allow controlled access by any user in the organization. As such, they provide the basis of workflow applications and collaboration for Exchange 2000 Server. Exchange 2000 boasts a variety of new features for public folders, including the capability to create many top-level folder hierarchies or folder trees, integration between the Exchange 2000 information store and Active Directory, the ability to secure items in public folders through ExIFS, accessibility from the Web, full-text indexing, and referrals enabled by default.

This chapter explored some important issues related to designing a public folder system in an organization. Each public folder tree uses a separate database on an Exchange server. Only the initial tree, however, is visible from within MAPI clients such as Microsoft Outlook. Other trees can be viewed only from OWA, Windows Explorer, or another application through the ExIFS.

Another key issue addressed in this chapter is that MAPI client permissions for the top-level hierarchy are the conventional MAPI permissions. Client permissions for the general-purpose hierarchies depend on the Windows ACLs. In Windows 2000 mixed mode, you can only have one MAPI public folder hierarchy for each organization. However, you can have multiple general-purpose hierarchies for an organization.

13

This chapter showed how to create and manage public folders using a client such as Outlook and the Exchange System Manager tool. It covered how to create multiple public folder trees in your Exchange organization and the issues involved with implementing multiple hierarchies. Remember that the multiple public folders feature of Exchange 2000 can dramatically affect your organization's strategy for public folder usage and implementation. This chapter showed how to set up replication so that your public folders can be copied to public folder stores on other servers.

As shown in this chapter, you can manage a public folder by simply right clicking on a folder and choosing Properties from the pop-up menu. The different tab components of the Properties page were explored in this chapter as well. The techniques involved in generating a new public folder tree as well as the configuration were also addressed. Only the Domain and Exchange Administrators groups have permissions to modify the root folder by default. If you decide to set permissions that determine which users can make changes to the root level of that tree, you can open the property sheet for the top-level folder and switch to the Security tab. Click the Add button to specify permissions for additional users.

This chapter presented several considerations to be addressed when setting up multiple public folder trees. First, additional hierarchies are replicated only to servers in which they are configured for replication, because the All Public Folders hierarchy is created on every public folder server and its list of folders are replicated throughout the organization. You may want to consider the suggestion to use additional public folder trees to make navigation easier for users as well as to make replication smoother.

Finally, remember some key issues of interest for MAPI. First, there can only be one MAPI top-level hierarchy per organization in mixed mode, although you can have multiple general-purpose top-level hierarchies per organization. Second, the MAPI top-level hierarchy folders are mail enabled by default. When you create additional hierarchies, they are not mail enabled.

The next chapter, Chapter 14, continues to empower the users of Exchange 2000 by exploring the design of an Exchange 2000 Server real-time collaboration solution.

Review Questions

1. Which of the following tools can be used to create and manage public folders within Exchange? [Check all correct answers]

   a. Netscape Messenger

   b. Microsoft Outlook

   c. Exchange System Manager

   d. User Manager for Domains

   e. Installable System Manager

2. What is another name for public folder hierarchies? [Check all correct answers]

   a. Top-level hierarchies

   b. Public branches

   c. Public folder trees

   d. General-purpose hierarchies

3. Which of the following client protocols are able to view all public folder hierarchies within Exchange 2000? [Check all correct answers]

   a. POP3

   b. IMAP

   c. MAPI

   d. NNTP

   e. Web-DAV browsers

4. In the Public Folders dialog box, which one of the following tabs would you access to input an administrative description of the public folder?

   a. General

   b. Replication

   c. Limits

   d. Details

   e. Permissions

5. Which of the following are valid steps to create a new public folder tree?

   a. Create a new top-level root folder that will contain the new tree structure.

   b. Create a new public folder store on the server to hold the contents of the new tree structure.

   c. Connect the new top-level folder to the new public folder store.

   d. All of the above.

6. The public store has subcontainers that allow you to view useful information. Which one of the following subcontainers allows you to view the folders in the public store, configure the properties of a folder, and replicate a public folder to a specific public store?

   a. Logons

   b. Public Folder Instances

   c. Replication Status

   d. Full-Text Indexing

13

7. The last step in creating the new public folder tree is to go back to the top-level root folder that you created and connect it with the new public folder store. Which of the following represents valid steps to perform this task?

   a. In the Exchange System Manager, right click on the top-level root folder in the main Folders container and choose Connect To from the menu.

   b. In the Exchange System Manager, double click on the top-level root folder in the main Folders container and choose Create Connection from the menu.

   c. In the Exchange System Manager, right click on the storage group, and choose New | Public Store from the menu.

   d. In the Exchange System Manager, right click on the storage group, and choose Create Connection from the menu.

8. Which one of the following factors should you take into consideration when planning multiple public folder trees?

   a. The size of the default public folder tree cannot be reduced; it can only be made larger.

   b. The All Public Folders hierarchy is created on every public folder server, and its list of folders is replicated throughout the organization.

   c. A mixed-mode organization can have multiple MAPI top-level hierarchies.

   d. You can have only one general-purpose top-level hierarchy per organization.

9. After you mail enable a folder, two settings are added to the General tab. Which two of the following represent these added settings? [Check the two best answers]

   a. A setting is added to the General tab that controls whether you want the public folder to be visible in the Global Address List (GAL) so that users can send mail to it.

   b. A setting is added to the General tab that allows you to set the delivery options and restrictions for your mail-enabled folder.

   c. A setting is added to the General tab that allows you to configure the way the name is displayed in the address list, whether it is the same name as the folder or a different name.

   d. A setting is added to the General tab that controls whether you can change the size, color, and appearance of the folders in your graphical interface.

10. At which two levels are public folders managed in Exchange System Manager? [Check the two best answers]

    a. At the private store level

    b. At the public folder store level

    c. At the public folder itself

    d. At the general store level

11. The settings on the public folder store Limits tab allow you to configure storage limits for all public folders in the public folder store. Which one of the following is *not* one of the three settings that you can configure for limits?

   a. Issue warning at (KB)

   b. Stop service at (KB)

   c. Prohibit post at (KB)

   d. Maximum item size (KB)

   e. Use public store defaults

12. Which one of the following public folders permissions allows a user to specify who can configure administrative rights, and is assigned to Organization, Administrative Group, and Public Folder Tree objects?

   a. Create Top Level Public Folder

   b. Modify Public Folder ACL

   c. Modify Public Folder Replica List

   d. Create Public Folder

   e. Administer Information Store

13. Exchange 2000 has four separate categories of permissions. What category allows you to determine which users can configure the mail-enabled Active Directory object?

   a. Folder rights

   b. Message rights

   c. Directory rights

   d. Administrators' rights

14. You are the Exchange 2000 administrator of a Windows 2000 forest that has one native mode domain present in the corporate infrastructure. In Exchange 5.5, you used distribution lists to apply permissions to public folders. What will you use in Exchange 2000 to accomplish this same task?

   a. Web storage groups

   b. Web distribution lists

   c. Universal distribution lists

   d. Universal security groups

15. In Exchange 2000, if an affinity exists between site A and site B and also between site B and site C, which of the following statements is true?

   a. Affinity must be manually configured between site A and site C.

   b. Exchange 2000 does not support transitive affinity.

   c. Affinity automatically exists between site A and site C.

   d. Public folder referrals will be restricted by default.

13

Real-World Projects

You are the system engineer in charge of planning the public folder implementation strategy of your organization. You have assembled your team and set goals, and you must now determine which features of Exchange 2000 will best serve your organization. Because the multiple public folders feature can affect your organization's strategy for public folder usage and implementation, you are going to focus your first report on this new feature.

Project 13.1

Produce a report for middle management that explains multiple public folders, including the advantages as well as some possible pitfalls for your organization.

Project 13.2

You are deciding whether to implement additional public folder hierarchies to minimize the general size of the default public folder hierarchy. Report on some of the other issues involved with this kind of optional implementation.

CHAPTER FOURTEEN

Designing an Exchange 2000 Server Real-Time Collaboration Solution

After completing this chapter, you will be able to:

✓ Understand the overall Exchange 2000 Server collaboration platform

✓ Understand various collaboration methods

✓ Plan your collaboration

✓ Design and deploy chat services

✓ Design and deploy instant messaging services

✓ Understand the Exchange collaboration development platform

M icrosoft Exchange 2000 Server is much more than just an email server—it is a collaboration platform that employs a number of technologies to enable a multitude of ways we can communicate and collaborate. Email is the primary one, but the Exchange platform also implements chat services, instant messaging services, data conferencing, and audio and video conferencing, as well as providing a collaborative application development framework. This chapter concentrates on chat services and instant messaging services, which will be important on your exam day, and it also overviews the other collaboration components of Exchange 2000.

Chat Service

A chat service is a very popular way to communicate and share a very broad range of information. Online realtime discussions are most commonly ongoing and span a huge variety of topics, with users freely joining and leaving. Online chat is a one-to-many forum, an open discussion. Users can go online and join chat sessions, which are known as channels or chat rooms. The topic of each room is usually reflected in the chat room name to make the nature of the discussion more obvious. Users join groups (chat rooms) based on topics; more common than not, this topic is maintained throughout the lifespan of the channel. In turn, chat rooms are grouped into chat communities based on interest, geography, age group, business organization, or other criteria.

Chat conversations may be private or public. A straightforward analogy to the chat service concept is a real-life room. People may enter and leave the room as they like; they can communicate to all of the members alike, hold a private conversation with someone, or they can ignore one another; they can even ask to leave the room. A teenager, for example, would probably not stay for a long time in the same room with a group of senior people. The same basic social rules apply to virtual chat rooms as are common in our everyday life.

Microsoft Exchange Chat Service relies on Active Directory (AD) to establish chat communities, channels, and other chat- and user-related settings. A single Exchange 2000 Server can host a variety of chat communities, which can be organized as business or public interests suggest. The basis of a chat service lies in technology called Internet Relay Chat (IRC), and its development dates back to the late 1980s. IRC protocol relies on Transmission Control Protocol/Internet Protocol (TCP/IP) for all transmission needs. IRC specifics are outlined in RFC 1459. Microsoft bases its implementation on IRCX as well as on IRC. IRCX is an extension to IRC that implements new commands for managing users and chat sessions, and other features.

Clients and Servers

As with email, online chat is a client-server application. To access chat services provided by Exchange or any other IRC server, you need to use client software. This can be any IRC-aware application, including desktop applications and Java applets built into a Web page, or downloadable ActiveX components that are presented on a Web page in the same manner as Java applets. Microsoft offers an application called Microsoft Chat that comes with Internet Explorer as an optional component.

In a chat service, client software connects to an Exchange server that hosts chat service using a standard IRC port (6667). Usually the first community that exists on the server reserves this port for itself. You can use port 7000 as well, or assign any other port number if these two are already taken by other services (only one service can be bound to any one port at a time). Clients have to be aware of your Exchange hostname or Internet Protocol (IP) address to successfully connect to your chat servers.

One Exchange 2000 Server can host up to 20,000 chat users and can have a number of communities defined. Servers maintain user lists (concurrently connected users) and community lists (defined chat room groups) independently of other servers and communities. Chat channels (rooms) can be registered or dynamic. Registered rooms are available at any time. Conversely, dynamic rooms are created as users desire, and as long as one user is present in that room the channel is maintained, but as soon as the last user abandons that dynamic channel, it is purged and is no longer present in the system. Client software passes messages to chat servers, and chat servers pass messages between users that are connected at the time of transmission. Chat servers operate independently of each other, and the same applies to chat communities. You can apply Access Control Lists (ACLs) to communities in AD to control access to your communities and deny access to staff who do not belong to certain communities or your chat service altogether. For hardware, Microsoft recommends using a quad CPU, 512MB RAM machine to support the full number (20,000) of users per server.

Server Extensions

Exchange Server supports server extensions. A server extension is a software module that enhances the features of an existing chat service. Just like most of the services, Exchange Chat Service has its own object model that is based on the Chat Server Extensibility Model. This model allows administrators to monitor and control chat service, and programmers to write extensions to enrich existing functionality. Keep in mind that each extension you add takes its toll on chat service performance.

Profanity Filter Extension

The profanity filter is based on a list of words that are considered offensive or otherwise inappropriate. It can filter out and/or kick/ban users who do not wish to comply with the rule to avoid using inappropriate or coarse language in their messages. To implement this feature, you need to define a list of restricted words and then apply it to either all dynamic channels or registered channels (you can apply different lists to different registered channels). When a user sends a message that contains one or more of the words from the profanity list applied to that channel, that message is blocked and is not re-sent to the members, and the sender receives a private warning that such language is considered inappropriate in this channel. This filter checks user nicknames, messages they type in private and public conversations, and warnings or greetings sent in the channels. Private conversations within a room are also called whispers. If you whisper to a member in that room, only that member will receive your message.

Transcription Extension

The transcription extension logs conversations into log files on the hard disk of your server. Once enabled, transcription extension logs all channel messages sent to the public into a file in the respective channel directory, and these logs are rotated automatically on a daily basis (00:00–23:59). You can enable one log for all dynamic channels, and a separate log for each registered channel. If you need this type of logging, be careful to monitor your disk space.

In-Band Commands

IRC chat client programs can be used to administer some aspects of your chat service. In-band commands are used in this case, and they require an administrative logon. An in-band command is an administrative instruction sent from a client program using chat protocol.

The following command enables or disables transcription of all dynamic channels:

```
EXTMSG  TSCRIPT  start | stop  DYNAMIC
```

The next command adds a specified filtered word into a profanity filter:

```
EXTMSG PFILTER ADD LIST=filter_name GWORD=word
```

This is just one of many in-band commands, provided as a sample.

Installing Microsoft Exchange Chat Service

Microsoft Exchange Chat Service is a standalone service component that has to be included during Exchange 2000 installation to provide chat services. If you have included the Chat Service component during initial installation, you are all set to configure the service. If you have not done so, then you will have to go to Add-Remove Programs and adjust the existing Exchange 2000 installed components to include Chat Services, as shown in Figure 14.1.

Microsoft Exchange Chat Service requires installation of Windows 2000 Server, Microsoft Exchange 2000 Server, and System Manager. The Windows 2000 Server may be either Domain Controller or Member Server. Exchange 2000 does not have to be installed on the same computer as Chat Service, but it must be installed

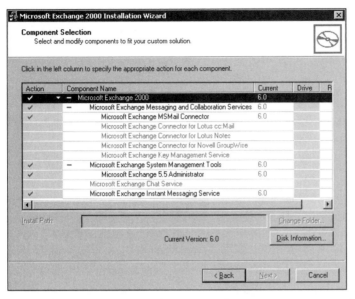

Figure 14.1 Exchange Server installation components with Chat Service missing.

within the same domain because Chat Service uses AD for its configuration and functioning. Finally, System Manager also does not have to be present on the same system, but make sure it is present on the machine from which you plan to administer your chat server.

Channels

Channels are a fundamental part of the infrastructure of a chat service. As mentioned previously, a channel is also known as a chat room, and it is a part of a chat community. To participate in a chat, you must first use your client software to bring up a list of active channels from the server to which you are connecting, and then select the channel you want, usually based on channel name and current member count. Permanent and temporary types of chat channels are available (see Table 14.1). All channels must adhere to the IRC naming standard by which the channel name must not be null and must be no longer than 200 American Standard Code for Information Interchange (ASCII) characters (except null, bell, linefeed, backslash, carriage return, space, and comma). If your clients support IRCX, the extended version of IRC proprietary to Microsoft, you can use between 1 and 100 double-byte character set (DBCS) symbols. All names follow a prefix, which defines the channel type. If your clients support IRCX, you can also use the Universal Character Set (UTF-8) encoding, which will allow your users to chat in any language they choose. You should not name channels with a number at the end due to issues that arise if you make this channel cloneable.

The properties of channels allow configuration of the channel mode (see Table 14.2).

14

Table 14.1   Channel type comparison chart.

Prefix	Type	Characteristics
#	IRC Registered	Permanent channel. This channel type is ASCII-based and supports all of the IRC clients. This channel must be created by an administrator and either starts up automatically when Chat Service initializes or waits for someone to enter it. The first person to enter is pronounced the host, who gains control over users of this particular channel. The host can share this status with other folks. This channel remains active regardless of user count. The administrator can modify the properties of each channel in System Manager.
&	IRC Dynamic	Temporary channel. This channel type is ASCII-based and supports all of the IRC clients. This channel is created by a user from an IRC client application and is maintained on the server until the last user exits the channel.
%#	IRCX Registered	Same as IRC Registered, but adheres to Microsoft's IRCX and supports UTF-8 universal encoding.
%&	IRCX Dynamic	Same as IRC Dynamic, but adheres to Microsoft's IRCX and supports UTF-8 universal encoding.

Table 14.2   Channel mode comparison chart.

Mode	Description
Public*	All information, except messages, is visible to nonmembers.
Private*	Only name, member count, and platform for Internet Content Selection PICS ratings property are visible to nonmembers.
Hidden*	Same as public except that you cannot list this channel in your software; you have to know the channel name to be able to join it.
Secret*	You cannot list or access this group if you are a nonmember.
Cloneable	This channel mode duplicates itself to accommodate more users than originally allowed. If the member count limit of, say, **#Toronto** channel, is set to 50, the next user who requests this channel will be placed into newly created **#channelname(+1)** channel, **#Toronto1** in our case. User number 101 will be placed into **#Toronto2** channel, and so on for up to 99 channels.
Moderated	This channel mode prevents participants from sending messages, effectively putting them into "read-only" mode. The host can assign speaker rights to a select few.
Auditorium	This channel mode is used for celebrity interview broadcasts and similar events. The host can elevate users into speaker position. Speakers can send messages to all members of the channel. Only the host is notified when the user leaves or enters the room. This mode helps to attain a certain level of control and still provide controlled interaction.

* Channel modes marked with an asterisk are configured on the Access tab of Channel Properties in System Manager. These four modes affect the visibility of the channel. Channel types not marked are configured on the Modes tab and affect functionality.

User Classes, Attacks, and Bans

Exchange 2000 Chat Service gives you plenty of control over your users' behaviors. You can specify user classes and user bans to help enforce your policies and prevent or reduce attack patterns and the chances that your service will incur some unwanted downtime. This section briefly discusses some risks that usually are associated with providing IRC chat services in your Exchange organization.

Certain popular attacks may compromise your uptime and availability; most commonly they have something to do with flooding your services with useless information to slow or even knock your server down, trying to attack your users, simply hacking your machine, or finding a bug in the software. The discussion here is not concerned with software bugs and hacking—those two factors are beyond your duties as Exchange administrator although you have to keep yourself current on the issues and advise individuals responsible for network and systems security. (You may be responsible, however, for implementing fixes and patches as Microsoft makes them available, but you are not the one who is actually writing them.) The following techniques may help to protect your chat service:

➤ *User identity masking*—This technique does not protect your service as much as it protects your users. By default, chat clients are identified on the screen when they join, and all members of the chat channel can see this information. By using the IP address or Domain Name System (DNS) name of an unsuspecting online chat visitor, other malicious users can exercise different attacks and hack other users. To reduce such activity, you can (and should) enable masking of on-screen client information so that only channel and system operators can see it in case they have to ban an offender. This masking will result in hiding parts of the real IP address the user is coming from—for example, instead of the last octet numbers in the IP address, you will see three crosses, or part of the DNS name will be crossed out as well.

➤ *Flooding attack protection*—Flooding is a denial-of-service type of attack accomplished by sending massive amounts of nonsense data to your chat sessions. Basically your server starts processing this data and, depending on the amount of data, either clients to which it was aimed are disconnecting due to the data flow to their side, or your server gets really busy and starts timing out and eventually dropping connections. This frustrates your legitimate users and disrupts the service, so of course you want to reduce the chances of it happening. You can do this by imposing delays on data processing and setting controls on data flow.

➤ *Cloning attack protection*—Cloning is a problem that relates also to denial-of-service attacks, and the effects are much the same as with the flooding attack—your server becomes less than responsive. The attacker establishes a multitude of client sessions and applies some load to each of them, resulting in a significant net load. By imposing a limit on the number of user connections allowed from a single IP address, you can reduce the chances that someone will compromise your availability. Exercise common sense when assessing the thresholds—if you set the threshold too low, chances are a few legitimate users will attempt a connection from the same IP network using the same network address translation (NAT) or proxy server, and your chat service will see them as a cloning attack if your threshold is exceeded.

14

The way to configure all of this is to employ user classes. In Systems Manager, you can define user classes, which are essentially some pattern that some users will match. User classes are similar to groups in user management, only there is no fixed membership in this case—users belong to classes if the class criterion matches the incoming user properties. For instance, if a user IP belongs to an IP subnet you defined, you have a match, and the user inherits that class membership and the settings you defined to go with that class. If a user matches with more than one class definition, the first alphanumerical match search will be applied. Criteria you can specify include hostname/IP address, IP address/subnet mask, nickname, username, authentication type, and active session time frame. In the class properties, after you define your matching criteria, you should impose some restrictions to control what users who match this profile can and cannot do. You can revoke logon rights, restrict channel creation or ownership, mask user identity, impose a maximum amount of connection a user can make or channels a user can join, impose bandwidth usage restrictions, impose message delays, and implement a nickname change delay. This is a powerful option you should consider when it comes to planning your Exchange environment.

If you have an offender that just does not "get it," and after repeated warnings continues to break your rules, you can get this user off your server and you can impose a ban. This ban may last until you grant administrative pardon to that user and revoke the ban, or you may set it to expire automatically after a period of time within 24 hours. You can use user groups in AD to impose a ban on a number of users based on their username. Keep in mind that bans are community-specific, and when you impose a ban it affects only the user's ability to connect to the community in which this ban is created. That same user can still connect to other communities on the same server, if such exist. After the ban expires or is revoked by the administrator, that user will regain his or her ability to participate in the channels that belong to the community on which the ban was imposed.

User Authentication and Connections

Exchange Chat Service supports three authentication types: anonymous (no authentication), basic authentication (clear-text authentication), and Windows Security Support Provider Interface (SSPI) authentication:

➤ *Anonymous*—This type of authentication requires no password and is the least restrictive and most accessible.

➤ *Basic authentication*—With basic authentication, a password is required and is transmitted in clear text on the wire (actually, it is encoded, so this text is not really clear, but decoding is a very simple process because no encryption is applied). This method is a reasonably secure way to authenticate all IRC-compliant clients regardless of the platform. Supplied credentials will be checked against AD user accounts.

➤ *Windows SSPI*—This method is the most secure way of authenticating your clients but should be used only when the entire client base supports some of the technologies involved (most of the Microsoft operating systems). If none of the technologies are supported, authentication will fail and the user will be rejected. The standard authentication method is New Technology LAN Manager (NTLM). Supplied credentials will be checked against AD user accounts.

User Roles

In the properties of every community, you will see a Security tab by which you can configure what kind of privileges authenticated users have. This is step two of the process—after configuring your authentication, you specify who should have administrator, system operator (or sysop), or user level access, or who should not be allowed into the community altogether. Unlike authentication, security can be applied on both community and channel levels. A corresponding access level exists on the channel level—user, host, or owner of the channel. You assign privileges by allowing or disallowing each access level to selected user accounts. If you disallow all three, the user will have no access rights to the community or channel. If you allow more than one right, the highest will take effect. Keep in mind that none of the nicknames can begin with or contain strings such as "system" or "service".

➤ *User*—User is the most restrictive permission; it allows authenticated or anonymous users to access chat channels and participate as members.

➤ *Sysop*—Sysop controls chat communities and monitors chat channels from IRC clients. These users can kill chat channels or ban users as they see appropriate. To enable special privileges within channels, the administrator assigns user accounts to the sysop category and enables the Chat Sysop Joins as Owner option. Only sysop nicknames start with the "sysop" string, as well as "CodeServ", "MemoServ", "HelpServ", "ChanServ", and "NickServ". Non-sysop nicknames must not start with a "sysop" string.

➤ *Administrator*—This elite group, as the name implies, has access to advanced features and has more privileges than anybody else. Administrators can execute commands from IRC clients and can override bans imposed by sysops. Only administrator nicknames start with the "admin" string.

14

Combined with user roles and authentication, user classes and user bans provide the Exchange Server administrator with powerful controls over Chat Service and its users. On the channel level, you can also specify user-, host-, and owner-level passwords and whether users must be authenticated or invited to join this particular channel. On the community level, you can specify how many users are allowed to join this community, and you can also select an option to disallow new connections. If you need to take a chat server offline for maintenance, do not disrupt conversations in progress. You should disallow new connections on the community level and wait until all existing connections are closed. This will ensure you have no downtime as far as user experience is concerned, providing that you have another server to take over incoming connections once the original community server is disabled.

Note: A classic question on the Exchange 5.5 Server exam was: "How do you take your chat server offline without disrupting chat service?"

Chat Protocols and Clients

As a brief recap, remember that default protocols used by chat service are IRC (industry standard) and IRCX (Microsoft-revised suggested standard). IRCX provides more functionality and multilingual support, whereas IRC supports a much broader range of client applications. The default IRC chat port is 6667, but as a chat service administrator, you have the ability to change this setting. It is the administrator's duty to select an appropriate type of client to use with your Exchange Chat Service deployment. If you have a need for broader support, you might be better off going with such popular third-party IRC clients as mIRC or PIRCH. If you require IRCX functionality, you may still have Microsoft Chat 2.1 or better as a requirement.

Instant Messaging

In the past few years, instant messaging (IM) has become one of the hottest applications, sparking a battle among a number of companies over the standards and protocols related to this technology as well as to its subscriber base. As we all know, supply needs demand, and demand was enormous. Thus, a natural move for Microsoft was to make its Instant Messenger technology available for public use under Microsoft Network (MSN) Messenger branding in its Exchange 2000 offering for corporate users and application service providers. IM combines the best qualities of email, telephone, and chat services, and enables users with instant and realtime collaboration that slashes the need for voice mail and overcomes the delays and response waiting times often associated with email. Also, the collaboration is instant, comparable to that of telephone service, but no long distance charges are involved in such collaboration. You can send and receive files while in conversation, and, more important, you have presence information right in your messenger client software, where just by looking at the user icons you easily determine who is available at this time and who is offline, away, busy, or out for lunch. This service beats chat services primarily because it is a collaboration- and communication-geared tool, by which you can determine if specific people who are of interest to you are available for interaction.

Chat rooms have a virtual crowd of people who share a common virtual interest, all sitting in one virtual room, and saying and doing all sorts of virtual things. At times, it is fairly difficult to find your room or user on crowded servers, and with the cloning of rooms, it is sometimes impossible to fit into the same channel, say, as your buddy, who you urgently need to contact. Even if you do locate your buddy, you have to whisper if you want some privacy, or create your own channel, which takes a little bit of time. Chat was created to meet people, but IM was created to keep in touch and collaborate with specific people, across the borders, instantly, and conveniently. In IM, you have a list of people in whom you are interested (and they are also interested in you, of course), and you are notified when they get online or go offline, as well as when you receive an instant message from them. If you have a multimedia computer, and your back-end Exchange is deployed to support conferencing, you can even initiate a voice conversation with a person overseas and pay for nothing but your local Internet connection cost. Next, we look at this concept from a technical perspective; Microsoft is likely to have instant collaboration questions on the exam.

Service Architecture and Components

To understand IM technology and be able to successfully plan and deploy it, one must understand the underlying structure first (see Figure 14.2). IM employs IM routers to carry out message routing decisions, IM homeservers to host actual users and maintain their presence information, IM clients to allow users to actually use the service and exchange instant messages, and AD for user information lookups.

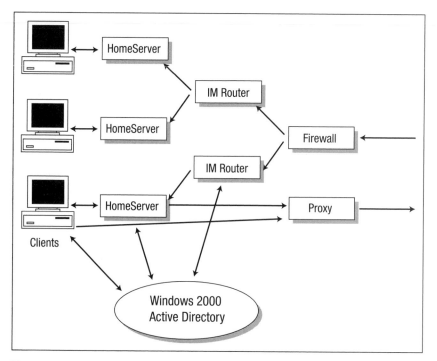

Figure 14.2 Instant messaging components.

This whole infrastructure may or may not have some security enhancements to firewall all incoming requests and proxy all outgoing ones; this is an option and not a requirement.

IM service can be either autonomous or public, and it can interact with other IM organizations, which makes IM an open platform much like email is (as long as you have Exchange servers on both ends)—regardless of your business affiliation, you can send email to anyone who has an email address, not only your intraorganization colleagues who reside on the same server or group of servers. Instant messages can be sent both intra- and interorganizational between separate Exchange Server 2000 IM Service implementations.

Technical implementation is based on Internet Information Server ISAPI (Internet Server Application Programming Interface) DLL (dynamic-link library). Exchange Server is needed to support the Extensible Storage Engine (ESE) IM node database, in which all user presence information is stored (see the discussion later in this chapter under the section "IM Addressing and IM Domains"). AD is tightly integrated into the design and is fundamental for its function because all user authentication and routing are carried out based on AD and the configuration information stored therein. Figure 14.3 shows the technical architecture of IM.

All communication between AD, the ESE node database, and Internet Information Services v. 5 (IIS5) is based on the server Application Programming Interface (API): for the IM client, server communication Rendezvous Protocol (RVP) is used. RVP

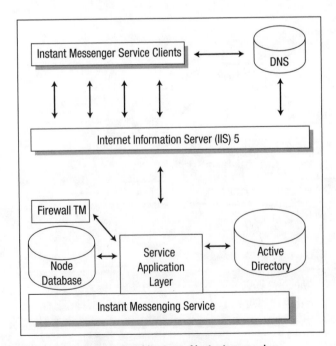

Figure 14.3 Technical architecture of instant messaging.

is an extension of Hypertext Transfer Protocol Distributed Authoring and Versioning (HTTP-DAV), which in turn, is an extension of HTTP 1.1 standard. RVP relies on port 80 and HTTP as its communication transport, and uses the Extensible Markup Language (XML) for formatting and information presentation instead of the Hypertext Markup Language (HTML). Microsoft developed RVP in accordance with the standards currently being outlined by the Internet Engineering Task Force (IETF), the technology standard development organization. This means that when the global community finalizes the standard specifications for instant messaging protocols and architectures, messaging clients and standards will no longer be vendor-specific, and your clients would eventually be able to interact with subscribers from different companies using whatever software they favor.

IM HomesServers

IM routers are used as connection points for remote clients, and they retain and update client presence information in the node database. They also maintain IM user accounts, and they communicate directly with connected clients to deliver messages and presence information as it changes. Homeservers authenticate users, and store their tracking lists. IM HomeServers do not store IM messages anywhere on the disk or in the node database; rather, all messages are kept in memory and are purged when the server is rebooted or service is stopped. Each IM HomeServer is capable of handling up to 10,000 concurrent users. When creating IM Home-Servers, an IIS virtual server must be created. By allowing user accounts to be hosted on this server, you make it a homeserver. Otherwise, the process of creating this server is identical to that of IM routers.

IM Routers

IM routers serve one purpose, that of instant message routing. They receive incoming messages, determine which homeserver hosts the user or users to whom these messages are addressed, and forward them to the respective homeservers. IM routers do not host actual recipients, or users, of the messages. IM specification does not allow the IM router to host users, and if you have only one homeserver, you do not need to implement any IM routers because all incoming messages will be destined to the same server. IM routers can support up to 20,000 concurrent connections. One IM router can service only one IM domain, so if you are hosting multiple IM domains, you will have to implement an IM router for each one of them, provided that domains have more than one homeserver. An IM router is an IIS virtual server. As time goes by, router information gets cached on clients and homeservers, and IM routers usage patterns decrease. When creating IM routers, you must first create an IIS virtual server. By not allowing user accounts to be hosted on this server, you make it a router. Otherwise, the process of creating this server is identical to that for IM HomeServers.

14

IM Addressing and IM Domains

Namespace planning is probably one of the most important topics when it comes to planning and designing the Exchange 2000 Instant Messaging Service. IM Addressing is based on IM domains that identify user accounts. As an analogy, an email address consists of a user information part, or alias, which precedes the @ in the address, and a domain name, which follows the @. When you send an email message, your SMTP mailserver will take the domain name of your destination address and query the DNS for MX (Mail eXchange) records. After the DNS returns an IP address for the mail server for that particular domain, your email message is sent directly to that IP address, and the receiving server delivers the message to the appropriate user mailbox.

In much the same way, you have an IM domain and an IM address. Users are identified by existing email address, the DNS lookup locates an SRV record (service locator) that points to an IM router server, and if that lookup fails, then the fallback mechanism tries to locate an A host record that corresponds to the email domain that follows an **im.** prefix. This is why Microsoft recommends having your email domains and IM domains match in namespace design, with IM domains bearing an **im.** prefix.

As an example, say you have a domain name registered with the DNS and in your AD as **somecompany.com**. Your mail server has an MX record in the DNS that points to **mail.somecompany.com**. At the same time, your email addresses do not contain a **mail.** prefix. All your emails look like **someuser@somecompany.com**. IM design guidelines suggest that you should use the same addressing namespace for your IM users whenever possible. In the case of IM, your clients will attempt to resolve the SRV record of the domain because all users are identified using an email address. An IM SRV record in the DNS looks like this:

```
_rvp._tcp.somecompany.com   SRV 0 0 80 im.somecompany.com.
```

In this example, the first part identifies the service type (RVP), followed by the record type (SRV), then two zeros are priority and weight values that allow control of the load-balancing round-robin feature of the DNS if more than one SRV record exists for this service, and finally port 80 and the hostname are specified. If SRV lookup is successful, the DNS server returns the hostname to which IM messages should be routed. After looking up the RVP SRV hostname, and then looking up the IP address of the returned hostname querying for the A hostname record (one of the DNS record types which maps a DNS name to IP address), your client collects all the information it needs to hand off the message to your server for further routing and delivery (see Figure 14.4).

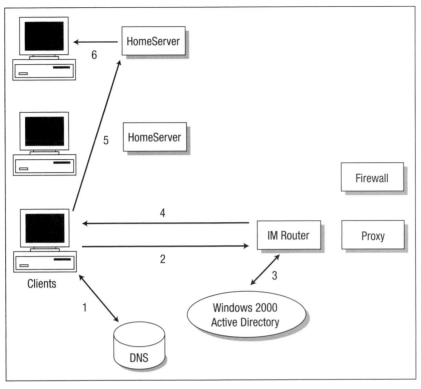

Figure 14.4   An attempt to deliver an instant message.

Therefore, if an SRV record lookup should fail, the client will resort to a fallback procedure and will attempt to resolve **im.somecompany.com** by querying the DNS for A host records. Say, for example, you had user **tanya@somecompany.com** and have defined an A host record in the DNS but not in the SRV. Client software will first attempt to look up the SRV record in the DNS, and if this process fails, the client assumes that the SRV would look like **im.somecompany.com** and your user's email address effectively becomes **tanya@im.somecompany.com**.

Remember to closely follow your email namespace when designing an IM service. Then, if your company has subdomains such as **acc.somecompany.com** and **dev.somecompany.com**, and users have email addresses that follow the DNS hierarchy (for example, **bob@acc.somecompany.com** and **john@dev.some-company.com**), you should have **im.acc.somecompany.com** and **im.dev.some-compny.com** A and SRV records created in the DNS and they should point to respective IM Routers. Recall from earlier in this chapter that you must have at least one IM Router per IM Domain. Although the strategy to follow **im.** prefix naming is suggested, it is not required as long as clients are able to resolve SRV records.

14

Uniform Resource Locator (URL)

RVP is an HTTP-based protocol that transfers XML contents on port 80. Whereas external addressing uses email addresses with which the user base is comfortable, internal addressing adheres to HTTP URL standards. Two types of URL addresses are assigned to every IM-enabled user in AD: server-specific and server-independent. Server-specific URLs are used when the IM router has to decide to which IM HomeServer an incoming message should be forwarded. Server-independent URLs are used when sending an outgoing message.

This distinction makes sense when you consider the following scenario (see Figure 14.5). Suppose you have two homeservers named A and B. On server A, user Sergey sends a message to Tanya, who is homed on server B. Recall from earlier in this chapter that homeservers do not carry out routing decisions; instead, these are the responsibility of routers. The homeserver would query AD for Tanya's server-independent URL and forward it to the IM router because all server-independent URLs contain server names of IM routers that have respective records in the DNS. After the IM router accepts this message, it will carry out a routing decision. The message will be delivered to homeserver B after the IM router looks up the homeserver for user Tanya in AD. If servers A and B are located in different organizations and on different networks, the message will be sent from server A to server B's IM routers because server A queries the DNS to resolve the recipient address first.

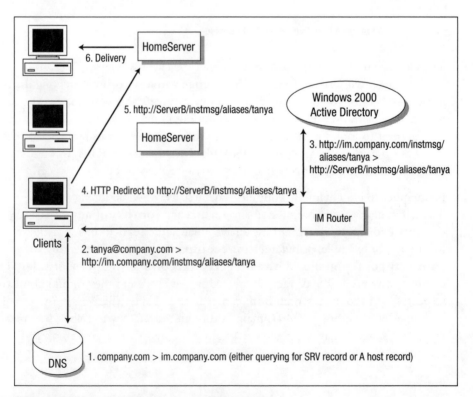

Figure 14.5   Message routing from server A to server B.

Conversion between URLs and Email Addressing

Email addresses, which essentially are IM addresses as well, are related to URLs that are actually used to send, route, and deliver messages in the following manner: IM client software converts an email address into a server-independent URL and then sends it to the IM router (remember that a server-independent URL always points to the IM router). The IM router receives this request, queries AD, and redirects this request back to the originator by using the standard HTTP 302 Redirect command, providing the originator with a server-specific URL. Then this XML message gets sent to the destination homeserver. This conversion from the email address in the user interface is a twofold process. First, the IM client takes the domain name and tries to find a record in the DNS—first an SRV record and then an A record, or, as a fallback, guessing that the A record hostname is the same as the email domain with the **im.** suffix added. Once the client has the IM router hostname, it formats the destination address according to the following pattern:

If the original email address is *user@domain.com*, it is translated to either of the following:

➤ **http://*im.domain.com*/instmsg/aliases/*user***—This is a server-independent, or logical, URL that is used when routing outgoing messages. It refers to the IM router.

➤ **http://*homeservername*/instmsg/aliases/*user***—This is a server-specific, or physical, URL that is issued by the IM router in response to client requests to send a message. It refers to the IM HomeServer.

Routing and Redirection

Microsoft's IM Service relies on two techniques to route messages. For requests originating externally that go into your network, IM Service uses a gateway, which protects your network from direct requests by putting them through firewalls and various security configurations. For requests originating internally, the standard HTTP 302 Redirect command is used. When the homeserver sends an HTTP request to transfer a message, the IM router responds with a redirect that forces re-addressing of the request to a destination server.

Administrative Privileges

When planning IM deployment, you must consider to whom you will give access to modify and manage different parts of the service. Two major security components need certain levels of administrative authority to allow you to make changes to your IM configuration. First, because user configuration data is stored in AD, you will need membership in the Domain Administrators security group to alter it. In addition, if you require access to manage a global IM configuration, you will need Exchange Administrators security group membership.

14

Active Directory

As mentioned previously in this chapter, AD is tightly integrated into the design of the service. IM routers query AD to determine IM HomeServers when making routing decisions. AD maps users to homeservers, and for each user that exists either on the homeserver or in AD, AD maintains server-specific and server-independent URLs. Every user need not have an account in AD, but if the user is already present in AD, then you can just enable IM in the account properties. When you install Exchange, one of the tabs that is added to the property sheets of user accounts is Exchange Features, and the IM status of the existing user is configured on that sheet. When you enable IM for a user, you can also select on which server you want the user to be hosted. Sometimes you will need to move users from one server to another—this is called re-homing. Re-homing does not affect the user's public (server-independent, or logical) URL.

To manage your users more efficiently, you can select a bulk of user accounts and invoke the Exchange Tasks Wizard, which will allow you to enable or disable the IM service on selected accounts, or to change the homeserver. To access your AD user accounts, go to the Active Directory Users and Computers MMC in Administrative Tools. AD and homeservers authenticate IM client logons.

IM Clients and Authentication

Use the MSN Messenger client as an RVP client application to connect to Microsoft Exchange 2000 Server. Client software ships with Exchange 2000 and is located in the \Instmsg\I386\Client directory on your CD.

Exchange Server 2000 provides two methods to authenticate its clients: HTTP Message Digest (MD) or Windows Integrated Authentication (WIA). Both methods operate by means of challenge-response sequences that do not send passwords over the wire, thereby reducing the risk of malicious spoofing or some other types of attacks. HTTP MD is the industry standard, and you should use it if you have to support clients that are other than Windows-based (Unix, for example). If you are serving only Windows machines, then WIA is the recommended authentication method. Remember that this authentication has to be secure enough to make your passwords unreadable if intercepted—those are the same passwords that your users have in AD!

Presence Information

IM Service provides a built-in ability to add users to a tracking list—a list that contains all your online "buddies." Depending on your activity in using the service, you may receive one of the online status categories, which you can also set manually. Status examples include Online, Away, Busy, On the Phone, Out to Lunch, or Appears Offline. Different colors and icons represent these status categories for all members on your tracking list, which makes it easy to determine if your colleague or friend is online and available for instant collaboration or is away or offline.

Presence information is maintained in the node database mentioned previously in this chapter under "Service Architecture and Components." When you add a person to your list, you subscribe to his or her presence information. Users who log on to IM Service, register themselves in the database, and automatic notification is sent to the people who are subscribed to their presence information. After a certain period of time, this information is updated and refreshed, and whenever a change is detected, another notification is sent to all the people who are on that tracking list. Privacy is not a concern here because IM Service provides Block List and Allow List, which can filter out unwanted subscribers. In addition, you can control your status manually, which comes in handy when there is more demand to collaborate than there is supply and you want to make it look as if you are away.

IM Protocols and Message Format

IM client-server communication is based on RVP, which is not yet a standard and is Microsoft-proprietary as of this writing. RVP is a derivative from HTTP1.1 extension HTTP-DAV, and as such it relies on port 80 and should not require any special accommodations when being deployed in an existing infrastructure. This is a very important concept to keep in mind when planning. It is the same as Internet browser traffic as far as your network security goes, and all specific information is conveyed in XML-formatted messages. XML is built around the concept that the server should only supply data, and the client then decides how to present it to the user. This will invariably create a very flexible platform for future enhancements and expansions into the handheld device market.

Firewall Topology Module

If you are exposed to clients from external networks, you are exposed to a great risk if you do not protect your network by a reverse proxy, firewall, or even a screened subnet. You should also mask your identity with a proxy server for all of your outgoing connections.

If you are using any kind of firewall technology, you have to define your internal network address ranges in the Firewall Topology property sheet of Instant Messaging Settings properties found in the Global Settings container. Once the Firewall Topology Module is enabled, you have to define what addresses are considered protected and can receive deliveries directly. Whatever is out of that defined range of addresses is considered external, and the proxy server specified on the same Firewall Topology sheet is used to make outgoing connections. This local address range works much the same way as LAT does in ISA 2000 and Proxy 2 servers—it defines which servers are located in the firewall protected area.

IM Planning Summary

When planning an IM Service rollout, you must carefully consider a few important aspects and the nature of this service. The first question on your agenda should be

14

whether to allow Internet connectivity. If the answer is yes, you are much more secure using firewall and proxy technologies. If you implement a firewall, you have to make sure that as many restrictions as possible are applied while also meeting your business requirements. Remember that IM and RVP messaging uses HTTP and default port 80. You also have to make sure that "miscellaneous" traffic, such as DNS queries that use User Datagram Protocol (UDP) port 53, gets through. If you disallow DNS traffic, you will not be able to resolve destination IM domains and routers outside your network. Also you may want to allow Internet Control Message Protocol (ICMP) traffic through if you want to have troubleshooting abilities and to use **ping**, **tracert**, and other ICMP-based utilities. You will have to think ahead and come up with a list of all your business needs well in advance.

When planning your incoming and outgoing connectivity, remember that an incoming firewall is optional. Incoming IM traffic uses port 80, and all packet filters should let it through. If you go with a screened subnet, or perimeter network configuration (known popularly as the DMZ, for demilitarized zone), beware that the IM router must be in the DMZ, it has to have access to AD, and authentication requests cannot be a gateway into a LAN. If you are using Winsock or Web Proxy for your outgoing connections, be aware that MSN Messenger adheres to the same technology as Internet Explorer 5 (IE5) as far as proxy server setup and functionality are concerned. You have to specify Firewall Topology in the IM Service properties for your solution to work.

While planning your IM domain and namespace, try to keep it as close to your email structure as possible because then your users need to memorize only one email address, which will be a focal point for both email and IM communication. Try to adhere to Microsoft's recommendation of having an **im.** prefix in front of your domain name when creating SRV and a Fully Qualified Domain Name (FQDN) records for your IM routers, to enable a client-side IM router name resolution fallback safety net. This prefix is not mandatory, but very much recommended. IM domain names should correspond to publicly visible SMTP domains.

When planning for hardware resources, keep in mind that IM routers can support up to 20,000 concurrently connected users, and IM homeservers support only up to 10,000 concurrently connected users. To maximize performance on such a heavy load, Microsoft recommends a dual 400MHz CPU, with 256MB RAM. The general guideline is the more resources you can allocate now, the less you will have to add in the foreseeable future. Upgrading involves downtime and often-unplanned difficulties.

When placing your IM routers and IM homeservers, remember that one IM router is required for each IM domain. If you have only one server, then the IM router and IM HomeServer will be the same physical server. If you have IM users (clients) in dispersed geographical areas crossing wide area networks (WANs), consider placing homeservers in those remote locations to minimize using WANs for traffic that may otherwise be local.

DNS Setup requires that at least one A entry per IM router exists in public portion of your DNS. You can use DNS round-robin features by mapping three different IP addresses to the same FQDN of the IM router. This will cause DNS to issue the first DNS IM router in response to the first request, the second in response to the second one, and so on. Keep in mind, though, that DNS query results get cached on the resolver side, so do not expect this to evenly balance your server usage. If another client goes through the same network to connect to your messaging service, chances are that cached DNS information will be used instead of a new query being issued. SRV records for IM routers are not required, but are strongly suggested.

On the client side, supported platforms at this time are Windows 9x, NT, and 2000. You have to install the client software that comes with the CD, and the Client Directory Service DS tool as well, for AD lookups and SRV DNS name support (for Windows 9x and NT).

To plan for bandwidth, have 56Kbps (kilobits per second) available for every 1,000 online users. This suggestion comes from Microsoft and is based on a corporate user profile (a corporate user is considered to be online 80 percent of the time). The more users are hosted on one server, the more traffic is concentrated on that server that does not need to be transferred. IM router information is looked up every now and then and is placed into the cache; nonetheless that information will have to travel the wire anyway.

Topologies

Having discussed the theory behind IM, let us now review a few classic configurations of IM networks. You must be comfortable with this type of charting to succeed on the exam.

Small Business

The small business profile has a relatively small user base, one location, and one HomeServer, and no IM router is needed (see Figure 14.6). An ISP provides network security and filtering functionality, so a small business need not have in-house firewalls.

14

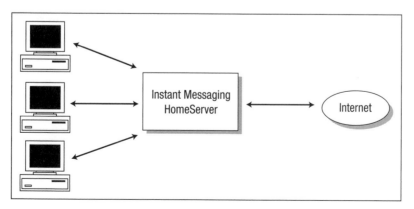

Figure 14.6   Small business topology.

Educational Institution

Educational institutions are characterized by heavy usage, no internal firewall protection, one IM router, and a number of IM HomeServers with a moderate amount of users populating each of them (see Figure 14.7).

Corporate Standard

Corporate standard deployments are enhanced over educational institutions primarily by the number of IM routers (see Figure 14.8). The corporate standard has a larger user base, requires more homeservers, and firewall protection is a must.

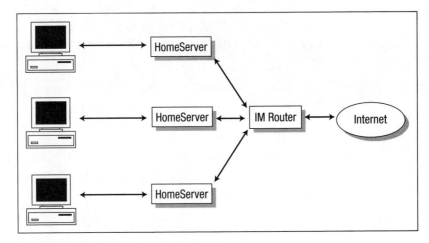

Figure 14.7   Educational institution topology.

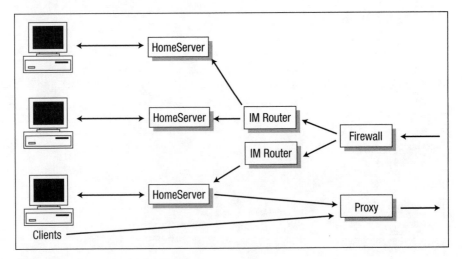

Figure 14.8   Corporate standard topology.

Variations of the Corporate Standard

The corporate DMZ has the same configuration as the corporate standard except that the IM routers are secluded in a DMZ zone (see Figure 14.9). The topologies for the reverse proxy and the packet filters are exactly the same as for the corporate standard employing a firewall solution. Utilized firewall technology is the only difference.

Corporate Multiple Email Domain

The corporate multiple email domain has the same configuration as the corporate standard, except for the use of multiple email and IM domains (see Figure 14.10).

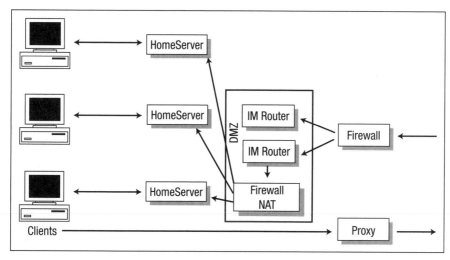

Figure 14.9   Corporate DMZ topology.

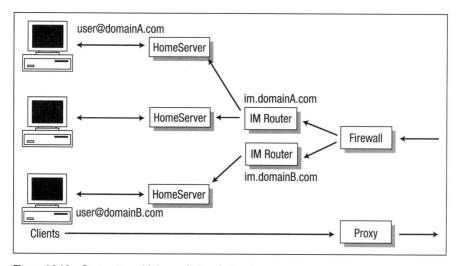

Figure 14.10   Corporate multiple email domain topology.

14

Multiple Win2K Forests

In multiple forest implementations, each forest is a completely separate IM installation because the forests do not share an AD structure. Each individual installation is much like that for the corporate standard communicating to the outside world.

ISP

The ISP configuration supports a very large user base but serves a different user profile with a relatively short online presence. This topology includes multiple IM routers and homeservers, and it may include different IM domains and the DNS round-robin feature.

Geographically Scattered Group

The geographically scattered group (see Figure 14.11) is categorized by a number of geographically dispersed regions that communicate over low-speed and often high-cost connections. Every location has a homeserver to minimize the network load.

Conferencing and Collaborative Solutions

Exchange 2000 Conferencing Server takes the entire collaborative Exchange platform to the next level. It incorporates Conference Management Service, Data Conferencing provider, and Video Conferencing provider to enable realtime user interaction, which includes live video and live audio in addition to chat, application sharing, shared whiteboard, and data (file) transfer services. Based on industry standards, Conferencing Server serves as a solid platform for enterprises to capitalize on advancements in realtime conferencing technology.

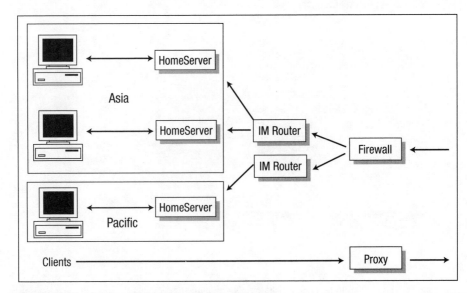

Figure 14.11　Geographically scattered group topology.

Conference Management Service

The main function of Conference Management, one of the three primary components of Conferencing Server, is to control access to and resources used by conference provider components. Conference Management Service is an extensible component upon which you can build third-party products, or use the ones provided by Microsoft.

Video Conferencing Provider

The Video Conferencing provider component enables realtime audio/video conferences and is built to utilize IP –multicast-enabled networks. Multicasting saves a lot of bandwidth by sending information to the next hop on the network path only once, and the hop router then distributes received content to the next hops to which they need to go all at once. As a result, instead of sending five 100Kbps streams between Exchange Server and its first hop, as in unicasting, it can be sent only once by utilizing multicasting. Hosts that need the contents must subscribe to receive the data. To take advantage of multicasting, the underlying network components have to be multicast-aware and configured appropriately. The Video Conferencing provider relies on the H.323 videoconferencing bridge service.

Data Conferencing Provider

The Data Conferencing provider is built on the ITU-T T.120 recommendation for multimedia conferencing. It incorporates technologies to enable application sharing, chat, shared whiteboard, and file transfer all in one conferencing environment.

H.323 Conferencing Bridge

Nonmulticast clients who want to join a multicast videoconference have to connect to the H.323 service that runs on the Conferencing Server and directly connects unicast clients to a conference. H.323 is a component of the T.120 Multipoint Control Unit (MCU).

T.120 MCU

You must install T.120 MCU to perform data conferencing. MCU is a subcomponent of the Data Conferencing provider, and it serves the purpose of connecting incoming requests for data conferencing with each other.

MADCAP Server

To participate in multicast communication, your devices must have a multicast IP address in addition to one of class A, B, or C. A multicast address is a class D address that falls within the range of 224.0.0.0–239.255.255.255 (first octet between 11100000 and 11101111in binary values). Your network devices (conferencing host,

14

end user, and all network devices such as routers in between) have to be IP-multicast aware for this communication to occur. Multicast Address Dynamic Client Allocation Protocol (MADCAP) Server serves as a Dynamic Host Configuration Protocol (DHCP) Server, issuing multicast IP addresses to clients. Microsoft DHCP Server, which ships with Windows 2000, supports the MADCAP specification and can be configured to serve multicast addresses to clients.

X.509 v3 Certificate Authority Certificates

In order to initiate a conferencing connection, your client has to authenticate to T.120 MCU. MCU uses X.509 certificates for authentication, and therefore a Certificate Authority must be incorporated in your infrastructure for certificate-based authentication to work. NetMeeting clients need to obtain certificates that prove their identity to enroll into a conference. Microsoft Certificate Services is used to issue certificates upon demand.

Exchange Server

Exchange Server 2000 is used to schedule conferences and allocate conference resources. Two types of system mailboxes serve conferencing needs: conference calendar mailbox and conference resources mailbox.

Conferencing Client

To participate in a multicast conference, you have to run your client on a multicast-enabled operating system, and Windows 2000 incorporates multicasting technology. Both Exchange and Windows clients rely on Telephony Application Programming Interface (TAPI) 3.0. In addition to the operating system, you need T.120-compliant conferencing software, such as Microsoft NetMeeting 3.x.

Outlook or Browser

To enroll or book a conference, you have to use either a Java-enabled browser, such as IE 4.01 (or better), or Netscape 4. Outlook Web Access must be installed to enable the Web-mailbox interface for browser clients. Besides scheduling, you can also participate in a conference through your Java browser. Outlook 2000 or a previous version is used to book conference time and attendance on the corporate network.

Planning Your Conferencing Solution Deployment

Software

To fully deploy Microsoft Exchange Conferencing Server, the following components must be installed on your network:

➤ Active Directory in the organization

➤ Microsoft IIS Server 5 for Exchange Server and Web access

➤ Microsoft Exchange 2000 Server installed in your domain

In addition, you may opt to incorporate Certificate Services in your organization to support certificate authentication as well as MADCAP Service to automatically distribute multicast IP addresses to multicast conference clients.

Hardware

Hardware requirements heavily depend on the load your Conferencing Server will be handling. Microsoft suggestions are as follows (but please keep in mind that these are minimum requirements that are just that—minimum requirements):

➤ 133MHz CPU (minimum required)

➤ 128MB of RAM (minimum required)

➤ 400MHz CPU (minimum recommended)

➤ 256MB of RAM (minimum recommended)

➤ 50MB of disk space

Collaboration Development in Exchange

Exchange Server historically is not just an out-of-the-box messaging and collaboration solution—it is also a flexible and feature-rich collaborative application development platform that allows developers to build highly productive company-specific solutions. Besides Collaborative Data Objects (CDO), Active Server Pages (ASP), HTML, Event sink, forms, and ActiveX Data Objects (ADO), have all been supported since Exchange 5.5. Now you can add Web Storage Schema (XML), Web Storage Event sink, and CDO for Exchange Management (CDOEXM) to that tally of incorporated programming object models and environments. Exchange 2000 provides several programming interfaces to make development easier, such as C++, Visual Basic and VBScript, and Java and JavaScript.

14

Through the CDO model, the Exchange platform can be used as a scheduling and messaging backbone to your desktop applications. You can programmatically implement as many of the features that Microsoft Outlook provides or as little as an ASP SendMail function for your Web site or mailing list functions in your client database. By combining public folders for data storage with custom forms and scripting either in Outlook or on the Web, you can develop virtually any kind of application that relies or incorporates messaging or scheduling functions; you can access any object or property stored in Exchange; and, with CDOEXM, you can manage Exchange.

Quite often, Microsoft and third-party companies come up with different solutions, such as the extension of scheduling notifications to mobile devices, or Human Resources/Order routing and tracking solutions. Exchange development is a topic well worth another book or two. For further information, please refer to the Microsoft Developer Network (MSDN) Web site at **http://msdn.microsoft.com**.

Chapter Summary

This chapter discussed realtime collaboration solutions provided by Exchange 2000 Server. Exchange employs chat and instant messaging to enable its users to interact with each other either in groups or individually, casually or for business purposes. Microsoft Chat Service adds IRC chat functionality to your messaging solution. Chat is an online community or place where people meet and discuss topics grouped by various criteria— geographic, age group, or any lifestyles or interests. Chat service hosts communities, and each chat community has chat channels, which are called chat rooms. Each channel has members who are online chat users. To participate in a chat session, you have to use IRC-compliant chat software. Microsoft implemented IRCX support in its service, so if you need to host multilingual chat rooms, you need to use the IRCX client software Microsoft Chat.

Instant messaging is new to Exchange and is a result of the enormous recent popularity of this realtime collaboration technology. IM is based on a proposed standard Rendezvous Protocol (RVP), and MSN Messenger is used as a client. Service functionality is based on XML as the formatting means and HTTP as the transfer means, and port 80 is used for message transfer. The service core is comprised of IM routers and IM homeservers, as well as DNS, AD, IIS virtual server, and clients In addition, various firewall technologies are employed to make sure you are not exposing your network to extreme security risks by making the service available externally. The IM router is an Exchange server that receives all incoming messages and makes routing decisions based on homeserver and user information stored in AD. The IM HomeServer is an Exchange server that hosts users and serves as an entry point for clients to access the service. IM Service can be either an autonomous deployment that is isolated to the needs of one company, or an interoperable deployment that interfaces with IM deployments in other organizations.

To maximize user-friendliness, email addresses are used on the client side for addressing and for user location/message routing functions. However, the client transfers messages to homeservers and onward by using HTTP as the message transfer protocol, so email addresses are translated into HTTP URLs that are either server-specific or server-independent. A server-independent URL is used to transfer messages to routers, which then redirect these messages using server-specific URLs. The address namespace of your IM design should be the same as your email namespace design so users have to remember only one email address for both IM messaging and email messaging. IM Service maintains the user presence information database. If user A adds user B into his or her "buddy list," user A is subscribing to the presence information of user B. When user B logs on, user B is registered with the presence database, and a status change notification is sent to subscribers for user B, and they can easily see if user B is busy, away, or offline.

Exchange also has a Conferencing Server solution that provides multimedia (audio/video/data) conferencing services. Bandwidth usage is minimized by multicasting, which means one data stream that needs to go to n different participants through the same router is sent only once to that router, and not n times. From that router onward, these streams are sent using the same approach, until data gets to the final point where individual clients subscribe to the multicast endpoint to receive the contents. Exchange Conferencing is built to embrace industry standards and recommended standards such as T.120 and H.323.

Finally, the Exchange collaborative development model exposes system objects and functions to programmers who can employ an array of technologies and several interfaces to build their own custom solutions.

Review Questions

1. Which of the following are the types of chat conversations that you can conduct? [Check all correct answers]

    a. Realtime

    b. Delayed

    c. Instant

    d. Private

    e. Public

2. On what technology does Microsoft rely to allow Microsoft Exchange Chat Service to establish chat communities, channels, and other chat and user-related settings?

    a. Instant Messaging

    b. Active Directory

    c. IRCX

    d. ADC

14

3. By default, client software connects to the Exchange Server hosting chat service using which standard IRC port?

   a. 7060

   b. 6700

   c. 6667

   d. 7000

4. Up to how many chat users can one Exchange 2000 Server host?

   a. Up to 12,000 chat users

   b. Up to 20,000 chat users

   c. Up to 22,000 chat users

   d. Up to 25,000 chat users

5. What are the two main types of chat channels (rooms). [Check the two correct answers]

   a. Public

   b. Private

   c. Registered

   d. Dynamic

   e. Synchronous

   f. Asynchronous

6. What is the name for the software module based on the Chat Server Extensibility Model that enhances the features of the existing chat service?

   a. Chat Connector

   b. Extensibility Component

   c. Chat Component

   d. Server Extension

7. Which one of the following in-band commands will disable the transcription of all dynamic channels?

   a. EXTMSG TSCRIPT start DYNAMIC

   b. EXTMSG TSCRIPT stop DYNAMIC

   c. EXTMSG TSCRIPT enable DYNAMIC

   d. EXTMSG TSCRIPT disable DYNAMIC

8. Which of the following components does Microsoft Chat Service absolutely require to be properly deployed? [Check all correct answers]

   a. Dynamic Host Configuration Protocol

   b. Windows 2000 Advanced Server

   c. Microsoft Exchange 2000 Server

   d. System Manager

   e. Domain Name Service

9. Which of the following attacks is a denial-of-service type of attack that sends massive amounts of nonsense data to a chat session?

   a. Flooding attack

   b. Cloning attack

   c. User identity masking

   d. Spoofing attack

10. Which one of the following is *not* an Exchange 2000 Chat Service-supported authentication type?

    a. Anonymous

    b. Basic Authentication

    c. Windows SSPI

    d. MS-CHAP

11. Which subcomponent of the Data Conferencing provider must you install to store data as well as connect incoming requests for data conferencing with each other?

    a. MADCAP Server

    b. T.120 Multipoint Control Unit

    c. X.509 v3 Certificate Authority certificates

    d. H.323 conferencing bridge

14

12. To participate in multicast communication, your devices must have a multicast IP address in addition to one of class A, B, or C. A multicast address is a class D address that falls within which of the following ranges of IP addresses?

    a. 168.0.0.0 to 198.255.255.255

    b. 192.0.0.0 to 224.255.255.255

    c. 224.0.0.0 to 240.255.255.255

    d. 226.0.0.0 to 242.255.255.255

13. You are planning to deploy your conferencing solution. To fully accomplish a deployment of Exchange Conferencing Server, you will need which of the following components installed on the network?

    a. Microsoft WINS Proxy

    b. Active Directory in your organization

    c. Microsoft IIS Server 5 for Exchange Server and Web access

    d. Microsoft Exchange 2000 Server installed in your domain

    e. DHCP Relay Agent

    f. b and d only

    g. b, c, and d only

    h. All of the above

14. You are planning the hardware for your conferencing solution deployment. Which one of the following is *not* a Microsoft suggested solution?

    a. 133MHz CPU minimum requirement

    b. 64MB of RAM minimum requirement

    c. 50MB of free disk space

    d. 400MHz CPU minimum recommended

15. Exchange Server provides a flexible and feature-rich collaborative application development platform that allows developers to build highly productive company-specific solutions. Which of the following components are supported in Exchange 2000? [Check all correct answers]

    a. CDO (Collaborative Data Objects)

    b. ASP (Active Server Pages)

    c. ADO (ActiveX Data Objects)

    d. Web Storage Schema (XML)

    e. Macromedia Generator Extensions

    f. CDOEXM (CDO for Exchange Management)

Real-World Projects

Project 14.1

In this project, you will create a chat community, a chat channel, classify users, and impose a user ban.

Step 1. Create a Chat Community

1. Open Microsoft Exchange System Manager by clicking on Start | Programs | Microsoft Exchange. System Manager will load.

2. Browse Console Tree on the left-hand side down to Servers container and locate the machine that will be hosting a chat community.

3. Expand Protocols, note whether the IRCX folder is there—if it is not present, then Chat Service is not installed and you need to add it from Add/Remove Programs, under the Exchange 2000 Change/Remove option.

4. Browse further down the Console Tree and locate the Chat Communities container. Note that it is not server-specific.

5. To create a new chat community, right-click the Chat Communities container and select New | Chat Community. A configuration page will appear.

6. On the General tab, assign your group a name and add a title if you wish (remember naming conventions). In the Connection Limits frame, you specify the user capacity of this community. Keep in mind that community is just a container for individual chat channels, and the maximum number of users allowed per server is 20,000. Select whether you require, attempt, or disable DNS resolution of the client IP addresses that are joining chat rooms. Finally, select whether you want to allow new connections. You want this checked for now, use this function when you have to take the server or community down for maintenance and want to prevent new connections for a defined span of time.

7. On the Channels tab, configure the default behavior of chat channels. Values include Channel defaults and Dynamic Channels defaults. Specify whether you want this community to provide dynamic rooms.

8. On the Messages tab, configure message of the day (MOTD), a message that is displayed right after a user joins a room in this chat community. Usually it is a short explanation of the purpose of this community and its general conduct rules. Also configure a separate message for users with administrative privileges.

9. On the Security tab, add user groups or individual accounts and assign appropriate permissions.

10. On the Authentication tab, choose your allowed methods of authentication. Remember to keep it on the basic authentication level if you have to support non-Windows clients.

11. Click OK. Your chat community is created. To finish the process, your chat community has to be assigned to a server that will be hosting it. To create this association, go up the console tree and browse to the server you want to assign.

14

Expand Protocols, right-click on IRCX, and click Properties. The IRCX protocol properties sheet will appear. Click on Add and choose the community you created from the drop-down list. Click OK to select it. On the next screen, check the Enable Server to Host this Chat Community checkbox to create your association. If you want to specify a port number other than the standard 6667 or to bind the service to a certain network interface only, configure it here. When you are done, click OK and then apply your changes. Your community is created and associated with the server.

Step 2. Create a Channel (Chat Room) within Your Chat Community

1. Browse your Console Tree to the Chat Communities container where you created a chat community in Step 1. Expand it, right-click on Channels, select New | Channel. A New Channel property sheet will appear.

2. Configure the General tab properties with information such as name, topic, subject, and language of the channel. Remember the chat room naming conventions from Table 14.2. This information is used by client software to search the channels available on your server. PICS is a rating system that defines the tolerance levels of coarse language, nudity, and violence. If you check the Create this Channel When Server Starts option, this registered channel will be starting up automatically without waiting for users to request connection.

3. Configure the Access, Security, and Modes tabs to reflect your security and access restriction guidelines and requirements.

4. On the Messages tab, define a MOTD for users entering and leaving the room. Entering the message is the most critical part and should always be used to advise the members of the conduct policy.

5. Click OK. Your chat channel is created.

Step 3. Create a Class and User Ban within Your Chat Community

1. In the console tree, right-click on Classes. Select New | Class.

2. On the General page, specify the scope of your class. This is a characteristic of users that should be exposed to certain rules as outlined in this class. Characteristics include nickname, username, and IP address or IP subnet address (using subnet mask).

3. On the Access tab, configure access limits to which all users that match this class will be exposed. Settings include logon, functionality, and time restrictions.

4. On the Settings tab, configure attack protection levels of this class by imposing various processing delays and bandwidth or connection restrictions.

5. Click OK when done. Your user class is created. When a user is compared to the class, the process goes from the top to the bottom of the classes list. Keep in mind that the effective class is the one that will match first.

6. Right-click on Bans. Click Properties. Select New | Ban.

7. Configure your ban based on chat nickname, Active Directory account username, or IP address. If you leave Start Time and End Time identical, this ban will be effective until revoked manually by the Administrator. Use Bans to deny access to users who are guilty of repeated misconduct or insult other members. Bans are imposed by sysops and chanops, as well as admins who are supervising chat members in the channels.

Your server is now ready to accept connections and you are prepared to manage your users.

Project 14.2

Create an IM router, IM homeserver, IIS Web server, and define firewall topology.

Step 1. Create a Virtual IIS WebServer for IM Router

1. Remember that IM service is HTTP-based, and to service HTTP requests we need an IIS virtual Web server first and then an Exchange Server. Go to Start | Settings | Control Panel. Double-click Administrative Tools, and then select Internet Service Manager. Internet Service Manager will now load.

2. Select the server on which you want to install IM router service, right-click on it, and select New | Web Server. Setup Wizard guides you through the virtual server creation process. Please remember that no more than one Web site can bind to default port 80 (or any other port, for that matter), so if your port 80 Web site already serves some other purposes, you will need to either reassign a port number or select a different computer. The Web site will not start if port 80 is in use, but on a port other than 80, IM Service will not install.

3. When you are done with the wizard, make sure your newly created Web site is running. By default it is stopped.

Step 2. Create a Virtual Web Server for the IM HomeServer on another PC

1. Repeat Step 1.

2. Remember that you do not need to have IM Router if you only have one homeserver.

14

Step 3. Create an IM Homeserver

1. Go back to Microsoft Exchange Systems Manager and browse to the server on which you plan to host your service. Expand the Server container, expand the Protocols container, right-click on Instant Messaging, and select New | Instant Messaging Virtual Server. A wizard will now appear that will guide you through the process.

2. You will have to select the Web server that will be assigned to service requests from the list of available port-80 Web servers. If your IIS Web server does not show up on the list, check what port it is binding to.

3. Check Allow this Server to Host User Accounts to make this server an IM homeserver.

Step 4. Create an IM Router

1. Repeat Step 3, but do not select the Allow this Server to Host User Accounts option. This will make this server an IM router. Create this router only if you have more than one homeserver. Router needs to be a different computer that has an IM virtual Web server bound to port 80.

Step 5. Define Firewall Topology

1. Firewall topology needs to be defined if you use any firewall solutions through which IM has to pass. Please note that this setting is server neutral and affects all servers in the organization.

2 Browse the Console Tree to Global Settings container. Expand it, right-click on Instant Messaging Settings, and select Properties.

3. On the property sheet that appears, select the Firewall Topology tab, and configure the protected (internal) IP address range and outgoing proxy configuration as it applies to your network. Click OK, and you are done.

CHAPTER FIFTEEN

Designing for Fault Tolerance and Data Recovery

After completing this chapter, you will be able to:

✓ Understand the overall Exchange 2000 Server database architecture

✓ Understand various backup types

✓ Plan your data fault tolerance

✓ Design backup solutions and perform backups

✓ Design recovery solutions and perform disaster recoveries

✓ Troubleshoot backup and restore processes

Overview of Data Storage in Exchange 2000

No matter how good your Active Directory (AD) and Exchange 2000 Server designs are, your career could be in danger if you have not thoroughly planned for disaster recovery. The planning and deployment of your Exchange organization is a sophisticated process. The minute your Exchange solution goes live, the entire corporation will depend on the service, so your duty, as an Exchange administrator, is to ensure reliability and availability. Without a proper backup plan in place, even such a small problem as a corrupted database page can lead to a disaster. At the very least, you will incur downtime or potentially lose vital business data. A proper backup strategy alone, however, is not enough. You must ensure that your backup strategy is reversible, meaning that you are able to regenerate the data and restore all the services in the least amount of time, thus minimizing production downtime. It is never enough to have only a backup strategy—the recovery strategy must also be planned and tested. You may never have to recover, but just in case you do, you must ensure that your solution actually works both ways. This testing may require additional hardware, which may be cost prohibitive for small businesses, but the cost of a catastrophic data loss could be devastating for a business of any size. You need to determine if you are ready to take this kind of gamble. By failing to test your backup and recovery, you are putting your entire data recovery strategy at risk. Therefore, you want to be sure to implement a step-by-step recovery process that is fully tested and documented.

Before we delve into planning for disaster recovery, we need to clarify a few important concepts that are relevant to the data storage architecture of Microsoft Exchange Server 2000. Although you could most likely successfully perform both backups and restores of data without having a total understanding of how Microsoft data storage functions, you should understand the process as a whole. The entire process is similar to and based on the same technology in Exchange 5.5.

Features such as transaction logging, checkpoint files, patch files, and other database fundamentals remain basically the same as those in Exchange 5.5. A few very important differences were introduced, however, that make Exchange 2000 a more scalable and flexible platform. For example, in Exchange 2000, the Directory Service database (dir.edb) no longer exists because it relies on Windows 2000 Active Directory instead. This new feature allows for more flexibility when designing fault-tolerant systems, which may either simplify or complicate matters when it comes to disaster recovery planning.

Format and Storage

Databases in Exchange 2000, just as in previous versions of Exchange, are built on Extensible Storage Engine (ESE) technology. Each database now consists of two files, .edb and .stm. Previously, there was only one .edb database file to store information for each of the three databases, which could store data only in Rich Text Format (RTF; in this case, Microsoft Database Exchange Format, or MDBEF). For Exchange to store non-MDBEF data, Information Store Service would have to first convert it to MDBEF format, which would consume central processing unit (CPU) cycles, random access memory (RAM), and disk space. This proved to be an inefficient format. In much the same way, Exchange 2000 stores MDBEF data in the .edb database file; however, now all of the non-MDBEF data goes into the second part of the database—the .stm database file—instead of being converted. Both of these databases are built on ESE technology. Microsoft refers to the .stm database by two names: Streaming File or Native Content Store.

In today's implementations, most email messages contain information that requires MDBEF conversion (graphics, audio, video, Hypertext Markup Language [HTML], and so on) without Native Content Store. This design eliminates the substantial overhead incurred by this conversion because non-MDBEF content is stored as raw bits. References to this content and overhead information are stored as RTF in the .edb file. The .stm file contains only raw data without the accompanying information. Every embedded database (EDB) is now accompanied by a (STM) database (usually with the same filename prefix). If you are performing a manual backup by simply copying the database files, you absolutely must treat the corresponding EDB and STM files as one single database because they are two parts of one database.

Content Conversion

Although content conversion is greatly reduced in Exchange 2000, it is not completely eliminated. Existing Messaging Application Programming Interface (MAPI) clients (e.g., Outlook 2000) are not aware of the Native Content Store and still write to the MDBEF database and request RTF contents. For example, when an Outlook client requests a picture that was stored in .stm Native Content Store(NCS), Exchange 2000 will fetch the raw data from the NCS, convert it to RTF in the server's memory, and pass this information on to the client. If the client does not modify and save this information, the server will dump it from the memory after it is no longer needed. Conversely, if the client wants to save this information, it must go through a conversion process and the requested file must be saved to the MDBEF database. When a client attempts to modify data that was presented from a raw data store, it must now be saved into the Rich Text Data Store. This process is known as promotion. Keep in mind that this applies only to MAPI clients.

15

Single Instance Store

Exchange 2000 supports the Single Instance Store (SIS) technology that was introduced in the earlier versions of the product. A result of this feature is that the same attachment sent to 50 people in your organization will not be stored in 50 separate mailboxes. Instead, the attachment is stored once in a transaction log in each storage group to which it is sent. It is also stored only once in every database that hosts the recipients of that message. As a result, if the message has a 5MB attachment, and all of the recipients are hosted within one storage group in one database, you will have two copies of this message, totaling 10MB, as opposed to 50 copies, totaling 250MB. If the recipients are located in three different databases within one storage group, you would end up with one copy in the transaction log, and three copies in each database, totaling 20 MB. The idea of this whole concept is to keep your database size as small as possible and at the same time keep performance optimized. This feature makes databases more manageable and reduces the time it takes to back up and restore.

Storage Groups

All data storage in Exchange 2000 is organized based on storage groups. A storage group is defined as a set of databases that share the same transaction log. In fact, Exchange 5.5 had the concept of storage groups as well, but very few users actually were aware of it because only one storage group was designed into the product, and there was no way of managing or altering it. Previous to Exchange 2000, the number of databases and their purpose was limited by design so that one storage group contained one database for the private mailboxes (priv.edb) and one database for public folders (pub.edb). Exchange 2000 supports up to four storage groups per server, and each storage group can contain up to five databases, making a maximum of 20 databases per single server. In addition, the naming convention is totally up to the administrator.

The storage group (see Figure 15.1) concept is key to the design of your Exchange fault-tolerance solution. Instead of having 20,000 users sitting in one database, as could be the case with Exchange 5.5, you can now have 20 databases hosting 1,000 users each. If one database becomes corrupt for any reason, or if one of the disks that hosts the particular database fails, your overall population is not affected. Only those users who had their mailboxes in that database, only 5 percent of the total

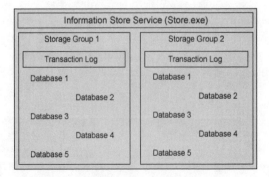

Figure 15.1   Exchange Server storage groups.

population in our example, will be affected. Restoring a single small database is obviously much faster and less troublesome than restoring the entire Data Store.

Each database within a storage group can be in one of the two states: mounted (initialized) or dismounted (stopped). By default, when you initialize Store.exe, databases are automatically mounted. The state of the database also has an impact on your backup and restore operations—a topic addressed in more detail in the section "How Backups Work" later in this chapter. By default, after installation, Microsoft Exchange Server 2000 will have two databases: one for private mailboxes and one for public folders, just as in Exchange 5.5.

Pages

The ESE database comprises chunks of data called pages. A page is a 4K unit of information contained in the database. Every page contains general information about itself, such as **checksum**, **timestamp**, and **page number**. Once a need arises to access certain pieces of information stored in the database, the pages of spanned information are read into memory. The pages are then marked in memory as "clean." If a page is modified, it is marked as "dirty," and a corresponding transaction gets written to the transaction log. Over time, dirty pages will get written (flushed) to the database. After all of the pages that constitute a transaction are flushed to the database, the transaction is marked as "committed" in the checkpoint file. Should a power outage or another catastrophic event occur during this process, the information that is being committed is not lost. The corresponding transaction will be replayed from the transaction log when the Information Store is initialized after a reboot.

Checksum is recalculated and verified on every page before it is accessed. This process will naturally introduce some latency to the process of reading data. The upside that justifies this technique is that data integrity is ensured. If the page **checksum** does not match the **checksum** that results in recalculation, the page is corrupt and you will have a problem.

In theory, one ESE database can support up to 16TB (terabytes) of data. An ESE database supports 2^{32} pages. That 4,294,967,296 pages multiplied by 4KB yields 17,179,869,184KB, or 16TB. This is merely theoretical because an average company is unlikely to have these kind of hardware resources. Besides, there are product limitations by design. The Standard Edition of Microsoft Exchange 2000 supports databases up to 16GB.

Transaction Logs

More often than not, your Exchange database will grow. Imagine that every single transaction you make (for example, sending a message) would have to be written straight to the database. Imagine further that the database is approximately 40GB—

15

not unusual for a mission-critical solution such as Exchange. This would obviously slow down the system; this is a good example of why you have transaction logs. Microsoft utilizes this technique to significantly reduce the amount of time needed for input/output (I/O) operations on the database when it comes to writing data.

Transaction logs are a group of relatively small files that store recent operations on the database. The transaction log is essentially a store of all recent changes that occurred to the database but have not yet been written to it. Single transactions usually consist of multiple operations, and until all these operations are successfully written to the database, the transaction is not considered successfully flushed to the database and is not marked as such in the checkpoint file. If the transaction flushing process commences a write operation just as a server crashes, the changes will be rolled back and later replayed after the Information Store is reinitialized.

Thus, instead of writing randomly to a huge database file, transactions are written to a much smaller transaction log file, which is later written to the actual database. Once a current transaction log reaches 5MB, it is turned over. The current log file is called a current generation, and every new log file created is a new generation. The filename of the current generation log is always E00.log. From there on, files are named E0000001.log and so on, with the numbers represented by a hexadecimal value.

Certain techniques ensure that transaction log data is written to the database in a consistent manner. These techniques are tests known as Atomic, Consistent, Isolated, and Durable, which are often referred to as ACID. You should never move or delete log files manually. Although the consequence of doing so may not surface until later, this action will corrupt the database and possibly cause severe problems and data loss. The full backup process purges transaction logs after a successful backup. Do not move or delete the transaction logs. Also, you should not run antivirus software on the logs. In certain circumstances, your antivirus application may detect a matching bit pattern and think that your log file is infected. Further, you should never enable the Windows NT file system (NTFS) or any other compression on the logs. This may result in data corruption and will most certainly decrease performance of your Exchange implementation. Last but not least, you should *not* use hard disk drive controllers that have write cache enabled on them. Doing so risks the chance that some data destined to the transaction log will get stuck on the controller should a power outage or hardware failure occur.

Circular Logging

Depending on the role of your Exchange server and the load it handles, you may want to consider circular logging. If your box has a lot of activity, transaction logs will start taking up a lot of space. If you have a critical need to control and reduce the amount of space consumed by the transaction logs, you may decide to enable circular logging. When enabled, circular logging produces only five logs of 5MB each, and after the fifth log is filled, Exchange starts overwriting transaction log number 1, after first committing its transactions to the database. Circular logging is generally not a recommended practice for most Exchange deployments, however. If your environment has mailboxes and/or public folders located on the server do not use circular logging. If a disaster occurs to a production server with circular logging enabled, you will be able to restore data only up to the last full backup. However, if you have a server dedicated to just forwarding mail (for example, a bridgehead server that stores nothing and exclusively forwards mail), circular logging may be a viable option, especially if this box is handling a significant load and backups are rarely done. Remember to disable circular logging when data recoverability is of the utmost importance.

Flushing or Committing Transactions

As discussed previously, all of the changes that happen on an Exchange database are occurring to the pages in RAM, located in server memory. You are not concerned about writing to the ESE database at this time, but just want to commit the transaction. Every transaction consists of one or more operations, and only when all of these operations have been written to the transaction log can the transaction be said to be committed.

Note: Committing transactions is not the same as flushing transactions from transaction logs to the actual ESE database, which will happen later after a full or incremental backup. Types of backups are discussed later in this chapter in the section "Types of Backups."

This entire commitment technique is known as "write-ahead." The ESE is based on this method so that the speed of transactions is significantly increased. Until you have executed a full or incremental backup, your transaction logs are much more than simply "logs." They are still the actual data that is supposed to be written to the main ESE database. The data is not yet written, however, because it would take entirely too much time, for example, to write transactions to a 30GB database on the fly. You need these logs to recover from a disaster because they represent all of the changes that were made to the database since the last backup. This is why transaction logs are so important in a production environment when you store data on your Exchange server.

Also, you should realize that transactions are not being committed from the memory to the transaction log at the very same moment they happen. The process actually takes some time, and you cannot really know the precise moment when a particular transaction gets committed. Exchange 2000 makes this decision on its own, although certain events may trigger commitment. For example, other processes may have started on the Exchange server that need some of the RAM taken by dirty Exchange pages (i.e., uncommitted transactions). Also, when you stop the

15

Store.exe (Information Store Service) process, the actual service shutdown may take a little bit of time because it makes sure that all transactions in the memory are committed and writes them to the transaction log as the service shuts down gracefully. RAM transactions are also committed to the log file during a full backup.

Version Store

Another component that relates to the process of committing transactions is the version store. The purpose of the version store is to keep track of transactions that have not yet been committed to the disk. Once a transaction is committed, information about it is purged from the version store. If hardware fails or a power failure occurs when a transaction is being committed, Store.exe will check the transaction log file next time it is initialized and verify that all of the transactions are fully committed. If Store.exe finds that some transactions were not completed successfully (or only a few operations within the transaction were written successfully), then the Information Store Service will roll these changes back. This process of starting Information Store and checking transaction logs can take a while, depending on the amount of data in the logs, but it helps to ensure the integrity of your databases.

Checkpoint Files

As mentioned in the "Pages" section earlier in this chapter, checkpoint files mark which transactions in the transaction log were flushed to the database and which transactions still need to be written to the database. It is important to understand that transactions are not committed directly from the transaction log. All write activity to the ESE database occurs from pages in memory. Therefore, at any given time, two copies of uncommitted transactions exist—one in the transaction log and one in the memory. There is one checkpoint file per transaction log file (and there is one transaction log file per storage group).

Patch Files

As your backup is chugging away, the larger your database is, the greater the chances are that someone will attempt to modify a page that is already stored in backed-up space. All such changes will be placed into the .pat patch file. After the backup is done, the size of the entire data store will be equivalent to the backup plus the patch file. If a need arises to restore a database, the patch file needs to be replayed against the restored database. If this does not occur (due perhaps to a missing or damaged patch file), you will have a serious issue on your hands. The chances are pretty good that some information in the database will be lost or your database may be entirely corrupted.

Exchange 2000 Backup Strategies

Now, with an understanding of the "big picture" of how Microsoft Exchange data storage is implemented, in this section you can explore some backup strategies as well as what information needs to be recovered if disaster strikes. This section also looks at the way AD affects the process. This section is absolutely critical for anyone who is not experienced with the NT and/or Exchange 5.5 backup process.

How Backup Works

As mentioned in the section "Storage Groups" earlier in this chapter, Exchange 2000 databases run in storage groups, and all storage groups run within the Store.exe process. Each database can be in either one of the two states: mounted (initialized) or dismounted (stopped). In addition, two major backup strategies exist: offline or online. These two options from Exchange 5.5 remain in Exchange 2000, although a slight modification has been made to the restoration process (which is covered later in this chapter in the "Recovering from Disaster" section). In most circumstances, you will be performing online backup; however, you may want to do an offline backup in some situations. Online backup essentially means that no service downtime or interruption occurs for the process to be executed, and all of the changes to the database being backed up are retained (see the discussion in the section "Patch Files"). With an offline backup, in contrast, you have to stop your databases and shut down your services, in which case transactions are flushed to the database. If you are doing an offline backup, you must manually select which databases you want to back up.

Although third-party Exchange 2000-aware software can be used for a disaster recovery strategy, for the purpose of this book you will use only Windows 2000 Ntbackup.exe to back up and restore. Upon initialization of the backup, **NTBACKUP** calls the necessary API procedures to inform Store.exe that database backup is on its way. Store.exe passes this information on to the ESE engine, which in turn enters backup mode. At this stage, a patch file is created for each database that is being backed up in any storage group, and a current-generation log file is turned over (renamed) in all affected storage groups. Remember that each storage group has its own transaction log file set. When all of these steps are successfully completed, **NTBACKUP** starts requesting all of the pages from the database currently being backed up in sequential order.

Note: Pages are not stored sequentially in most cases. This can take a toll on performance, so to avoid fragmentation you should maintain and defragment databases.

Backup also recalculates all of the **checksum**s on all the pages that are being read to ensure data and hard disk drive subsystem integrity. You can back up multiple databases or individual databases, serially or simultaneously. Storage groups provide

15

you with more granular control over the data that you store. Microsoft recommends backing up entire storage groups as a more reasonable approach. Remember that transaction logs are shared across all databases in the storage group, and they are crucial when it comes to data recoverability.

If you have multiple storage groups and multiple tape drives, you can back up several storage groups simultaneously to different tapes or file dumps, which can prove to be a great time-saver for high-end solutions. However, you cannot back up different databases in the same storage group simultaneously. To back up several databases within one group, you have to either run one backup job that would back them up serially, or schedule different backup jobs to run at different times. After database backup is done, patch files are copied to the tape (or dumped on the disk, depending on how you back up) along with all relevant transaction logs that are purged from Exchange data store directories. All three—database, patch file, and transaction logs—are necessary to restore your databases in case of a disaster. Depending on the type of backup, the actual database may not necessarily be backed up every time the process is triggered.

Types of Backup

Five different backup types are available to implement your disaster recovery strategy (see Table 15.1). Regardless of the option you choose, the objective remains the same and must be attainable—complete disaster recovery with no or minimum impact. Your backup and/or restore times and required capacities will be affected by the type of backup you choose. Keep in mind that there is no "one-size-fits-all" solution as far as backup strategy is concerned. Table 15.1 presents the different backup methods and their respective capabilities applicable to Exchange 2000 data storage system. Please note that "?" marks mean that operation may or may not be performed based on database state. If even a single change was made, which will represent most of the cases, database and log backup will be performed.

Full Backup

The full backup option (also called normal backup) backs up the entire database, including transaction logs (except the current generation, which is essentially contained in a patch file) and patch file itself. After full backup completes, it purges all backed up transaction log files and frees up space on your disk. A very practical

Table 15.1   Backup types in Exchange 2000.

Backup Type	Database Copy	Log Copy	Log Delete
Full (normal) Backup	V	V	V
Incremental Backup	X	V	V
Differential Backup	X	V	X
Copy Backup	?	?	X
Offline Backup	V	—	—

approach to data management is to run this type of backup every night to keep the space taken by transaction logs down to a minimum. Although you can use circular logging with this type of backup, circular logging is not recommended in any production environment in which data recoverability is of the utmost importance.

Full backup sets a marker on all files that were backed up. If you later have to restore data from full backup, the process is straightforward: you just restore the latest full backup. This backup process has the disadvantage, however, of being time and capacity consuming, because the entire database is backed up on every run, However, full backup is the fastest way to restore because all you have to restore is one database that was fully backed up.

Incremental Backup

Incremental backup works only with transaction logs, and therefore circular logging is impossible when implementing this option. Incremental backup is another way to get rid of ever-growing transaction logs and freeing up some space on the disk subsystem, but it does not really back up the database. All it backs up is the portion of the transaction logs that have their checkpoint set (transactions that were flushed to the ESE database).

Incremental backup is perhaps the most optimal approach to ensure your data integrity requirements are met for time and capacity usage. An incremental backup backs up only the changes that occurred since the last incremental or normal backup, whichever was the most recent. This type of backup is useless by itself without a full backup preceding it. Usually, a full backup is run in the beginning of the week, say on a Sunday, and an incremental backup is run every night. Then, if a disaster should happen on Thursday, you would have to restore full backup from Monday first, and then sequentially restore all incremental backups. After restoration is completed, you can mount the database and it will replay transaction logs restored from incremental backups, so it is important not to initialize the database until all tapes are run. This strategy allows for the fastest backup routines possible, but the restoration time is the longest because you have to restore the normal set plus all incremental backups that ran after normal backup was made. Downside of this method is that you have to be absolutely sure that backup media is reliable because if you have to restore your database on Friday and one of the incremental tapes from Tuesday become damaged—Monday will be as far as you would be able to go. Ensuring reliability of the media is a must with every type of backup.

Differential Backup

A differential backup works exclusively with transaction logs in the same way as an incremental backup. Therefore, circular logging must be disabled and cannot be used with this strategy either. The difference between incremental and differential backups is that differential backups do not purge the logs that are backed up. Differential backup takes all of the logs between the last full backup and the current

15

checkpoint and backs up the transaction logs. Restoring with the differential backup is faster than with the incremental backup because all you have to restore is the last full backup set and the latest differential backup. Backing up takes increasingly longer with every backup because all the changes that were made since the last normal backup have to be backed up. As mentioned, logs are not deleted, so you must ensure you have enough hard disk drive space for your database to grow. When restoring, keep in mind not to mount the database until both the full and the latest differential backups are restored because transaction logs from the differential set will have to be replayed upon initialization.

Copy Backup

Copy backup is similar to full backup in that it does not purge the logs from your system; it only takes a current snapshot of it. Copy backup does back up those files that were changed or added since full backup ran, so in most scenarios, this will include your databases as well. This backup type is not normally used in your day-to-day automated routine, and files that need to be backed up have to be specified manually.

Copy backup is for taking a system snapshot prior to doing some minor or major changes to the server, such as installing some hardware or system software (such as a service pack). Copy backup does not interfere with your scheduled backup routines in any way because it does not reset any checkpoint information and does nothing in terms of flushing transactions to the database—it simply copies information. Always back up your system before doing any kind of changes to the functioning production system.

Offline Backup

All previous backup types were online backup routines. An offline backup is in a class of its own. Whereas online backups require Store.exe to be started and the databases mounted, offline backup requires exactly the opposite. Store.exe must be stopped. When you stop services, all dirty pages (RAM pages) are written to the database and the database is said to be consistent. After services are stopped, the rest of the process is file-level, so you could use any backup software to just copy it somewhere on the network or to multiple CDs using the file splitting utility. You must select files manually if you are using **NTBACKUP**. Offline backup is not recommended for daily operations; however, it may come in handy if your full backup copy gets corrupted or misplaced.

Time and Capacity Planning

More often than not, when disaster does happen, the time to recover needs to be minimized. Table 15.2 shows a time planning comparison. This table does not apply to each and every situation, but it presents an overall idea of the strengths and weaknesses of each method.

Table 15.2 Time planning comparison based on weekly rotation.

Backup Type	Time to Backup	Time to Restore	Capacity Need
Normal daily (same tape)	Maximum	Minimum	Minimum
Normal and incremental	Minimum	Maximum	Average
Normal and differential	Average	Average	Average

Planning Your AD Backup Strategy

The previous section focused on backing up your Exchange 2000 databases (Information Store). Unfortunately, this is far from everything you will need to fully recover from a total disaster as quickly as possible. Every systems administrator must have an up-to-date backup of AD and other important components that constitute Exchange environment, including the following:

➤ System State (registry and COM+ objects and registrations)

➤ System partition contents of Exchange Server

➤ Active Directory (AD)

➤ Site Replication Service database (SRS database)

➤ Internet Information Service metabase (IIS metabase)

➤ Key Management Service database (KMS database)

Active Directory

Previous chapters showed how Exchange 2000 moved from server-centric design and that in version 2000 all configuration data is stored in AD and is propagated through the AD forest to all domain controllers (DCs). AD design of your organization has a direct impact on planning and implementing recoverability of your Exchange solution. You can deploy your AD—as well as ensure that you have a backup in case the DC goes down—in several ways, depending on several factors.

The first important factor is the manner in which you deploy your solution. In a small organization, one powerful machine may be "all things to everybody." Perhaps it is a DC that holds a master replica of AD and the Exchange Server 2000 that is fully reliant upon it. Although this situation would be easier for backups, it is not a recommended configuration. A more reliable and fault-tolerant solution would be to have a couple of dedicated DCs holding more than one copy of AD, and a stand-alone Windows 2000 Server or Advanced Server dedicated to Exchange Server 2000. In this scenario, the backup and disaster recovery will be more complex, but at the same time, the load is spread over several servers. The DC may still crash along with your Exchange Server, but the chances are in your favor that you will need to worry only about losing one or the other.

15

Apart from the performance gains, having at least two replicas of AD, no matter how small your organization, is a very good practice. You will have more available recovery options in case of a disaster, and downtime is either minimized or eliminated. Back-ups of the AD should be performed regularly, and a backup copy should be stored off-site. Remember to do an AD backup each time before and after making a change to AD or installing a major application. You may want to roll back in case the result is not favorable. Even though having an AD backup can be a lifesaver, you can still restore individual mailboxes from your Exchange 2000 backup tapes.

System State of Exchange Server and Domain Controller

Windows 2000 introduces a new backup type called the System State backup. This backup type exists universally in all products of the Windows 2000 family and is available in **NTBACKUP**. It is much the same as backing up system registry in Windows NT, but it goes further by saving the IIS metabase, as well as COM+ objects and registrations. System State is a complete snapshot of system-specific information that is imperative to have for each and every machine in your network that you would regret losing. System State backup is indispensable when it comes to rebuilding your Exchange box from scratch because it saves you a vast amount of time and effort by not having to go through system configuration and tune-up from the ground up. System State is pretty much useless without a system partition backup because it reflects the configuration based on then-existing files. If you do not restore first, you may actually cause yourself more problems and find that a total reinstall of Windows 2000 is your last resort.

System Partitions of Exchange Server and Domain Controller

You can also back up your system partitions and other partitions that contain vital product data by using **NTBACKUP**. You can use any software you prefer, but you must have a system partition of every production server backed up and available in times of trouble. Combined with System State backup, this strategy gives you a complete snapshot of the system. If there were a need to rebuild a box, you would simply need to reinstall Windows 2000 with default options and settings, restore the system partition, and restore the System State. You could save even more time by using third-party cloning solutions. This topic is beyond the scope of this book as well as the exam. Just be aware that it is a very viable and efficient way to save time and effort.

Site Replication Service Database

The SRS database is an Exchange 2000 database that stores a replica of Exchange 5.5 directory information for coexistence purposes in mixed site implementations. SRS database replicates with Exchange 5.5 servers on a regular basis and is treated just as if it were another Exchange 5.5 box in the network. It complies with the same rules as other Exchange 2000 databases, and therefore it should be treated the same way.

An updated version of SRS database is not critical as long as healthy Exchange 5.5 boxes are running in the network. SRS, AD, and Exchange 5.5 directory are all designed to have a functionality of backfilling out-of-date replication partners. If you ever run into difficulties and have to restore SRS from an outdated backup, Exchange 5.5 computers will quickly bring your SRS up to speed. Replication is also an important concept to keep in mind. As long as you have one replication partner still alive and functioning well, you can reestablish the process. All you need to do is ensure that this information is backed up on at least one of the machines.

Internet Information Server Metabase

As shown in previous chapters, Exchange 2000 still supports Message Transfer Agent (MTA)-based X.400 communication for backward compatibility with Exchange 5.5. Its native communication protocol, however, has changed from X.400 to Simple Mail Transfer Protocol (SMTP). Exchange 2000 relies completely on the native Windows 2000 SMTP stack for its messaging needs. For Exchange 2000 to run, IIS 5 components (namely SMTP for message transfer and NNTP [Network News Transfer Protocol] for news transfer) must be installed and running. NNTP is not a requirement if you are not servicing newsgroups.

All IIS configuration is stored in the registry-like format and is called the IIS metabase. All the changes that you make through the Microsoft Management Console (MMC) are written to the metabase. That is the recommended way to make modifications, although a **regedit**-like tool called **metaedit** is available from Microsoft that allows direct access to the configuration storage. Without the IIS metabase, or with a corrupted one, neither IIS nor SMTP can function. This is why the IIS metabase should be on your backup list. Although metabase is a database, it has no fancy features such as transaction logs. It is a plain file that can be backed up either by right-clicking the computer icon in IIS MMC and choosing the Backup/Restore configuration, or by running System State backup to do it automatically. The default path of this vital configuration file is %systemroot%/system32/inetserv/metabase.bin.

Key Management Service

Undoubtedly, one of the most important steps in your disaster recovery plan is to include KMS and the certification authority (CA) service and their related information. Your best recovery efforts may well become futile if the security information is irrevocably lost along with all of the encrypted business correspondence throughout your entire Exchange 2000 organization. The KMS database stores the private keys of your users, whereas the directory has the public keys. To be able to recover the security context of your Exchange 2000 deployment, you must make sure that the following items are in your backup strategy:

➤ Active Directory database (contains user accounts that have KMS authority)

➤ KMS database (available for online backup in **NTBACKUP**)

15

➤ KMS start-up password (database will not start without it)

➤ CA certificates for each CA server (.p12 files)

➤ CA certificate passwords for each CA certificate

Some of this information can be backed up using a generic approach with **NTBACKUP**. The person who installed and configured these services usually knows other information, such as passwords. This information should be kept strictly confidential because these passwords essentially control the entire encrypted messaging. It is simply not enough that your databases are backed up. Some of the "supporting" services may prove critical to restore, and therefore they, too, must have their own rigorous backup strategy. All of this information will be needed if you happen to run into a total disaster for which full recovery would have to be performed.

Planning Your Backup Strategy

As discussed in the section "Type of Backups" earlier in this chapter, granular control over the backup strategy that is chosen depends on which of the five backup types are selected. The following sections look at some of the most popular strategies.

Normal Daily Backup

From an administrative point of view, the normal daily strategy is perhaps the most simple and convenient choice for backing up your data. It is also the fastest to restore. Downtime is minimal, and this is often an overriding factor. With this strategy, every night a full backup is performed and all of the logs are purged. All of the critical data is stored on one tape (or a disk dump). From the backup perspective, in contrast, the normal daily backup is the most stressful on the system and should be scheduled during off-hours, when user activity is minimal. This is sometimes difficult to achieve for a service provider or the headquarters of an international corporation. The process is greatly improved if you have advanced hardware, such as fiber-channel hard disks. Depending on the particular situation, you could be better off performing a normal backup using high-throughput disk subsystem as your backup media, and later copy the backup file off the production machine and dump it on a tape. This may potentially create serious network congestions as these files can be measured in gigabytes. You have to evaluate your particular scenario to see if this might work for you.

Normal with Incremental Backup

The normal with incremental backup option has a weekly rotation in its classic implementation. Typically, on Sunday night a full backup is performed and transaction logs are purged. Every weekday night afterward, an incremental backup is performed, purging the log files and saving "checkpointed" transactions. This strategy ensures that performance impact is minimized during the week. If a disaster should happen on Friday, you would need to restore the full backup set first, and then each incremental set starting with Monday and working forward. After that, you would mount your database, and the transaction log would be replayed. If one of the backup sets is gone or becomes corrupted on Wednesday, for instance, Tuesday night is as far as you can go in terms of recoverability. Normal with incremental backup is the most time-efficient method because only the changes for the day are backed up. The downside to this strategy is that because you have to keep all of the increments throughout the weekly cycle, it takes the most time.

Normal with Differential Backup

Just like the normal with incremental backup, the normal with differential backup plan works faster than the normal daily and puts less stress on the system because it does not actually back up the database, only the logs. With this option, however, logs are not purged but rather retained. As you progress through the week, differential backup takes progressively longer to complete because the changes accrue throughout the week and the transaction logs get bigger. To restore a database that failed on Friday, for example, you would have to restore a full Sunday backup and differential Thursday backup. After you mount the database, transaction logs will be replayed. This is a moderate approach as far as restoration time and capacity are concerned.

Other Backup Options

Sometimes it makes sense to combine the classic approaches or even implement a copy backup in the middle of the selected cycle. For example, you could perform a full backup on Sunday, and an incremental or differential backup on Monday, Tuesday, and Wednesday. On Wednesday, which is statistically the busiest day of the week, you would run a copy backup (which does not interfere with your incremental or differential strategies) to back up your database. You would then resume with your day-to-day strategy. This scenario gives you a sort of safety net—a failover process that guarantees that you can still recover as much data as possible in case a mainstream backup plan is compromised.

Tape Rotation

It is a good idea to reuse tapes and cycle them. Keep in mind that it is always good practice to keep the last and penultimate copies of the backup in case there is a total disaster and the current backup set is lost or damaged. Tapes and cassettes themselves have their own life cycles and are not designed to last forever. In the case of a weekly rotation, you may want to have two last full backups and to rotate tapes on a weekly basis.

15

Verify, Test, and Practice

A reliable backup strategy involves, first of all, that you perform a backup of *all* vital components, as discussed previously. Second, you should verify that the backup actually works. Third, you should be sure that it is reversible, incurring the least amount of downtime. Several tools are available to ensure the first two steps, but the third step should be done away from the production network in a lab. This will ensure that the backup strategy is effective, that skills of personnel are adequate, and that the production disaster recovery is not the first recovery performed. All of these steps should be documented and tested.

To make sure that the backup process completes successfully, you should take two steps. The first is to provide data tapes or disk storage of adequate capacity, and the second is to monitor your backup logs and system events. System Event Viewer is accessible through the Users and Computers management snap-in of MMC, or by simply typing "eventvwr" (without quotes) in the Start | Run window. Once there, you can select the Application log and filter all events by **NTBACKUP** source, so that only relevant information is displayed. If something goes wrong and the backup process fails, this situation will be reflected in the Event Viewer. To get even more granular details, you can examine the backup log. The location of this log is configured during the job creation process in Windows NT Backup (accessed through **NTBACKUP**).

NTBACKUP Switches—Automation

Windows 2000 introduced a widespread component—the wizard—that disappointed some veteran system administrators. Wizard components are everywhere in Exchange/Windows 2000, and **NTBACKUP** is no exception. To easily create a job, you can turn to the wizards for a convenient walk-through. It actually does not matter which process you choose as long as the backup job is scheduled and is successful. For those in Exchange 5.5 and Windows NT 4.0, the **NTBACKUP/AT (WINAT)** command, a familiar and powerful command prompt, is still available.

You can still use the **NTBACKUP** user interface to manually configure and schedule recurring jobs. You can also create batch files to run the **NTBACKUP** command with appropriate switches, and schedule these batch files to run automatically using the **AT** command or **WINAT** user interface. **NTBACKUP** and **AT** commands come with Windows2000, and an extended version of NTBACKUP program that supports Exchange backup commands—with Exchange 2000. WINAT tool is the same as **AT** utility, only gives you a user interface instead of being command-prompt based, it is available in the NT Resource Kit. You can also use Scheduled Tasks (Start | Programs | Accessories | System Tools) component to schedule your batch files. You should be aware of all of these methods.

Planning for Fault Tolerance

Chapter 3 addressed some of the important factors for choosing the appropriate disk subsystem to provide an acceptable level of performance. This also applies to fault tolerance. A good fault-tolerant system design always begins with quality hardware. A RAID (Redundant Array of Independent Disks) subsystem goes beyond the scope of this book, but you should be aware of some aspects of this topic and what impact it has on your Exchange recoverability. Windows 2000 supports three basic types of RAID disk systems through software drivers: RAID-0, RAID-1, and RAID-5.

RAID-0, known as disk striping, does not provide fault tolerance. Disk striping only improves the read/write performance. It comprises at least 2 disks and can span up to 32 disks. Data is written in 64K increments across all of the disks that participate in the array. Should one of the disks fail, data across the entire array is lost. This solution is cheaper than the others because 100 percent of the data capacity is used for storing data.

RAID-1, called disk mirroring, provides fault tolerance by writing (and reading) data to (and from) two disks simultaneously, creating an exact copy of the information. This solution is more expensive than RAID-0, measured by cost-per-megabyte. Due to the inherent duplication in mirroring, only 50 percent of the disk space can be used to write one copy. Write performance is a bit sluggish because two copies of information must be written to two disks by a single DC. Read performance is improved, however, because read operations are balanced over two disks. If one disk fails, an exact copy exists on the other disk. If the DC fails, however, that mirror set also is lost. An enhanced version of disk mirroring, known as disk duplexing, has two separate controllers for each disk. This duplexing feature makes the configuration more fault tolerant by providing an additional controller.

RAID-5 is the fault-tolerant solution you would use for your transaction logs in Exchange 2000. It is the same as RAID-0 with a fault-tolerant design. Stripe Set with Parity calculates parity information on the data written to an array member. This information is stored across all array members. Remember that no matter how many drives participate in this array (3 to 32), if one array member (disk) fails, the information in the entire array is not lost and can be easily regenerated. If more than one disk fails in any configuration, however, the entire array is lost.

By placing transaction logs and/or the database on a RAID-5 subsystem—be it hardware or software implementation—you may be able to protect your organization from the data recovery process. In a failure, you can simply proceed to regenerate the data that was located on the failed disk. Again, if more than one disk fails, which is statistically difficult but possible, you will still need to have a reliable backup in place. Placing logs on RAID-0 or RAID-5 subsystems also improves I/O performance.

15

A common disaster scenario is a power outage and crashed server with several uncommitted transactions. As a result of this unfortunate situation, you may have missing data, corrupted databases, corrupted system files, or even damage to vital and expensive server hardware. A much cheaper solution to prevent this type of disaster is to purchase one midrange uninterruptible power supply (UPS) unit and set it up so that if a power outage occurs, it informs the system and orders a prompt and graceful shutdown. This is a must for any production server, regardless of whether power outages are anticipated or impossible. In any situation, spikes and dips occur in electrical voltage, which can be disastrous for your production machines. A UPS balances them out and provides a stable current.

Replication

Another method of adding fault tolerance to your configuration is to replicate the public folder information and data across your Exchange 2000 servers. With this method, should one replication partner go down, information would still be available from a different source. The most important disadvantages to this method, however, are the replication traffic and processing overhead. Depending on how vital this data is for business, the requirement for availability may outweigh some additional replication traffic on the network. Use this feature wisely.

Fault Tolerance with Storage Groups

Storage groups need to be considered again in relation to planning for fault tolerance. Huge databases as a result of increased message flow are nothing new in modern organizations. A corrupt page in a 10GB database may eventually render this database unusable and a candidate for recovery. Two issues are associated with recovering large databases. One is that all of the user mailboxes stored in this database are inaccessible. The second is that, depending on the hardware, restoring the database may take quite a lot of time and money. In many cases, restoration can take hours. Storage groups allow you to create 10 1GB databases instead of having to use one 10GB database. In this case, only one database would be down, only one-tenth of the users would be affected, and 10 times less time would be needed to restore from tape backup. You can also place your databases on different disks to balance the chances of hardware failure affecting all of the users.

Antivirus Software

Antivirus applications that provide virus detection logic are imperative for all computer systems worldwide. Just as necessary is using an Exchange 2000–aware antivirus solution for your messaging and collaboration needs. Antivirus software operates by searching for certain bit patterns. Considering the amount and content of email that an organization exchanges, a clean email can easily become suspect and be destroyed. This may potentially lead to unpredictable problems when it comes to Exchange databases and transaction logs. As a result, an antivirus package that is not customized for Exchange 2000 is almost as bad as having no antivirus solution. Either way, you may end up recovering data on a machine that has become damaged due to a virus or data corruption.

Operating System Configuration Audits and Documentation

Every single organization, no matter the size, must document and audit all of the configuration information for production machines. This will help to ensure that your Exchange servers are configured the way they should be. Documentation will also be valuable when you need to perform full data recovery. The price that you will pay for not having this information is serious downtime and severe restoration problems. This documentation should include all of the driver names and version numbers, operating system configuration settings (pagefile, services, partitions, and so forth), application versions, settings, and other vital vendor information.

Recovering from Disaster

Whereas Exchange 5.5 Information Store Service (Store.exe) must be stopped for the database to restore, this is no longer true in Exchange 2000. The Information Store process must be running, but databases that you are restoring must be taken offline by the dismount process. The first part of this chapter stated that all databases in a storage group can be either mounted or dismounted (in other words, started or stopped). This ability to restore individual databases without affecting others in the group comes in very handy when you have planned your fault tolerance and distributed all the users and 10GB databases into several smaller databases then you can have the remainder of the databases running and accessible while you are repairing the one affected database.

Upon installation of Exchange 2000, when you start Store.exe, all existing and new databases will be mounted by default. This is the case unless this behavior is changed administratively (in Exchange System Manager) or there is a corrupted database. Be aware that a successful startup of Information Store does not necessarily mean that your databases are running. Such a design does ensure that you can always start Store.exe no matter what happens to your databases so that you are able to restore them.

In Exchange 2000, you can no longer have your disaster recovery test machines running in the same production network, as was the case with Exchange 5.5. The reasoning behind this is that Exchange 2000 relies on AD to store its configuration information. AD propagates this information globally throughout the entire AD forest. To perform database recoveries on a separate Exchange 2000 server, the

15

machine must be taken to another AD forest, although it can remain in the same physical network. This requirement is not really problematic because you can use the **dcpromo** command to demote (and promote) servers to (and from) domain controller status in any AD. If a database becomes corrupted, you can simply dismount and restore it from backup. If a disaster occurs and your Exchange 2000 box is completely destroyed, you will have to perform the following tasks:

➤ Find replacement hardware

➤ Configure the hardware to closely match the destroyed box (including hard disk partitioning)

➤ Reinstall Windows 2000

➤ Restore system partition and System State (which includes IIS metabase)

➤ Reinstall Exchange

➤ Restore vital data from backup tapes

Remember that no configuration information is stored on an Exchange machine itself. All of this information is stored in AD. To effectively perform this restoration, you would have to use a new installation switch, /disasterrecovery. When implemented, this switch will install Exchange 2000 software with all of the configuration data that is still stored in AD and is not damaged or lost. This is another reason to take good care of AD and treat DCs (or one DC, at least) as if they were your Exchange 2000 machine.

KMS and SRS services are built on the same principle as databases in that they can be in a semirunning state. In other words, the service is started and the database of the service is dismounted. Just as with databases, this is the only state that allows restoration. Do not forget to restore these services when recovering from a total disaster.

Hard Recovery

After database information has been restored, it is equally as important to perform so-called "hard recovery" on the databases before initializing them. This process replays transaction logs and applies patch files, thus bringing the database to a consistent state. The hard recovery process runs automatically when restoring with the Last Backup Set option enabled. To prevent further corruption, you must complete this task before mounting the restored databases. You should never select this option if you still have to restore incremental or differential tapes after full backup is finished. If you find that you need to run a hard recovery manually, you can use the following command:

```
eseutil /cc [path to restore.env]
```

ESEUTIL is a critical tool in maintaining your databases (defragment, check consistency, run hard recoveries, and so forth).

The Restore.env file is a new addition to the recovery process in Exchange 2000, or a slight modification from Exchange 5.5. Previous versions of Exchange would mark the registry with a Restore in Progress key. Exchange 2000 has the Restore.env binary file to control hard recovery and assure that patch and logs are applied and replayed correctly. You can view the contents of this file by running the following command in the folder where restore.env is located:

```
eseutil /cm
```

Tip: Remember that hard recovery in **NTBACKUP** is controlled by the Last Backup Set option.

In Exchange 2000 you can restore multiple storage groups from different tapes simultaneously. You must specify different temporary file locations if you are attempting a restore from multiple full backups to the same storage group.

Restoring to Alternate Exchange Server

The process of restoring your Exchange 2000 backup tapes is similar to the process of restoring an Exchange 2000 server machine from scratch. The following are a few factors to consider when restoring backup tapes:

➤ You cannot install recovery server into the same AD forest. Only one Exchange organization is allowed per one AD forest.

➤ Recovery server must be installed using the exact same organization name as that of the original server.

➤ Storage group and database names must match the original names.

➤ The database must be recovered in an administrative group in which LegacyExchangeDN stem values are the same as the original server.

15

LegacyExchangeDN

LegacyExchangeDN is a parameter that is used for legacy Exchange 5.5 coexistence; hence, if you are not maintaining such servers in your environment, chances are you won't need to worry about it. Every object in Exchange 5.5 organizations has a distinguished X.500 directory name. To fully restore functionality in the mixed environment, a newly recovered Exchange 2000 server must be in the same hierarchical context within AD so that all of its objects have the same DN (Distinguished Name).

Restoring and Reconnecting Individual Mailboxes

Situations may come up for which you will need to perform a restore on one
Exchange 2000 server mailbox. This may occur, for example, because you need to
restore some important correspondence or because of other political or technical
reasons. If AD is completely lost, individual mailboxes can still be recovered from
the Exchange 2000 backup set and reconnected to newly created user objects. The
Mbconn tool that comes with the Exchange 2000 CD-ROM allows you to do a
mass recovery and reconnection of individual mailboxes.

Restoring Deleted Items

When you delete a mailbox in Exchange 2000, the contents of the mailbox and the
mailbox object itself are not deleted, they simply become disconnected. Within 30
days (by default, although configurable), you can go back into Exchange System
Manager (ESM), go to the disconnected mailboxes list, and manually reconnect
deleted mailboxes if necessary. If the mailbox to which you are trying to reconnect
is not yet marked as disconnected, you can run Mailbox Cleanup Agent from ESM.

A Deleted Items Retention Period setting allows for deleted messages and mailbox
content items to be retained in the database for a certain number of days
(configurable). This setting has a trade-off: the more days you retain deleted items,
the more storage you need to support it, and the chances are less that you will be
restoring a mailbox from a backup to recover deleted items. If Deleted Items
Retention is enabled, Outlook clients can go into Tools | Deleted Items to attempt
to recover deleted items from the server database.

Chapter Summary

This chapter reviewed critical strategies that should be included or at least considered in disaster recovery planning. These strategies are not limited to just backing
up the Exchange 2000 data store, but also include underlying configuration and
directory backup as well as designing your entire messaging organization with fault
tolerance in mind.

This process has much in common with previous versions of Exchange Server,
although some important differences exist. For example, data store organization is
completely different. In addition, you can now plan your database locations and
purposes to better fit your organizational needs. This is a significant improvement
over Exchange 5.5 in terms of fault tolerance and load balancing because it relates
to backing up, maintaining, and restoring databases. Instead of one huge 16GB
database, for example, you can have 16 smaller 1GB databases. Even if a few pages
become corrupted and render one of the databases unusable, it is statistically
impossible that the same thing will happen at the same time to all 16 databases,
unless, of course, underlying hardware is the problem.

In terms of underlying hardware, the situation is similar to previous iterations of Exchange. You still have three RAID levels implemented by the ftdisk.sys software driver that ships with Windows 2000. Depending on how critical the data is, you may decide to spend money on high-end hardware RAID solutions that are more robust and reliable.

Configuration information is no longer server-centric but instead is stored in Active Directory. Multiple Exchange servers are easier to back up and restore. This design requires that AD domain controllers be backed up regularly and that enough replicas exist in the network to avoid Exchange downtime should one of the replicas become unavailable.

To recover from a total disaster, you should have all of the backups in place to restore system partitions on domain controllers and Exchange servers, the system state of both machines (including registry, metabase, and COM+ information), Active Directory backup, and Exchange Server database backups. A plethora of data recovery strategies could and should be implemented in any organization, but what is very important to understand is that regular backup is not the only step that needs to be taken to ensure quick and easy recovery. Proper safeguard practices may save you from losing or corrupting your data in the first place. As Exchange administrator, you must make sure that all possible causes of data loss are eliminated, and if something still happens, then it would be time to get your tapes. Real-world data recovery in production environments should never be your first experience. Without ongoing skill drills and practice, one may do more damage than good when it comes to recovery of vital business data.

Review Questions

1. Which one of the following database fundamentals has changed dramatically in the upgrade from Exchange 5.5 to Exchange 2000?

   a. Transaction logging

   b. Checkpoint file

   c. Patch files

   d. Dir.edb

2. Exchange 2000 stores MDBEF data in the .edb database file. Instead of being converted, all non-MDBEF data goes into the second part of the database, which is also built on ESE technology. What is the file extension of this other database file?

   a. .ebd

   b. .stm

   c. .mdb

   d. .ese

15

3. Which of the following is the parameter that represents the distinguished names used for legacy Exchange 5.5 coexistence?

   a. LegacyExchangeDN

   b. Exchange55DN

   c. LegacyDistinguishedName

   d. ExchangeLegacyDN

4. You need to manually perform a hard recovery from the command line. Which one of the following commands will accomplish this task?

   a. **ntbackup backup [*systemstate*]**

   b. **eseutil /cm**

   c. **eseutil /cc [*path to restore*.env]**

   d. **setup /disasterrecovery**

5. You want to perform a restoration that will install Exchange 2000 software with all the configuration data that is still stored in Active Directory and is not damaged or lost. Which one of the following commands will accomplish this task?

   a. **ntbackup backup [*systemstate*]**

   b. **eseutil /cm**

   c. **eseutil /cc [*path to restore*.env]**

   d. **setup /disasterrecovery**

6. The virus detection logic used by your antivirus software should be Exchange 2000–aware because antivirus software operates by searching for certain bit patterns. Considering the amount of email in Exchange, a clean email may possibly become suspect and be destroyed. Also, unpredictable problems can occur in Exchange databases and transaction logs. Is this true or false?

   a. True

   b. False

7. You have sent a 5MB attachment to 50 people in your Exchange 2000 organization. If that message had a 5MB attachment, and all of the recipients were hosted within one storage group in one database, what would be the total storage size of this message on your system?

   a. 5MB

   b. 10MB

   c. 50MB

   d. 250MB

8. The state of your database has an impact on your backup and restore operations. Each database within a storage group can be in one of the two states. Which of the following are actual database states? [Check the two best answers]

   a. private

   b. public

   c. mounted

   d. loaded

   e. unmounted

   f. dismounted

9. What are the units of storage that comprise an ESE database?

   a. Blocks

   b. Chunks

   c. Units

   d. Pages

10. The Standard Edition of Microsoft Exchange 2000 supports databases up to which size?

    a. 16MB

    b. 16GB

    c. 64MB

    d. 64GB

11. What term best describes the process by which Exchange 2000 produces five logs of 5MB each, and after the fifth log is filled, it starts overwriting transaction log number 1 after first committing its transactions to the database?

    a. Flushing transactions

    b. Transaction logging

    c. Circular logging

    d. Committing transactions

12. When you initialize the backup program **NTBACKUP**, it will call the necessary Application Programming Interface (API) procedures to inform Store.exe of the fact that database backup is about to commence. Store.exe passes this information on to what Exchange 2000 component, which in turn enters backup mode?

    a. The ESE engine

    b. The storage group

    c. The transaction log

    d. The hard disk drive subsystem

15

13. Which type of backup procedure will include a database copy and a log copy, as well as a log delete?

    a. Incremental backup

    b. Differential backup

    c. Copy backup

    d. Full (normal) backup

14. Whereas online backups require Store.exe to be started and databases mounted, offline backups require that Store.exe must be stopped. Which of the following is most accurate?

    a. The is a true statement.

    b. This is a false statement.

    c. There are too many other factors to consider before determining the accuracy of this statement.

    d. You cannot perform offline backups in Exchange 2000.

15. Which new backup type in Windows 2000 is similar to backing up the Windows NT system registry but goes further by saving the IIS metabase, as well as COM+ objects and registrations, thereby giving a complete snapshot of system-specific information?

    a. Differential backup

    b. Copy backup

    c. Full (normal) backup

    d. System State backup

Real-World Projects

You are the system administrator for the human resources department at a health care organization. In your small department, you are planning to run Exchange 2000 on your Active Directory domain controller. You would like to test the backup and restore features available through the **NTBACKUP** interface to determine whether it meets your departmental requirements. Due to budgetary issues, you wish to avoid having to request additional funds for a third-party backup application. In the following three projects, you will experiment on your own test/lab machines.

Project 10.1

Back up the database/System State. Take a survey of all of the backup features that are available in the **NTBACKUP** graphical user interface.

Project 10.2

Restore the database/System State of your system and familiarize yourself with the Restore features of the **NTBACKUP** tool.

Project 10.3

Create a batch file that performs a backup of system files of your choice. Schedule the batch file to run from a command prompt.

15

CHAPTER SIXTEEN

Deploying an Exchange 2000 Server Messaging Cluster Solution

After completing this chapter, you will be able to:

✓ Define high-availability architecture

✓ Understand and deploy Microsoft Cluster Server (MSCS)

✓ Compare Exchange 5.5 clustering with Exchange 2000 clustering

✓ Realize several client perspectives

✓ Explain front-end and back-end architectures

An Overview of Email Problems

Email is a tremendously vital function for most organizations. As a general rule, users will insist that this messaging system always be accessible. Your servers may be storing a hefty amount of Web documentation for your organization as well. From time to time, events such as operating system upgrades, service pack deployments, hardware failures, and application errors will demand scheduled and unscheduled downtime. If your organization is like many others, downtime may be deemed completely intolerable. If a server operating system in your company fails, the consequences can be ruinous. A system failure can result in vanishing revenues, interruption in service to customers and partners, and interruption of vendor relationships, all the way down to an idle and inefficient workforce. Whatever the scenario, recovery from a system failure can involve huge potential outlays to many areas of your organization. Other hidden costs may be involved as well, including the loss of corporate goodwill; injury to your corporate reputation with customers, suppliers, and partners; and the notion that your organization is not able to meet the requests of customers. This chapter explores the requirements and strategies for deploying a high-availability solution through an Exchange 2000 Server messaging cluster solution.

Defining a High-Availability Architecture

Downtime is often defined by a solitary event, such as when an Exchange server is out of commission for six to eight hours. However, you must look inside the entire downtime event and single out the costs and subcomponents of the downtime. This high-availability architecture is what is examined in this section. First of all, in terms of downtime, you need to recognize that there is a distinct difference between the concepts of fault tolerance and high availability. The distinction comes down to whether you are attempting to eradicate or merely minimize downtime. The goal of *high availability* is to curtail the amount of downtime. *Fault-tolerant* solutions, in contrast, look for the elimination of downtime. This chapter focuses on the Microsoft Cluster Server (MSCS) as it relates to Exchange 2000 Server. MSCS is a high-availability solution.

Clustering can offer the users in your organization a highly available infrastructure by reducing, or completely eliminating, single points of failure. A *cluster* can be defined as a group of independent servers that share a common disk subsystem, act as a single unit, and have a common network name and IP address. The hardware configuration of the server is identical for each server in the cluster. In a cluster, if one server is nominated with the active node, this active node will have absolute control of the shared disk and all of the cluster resources. The other node(s) in the cluster will exist in a passive (or standby) state in anticipation of an active node failure. Whenever a failure occurs, the passive node will assume the role of the active node. This method of clustering allows administrators to apply upgrades during the day without interrupting user productivity. The administrator can apply the upgrades to the passive node and then transfer this passive node to the active node. This course of action has low impact on users and is completely transparent. Quite commonly, Exchange mailbox servers are deployed in a cluster.

Concepts of Availability

Before the details of deploying Microsoft clusters are explored, you should fully understand the larger concepts and terminology of availability. This knowledge will be vital to help you determine if a clustering solution is right for your organization. Your job may well depend on it. One of the main goals of availability is to safeguard the mission-critical systems in your infrastructure. Mission-critical systems are defined as information systems that are indispensable to the operation and success of an organization. Many organizations consider messaging a mission-critical application. Exchange 2000 Server is particularly critical because it is commonly the platform for teamwork, workflow, knowledge management, and line-of-business applications.

Availability can be thought of as the proportion of time that a system is functioning, which is often expressed by a percentage value. Table 16.1 displays some common availability statistics accepted by the industry.

A key concept of availability is the *mean time between failures*. This factor is the statistically resultant length of time that a user may realistically expect a component, device, or system to work between two catastrophic failures. Another factor that will be part of your analysis is the notion of reliability. *Reliability* is a determinant of how dependable your system is. Reliability is also defined as a combination of availability and data integrity.

Another significant factor is the *recovery point*, or the amount of data lost due to a system failure. A common aim of many organizations is to provide a recovery point of zero, meaning absolutely no loss of data. A further concept, which relates to the recovery point, is the recovery time. *Recovery time* is the amount of time required to return a system to full operation. A major objective in your organization should be to reduce the recovery time for particular types of failures.

16

Table 16.1   Availability statistics.

Availability	Amount of Downtime per Year
99%	3 days, 15 hours, 21 minutes
99.9%	8 hours, 44 minutes
99.99%	52 minutes
99.999%	5 minutes

Components of Downtime

Downtime comprises the time it takes to make the system operational again. Suppose, for example, that your system experiences eight hours of downtime. This could be broken down as follows. It may be at least two hours before someone realizes the server was down. Once that insight is made, it may take four more hours to determine that the database was corrupted. It subsequently may take another hour to locate a good backup tape and then finally one more to restore the database. This is just one scenario that has a variety of events, costs, and sub-events. We explore the cost factors of these events later in this section.

Many events can prevent you from keeping the system in operation. One of the most common downtime events is actually planned downtime. This premeditated event allows you to perform hardware upgrades and software upgrades, as well as configuration changes to your design. Your organization may also come into contact with component failure due to hardware or software issues. Although product vendors have been struggling in a very competitive marketplace to improve the mean time between failure rates for individual components, the complexity of today's hardware and software components will still render occasional failures.

Recent studies have indicated that human intervention or programmatic errors cause approximately 80 percent of all unplanned outages. Many circumstances exist by which inadvertent or malevolent actions by people can have a negative impact on your computing environment. Planned administration of systems can even lead to problems as well. The remaining 20 percent of failures are typically related to hardware, operating systems, or environmental factors. Operator errors include incorrectly applying measures in a particular situation, performing a task inappropriately, or failing to perform a necessary task at all. Application failures include errors in software, performance issues, and incompatibility problems.

Building-level incidents and disasters can disturb a room, building, or even an entire campus. If you decide to physically move a server between sites, a hardware failure can result when that server is restarted. Catastrophes such as fire, flood, power outages, or even governmental actions can disrupt service by physically damaging or destroying hardware, terminating power to critical systems, or preventing access to systems. For example, metropolitan area disasters such as fire, flood, blackouts, and riots that affect entire towns and cities, can affect systems in the locality. Regional events, such as earthquakes, hurricanes, and military/political upheavals, can have a bearing on the operation of your Exchange 2000 environment over hundreds of square miles.

Isolating the Target of Failures

Quite likely, many areas of your organization will rely on Exchange 2000 for more than just email. Many organizations use Exchange 2000 for collaborative and knowledge management applications, secure storage for Web sites, or document and multimedia data repositories. To establish the level of availability needed for Exchange 2000, you will want to isolate the effective targets of different system failures. You should survey your departments to find out who or what is negatively affected when a mailbox server fails. For example, a mailbox server going down will halt communication between individuals, groups, and external contacts. In addition, information stored on the server will not be accessible. Also, operational processes can stall because managers cannot carry out authorization, certification, and endorsement of various business processes. Finally, personal efficiency, workflow, collaboration, knowledge management, and line-of-business applications that rely on user interaction or message storage are affected as well.

When a public folder server fails, critical business data coming into your organization can cease, and personal productivity suffers. In addition, applications, document repositories, Web sites, and knowledge management systems stop working. You may also suffer a network failure, and, depending on what type of failure it is and where it occurs, a multiplicity of actions can take place. Message delivery between Exchange 2000 components slows down or stops, and unpredictable access from clients and servers to the Active Directory service may manufacture logon failures. Communications to customers and partners may be affected as well. If a connector server fails, message delivery between internal and external systems can languish. Virus and content scanning also may not occur. More important, critical business processes may break up, and external customers may be prevented from communicating with your organization. The bottom line of these events can have a devastating effect on sales and revenue.

Global catalog servers perform as the Global Address List (GAL) for both clients and Exchange 2000 servers. More than 90 percent of all interactions with Active Directory occur with the global catalog. If one or more Active Directory global catalog servers fail, the corporate address list cannot be obtained. Moreover, users may not be able to log on to Windows 2000. Exchange 2000 uses Active Directory to store configuration information. If one or more Active Directory domain controllers fail, it will not be possible to manage Exchange. Consequently, queries for directory information by Exchange 2000 servers can fail, producing communication errors as well as a diminution in global stability.

Determining the Costs of Downtime

16

Before investing time and money to design and deploy a high-availability solution for Exchange, you need to determine the cost of downtime. Losses can be measured in many different ways, and if money is the measure, the figures can be astonishing. A recent highly regarded study found that costs of downtime can range from $1,000 to $27,000 per minute. Furthermore, in some organizations, the cost of downtime for a single incident can exceed $10,000,000.

It is imperative that you ascertain and comprehend the events that can have a negative impact on both Exchange 2000 Server and the services and systems that rely upon it. Realize the vulnerabilities of the components, processes, and systems that rely on Exchange 2000. After you consider these factors, determine which technology and processes you can use to realize the availability you need. After you complete these actions, you will have a better understanding of the financial costs and impacts of a failure within your Exchange organization.

System Vulnerability

You should also determine the risks and other events peculiar to your business environment that can cause a failure of Exchange. Identify other software applications within the Exchange infrastructure and organization that can crash as well as the types of failures they can generate. Perform a complete examination and assessment of the technologies and systems that you use to supply high availability to your organization. For example, what would happen if your internal telephone system failed, and what bearing would this have on your business operations? The cumulative effects on communications among individuals, departments, customers, and partners should be analyzed in advance of a catastrophe.

Many organizations find themselves in an awkward situation by underestimating the importance of messaging services to the internal and external communications infrastructure. Email is also often implemented for routing in workflow applications, and the business functions provided by email services can be rather far-reaching. A possibility of incompatibility between components always exists. This occurs due to the huge marketplace of independent vendors that produce hardware components.

Vulnerabilities and Your Environment

You should know to what degree your environment is vulnerable to failures. Hardware is the first main factor, and it relates to servers and the components that are needed to support the services of Exchange 2000. Typical considerations are the uninterruptible power supply (UPS), processor failure, bad memory, and the performance or reliability of the disk subsystem. Another key area of hardware exposure involves the networking components. This can range from the physical cabling and NICs to the switches and routers. In most environments, these devices are critical to offering consistency and robustness to Exchange 2000 users.

Due to the range and intricacy of today's application software, you will inevitably have some problems. These issues can occur with solitary processes or with the interaction between two or more components. You need to resolve how well you are you able to repair software errors or application conflicts with the use of hot fixes, updates, and service packs. This topic is covered in greater detail in Chapter 17, which addresses troubleshooting Exchange 2000 Server. You should determine, as well, the efficacy of your service management techniques and measures that support recovery work in instances of failure. Make sure that factors such as configuration management, capacity planning, and modification control are definite and implicit to provide a safety net for disaster recovery and the ongoing success of Exchange 2000 services.

Recovery Point and Recovery Time

Earlier in this chapter, the section "Concepts of Availability" introduced the terms recovery point and recovery time. Another aspect in determining the downtime cost for your organization is to define the recovery point objective and the recovery time objective. You need to know the expected recovery time and recovery point if a disaster occurs. The recovery point focuses on the data that must be restored in the event of a failure. The recovery time refers to the amount of time required to return the affected Exchange 2000 system to operation. A definite trade-off exists between time and data, and you must contemplate this trade-off when determining the availability of your Exchange 2000 environment.

As discussed previously in this book, you can distribute components of your Exchange 2000 infrastructure, such as connector servers, global catalog servers, and mailbox servers, over a large geographical area. These components can offer numerous functions or dedicated services to your entire Exchange infrastructure. You will probably need to put into operation different layers of availability for the contrasting aspects of Exchange 2000. For instance, you can have alternative routes for message delivery routing by implementing a group of Exchange 2000 servers. When one of these servers fails, the messaging stream can carry on if alternate routes have been built into the infrastructure. As a result, however, recovery time for this particular architecture could be longer than that of a mailbox server system. In similar fashion, because server data consists mainly of queued messages, the recovery point would not be critical. Some of the methods that can be implemented to reduce recovery time and recovery point in an Exchange 2000 environment are:

➤ Replicating the data

➤ Deploying several databases and storage groups

➤ Introducing resilient message routing

➤ Backing up and restoring data online simultaneously

Implementing Availability Technologies

The following sections highlight some of the technologies that can be used to develop a high-availability architecture. You should consider several architectural and component-level design issues to improve resilience and introduce systemic redundancy.

16

Power Supplies

Many ways exist to make certain that an adequate power supply is provided. Many server configurations support redundant power supplies inside the server itself. This allows the secondary unit to take over in the event of a failure. Another common scheme for protecting electrical input is to employ a UPS. A single-server UPS option will offer backup power for minutes all the way up to several hours. This allows for ample time to appropriately shut down the server. A UPS can be a powerful ally in your corporate data loss and corruption prevention strategy. Beyond this, backup generators can be employed for larger data centers to provide maximum protection in the case of power failure, brownouts, or surges.

Distributed Environments

Exchange 2000 is often installed on several servers in an organizational infrastructure. If your company has more than one physical location, you should take advantage of routing groups. You can appoint connector servers to reduce the single points of failure and expand overall system availability. In addition, public folder stores can also be dispersed over a wide geographical area to improve user and application performance. This technique will also serve as an alternative method for reducing data loss in case of an emergency or hardware crash. Having a powerful server is a total waste if your users (or other servers) cannot access it. You can make a nice down payment toward your high-availability scenario by simply deploying two network interface cards. One of them can be reserved as an extra interface, connect two separate local area network (LAN) segments, create redundant links, and implement intelligent routing schemes. You must define a robust message routing topology through the placement of routing groups, routing group connectors, and connector servers in order to eliminate as many single points of failure as you can. This focus on message routing can make it possible to provide better high availability for your organization.

Databases and Replication

You can put multiple databases into service in your Exchange 2000 design. This is a critical improvement over previous versions of Exchange, which support only one private and one public database for each server. In Exchange 2000, you can further data availability by defining a database for use as either a public folder store or a mailbox store. You can back up, restore, mount, and dismount databases independently of each other, as well as allocate a user's mailbox to a mailbox store. You may choose to keep a copy of information in other locations as well. Public folder replication allows public folder stores to replicate to other servers in the organization. This availability enrichment can enhance response time and offer an effective backup of public folder data.

Storage Groups

Storage groups are a collection of Exchange databases that share a set of transaction logs. Availability can be improved because a maximum of five databases per storage group can consist of any combination of mailbox and public folder stores. A single node running Exchange can support up to four storage groups. In a Windows 2000 cluster, the total number of storage groups on a single node must be four or less, despite the number of Exchange virtual servers that exist on the node.

RAID

The most common fault-tolerant solution, which also increases the data storage in a single machine, is to deploy a RAID configuration. RAID is an acronym for Redundant Array of Independent (or Inexpensive) Disks. It is technically a system of hard disk drives that uses two or more drives in combination. The ultimate goal of RAID is to provide for fault tolerance and performance gain. RAID disk drive implementations include simple mirroring between two disks (RAID 1) and mirrored stripes or striped mirrors (RAID 0+1 and RAID 5). Even with the fault tolerance and performance gains, a reduction in the storage requirements on the Exchange 2000 server is not achieved.

Microsoft Cluster Server

As mentioned previously, clustering is the process whereby two or more servers are coupled together so that they perform and appear as a single computer. Clustering is a popular strategy used for parallel processing applications, load balancing, and fault-tolerance solutions. Exchange 2000 Server enhances this ability by allowing you to establish a logical unit of file storage on a cluster consisting of multiple Exchange Server computers. By utilizing all servers at all times, you can reduce system costs and increase reliability. This eliminates the need for dedicated failover-only servers. After reviewing the previous information in this chapter and applying it to your organization, you should have a pretty good idea if clustering is the right solution for you. However, to accurately determine if clustering can help your organization, you need to isolate and document all of the events that occur during a downtime event. This was the main purpose for the preceding sections of this chapter. You are now prepared to move into the clustering world with confidence that it is the right solution for your networked environment.

Clustering Models

In general, two prime clustering models exist. The first type is the Shared Disk model. In this arrangement, disk resources can be owned by all of the nodes in the cluster at any one point in time. Any node can write or access those resources as well. To employ this architecture, some class of distributed lock management

16

component must be implemented between the nodes to control locking. This typically requires deploying proprietary software.

The second primary clustering model is the Shared Nothing model. In the Shared Nothing model, any one node in the cluster can own any available resource; however, a node can be the owner of only one resource at a time. This means that none of the resources in your cluster are shared. The Shared Nothing model is easier than the Shared Disk model to implement as well as troubleshoot, and it does not require a proprietary hardware solution. Microsoft went with the Shared Nothing model in MSCS because of industry standard hardware support and the ease at which third-party applications run on top of it. Figure 16.1 is a graphic representation of the Shared Nothing model.

MSCS first shipped in 1997 with Windows NT 4.0 Enterprise Edition, within just a few months of the availability of Exchange 2000. A multitude of original equipment manufacturers (OEMs) and vendors signed on with MSCS to furnish a large number of storage server combinations. Many of these organizations have become and continue to become certified for the Cluster Hardware Compatibility List (HCL). The Windows 2000 version is in all actuality just a minor upgrade to MSCS. Windows 2000 Cluster Services includes many bug fixes over MSCS, as well as additional minor support for components such as Domain Name System (DNS) and Dynamic Host Configuration Protocol (DHCP) in a cluster infrastructure. Also included are additional application programming interfaces (APIs) for third-party cluster backups and restoration of the cluster quorum disk.

MSCS Failover Modes

MSCS has two different failover modes. The first mode is the service failover mode, which is also known as active/passive mode. Active/passive means that you can run that instance of service or resource on only one mode of the cluster at a time. An instance of resource could be an occurrence of a database or even an instance of

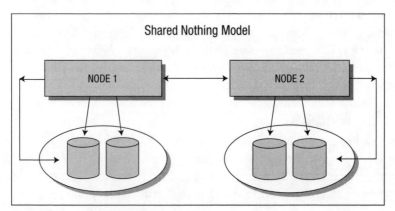

Figure 16.1 The Shared Nothing model.

Internet Information Services (IIS). True intelligence is available neither for the application that you are running nor real exposure to the cluster itself. MSCS does not know anything about the application and vice versa. The other failover mode is the resource failover mode, otherwise known as active/active. With active/active failover, services can run on more than one cluster node at a time. Active/active is cost effective because you are using all of the capacity of your machine, as opposed to active/passive where you only actively use 50% of your inversion. All of the computers in a cluster can be aggressively and robustly processing the messaging requests until a failure happens that triggers rollover recovery.

Active/active clustering can also be described as a scenario in which both members of the cluster are online and accepting user requests for various services. The active/active clustering model offers fault tolerance in case a server goes down and assures the minimum possible undesirable effect on the user. The capability of using all your servers at all times reduces system costs and increases reliability. This also eliminates the need for dedicated failover-only servers. When a stoppage does occur, as is theoretically inevitable, it will trigger a rollover to recovery mode. This active/active clustering support also allows you to allocate storage groups to be on clustering nodes so that they will fail over to other servers if necessary. In addition, the Exchange servers in the cluster do not have to be configured the same way or even be the same size. This feature increases your range of configuration options as a system administrator. Server clusters can also be used in concert with front-end load-balanced clustered servers to provide additional scalability and reliability. Exchange 2000 Enterprise Server provides the dependability and scalability requirements of the most demanding enterprise customers for messaging and collaboration. It uses an unlimited data store as well as active/active clustering solutions.

Two-Way and Four-Way Clustering

Another way that Microsoft Exchange 2000 Server delivers enhanced scalability and reliability for your messaging infrastructure is by supporting two-way (two-node) and four-way (four-node) active/active clustering. Exchange 2000 supports two-node clusters in Windows 2000 Advanced Server. Four-node clustering is supported only in Microsoft Datacenter Server. The Datacenter edition is an OEM-only version that is installed with or provided with your actual hardware vendor. Support for four-node Exchange cluster will vary from vendor to vendor. This capability to implement multiple servers at all times can radically lessen system costs. Additionally, reliability will be greater than before because no dedicated servers are necessary to help recover from system failures.

Key Cluster Concepts

A resource in a cluster is technically the smallest manageable unit with that cluster. This unit can be can be physical or logical. For example, an Internet Protocol (IP) address would represent a logical unit, and a disk device would be a physical unit in the cluster. With the MSCS Shared Nothing model, these resources are owned by

16

only one node at a time. Nodes can preserve ownership of the resources, and this activity is managed by the cluster services. A resource can depend on another resource as well and generally occurs within a resource group. A resource group is a collection of resources that are gathered to accomplish some purpose. These resources can gracefully be brought online or taken offline. MSCS is really a set of dynamic-link libraries (DLLs) and APIs for Windows 2000. The main DLL files are EXCLUADM.DLL and EXRES.DLL, as represented in Figure 16.2.

From a Shared Nothing perspective, the hardware is really the driver itself. You must choose hardware that can support the Shared Nothing driver model. A cluster interconnects the two nodes, and this interconnect can be anything from an Ethernet card to a complex, high-performance proprietary component for Windows 2000 Datacenter Server. In addition, shared storage is required for MSCS and can be in the form of a shared small computer system interface (SCSI) or Fibre Channel.

SCSI and Fibre Channel

SCSI is a parallel interface standard used to affix peripheral devices to computers. Shared SCSI interfaces offer faster data transmission rates than standard serial and parallel ports. You can also connect many devices to a single SCSI port, making SCSI an input/output (I/O) bus instead of just an interface. SCSI comes in many different flavors and supports several types of connectors.

Fibre Channel is a serial data transfer architecture. The most widely established standard is Fibre Channel Arbitrated Loop (FC-AL). It uses optical fibers and was designed for the newer brands of mass storage devices and other peripheral devices that need very high bandwidth. FC-AL will eventually replace SCSI for high-performance storage systems.

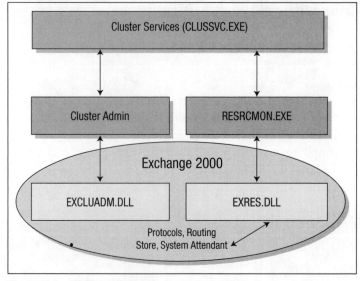

Figure 16.2 MSCS architecture.

Exchange 5.5 versus Exchange 2000 Clustering

Microsoft's first attempt at cluster support came through its Exchange 5.5 application. The main design goal was simply to get some clustering support into Exchange 5.5 to provide additional functionality.

Exchange 5.5 Clustering

Microsoft did not support active/active mode in Exchange 5.5; it supported only active/passive mode. If there was a node failure in Exchange 5.5, therefore, you basically had to kill the services on one node and bring them up on the other node. The only part of Exchange 5.5 that is "cluster aware" is the setup program when it recognizes for a split second that it is on a cluster. So, technically, Exchange 5.5 is not cluster aware and it also utilizes a generic resource DLL. Generally speaking, this legacy version of cluster support offers a low return on investment (ROI).

When Microsoft set out to provide clustering support in Exchange Server 5.5, the development team had two primary goals. First, they wanted to boost the availability features of Exchange Server by adding clustering support. Second, they needed to provide protection from hardware failures. This earliest clustering model did not include support for distributed processing, load balancing, and data backup. As a result, Exchange Server 5.5 provided only straightforward failover capabilities when paired with MSCS. Figure 16.3 displays the Exchange 5.5 clustering architecture.

In Exchange Server 5.5 active/passive clustering, only one node of a cluster provides service to users at any given time. This type of clustering runs on one

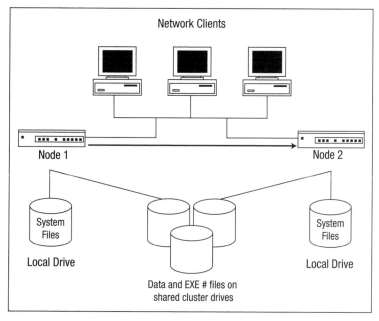

16

Figure 16.3   The Exchange 5.5 clustering architecture.

clustered server, but it cannot be restarted automatically on the other server if there is a system failure. Active/passive schemes require dedicated failover servers, and therefore hardware is used less efficiently than with active/active technologies.

Exchange 2000 Clustering

An Exchange 2000 server cluster commonly consists of one or two server nodes, each typically holding two network cards; an internal disk subsystem for the operating system plus application executables; and a SCSI interface attached to one or more shared storage devices. When Exchange 2000 is installed on a Windows 2000 cluster, virtual servers are configured on each node. Each Exchange virtual server (EVS) is accountable for one or more storage groups. (A later section of this chapter, "Virtual Servers," presents more about the implementation of virtual server clusters.) When a stoppage occurs in a server cluster that runs Exchange 2000, the Exchange virtual server fails over to another node. Each node starts out with one virtual server that has one or more storage groups. When a node fails, the duties for the virtual server on that node are transferred to another node in the server cluster.

Keep in mind that a node or standalone server can function with a maximum of four storage groups; therefore, in the event of a failure, you must ensure that the remaining nodes do not support more than four storage groups. Exchange 2000 MSCS provides up to four-way active/active clustering, enabling all the computers used in a cluster to be actively processing messaging requests in anticipation of a failure that triggers rollover recovery. Exchange 2000 can maintain access equilibrium to all servers (also called nodes) in a server cluster, thereby making more resourceful use of hardware. The preservation and up-grade features are also a big benefit in Exchange 2000 clustering.

A number of significant Exchange 5.5 workings have been incorporated into the Windows 2000 operating system. These components include the directory as well as such transports as Hypertext Transfer Protocol (HTTP), Network News Transfer Protocol (NNTP), and Simple Mail Transfer Protocol (SMTP). Because of this assimilation, you must install Windows 2000 before you install Exchange 2000. One standard resource DLL is used for each Exchange service (Directory Service, Information Store Service, Message Transfer Agent, and System Attendant). This allows distinct services to be brought down without causing a total failover. Services are also isolated, which helps to improve troubleshooting.

Although your organization can appreciably increase Exchange 2000 Server availability and resources dependencies through MSCS, the advantages come with several caveats. Based on Microsoft's fundamental goals for providing MSCS support to Exchange 2000 Server, deployment in a clustered environment has the following advantages and disadvantages.

Advantages:

➤ MSCS offers defense from hardware-related failures.

➤ Clustering provides added means to carry out preventive maintenance operations on cluster nodes.

➤ MSCS in Exchange 2000 gives your organization shelter from outages isolated to the primary cluster node.

Disadvantages:

➤ Exchange 2000 provides support for the MSCS (active/passive) service failover mode only.

➤ Support is restricted to the MSCS generic resource DLL with no Exchange Server–specific failure detection.

➤ MSCS is not cluster-aware.

➤ Failover times can fluctuate, depending on a number of factors, including information store size, server load, and hardware I/O capabilities.

By working within the parameters of the confines of available technology, you can effectively deploy Exchange 2000 Server on MSCS. This deployment will offer your organization significantly amplified system availability and protection from hardware failures. Clustering Exchange 2000 Server can help your organization meet its high availability requirements by protecting servers from critical failures that could not be tolerated in a nonclustered scenario. Figure 16.4 shows the Exchange 2000 clustering architecture.

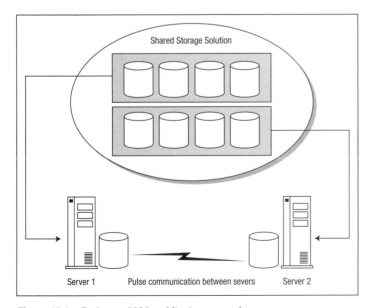

Figure 16.4 Exchange 2000 architecture example.

HCL

You can view the MSCS Hardware Compatibility List at the following Web site:

http://www.microsoft.com/hwtest/hcl

Exchange 2000 Services under MSCS

Several key features relate to Exchange 2000 services and clustering, as shown in the following list:

➤ Services are all still running in inactive mode.

➤ The active/active services are always running.

➤ The Exchange service is controlled through Cluster Admin only.

➤ The active/passive services stop and start when going offline or online, respectively.

Virtual Servers

MSCS supports active/active resource failover mode in addition to virtual server technology. A virtual server can be defined as a server that resides on a physical server yet appears to the user as a separate server or an autonomous standalone individual Web site. A virtual server is actually a resource group within Exchange 2000. In the Windows 2000 server cluster is a resource group that will become the Exchange virtual server. The Exchange virtual server represents the finest granularity of failover obtainable with MSCS. Each virtual server will have its own autonomous configuration information such as domain name, IP address, port number, and authentication.

Each virtual server can hold a different layer of security as well as connect to a different network as an independent host. For instance, you could configure one virtual server to deliver messages solely between the Exchange 2000 computers in your organization. Subsequently, you could configure another virtual server to externally connect to the Internet. This design allows you to set a higher level of security for incoming messages from the Internet or an extranet. Also, you may decide to prevent anonymous access by placing a restriction on a virtual server. By default, in Exchange 2000, only one virtual server per protocol can be present on each server. The Exchange System Manager is the tool you will use to configure this attribute.

Exchange 2000 can operate one or more virtual servers on each computer node in the cluster. Every Exchange virtual server can run its own programs with discrete access to devices and peripherals. Subsequently, clients will link to the virtual servers in the same manner in which they connect to a standalone server. The cluster service monitors and controls the virtual servers in the cluster. If a failure occurs, the cluster service will restart or will move the virtual servers on the failed computer to a node that is entirely functional. If you are conducting a planned outage, you can move the virtual servers to other computers manually. Regardless, the user will observe a disruption in service only during the brief time that the virtual server is in conversion.

In Windows 2000, whether you are in a cluster scenario or not, you are limited to four storage groups on a virtual server. On any one node of the cluster, whether during production run time or during failover conditions, you can have a maximum of only four storage groups running on the cluster You could configure one node with one storage group of four virtual servers, two virtual servers with two storage groups, and so on. If you have a virtual server that has four storage groups on one node, and you try to fail that server over to another virtual server that already has four storage groups, the failover is not going to happen. Table 16.2 shows the various storage group configuration possibilities.

Cluster Setup Issues

If you propose to install clustered Exchange servers, you must install or upgrade another server in your Exchange site before you can install the clustered server. This is obligatory because the Site Replication Service (SRS) cannot run on a cluster. The SRS is essential for coexistence with down-level Exchange servers. The hardware on which down-level Exchange servers are installed may not be able to run Exchange 2000 and must be replaced rather than upgraded.

You can perform what is known as a "rolling upgrade" of an MSCS cluster. This course of action upgrades the operating system from Windows NT 4 Server

Table 16.2 Storage group configurations.

Exchange Virtual Server Names	Number of Storage Groups
EVS1	1
EVS2	1
EVS1	2
EVS2	2
EVS1	1
EVS2	2
EVS1	1
EVS2	3

16

Enterprise Edition to Windows 2000 Advanced Server separately on each node in the cluster. When this process is complete, you have a Windows 2000 cluster. Keep in mind that not all applications will automatically support this upgrade. You must be certain that all of the software running on the cluster is fully compatible with Windows 2000. Exchange Server 5.5 will run on the Windows 2000 cluster, but applications such as backup software, virus checking, or messaging connectors may need upgrades or replacement. Some of the events that occur in Windows 2000 during the cluster setup process are the following:

➤ Setup auto-senses the cluster installation.

➤ Setup installs the cluster resources and services.

➤ Binary files are copied to the local mode.

➤ The process updates the cluster registry.

Tip: You can configure the Exchange virtual server with Cluster Admin.

Microsoft provides a set of documented steps for carefully preserving databases while you remove Exchange and then install and rebuild it on the Windows 2000 cluster. These steps can take days to accomplish. You must perform backups, get rid of any components (such as connectors), remove Exchange Server 5.5, install Exchange 2000, restore the databases, check that the whole lot is functional, bring the cluster back online, and then conclude the process by doing more backups. In addition, the messaging service is not accessible to users while these operations are happening. This routine can appreciably influence service level agreements (SLAs), as well as uptime statistics. Also, you should do this in a test lab environment before attempting to upgrade a production cluster, so you can be certain that you can perform the steps correctly.

An alternative approach, however, is to install a new Exchange 2000 cluster into the same site as the existing Exchange Server 5.5 cluster and then shuffle mailboxes from the old cluster to the new one. This is a more appealing methodology because it restricts the burden of the migration on the user whose mailbox is being moved at a given time. Ultimately, when you have moved all of the mailboxes to the Exchange 2000 cluster, you can decommission the Exchange Server 5.5 cluster by removing it from the organization. You can then reallocate the old cluster hardware for other functions, such as for a new Windows 2000 domain controller.

Client Perspectives

The upshot of clustering on the client depends on the category of client and the client responsibilities. Messaging Application Programming Interface (MAPI) clients (Outlook, for example) are different from some of the Internet protocol clients in that they will reconnect if the server goes away. When the server comes back, it will re-establish the connection by design. Also, MAPI clients will engender an error when a virtual server fails over. Generally, with Outlook, the worst that will happen is that you will get a network error and you will need to retry so MAPI can re-establish the connection. Post Office Protocol version 3 (POP3) clients, however, are just sitting and waiting to retrieve email and may not know that a virtual server has failed.

Front-End and Back-End Architecture

Exchange 2000 also makes available a method for sorting out client access from client data for non-MAPI clients, such as Outlook Web Access, Internet Message Access Protocol (IMAP), and POP3 clients. This feature is supplemental to providing a flexible architecture for routing, public folder stores, and mailbox stores. You can attain this by deploying front-end and back-end server architectures. This design will define a set of Exchange servers for data and another set of Exchange servers as protocol servers that service HTTP, IMAP, and POP3 protocols. Your MAPI clients must join directly to a back-end mailbox server. The chief payback for front-end and back-end architecture is a unified namespace, the capacity to isolate mailbox servers, and lower overhead for Secure Sockets Layer (SSL) encryption.

Improved Security

A front-end and back-end architecture allows you to set out a more secure system. For example, back-end servers can sit behind a firewall or on a different subnet in a private, inaccessible network. The front-end servers can have two network cards and reside in both the external network and the secure, internal LAN. As Chapter 8 showed, you can configure the front-end server by using Transmission Control Protocol/Internet Protocol (TCP/IP) filtering to listen only to select protocol ports, thereby controlling the frequency of malicious attacks on your infrastructure.

SSL connections need to execute processor-intensive encryption and decryption operations that can affect system performance. If your organization is using a front-end and back-end architecture, the front-end server can deal with the encryption for the client. The front-end server and back-end server can then communicate without the overhead of SSL encryption. This will allow you to create a more safe and resourceful clustering topology.

16

Improved Fault Tolerance

When an Outlook Web Access client exchanges data with a front-end server, for example, the server queries Active Directory for that user's home server and database. The query is then passed on to the appropriate back-end server, and a session is established. The Outlook Web Access client communicates with the front-end server by means of HTTP. The front-end server then uses HTTP to communicate to the back-end server. Your clients have the facility to always hook up the same way, despite the Exchange server on which their inbox resides. This is made feasible by deploying network load balancing with an arrangement of front-end servers. This provides further fault tolerance when accessing user data and offers separation between users and their mailboxes. Network load-balancing will not confirm that an application has failed, however, only that the hardware has failed. This can permit some connections to appear operational even when there is no access to data. It can also result in the ability to move a mailbox between different back-end servers without impacting the user. You can also supply fault tolerance by using a mutual IP hostname for all of the front-end servers, and then letting the round-robin mechanism of the DNS server make a specific IP address available for each request. Because the front-end servers do not accumulate any state information, another front-end server can handle the request if the first one fails.

Note: Front-end and back-end architecture is best suited to non-MAPI clients such as Outlook Web Access. If you use a MAPI client in this configuration, direct connection between the Outlook (MAPI) client and the back-end server would take place.

Unified Namespace

A unified namespace provides easier administration of multiple servers. If all servers are part of a front-end and back-end architecture, a single server name provides user access to multiple servers in your establishment. You can configure clients to connect using the same name, and software or hardware load balancing will indiscriminately dispense the load among the three front-end servers. The front-end server queries Active Directory, and sends the call to the right back-end server. Furthermore, when you intend to move mailboxes from one server to another, clients do not need to reconfigure the name of the server to which they log on. As your user population increases, you can include front-end servers without reconfiguring clients.

Improved Scalability

Horizontal scalability is another added feature of the front-end and back-end architecture. If front-end servers cannot manage the demand, you can merely place a new front-end server into production. The front-end servers do not accumulate data, and they operate only as protocol converters. Therefore, you need only to install Exchange 2000 and update DNS to include the new server name. The arrangement of multiple storage groups and databases in a server cluster, deployment of a front-end and back-end architecture supported by network load-balancing schemes, and public folder stores replicated across both server clusters present a high-availability resolution for Exchange 2000. In addition to these technologies, the redundant and distributed nature of Active Directory reduces single points of failure in the system.

Chapter Summary

This chapter has explored the necessities and strategies for deploying a high-availability design through an Exchange 2000 Server messaging cluster solution. The outcome of not implementing a high-availability solution can include lost revenue, disruption in customer service, and trouble with corporate relationships, as well as an unproductive workforce. Huge costs accrue in many areas of your organization for recovering from a system failure. The hidden costs may include the loss of good will; damage to your corporate status among customers, suppliers, and partners; and the notion that your business is not able to meet the needs of customers.

This chapter also revealed a difference between fault tolerance and high availability. The difference comes down to whether you are attempting to eliminate or merely minimize downtime. High availability seeks to minimize the amount of downtime. Fault-tolerant solutions, in contrast, seek to eliminate downtime. This chapter focused on the high-availability solution of Microsoft Cluster Server as it relates to Exchange 2000 Server.

The key term "availability" is defined as a ratio of time that a system is operating, which is often expressed as a percentage. Another key term is the "recovery point," the amount of data that is lost due to a system failure. A common objective of many organizations is to provide a recovery point of zero, meaning absolutely no loss of data. Another key concept that relates to the recovery point is the recovery time, or the amount of time necessary to return a system to full operation. A top objective of your organization should be to reduce the recovery time for a particular type of failure.

Human intervention or programmatic errors cause 80 percent of all unplanned outages. Operator errors include applying procedures incorrectly to a given scenario, performing a task improperly, or not performing a task at all. Application failures include errors in software, performance issues, and incompatibility problems. Building-level incidents and disasters can affect a room, building, or an entire location. Physically moving a server between sites can result in a hardware failure when that server is restarted. Problems such as fire, flood, power outages, earthquakes, hurricanes, and military or political disorders can interrupt service by physically injuring or destroying hardware, terminating power to critical computer systems, and preventing access to systems. These events can affect a metropolitan area or can be regional events that occur on an even wider magnitude of hundreds of square miles.

16

Hardware is the first main factor that relates to servers and the components needed to support the services of Exchange 2000. Typical issues are the uninterruptible power supply (UPS), processor failure, bad memory, and the performance and reliability of the disk subsystem. Another key area of hardware vulnerability involves the networking components.

Clustering is the process whereby two or more servers are linked together so that they perform as a single computer. Clustering is a popular strategy used for parallel processing applications, load-balancing, and fault tolerance. With the Shared Nothing model of clustering, any one node in the cluster can own any available resource; however, a node can own only one resource at a time. This means that none of the resources in your cluster are shared, as they would be in the contrasting Shared Disk model. The Shared Nothing model is easier to implement as well as troubleshoot and it does not require a proprietary hardware solution. Microsoft uses the Shared Nothing model in their cluster services due to industry standard hardware support and the ease at which third-party applications run on top of it.

Two different failover modes are active/passive and active/active. The active/passive mode is the Service Failover Mode. Active/passive means that you can run that instance of service or resource on only one node of the cluster at a time. With active/active failover, services can run on more than one cluster node at a time. Another way that Microsoft Exchange 2000 Server delivers enhanced scalability and reliability for your messaging infrastructure is by supporting two-way (two-node) and four-way (four-node) active/active clustering. Exchange 2000 supports two-node clusters in Windows 2000 Advanced Server. Four-way, or four-node, clustering is supported only in Microsoft Datacenter Server. The Datacenter edition is an OEM-only version that is installed or provided by your hardware vendor.

You can successfully deploy Exchange 2000 Server on MSCS by working within the parameters of the limitations of the available technology. This provides your organization with significantly increased system availability and system protection from hardware failures. Clustering Exchange 2000 Server can help your organization meet its high-availability requirements by protecting servers from critical failures that could not be tolerated in a nonclustered scenario. The combination of multiple storage groups and databases in a server cluster, deployment of a front-end and back-end architecture supported by network load-balancing, and public folder stores replicated across both server clusters provide a high-availability solution for Exchange 2000. In addition to these technologies, the redundant and distributed nature of Active Directory reduces single points of failure in the system. Chapter 17, the next and final chapter, explores the common troubleshooting techniques and scenarios of Exchange 2000.

Review Questions

1. Which one of the following solutions is designed to merely minimize downtime as opposed to totally eradicating downtime?

   a. Fault tolerance

   b. High availability

   c. Flaw acceptance

   d. Checksum systems

2. Which one of the following factors is the statistically ensuing length of time that a user may reasonably expect a component, device, or system to work between two catastrophic failures?

   a. Recovery point

   b. Recovery time

   c. Availability ratio

   d. Mean time between failures

3. Which of these percentages represents a commonly accepted availability figure associated with a total of approximately 8 hours of downtime per year?

   a. 99%

   b. 99.9%

   c. 99.99%

   d. 99.999%

4. Recent studies have indicated that approximately 80 percent of all unplanned outages are due to which of the following factors?

   a. Operating systems failure

   b. Hardware issues

   c. Human intervention

   d. Environmental factors

5. Which of the following events can happen in your organization when a public folder server fails? [Check all correct answers]

   a. Critical business data coming into your organization can cease.

   b. Personal productivity may suffer.

   c. Web sites and knowledge management systems can stop working.

   d. None of the above.

16

6. More than 90 percent of all interactions with Active Directory occur with which component?

   a. DNS service

   b. DHCP

   c. Group policy

   d. Global catalog

7. Losses can be measured in many different ways, and if money is the measure, then the figures can be astonishing. A recent highly regarded study found that costs of downtime normally fall into what monetary range?

   a. $1,000 to $27,000 per minute

   b. $5,000 to $35,000 per minute

   c. $10,000 to $47,000 per minute

   d. $20,000 to $57,000 per minute

8. Hardware is the main environmental factor that is vulnerable to failure. Which of the following are typical hardware considerations?

   a. Uninterruptible power supply

   b. Processor failure

   c. Disk subsystem reliability

   d. Networking component problems

   e. a and c only

   f. All of the above

9. Which of the following represent methods that can be implemented to reduce recovery time and recovery point in an Exchange 2000 environment? [Check all correct answers]

   a. Replicating the data

   b. Deploying several databases and storage groups

   c. Introducing resilient message routing

   d. Backing up and restoring data online simultaneously

10. Regardless of the number of Exchange virtual servers that exist on a node, in a Windows 2000 cluster, what is the maximum number of storage groups allowed on a single node?

   a. 2

   b. 3

   c. 4

   d. 8

11. What is the name of the strategy used for parallel processing applications, load balancing, and fault tolerance in which two or more servers are tied together so that they perform and appear as a single computer?

    a. Virtual servers

    b. Front-end and back-end architecture

    c. Routing groups

    d. Clustering

12. Which of the following is a primary clustering model? [Check the two best answers]

    a. Shared Storage model

    b. Shared Disk model

    c. Shared Nothing model

    d. Shared Cluster model

13. Which failover mode of Exchange 2000 is a scenario in which both members of the cluster are online and accepting user requests for various services?

    a. Active/passive clustering

    b. Passive/active clustering

    c. Active/active clustering

    d. None of the above

14. Microsoft Cluster Services is really a set of DLLs and APIs for Windows 2000. Which one of the following is a main DLL file?

    a. EXCLUADM.DLL

    b. EXPRESS.DLL

    c. MSCSEXC.DLL

    d. MSCSADM.DLL

15. Each virtual server will have its own autonomous configuration information that includes which the following? [Check all correct answers]

    a. Domain name

    b. IP address

    c. Port number

    d. Authentication

16

Real-World Projects

Project 16.1

You are the network administrator in your small software firm. To minimize the impact of an upgrade, you decide to upgrade the operating system of Exchange 5.5 member servers in a Windows NT 4 domain to Windows 2000. These servers will still be members of the Windows NT 4 domain. Using your own company, a friend's organization, or imaginary case study, submit a report that addresses the following questions:

➤ What version of Windows NT is currently installed?

➤ What service packs have been installed?

➤ Where are the page files located and what size are they?

➤ What necessary upgrades must be performed before Exchange 2000 is deployed?

Project 16.2

Plus Ultra Group has a single Exchange 5.5 server that services 2,500 user mailboxes and another server in the organization that handles public folders. Each mailbox has a limit of 35MB of data, thereby making the maximum mailbox store size 87.5GB of data (not accounting for disk space savings based on single-instance message storage). Therefore, every backup and restore handles 87.5GB of data; all 2,500 users will be affected if a corruption occurs in the database and offline recovery utilities are used, or if the database must be recovered in its entirety. Write a proposal that includes steps that Plus Ultra Group should take in this scenario when implementing Exchange 2000.

Possible Solution:

When Plus Ultra Group implements Exchange 2000, it could break up the 2,500-user load across a number of databases. They may decide that a 20GB maximum for a single database is a good goal. The more important factor in splitting the load, however, would be to reduce the impact to users in the case of database corruption. They could go with a 300-user maximum for each database. The split diminishes the effect of a single database corruption to a maximum of 300 users. All of the other users will still be able to use the system. The decision to split up the 2,500-user load across a number of databases also shrinks the backup time by implementing a parallel backup strategy. In addition, the split allows for an increase in the mailbox size limit to 60MB per mailbox and the mailbox store size limit to 20GB.

CHAPTER SEVENTEEN

Troubleshooting Exchange 2000 Server

After completing this chapter, you will be able to:

✓ Take preventive maintenance measures in Exchange 2000

✓ Review general troubleshooting strategies

✓ Understand Exchange 2000 installation and setup issues

✓ Solve common connectivity problems

✓ Address Web Storage System issues

✓ Investigate problems with Active Directory and Active Directory Connector

✓ Identify Exchange 2000 backup and restore challenges

✓ Be aware of common performance issues

Preventive Maintenance

No matter what operating system, architecture, infrastructure, or networking environment you have, genuine "from-the-bottom-up" strategies are available to assist you in troubleshooting problems in your Exchange 2000 organization. Even though the layered nature of networking has not been covered in this book, you should consider a solid investigation of the Open Systems Interconnection (OSI) networking model. Reviewing the OSI model and the network architecture will help you determine if a problem at a lower layer is preventing the upper-layer components from functioning properly. When you encounter a connectivity problem on a client computer, your first troubleshooting action should be to check the physical cabling. This translates into verifying that the bottom two layers of the OSI model are working properly. A next step would be to run **ipconfig /all** to confirm your network configuration. If you do not see a valid Internet Protocol (IP) address, then you can be relatively certain the problem resides in the IP layer. After this, you can **ping** the loopback address 127.0.0.1 and then **ping** the IP address of a computer on your client or server's local subnet. Normally, this IP address will be the default gateway for that subnet; if one exists. These two tests will conclude if the code for the network stack is being loaded and the IP layer is operating. What you are doing here is simply testing the network from the bottom of the OSI model up to the top.

A key facet of your troubleshooting design should involve the development of a repair strategy for your organization. This includes a number of factors, for example, designing an Exchange 2000 system that allows for replicas of components so that operations can be carried on during repair downtime. You need to devise courses of action and to construct topology maps to catalog the most important components in your messaging environment. Along with topology maps, you should document a sequential description of all finished repairs, an agenda for required maintenance, and tracking mechanisms for all of your troubleshooting and repair activities. By taking the proper preventive maintenance and planning steps, you will be better able to ward off disasters.

You can also put into action other precautionary measures that can help minimize the risk and impact of disasters on your Exchange 2000 servers. One good idea is to avoid making an Exchange 2000 Server system perform as a domain controller. Also, make sure that you keep a precise record of changes and document all configurations on your Exchange servers. Furnish your servers with ample hard disk space to allow for system recovery. Always install your servers in a suitable and secure environment. Preserve your transaction log files for the directory as well as the information stores on separate hard disks, and use uninterruptible power supplies (UPSs) for server protection. Lastly, implement hardware RAID (Redundant Array of Independent Disks) level 5 mirroring whenever feasible, and be sure that the circular logging feature of Exchange 2000 is disabled.

Note: Circular logging is disabled by default in Exchange 2000. The use of transaction log files will vastly improve the recovery capabilities of Exchange Server. Because databases contained in a storage group share transaction log files, the circular logging configuration applies to one storage group at a time.

In addition to server and configuration planning, you should be certain that you routinely finalize a set of preventive measures to ensure reliability of your Exchange 2000 Server data. This series of tasks should include allocating the information store resources; clearing out mailboxes; generating, adjusting, and removing email addresses and mailboxes; maintaining the information store; making global batch modifications to mailboxes, distribution lists, and custom recipients; verifying replicated directory information; and performing backups. When preparing your preventive maintenance plan, be sure to create a training curriculum for administrators and other members of your information technology (IT) staff concerning repair steps, preventive processes, and restorative processes, as well as disaster recovery plans. This should comprise qualification training on procedures and intermittent drills that simulate disaster recovery scenarios.

Microsoft Exchange 2000 Server provides a number of resident utilities and resources to simplify troubleshooting tasks. Several of these tools can also be used remotely to analyze and repair problems throughout the organization. Between Windows 2000 Server and Exchange 2000 Server, you have a wide array of troubleshooting components available. Troubleshooting involves more than simply one source, typically requiring a combination of diagnostic tools. Diagnostic logs for connectors and services can alert you to possible troubles associated with connection and service failures (see Figure 17.1). The Link monitor display and log allows you to corroborate the fact that test messages sent to servers are making the round-trip within a particular length of time. Message queues such as the Message Transfer Agent (MTA), Internet Mail Service (IMS), and Microsoft Mail Connector

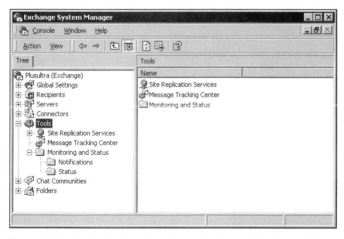

Figure 17.1 Monitoring Tools interface in Exchange 2000 System Manager.

can be analyzed as well. You can exhibit these queues, delete messages, and actually change the order of the messages in the queue with some MTA queues.

In addition to these components, the message tracking log will monitor all messaging being generated by the information store and directory services. The Server Monitor display and log will decide whether Exchange 2000 Server components are running. They test all elemental and discretionary server components as well as installed connectors. Once you are alerted to a problem by Server Monitor, you can use this data to perform further research as to the cause of the problem. The old standby Windows NT/2000 application, Event Viewer, is another valuable tool that can be used to measure server performance (Figure 17.2). As previously mentioned, you will need to generate a complete network topology or routing map. The network topology diagram gives an all-purpose topology of your Exchange 2000 system by displaying the positioning of the routers, servers, and gateways. The routing map will display the information flow as it arrives and exits your site.

General Troubleshooting Strategies

When troubleshooting Exchange 2000 clients, you should implement the following basic fundamentals. Obviously, you first need to identify the problem. The tools and components referenced in the preceding section are key to recognizing and analyzing system problems. The next step is to verify whether the problem is a common one by finding the most current deployment guides, read me files, and updates from Microsoft. Consider subscribing to Microsoft TechNet at **www.microsoft.com/technet**. A good alternative is to use the support site, **http://support.microsoft.com/support** because it is focused on more problem solving. By using all of the tools and documentation at your disposal (including the remainder of this chapter), you can attempt to isolate and test the error conditions that are surfacing.

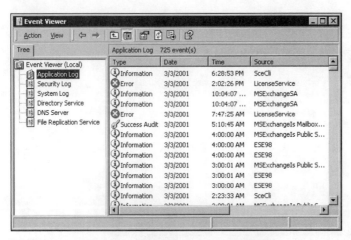

Figure 17.2 Windows 2000 Application Log in Event Viewer.

When you begin the troubleshooting process by analyzing symptoms to determine a strategy for resolution, reflect on several factors. First, see whether any error messages are being generated, and if so, determine when the problem arises. Is this a problem that is entirely random, or can you replicate the scenario? Determine if the issue is particular to a certain component or function of Exchange 2000, such as a connector or the directory. Find out if the difficulty occurs within any other area of Exchange, or if it is a function of the Windows 2000 operating system. Ask yourself if you—or another IT staff member—have made any current changes to the environment, configuration, or other conditions. For example, have you modified any of the programs, components, or settings on your server or client computer, such as adding or removing programs or new hardware? Determine further if the problem is taking place on more than one client or server.

Remember that you can access the Help menu in System Manager and get context-sensitive help, as seen in Figure 17.3. If you cannot fix the issue, you may want to consider consulting online troubleshooting and support options (see, for example, Figure 17.4). Check with an appropriate online forum or support group, where available. Quite likely, other users have discovered problems, reported them, and possibly found fixes or workarounds for your particular scenario. By leveraging the time and experiences of others, you can save time finding the cause of the problem and troubleshooting the issue.

The best way to quickly sort out a problem is to methodically isolate and test the error conditions. Remove all variables to help determine the cause of a problem. Close all other applications and running processes, if possible, to eliminate other components as possible causes of the issue. You can then isolate the cause by modifying a certain value and then testing to see if the problem is fixed. If a

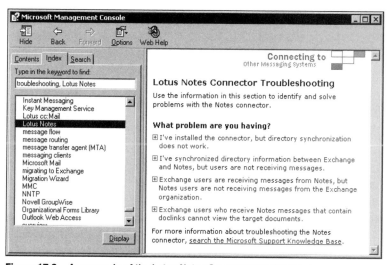

Figure 17.3   An example of the Lotus Notes Connector troubleshooter.

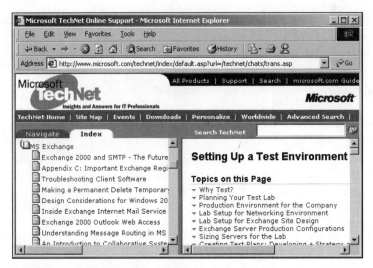

Figure 17.4   Microsoft TechNet online support.

component does not function in a lab system after upgrading to new hardware or software, revert back to the original hardware or software and then retest it. Check each change independently to verify if it solves the problem. Document all changes and their resulting effects on the system. This information will offer a superb resource for any troubleshooting sessions in the future. If you must eventually turn to product support personnel, this data will facilitate the troubleshooting of your problem.

Another excellent practice is to employ active event and error log scanning and reporting. Remember that you should not only monitor, but also implement alerting. It does not really help if your backup server is the only entity that is aware of a hitch in your environment. You should have, at the very least, some basic monitoring that alerts you through email when errors occur or when backup operations are not successful. The best practice is to have monitoring in place that accurately notifies system managers of any error or failure conditions in daily backups. Because most types of issues, such as database corruption, terminate the backup job, it is better to be proactive with these types of problems rather than reactive after it is too late to prevent catastrophe.

Exchange 2000 Installation and Setup Issues

No discussion of installation and deployment would be complete without address-ing possible issues related to the configuration of Exchange 2000. When you install and set up Exchange 2000, you probably will run into error messages and command failures. Network problems often spawn a setup failure. If this happens during your installation, you should make sure that the network link is working properly. Your best solution, if installation stalls, is to perform a complete reinstall of the Exchange components. To effectively reinstall Exchange components, simply shut down all of the Exchange services, restart the server, and execute the Setup program. Reinstall any components that Setup did not properly install during the initial installation process.

One of the most common issues occurs when the setup command has problems executing the ForestPrep switch. ForestPrep, as discussed in Chapter 3, updates the Active Directory schema for Exchange 2000. The syntax for this command is **Setup/forestprep**. Check to see if the account has the Schema Admins, Enterprise Admins, and Local Administrator rights to the server permissions. DomainPrep is run to set appropriate permissions in preparation for Exchange 2000. If you run the command **Setup/domainprep** and it fails to execute, you need to make sure that the account has the Domain Admins and Local Administrator rights to the server permissions.

When you are running Setup and you see a message that the directory service is busy, you are probably installing Exchange 2000 Server into a child domain. This scenario can raise a peculiar problem due to the manner in which the named pipe transport functions. The server side generates an instance of the named pipe for the express purpose of being used by the clients. The first client that attempts to make a connection becomes coupled to that instance. Because of this, the server must generate another instance of the named pipe to permit other clients the ability to connect. If another client tries to connect before the creation of the new instance, Exchange Server will appear to the second client not to accept a connection. There is a solution for this issue that goes back to what was mentioned earlier in this chapter. You need to initiate the Exchange 2000 Setup again and install the components that did not install the first time around. Once you do this, Exchange 2000 Setup will complete successfully.

If you install Exchange 2000 Server and you receive this error message,

```
Setup Fails: Error 0xC103798A
```

it could be that the Setup failed while configuring the registry entries for the Exchange System Management snap-ins. In addition, if any component of Exchange Server 5.5 that was previously installed on a server does not completely uninstall, you may have a versioning conflict with the exchmem.dll file. Before running Exchange 2000 Setup, consider renaming the existing file to exchmem.old. Exchange 2000 will then duplicate the appropriate exchmem.dll file during setup, thereby eliminating the problem. You can see this directory location in Figure 17.5.

17

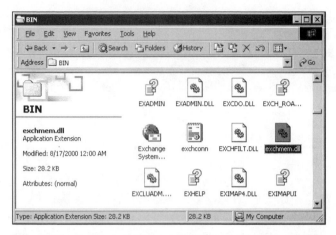

Figure 17.5   Exchmem.dll file located in Program Files\Exchsvr\BIN.

Setup Failures When Attempting to Join an Existing Site

If your Setup crashes when you attempt to join an Exchange 2000 Server to an existing Exchange Server 5.5 site, you may see an error message stating:

```
Setup Was Unable to Bind to the Exchange Server.
```

This error message shows up when the account that you are using to initiate the Setup procedure has insufficient or faulty permissions configured for the target server's Exchange Server 5.5 directory. The best way to crack this problem is to grant this account the Administrator permissions at the Site and Configuration levels of your Exchange 5.5 Server.

In large organizations, attempts to install Exchange 2000 Server to an existing site with numerous servers or sites have caused Setup to stop working in certain situations. In this type of scenario, you may often get the following message:

```
Idispatch not found for [Microsoft Exchange conferencing MMC snap-in].
```

The best solution to this predicament is to take some preventive steps on your Exchange 5.5 server before attempting the installation. Before you install Exchange 2000, complete these steps on the existing Exchange 5.5 server:

1. Run Exchange Server Administrator.

2. Expand the Organization component, click to expand Site, click to expand Configuration, and then click to expand Protocols.

3. Double-click the LDAP (Lightweight Directory Access Protocol) and open the Properties page.

4. Click the Search tab and change the "Maximum number of search results returned" value to equal to or greater than the number of servers in your organization.

Note: If the LDAP protocol object at the server level is not configured to use the site defaults, you should modify this value at the server level.

You may run into a situation in which the Setup procedure fails while you are joining an Exchange Server 5.5 site on a Windows 2000 domain controller. For instance, you run Exchange 2000 Server Setup on a member server in a Microsoft Windows 2000 Server domain, and Setup does not function when the Windows 2000 Server domain controller is upgraded from Windows NT 4 and has Exchange Server 5.5 installed. Setup fails when you attempt to unite with the existing Exchange Server 5.5 site. This issue surfaces because Exchange Server 5.5 and the Windows 2000 domain controller are both attempting to use port 389 to contact the LDAP. The resolution to this predicament is to use the Exchange Server Administrator program, under the Protocols section, to alter the Exchange LDAP port number before you run Exchange Server 5.5 on a Windows 2000 Server domain controller. Change the Exchange LDAP port number before you upgrade Windows NT 4 to Windows 2000 Server.

Note: You will have to restart the Exchange 5.5 directory service after modifying the port number.

Assume that you are upgrading an Exchange 5.5 server to an Exchange 2000 server, and Exchange 2000 gives false alerts, or attempts to restart services that do not exist in Exchange 2000, or tries to restart the server. These actions can occur when the Exchange 5.5 servers that you configured for monitoring attempt to find services that previously existed in Exchange 5.5 but do not exist in Exchange 2000. To unravel this situation, prior to upgrading a server from Exchange 5.5 to Exchange 2000, eliminate the configuration on other Exchange 5.5 servers that cause them to monitor the server you want to upgrade. To remove the configuration on Exchange 5.5 servers, follow these steps:

1. Place the monitoring servers in maintenance mode for the period of the upgrade to make certain that no monitoring occurs until those servers are brought out of maintenance mode.

2. Upgrade the server. When you do this, however, all monitoring configurations on the newly upgraded server will be lost. If that server monitors other servers, it will not be able to do so after you upgrade.

3. When the server comes back online, it is configured just like a new Exchange 2000 install. No notifications will be configured. Also, the Status will show that the server is in a serious state if any of the following services are stopped: Web Storage System, Microsoft Exchange MTA stacks, Microsoft Exchange Routing Engine, Microsoft Exchange System Attendant, Simple Mail Transfer

17

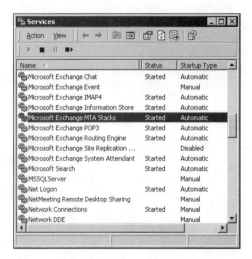

Figure 17.6   The Services status, after new installation.

Protocol (SMTP), or World Wide Web Publishing Service. Figure 17.6 displays an example of the System Services component after setup. In addition, there is no default warning state.

4. Configure notifications, and then set up other Exchange 2000 servers to monitor resources on the upgraded server. Exchange 5.5 servers should monitor only Exchange 5.5 servers; Exchange 2000 servers should monitor only Exchange 2000 servers.

When attempting to include a new server at a site, Setup may fail. To install Exchange fittingly on the new server, you must reinstall Exchange or the components that failed. Information about the new server may be replicated to other servers on the site. To prevent the site's directory from becoming corrupted, eliminate the new server from the site's directory before you reinstall the server. To guarantee that Exchange is installed appropriately on the site, delete the server object for the new server on the Administrator program on the remote server that you specified during setup. Next, run Setup again on the new server, and select Remove All. Finally, run Setup again on the new server, and reinstall Exchange.

Replication Issues during Installation

Public folder replication does not take place until the Active Directory replicates. If the gap between directory replications is lengthy, the Web Storage System may seek to replicate public folders before the new site is added to the directory. A resolution is merely to wait for the directory to replicate the new site information or force directory replication to occur. To ensure that public folders replicate effectively, click the General tab for the server directory and click Update Now. If you choose to force directory replication, do it when the server's performance is not critical and connection costs are low.

Solving Connectivity Issues

Connectivity problems can include client connectivity, protocol troubles, and problems with public folders, as well as email and Instant Messaging issues. For example, a virus can attack Outlook rendering it impossible to send an email or even close the program. Sometimes, Outlook client messages can be lost. If you send messages using Exchange 2000 with a Microsoft Outlook 2000 client and message failures occur, fixes are available. When you use an Outlook 2000 client with Exchange 2000, you can track messages by using Message Tracking Center (see Figure 17.7), located on the Tools menu in System Manager, and Queue Viewer (see Figure 17.8), found on the SMTP and X.400 protocol nodes for each server.

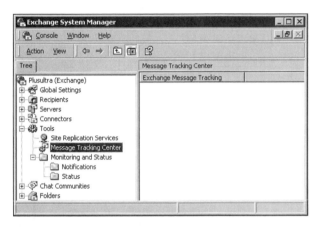

Figure 17.7   Example of the Message Tracking Center.

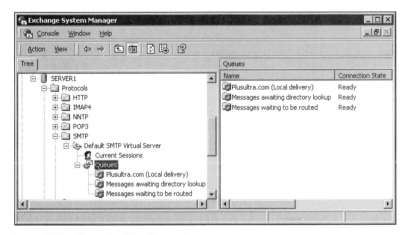

Figure 17.8   Example of the Queue Viewer.

17

Queue Viewer

The Exchange 2000 System Manager also offers a new module, called the Queue Viewer, which can be used to scrutinize the status of all queues. Messages in the queue can be frozen, sent back to the sender, or deleted. You can also use this utility to identify a problem and troubleshoot it after the Exchange Monitoring and Status tool focuses on one.

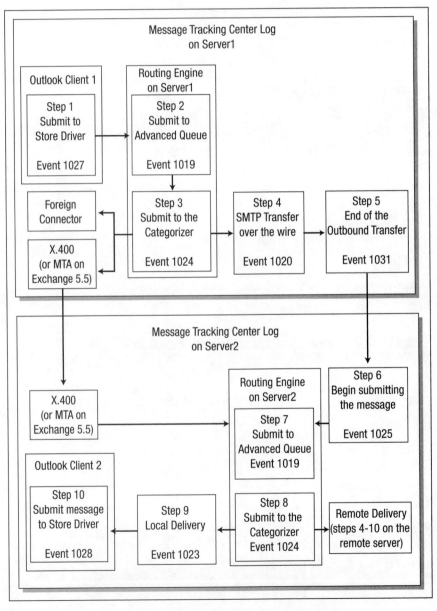

Figure 17.9   Steps of an Outlook message from Server1 to Server2.

To determine the source of a message routing problem between Outlook clients in an Exchange 2000 messaging system, use the flowchart in Figure 17.9 to help troubleshooting by using the event ID codes. These event codes will show up for each step in the associated log in the Message Tracking Center. The steps in the Server1 log appear on the server that sends the message, whereas the steps in the Server2 log appear on the recipient server. Use Table 17.1 to help troubleshoot Outlook 2000 messaging issues.

The Internet News Service creates a file called Ics.dat that it places in the Insdata directory. If the Ics.dat file is corrupted or missing, Internet News Service creates a new Ics.dat file. During the next Network News Transfer Protocol (NNTP) connection, Internet News Service attempts to replicate all the messages in the

Table 17.1   Steps of an Outlook message with troubleshooting options.

Step Number	Event ID code	Event	Troubleshooting Options
1	1027	The message goes from the Outlook 2000 outbox and is submitted to the store driver.	Verify if the message left the Outlook 2000 outbox.
2	1019	The message goes from the store driver to the Advanced Queue.	The SMTP service may be stopped. Make sure that the SMTP service is running on the sender's main server.
3	1024	The message is transferred from the Advanced Queue to the Categorizer.	Use Queue Viewer to find out if the message stopped in the Advanced Queue. Exchange also decides at this point whether to use the SMTP connector or a foreign connector. The message flow returns to the Exchange 2000 sequence at Step 7.
4	1020	The message transfers over the wire using SMTP.	The SMTP service may have been stopped or Active Directory/domain controller may not be functioning. Use the Queue Viewer to search for a Lookup Queue backlog.
5	1031	End Outbound Transfer.	The remote end server may not be functioning.
6	1025	The message begins the transfer to the remote server over port 25.	The SMTP service may be stopped. Verify to see if the SMTP service is running.
7	1019	The message moves from the store driver to the Advanced Queue.	The SMTP service may be stopped. Make sure that the SMTP service is running on the remote server.
8	1024	The message transfers from the Advanced Queue to the Categorizer.	Use the Queue Viewer to find out if the message stopped in the Advanced Queue.
9	1023	Local Delivery.	The Web Storage System may be stopped. Users will also have problems logging on.
10	1028	The message goes from SMTP Internet Information Services to the store.	Not applicable.

17

newsgroup public folders included in the news feed. To prevent this from occurring, select "Mark All as Delivered" on the Advanced tab for that news feed.

Sometimes you may experience a situation in which the Site Replication Service
(SRS) will not run in a native Exchange 2000 environment. For example, you
attempt to create a new SRS when your Exchange 2000 Server organization
consists exclusively of Exchange 2000 servers, and the following error message
occurs:

```
Microsoft Exchange Administrator
This operation cannot be run in a Native Mode Exchange organization.
   ID no: c1037d38
```

The SRS provides support for previous versions of Exchange Server and is not
relevant in a native Exchange 2000 environment. The solution is to run STS not in
native mode, but rather in mixed mode.

Another problem that you may encounter is that the Instant Messaging logon may
fail in Exchange 2000, yet it works in Windows 2000. For example, a user enabled
for Instant Messaging attempts to log on to an Instant Messaging home server and
receives the authentication failure dialog box. The credentials, however, allow the
user to log on to Windows 2000. The user is denied access by Exchange 2000
Internet Information Services (IIS). This problem happens because the password
isn't correct, the user account is not functioning, or the password policy for the user
is not set correctly (enable password encryption). To solve this problem, be sure that
the password is valid. Also, check to see that the user account is valid and functioning and the password policy for the user is set appropriately.

In addition, an attempt to view Instant Messaging contacts during an online
conference can fail. In Exchange 2000, Instant Messaging and Conferencing
technologies are not incorporated; therefore, a client's Instant Messaging contacts
will not show in an online conference session. This occurs because the Microsoft
Network (MSN) Messenger client has a user object syntax with the
User.LogonName that is different than User.FriendlyName. This will cause an
Instant Messaging display problem. To repair this, you can display current Instant
Messaging contacts whenever a user joins an online conference by making changes
in Active Directory.

Navigate to the Exchsrvr|Conferencing|Usa folder and find the file called
Confpanel.asp. Seek out the Confpanel.asp file for User.FriendlyName, substitute it
with User.LogonName, and then save it. After you swap this text, all Instant Messaging client-defined contacts materialize in your online conference Web page in
the console tree near the bottom. Also, from time to time, an Instant Messaging
client may disengage when the status changes. An Instant Messaging client changes
status swiftly among one or more different states, and the client automatically

disconnects. This occurs when the Instant Messaging server is busy and discards client requests such as calls for changing status. If a client cannot retain its status, it automatically logs off from the Instant Messaging server. There is actually no resolution to this supposed quandary because this client behavior is by design.

If you are using Word 2000 as your email editor, an error message of

```
Conference not found.
```

might appear when you attempt to join an online conference. This is a signal that the Conference Management Service cannot find the conference that you are trying to join. In Exchange 2000, you can join an online conference in a variety of ways. However, when you have Word 2000 defined as your default editor for email messages, and you open an email message and click the conference URL, this error message will show on the Web page. This occurs because when Word 2000 is used as your default email editor, the URL does not include the equal sign (=), which is augmented to the end of each conferencing URL. To fix this bug, join the conference by clicking the conferencing URL from the Preview pane.

Tip: You should not use Word 2000 as your email editor if you regularly join online conferences.

Another troubleshooting scenario that can emerge when dealing with newsgroups occurs when a deleted newsgroup is retained in the Exchange 2000 public store. When you install Exchange 2000 Server on a computer running Windows 2000 Server, you have the alternative to store your newsgroup content on the local hard disk, a remote share, or in the Exchange public folder database. When you store newsgroups in the Exchange public store, you might observe that the corresponding public folder is not removed when you delete the newsgroup through the Exchange System Manager Microsoft Management Console (MMC) snap-in. This occurs because Exchange System Manager deletes the newsgroup from the Newsgroups list, but the NNTP service does not delete the public folder from the store. To delete the public folder from the store, you must delete it manually from the Public Folders node in Exchange System Manager.

In Exchange System Manager, you can remove newsgroups that exist in the Web Storage System. After you expand the NNTP virtual server's node, you can opt for the Newsgroups node. A list of newsgroups displays in the Details pane. You can then choose a newsgroup and delete it by clicking Delete on the Action menu. When you delete a newsgroup in this way, however, its matching public folder is not deleted.

17

When a newly demoted domain controller is replicating, ReplMon might display the Deleted Server error message. This occurs because Exchange continues to attempt inbound replication from deleted servers for a designated period of time (the default is two weeks) to allow you to restore domain controllers that are accidentally deleted. After that interval passes, the tombstone is deleted, and the Deleted Server message no longer appears. For this particular situation, no action is necessary.

If you are configuring an SMTP connector to operate on a nonstandard port to enhance security to prevent sniffing, the SMTP connector will not function. This occurs because Exchange System Manager does not support connections to a remote port other than port 25. You should use SMTP authentication or encryption between the configured two servers using Exchange System Manager, and use only port 25 for the SMTP connector.

Packet Sniffers

A "sniffer" is a program can be used both for legitimate network monitoring functions and for stealing information off a network. Unauthorized sniffers can be catastrophic for networked security since they are almost impossible to detect. They are popular with hacker's on TCP/IP networks.

Routing Connectivity Issues

Assuming that you are running Domain Name System (DNS) resolution, the SMTP service may generate the following error message:

```
The following recipient could not be reached: jdoe@server.whatever.com on
    5/18/2000 5:26 PM.
```

Sometimes the email system is incapable of delivering the message, but will not report it for a specific reason. Check the address and try again. Verify that the server is configured to use a valid DNS server or servers and also make sure the domain is valid. You can check domain validity by using the **nslookup** utility. A good practice with this kind of error is to determine if this is the only email address from this domain that is having problems and if there are any other domains having the same problem.

After you create multiple routing groups and shift servers into these routing groups, messages may no longer stream between the servers of the different routing groups. These messages are returned immediately to their senders with a **5.0.0** error code in the non-delivery report (NDR). This happens because connectors must be configured between routing groups for mail to flow between them. You may also get the following error until you have configured the routing group connectors for the routing groups:

```
SMTP Protocol Error "454 Client Must Be Authenticated"
```

In addition to these errors, clients can have difficulties sending email to an Exchange 2000 server because the following SMTP protocol error occurs:

```
454 Client must be authenticated.
```

This will happen because the server does not allow anonymous SMTP connections and requires the client to authenticate. SMTP clients that have not been configured for SMTP authentication or do not have this capacity cannot tender email to a server that is set to prohibit anonymous connections. A couple of solutions to this problem exist: The first is to configure the SMTP client to perform SMTP authentication to the server; the second is to configure the Exchange 2000 server to allow anonymous connections.

The final connectivity issue explored here occurs when you are not capable of accessing an accompanying Hypertext Transfer Protocol (HTTP) virtual server on an Exchange 2000 cluster. This inaccessibility can occur when you make use of System Manager to create an additional HTTP virtual server in a Windows 2000 cluster server. The problem here is that Exchange 2000 Setup does not create the correct HostName for Distributed Authoring and Versioning (DAV). The solution is to simply not create additional HTTP virtual servers in an active/passive Exchange 2000 Server cluster environment.

Web Storage System Issues

You might have problems with your data storage in Web Storage System, together with those related to the Exchange Installable File System (ExIFS), mailboxes, and databases. For example, if you stop the ExIFS service and then endeavor to restart it, the following error message may occur:

```
System error 2 has occurred. The system cannot find the file specified.
```

The ExIFS installs with Exchange 2000 Server and runs as a hidden service on an Exchange 2000 server. It allows file-level access to a range of items within a private or public store. On an Exchange 2000 server, the ExIFS service characteristically maps as drive M in Windows Explorer. Because the ExIFS runs as a hidden service, it is not visible in the Services dialog box in Administrative Tools. However, you can still issue a **net stop** or **net start** command to start or stop the ExIFS service. Halting the ExIFS service does not make the mapping to drive M disappear. The fix for this issue is to manually stop the ExIFS service by issuing a **net stop** command; you must issue the following command at the command line before restarting the ExIFS:

```
Subst m: /d
```

17

You can then launch the ExIFS service by issuing the **net start** command as shown:

```
Net start exifs
```

If ExIFS still does not start, confirm that none of the users have an open file on drive M or are accessing this drive by using a share. On the other hand, you can stop all links to the server by issuing the following command at the command prompt:

```
Netses/ed
```

*Note: Be careful in using the **netses/ed** command because it will disconnect all users from the server.*

If you carry out operations on a network drive that is mapped to an ExIFS share, and the remote file operation against an Installable File System (IFS) share fails with the error **0xEFAD2521**, the error may persist even after the server restarts. This error occurs because Exchange does not recognize the mapped network drive. To fix this, delete the mapped network drive and then re-create it. You can do this at the command prompt by typing:

```
net use <drive> /d
net use <drive> \\<server>\<share>
```

Also, the error message

```
System Cannot Find the Path Specified or x:\mailbox is Not Accessible.
```

may occur in Internet Explorer when you try to remotely access a mailbox via the MBX (mailbox) share, even though you can effectively access the contents of the MBX directory. This occurs when the administrator has shared the MBX directory using a net share command and has erroneously typed the domain name. The fix for this is to delete the MBX share and then re-create it with the correct domain name.

Another problem scenario relates to the last access time not being updated on files. For example, suppose you need to find out the last time a file was accessed, but the "last access time" field has not been updated. The last access time field on files accessed for read-only purposes is disabled by default for performance reasons. The remedy for this is to enable last access time update by creating the following DWORD registry key and setting it to 1: HKEY_LOCAL_MACHINE | System | CurrentControlSet | Services | MSExchangeIS | ParametersSystem | UpdateLastAccessTime. In another Web Storage predicament, you may attempt to generate an extra Web

Storage System on your Exchange 2000 server and try to mount the store, only to get the following message:

```
The store could not be mounted because the Active Directory information
    was not replicated yet.
```

Three possible solutions exist for this problem: First, you can press Cancel and mount the store afterward from its Context menu. Second, you can press Retry to keep attempting to mount Web Storage System. If you click Retry, Exchange 2000 tries to mount Web Storage System after the next Active Directory replication cycle, and the following progress bar displays:

```
Waiting for the replication of Active Directory information on server
    [your server].
```

With the third resolution, you can think about forcing the process by manually making the Active Directory replicate. To manually compel Active Directory to replicate, take the following steps:

1. Open Active Directory Sites and Services in Administrative Tools.

2. Click to expand the following objects:

   ➤ Active Directory Sites and Services—**servername**

   ➤ Sites

   ➤ Default-First-Site-Name

   ➤ Servers

   ➤ Any domain controller in your Exchange 2000 Server domain

   ➤ New Technology Directory Service (NTDS) settings

3. Right-click the object in the details pane, then select Replicate Now.

More Storage Failure Scenarios

When attempting to move a mailbox from Exchange 5.5 to Exchange 2000, the following error message may occur:

```
Exchange 5.5 to Exchange 2000 Mailbox Move Failed.
```

This happens because Web Storage System cannot find the specified object. Either the object does not have Read permissions or it is not completely replicating. Your solutions are either to grant the object permission to Read Web Storage System or make certain that it fully replicates.

17

Another storage issue can occur when the client displays the wrong public folders after modifying the public database. In this scenario, you modify the public store attribute of an Exchange 2000 mailbox to point to Exchange Server 5.5 Public Database. Then you modify the public store attribute to point back to the Exchange 2000 server, and the Exchange 2000 mailbox still reflects the Exchange Server 5.5 computer. This occurs because the store provider on the client computer caches the PR_PROFILE_SERVER and PR_PROFILE_SERVER_DN attributes in the registry as Messaging Application Programming Interface (MAPI)-profile–stored data. This information is updated only for Exchange 2000 to Exchange Server 5.5 but not for Exchange Server 5.5 to Exchange 2000. The solution here is to remove the MAPI profile on the Exchange 2000 client, and then re-create the MAPI profile. Take the following steps to accomplish this:

1. Create an Exchange 2000 mailbox.

2. On the private store object of the Exchange 2000 mailbox, alter the default-associated MAPI top-level hierarchy from the Exchange 2000 public store to the public store attribute of an Exchange 5.5 server.

3. Change from the Exchange Server 5.5 public store attribute to the Exchange 2000 public store attribute on the Exchange 2000 mailbox.

The Exchange 2000 mailbox displays the Exchange 2000 public folders after the public mailbox store attribute changes back to reflect the Exchange 2000 server. In Exchange 2000, you can have several databases in a storage group. You must mount or dismount each database individually. To individually mount or dismount each database, take the following actions:

1. Start Exchange 2000 Server System Manager.

2. Choose Organization, then choose Servers, and then select the name of the server you want.

3. Click Information Store, click Storage Group, and then click the database you want to mount or dismount.

4. Right-click the database, then choose All Tasks, and then mount or dismount Web Storage System.

Problems with Active Directory and Active Directory Connector

Because Exchange 2000 depends on Active Directory and the Active Directory Connector (ADC) for communications with older versions of Exchange, you may have to troubleshoot Active Directory and the ADC from time to time. You may not be able to modify Active Directory objects effectively. For example, you may not be able to modify a directory object because the object is read-only or because you are logged on under an account that does not have permission to modify objects. To remedy such situations, make sure that you have permission to modify objects for the site. Because some objects make reference to objects in another site, you might also need permission to another site to modify those objects.

The Exchange 2000 options can also be unavailable to you in the Active Directory Users and Computers component, so that you cannot add, delete, or move an Exchange 2000 mailbox while using Active Directory Users and Computers. This occurs when you administer users from a system for which the Exchange System Management tools are not installed. For example, suppose you load Exchange 2000 Server on to a computer as a member server and then attempt to administer this server from Active Directory Users and Computers in MMC on a domain controller, but you do not see the Exchange 2000 extensions. A first problem-solver would be to start Active Directory Users and Computers from the Exchange 2000 member server. A second alternative would be to install the Exchange 2000 System Management tools on the domain controller.

Another issue is that hidden objects in Exchange 5.5 are suddenly visible in Exchange 2000. Suppose that you have Exchange Server 5.5 and Exchange 2000 Server installed on the same site and have configured an Active Directory connection agreement between them. To your dismay, you have the ability to view replicated hidden objects in Exchange Server 5.5 via the Exchange 2000 System Manager. By using the Exchange Server 5.5 Administrator program, you can mark objects as hidden. To view these objects through the Administrator program, click Hidden Recipients on the View menu. Exchange 2000 allows you to hide objects from the client view also, but there is no special view in System Manager. Objects that replicate from Exchange Server 5.5 and are marked as hidden remain hidden from the client view but can be seen in the Exchange 2000 System Manager.

The Configuration Connection Agreement

If you are upgrading Exchange Server 5.5 to Exchange 2000 Server, the installation process will entail having an ADC between Windows 2000 Active Directory and the Exchange Server 5.5 directory service. This generates a sort of connection agreement, known as a configuration connection agreement, placed on the ADC. The agreement then reads the site information from Exchange Server 5.5 and writes it into the Active Directory configuration naming context. In addition to having the ADC in place, you must also have connection agreements for the Exchange Server 5.5 containers that hold the mailboxes, as well as any other items that you need to upgrade to their Exchange 2000 equivalents. Each connection agreement points to a particular organizational unit in Active Directory. To access both directories, the connection agreement uses LDAP on port 389. If Exchange

17

5.5 Server is operating on a global catalog or Windows 2000 Server domain controller, you need to alter the LDAP port of the Exchange 5.5 Directory Service to a value separate from the default value.

To work out this problem, you should first check to see if the server is a domain controller. Accomplish this by opening Active Directory Users and Computers and expanding the Domain Controller folder. If the server is visible in the right pane then it is a domain controller. In this case, you should change the LDAP port in Exchange 5.5. Launch the Exchange Administrator program, expand the Site, Configuration, and Protocols containers, and then double-click LDAP (Directory) Site Defaults. Next, on the General tab in the Port Number box, change the port number value to something other than 389. Once you conclude these actions, click OK and close the Administrator program. Finally, you will open the MMC Services tool and restart the directory service. This interface is shown in Figure 17.10.

Another situation related to Active Directory can occur while attempting to run Active Directory Connector Setup. If you are logged on as a user in the Administrator group, the operation will fail to update the schema. The reason for this is that you must be an Enterprise Administrator to control the Active Directory Connector Setup. Some operations (during install or reinstall) will break down if the user running Active Directory Connector Setup is not an Enterprise Administrator. To handle this problem, simply give this account Administrator permissions at the Site and Configuration level of your Exchange 5.5 Server.

Backup and Restore Issues

Backup and restore are important functions for maintaining Exchange 2000 servers; therefore, you may find it necessary to troubleshoot these functions. Consider returning to Chapter 15 for a review before moving into this section.

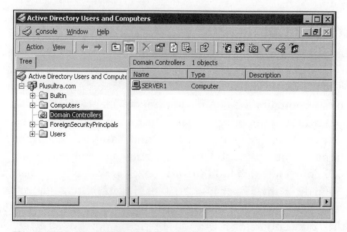

Figure 17.10   Troubleshooting the ADC.

One of the first issues that you may encounter is the inability to create an identical server or identical mailboxes in a site or organization for backup. This will become evident if, for some reason, you attempt to create a copy of an Exchange 2000 server within the same organization as the original for backup or restore purposes. This is by design, because Exchange 2000 demands that you have a unique Exchange distinguished name. Also, when performing backup and restore, you may receive the error message:

```
Event ID 1018, 1019, or 1022: Database is damaged.
```

This is an indication that online backup cannot be accomplished because the database is damaged. Remedy this situation by checking out the hardware for errors and carrying out a restore of this database as soon as possible. You can perform an offline backup so that you have a recent copy of the database even though it is damaged. Be careful, however, to never delete logs from the system while executing an offline backup. These logs are essential if you decide to restore from the online backups.

Another common error that you may encounter occurs when you are mounting a storage group with a missing database in an effort to recoup after an unanticipated system shutdown. This will generate one or both of the following errors in the Event Viewer application log:

```
1216 error
0xfffffb40 error
```

This happens because the Extensible Storage Engine (ESE) is working to bring all of the databases in a storage group to a uniform state during the recovery process. The ESE tracks all databases in the log files for the storage group to accomplish this task. If a database is omitted, the ESE will generate a 1216 error and will not start the storage group. This issue can be resolved by finding the missing database files and inserting them in the proper locations. If the missing database was deleted or lost, you can restore the missing database from backup. The other databases in the storage group can still be mounted and accessed while you are restoring this database. This can be accomplished by taking the following actions:

1. Run the command – **eseutil /r Log Base Name /I** to enable the ESE to mount the databases at hand while ignoring the missing databases. To run this command you must be logged on with the proper exchange permissions. After executing **eseutil**, all databases that are not present will need to be restored from backup.

2. Mount the databases in the storage group that are now existing and constant.

3. Permit users on the running databases to retrieve their email messages.

4. Restore the missing database from backup.

17

Performance Issues

When you notice that an Exchange 2000 system resource is operating outside suggested performance thresholds, you need to probe that resource in greater detail. This can include the following actions:

➤ Scrutinize the components that you are running and the resources that they require in order to establish if they are satisfactory.

➤ Investigate your hardware and software configurations. The settings should meet or exceed the Microsoft recommendations for the operating system and the supported services.

➤ Think about varying the workload. You may want to process assorted tasks at different times of the day. For a more effective analysis when investigating a particular problem, limit your charting and reporting to specific events occurring at known times.

➤ Examine entries in the event log for the time period when you began to notice the irregular counter values. This information may offer insight into the cause of system performance problems.

For instantaneous diagnosis and problem solving of situations such as shutdowns or logon failures, consider monitoring and logging for a shorter duration. You should repeatedly sample when monitoring over a short time period. Likewise, for long-term forecasting and analysis, you should log for a longer period and set the update interval accordingly. Consider network utilization or hard disk usage as well as other activities that transpire at the times when you see increased resource consumption. Do your best to truly comprehend the usage patterns. They might be associated with specific protocols or computers. Set about making corrections with a scientific approach. For example, do not make more than one modification at a time. Always repeat monitoring after a change so you can corroborate the results and do away with results that are questionable. Be sure to keep precise records of what you accomplish as well as what you discover. When looking at resource bottlenecks, concentrate on the performance objects and counters that relate to the identifiable resource where you believe the issue exists.

Bottlenecks

A bottleneck is simply a hindrance to data transmission through a system's processor or over a Transmission Control Protocol/Internet Protocol (TCP/IP) network. Bottlenecks usually occur when a system's bandwidth will not support the amount of data being relayed at the speed that it is being processed. Bottlenecks affect processor performance by slowing not only the flow of information back and forth between the central processing unit (CPU) and the memory, but also the data transmitted across networks.

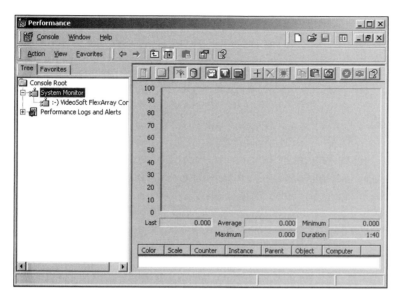

Figure 17.11   The System Monitor.

Windows 2000 System Monitor (Figure 17.11) provides valuable information about performance statistics relating to memory usage, processor usage, server throughput, queue size, and the number of write/read operations per second. You can simply take advantage of System Monitor's preconfigured chart views, which are incorporated into Exchange 2000, to assist your information gathering. The System Monitor will allow you to better enhance system performance and detect resource bottlenecks.

Another basis for using the System Monitor MMC snap-in is to ascertain whether you have a memory leak in the LDAP service when using the Exchange 2000 Migration Wizard, which is a known issue in Exchange 2000. For example, you are using LDAP Migration Wizard to execute multiple scans on large containers; however, the LDAP service will not release memory. For every container that you scan, the service will consume more memory until sooner or later all of the available memory is stolen and CPU usage is throttled at 100 percent. A message from Windows 2000 Server will alert you about low virtual memory when memory gets low. The system will request that you close some noncritical applications to assuage the memory problem.

Issues with Windows 2000 Server Tools

17

Exchange 2000 relies on a number of kernal Windows 2000 Server features and tools to operate. Ironically, you might find it necessary to troubleshoot some of these Windows 2000 Server tools themselves, as seen in the previous paragraph.

Sometimes you may run into a circumstance in which you get an error message signifying that Exchange cannot access the registry because, in this single instance, an incorrect value is detected and the registry cannot update. A solution to this problem is to delete the instance and then add it back. Deleting the instance removes the old instance and allows you to start over. Deleting an instance that has a corrupt registry entry might not be successful, however. You can continue by performing the following procedure.

Warning: Do not use a registry editor to directly edit the registry unless you have no other alternative. The registry editor bypasses the standard safeguards provided by administrative tools. These safeguards are in place to thwart you from entering inconsistent settings or entries that could degrade performance or even harm your system. Direct editing of the registry can have grave and unforeseen consequences that can prevent your system from starting and possibly involve the reinstall of Exchange 2000. To configure or customize Exchange 2000, you should use the applets in Control Panel or MMC whenever feasible.

The proper procedure for removing the external instance completely is as follows:

1. Stop the external instance in the Control Panel | Services dialog box.

2. Remove the instance name from the following registry value:
   HKLM | Software | CurrentControlSet | NT External | Linkage | Export"
   MULTI_SZ

3. Delete the following instance key from the registry:
   HKLM | Software | CurrentControlSet | <Instance Name>

Chapter Summary

This final chapter has introduced not only some powerful troubleshooting methods and strategies, but also specific problems and errors that are documented in Exchange 2000. Whatever your operating system, architecture, infrastructure, or networking environment, some fundamental strategies should be implemented to assist in preventing costly disasters as well as troubleshooting problems. Remember to take the time to study the OSI networking model and your present network architecture to help determine if a lower-layer problem is preventing the upper-layer components from functioning within specifications. When you encounter a connectivity problem on a client computer, your first troubleshooting step should be to check the physical cabling.

Design your Exchange 2000 system to provide replicas of components so that operations can continue even during repair downtime. Formulate an action plan as well as a topology map to identify the most vital components in your messaging system. Along with the topology maps, you will need to document a chronological account of all completed repairs, a schedule of needed maintenance, and tracking mechanisms for all troubleshooting and repair activities.

This chapter provided some excellent measures to take for preventive medicine. It is optimal to avoid making an Exchange 2000 Server system a domain controller. It is also important to keep an accurate record of modifications as well as to document all Exchange server configurations. Furnish your servers with adequate hard disk space to allow for system recovery. Install your servers in a proper and secure environment at all times whenever feasible. Preserve your transaction log files for the directory as well as the information stores on separate hard disks, and use UPSs for server protection. Implement hardware RAID level 5 mirroring whenever feasible, and make sure that the circular logging feature of Exchange 2000 is disabled.

Exchange 2000 Server and Windows 2000 provide a wide array of tools and resource components to assist you in troubleshooting. Several of these tools can also be used remotely to analyze and repair issues throughout the organization. In addition, this chapter explored many solutions and explanations for known issues, errors, and troubleshooting hotspots in Exchange 2000 with regard to installation and setup, common connectivity problems, the Web Storage System, Active Directory and the Active Directory Connector, backup and restore, and performance issues.

Review Questions

1. The use of transaction log files can greatly improve the recovery capabilities of Exchange Server. Therefore, which feature, disabled by default in Exchange 2000, should you verify is turned off as a troubleshooting measure?

   a. Circumference logging

   b. Consistency logging

   c. Circular logging

   d. Capable logging

2. What set of tools will you implement in Exchange 2000 to verify if test messages sent to servers are making the round-trip within a particular length of time?

   a. Diagnostic logs for connectors and services

   b. The Link monitor display and log

   c. The Message Tracking log

   d. Event Viewer

17

3. One of the most common problems during installation occurs when the component used to update the Active Directory schema for Exchange 2000 has problems executing. Which one of the following switches used with the **setup** command can cause this issue?

   a. /adprep

   b. /schemaprep

   c. /domainprep

   d. /forestprep

4. During the installation of Exchange 2000 Server, you receive the following error message:

   ```
   Setup Fails: Error 0xC103798A.
   ```

   What could be the problem?

   a. Setup failed while configuring the registry entries for the Exchange System Management snap-ins.

   b. A component of Exchange Server 5.5 that was previously installed on the server did not completely uninstall.

   c. You are installing Exchange 2000 Server into a child domain.

   d. You ran the Setup/domainprep command, and it failed to execute.

5. You are running Exchange 2000 Setup and you see a message telling you that the directory service is busy. What could be the issue in this scenario?

   a. Setup failed while configuring the registry entries for the Exchange System Management snap-ins.

   b. A component of Exchange Server 5.5 that was previously installed on the server did not completely uninstall.

   c. You are installing Exchange 2000 Server into a child domain.

   d. You ran the Setup/domainprep command, and it failed to execute.

6. Setup crashes when you try to join an Exchange 2000 Server to an existing Exchange Server 5.5 site. You see an error message that states the following:

   ```
   Setup Was Unable to Bind to the Exchange Server.
   ```

   You discover, through troubleshooting, that this error message is typically generated when the account that you are using to initiate the Setup procedure has inadequate or incorrect permissions configured for the target server's Exchange Server 5.5 directory. Which one of the following is a solution to this problem?

    a. Grant your account the Administrator permissions at the Site and Configuration levels of your Exchange 5.5 server.

    b. Run the DomainPrep tool on the Exchange 2000 Server before attempting to join the existing Exchange Server 5.5 site.

    c. Run the ForestPrep tool on the Exchange 2000 Server before attempting to join the existing Exchange Server 5.5 site.

    d. All of the above.

7. While attempting to add a new server to a site, the setup process fails. You reinstall Exchange on the new server to refresh the components that failed when attempting to add the new server. You notice soon after, however, that information about the new server is being replicated to other servers on the site. How do you prevent this from happening?

    a. This replication cannot be prevented because it is by design.

    b. Remove the new server from the site's directory after you reinstall the server.

    c. Remove the new server from the site's directory before you reinstall the server.

    d. You cannot add a new server to an existing site.

8. You are using an Outlook 2000 client with Exchange 2000. You can monitor the path of messages with an Exchange 2000 tool that is located on the Tools menu in System Manager. What is the name of this component?

    a. Queue Viewer

    b. Event Viewer

    c. Message Tracking Center

    d. SMTP node monitor

9. The Internet News Service creates an important special file that it places in the Insdata directory. This file can be the cause of troubleshooting issues with NNTP connectivity in Exchange 2000. If this file is corrupted or lost, Internet News Service creates a new one by default. What is the name of this key file?

    a. Ntp.dat

    b. Nntp.dat

    c. Ins.dat

    d. Ics.dat

17

10. After creating multiple routing groups and subsequently moving servers into these routing groups, messages may no longer flow between the servers in the different routing groups. These messages are immediately returned to their sender with a 5.0.0 error code in a report. What is this report called?

    a. Undeliverable report (UDR)

    b. Nondelivery report (NDR)

    c. Message Undeliverable report (MUR)

    d. Canceled Delivery report (CDR)

11. You suspect that you are having problems with your data storage in the Web Storage System. You need to stop the ExIFS service and then restart it. How can you accomplish this?

    a. Use the Internet Services Manager

    b. Use the Services dialog box in Administrative Tools

    c. Use the net stop and net start commands

    d. Use the Microsoft Internet Explorer

12. You are administering users through Active Directory Users and Computers on a system in which the Exchange System Management tools are not installed. Which of these scenarios is likely to be true under these circumstances? [Check all correct answers]

    a. The Exchange 2000 options may not all be available.

    b. You cannot add, delete, or move an Exchange 2000 mailbox.

    c. You do not see all of the Exchange 2000 extensions.

    d. None of the above.

    e. a, b, and c are correct.

13. You have decided to run Exchange 5.5 Server on a global catalog server or Windows 2000 Server domain controller in a Windows 2000 environment. What must you do to accomplish this?

    a. You must change the LDAP port of the Exchange 5.5 Directory Service to a value different from the default value.

    b. You must change the LDAP port of the Exchange 5.5 Directory Service to 389.

    c. You don't have to do anything; everything should work fine in this scenario.

    d. You cannot run Exchange 5.5 Server on a Windows 2000 global catalog server.

14. You are attempting to perform a backup in your Exchange 2000 infrastructure when you receive the error message:

```
Event ID 1018, 1019, or 1022: Database is damaged.
```

What is this error indicating?

   a. You have deleted logs from the system when performing an offline backup.

   b. You are not using a unique Exchange distinguished name.

   c. You are attempting to mount a storage group with a missing database in an attempt to recover after an unexpected shutdown.

   d. The online backup cannot complete because the database is damaged.

15. What Windows 2000 tool provides information about such performance statistics as processor use, memory use, server throughput, queue size, and number of write/read operations per second?

   a. Event Viewer

   b. System Manager

   c. System Monitor

   d. Active Directory Cleanup Wizard.

Real-World Projects

You are the network administrator in charge of integrating your Windows 2000 troubleshooting processes into the Exchange 2000 deployment. Your management has asked you to lead a team of people on determining solutions for troubleshooting issues.

Project 17.1

Microsoft has released a patch for Exchange 2000 to resolve problems found in the HTTP-DAV protocol implementation. As the Exchange 2000 administrator in charge of troubleshooting, you should also install the related "malformed URL" patch for Internet Information Server 5. A patch for a second WebDAV denial of service vulnerability is now available. Use the Internet to find these fixes.

Project 17.2

The MDB Viewer tool is a 32-bit MAPI 1.0 program that you can utilize to view or modify object properties in a MAPI 1.0 message store. The Exchange Server information store, personal folder files (.pst files), and offline folder files (.ost files) are just a few examples of message stores that you can gain access to by using the

17

MDB Viewer utility. Write a brief report for your team on this tool. You can find more information at **www.microsoft.com/technet/exchange/technote/mdbview.asp**.

Project 17.3

You have discovered that mailboxes are not accessible after your upgrade to Exchange 2000. Locate knowledge base article #Q288840 on the World Wide Web and briefly explain a possible fix for the problem.

CHAPTER EIGHTEEN

Designing Messaging Infrastructure with Microsoft Exchange Server 2000 Sample Exam

Real-world Designing Exchange Server 2000 exam is based on six case studies and a batch of questions following each of them. The number of questions in each scenario may vary, but the total number of questions on the exam is 60, and passing score is set at 690 points. This is a four-hour exam, and for each scenario you will have approximately between 20 and 50 minutes to read the scenario and answer a batch of questions. If you run out of time on one of the scenarios, you will be forced into the next scenario regardless of how many questions you have yet to answer, so be sure to time yourself and mark questions you do not know the answers to for later review if you have some time left. You can move between questions in one scenario, but once you move on to the next scenario you will not be able to return to the previous ones. If you finish any scenario ahead of time, your remaining time will not be transferred to the next scenario, so think of each scenario as a separate little exam within a bigger exam. As you move along in this chapter, try to time yourself, allowing an average of 30-40 minutes per scenario.

Case Study 1: Smoke on Water Corporation—A Leader in Corporate IT Outsourcing

Company Overview

Smoke on Water Corporation is an established leader in computer consulting that primarily serves other businesses, headquartered in Indianapolis, Indiana. It is quickly acquiring other private consulting businesses nationwide. Because of a large influx of cash and other assets, as well as a softening economy, Smoke on Water Corporation has decided to leverage these assets to make mergers and acquisitions a primary corporate goal for the next year. Because Smoke on Water Corporation plans on acquiring dozens of other companies over a relatively short time, the complexity will grow exponentially. Smoke on Water Corporation needs a technology that will enable secure, customizable communications and collaboration within the company, as well as numerous outside partners, advisors, and regulators.

Current Technology Infrastructure

The current technology infrastructure demands sophisticated networking tools that can ensure both high levels of security and maximum openness to enable smooth communications and collaboration. A team of developers at Smoke on Water Corporation has developed a range of tools based on Exchange collaboration platform. Most of these applications are mission-critical, Web-centric, and built on Exchange and other components. Exchange 2000 Server provides Corporation's clients with a range of powerful MIS tools, such as common collaboration areas, secure business process workflow, and integration with Microsoft Office applications.

Smoke on Water Corporation had to produce an application that would grant uninterrupted access to communications, a means for locking down data at the document level to guarantee that private information is protected, and a common "meeting place" where negotiating parties and their advisors could easily work together. Exchange 2000 provides the assimilation of the different components, such as the Web functionality, the data-storage tools, and a user-friendly environment for every task from sharing documents to organizing meetings. With Exchange 2000, it is much easier and faster to develop a fully customized and secure Web application. Because Smoke on Water Corporation has been creating collaborative solutions for business since 1998, it is able to leverage the power of the new and enhanced features in Exchange 2000 to develop an entirely new and rich application for the merger and acquisition process. These features include areas described in the following paragraphs.

Network and User Base

Currently, Smoke on Water Corporation has offices in 10 locations across North America, headquartered in Indianapolis. Most of these locations are connected to corporate Frame Relay network of 512 Kbps with a CIR of 64 Mbps, but certain high-volume offices are connected over a T1. WAN upgrade hasn't been budgeted, despite phenomenal growth that the Corporation is experiencing. Management believes that it's more cost-effective to consolidate WAN resources of the companies that Smoke on Water Corporation is acquiring. Current user base is approximately 27,500 email and public folder users, and is broken down as follows:

➤ Indianapolis, Indiana—8,000 users

➤ New York, New York—2,000 users

➤ Toronto, Ontario—5,000 users

➤ Montreal, Quebec—2,000 users

➤ Vancouver, British Columbia—500 users

➤ Seattle, Washington—1,500 users

➤ San Francisco, California—2,500 users

➤ Los Angeles, California—4,500 users

➤ Houston, Texas—1,200 users

➤ Miami, Florida—300 users

Most of the messaging needs of Smoke on Water Corporation are contained within individual offices' locations, although a fair amount of traffic constantly travels across corporate WAN. At each location, there are services to provide dial-in connectivity, and roaming users must be able to use the system in realtime (including messaging, calendaring and scheduling, and public folders) while on business trips. In each location, there is a local administrative team that is responsible for all day-to-day administration, and a central HQ IT team is managing all the AD and security-related matters.

Active Directory Integration

The combination of Exchange 2000 with the Microsoft Windows 2000 Active Directory service simplifies management of Exchange. This is definitely a major concern for anyone using these tools. Smoke on Water Corporation has successfully migrated to Windows 2000 platform last month. Their AD design is a single forest, single domain, with multiple sites that are mapped to regional offices.

Hardware

Smoke on Water Corporation ran lab stress-tests and determined that their current hardware is capable of providing adequate response times when hosting up to 1,500 mailbox-enabled users per server. They also concluded that each server would generate on average 35 global catalog queries per second. Their GC servers can handle close to 150 queries per second each.

Item-Level Security

The capability to institute granular security settings at the individual document level results in firm control of access to information. Item-level security is one of the key enhancements that makes Exchange 2000 a powerful platform for enabling collaboration among varying persons and parties in mergers and acquisitions.

Integration with Microsoft Office

Office 2000 users will store and retrieve Office documents directly to and from the Microsoft Web Storage System, using the standard Save As and Open commands. This is valuable for Smoke on Water because most users have standardized on Microsoft Office. This standardization provides a dependable design as well as a toolkit for administering email and documents in concert. The main Microsoft application being deployed includes the following:

➤ Microsoft Office 2000

➤ Microsoft Visual Studio 6

➤ Microsoft Visio

18

Interview with the Network Administrator

"The goal behind our web-based tools is to create a solid, Web-based component that could be used by all the various industry professionals who want to expand their organizations. The logic behind it is to offer a method for assisting all the parties in acquiring, storing and sharing critical information in the IT cycles, so that they can more completely manage the process of successfully integrating new technologies. Exchange 2000 looks like the best of the breed for our collaboration development at Smoke on Water Corporation."

"We are looking at a number of likely strategies for our new infrastructure, including implementing multiple Exchange servers that are dedicated to conferencing and mail, as well as implementing MADCAP technology. The tight integration of Exchange 2000 and the other Microsoft applications and technologies is allowing us to craft an extremely useful, customizable, and secure program that meets the rigid needs of the merger and acquisition processes. It also enables highly effective collaboration and communication within our company and with our partners and advisors."

Your Role

You are employed as the chief systems architect. You have put together an IT team to integrate all the tools into the present system. Your team is responsible for the corporate network infrastructure and for the servers at the corporate office in Indianapolis. Your team will also be responsible for the huge task of integrating the systems of other mergers and acquisitions.

Your team has three tasks before it. First, your team's primary short-term task is to develop a migration platform for this new acquisition to an Exchange 2000 solution. Second, you need to deploy collaboration services between your organizations. The third, and main, objective will be to implement reliable data archiving and disaster recovery plan.

Question:: 1.1

You are considering Exchange 2000 client planning for Smoke on Water Corporation. When deploying clients for roaming users, what software should you select to meet Smoke on Water's requirements?

○ a.   Microsoft Outlook 2000 in corporate mode

○ b.   Microsoft Outlook Express with IMAP4 and NNTP

○ c.   Microsoft Outlook Web Access

○ d.   Microsoft Outlook 98

Question:: 1.2

Smoke on Water Corporation is entering the final stage of acquiring another company, and the deal is likely to close in a couple of days. You were assigned to provision for Exchange deployment in the new location. Network engineering team established ISDN BRI (128 Kbps) connectivity between the new office and the HQ. Proposed solution is to have 20 clients run Outlook 2000 on remote end and connect to HQ Exchange servers using MAPI.

○ a. This solution is the preferred way and satisfies the requirements of Smoke on Water Corporation.

○ b. This solution does not provide adequate performance for end-users because there is not enough bandwidth.

○ c. This solution does not provide adequate security to satisfy company requirements.

○ d. This solution does not provide access to scheduling information.

Question:: 1.3

How many Exchange 2000 mailbox servers should you deploy to serve users in Indianapolis?

○ a. 4

○ b. 6

○ c. 7

○ d. 8

Question:: 1.4

How would you deploy Exchange 2000 routing groups?

○ a. In accord with corporation requirements for centralized security and routing administration, create one routing group for the entire corporation in Indianapolis.

○ b. Create one routing group for each remote location. Add remote servers to corresponding routing groups.

○ c. Create one routing group for each remote location. Add remote servers to corresponding routing groups. Create one routing group for HQ location and add HQ servers to that group. Place all routing groups in one administrative group and delegate control to centralized management team in HQ.

○ d. Create one routing group for each remote location. Add remote servers to corresponding routing groups. Create one routing group for HQ location and add HQ servers to that group. Place all routing groups in one administrative group and delegate control to remote locations on a group-by-group basis.

18

Question:: 1.5

You want to ensure database recoverability to the point of failure. You want to make sure you are able to restore databases in the least amount of time. How should you design your backup strategy?

- ○ a. Enable circular logging. Backup individual databases.
- ○ b. Disable circular logging. Backup individual databases.
- ○ c. Enable circular logging. Backup individual storage groups.
- ○ d. Disable circular logging. Backup individual storage groups.

Question:: 1.6

You want to use mail-enabled groups to provide management with an easy way of communicating information to employees and partners. How would you implement this in the most efficient and convenient way?

- ○ a. Create mail-enabled Global Groups that are mapped to departments and populate them with employees. Nest these groups in a hierarchical manner.
- ○ b. Create mail-enabled Local Groups that are mapped to departments and populate them with employees.
- ○ c. Create mail-enabled USG groups that are mapped to departments and populate them with employees. Nest these groups in a hierarchical manner.
- ○ d. Create mail-enabled UDG groups that are mapped to departments and populate them with employees.

Question:: 1.7

You want to implement Exchange 2000 servers in Smoke on Water's headquarters so that the infrastructure becomes less susceptible to Denial-of-Service attacks to ensure email service is available at all times. How should you do that?

- ○ a. Implement clustering solution and make two servers host the same storage groups.
- ○ b. Implement several storage groups and spread users across several databases within those storage groups.
- ○ c. Accept all incoming email messages to a UNIX server and have it as a smarthost that will be relaying mail to your Exchange 2000 servers.
- ○ d. Implement several front-end servers to accept incoming connections.

Question:: 1.8

You are deploying Outlook Web Access infrastructure for the Smoke on Water Corporation. Which ports should you open on the firewall between OWA clients and OWA server to enable client access to email, scheduling, and public folder information?

○ a. HTTP, SSL

○ b. HTTP, SSL, IMAP4, RPC

○ c. HTTP, SSL, POP3, SMTP, IMAP4

○ d. HTTP, MAPI

Question:: 1.9

You are configuring ADC connection agreements for Smoke on Water Corporation and your assignment is to ensure that both Exchange 5.5 and Exchange 2000 directories can be managed throughout migration phase from a single location. How would you set up your ADC?

○ a. Configure one-way connection agreement to one Exchange 5.5 site in Indianapolis.

○ b. Configure two-way connection agreement to one Exchange 5.5 site in Indianapolis.

○ c. Configure one-way connection agreement to each Exchange 5.5 site.

○ d. Configure two-way connection agreement to each Exchange 5.5 site.

Question:: 1.10

When installing your first Exchange 2000 server in Smoke on Water Corporation, there are a few necessary steps that you must take to prepare Active Directory for Exchange and extend its schema. What steps must you take to deploy your first Exchange 2000 server? [Check all correct answers]

❏ a. Run setup.exe with /forestprep switch.

❏ b. Run setup.exe with /domainprep switch.

❏ c. Run setup.exe to install Exchange 2000 Server.

❏ d. Configure ADC to replicate between Exchange 2000 and Exchange 5.5.

18

Case Study 2: TechnoGrip University

Company Overview

TechnoGrip University of Scottsdale, Arizona offers undergraduate and graduate programs and certificates targeted chiefly to mid-career IT professionals. The university's 85,000 students spend three weeks a year on campus and the remainder of their studies are made up of online learning from their home or office. The business scenario of TechnoGrip University is to create a compelling distance-learning program, featuring online chat communities and Instant Messaging. These capabilities must be built on familiar productivity tools and they must be secure enough to allow for anywhere, anytime learning.

Current Technology Infrastructure

The solution that has been implemented is a Windows 2000 Advanced Server operating system platform, Microsoft Exchange Server 2000 for online collaboration, a SQL Server 7 database as the knowledge object engine, and Active Server Pages to provide the templates. TechnoGrip will also use Office 2000 and Outlook 2000 as a client-side solution.

The solution is built completely on the Microsoft platform: Microsoft Exchange Server 2000 will provide the secure and robust infrastructure for collaborative assignments, calendars, and general communications. A custom Office 2000 application delivers information to desktops in a simple, consolidated view. Students are capable of working at their own pace. They can also access course material anywhere and at anytime, 24 hours a day and 7 days a week (in theory), from home or workplace. They can collaborate with other students in realtime to complete assignments, share ideas and strategies, debate concepts as a team, and—when necessary—collaborate with instructors.

Interview with the Vice President and Network Administrator

"We need our online course material to function in similar fashion to an e-commerce solution. We decided to drive it from a SQL database and then modify and deliver according to the students' needs and preferences. Students must be able to work at their own pace and be able to access the course material at a convenient time and place, whether that is during the day or late at night, at home or at their workplace. This is key to the success of our business model. Our online learning community needs to assist learners in collaborating with other students in realtime to complete assignments, share ideas and strategies, debate issues as a team, and counsel with instructors."

"We chose Exchange Server 2000 because it integrates with the Windows 2000 operating system Active Directory service, provides coordinated administration using the Microsoft Windows 2000 MMC, and provides native access to Internet mail content. We must be able to allow our instructors, many of whom do not have the network technical expertise to use these tools, with a way to access and manage students and content using a Web browser interface. This is going to be made possible by Active Server Page technology, stored procedures in the database, and WBEM."

"We need to create drop boxes where students can post assignments, or post reviews of other people's assignments, and have those be anonymous to other students. Our Exchange 2000 Server solution should also allow students to incorporate course deadlines into electronic journals and handheld computers so their personal, professional and educational lives are always in sync. What we hope to end up with is a robust, secure platform that is flexible enough for students to use at their convenience, whether from a Web interface or an Outlook client."

Your Role

Your role is that of a private consultant who has been hired after a previous company was unable to meet the needs or live up to their promises to TechnoGrip University. All of the software and hardware solutions are purchased and in place—for the most part. Your immediate role is to turn a collection of Exchange 2000 servers into a robust Instant Messaging and realtime collaboration platform.

Question:: 2.1

You are designing Microsoft Chat Service and considering what client requirements you should impose. TechnoGrip University is an e-commerce initiative that will become open to international students in many languages. You want to have an ability to enable chat sessions in various languages. What requirement must your chat clients meet to support it?

○ a. Client software must adhere to IRCX specification proposed by Microsoft.

○ b. You cannot do this in Chat Service.

○ c. Client software must adhere to IRC industry standards.

○ d. Client software must adhere to IRCE specification proposed by Microsoft.

Question:: 2.2

Based on current user base, how many chat servers should you deploy?

○ a. 2

○ b. 3

○ c. 4

○ d. 5

18

Question:: 2.3

What hardware must you ensure is available for each of the planned chat service servers to provide adequate response times?

○ a. One CPU, 256MB RAM

○ b. Two CPU, 512MB RAM

○ c. Three CPU, 512MB RAM

○ d. Four CPU, 1GB RAM

Question:: 2.4

What channel mode is the most appropriate when lecturing to a large number of students simultaneously?

○ a. Cloneable

○ b. Auditorium

○ c. Moderated

○ d. Classroom

Question:: 2.5

Which ports must you enable on the University firewall so that students will be able to access chat channels? [Check all correct answers]

❑ a. 667

❑ b. 6667

❑ c. Any IRC port(s) that is (are) assigned to existing channel(s)

❑ d. HTTP

Question:: 2.6

How would you protect your chat service from cloning attacks?

- ○ a. Impose bandwidth limits
- ○ b. Impose message-processing delays
- ○ c. Impose maximum IP connections limit
- ○ d. Impose masking of DNS names and IP addresses

Question:: 2.7

Based on Microsoft's IM specification, how many HomeServers should you deploy to host instant messaging clients?

- ○ a. 3
- ○ b. 5
- ○ c. 7
- ○ d. 9

Question:: 2.8

Based on Microsoft's specification and your single-domain design of TechnoGrip University, how many IM Router servers would you need to support your IM infrastructure? [Check all correct answers]

- ❑ a. 3
- ❑ b. 5
- ❑ c. 7
- ❑ d. 9

18

Question:: 2.9

What default port(s) should you allow in and out of your secure network to enable RVP instant messaging protocol communication?

○ a. XML, HTTP

○ b. HTTP

○ c. HTTP, RVP

○ d. RVP, XML

Question:: 2.10

Your instant messaging service DNS records should exist for each IM Router in order to enable direct email namespace to map to IM namespace and to load-balance your IM servers. What is the format of this record?

○ a. _rvp._tcp.technogripu.com SRV 0 0 80 im.technogripu.com

○ b. _xml._tcp.technogripu.com SRV 0 0 80 im.technogripu.com

○ c. _http._tcp.technogripu.com SRV 0 0 80 im.technogripu.com

○ d. _im._tcp.technogripu.com SRV 0 0 80 im.technogripu.com

Case Study 3: Springfield Fashion Ltd.

Company Overview

Springfield Fashion Ltd. is a retail department store chain that concentrates on selling moderately priced clothing and household goods from 80 stores throughout the world. The corporation has grown at an average rate of three new stores every year since the company's inception. The Springfield Fashion Ltd. corporate management team requires a computing environment that is flexible enough to support this level of growth. All operations are managed from the corporate office in Oakville, Ontario. The corporate officers include a President and three Executive Vice-Presidents (EVPs). One EVP is in charge of the Clothing division, another EVP is accountable for the Household Goods division, and the third EVP is responsible for the Facilities and Transport (F&T) division. Each division has approximately 2,000 employees. Of these 2,000 employees, there are about 200 managerial positions, roughly the same amount of lawyers, and the same amount of accountants. In case of disaster, it is required that managerial positions are restored and brought back online in less then an hour, lawyers in less then two hours, accountants in less then three hours, and all the rest in less than four hours.

Buyers who belong to one of the departments in each division are responsible for purchasing merchandise to be sold at the company's stores. These buyers are based out of the corporate office. Springfield Fashion has agreements with a core group of vendors from whom the buyers purchase merchandise. Members of the F&T Division are responsible for acquiring property for new stores, coordinating the construction of new stores, maintaining the existing store facilities, and transporting goods from distribution centers to each of the stores. There is a distribution center in each region.

Current Technology Infrastructure

Each division has one or more Information Technology (IT) teams. The IT department in the F&T Division is responsible for the corporate network and for implementing applications that are common to all stores, such as the Point of Sale (POS) and Inventory applications. There are five IT teams in the F&T division. One of the teams works at the corporate office and each of the other four teams works in one of the regions.

There are six servers at the corporate office that run Novell NetWare version 4.11. There are also two servers at the corporate office that run Windows NT Server 4. There are approximately 500 client computers at the corporate office running Windows 98. The computers at each store run Windows 98. There is a computer terminal at each checkout counter on which the POS application is installed. There are 50 to 100 computers per store, including the computers used for the checkout counters. A NetWare server is in place at each distribution center, and approximately 125 client computers are running Windows 98. The cashiers who operate the computer terminals at the checkout counters are members of the F&T division.

Interview with the Senior IT Manager

"We have some very detailed plans for growing our computing infrastructure here at Springfield Fashion. We want all computers running Windows 98 to be upgraded to Windows 2000 Professional or replaced with computers running Windows 2000 Professional. Our existing NetWare servers running GroupWise will continue to be used for the next year, but new servers running Windows 2000 Advanced Server will be purchased. All applications will eventually be installed on the computers running Windows 2000 Advanced Server, and existing data and mail will be moved from the NetWare servers running GroupWise to the new Windows 2000 servers and migrated to an Exchange 2000 mail and collaboration solution.

We do not currently have a Web site on the Internet, but management wants to implement one as part of the upgrade. The Web site will not be used for electronic commerce but will instead serve as a source of general information about Springfield Fashion and its stores. As Springfield Fashion Ltd transitions from a NetWare/GroupWise-based network to a Windows 2000/Exchange 2000-based network, we want to minimize the impact on users and overall productivity.

18

Your Role

You are one of the several IT consultants hired by Springfield Fashion Ltd to implement Exchange 2000 environment. You are not responsible for Novell GroupWise migration; however, you must ensure that highest data fault tolerance and recoverability standards are met. Company has ideas about leveraging the features of Exchange 2000, such as public folders and Outlook Web Access to increase overall productivity—and you were asked to help evaluate these features.

Question: 3.1

You have a disaster-recovery plan in place. You placed transaction logs on one disk subsystem, and databases on another one. On Sunday night, full backup was performed successfully, and then incremental backups were performed on Monday, Tuesday, Wednesday, Thursday, and Friday. On Saturday, one of the databases became corrupted. How would you restore your database to the point of failure?

- a. You cannot restore this database to the point of failure because Incremental backup purges transaction logs.

- b. You should restore this database from the last full backup and then restore the latest incremental backup tape.

- c. You should restore this database from the last full backup, then restore all the tapes made on Monday through Friday.

- d. You should restore this database from the last full backup, then restore all the tapes made on Monday through Friday, and finally replay transaction logs between last incremental backup and database disaster.

Question: 3.2

How should you design your disk subsystem to ensure maximum reliability and performance?

- a. Place the system partition on duplexed RAID-1 subsystem, transaction logs on a RAID-5 subsystem, and databases on a different RAID-5 subsystem. Enable circular logging.

- b. Place the system partition on duplexed RAID-1 subsystem, transaction logs on a RAID-5 subsystem, and databases on a different RAID-5 subsystem. Disable circular logging.

- c. Place the system partition on RAID-0 subsystem, transaction logs on a RAID-5 subsystem, and databases on a different RAID-5 subsystem. Disable circular logging.

- d. Place the system partition on duplexed RAID-1 subsystem, transaction logs on a RAID-0 subsystem, and databases on a different RAID-0 subsystem. Disable circular logging.

Question: 3.3

To meet Springfield Fashion's internal SLA requirements, how should you design storage groups in each location to ensure that user mailboxes can be restored in a limited amount of time and in order of priority?

○ a.   Create four storage groups for each of the four employee categories. Split employees in smaller groups within storage groups and put them in separate databases.

○ b.   Create one database per each of the four employee categories within one storage group.

○ c.   Create one database to simplify backup and restore procedures and place all your users in that database.

○ d.   Create four storage groups for each of the four employee categories. Put all employees in one database within each storage group.

Question: 3.4

You are designing backup strategy for Springfield Fashion. You want to ensure that database recovery reliability and time requirements are met. What must you backup besides your Exchange 2000 databases to ensure that you can recover the system in the quickest time? [Check all correct answers]

❑ a.   System state

❑ b.   System partition

❑ c.   pagefile.sys file

❑ d.   Windows Metabase

Question: 3.5

You want to ensure that Springfield Fashion managers communicate among themselves in a secure way. How would you do this?

○ a.   Implement VPN solution

○ b.   Implement IPSec in your network

○ c.   Use digital certificates in Outlook to encrypt email messages

○ d.   Implement SSL in your network

18

Question: 3.6

How should you place your OWA servers to provide maximum security from inbound connections that come from the Internet?

○ a. To ease administration, place OWA servers on the same network segment as Exchange 2000 servers.

○ b. Place OWA servers outside your network directly connected to the Internet so that your clients are able to access it.

○ c. Place OWA servers between your external firewall and Exchange 2000 servers.

○ d. Place OWA servers into the DMZ zone.

Question: 3.7

You come in early on Monday morning and discover that one of your main Exchange 2000 servers crashed during the night and cannot be booted up due to a major software problem. How would you rectify this situation?

○ a. Blame it on the power surges and unreliable power supply from the local power station.

○ b. Get a replacement box similar in terms of hardware to the one that failed. Install Windows 2000 on it, perform system state restore, perform Exchange installation, restore databases, and—if possible—replay logs from the failed server's disks.

○ c. Get a replacement box similar in terms of hardware to the one that failed. Install Windows 2000 on it, perform system partition restore, perform system state restore, perform Exchange installation with the /disasterrecovery switch, restore databases, and—if possible—replay logs from the failed server's disks.

○ d. Get a replacement box similar in terms of hardware to the one that failed. Install Windows 2000 on it, perform system partition restore, perform system state restore, perform Exchange installation, restore databases, and—if possible—replay logs from the failed server's disks.

Question: 3.8

Your central location suffered a disaster that resulted in a complete loss of existing Windows 2000 DC and Exchange servers. Luckily, the company followed your recommendation and stored updated copies of backup tapes off-site. What are your steps in rectifying this situation?

- a. Order replacement boxes, install Windows 2000 on DC server and Exchange server(s), restore system partition and system state, and restore Exchange server databases.

- b. Order replacement boxes, install Windows 2000 on DC server and Exchange server(s), restore system partition and system state, reinstall Exchange server, and restore databases.

- c. Order replacement boxes, install Exchange server(s), restore system partition and system state, reinstall Exchange server with /disasterrecovery switch, re-create Windows 2000 on DC server and restore AD, restore databases, and replay logs—if possible—to recover them from the old disks.

- d. Order replacement boxes, install Windows 2000 on DC server and Exchange server(s), restore AD, system partition, and system state, reinstall Exchange server with /disasterrecovery switch, restore databases, and replay logs—if possible—to recover them from the old disks.

Question: 3.9

You are proposing public folder design, and among the requirements of Springfield Fashion are performance and capability to conduct effective searches on the contents of public stores. The company plans to use public folders extensively within its HQ location to support decision-making and store company data in the organized manner. What would be the best solution to meet these needs?

- a. Place public folder store on the mail servers in Exchange, but ensure it is defined in a different storage group. To enable searches within attachments stored in the messages of public folders you will have to program an application that will be taking the contents and indexing it in a SQL server on a regular basis.

- b. Place public folder store on the mail servers in Exchange, but ensure it is defined in a different storage group. Enable full-text indexing to make the contents searchable.

- c. Place public folder store on a separate dedicated Exchange server. To enable searches within attachments stored in the messages of public folders you will have to program an application that will be taking the contents and indexing it in a SQL server on a regular basis.

- d. Place public folder store on a separate dedicated Exchange server. Enable full-text indexing to make the contents searchable.

18

Question: 3.10

Certain portions of public folder tree in the corporate headquarters should be made accessible to remote branches—these branches use only a limited amount of information within that folder, but they use it heavily. This information changes several times a week. How should you design for this?

○ a. Have all remote offices access central location.

○ b. Replicate all public folders on a regular basis to remote servers.

○ c. Replicate regularly only those public folders to remote locations that are needed.

○ d. You cannot replicate public folder content; you have to upgrade WAN connection speeds.

Case Study 4: Plus Ultra Group Entertainment

Company Overview

Plus Ultra Group Entertainment administers 15 different Web sites around the world as part of the operations of their online entertainment venture that offers customers music information, chat sites, and other online entertainment. When Plus Ultra Group Entertainment split off from its parent company, it had to decide about a messaging platform that would be easy to deploy and manage; yet it still had to supply commanding communications capabilities for 24 × 7 global operations.

In its push to become one of the biggest entertainment brands around, Plus Ultra Group Entertainment has followed many different technology and marketing options to draw in customers in the dynamic music entertainment industry.

Plus Ultra Group Entertainment has built a strong global presence on the Internet, operating a variety of entertainment Web portals. To keep the Web presence running in top form and to produce the advertising sales that keep the sites going, Plus Ultra Group Entertainment employs about 8,000 people in several offices around the planet. Its main office is in New York, and satellite operations are in Los Angeles, Toronto, London, and Tokyo. With such a detached workforce, the company's messaging infrastructure is essential to the efficient operation of a competitive enterprise in a swiftly evolving industry.

To keep its employees in continuous communications with each another, the leaders of Plus Ultra Group Entertainment made a strategic resolution to deploy Exchange 2000 Server as its messaging and collaboration platform. Exchange 2000 Server will provide performance and stability for the company's infrastructure. It will also provide advanced features like enhanced Web access and Instant Messaging that will ultimately help Plus Ultra Group Entertainment employees do their jobs more easily and efficiently.

Current Technology Infrastructure

Within any given week, the message flow at Plus Ultra Group Entertainment can exceed 1.5GB inbound and 3GB outbound. This number is a lot of messaging traffic for a company of around 8,000 employees. Exchange 2000 Server provides a number of features that will be needed to improve the communications and collaborations throughout Plus Ultra Group Entertainment. The company plans on implementing the following technologies:

➤ Enhanced Web Access and WebDAV—These technologies will offer support for documents formatted in Extensible Markup Language (XML) and HTML as well as other data. Exchange 2000 support for Microsoft Web Distributed Authoring and Versioning (WebDAV) will be necessary because Plus Ultra Group Entertainment needs this HTTP-based protocol to allow users to collaborate on documents via the Web, regardless of the applications used to create the content. Also, WebDAV support in Exchange 2000 will let Plus Ultra Group Entertainment store documents directly into Exchange, which makes replicated document management and team-based authoring possible.

➤ Microsoft Web Storage System—This will also be implemented by Plus Ultra Group so that the Exchange 2000 Web support can improve workflow through the use of the Web and public folders to simplify the flow and management of project-related data and documents.

➤ Integration with Microsoft Windows 2000 Microsoft Active Directory Service—This addition is also a must for the company. In the past, they had a user management utility and a directory service inside Exchange, which demanded making the same change to a user profile twice. They now need to have the user account and other information in the same directory so that it will be easier and faster to create and modify user accounts. They will also be using Active Directory Connector, which is included in both Exchange 2000 and Windows 2000, to create an entirely new messaging infrastructure while easily linking messaging systems.

➤ Policy-Based Administration—Coriolis Entertainment also wants to employ this feature, which will allow them to easily establish policies for people at various levels in the management structure.

➤ Instant Messaging Services—This feature will help reduce the strain on network resources while providing a channel for fast intradepartmental communications. Because Instant Messaging relies on a federated architecture, IM will reduce the overall load on the Exchange Server. Support for Multi-user Conferencing will also be necessary. Plus Ultra Group Entertainment needs Exchange 2000's support of on-demand sharing of data and information using any T.120-compliant client is helping improve their communications with the deployment of Microsoft NetMeeting conferencing software.

18

Plus Ultra Group Entertainment is implementing Exchange 2000 Server, using features such as Web support, Active Directory integration, and Instant Messaging. Exchange 2000 Server is highly stable and scalable, ensuring 24×7 messaging for employees in different offices and time zones. Instant Messaging will reduce the strain on system resources, while Web support will provide easy access to the Plus Ultra Group Entertainment messaging system. Plus Ultra Group is still relying on Exchange 5.5 during the transition period to Exchange 2000. Here is the other software that is being used:

➤ Microsoft Exchange 2000 Server

➤ Microsoft Windows 2000 Server

➤ Microsoft Internet Information Services 5

➤ Microsoft Visual Studio 6

Interview with the Vice President of Operations

"We looked at the best options in a messaging platform and decided that it would have to be fast, reliable, and enhance good communications throughout the company. Our previous parent company had already implemented Exchange 5.5, and we saw that continuing with Exchange for Plus Ultra Group Entertainment would be appropriate for ensuring seamless company-wide communications. Exchange 5.5 has worked well for Plus Ultra Group Entertainment, and the IT team's decision to migrate to Exchange 2000 Server is a sound one that is fully supported by the rest of the management."

"We wanted to be a leader in all categories, including our technology. We realized that one of the best ways to make our users more productive was to improve their experience at their desktops and communications between individuals and groups, regardless of where they were physically located. We are a Web- and technology-focused company, and we didn't want the limitations of a 9-to-5 company. Exchange 2000 Server offered almost everything we could imagine to improve the users' experience and productivity, both in and out of the office."

Your Role

You are the manager of messaging technology and operational systems for Plus Ultra Group Entertainment. It is your job to have a comprehensive understanding of all the new technologies to be deployed in this design. You are the head of the Exchange 5.5-to-Exchange 2000 upgrade/migration campaign. You are also responsible for selecting team leaders to assist you with the many new technology implementations. The Web Development department also answers to you, and you answer to the Vice President of Operations.

Question: 4.1

After careful consideration, you have decided to implement USG groups to enable broadcast communications. How do you ensure that its use is controlled and managed in an effective manner? [Check all correct answers]

❏ a. In Exchange System Manager, designate who can send messages to this group.

❏ b. In Active Directory, designate who can send messages to this group.

❏ c. In Exchange System Manager, designate size limits of the message that can be sent.

❏ d. In Active Directory, designate size limits of the message that can be sent.

Question: 4.2

You have only one domain in Plus Ultra Group Entertainment that uses Exchange 5.5 and 2000 and Windows 2000 and NT domain controllers, and you want to deploy Universal Security Groups but cannot. What is the reason?

○ a. Universal groups are not available in mixed mode.

○ b. USG groups are not available in mixed mode.

○ c. UDG groups are not available in mixed mode.

○ d. Universal groups are not available in migration mode.

Question: 4.3

Departments that used NT 4 had many NT domains. Plus Ultra Group Entertainment has implemented a separate resource domain strictly for Exchange servers. These resource domains will not be necessary in Windows 2000. What design characteristic of Windows 2000 will effectively deal with this?

○ a. In the Windows 2000 architecture, enterprise domains take the place of resource domains eliminating the need for separate resource domains that form administrative and security boundaries.

○ b. In the Windows 2000 architecture, all of your resource domains will actually stay intact and will be seamlessly integrated into Active Directory.

○ c. In the Windows 2000 architecture, child domains will substitute for resource domains and will remove the need for separate resource domains.

○ d. None of the above answers are correct.

Question: 4.4

With Exchange 2000, Plus Ultra Group Entertainment employees have the ability to use the Exchange information Web Store as the single location for managing documents and versioning because of which of the following specifications?

○ a. XML

○ b. HTTP WebDAV

○ c. ASP

○ d. Storage Groups

Question: 4.5

Which of the following components is the Windows 2000/Exchange 2000 equivalent of the Exchange 5.5 Distribution List?

○ a. Active Directory public folder

○ b. Active Directory mail-enabled contact or user

○ c. Active Directory mail-enabled group

○ d. Active Directory mailbox-enabled group

Question: 4.6

You want to protect areas of your organization from the data-recovery process by placing transaction logs and databases on a RAID configuration. Which of the following RAID solutions would work best for this scenario?

○ a. RAID-0

○ b. RAID-1

○ c. RAID-3

○ d. RAID-5

Question: 4.7

Which of the following are the general types of policies that are implemented in Exchange 2000? [Check all correct answers]

❑ a. System policies

❑ b. Server policies

❑ c. Public folder policies

❑ d. Recipient policies

Question: 4.8

Which of the following supplemental components is a customized Exchange 5.5 directory that works on the Exchange 2000 server to assist replication between Exchange 2000 and the residual Exchange 5.5 servers?

○ a. SNMP

○ b. SMS

○ c. SRS

○ d. SMTP

Question: 4.9

Which of the following represent the different types of Active Directory connectors? [Check all correct answers]

❑ a. Supplemental ADC

❑ b. Enhanced ADC for Exchange 2000

❑ c. ADC for Windows 2000

❑ d. Enhanced ADC for Windows 2000

Question: 4.10

With Exchange 2000, the post-migration organization will have far fewer replication partners. Why is this so?

○ a. Every Exchange Server 5.5 server takes part in the Active Directory information-replication process.

○ b. Windows 2000 replicates much less data than a typical Exchange 5.5 design.

○ c. Exchange 2000 exists in a native mode organization to work with all Exchange 5.5 servers as if they were still in an Exchange Server 5.5 organization.

○ d. Exchange 2000 uses Windows 2000 Active Directory instead of a separate Directory Store.

Case Study 5: IT Professional Consulting Corporation

Company Overview

Headquartered in Monaco, IT Professional Consulting Corp is one of the largest European consultants, employing more than 16,000 employees in 50 offices in Western Europe, with more than 50,000 customers. Additionally, IT Professional Consulting has acted as a true business partner to help organizations of all sizes manage their existing technology investments, take advantage of new technologies, and maintain control of their business from a technological perspective. IT Professional Consulting produces various customized enterprise software for critical core-business processes in the areas of finance, manufacturing, distribution/logistics, and human resources. The company also provides industry-specific technology solutions for a number of complex business sectors.

Current Technology Infrastructure

Historically, IT Professional Consulting has implemented a variety of messaging systems, and the most recent is Lotus Notes. This has made it challenging for IT Professional Consulting to keep support and training costs low as well as to maximize internal or external communications. The company upgraded to Exchange 5.5 in most areas several years back, while keeping Human Resources and other areas on Notes. Because messaging is mission-critical at IT Professional Consulting, the company is implementing Exchange 2000 Server, which will allow the organization to centralize everything and better meet their service-level needs.

By implementing Exchange 2000, IT Professional Consulting should be able to reduce support and training costs caused by multiple email systems. IT Professional Consulting decided to move to a single infrastructure based on Microsoft products: Exchange 2000 Server, Microsoft Office XP, and Microsoft Windows 2000 Professional.

Many groups within IT Professional Consulting will benefit from Exchange Server. In particular will be the Training Department. The Training group would like to move from Notes to Exchange calendaring to manage its training schedules. A large percentage of business communications that are with external customers and business partners now takes place through email. Combining everything into Exchange 2000 will be a tremendous benefit to an organization that will need to quickly disseminate information to customers as well as internal employees.

IT Professional Consulting Corporation plans on using the Public Folders feature of the Outlook and Exchange platform extensively. The company will use Public Folders to support many IT project management efforts, as well as Human Resource documentation. Eventually, the majority (if not all) of the company's users will always have Outlook running so they will have an integrated interface to manage information. The company's executives will also employ Public Folders to gather and organize meeting agenda items and manage daily business activities.

Cost of ownership is an increasingly important variable in corporate-messaging decisions for IT Professional Consulting. It expects this new Exchange 2000 solution to eventually decrease cost of ownership. Also, the clustering capability of Exchange 2000 should increase reliability and decrease required downtime, while the single Active Directory service will reduce current administration costs associated with maintaining both Windows 2000 and Exchange directories. Dial-up costs associated with Outlook Web Access usage will also be reduced.

The most critical ingredient for Exchange 2000 is a well-implemented Windows 2000 operating system. This is because the two systems are so integrated. Training administration personnel on Windows 2000 and involving them in Exchange 2000 planning and testing from the beginning is a key strategy for IT Professional Consulting.

Interview with the Senior Network Architect

"Since we have an assortment of different messaging systems in place, this decision to migrate to Exchange 2000 should hopefully reduce the long-term support and training costs. Consolidation will also help IT Professional Consulting to limit the number of interoperability issues. Messaging has become a mission-critical application at IT Professional Consulting; therefore, Exchange 2000 Server will provide many enhancements to better meet our service-level agreements. That is the real benefit of Exchange 2000."

"We plan to implement Instant Messaging as a possible value-added feature for our users when rolling out Exchange 2000. The company is also contemplating how to best implement Web pages as a front end to Public Folders. There is a lot of potential here, and we plan to initially roll this technology into Human Resources and, possibly, the Training Department. I expect to see a union of voice and data occurring pretty rapidly at IT Professional Consulting as well. We have a large number of

18

remote users, and we need to make email access more effective and efficient, which will boost productivity. Finally, reliability and security are vital goals in the design of the new IT Professional Consulting Windows/Exchange 2000 solution."

Your Role

You have been chosen by the senior Network Architect to lead several deployment teams at IT Professional Consulting. For the deployment, you must manage the following main areas:

➤ Hardware planning

➤ Storage group configuration

➤ Administrative group deployment

➤ Routing group architecture

➤ Client access administration

➤ Data recoverability plan

Question: 5.1

You have deleted a user in active directory by mistake, and you want to re-create the user. What steps should you take to restore the user mailbox?

○ a. Restore database from the last backup tape.

○ b. Restore individual mailbox from the tape.

○ c. Restore AD user from the tape.

○ d. Reconnect disconnected mailbox to a newly created AD account.

Question: 5.2

After you have defined the boundaries of routing groups, what else should you do to enable routing between these groups?

○ a. Install SMTP stack from Windows 2000 CD-ROM

○ b. Configure routing group connectors

○ c. Configure GWART group connectors

○ d. Configure ADC group connectors

Question: 5.3

You have three storage groups defined on one of the IT Professional Consulting Exchange 2000 servers with five databases in each one. One of the managers sends a broadcast to all employees, and 1,500 user mailboxes are stored within these databases. Users are split equally 500 per storage group, 100 per database. Size of the broadcasted message was 135KB. How much storage will this message consume on the server in question?

- ○ a. 405KB
- ○ b. 2,025KB
- ○ c. 2,430KB
- ○ d. 202,500KB

Question: 5.4

Why is it important to have one of your IM Router servers named 'im.ITproConsult.com' and have appropriate host record in DNS?

- ○ a. Information technology community would notice your IM record in the DNS system and would reckon with your company being on the technological cutting-edge—having all recent advances in realtime collaboration implemented.
- ○ b. Instant Messaging relies solely on this record to deliver IM messages between organizations.
- ○ c. Instant Messaging uses im. records in DNS as a fallback name-resolution mechanism.
- ○ d. There is no need to have im. record in DNS.

Question: 5.5

By default, what would neo@itproconsult.com be translated to when attempting to deliver an IM message to the user Neo?

- ○ a. http://im.itproconsult.com/instmsg/aliases/neo server-independent URL, http://SomeHomeServer/instmsg/aliases/neo server-specific URL.
- ○ b. http://im.itproconsult.com/instmsg/aliases/neo server-specific URL, http://SomeHomeServer/instmsg/aliases/neo server-independent URL.
- ○ c. http://im.itproconsult.com/instmsg/aliases/neo domain-independent URL, http://SomeHomeServer/instmsg/aliases/neo domain-specific URL.
- ○ d. This email address will not be translated; it can be used as-is to deliver IM message.

18

Question: 5.6

What is FTM, and what is its purpose in Exchange 2000?

○ a. It stands for File Transfer Mode and is used to transfer files between IM clients.

○ b. It stands for Firewall Topology Module and is used to configure firewall topology for Chat Service to function in a secure fashion.

○ c. It stands for Firewall Topology Module and is used to configure firewall topology for IM to function in a secure fashion.

○ d. It stands for Firewall Topology Module and is used to configure Information Stores to function in a secure fashion.

Question: 5.7

It has been estimated that your GC servers can handle approximately 120 LDAP queries per second and it is estimated that each Exchange 2000 server will be generating roughly 30 queries per second during peak hours. Your Exchange 2000 deployment is 30 Exchange 2000 servers, concentrated in 16 remote locations, no more than 4 servers per location. Your WAN is highly congested during the peak hours. How should you design your GC server allocation strategy?

○ a. Configure GC replication to occur every 2 hours. Place one GC server in each remote location.

○ b. Configure GC replication to occur every 6 hours. Place one GC server in each remote location.

○ c. Configure GC replication to occur at midnight. Place all your servers on a high-bandwidth LAN segment in Monaco.

○ d. Configure GC replication to occur at midnight. Place one GC server in each remote location.

Question: 5.8

You have a cluster Exchange 5.5 server. What migration/upgrade strategy should you take to move to Exchange 2000 platform seamlessly?

○ a. Either migration or in-place upgrade strategy would be suitable.

○ b. You cannot migrate cluster solutions; you have to upgrade.

○ c. You cannot upgrade cluster solutions; you have to migrate.

○ d. There is no way you can move data from this server to the new platform.

Question: 5.9

What is the purpose and functionality of KMS in Exchange 2000?

O a. KMS stands for Key Management Service; it relies on Windows 2000 Certificate Services, and it provides communication encryption on application level for Exchange messaging using X.509 certificates.

O b. KMS stands for Key Management Server; it relies on Windows 2000 Certificate Services, and it provides communication encryption on application level for Exchange messaging using X.509 certificates.

O c. KMS stands for Key Management Service; it relies on Windows 2000 Certificate Services, and it provides communication encryption on application level for Exchange messaging using X.500 certificates.

O d. KMS stands for Key Management Server; it relies on Windows 2000 Certificate Services, and it provides communication encryption on application level for Exchange messaging using X.500 certificates.

Question: 5.10

You are using KMS to secure communications between the offices of IT Professional Consulting Corporation. What must you make sure to include in your backup strategy not to lose any encrypted information organization-wide in case disaster strikes one of the servers that manage encryption and certificates? [Check all correct answers]

❑ a. KMS Database to restore certificate mappings

❑ b. CA certificates for each CA server to restore identity of the servers

❑ c. KMS-CA to synchronize revocation lists

❑ d. Active Directory to recover your security contexts and server/user database

18

Designing Messaging Infrastructure with Microsoft Exchange Server 2000 Exam Answers

Question: 1.1

Correct answer(s): c. Microsoft Outlook Web Access is the only choice that allows accessing emailing and scheduling information with an acceptable level of performance over a dial-up connection.

Wrong: a. Answer a is possible, but amount of bandwidth needed will make this solution very slow in terms of end-user experience. Therefore, this is not recommended.

Wrong: b. Answer b is incorrect because Outlook Express has no means of accessing scheduling information.

Wrong: d. Answer d is incorrect (see answer a).

For more information on this topic, see MCSE Exchange 2000 Design Exam Prep Chapter 5, the section titled "Implementing Outlook Web Access."

Question: 1.2

Correct answers: b. To provide satisfactory level of performance when consolidating servers you must ensure sufficient bandwidth is available. 256 Kbps is the recommended connection speed.

Wrong: a. Because there is not enough bandwidth available, this solution does not satisfy the requirements of Smoke on Water.

Wrong: c. Microsoft Outlook can be used with digital certificates to encrypt communication; therefore, answer c is incorrect.

Wrong: d. Microsoft Outlook is the most feature-rich client for Exchange and does provide access to scheduling information; therefore, answer d is incorrect.

For more information on this topic, see MCSE Exchange 2000 Design Exam Prep Chapter 7, the section titled "Examining Current Exchange 5.5 System."

Question: 1.3

Correct answer: b. Based on the lab tests of Smoke on Water Corporation it has been determined that adequate performance level is maintained by placing as many as 1,500 mailbox–enabled users per server. Six servers can accommodate up to 9,000 users.

Wrong: a, c, and d. These answers are incorrect because they either suggest inadequate performance levels or unwise use of hardware resources.

For more information on this topic, see MCSE Exchange 2000 Design Exam Prep Chapter 3, the section titled "Mailbox Servers."

Question: 1.4

Correct answer(s): c. Consistent with the definition and purpose of routing groups, you should place local servers into separate routing group. These groups should be defined in one administrative group for administrative purposes of Smoke on Water Corporation and associated with the servers found in remote location for which routing group is created.

Wrong: a. Routing group should be local for the servers connected via high-bandwidth, reliable connections such as LAN. Smoke on Water Corporation's network spans many remote locations connected via slower and less reliable WAN links; therefore, answer a is incorrect.

Wrong: b. Smoke on Water Corporation has one HQ location that needs its own routing group; therefore, answer b is incorrect.

Wrong: d. First, you cannot delegate control on a routing group basis, you can only delegate control at administrative group or organization level. Second, Smoke on Water Corporation envisions central management of routing groups; therefore, answer d is incorrect.

For more information on this topic, see MCSE Exchange 2000 Design Exam Prep Chapter 9, the section titled "Routing Groups."

Question: 1.5

Correct answer(s): d. Disabling circular logging is a must for environments where data recoverability is important. Backing up individual storage groups is more efficient than backing up individual databases.

Wrong: a and c. Enabling circular logging prevents recoverability to the point of failure because transaction logs will be overwritten as needed and you will not be able to replay them. Therefore, both answers a and c are incorrect.

Wrong: b. This answer is correct, but is less efficient than backing up storage groups. Therefore, answer b is not the best answer to this question.

For more information on this topic, see *MCSE Exchange 2000 Design Exam Prep* Chapter 15, the section titled "Circular Logging" and "Storage Groups."

Question: 1.6

Correct answer(s): c. Creating Universal Security Groups and nesting them within each other based on departmental structure is the most efficient approach because changes made to individual groups will not force entire structure to replicate between GCs, and Outlook users will be able to see who are members of each group. Also, USGs have their own SID and can be used to define permissions in ACLs on objects.

Wrong: a. This approach is possible, however Outlook clients will not be able to see memberships of these groups. Also, global groups cannot be nested deeper than one level. Global groups are not recommended as email distribution vehicles.

Wrong: b. It is not recommended to use domain local groups as email distribution mechanisms due to their limitations and AD/GC replication issues.

Wrong: d. USG is a preferred way over UDG because it allows you to better manage your users by combining email distribution and security contexts.

For more information on this topic, see *MCSE Exchange 2000 Design Exam Prep* Chapter 12, the section titled "Windows2000 Groups Overview."

Question: 1.7

Correct answer(s): d. Front-end servers are used to balance incoming connection load and deliver messages to the back-end servers that have storage groups defined. If one server falls victim to a DoS attack, there will be others to accept mail.

Wrong: a. Clustering solution is the recommended way of providing fault-tolerance on the back-end server side where databases are defined, but not to load-balance incoming connections; therefore, answer a is incorrect.

Wrong: b. This approach does not affect the server's ability to handle incoming connections in any way and, therefore, answer b is incorrect.

Wrong: c. This approach does not address the problem of denial-of-service attack; you still have one physical host that accepts incoming connections; therefore, answer c is incorrect.

For more information on this topic, see *MCSE Exchange 2000 Design Exam Prep* Chapter 1, the section titled "Enhancements to Reliability and Scalability."

Question: 1.8

Correct answer(s): a. Outlook Web Access uses ASP pages transferred over HTTP and secured with SSL to communicate all types of Exchange 2000 information to the client, therefore answer a is correct because it allows only necessary protocols in or out of the secured network.

Wrong: b. IMAP4, RPC are not needed for OWA and should not be allowed in this particular scenario; therefore, answer b is incorrect.

Wrong: c. POP3, SMTP, IMAP4 are not necessary for OWA to function and therefore should not be allowed on the firewall in this case. Answer c is incorrect.

Wrong: d. MAPI stands for Mail Application Programming Interface and is not a protocol in itself, it is rather an object model that programmers use to write mail-enabled applications. Therefore, answer d is incorrect.

For more information on this topic, see *MCSE Exchange 2000 Design Exam Prep* Chapter 5, the section titled "Implementing Outlook Web Access."

Question: 1.9

Correct answer(s): d. To manage Exchange 5.5 and Exchange 2000 from one central location you have to set up two-way ADC connection agreements to each Exchange 5.5 site.

Wrong: a and c. These two answers are incorrect because one-way connection agreement replicates data from one directory, but not from both.

Wrong: b. This answer is incorrect because this configuration will cause excessive replication traffic between Exchange 5.5 site that you are replicating to and the rest of your Exchange 5.5 organization.

For more information on this topic, see *MCSE Exchange 2000 Design Exam Prep* Chapter 10, the section titled "Exploring Connection Agreements."

Question: 1.10

Correct answer(s): a, b, and c. Before you rollout your Exchange 2000 Server, you have to prepare your forest and domain for the installation.

Wrong: d. This answer is not required to install Exchange 2000 and extend AD, but may as well be included in your Exchange 2000 rollout depending on the migration plan. Therefore, answer d is incorrect.

For more information on this topic, see *MCSE Exchange 2000 Design Exam Prep* Chapter 10, the section titled "ForestPrep and DomainPrep."

Question: 2.1

Correct answer(s): a. To support communication in different languages your software must adhere to IRCX protocol specification proposed by Microsoft.

Wrong: b. This answer is incorrect because it is possible to provide chat service in various languages.

Wrong: c. This answer is incorrect because IRC standard has no support for multilingual service.

Wrong: d. This answer is incorrect because there is no such specification.

For more information on this topic, see *MCSE Exchange 2000 Design Exam Prep* Chapter 14, section titled "Chat Service."

Question: 2.2

Correct answer(s): d. Microsoft recommends to host up to 20,000 users per chat server. Minimum number of servers you have to deploy to meet this recommendation is 5.

Wrong: Answers a, b, and c. These answers are all incorrect because they do not provide adequate performance to host such a vast user base.

For more information on this topic, see *MCSE Exchange 2000 Design Exam Prep* Chapter 14, the section titled "Clients and Servers."

Question: 2.3

Correct answer(s): d. Microsoft recommends 4 CPU, 512 MB per machine to handle full amount of 20,000 chat user connections. d is the best-suited answer from the pool of proposed configurations and exceeds this recommendation.

Wrong: a. This configuration is inadequate to support 20,000 users per server.

Wrong: b. This configuration does not have enough CPUs to warrant efficient connection management.

Wrong: c. It is not possible to have three processors per machine.

For more information on this topic, see *MCSE Exchange 2000 Design Exam Prep* Chapter 14, the section titled "Clients and Servers."

Question: 2.4

Correct answer(s): b. In this mode, class can "listen" to the speaker and host can assign certain members a right to ask questions. Users are not notified when members are entering or leaving.

Wrong: a. If you make this cloneable, users who connect over the set limit of maximum connections will end up in a cloned chat room without a lecturer.

Wrong: c. In moderated chat room, members will be notified when other members are joining or leaving therefore creating distraction.

Wrong: d. Classroom channel mode does not exist.

For more information on this topic, see *MCSE Exchange 2000 Design Exam Prep* Chapter 14, the section titled "Channels."

Question: 2.5

Correct answer(s): c and d. You should allow any IRC ports that you have assigned to chat communities (including default port 6667, if it is used). HTTP must be enabled to access chat channels via the website.

Wrong: a and b. These answers may or may not be used in your implementation and if they are used, they fall under answer c.

For more information on this topic, see *MCSE Exchange 2000 Design Exam Prep* Chapter 14, the section titled "Chat Protocols and Clients."

Question: 2.6

Correct answer(s): c. By imposing maximum IP connections limits you are restricting a number of connections allowed from one IP address. This method is used to limit the possibility of clone attacks.

Wrong: a and b. Bandwidth limits and message-processing delays are used to combat flooding attacks.

Wrong: d. Masking of DNS names and IP addresses are used to protect your chat clients from direct attacks by other chat clients.

For more information on this topic, see *MCSE Exchange 2000 Design Exam Prep* Chapter 14, the section titled "User Classes, Attacks and Bans."

Question: 2.7

Correct answer(s): d. Microsoft suggests using one homeserver per each 10,000 active online users. You should always plan for the worst-case scenario when all users are online.

Wrong: a, b, and c. These answers do not meet performance requirements.

For more information on this topic, see *MCSE Exchange 2000 Design Exam Prep* Chapter 14, the section titled "IM HomeServers."

Question: 2.8

Correct answer(s): b. Microsoft's suggestion is to use one IM Router per every 20,000 active online users per domain. Because the University has 85,000 students, you'll need five IM Routers. You should always plan for the worst-case scenario, when all users are online.

Wrong: a, c, and d. These answers either do not suffice to handle the maximum possible load or are more than necessary therefore resulting in wasteful hardware allocation and management overhead.

For more information on this topic, see *MCSE Exchange 2000 Design Exam Prep* Chapter 14, the section titled "IM Routers."

Question: 2.9

Correct answer(s): b. HTTP port 80 is the only port from the listed options that you have to allow for instant messaging to work.

Wrong: a and d. These answers are incorrect because XML is not a port, it is a content type that is transferred over HTTP port.

Wrong: c. This answer is incorrect because RVP works over default HTTP port 80 and uses HTTP as a communication means.

For more information on this topic, see *MCSE Exchange 2000 Design Exam Prep* Chapter 14, the section titled "Service Architecture and Components."

Question: 2.10

Correct answer(s): a. _rvp._tcp.technogripu.com SRV 0 0 80 im.technogripu.com is the correct instant messaging DNS service record.

Wrong: b, c, and d. These answers are all examples of incorrect instant messaging DNS service records.

For more information on this topic, see *MCSE Exchange 2000 Design Exam Prep* Chapter 14, the section titled "IM Addressing, IM Domains, DNS."

Question: 3.1

Correct answer(s): d. This method will restore your database to the point of failure.

Wrong: a. Incremental backup does purge transaction logs that were flushed to the database, and this is why you have to restore each tape of incremental backup cycle. But this is possible, and therefore, answer a is incorrect.

Wrong: b. You will corrupt your restored from full backup database if you restore only certain incremental backups but not the ones that preceded them. Therefore, answer b is incorrect.

Wrong: c. This method will restore the database only till the last incremental backup but not to the point of failure. Therefore, answer c is incorrect.

For more information on this topic, see *MCSE Exchange 2000 Design Exam Prep* Chapter 15, the section titled "Incremental Backup."

Question: 3.2

Correct answer(s): b. Placing system partition on a duplexed mirror set RAID-1 array will ensure you have two identical copies of the system. Placing databases and transaction logs on separate stripe sets with parity RAID-5 arrays will ensure you have maximum performance and recoverability. Circular logging must be disabled where data recoverability is of importance.

Wrong: a. "Enable circular logging" at the end of the answer automatically makes it a wrong choice.

Wrong: c. You cannot place system partition on RAID-0 stripe set, it only makes a disk subsystem more vulnerable to failures. Therefore, answer c is incorrect.

Wrong: d. By placing transaction logs and databases on RAID-0 volumes, you are compromising your ability to recover in case one of the disks fails. Therefore, answer d is incorrect.

For more information on this topic, see *MCSE Exchange 2000 Design Exam Prep* Chapter 15, the section titled "Planning for Fault Tolerance."

19

Question: 3.3

Correct answer(s): a. This design would ensure that you can restore smaller groups of users from different departments in the shortest amount of time and meet your SLA requirements.

Wrong: b. This design is less fault-tolerant and will require more time to restore each of the databases. Also, you cannot restore multiple databases within one storage group at the same time. Therefore, answer b is incorrect.

Wrong: c. This solution will definitely simplify restore and backup routines, but this is not the objective you are required to achieve. Therefore, answer c is incorrect.

Wrong: d. This design is close to ideal but answer a provides smaller databases and more distributed user base, therefore making your solution more fault-tolerant and answer d incorrect.

For more information on this topic, see *MCSE Exchange 2000 Design Exam Prep* Chapter 15, the section titled "Planning for Fault Tolerance."

Question: 3.4

Correct answer(s): a and b. You need to have system partition and system state to restore your system in the least amount of time.

Wrong: c. The pagefile.sys file is a memory swap file, and it has no relevance to ensuring your system recoverability.

Wrong: d. There is no such thing as Windows Metabase, Windows uses registry to store its configuration. IIS stores its configuration in the metabase, and IIS metabase is backed up as part of the system state backup.

For more information on this topic, see *MCSE Exchange 2000 Design Exam Prep* Chapter 15, the section titled "Planning Your Backup Strategy."

Question: 3.5

Correct answer(s): c. This method will ensure that a secure email communication requirement is met.

Wrong: a. VPN solution is not feasible to implement for intra-company use, it is used to provide secure connection over the Internet. Therefore, answer a is incorrect.

Wrong: b. Although IPSec would meet the requirement of securing email communication, this method requires underlying infrastructure, and might require network hardware upgrade to offload encryption-decryption from the CPU. This is not the preferred way of doing it, although eventually you should consider implementing it to secure all communications; therefore, answer b is incorrect.

Wrong: d. You cannot use Secure Sockets Layer to achieve the required result.

For more information on this topic, see *MCSE Exchange 2000 Design Exam Prep* Chapter 5, the section titled "More Advantages of Outlook 2000."

Question: 3.6

Correct answer(s): d. Placing your OWA servers in the DMZ zone will ensure maximum security by protecting your OWA servers from the incoming connections, and placing a firewall between OWA servers and Exchange 2000/LAN will ensure that even if OWA servers are compromised this has much less chance of spreading into your internal network.

Wrong: a. This is the most dangerous way of designing your public access network.

Wrong: b. In this scenario your OWA servers are fully exposed to hackers on the Internet. This is not how you design for security.

Wrong: c. This will protect your OWA servers from external attacks to some extent but external user connections will still have to be allowed into your internal network, which is not the best way of designing for security.

For more information on this topic, see *MCSE Exchange 2000 Design Exam Prep* Chapter 5, the section titled "Implementing Outlook Web Access."

Question: 3.7

Correct answer(s): c. Indicated steps will ensure that you have cloned the failed system.

Wrong: a. Blaming it on power surges will not rectify the situation; just the opposite, it will make it look worse because you have not provisioned for UPS and power surge protection in the first place.

Wrong: b. This sequence of recovery steps will fail because restoring system state over a fresh installation of Windows will corrupt it without first restoring system partition.

Wrong: d. This sequence of recovery steps will not result in a seamless restoration because you will end up with a brand new Exchange server, configuration-wise. You should use /disasterrecovery installation switch to install Exchange anew using existing configuration stored in AD.

For more information on this topic, see *MCSE Exchange 2000 Design Exam Prep* Chapter 15, the section titled "Recovering from Disaster."

Question: 3.8

Correct answer(s): d. This sequence of actions will recover your data from the disaster.

Wrong: a. You cannot restore Exchange server databases without having an Exchange server first.

Wrong: b. This method will result in Exchange server having a different security and AD context than previously and will require a lot of administrative overhead to reconfigure the rest of your organization accordingly.

Wrong: c. You cannot use /disasterrecovery switch before having active directory installed.

For more information on this topic, see *MCSE Exchange 2000 Design Exam Prep* Chapter 15, the section titled "Recovering from Disaster."

Question: 3.9

Correct answer(s): d. Placing public folders on a separate server if a heavy load is expected is a good design practice. Full-text indexing service will index certain most popular types of attachments such as DOC, PPT, and HTML.

Wrong: a, b. This is not a good practice to mix mail and public folder server functions when heavy load is expected.

Wrong: c. You could program such a solution, but this is time-consuming, not very user-friendly, and needless because full-text indexing is capable of retrieving the contents of most popular attachments.

For more information on this topic, see *MCSE Exchange 2000 Design Exam Prep* Chapter 13, the section titled "Full Content Indexing."

Question: 3.10

Correct answer(s): c. This solution satisfies the requirements, maintains a solid level of performance, and reduces WAN usage.

Wrong: a. This method is not optimal because of WAN speeds and usage

Wrong: b. This method is wasteful in terms of WAN bandwidth usage. Remote locations do not need all the content.

Wrong: d. You can replicate public folder content.

For more information on this topic, see *MCSE Exchange 2000 Design Exam Prep* Chapter 13, the section titled "Replicating Public Folders."

Question: 4.1

Correct answer(s): b and d. These answers are correct ways of ensuring that your groups are used consistently with their design purpose.

Wrong: a and c. Group management is not in Exchange anymore, it is managed through Active Directory Users and Computers.

For more information on this topic, see *MCSE Exchange 2000 Design Exam Prep* Chapter 12, the section titled "Windows 2000 Groups Overview."

Question: 4.2

Correct answer(s): b. USG groups are not available in mixed mode.

Wrong: a and c. These answers are incorrect because UDG groups are available in mixed mode domains.

Wrong: d. There is no such thing as migration mode.

For more information on this topic, see *MCSE Exchange 2000 Design Exam Prep* Chapter 12, the section titled "Windows 2000 Groups with Universal Scope."

Question: 4.3

Correct answer(s): c. In Windows 2000 architectures, child domains will substitute for resource domains and will remove the need for separate resource domains that form administrative and security boundaries.

Wrong: a. In the Windows 2000 architecture, child domains, not enterprise domains, take the place of resource domains.

Wrong: b. This is not an accurate statement. See the answer for c.

Wrong: d. Answer c is a correct answer.

For more information on this topic, see *MCSE Exchange 2000 Design Exam Prep* Chapter 7, the section titled "Hindrances to a Smooth Upgrade/Migration."

Question: 4.4

Correct answer(s): b. Users have the ability to use the Exchange information Web Store as the single location for managing documents and versioning through the WebDAV specification.

Wrong: a. XML governs content format that is travelling the network by means of HTTP. XML delivers tagged content and leaves the formatting and presentation functions to particular consumer software thereby enabling unified data-driven solutions.

Wrong: c. ASP is much like XML and is used to deliver dynamic content in web pages.

Wrong: d. A storage group is a collection of mailbox stores and public folder stores that share a set of transaction log files. Exchange manages each storage group with a separate server process.

For more information on this topic, see *MCSE Exchange 2000 Design Exam Prep* Chapter 1, the section titled "Microsoft Outlook Web Access."

Question: 4.5

Correct answer(s): c. An Active Directory mail-enabled group is the Exchange 2000 equivalent of the Exchange 5.5 Distribution List.

Wrong: a. Active Directory public folder is not the Exchange 2000 equivalent of the Exchange 5.5 Distribution List.

Wrong: b. Active Directory mail-enabled contact or user is not the Exchange 2000 equivalent of the Exchange 5.5 Distribution List.

Wrong: d. Active Directory mailbox-enabled groups do not exist.

For more information on this topic, see *MCSE Exchange 2000 Design Exam Prep* Chapter 12, the section titled "Windows 2000 Groups Overview."

Question: 4.6

Correct answer(s): d. RAID-5 is the fault tolerant solution that you would use for your transaction logs and possibly databases in this Exchange 2000 cost-saving scenario. In a failure, on RAID-5 you can simply proceed to regenerate the data that was located on the failed disk.

Wrong: a. RAID-0 does not provide fault tolerance.

Wrong: b. RAID-1 is generally for mirroring the operating systems and other critical files.

Wrong: c. RAID-3 is not supported in Windows 2000.

For more information on this topic, see *MCSE Exchange 2000 Design Exam Prep* Chapter 15, the section titled "Planning for Fault Tolerance."

Question: 4.7

Correct answer(s): a and d. The two general types of policies that are available in Exchange 2000 are system policies and recipient policies.

Wrong: b. There are no server policies; they are part of system policies.

Wrong: c. Public folder policy is not one of the two general types of policies that are available in Exchange 2000.

For more information on this topic, see *MCSE Exchange 2000 Design Exam Prep* Chapter 5, the section titled "Exploring Policies."

19

Question: 4.8

Correct answer(s): c. Site Replication Service (SRS) is a customized Exchange 5.5 directory that works on the Exchange 2000 server to assist replication between Exchange 2000 SRS and the residual Exchange 5.5 servers.

Wrong: a. SNMP is Simple Network Management Protocol and is the network management protocol of TCP/IP.

Wrong: b. SMS is Microsoft Systems Management Server and is used to manage large-scale deployments of software and keep inventory.

Wrong: d. Simple Mail Transfer Protocol (SMTP) is used for the transfer of mail messages and attachments.

For more information on this topic, see *MCSE Exchange 2000 Design Exam Prep* Chapter 10, the section titled "Replication and Synchronization with ADC."

Question: 4.9

Correct answer(s): b and c. There are two editions of the Active Directory Connector. One connector is the ADC for Windows 2000, which ships with Windows 2000 Server. A second type of AD connector is the Enhanced ADC for Exchange 2000 that ships with Exchange 2000 Server.

Wrong: a. This is not an ADC.

Wrong: d. A second type of AD connector is the Enhanced ADC for Exchange 2000 that ships with Exchange 2000 Server, not Enhanced ADC for Windows 2000.

For more information on this topic, see *MCSE Exchange 2000 Design Exam Prep* Chapter 10, the section titled "Replication and Synchronization with ADC."

Question: 4.10

Correct answer(s): d. Exchange 2000 has fewer replication partners since only domain controllers replicate Active Directory information.

Wrong: a. Although every Exchange Server 5.5 server takes part in the directory replication process, only domain controllers replicate Active Directory information.

Wrong: b. You will need to make sure that replication is functioning well because Windows 2000 replicates much more data than Exchange 5.5 typically requires.

Wrong: c. Exchange 2000 can exist in a mixed mode, not native mode, organization working with legacy servers as if they all resided in an Exchange Server 5.5 organization.

For more information on this topic, see *MCSE Exchange 2000 Design Exam Prep* Chapter 7, the section titled "Hindrances to a Smooth Upgrade/Migration."

Question: 5.1

Correct answer(s): d. This would be the right way of re-creating the mailbox. User in AD will not have the same SID, but you can reconnect the mailbox because by default nothing is deleted in Exchange until after 30 days from the time when the mailbox was deleted.

Wrong: a. This will not rectify the problem because user account is what's missing.

Wrong: b. You cannot restore an individual mailbox from the tape without restoring the entire database to a different location and moving the individual mailbox.

Wrong: c. You cannot restore a user from the tape.

For more information on this topic, see *MCSE Exchange 2000 Design Exam Prep* Chapter 15, the section titled "Restoring Deleted Items."

Question: 5.2

Correct answer(s): b. After you define the boundaries of your routing groups, you have to configure routing group connectors for these groups to communicate.

Wrong: a. SMTP is required to install Exchange 2000 in the first place.

Wrong: c. GWART is a routing table that was used in Exchange 5.5 to carry out routing decisions, replaced by link-state routing table in Exchange 2000.

Wrong: d. ADC connector is used to replicate directory information between Exchange 5.5 and Exchange 2000.

For more information on this topic, see *MCSE Exchange 2000 Design Exam Prep* Chapter 4, the section titled "Routing Group Connectors."

Question: 5.3

Correct answer(s): c. Single Instance Storage algorithm will store one copy of this message in transaction log per storage group, and once per each database, therefore making it 18 instances in total, and 18 time 135KB equals 2,430 KB.

Wrong: a, b, d. These answer are all incorrect because they are not calculated using the formula presented in answer c.

For more information on this topic, see *MCSE Exchange 2000 Design Exam Prep* Chapter 15, the section titled "Single Instance Store."

Question: 5.4

Correct answer(s): c. IM uses im. records in DNS as a fallback name resolution procedure.

Wrong: a and d. These answers are incorrect because these statements are not true.

Wrong: b. Instant messaging does not rely solely on im. records and, therefore, this answer is incorrect.

For more information on this topic, see *MCSE Exchange 2000 Design Exam Prep* Chapter 14, the section titled "IM Addressing, IM Domains, DNS."

Question: 5.5

Correct answer(s): a. This answer provides correct URLs that given email address would be translated to when attempting to deliver an IM message.

Wrong: b. Server-specific and server-independent URLs are shown in the reverse order incorrectly.

Wrong: c. There are no domain-specific or domain-independent URLs in the IM namespace terminology.

Wrong: d. IM messages are delivered using URLs, HTTP protocol, not SMTP, therefore this translation is necessary and this answer is incorrect.

For more information on this topic, see *MCSE Exchange 2000 Design Exam Prep* Chapter 14, the section titled "URL and Email Addressing Put Together."

Question: 5.6

Correct answer(s): c. FTM stands for Firewall Topology Module and is used to configure IM messaging properties to secure incoming and outgoing communications.

Wrong: a. FTM does not stand for File Transfer Mode.

Wrong: b and d. FTM is used when configuring IM, not Chat Service or Information Store.

For more information on this topic, see *MCSE Exchange 2000 Design Exam Prep* Chapter 14, the section titled "Firewall Topology Module."

Question: 5.7

Correct answer(s): d. This strategy ensures high performance requirements are met and does not congest WAN links during business hours.

Wrong: a and b. This strategy will interfere with normal business hours and is not a recommended approach.

Wrong: c. This strategy doesn't warrant adequate user response times resulting in delays and frustration.

Question: 5.8

Correct answer(s): c. You cannot upgrade this server, you have to migrate.

Wrong: a and b. You cannot upgrade and therefore, answer a is incorrect. Migration is the only strategy available; therefore, answer b is incorrect.

Wrong: d. There are several ways in which you can migrate your data from clustered solution; therefore, answer d is incorrect.

For more information on this topic, see *MCSE Exchange 2/000 Design Exam Prep* Chapter 7, the section titled "Exchange 2000: Upgrade or Migration?"

Question: 5.9

Correct answer(s): a. KMS stands for Key Management Service; it uses X.509 certificates.

Wrong: b. KMS does not stand for Key Management Server and, therefore, this answer is incorrect.

Wrong: c and d. X.500 is the specification of an AD-like directory, not digital certificates that are used to encrypt electronic transmissions.

For more information on this topic, see *MCSE Exchange 2000 Design Exam Prep* Chapter 8, the section titled "Certificate Services and the KMS."

Question: 5.10

Correct answer(s): a, b, c, and d. You need all four components to successfully recover from a disaster.

For more information on this topic, see *MCSE Exchange 2000 Design Exam Prep* Chapter 15, the section titled "Key Management Service" and Chapter 8 in the section titled "KMS Installation and Administration."

19

Appendix A
Answers to Review Questions

Chapter 1 Solutions

1. **a, c,** and **d**. Exchange 2000 has three versions. Exchange 2000 Server is well suited for the messaging and collaboration needs of small to medium organizations. The next version, Exchange 2000 Enterprise Server, provides the dependability and scalability requirements of demanding enterprises for messaging and collaboration through its unlimited data store and active/active clustering solutions. Finally, Exchange 2000 Conferencing Server allows workers to arrange, manage, and take part in data, voice, and videoconferencing sessions across both the intranet and the Internet. Answers b and e are incorrect because Exchange 2000 Datacenter Server and Exchange 2000 Instant Messaging Server are not versions of Exchange 2000.

2. **d**. Exchange 2000 Conferencing Server allows workers to arrange, manage, and take part in data, voice, and videoconferencing sessions across both the intranet and the Internet.

3. **c**. Because it is Active Directory-based, Exchange offers a high degree of security through the use of the Windows 2000 operating system Access Control Lists (ACLs).

4. **d**. The Active Directory Connector (ADC) allows you to populate the Active Directory from directory information held in Exchange 5.5. You can also manage Exchange 5.5 directory information from the Active Directory and replicate information about directory objects between the Exchange directory and Active Directory Services.

5. **b**. The LDIF text file format allows you to perform a bulk import/export from Active Directory.

6. **c**. Individual mailboxes and public folders can be recovered in Exchange 2000.

7. **e**. All of the above are correct.

8. **d**. With active/active clustering, two servers work together to actively process messaging requests until a failure occurs that triggers the rollover recovery

mode. Exchange 2000 can run at the same time on more than one server and can simultaneously process requests. Another feature is that the Exchange servers in the cluster do not have to be the same size or be configured in the same manner. Keep in mind that while using only one node of the cluster, the performance of the system will experience some decrease.

9. **a**. The monitoring infrastructure and user interface for system monitoring in Exchange 2000 is built on Windows Management Instrumentation (WMI).

10. **b**. Users have the ability to use the Exchange Information Web Store as the single location for managing documents and versioning through the Web-DAV specification.

11. **a**, **b**, **d**, and **e**. Valid file types for full-text indexing are Microsoft Word (.doc), Microsoft Excel (.xls), Microsoft PowerPoint (.ppt), HTML (.htm, .html, .asp), text files (.txt), and Embedded MIME (.eml).

12. **d**. Exchange 2000 uses a link state table to determine the shortest path between two routing groups for a given message routing and selection process. A link state table is the database of information on each Exchange 2000 Server that stores the status of a server, the link state information propagated by the link state algorithm, and the costs of the connections between servers to determine the most efficient route for a message.

13. **c**. IPSec is a security design framework consisting of open standards that guarantee secure, private communications over IP networks. IPSec takes advantage of several cryptographic security services developed by the Internet Engineering Task Force (IETF) IPSec working group to accomplish this goal. Certificate services and Key Management Services (KMS) provide security on the application layer; IPSec offers security at the IP transport layer (Layer 3).

14. **e**. The Web Storage System is a platform that provides a single storage repository for organizing many types of information within one Exchange 2000 infrastructure. The Exchange 2000 Web Storage System merges the functionality of a file system with the technology of the Web to access and manage information through a single, URL-addressable locality. It also provides a platform for both Web and workflow applications, and supports DHTML and XML standard interfaces to link Exchange into your e-commerce and Internet infrastructure.

15. **d**. The T.120 standard contains a series of communication and application protocols and services that provide support for realtime, multipoint data communications. These multipoint facilities are the building blocks for a new range of collaborative applications, including desktop data conferencing, multiuser applications, and multiplayer gaming.

Chapter 2 Solutions

1. **e.** All of the above answers can have an influence on your organizational deployment of an Exchange solution.

2. **b.** This information is distributed as the Microsoft Solutions Framework (MSF), a systematic collection of data from customers, partners, IT organizations, product managers, and consultants to generate detailed analyses that organizes this data into practical models.

3. **b.** The Development phase is the phase that will involve the actual pilot testing of all the organizational and physical aspects of the migration and deployment development plan.

4. **d.** The Scope phase of the Microsoft Solutions Framework Infrastructure Deployment Process is where all of the issues should be addressed. You will create a Scope document that covers issues such as customer service; impact on the IT personnel, sales, marketing, and operations departments; effect on the executives; and other issues that are specific to your organization in general.

5. **c.** A large multinational organization (LMO) has a central organization with a considerable global presence. This type of organization may have a large corporate headquarters with international regional offices and national branch offices. The LMO has a more centralized administrative structure than the large international conglomerate, but the larger branch offices will have their own dedicated IT departments. The regional and branch offices are joined to the headquarters by a network of various WAN links, and the LMO usually has more than 10,000 employees. LMO examples include Microsoft and Compaq.

6. **b.** The small autonomous organization (SAO) resides in a single locality and has no branch offices. Administrative management is totally centralized or often outsourced to another vendor. The workforce is usually made up of 50 or more employees; however, SAOs with fewer than 50 people in the workforce may want to follow Microsoft's recommendation and consider putting Exchange 2000 into operation as part of a Small Business Server (SBS) solution.

7. **c.** A medium branch office (MBO) has no down-level connections, similar to a large branch office, and is often linked to either the global headquarters or a regional branch. The number of users in the medium branch office is generally considerably smaller than that in a large branch office. The MBO will characteristically have 5 to 20 people implementing one or two servers. The servers will carry out multipurpose roles, one of which will be the Exchange 2000 Server function. Connections to the global headquarters or a regional office are usually by way of an asynchronous dial-up, ISDN, or ADSL. MBOs will rarely have the luxury of a T1 connection.

8. **b.** Organizations that are planning for sudden growth due to a company takeover or merger in the near term are referred to as planning expansion (PE) types. Considerations will include, for example, whether you should proceed as two distinctive operations with separate directory spaces and Exchange implementations, or merge the directories as well as administrative duties.

9. **a.** The three general categories of business models are centralized, decentralized, and outsourced. Distributed is not a category of an IT business model.

10. **d.** An outsourced IT business model relies on an outside group for IT management. Systems administrators who are not employees of the company will design and maintain the network. In such a model, external systems administrators will also design the Exchange 2000 structure. In an outsourced IT business model, the structure must be planned so that users are able to access the necessary network resources, but only external systems administrators can manage the network.

11. **b.** The element of the business infrastructure is the current geographical scope or geographical presence of an organization. An analysis of the geographical scope of an organization provides an insight into the number of Active Directory forests and domains you need to create. It also assists you in planning your Exchange database and administrative solutions. The future geographical scope refers to the expansion plans of an organization, including new offices and future acquisitions and mergers.

12. **c.** The 80-20 rule can be applied to get a general feel for the flow of electronic mail that already exists between workgroups or business units of an organization following measurable communication patterns. To be more precise, 80 percent of communication stays within an individual's workgroup, and the remaining 20 percent flows outside of the unit or workgroup.

13. **c.** A key aspect of creating your overall deployment of Exchange 2000 is risk assessment. After reviewing the many advantages and technological features of Exchange for your enterprise, you need to assess the possible problem areas that may surface during your deployment project.

14. **d.** System policies are a way for administrators to define properties on a large number of objects by defining properties on a single policy object. The most important principle behind policies is to allow administrators the ability to define settings and parameters for the Exchange 2000 organization on a grand scale.

15. **b.** Address lists allow users to effortlessly view a list of available recipients. This greatly simplifies the process of sending messages.

Chapter 3 Solutions

1. **g.** All of the above statements are true regarding the prerequisites that must be in place prior to the installation of Exchange 2000.

2. **a** and **c.** The minimum requirements for an Exchange 2000 deployment are (1) Intel Pentium or compatible 133MHz or higher processor; (2) 128MB RAM (supported minimum), 256MB RAM (recommended minimum); (3) 500MB available disk space for the drive on which Exchange is installed; (4) 200MB available disk space on the system drive; (5) CD-ROM drive; and (6) VGA or better monitor.

3. **a.** This is known as the leapfrog method.

4. **c.** Conferencing services is an optional software component that can be run with Exchange 2000 Server.

5. **a.** When you choose to install all of the Exchange services on a single machine during installation, you are configuring what is technically known as an all-in-one server.

6. **d.** If your organization has more than 1,000 users, your dedicated mailbox server should have two to four processors and at least 1GB of memory.

7. **a**, **b**, and **c.** A dedicated Internet mail server is deployed as part of the standard Exchange Messaging and Collaboration installation option and will use virtual servers to provide IMAP4, NNTP, and POP3 services.

8. **e.** All of the above. Dedicated public folder servers hold public folders and provide public folder data to clients. Public folder servers will use any one of several protocols, including MAPI, HTTP, HTTP-DAV, and IMAP4.

9. **d.** AppleTalk connector is not a connector that Exchange 2000 Server supports.

10. **c.** In previous versions of Exchange, systems that have one or more connectors linking two Exchange sites or connecting Exchange to the Internet are referred to as bridgehead servers. These servers are in charge of sending mail and public folder information as well as replicating the Exchange directory between sites.

11. **c.** If the usage of the server is going to be similar after the upgrade, look for CPU usage running at about 30 percent or less to signal ample processing for Exchange 2000. You should strongly think about either upgrading the processor or even migrating the Exchange 5.5 server if the processor is being pushed beyond 30 percent.

12. **a**. Mailbox and public folder servers place a high necessity for memory on the server. For a mailbox server with fewer than 500 users, a memory configuration of 256MB RAM is recommended. You should double the RAM to 512MB for up to 1,000 users, and move up to 1GB RAM for 1,000 to 2,500 users. If your mailbox server scales to handle more than 2,500 mailboxes, you will want to configure your server with 2GB RAM.

13. **d**. You would need to install and configure the TCP/IP network software for Windows 2000 server before configuring an X.400 transport stack and an X.400 connector to talk to another X.400 system over TCP/IP.

14. **c**. This is false. An advantage of RAID 0+1 is fast read and writes. A distinct disadvantage of RAID 5 is that it can be slow for read and write.

15. **c**. Regardless of the hardware platform your organization is using, a considerable performance gain can be made from separating the log files from the STM files. The log files write sequentially from the database to the hard disk, whereas the STM files randomly carry out input/output. In addition, separating these files will help you to analyze the I/O load from specific user actions by isolating different functions.

Chapter 4 Solutions

1. **d**. All answers are correct. To be included in a routing group, Exchange servers must belong to the same Windows 2000 forest, the servers must have permanent and direct SMTP connectivity to one another, and all servers within a routing group should always be able to contact the routing group master.

2. **c** and **d**. Microsoft Visio 2000 and Exchange Server Topology Diagramming Tool can be used to assess your current organizational infrastructure and construct an illustration of it. (To get more information, navigate your Web browser to **www.visiopartners.com**.)

3. **c**. SMTP is the native communications protocol used between servers running Microsoft Exchange 2000 Server.

4. **b**. Administrative groups and routing groups will also substitute for your existing Exchange 5.5 sites. Administrative groups are sets of Exchange 2000 servers that share a common administrative design.

5. **True**. After you install a server in an administrative group, it cannot be moved. Therefore, you must establish the administrative group before you install Exchange 2000.

6. **b** and **d**. Setting up multiple Exchange organizations will require synchronization because recipients in other forests will not be security principals in the local forest. You will lose access to public folders, access to calendar free and busy information, and access to other users' appointment books as well. The other recipients can indeed be retained as contacts, and you can use the Active Directory connector to synchronize between forests.

7. **d**. You would use the Move Server Wizard.

8. **c**. You cannot migrate Exchange databases between forests.

9. **b**. The message transfer agents for Exchange 5.5 and earlier are built upon the X.400 standard for addressing and carrying email messages.

10. **b**. Message journaling is configured on a database to create a copy of every message received by users on that database and to send the copy to a folder for archival purposes.

11. **d**. All enterprise-messaging systems require a way of passing routing data to one another. In Exchange 2000, when a connector is placed between two routing groups, a cost is associated with the link. A cost represents route preference when multiple routes are available; the lower the cost, the more preferable the route.

12. **a**. Your earlier version of Exchange may use a routing calculation server that composes the available routes and costs from the directory and forms a Gateway Address Resolution Table. This table is designed to circulate the routing topology for the organization to all the other servers in the Exchange site.

13. **c**. In earlier versions of Exchange, Internet Mail Service, previously named the Internet Mail Connector, stored this outbound message content configuration information.

14. **c**. Microsoft would categorize this as Medium usage.

15. **c**. Public Folders sharing information among users are always stored in the Information Store (IS), although you can select the store where you want to place the Public Folders.

Chapter 5 Solutions

1. **a**. The correct format that is supported is RFC 822, not RFC 804. RFCs are a series of reports and notes concerning the Internet. Each "Request for Comment" is assigned an RFC number—which, once published, never changes.

2. **b**. MAPI, an acronym for Messaging Application Programming Interface, is a structure built into Exchange 2000 that allows different email applications to work together to distribute mail. Applications can share mail messages as long as both are MAPI enabled. Extended MAPI version 1 is an industry-wide standard for writing messages and email and for workflow applications.

3. **c**. An Active Directory mail-enabled group is the Exchange 2000 equivalent of the Exchange 5.5 distribution list.

4. **b**. The Recipient Update Service is the Exchange 2000 service that updates the recipient objects within a domain with explicit types of information. This service can update recipient objects with address list membership and email addresses at intervals scheduled by the administrator.

5. **b** and **c**. The two general types of policies that are available in Exchange 2000 are system policies and recipient policies.

6. **b**, **d**, and **e**. Client applications are generally placed into one of the following three categories: messaging-aware applications, messaging-enabled applications, and messaging-based workgroup applications.

7. **a**. Only users with Windows 2000 accounts will be able to have a mailbox and send or receive mail. If the account is mail enabled but not mailbox enabled, users will be allowed only to send mail. Clients that are mailbox enabled can also receive mail and configure further settings and properties.

8. **c**. POP3 does provide access to the inbox on the mail server. Although POP3 messages are normally not centrally stored, it is possible to configure this for your environment.

9. **c**. Although Exchange 2000 Server supports both POP3 and IMAP4 protocols, your organization will have to incorporate an IMAP4-compliant client to receive all of the benefits of Exchange 2000. Using only a POP3 client will allow users to access Exchange 2000 Server email, but not the contacts, calendar, notes, or journal folders.

10. **d**. The Outlook Web Access feature allows Exchange 2000 to integrate with an IIS server to connect to the Internet. This feature provides the capability for users to access email and public folders in the Web Storage System using an ordinary Web browser.

11. **c**. The Web Distributed Authoring and Versioning (Web-DAV) protocol provides further access to an extensible collection of related properties. Web-DAV defines commands that are used to copy, move, delete, search, lock, and unlock resources, as well as to create new folders. These capabilities make Web-DAV an excellent tool for creating interoperable, shared applications.

12. **c**. Outlook Web Access has an intuitive interface for access to such specialized folders as those that store appointments on calendars and those that store contact information. It also provides URL access to the private message store. The other statements are false.

13. **a**, **b**, **c**, and **d**. All these technologies—PIM, Microsoft Office 2000, IE5, and the Internet—are compatible with Outlook 2000.

14. **a**. The vCard technology automates the trading of personal information that would normally be found on a conventional business card.

15. **a** and **d**. Outlook Express offers very limited functionality. It supports only the email and contact features available on Exchange 2000 Server. Furthermore, Outlook Express does not let users access several other capabilities, such as tasks and calendars.

Chapter 6 Solutions

1. **a**, **c**, **d**, **f**, and **g**. The Professional Office System (PROFS) or Office Vision connector is not supported in Exchange 2000. The SNA Distribution System (SNADS) connector is also not supported in Exchange 2000. Directory synchronization is important for moving mail between dissimilar systems. As a result, the Exchange PROFS connector and the Exchange SNADS connector must stay on your Exchange 5.5 servers.

2. **c**. If you have multiple directories from a variety of systems, you might want to think about using Microsoft Metadirectory Services.

3. **a**, **b**, **c**, **d**, and **e**. All of the above are important factors.

4. **b**. Link monitors view the roundtrip time of PING messages that are sent between a computer running Exchange 2000 Server and a GroupWise system. A notification is triggered if the roundtrip exceeds certain selected parameters.

5. **c**. A fair number of organizations are still deploying Microsoft Mail, although larger organizations usually have it in just a few departments. Because of the limitations due, in part, to Mail's reliance on the Shared File System (SFS), most organizations will be performing a migration to Exchange 2000 as opposed to coexistence.

6. **b**. The Exchange Calendar Connector gives Exchange 2000 and GroupWise users the ability for near real-time access to free/busy calendar data. Exchange Calendar Connector runs on a computer as an Exchange 2000 Server service and extends the calendar interoperability features of Exchange Server.

7. **d**. Microsoft Mail for PC Networks uses Message Transfer Agents (MTAs) to move mail between Mail for PC Networks post offices.

8. **b.** A Message that cannot be mapped to a corresponding message type in the target domain will be automatically converted to an email message.

9. **a.** The Microsoft Mail connector directory on the Exchange server is in the \Exchsrvr\Connect\Msmcon folder. You can configure the Microsoft Mail connector with MMC.

10. **d.** The basic GroupWise components are the Message Transfer Agent (MTA), which routes messages between domains, post offices, and gateways; The Post Office Agent (POA), which delivers messages to users' mailboxes; and a Domain, which offers a logical grouping for the functions of addressing and routing.

11. **d.** The mapping files with default mapping rules for your attributes are located in the \exchsrvr\conndata\dxamex and \Exchsrvr\Conndata\Dxanotes folders. The Notes connector uses both of these directories during the directory synchronization process. The dxamex folder contains the Mapnotes.tbl file, which holds the mapping rules for the entries going from Notes to Exchange.

12. **c.** This is true. Exchange Server DXA servers and requestors will immediately apply changes.

13. **d.** All of the above are true statements.

14. **a** and **d.** You must check the database version cc:Mail is using. You must have Lotus cc:Mail Post Office Database version 6, with cc:Mail Import version 5.15 and Export version 5.14 or Lotus cc:Mail Post Office Database version 8, with cc:Mail Import version 6, Export version 6, and the Ie.ri file.

15. **c.** You can convert Notes Doc-links to OLE documents, Rich Text Format (RTF) attachments, or URL shortcuts. Convert Doc-links to URL shortcuts if all of the Lotus Notes servers in the organization are Domino servers and are configured to support Web-enabled applications. If they are not, convert them to RTF attachments, which is the default.

Chapter 7 Solutions

1. **b.** A large organization will often choose multiphase migration because it has a more complex and far-reaching design. It is usually impossible for all of their MSMail departments to upgrade at once. In addition, hardware must be made available in the early phases so that it can be redeployed later. Also, the Exchange Server implementation group will not be able migrate all of the users within an acceptable downtime to employ a single-phase migration.

2. **b.** Consider examining your organization on three levels, if applicable: the data center level, the infrastructure at an Exchange site level, and at each individual server level. The domain is technically a security boundary and does not apply.

3. **c.** This is not one of the migration steps. Valid migration steps are to migrate the hub post offices, the Dirsync components, and the gateways to connectors.

4. **b.** When upgrading Exchange servers that host directory replication connectors, the upgrade will generate the Site Replication Service (SRS). The role of the SRS is to replicate the Exchange 2000 configuration information to the down-level Exchange environment.

5. **a.** Servers with unsupported connectors must coexist because they cannot be migrated to Exchange 2000 and must stay on down-level versions of Exchange.

6. **a**, **b**, **c**, and **d.** All of the statements are correct in this scenario. An in-place domain upgrade is a relatively clear-cut process where all of the Windows NT 4.0 account domains are upgraded to Windows 2000. At the very least, the PDC in each applicable domain must be upgraded. All of the domains must be in the same forest. A maximum of one of the upgrades can create a new forest, and the remainder of the upgrades must join their domains to the existing forest either as child domains of an existing domain or as root domains of a new tree.

7. **b**, **c**, and **d.** The options for conflict handling are as follows: Ignore (this option does nothing); Replace (this option merges the accounts); and Rename (this option creates a separate account using a prefix or suffix supplied by the administrator).

8. **a** and **c.** You are choosing to run the Active Directory Migration Tool without sIDHistory, recreating Access Control Lists (ACLs), and then running the ADC. Without sIDHistory, a recently migrated account cannot access any of the resources to which the old account had access. This is why the migration process needs to comprise steps to reapply the new SID to all of the resources to which the old SID had permissions. You must carry out this step before transferring the user over to the new account so that users will always be able to access resources. For this scenario to work well with the ADC, you need to update the permissions on the Exchange 5.5 mailboxes before you run the ADC. This will make it simple for the ADC to match mailboxes and accounts after you are finished. You can update the permissions manually, although this is not practical for a lot of users. The Active Directory Migration Tool has an option to re-create ACLs that set permissions on Exchange mailboxes.

9. **c.** The three basic levels of migration for Microsoft Exchange Server are coexistence, new mailbox deployment, and full migration. Partial migration is not a level of migration.

10. **b.** The Migration Wizard may generate duplicate accounts in Active Directory, and the Active Directory Account Cleanup Wizard can simplify the process of deleting these duplicate accounts.

11. **c** and **e**. Microsoft offers the Microsoft Application Services for Lotus Notes, which is a migration toolset consisting of two applications: Microsoft Exchange Application Analyzer for Lotus Notes and Microsoft Exchange Application Converter for Lotus Notes. These utilities will help you migrate your Notes application to Exchange and Outlook. The Exchange Server Management Tool and the Active Directory Reconciliation Wizard do not exist.

12. **b**. The Lotus Notes Connector offers functionality for bidirectional mail transfer, directory synchronization, and scheduling processes.

13. **b** and **c**. The Exchange Server Migration Wizard comprises two primary pieces: the source extractor and the migration file importer. The source extractor component copies directory information, messages, calendar information, and collaboration data from an existing message system. It then stores the data in an Exchange Server Migration Wizard importable format. The migration file importer imports the directory, calendar, and collaboration information to Exchange 2000.

14. **c**. In the Account Creation Options dialog box, you select a method to create passwords for new user accounts. If you are using a template to facilitate setting up nonpersonal attributes, in the Template "object to be used for nonpersonal attributes" box, click Browse, select the template, and then click OK. When you complete the selection, click on Next.

15. **b** and **c**. Lotus cc:Mail clients can also use an Exchange 2000 Server as a gateway to other messaging environments such as SMTP and X.400. Exchange Server offers a dependable, robust, and low-cost solution because these components are built in. The most important requirement is probably for cc:Mail users to have full inbound and outbound Internet mail. You can do this by simply configuring the Internet Mail Service (IMS) on one of the Exchange servers.

Chapter 8 Solutions

1. **d**. The mode that you will implement in combination with the Exchange Server KMS to provide the highest level of automation for Outlook 2000 is the Corporate/Workgroup mode.

2. **a**, **b**, **c**, and **d**. To protect against internal attacks, these permissions should be applied to the Active Directory Connector service account: Built-in\ Administrators group, Enterprise Admins if used only with Windows 2000, Enterprise Admins if used with Exchange 2000 Server, and Exchange Full Administrator role if used with Exchange 2000 Server.

3. **a**, **b**, **c**, and **d**. All of the answers represent administrative tasks that can be performed in Exchange 2000.

4. **a** and **b**. filename.explog and filename.implog are the files that the Exchange KMS Key Export Wizard uses to log the results of the export and import processes.

5. **c**. The NT Event Viewer's application folder is the primary source of Key Management Services troubleshooting information.

6. **b** and **c**. You can implement the MMC Exchange System Manager snap-in or invoke Advanced Security as a standalone snap-in to administer the KMS.

7. **d**. The Certificate Revocation List (CRL) lists the users whose security tokens has been revoked, and therefore should not be authenticated as secure.

8. **b**. The Web Server Certificate for IIS will be needed to get this added functionality.

9. **a**. High Encryption Pack for Windows supports the Microsoft Enhanced Cryptographic Provider on your CA server in your Exchange 2000 infrastructure.

10. **c**. Exchange 2000 Key Management Service generates X.509 version 3 user certificates for digital signature and encryption employed by Exchange 2000 and Outlook 2000 at the application layer of the networking message architecture.

11. **d**. Audits is not a feature of the Key Management Service.

12. **b**. MD5 is an algorithm created in 1991 by Professor Ronald Rivest that is used to create digital signatures and is intended for use with 32-bit machines.

13. **b** and **c**. IPSec supports the Transport and Tunnel encryption modes.

14. **d**. S/MIME is the de facto standard for secure messaging on the Internet and as the foundation for many public key infrastructure (PKI) deployments in organizations.

15. **b**. Asymmetric ciphers are also called public-key ciphers and they use a key for encryption and another key for decryption.

Chapter 9 Solutions

1. **d.** The best way to allow public folder referrals to servers in another routing group is to implement and configure a Routing Group Connector between the two routing groups.

2. **b.** The Events Root system folder contains scripts for an Exchange Server 5.5–compatible event service and is created on a server when it is installed as the first server in an administrative group.

3. **b.** When a connection fails, the bridgehead server with the failed connector continues to repeat the connection 3 times at 60-second intervals.

4. **d.** When you map out your routing topology, you should take into consideration the physical locations that you have, how they are connected, and whether you want to control the message flow. This task is similar to designing Exchange sites in earlier versions of Exchange as well as designing Windows 2000 Active Directory sites.

5. **c.** When you have only a single group of servers with full-time high-bandwidth connectivity, no special routing groups are required. However, as an option, you might consider generating routing groups between these servers to control the message flow across political or departmental boundaries.

6. **d.** A routing group name can have up to 64 characters.

7. **b.** All Exchange servers will attempt to use global catalogs from their local domain and site by default. However, if not enough global catalogs exist in the local domain and site, Exchange will expand the scope and request global catalogs from the local site only.

8. **c.** The message goes next to the advanced queuing engine regardless of whether the message is local or remote. When an Exchange 2000 server figures out that a recipient is on the same server as the sender, Exchange 2000 delivers the message to the recipient's mailbox in the following manner:

    1. MAPI client transmits the message.

    2. The message goes to the advanced queuing engine regardless of whether it is local or remote.

    3. The advanced queuing engine deposits the messages in the "pre-categorizer" queue.

    4. The message "categorizer" grabs the message from the pre-categorizer queue and processes the message. The categorizer expands groups when necessary and checks the sender and recipient limits.

    5. The message categorizer drops the message in the local delivery queue if the recipient is local.

    6. The Web Storage System associates the message with the recipient's mailbox.

9. **a** and **d.** To offer a more flexible deployment and administration configuration, in Exchange 2000 Server, all three boundaries are separate. Also, the namespace hierarchy exists in Active Directory in the form of a domain.

10. **b.** Servers running Exchange must belong to the identical Active Directory forest. Other rules that apply to servers within the same routing group are that *all* servers running Exchange must have permanent and stable direct connectivity to one another. Also, *all* servers within a routing group need to be able to make contact with the routing group master.

11. **c.** If multiple routing groups exist within an organization, the sending server uses the link state table to determine the best route based on connection cost and status.

12. **a.** You designate a server to be the routing group master for a routing group. The routing group master maintains the link state information received from different sources. The routing group master collates this data and makes it available to other servers within the routing group using propagation algorithms.

13. **b, c,** and **d.** You can use SMTP Connectors to connect routing groups. You should use them when the remote server connector is the Internet Mail Service from earlier versions of Exchange; when a pull relationship is required between servers in which one side queues messages and the other side pulls them by using the **TRN** or **ETRN** command; and when you want to define Transport Layer Security (TLS) or other security parameters.

14. **a, b, c,** and **d.** The following are reasons to divide Exchange 2000 servers into multiple routing groups:

   ➤ Routing group prerequisites are incompatible.

   ➤ Network connections are unreliable.

   ➤ The messaging path must be altered from single-hop to multi-hop.

   ➤ Messages must be queued and sent on a schedule.

   ➤ Low-bandwidth network connections exist for which X.400 connectivity is more appropriate.

   ➤ Client connections to public folders exist.

15. **b.** Exchange 2000 server does perform mail exchange (MX) record resolution for SMTP, but more often than not it resolves the target server by using an A (host) record. This simplifies the arrangement of the Routing Group Connector because an Exchange or DNS administrator does not have to create or manage MX records.

Chapter 10 Solutions

1. **d.** If the Active Directory Connector experiences a failure, perform the following steps to revert back to an operational state:

   1. Disable the connection agreement.

   2. If this does not solve the issue then shut down the ADC service.

   3. If data is corrupted, remove the organizational unit where the data was stored and perform a restore from a tape with a known good state.

   4. Finally, use the Windows 2000 LDP tool to edit data in Active Directory.

2. **b.** This is the role of a Virtual Private Network, not SMTP. VPNs offer a scheme for encapsulating private data packets with a header, enabling it to confidentially move over the network.

3. **a.** The administration of Windows 2000 remote access VPN connections is accomplished through the Dial-In Properties page on user accounts. To control remote access on a per-user basis, simply enable the Grant Dial-In Permission To User setting on the Dial-in Properties tab of the user accounts that are able to make remote access connections.

4. **d.** A firewall uses packet-filtering technologies to sort out particular types of data traffic. IP packet filtering offers a method to define precisely what IP traffic you want to cross your firewall. This technology is essential for organizations linking private intranets with public networks like the Internet.

5. **c.** Although it can be configured to use another port, by default, a virtual server uses Port 25 to take delivery of SMTP connections and listen in on all of the network interfaces.

6. **a.** A relatively simple approach for preventing this type of infringement is to set up a virtual server to do a reverse DNS lookup against the sender of a message. Performance factors should be considered as well when using this solution.

7. **d.** The following list includes some default configurations that you may consider restricting to prevent servers from being inundated:

   ➤ The SMTP session size is limited to 10,240KB.

   ➤ The message size is limited to 2,048KB.

   ➤ The number of messages for each connection is limited to 20.

   ➤ The number of recipients for each message is limited to 100.

8. **b.** The default period that a message will remain in the Exchange 2000 queue is 12 hours. After two days, if the message has still been cleared from the queue, a nondelivery report is sent to the sender.

9. **a, b**, and **d.** ADC doesn't host the active replication components on a foreign system. It only hosts the components on Active Directory.

10. **c** and **d.** There are two editions of the Active Directory Connector. One connector is the ADC for Windows 2000, which ships with Windows 2000 Server. The second type of AD connector is the Enhanced ADC for Exchange 2000 that ships with Exchange 2000 Server.

11. **d.** The SRS is a customized Exchange 5.5 directory that works on the Exchange 2000 server to assist replication between Exchange 2000 SRS and the residual Exchange 5.5 servers. SRS allows for integration with Exchange 5.x sites that use both RPC and mail-based replication processes.

12. **a**, **b**, **c**, and **d**. All of the items are common information held by the connection agreement: The names of servers to contact for replication; the object classes to replicate; target containers; the replication schedule.

13. **a** and **c**. The two types of ADC connection agreements are the user connection agreement and the configuration connection agreement.

14. **b** and **c**. The mail-enabled distribution group and the mail-enabled security group will match up to Exchange Directory Service distribution list object.

15. **c**. LDP is a graphical tool that allows LDAP operations like search, modify, add, and delete. You can use LDP to see objects and object metadata in Active Directory. You can also use LDP to observe attributes but realize that the rules format for matching attributes is very specific.

Chapter 11 Solutions

1. **a**. In Exchange 2000, Outlook is no longer a requirement for accessing public folders. This can be achieved through the WebAccess component.

2. **a**, **b**, **c**, and **d**. The administrative model is comprised of administrative groups, routing groups, policies, and permissions.

3. **c**. In Exchange 2000, all configuration and objects are based on and included into Active Directory. Administration is no longer server- or site-centric, and, as a result of AD integration, it is much more flexible.

4. **d**. The three types of administrative models are the centralized administration model, decentralized administration model, and mixed administration model. In most cases, Exchange administrative models mirror the information technology support team structure within an organization.

5. **b**. The decentralized administration model is the most effective option for large organizations, and it has the same effect as sites in Exchange 5.5.

6. **b** and **c**. You cannot nest administrative groups within administrative groups. The administrative group's parent node can contain individual administrative group child nodes, and within those nodes you create task-specific objects, such as a servers group, chat communities group, and routing group, among others. You cannot create another general administrative group where you have to create task-specific groups. Also very important, when you first install Exchange 2000 server it runs in mixed mode. In mixed mode, not native mode, administrative groups are treated as Exchange 5.5 sites for compatibility reasons.

7. **d**. Public store policies cover the functions of all the other policies with the addition of such replication settings as replication interval and message size limits. Clint policy is not an actual system policy type.

8. **a**, **d**, and **e**. Exchange 2000 configuration is organized in a hierarchy of objects of different types. Some of these objects such as administrative group folders can contain other objects and are referred to as container objects. Some objects cannot contain other objects and are referred to as items, or leaf objects—these are server objects, policy objects, database objects, and so forth. Administrative groups (containers) are called parent objects in relation to the objects they contain, which are referred to as child objects.

9. **b**. Parent Object Only is not one of the inheritance configuration options.

10. **a** and **c**. When the first Exchange 2000 server is installed, it creates two default administrative groups in Active Directory Users and Computers: Exchange domain servers and Exchange enterprise servers.

11. **d**. All of these objects in Exchange hierarchy have extended permissions.

12. **c**. Organizational units are logical units, or containers, used to organize objects such as users, computers, printers, groups, applications, file sharing, and other objects.

13. **b**. Native mode, as the name implies, is used when the organization has moved completely to the Exchange 2000 platform and there is no need to maintain Exchange 5.5 sites.

14. **a**. True. In Exchange 5.5, user administration was a separate process from administering recipient mailboxes.

15. **d**. The three standard administrator types in Exchange 2000 are the view-only administrator, the administrator, and the full administrator.

Chapter 12 Solutions

1. **a**, **b**, and **d**. In Exchange 5.5, administrators had to deal with three major organizational units when managing recipients: NT domain local groups, NT domain global groups, and Exchange distribution lists (DLs).

2. **a**. One of the major planning and deployment advancements that Windows 2000 has to offer is that one group can be used for both security and mail-distribution purposes.

3. **b**. Global groups in Windows 2000 allow one level of nesting.

4. **d**. In native mode, not mixed node, global groups can contain other global groups and user accounts from the same domain. In mixed mode, global groups can contain only user accounts.

5. **c**. Windows 2000 has introduced a group with a new scope—the universal group. It can be implemented only in Windows 2000 running native mode (where no Windows NT domain controllers coexist).

6. **a.** There are two types of universal groups: universal distribution groups (UDGs) and universal security groups (USGs). USGs require the native mode environment, but UDGs exist in both mixed mode and native mode environments.

7. **b** and **d.** In Windows 2000 and Exchange 2000, use universal distribution groups (UDGs) to provide mail distribution functionality, and universal security groups (USGs) to control access to public folders.

8. **b.** When deploying Windows 2000 groups in Exchange 2000 organization, try to use universal security groups (USGs) as much as possible because they provide maximum membership and reference flexibility within the AD forest.

9. **d.** When you send a message to a group, if the group is USG or UDG, group membership is taken from a local global catalog server. On the contrary, if it is a domain local group or domain global group, then members are looked up on one of the local domain controllers.

10. **c.** A Microsoft tool called LoadSim can help you test your system responsiveness and measure baselines.

11. **b.** An object can be mail-enabled, which means this object can accept mail but does not have its own storage to send mail to. An example of a mail-enabled recipient is a Windows 2000 distribution group or mail-enabled security group.

12. **a** and **c.** A distribution group is a distribution list by design a security group can be mail-enabled by configuring an email address in its properties. The major difference between the two is the security identifier (SID). Distribution lists do not have SIDs, and therefore cannot be referenced on ACLs (they cannot be used to assign permissions). On the contrary; security groups have SIDs and are designed to participate in ACL definitions.

13. **a.** Use delegation wizards to delegate administrative privileges in your Exchange 2000 environment.

14. **d.** The access control model (ACM) in Exchange 2000 is completely redesigned from that of Exchange 5.5, and this time it closely matches the Windows 2000 ACM. Permission management is no longer container-based—it is object-based and even property-based, and as a result of this major change, ACM in Exchange 2000 is much more granular and flexible.

15. **a**, **c**, and **d.** Other methods at this time are Windows Scripting Host (WSH) VBScripts and JavaScript that use the ADSI model, and ASP pages through Web-based administration.

Chapter 13 Solutions

1. **b** and **c**. Microsoft Outlook and Exchange System Manager can be used to create and manage public folders within Exchange.

2. **a** and **c**. Top-level hierarchies and public folder trees are other names for public folder hierarchies.

3. **b**, **c**, and **e**. IMAP, MAPI and Web-DAV clients are able to view all public folder hierarchies within Exchange 2000.

4. **d**. In the Public Folders dialog box, the Details tab will allow you to input an administrative description of the public folder.

5. **d**. All of the above are valid steps to create a new public folder tree.

6. **b**. The Public Folder Instances subcontainer allows you to view the folders in the public store, configure the properties of a folder, and replicate a public folder to a specific public store.

7. **a**. To go back to the top-level root folder that you earlier created and connect it with the new public folder store, you should go to the Exchange System Manager, right click on the top-level root folder in the main Folders container and choose Connect To from the menu.

8. **b**. When planning multiple public folder trees, you should take into consideration the fact that the All Public Folders hierarchy is created on every public folder server, and its list of folders is replicated throughout the organization.

9. **a** and **c**. Once you mail-enable a folder, a setting is added to the General tab that controls whether you want the public folder to be visible in the Global Address List, or GAL, so that users can send mail to it. Also a setting is added to the General tab that allows you to configure the way the name is displayed in the address list, whether it is the same name as the folder or a different name.

10. **b** and **c**. Public folders are managed at the public folder store level and at the public folder itself in Exchange System Manager.

11. **b**. "Stop service at (KB)" is fabricated and is not one of the three settings that you can configure for limits.

12. **b**. The "Modify Public Folder ACL" public folders permission allows a user to specify who can configure administrative rights, and is assigned to Organization, Administrative Group, and Public Folder Tree objects.

13. **c**. The directory rights category of permissions allows you to determine which users can configure the mail-enabled Active Directory object.

14. **d**. You will use universal security groups in Exchange 2000.

15. **c**. If an affinity exists between site A and site B and also between site B and site C, affinity automatically exists between site A and site C.

Chapter 14 Solutions

1. **d** and **e**. Chat conversations may be private or public.

2. **b**. Microsoft Exchange chat service relies on Active Directory to establish chat communities, channels, and other chat and user-related settings.

3. **c**. Client software connects to the Exchange server that hosts Chat Service by using the standard IRC port (6667). Usually the first community that exists on the server reserves this port for itself.

4. **b**. One Exchange 2000 Server can host up to 20,000 chat users.

5. **c** and **d**. Chat channels (rooms) can be registered or dynamic.

6. **d**. Server Extension is the name for the software module based on the Chat Server Extensibility Model that enhances the features of the existing chat service.

7. **b**. It is possible to use IRC chat client programs to administer some aspects of your chat service. In-band commands are used in this case, with a requirement of administrative logon. An in-band command is an administrative instruction sent from a client program using chat protocol. The following command disables transcription of all dynamic channels:

   EXTMSG TSCRIPT stop DYNAMIC

8. **c** and **d**. Microsoft Chat Service requires installation of Windows 2000 Server (not necessarily Domain Controller), Microsoft Exchange 2000 Server, and System Manager.

9. **a**. A flooding attack is a denial-of-service type of attack that sends massive amounts of nonsense data to a chat session.

10. **d**. Exchange Chat Service supports three authentication types: Anonymous (no authentication), Basic Authentication (clear-text authentication), and Windows Security Support Provider Interface (SSPI) authentication.

11. **b**. You must install a Multipoint Control Unit to hold data conferencing. MCU is a subcomponent of the Data Conferencing provider, and it serves the purpose of connecting incoming requests for data conferencing with each other.

12. **c**. To participate in multicast communication, your devices must have a class D multicast IP address that falls within the range of 224.0.0.0 – 239.255.255.255.

13. **g.** To fully deploy Microsoft Exchange Conferencing Server, you need Active Directory in the organization, Microsoft IIS Server 5 for Exchange Server and Web access, and Microsoft Exchange 2000 Server installed in your domain.

14. **b.** Although hardware requirements depend heavily on the load of your conferencing server, Microsoft suggests a minimum requirement of 128MB of RAM.

15. **a**, **b**, **c**, **d**, and **f.** Exchange Server allows developers the support for Collaborative Data Objects (CDO), Active Server Pages (ASP), (Hypertext Markup Language (HTML), Event sink, forms, ActiveX Data Objects (ADO), Web Storage Schema (XML), Web Storage Event sink, and CDO for Exchange Management (CDOEXM).

Chapter 15 Solutions

1. **d.** Basically, transaction logging, checkpoint file, patch files and other database fundamentals remain the same in Exchange 2000. The Directory Service database (dir.edb) does not exist in Exchange 2000, because it relies on Windows 2000 Active Directory instead.

2. **b.** In much the same way as in Exchange 5.5, Exchange 2000 stores MDBEF data in the .edb database file, only now all non-MDBEF data goes into the second part of the database, the .stm database file. Both of these databases are built on ESE technology.

3. **a.** LegacyExchangeDN is a parameter that is used for legacy Exchange 5.5 coexistence.

4. **c.** Sometimes you will have to run hard recovery manually, and this is done using this command: **eseutil /cc [*path to restore*.env]**.

   You should be aware that **ESEUTIL** exists as a critical tool, but it is not a topic of this chapter. This tool is used to maintain your databases (defragment, check consistency, run hard recoveries, and so on).

5. **d.** You can reinstall Exchange 2000 using the setup/disaster recovery option. This option allows you to run Setup in Disaster Recovery mode to rebuild a server previously lost in the Exchange topology.

6. **a.** Every computer system worldwide should have some sort of virus detection logic. Just as important is using an Exchange 2000-aware antivirus solution for your messaging and collaboration needs. Antivirus software operates by searching for certain bit patterns. Considering the amount and content of email coming in these days, a clean email can become suspect and be destroyed. Software that is not Exchange 2000-aware may potentially lead to unpredictable problems when it comes to Exchange databases and transaction logs.

7. **b.** This means that the same 5MB attachment sent to 50 people in your organization is not going to be stored in 50 mailboxes. Instead, it is going to be stored once in a transaction log in each storage group to which it was sent, and once in every database that hosts recipients of that message. Therefore, if there was a 5MB attachment in that message, and all recipients were hosted within one storage group in one database, you would end up with two copies of this message, totaling 10MB as opposed to 250MB.

8. **c** and **f.** Each database within a storage group can be in one of the two states: mounted or dismounted. By default, when you initialize Store.exe, databases are mounted automatically. The state of the database has an impact on your backup and restore operations.

9. **d.** The ESE database is comprised of chunks of data called pages. A page is a 4K unit of information contained in the database.

10. **b.** The Standard Edition of Microsoft Exchange 2000 supports up to 16GB databases.

11. **c.** If there is a critical need to control and reduce the amount of space taken by transaction logs, you might want to enable circular logging. When enabled, it produces only five logs of 5MB each, and after the fifth log is filled Exchange starts overwriting transaction log number 1, first committing its transactions to the database. This is not a good practice for most Exchange deployments, however.

12. **a.** Upon initialization of the backup, **NTBACKUP** calls the necessary API procedures to inform Store.exe of the fact that database backup is on its way. Store.exe passes this information on to the ESE engine, which in turn enters backup mode.

13. **d.** The full (normal) backup procedure will include a database copy and a log copy, as well as a log delete.

14. **a.** This is a true statement. Whereas online backups require Store.exe to be started and databases mounted, offline backups require exactly the opposite—Store.exe must be stopped.

15. **d.** System State is a new backup type in Windows 2000 that goes further by saving the IIS metabase, as well as COM+ objects and registrations. It provides a complete snapshot of system-specific information.

Chapter 16 Solutions

1. **b.** The distinction comes down to whether you are attempting to eradicate downtime or merely minimize downtime. The goal of high availability is to curtail the amount of downtime. Fault-tolerant solutions, in contrast, look for the elimination of downtime.

2. **d.** A key concept of availability is the mean time between failures. This factor is the statistically resultant length of time that a user may realistically expect a component, device, or system to work between two catastrophic failures.

3. **b.** The common availability statistic accepted by the industry for 99.9 percent downtime is 8 hours, 44 minutes.

4. **c.** Recent studies have indicated that human intervention cause approximately 80 percent of all unplanned outages.

5. **a, b,** and **c.** When a public folder server fails, critical business data coming into your organization can cease, and personal productivity may suffer. In addition, applications, document repositories, Web sites, and knowledge management systems can stop working.

6. **d.** More than 90 percent of all interactions with Active Directory occur with the global catalog.

7. **a.** A recent highly regarded study found that the monetary costs of downtime by and large range from $1,000 to $27,000 per minute.

8. **f.** Typical considerations are the uninterruptible power supply (UPS), processor failure, bad memory, and the performance and reliability of the disk subsystem. Another key area of hardware exposure involves the networking components, which can range from the physical cabling to switches and routers. In most environments, these devices are critical to offering consistency and robustness to Exchange 2000 users.

9. **a, b, c,** and **d.** All of these are methods that can be implemented to reduce recovery time and recovery point in an Exchange 2000 environment: replicating the data, deploying several databases and storage groups, resilient message routing, and backing up and restoring data online simultaneously.

10. **c.** In a Windows 2000 cluster, the total number of storage groups on a single node must be four or less, despite the number of Exchange virtual servers that exist on the node.

11. **d.** Clustering is the process whereby two or more servers are coupled so that they perform and appear as a single computer. Clustering is a popular strategy used for parallel processing applications, load-balancing and fault-tolerance solutions.

12. **b** and **c.** Generally speaking, the two prime clustering models are the Shared Disk model and the Shared Nothing model.

13. **c.** Active/active clustering can be described as a scenario in which both members of the cluster are online and accepting user requests for various services. The active/active clustering model offers fault tolerance in case a server goes down and assures the possible minimum undesirable effect on the user.

14. **a**. Microsoft Cluster Services is really a set of DLLs and APIs for Windows 2000. The main DLL files are EXCLUADM.DLL and EXRES.DLL.

15. **a**, **b**, **c**, and **d**. Each virtual server will have its own autonomous configuration information such as domain name, Internet Protocol (IP) address, port number, and authentication.

Chapter 17 Solutions

1. **c.** Circular logging is disabled by default in Exchange 2000. You may need to verify that it is turned off as a troubleshooting measure.

2. **b.** The Link monitor display and log tools will help you verify if test messages sent to servers are making the round-trip within a particular length of time.

3. **d.** the ForestPrep component is used to update the Active Directory schema for Exchange 2000. The command to run the program is **setup/forestprep**.

4. **a.** During the installation of Exchange 2000 Server, the error message

```
Setup Fails: Error 0xC103798A
```

indicates that the setup failed while configuring the registry entries for the Exchange System Management snap-ins.

5. **c.** If you see a message telling you that the directory service is busy while running the Exchange 2000 Setup, you are likely installing Exchange 2000 Server into a child domain.

6. **a.** If an error message is generated when the account that you are using to initiate the setup procedure has inadequate or incorrect permissions configured for the target server's Exchange Server 5.5 directory, you should grant your account the Exchange Administrator permissions at the Site and Configuration levels of your Exchange 5.5 server.

7. **b.** In this scenario, when you notice that information about a new server is being replicated to other servers on the site, you should remove the new server from the site's directory after you reinstall the server.

8. **c.** You can monitor the path of messages with the Message Tracking Center component in Exchange 2000.

9. **d.** The Internet News Service creates an important special file called Ics.dat that it places in Insdata directory. If this file is corrupted or lost, Internet News Service creates a new one by default.

10. **b.** These messages are immediately returned to their sender with a **5.0.0** error code in a Non–delivery report (NDR).

11. **c.** Problems may arise with your data storage in Web Storage System, including those with the Exchange Installable File System (ExIFS), mailboxes, and databases. For example, if you stop the ExIFS service and then attempt to restart it, the error message

    ```
    System error 2 has occurred. The system cannot find the file specified
    ```

    may pop up. The ExIFS installs with Exchange 2000 Server and runs as a hidden service on an Exchange 2000 server; therefore, it is not visible in the Services dialog box in Administrative Tools. However, you can still issue a **net stop** or a **net start** command to stop or start the ExIFS service, as well as other tools from the Windows 2000 Resource Kit.

12. **a, b**, and **c.** If you are administering users through Active Directory Users and Computers on a system where the Exchange System Management tools are not installed, all the Exchange 2000 options may not be available; you will not be able to add, delete, or move an Exchange 2000 mailbox; and you will not see all of the Exchange 2000 extensions.

13. **a.** If you decide to run Exchange 5.5 Server on a global catalog server or Windows 2000 Server domain controller in a Windows 2000 environment, you must change the LDAP port of the Exchange 5.5 Directory Service to a value different from the default value of 389.

14 **d.** When attempting to perform a backup in your Exchange 2000 infrastructure and the error message

    ```
    Event ID 1018, 1019, or 1022: Database is damaged
    ```

    is received, the online backup cannot finish because the database is damaged.

15. **c.** System Monitor is the Windows 2000 tool that provides data regarding such performance statistics as processor use, memory use, server throughput, queue size, and number of write/read operations per second.

Appendix B
Objectives for Exam [70-225]

Analyzing Business Requirements	See Chapter(s):
Analyze factors that influence organizational policy requirements.	2
Analyze the existing and planned business models.	2
Analyze the existing and planned business-security model.	2, 8
Analyze the existing and planned administrative model.	2, 11

Analyzing Existing and Planned Resources	See Chapter(s):
Analyze existing server roles.	3
Analyze existing and planned network resources.	3
Analyze existing directory- and name-resolution configurations.	3
Analyze the impact of Exchange 2000 Server on the existing and planned network.	3
Analyze the existing messaging system architecture and potential changes to this architecture.	3,4
Analyze existing messaging client configurations.	3,4

Designing an Exchange 2000 Server Messaging Solution	See Chapter(s):
Design an Exchange 2000 Server routing group topology.	4, 9
Design an Exchange 2000 Server administrative model.	4,10
Design an Exchange 2000 Server realtime collaboration solution that uses Chat Service, and/or Instant Messaging.	14
Plan public folder usage and implementation.	13
Design an Exchange 2000 Server security plan.	8
Secure the Exchange 2000 Server infrastructure against external attacks.	8
Secure the Exchange 2000 Server infrastructure against internal attacks.	8
Design an authentication and encryption strategy.	8
Plan for coexistence of Exchange 2000 Server with other messaging systems.	6
Plan for coexistence with foreign mail systems, such as Notes, cc:Mail, GroupWise, MS Mail, PROFS, TAO, and SNADS.	6
Plan for coexistence with Exchange Server 5.5.	7,10
Design interorganizational connectivity and synchronization.	10
Designate and design servers.	3,10
Plan traffic flow.	3,10
Design server hardware and disk configurations to achieve fault tolerance and increased performance and to provide for a backup strategy, based on server role.	3, 15
Design an upgrade or migration strategy.	7
Design ADC connection agreements.	6,10
Plan a migration that uses ADMT.	7
Design connection agreements to support container synchronization.	6,10
Decide direction of synchronization.	6,10
Design a strategy for mail access. Messaging clients include MAPI, IMAP4, POP3, and HTTP mail.	5

Designing for Fault Tolerance and Data Recovery	See Chapter(s):
Design a backup solution.	15
Design a recovery solution.	15
Design fault-tolerance solutions.	15

Deploying an Exchange 2000 Server Messaging Solution	See Chapter(s):
Deploy routing groups and foreign connectors.	9,10
Deploy administrative groups.	11,12
Plan deployments of messaging clients, such as MAPI, IMAP4, POP3, and HTTP mail.	5
Deploy an Exchange 2000 Server messaging solution in a cluster.	16
Diagnose and resolve coexistence problems.	17
Resolve email delivery problems.	17
Resolve problems with foreign connections.	17
Resolve address synchronization problems.	17
Resolve problems with address and name resolution	17
Diagnose and resolve other deployment problems.	17
Resolve failed deployments that require a rollback to Exchange Server 5.5.	17
Resolve permissions problems.	17
Resolve problems with sending and receiving email.	17
Resolve security problems.	8,17
Resolve DNS name-resolution problems.	17
Resolve problems involving resource limitations.	17

Appendix C
Exchange 2000 Server
Design Resources

Books

Exchange 2000 .NET Server Black Book, Phillip Schein and Evan Benjamin, The Coriolis Group. ISBN: 1-57610-997-6. *.NET Server Black Book* is a comprehensive reference to administering, configuring, and troubleshooting Exchange 2000. The book teaches how to utilize the new features of Exchange 2000 and SMTP. It covers migrations issues and planning for design and integration, site topology and organization, corporate and user's needs, Exchange Service selection, and disaster recovery.

MCSE Exchange 2000 Administration Exam Cram, Will Willis and David Watts, The Coriolis Group. ISBN: 1-57610-980-1. This intense study guide is for IT professionals who are serious about passing the popular MCSE Windows 2000 elective exam "Installing, Configuring, and Administering Microsoft Exchange 2000 Server" (70-224).

MCSE Exchange 2000 Administration Exam Prep, Phillip Schein and Evan Benjamin, The Coriolis Group. ISBN: 1-57610-919-4. This guide prepares you for the Microsoft Exchange 2000 Administration certification exam (70-224). The book covers Windows 2000, Active Directory, and the component architecture of Exchange 2000, and the new version of Microsoft Outlook Web Access as well as support for instant messaging, chat services, and data conferencing services.

MCSE Exchange 2000 Design Exam Cram, William Baldwin, The Coriolis Group. ISBN: 1-58880-032-6. This focused study program will help you prepare to pass the MCSE Designing and Deploying a Messaging Infrastructure with Microsoft Exchange 2000 Server exam (70-225). All of the pertinent test concepts, such as analyzing business requirements and resources for Exchange 2000, designing and deploying Exchange 2000 Server messaging solutions, fault tolerance and data recovery, and managing Active Directory and Internet Information Server (IIS) are covered.

Microsoft Exchange 2000 Server Administrator's Companion, Walter J. Glen and Bill English, Microsoft Press. ISBN: 0-73560-938-1. This book is the IT implementer's guide to deploying and maintaining Exchange 2000 Server. The topics covered include: Outlook Web Access and SMTP, Chat Service and Instant Messaging, plus integration with Microsoft Windows 2000 Server Active Directory services and

Microsoft Outlook 2000. The companion CD-ROM includes a fully searchable electronic version of the book and useful white papers by Exchange experts.

Microsoft Exchange 2000 Server Administrator's Pocket Consultant, William R. Stanek, Microsoft Press. ISBN: 0-73560-962-4. This concise and easy-to-use pocket reference includes tables, lists, and step-by-step instructions and presents fast answers to help the user complete fundamental tasks, work with Active Directory services (ADS), administer and troubleshoot data storage, and administer servers and groups. You'll find the following topics covered: Microsoft Exchange 2000 Server, from the administrator's perspective; the relationship between Exchange 2000 Server and Active Directory; management of users and groups; management of online and offline address lists; database design and upkeep; server optimization; and message routing.

Microsoft Exchange 2000 Server Resource Kit, Microsoft Press. ISBN: 0-73561-017-7. This kit backs up its valuable collection of administration utilities with some solid technical advice, "official" wisdom, and precise writing. The authors, members of the development team and Microsoft's consulting arm, explain the options, and the appropriateness of the options, that are available to the administrator.

Windows 2000 Security Little Black Book, The Hands-On Reference Guide for Establishing a Secure Windows 2000 Network, Ian McLean, The Coriolis Group. ISBN: 1-57610-387-0. This book discusses potential security holes in the Windows 2000 system and how to prevent them. It covers both desktop and server security. Finally, this book emphasizes security issues raised by high-bandwidth connections to the Internet with and without firewalls.

Magazines

Microsoft Certified Professional Magazine, Microsoft Corporation, Irvine, CA. This monthly magazine for certified professionals is a good resource for general certification information.

Certification Magazine, MediaTec Publishing, Oakland, CA. This monthly magazine is slanted toward certified professionals of information technology. This magazine's aim is to provide IT pros and technical trainers with a comprehensive look at all platforms of IS/IT certification and training.

Online Resources

Web Sites

www.microsoft.com/exchange—Microsoft Exchange Server Home Page. This site presents the latest news, product overviews, and updates on Exchange 2000. You'll also find links to various white papers, online seminars, and other resources.

www.email-software.com—Microsoft Exchange Server 2000 and Outlook Resource Site. This site offers a wealth of information on integration between Exchange and Outlook.

www.win2000mag.net/channels/exchange—Windows 2000 Magazine Exchange & Outlook Channel. This online Windows magazine offers a large number of pertinent articles for subscribers and non-subscribers.

www.exchange-mail.org—Exchange-mail.org. This is a nonprofit Web site for general information, forums, news, and updates on the world of Exchange 2000.

Trial Software

www.microsoft.com/exchange/evaluation/trial—Exchange 2000 Server Trial Software. Here, you can download an evaluation copy of Exchange 2000 Server.

Appendix C

Glossary

access
Information exchanged within a computer system or over a network.

access control
When the access to a system or network resource is restricted. Authorized users are the only participants allowed access. It is also a security feature in Windows 2000 that controls access to information, objects, or components for specified users and groups.

Access Control Entry (ACE)
An entry in an access control list (ACL) that holds the security identifier (SID) for a user or group. Also contains an access mask that permits, denies, or audits operations by users or groups.

Access Control List (ACL)
A list of Windows 2000 security principals, user accounts, and groups associated to an object. It is used to decide whether a user or a process has access to an object.

access permission
A designation associated with an object, such as a folder or file, that controls which users have access to the object and the manner of that access.

access token
A data-structure object that contains the security identifier of an active process. It stores security information that identifies a user to the security subsystem on a computer running Windows 2000. These tokens establish the security context of a process and include a user's security ID, the security IDs for groups that the user belongs to, as well as a set of the privileges the user was given on the local computer.

account domain
This domain exists for the purpose of controlling a user account and the security database for other domains.

account lockout
A feature of NT Server security that locks a user account if a number of failed logon attempts happens in a certain period of time. It is based on account policy-lockout settings.

account lockout policy
Configuration setting that determines the results of a user account being locked out.

account policy
A setting that controls the way in which the user employs passwords. It is set for all user accounts in a domain or for all user accounts of a single workstation or member server when administering a computer. An account policy can control minimum password lengths, how often users must change passwords, and how often users can reuse their old passwords.

Active Data Objects (ADO)
A programming interface that resides on top of OLE/DB that allows high-level

programming languages the ability to access an underlying data store with a common query language. In Exchange 2000, a data store would be Active Directory, the Exchange 2000 store, or a SQL database.

Active Directory (AD)

The Windows 2000 Directory Service that replaces the Security Accounts Manager in Windows NT 4. AD consists of a forest, domain(s), organization units, containers, and objects. Within Active Directory, multiple classes of objects can be defined. These classes may include users, groups, computers, printers, and applications. AD makes available the information about objects on the network for authorized administrators and users. Active Directory allows qualified network users to access resources anywhere on the network through a single logon process. AD also gives administrators a single hierarchical view of the network along with a single point of control over all network objects.

Active Directory Connector (ADC)

The ADC replicates information between an Exchange Server 5.5 directory and Active Directory. This information can include mailboxes, custom recipients, and distribution lists. ADC deploys connection agreements to define individual replication configurations. ADC functionality provides a method of administration of a directory from either Active Directory or the Exchange 5.5 directory service.

Active Directory Service Interfaces (ADSI)

An abstraction interface that provides programming languages compatible with the Component Object Model (COM). These languages include Visual Basic, VBScript, JavaScript, C, and C++. The purpose of ADSI is to allow for a common command set of directory calls to an underlying Directory Service. ADSI components include Lightweight Directory Access Protocol (LDAP), NDS, Bindery, and Windows NT (SAM).

Active Directory Users and Computers

A MMC snap-in that allows administrators to manage objects in the Active Directory.

active partition

A primary partition marked as "active" when it contains the operating-system boot files.

Active Server Page (ASP)

A Web page that includes scripts or programs that can be processed on a Web server before they are sent to the user. This scripting environment also runs ActiveX scripts and ActiveX components on a server. Developers combine scripts and components to create Web-based applications.

ActiveX

A set of programming components from Microsoft that are used make Web pages and applications interactive.

address list

A collection of recipient objects that can contain one or more kinds of objects, such as users, contacts, groups, public folders, conferencing, and other resources. Exchange 2000 address lists also offer a way to partition mail-enabled objects in Active Directory for the benefit of certain user groups.

address list service

A service of the Exchange System Attendant that populates address list containers in Active Directory. This mechanism is based on filtering rules found in RFC 2254 Lightweight Directory Access Protocol (LDAP).

address mask

A bit mask used to select bits from an Internet address to determine the network number and subnet parts of an address. The procedure is referred to as the subnet mask.

address resolution

The one-to-one mapping of an IP address to a physical address.

Address Resolution Protocol (ARP)

A protocol used to dynamically bind an Internet address to physical address in an Ethernet or token ring network topology.

address space

A set of address information that identifies certain kinds of messages. The address space is linked with a connector or gateway and is usually a subset of a complete address.

administration group

A grouping of Exchange 2000 Servers that can be administered as a single entity. An administration group can include policies, routing groups, Public Folder hierarchies, monitors, servers, conferencing services, and also chat networks. It can also be defined as a collection of Active Directory objects that are grouped together for the purpose of permissions management. The content of an administrative group depends on choices made during the installation process.

administrator

The Windows 2000 account that was designed to perform network-management and system-maintenance duties.

advanced security

A technique that allows users to digitally sign or encrypt messages. When signing messages, the sender provides an advanced security password. When decrypting messages, recipients must give an advanced security password.

applet

A small program built into either an operating system or a larger application. It can also be a separate tool or utility found in the Control Panel of Windows 2000. Applets usually have only one purpose or function.

Application Programming Interface (API)

A structure provided by vendors for an interface to applications.

architecture

The design and structure of operating system components or other systems and their relationships to each other.

asynchronous event

A circumstance that occurs after an item is saved or deleted. Asynchronous events do not happen in any particular sequence along with other events.

attack

An attempt to bypass a set of security controls or firewalls with the intent to disrupt performance, destroy systems, or steal data. An active attack alters data on the system; a passive attack releases data into the system.

attribute

Information about a file that determines if it is read-only, hidden, system, or compressed. It can also designate if the file has been modified since a backup copy was generated. In object-oriented application design, an attribute represents an individual characteristic of the object.

audit

To track user actions on a server or workstation by monitoring and recording specified events in an event log.

audit policy

Configuration for a domain's server or individual computer that determines the type of events that will be logged.

Glossary

authentication

In Windows 2000, authentication is the validation of a user's logon information. In Exchange 2000 it can be the process of verifying user identity by establishing a connection to a chat server.

author mode

The console setting that permits a user to add and remove snap-ins, generate new windows, view the whole console tree, and save new versions of the console.

authorization

The granting of rights to a user, program, or process.

autonomous system

A group of routers and/or networks that are controlled by a single administrative unit and work in concert to propagate network information via an Interior Gateway Protocol.

backbone

The main network connection between segments of a local area network.

back-end server

A server that hosts at least one database that other servers can connect to in order to transfer data or requests from clients.

Backup Domain Controller (BDC)

An NT Server computer that stores in read-only mode a copy of the account and security databases.

baseband

A network specification that uses a single carrier frequency. Baseband transmissions demand that all stations on the network participate in every transmission. Ethernet is an example of a baseband technology.

bastion host

A host computer that must be secure. This is mandatory because it is available from the Internet and, therefore, exposed to attack. It serves as a protective relay agent between Internet mail internal users in an organization.

binding

A method of establishing a communication channel between a protocol driver and a network card.

bottleneck

A scenario created when a system resource or device limits overall performance.

bridgehead

A server designated to perform as a point of transfer between Exchange 2000 routing groups. It may also be a server nominated to be the initial point of contact for an instant messaging organization.

bridgehead server

In Exchange 2000, a connection point from a routing group to another routing group, remote system, or other external system. Generally speaking, a bridgehead server is a server system that links servers through the same protocols so that data can be transferred successfully from one server to another.

broadband

As opposed to *baseband*, broadband is a network structure that multiplexes independent, multiple network carriers on a single cable. Broadband technology can carry voice, video, and data over the same cable.

broadcast

A data message meant to be delivered to all nodes on a network. These messages may be hardware broadcasts or from higher transport layers like an IP-directed broadcast (126.255.255) that is delivered to all nodes in a particular subnet.

cache

An area of hard drive storage space or part of hardware such as DRAM that is designated to repeatedly write and/or retrieve the same data. System operations occur much quicker because cache memory is faster than a computer system's SRAM. Caching also refers to a local area where information about the Active Directory domain name space is stored.

CDO System Management

An API that allows administrators to access management information on an Exchange 2000 Server through programming. This API can include message queues and mailbox storage data. CDO System Management was formerly known as Exchange Management Objects (EMO).

certificate

A digital credential that authenticates a user on the Internet, intranets, or both. These components ensure the genuine transfer of confidential information (or other sensitive material) on a network using public encryption technology. In Exchange 2000, certificates store information used for digital signatures and encryption that binds a users public key to a mailbox.

Certificate Authority (CA)

An authority in a network that issues and administers security credentials (and public keys) for the encryption and decryption of messages.

certificate revocation list (CRL)

A list of users whose security tokens were revoked and cannot be authenticated as secure.

Certificate Services (CS)

CS provides support for the authentication of secure email, Web-based objects, and smart cards.

certificate template

A Windows 2000 data structure that determines, in advance, the format and content of a certificate, depending on its planned usage.

certificate trust list (CTL)

A digitally signed list of root certification authority certificates that administrators consider trustworthy for selected purposes. Examples can include client authentication or secure email.

certification

This is a procedural assessment that determines whether a certain computer system or network meets a set of security requirements that have been previously specified.

certification authority (CA)

A CA is a server component that issues certificates to clients and servers. A certification authority confirms the identity of a public key user. A CA can also withdraw certificates when the private key related to the certificate is compromised or the subject of the certificate is no longer part of the system.

Challenge Handshake Authentication Protocol (CHAP)

A protocol employed by Microsoft remote access service to negotiate for the most secure method of encrypted authentication that both the client and server support.

channel

A channel is also known as a *chat room* in Exchange 2000. The channel is the platform for Chat Service communication.

checkpoint file

A file that contains a list of transactions that have been saved to disk successfully. The Edb.chk file points to the log file of all transactions that have been successfully committed to the database file. Separate checkpoint files exist for each storage group.

circular logging

A transaction logging technique used in the Web Storage System where older log files are overwritten after transactions in the log file are committed to the database.

client

A computer system used to access server computers and other network resources.

client/server model

A design of the interaction that occurs in a distributed computing environment where a component at one node sends a request to a component on another site and then waits for a response. The client application will rely on server processing power.

coexistence

The situation that occurs when you connect Exchange 2000 to another messaging system so that the two systems operate in tandem. This could be a previous version of Exchange. Coexistence periods can be short-term or long-term.

Collaboration Data Objects 1.21 (CDO 1.21)

An application programming interface that lets users and programs access data objects within an Exchange Server. CDO 1.21 is also known as Active Messaging and OLE Messaging.

Collaboration Data Objects 2 (CDO 2)

A high-level application programming interface that lets applications programmatically access Simple Mail Transport Protocol (SMTP) and Network News

Transport Protocol (NNTP) stacks on a Windows 2000 system.

Collaboration Data Objects For Exchange 2000 (CDO For Exchange 2000)

An application programming interface that is a superset of CDO 2. In addition to gaining programmatic access to the Simple Mail Transport Protocol (SMTP) and Network News Transport Protocol (NNTP) stacks, CDO For Exchange 2000 offers support for generating and manipulating of messages, appointments, and contact cards.

complete trust domain

A domain model that determines how domains are managed in a Windows NT environment.

Conference Management Service

The component of Exchange 2000 Conferencing Server that reserves and schedules online meetings.

conference resource

When scheduling an online meeting, a conference resource is an Exchange 2000 mailbox that users give an invitation to.

Conference Technology Provider (CTP)

A firm that offers data conferencing integration services for components such as realtime video, audio, and telephony.

Conferencing Management Service (CMS)

A network service that "books" virtual resources for Exchange Conference Service online meetings. Each site will typically have an active Conferencing Management Service providing rapid connections for the data conferencing users.

Configuration Connection Agreement (ConfigCA)

A unique connection agreement deployed as part of the Active Directory Connector that replicates configuration naming context information from down level Exchange 5.x sites to the administration groups in Active Directory (and vice versa). This special type of connection agreement is automatically generated the first time an Exchange 2000 server is introduced into an Exchange 5.5 site and cannot be created manually.

connection agreement
These are implemented by Active Directory Connectors (ADC) to manage the replication between an Exchange 5.x (or earlier) site and Active Directory. The standard connection agreement replicates Exchange recipient objects (mailboxes, distribution lists, custom recipients, and public folder proxies) and Active Directory objects (users, groups, contacts, and public folder proxies) between the Exchange 5.5 directory and Active Directory.

console
A control interface where a user communicates with a computer screen through a keyboard or mouse. A console integrates all the utilities, information, and Web pages that an administrator needs to perform certain tasks.

contact
An object of Active Directory that symbolizes a user without a Windows logon account or mailbox. A contact often represents a user outside of the organization. A contact in Windows 2000 is the same as a custom recipient in earlier versions of Exchange.

container
An object that contains other objects.

contiguous namespace
A data structure that contains names that share a common root.

Control Panel
The collection of applets within Windows 2000 (and also within Windows 95, 98, ME, XP, and NT) where the majority of system- and hardware-level installation and configuration changes occur.

counter
A data object used for monitoring by the Windows 2000 Performance tool. Performance counters are used to measure or monitor some facet of a registered system or program object.

custom address list
An address list generated for users who need a customized view of recipients within an Exchange organization.

custom recipient
A custom recipient is implemented in legacy versions of Exchange and represents a user who is not hosted by Exchange. In Exchange 2000, these users can be added to Active Directory as contacts, Windows 2000 users, or users whose Windows 2000 accounts are disabled.

data conference
An online conference where members share data in real time.

Data Conferencing Provider (DCP)
An Exchange 2000 Conferencing Server conference technology provider that allows for hosting of data conferences.

decryption
The conversion of encrypted text into human-readable text (also called *plaintext*).

default address list
A list of addresses that are generated automatically depending on the values of specific attributes of Active Directory objects.

Glossary

demand paging
The process whereby an active application requests free pages of memory from RAM.

Desktop Management Interface (DMI)
An industry framework for centrally managing and tracking hardware and software components in a PC system. DMI was created by the Desktop Management Task Force (DMTF) to automate system management.

dial-up networking
The process of making connections at the Digital Data Link layer over various serial-based media. Dial-up refers to brief connections instead of leased connections.

digital signature
A tool for authenticating the origin of a message as well as the identity of a sender and receiver. It is a personal authentication technique based on encryption and secret authorization codes used for signing electronic documents.

directory partition
A self-contained portion of a directory hierarchy that can have its own properties. Active Directory includes the domain, configuration, and schema directory partitions.

directory replication
The method of updating the directories of all servers between and within sites.

Directory Replicator Service
A service that replicates directories and the files in those directories among computer systems.

discretionary access control
An access control policy that governs access to resources based on the identity of a user.

Disk Management
The MMC snap-in used to administer disk drives.

Distributed Authoring and Versioning (DAV)
An extension of the Hypertext Transfer Protocol (HTTP) that provides for manipulation of objects and attributes.

Distributed File System (DFS)
A Windows 2000 Server service that manages and modifies shared resources from various locations on a network in a single hierarchical system.

distribution list
A group of recipients that are generated to facilitate the mass mailing of messages. All members of a list will receive a copy of the message when email is sent to a distribution list.

domain
In Windows 2000, a domain is a logical security boundary. Permissions that are granted in one domain are not transferable to another domains.

domain controller (DC)
A DC is a designated computer role on a Windows 2000 Server that authenticates domain logons and controls security policies and the account database for a domain. A domain controller manages user access to a network, including logging on, authentication, and access to Active Directory and shared resources. Every Windows 2000 domain controller holds a complete replica of the domain-naming context that the server is in as well as a complete copy of the configuration/schema naming contexts for the forest.

domain controller locator

An algorithm designed to locate domain controllers on a Windows 2000 network. It runs in the context of the Net Logon service and can find domain controllers via DNS or NetBIOS names. It can also be implemented on a network where Internet Protocol transport is unavailable.

domain local group

A Windows 2000 group that exists only in native-mode domains. They can contain members from anywhere in the forest, trusted forests, or trusted pre Windows 2000 domain. Domain local groups grant permissions only to resources within the domain in which they exist.

domain mode

A sphere of control for the Active Directory domain, which is either mixed-mode or native-mode.

Domain Name System, or Service (DNS)

A TCP/IP standard naming service that enables clients and servers to resolve names into IP addresses and vice versa. Windows 2000 uses dynamic DNS, which allows clients and servers to automatically register and define records with no manual assistance from an administrator.

domain naming master

Only the domain naming master domain controller has the capability to add new domains to the forest, remove domains from the forest, and add or remove cross-reference objects to external directories.

domain user account

A user account that can be used throughout a domain.

driver

A software component used by an operating system to control a device. They are usually device specific.

DSAccess

The Exchange 2000 component that delivers the directory-lookup services for other components like SMTP and the Message Transfer Agent.

DSProxy

The Exchange 2000 component that can refer and proxy MAPI DS requests from Outlook clients to Active Directory for address book query and name resolution.

dual key pair system

A security design that implements two separate key pairs. Each key pair has its own distinct usage restrictions. One key pair is for message encryption and the other is for creating and validating digital signatures.

dynamic distribution list

A set of recipients that can receive sent email via an LDAP query submission. Dynamic distribution lists are feature of the transport in Exchange 2000.

Dynamic Host Configuration Protocol (DHCPP)

A standard set of guidelines for automatically assigning IP addresses to nodes on a TCP/IP network. The dynamic addressing mechanism allows a computer to have a different address each time it logs on to a network.

dynamic storage

A new Windows 2000 standard technique of dividing a drive by using volumes.

effective policy

The increasing result of the priority application of group policies.

Glossary

encapsulation

The process of wrapping one protocol inside another protocol.

Encrypted File System (EFS)

A Windows 2000 NTFS5 security feature that allows files, folders, and entire drives to be encrypted. With EFS encryption, only the user account that performed the encryption has the private key to decrypt and access the secured objects.

encryption

The conversion of human-readable text (plaintext) into a form that is indecipherable to a person. This advanced security feature offers confidentiality by allowing users to conceal data.

event

From a programming viewpoint, an event is a particular action or occurrence of a changing state that triggers an event sink. For example, the arrival of a message to the SMTP service is an event that can trigger event sinks.

event log

A tool that records events in System, Security, and Application logs located in the Event Viewer component of Windows 2000.

event sink

A segment of code that activates upon a defined trigger, such as receiving a new message. In Exchange 2000, event sinks on the store can be synchronous (code executes as the event is triggered) or asynchronous (code executes sometime after the event).

Event Viewer

A system component of Windows NT/ 2000 that displays logged or audited events in logs called System, Security, and Application.

Exchange 2000 Conferencing Server

A program that offers reliable, scalable online data and video conferencing.

Exchange Administrator

An Exchange Administration Delegation Wizard role that gives a user permissions to fully administer Exchange system information. However, the user cannot modify permissions.

Exchange Conferencing Services (ECS)

An Exchange 2000 service that permits users to meet in Exchange Server-hosted virtual rooms. ECS defines the use of a Conferencing Management Service to coordinate bookings and a T.120 Multipoint Control Unit (MCU) for the connection of clients to a conferencing session.

Exchange Full Administrator

An Exchange Administration Delegation Wizard role that gives a user the permission to fully administer Exchange system information as well as modify permissions.

Exchange View Only Administrator

An Exchange Administration Delegation Wizard role that gives a user permissions to view Exchange configuration information.

EXIPC

A queuing layer that facilitates the Internet Information Server and store processes to transfer data back and forth quickly. This process is necessary on an Exchange 2000 Server to realize the best possible performance between protocols and database services.

extended Instant Messaging address

A more fully qualified Instant Messaging address, which is based on the standard Simple Mail Transfer Protocol (SMTP) format, **someone@im.coriolis.com**.

Extensible Storage Engine (ESE)

ESE is often referred to as JET. The ESE is a process that defines a low-level application-programming interface to the underlying database structures in Exchange 2000 Server. Exchange 2000 uses ESE98. Extensible Storage Engine is also used by other databases like the Active Directory database.

extranet

A shared network that uses Internet technology to connect businesses with their suppliers, customers, and other partners that share common goals.

failover

The method used for taking resources offline, either individually or in a group, on one system and bringing them back online on another system.

File Allocation Table (FAT)

The 16-bit file allocation system that was introduced with DOS. FAT16 is supported in Windows 2000 and is used to format partitions or volumes up to 4G.

FAT32

The enhanced version of FAT introduced by Windows 95 Service Release 2. It is supported by Windows 2000 and expands the file and volume size of FAT to 32G.

fault tolerance

The preservation of data integrity when a hardware failure occurs. In Disk Administrator, fault tolerance is provided using mirror sets, stripe sets with parity, and volume sets.

FDISK

A DOS tool used to partition a hard disk. This utility can only see and manipulate primary NTFS partitions. FDISK cannot view logical drives in an extended partition formatted with NTFS.

file security

The protection of files by using discretionary (or mandatory) access control methods.

file system

The technique used to organize files on disk to read and write them. Windows 2000 supports NTFS, FAT, and FAT32 disk file systems.

firewall

A system designed as the first defense against unauthorized access to a network. A firewall also grants access to authorized users. A firewall prevents direct communication between an internal network and external computers by routing messages through a proxy server outside the network design.

forest

A set of domains and domain trees with the implicit name of the first domain installed. All domain controllers within a forest share the same configuration and schema naming contexts. A forest is also known as an *enterprise*. Forests permit organizations to group divisions that operate independently yet still need to inter-communicate.

fragmentation

The dividing by the operating system of a file into two or more parts, where each part is stored in a different location on the hard drive.

front-end/back-end

An Exchange 2000 design infrastructure where clients access a group of protocol servers (the front-end) for collaboration information. These same protocol servers communicate with the data stores on a separate server (the back-end) to gather the physical data. The front-end and back-end design offers a scalable, single point of contact for all data requests.

Glossary

front-end server

A server that receives requests from clients and passes them on to the suitable back-end server.

full-text indexing

An indexing algorithm that lets users deploy the Microsoft Outlook Advanced Find feature to rapidly locate mail messages, message properties, body text, attachments and documents in the Microsoft Web Storage System.

gateway

A network device that enables communication between two networks or systems.

global address list (GAL)

A list that stores all Exchange users, contacts, groups, conferencing resources, and public folders in an organization. The GAL is retrieved from the global catalog servers in Active Directory and is used by Outlook clients to address messages or find information about recipients within the organization.

global catalog

A server that holds a complete replica of the configuration and schema naming contexts for a forest, a complete replica of the domain naming context in which the server is installed, and a partial replica of all other domains in the forest. The global catalog is the central repository for information about objects in the forest.

global group

A group that exists throughout a domain and can be generated only on a Windows 2000 Server system. A global group can contain user accounts only from its own domain.

Graphical User Interface (GUI)

A graphical operating structure that resides atop a command-line-based operating system.

group

An object defined in Active Directory that contains members of other objects, such as users, contacts, and even other groups. It can be a distribution group or security group depending on the requirement. It can have a scope of local, domain, or universal. A group is akin to a distribution list in Exchange Server 5.5.

Group Policy

A Windows 2000 Microsoft Management Console (MMC) snap-in that designates the desktop settings and behavior for users.

Group Policy Object (GPO)

A set of Group Policy configuration information, stored at the domain level., that basically affects users and computers contained in sites, domains, and organizational units. Group Policy objects are fundamentally the documents created by the Windows 2000 Group Policy MMC snap-in.

hash

A fixed-size product of a one-way mathematical message digest function to an arbitrary amount of data. A hash is also called a message digest.

Hypertext Transfer Protocol (HTTP)

A standard client/server protocol used to retrieve multiple data types on the Internet via the Web and hypertext (HTML) files, which contain embedded links to other files. HTTP is based on the TCP/IP protocol.

identification

The method of establishing a valid account identity on a Windows 2000 system by supplying a working domain name and account name.

imported user account

A local account generated from the duplication of the name and password of an existing domain account. It can be implemented only when the Windows 2000 Professional system is able to communicate with the original account's domain.

in-place upgrade

A process of upgrading to Exchange 2000 Server where you run Exchange 2000 Setup on a server with Exchange Server 5.5 with Service Pack 3.

infrastructure master

A domain controller that updates cross-domain group-to-user references to reflect a user's new name. This domain controller role locally updates these references and uses replication to update all other replicas in the domain.

Installable File System (IFS)

A storage technology that works like a filing system by making mailboxes and public folders appear as conventional folders and files. IFS employs customary Microsoft Win32 applications like Internet Explorer and the command prompt.

Instant Messaging (IM)

An Exchange 2000 service that provides realtime messaging and collaboration between users. The MSN Messenger client is typically used to log on to Instant Messaging.

Instant Messaging address

Instant Messaging uses SMTP email addresses for addressing, although some scenarios require a more fully qualified Instant Messaging address. This is known as an extended Instant Messaging address.

Instant Messaging domain

A DNS name that designates a logical collection of Instant Messaging user accounts and home servers. The IM domain is represented by a virtual server called an Instant Messaging router.

Instant Messaging home server

A virtual server that hosts Instant Messaging user accounts and communicates directly with clients to send and deliver instant messages and presence information.

Instant Messaging Presence Protocol (IMPP)

A standards-based protocol that clients use to communicate with an Instant Messaging server.

Instant Messaging router

An Instant Messaging router that accepts incoming messages, finds a recipient's home server, and relays the message on to that server for delivery.

Instant Messaging Service

A service that provides realtime messaging and collaboration between users.

Internet Information Server (ISS)

A component of Exchange 2000 and Windows 2000 that identifies a computer as an Internet server. It is Microsoft's Web service for publishing information on an intranet or the Internet, and for developing server-based Web applications. Exchange 2000 extends the messaging features of IIS during installation and merges them into the Exchange message routing architecture.

Internet Key Exchange

A protocol that establishes the security association and shared keys needed for two entities to communicate with Internet Protocol security (IPSec).

Glossary

Internet locator service

Active Directory uses DNS as an Internet locator service to resolve Active Directory domain, site, and service names to an IP address.

Internet Messaging Access Protocol version 4 (IMAP4)

A standards-based protocol that provides access to mailbox information. This protocol is considered more sophisticated than POP3, as it supports essential online capabilities and access to more than simply the Inbox folder. IMAP4 lets a client access mail on a server rather than downloading it to the user's computer and is designed for situations where users log on to the server from a array of different systems.

Internetwork Packet Exchange/Sequenced Packet Exchange (IPX/SPX)

A networking protocol from Novell that interconnects networks using NetWare clients and servers. IPX is a connectionless datagram (or packet) protocol that functions at the network layer of OSI model.

Internet Protocol (IP)

The process by which data is sent from one computer to another computer on the Internet. Each host on the Internet has at least one unique address that identifies it from all other hosts on the Internet.

Internet Service Provider (ISP)

A business that provides Internet connectivity to individuals, businesses, and other organizations.

interprocess communication (IPC)

The capability where one task or process exchanges data with another in a multitasking operating system environment. IPC generates a communication process between two processes in the form of pipes, semaphores, shared memory, queues, signals, and mailboxes.

IP address

An address used to uniquely identify a TCP/IP network and node.

IP datagram

A chunk of data transferred across a network by Internet Protocol. The IP datagram includes a header that contains the Internet source and destination addresses.

IP Security (IPSEC)

An encrypted communication system for TCP/IP used to create protected communication sessions.

Joint Engine Technology (JET)

A technology that defines the low-level access to underlying database structures in Exchange Server 4 and 5. The ESE in Exchange Server 5.5 and Exchange 2000 replace the forms of the JET technology.

Kerberos

An encryption authentication design in use by Windows 2000 that verifies the identity of a client and server before the data is actually transferred.

Kerberos V5

Kerberos V5 authentication protocol is the default authentication service for Windows 2000 and is used to verify user or host identity.

key

A secret code or number used to digitally sign, encrypt and decrypt data. The key is usually known only by the sender and the receiver of the information, and often occur in pairs (key pairs). An example of this mechanism is the public key and a private key.

Key Distribution Center (KDC)

A network service that provides session tickets and temporary session keys used in the Kerberos authentication protocol. The

KDC runs as a privileged process on all domain controllers under Windows 2000 and uses the Active Directory to direct sensitive account information.

Key Management server

The Exchange server on which the Key Management Service has been installed and is running. There can be one Key Management server per administrative group.

Key Management Service (KMS)

An elective Microsoft Exchange 2000 Server component that is installed on a selected server in an administrative group. It provides centralized management and archiving of private keys. The KMS also maintains every user's private encryption key in an encrypted database. The keys are used to encrypt email messages as well as sign messages with digital signatures.

key pair

A cryptographic structure used in messaging security that consists of a public key and a private key. A public key is connected with a user through a readily available, published certificate and the corresponding private key is stored in a secure location on the user's client computer.

Knowledge Consistency Checker (KCC)

A built-in component running on all domain controllers that generates the replication topology for the Active Directory forest. The Knowledge Consistency Checker reviews and modifies the replication topology at specified intervals. This is done to ensure direct or transitive propagation of data.

Layer 2 Tunneling Protocol (L2TP)

A virtual private network (VPN) protocol that was developed by Cisco to improve security over Internet connections through IPSec integration.

LDAP Data Interchange Format (LDIF)

A draft of an Internet standard for a file format that can be used to carry out batch operations on directories that obey the rules of Lightweight Directory Access Protocol.

leapfrog upgrade

A method of upgrading to Exchange 2000 Server on a new server. Users are transported from a legacy Exchange server to a new server. Exchange is then installed on the server running the earlier version of Exchange. This move and upgrade cycle is repeated until all of the servers are upgraded.

Licensing Services API (LSAPI)

An interface that offers routines for controlling software licensing.

Lightweight Directory Access Protocol (LDAP)

A standards-based protocol that can be used to interact with Directory Services that are in conformance. LDAP version 2 provides for reading a directory database. LDAP version 3 enables users and applications to read and write to a directory database. LDAP is designed to work on TCP/IP stacks so that information can be extracted from a hierarchical directory like X.500.

link state algorithm (LSA)

The formula used to distribute routing status data between Exchange 2000 Servers. LSA is based on the Open Shortest Path First (OSPF) networking technology. Link state information is transferred among routing groups using the X-LSA-2 command verb over SMTP and within a routing group using a TCP connection to port 3044.

link state information

Data about the condition of the links in an Exchange 2000 messaging system based on the link state algorithm. The structure rapidly and frequently calculates the state of system links for up-to-date route status. Exchange 2000 servers use link state information to make the most efficient routing decision. This effectively eliminates message bounce and looping.

link state table

The database stored in memory that is used on each Exchange 2000 Server. The table stores link state information distributed by the link state algorithm. It is used to evaluate the most efficient route for a message based on cost and connection availability.

local account

A user account provided on a server in an NT domain for a user whose global account is not in a trusted domain. Local accounts are unnecessary where trust relationships exist between domains.

local bridgehead server

A server within a routing group that manages transport of email between connector and the routing group. Routing group connectors can have multiple local bridgehead servers. If a routing group has no local bridgehead server then every server in the routing group assumes the role of a local bridgehead server.

local computer policy

A Windows 2000 security management attribute implemented to classify and control security-related functions.

local group

A group created on an NT workstation or NT Server. Local groups cannot be used by trusted domains.

local profile

A collection of requirements and preferences for an individual user that is stored on a local machine.

Local Security Authority (LSA)

A protected subsystem that authenticates and logs users onto the local system. The LSA also preserves information about all facets of local security on a system and supplies a range of services for translation between identifiers and names.

local security policy

The centralized management device that controls password, account lockout, audit, user rights, security options, public key, and IP security.

local user account

A user account that exists on a single computer.

locked out

The state of a user account when it is disabled. Generally as a result of repeated failed logon attempts.

logon authentication

The prerequisite to give a name and password to get access to a computer system.

logon script

A code string that performs tasks such as mapping drive letters, launching programs, or performing other command-line operations every time the system boots.

mail-based replication

A structure that distributes directory information over a messaging transport. This mechanism applies to Exchange 5.x intersite directory replication as well as Active Directory replication via SMTP.

mail exchanger resource record

The MX resource record is a DNS record that designates a mail exchange server for a DNS domain name. A mail exchange server is a host that processes and/or forwards mail for the DNS domain name.

mail-enabled
An Active Directory object that has at least one email address defined for it. A mail-enabled user has an associated email address, but not an associated Exchange mailbox.

mailbox
The location set up by an administrator where email is delivered. If a collection of personal folders is specified as the email delivery location, the email is routed from the mailbox to this location.

mailbox store
The portion of the Web Storage System that controls data in mailboxes. It consists of a rich-text .edb file in addition to a streaming native Internet content .stm file.

mailbox-enabled
An Active Directory object that has an Exchange mailbox associated with it. This mail-enabled object can both send and receive messages throughout the Exchange infrastructure.

mandatory access control
A policy that restricts access to files and resources based on the class of information as well as on the defined security level.

mandatory profile
A user profile that does not preserve the changes after a user logs out. Mandatory profiles are employed to manage a common user desktop environment.

master domain
A domain model that determines how domains are administered.

memory bottleneck
A system blockage caused by a lack of available physical or virtual memory resources, resulting in system slowdown or even crashes.

Message Transfer Agent (MTA)
The Exchange Server component that transports messages between other information stores, connectors, third-party gateways, and other server MTAs by way of the X.400 protocol. It is also referred to as X.400 protocol in Exchange 2000 System Manager.

Messaging Application Programming Interface (MAPI)
The application-programming interface implemented by Microsoft messaging applications, such as Outlook and Outlook Express, to access collaboration data. MAPI Remote Procedure Calls (RPC) are used as the transport protocol between Outlook clients and Exchange servers.

metabase
A unit of storage that holds information similar to IIS. It can be viewed through tools like Metaedit.

metabase update service
A component of Exchange 2000 that reads data from Active Directory and converts it to the local IIS metabase. This service enables an administrator to make configuration changes to virtual servers remotely without sustaining a permanent link to each system.

metadata
Simply, data about data. In Exchange 2000, metadata can be used in the context of Active Directory and also the process of describing the structure within the store or the Message Transfer Agent.

Microsoft Database (MDB)
An instance of a database used in Exchange Server. A single MDB is usually defined as public or private depending on the type of data that it stores.

Microsoft Management Console (MMC)

The standardized interface into which consoles, snap-ins, and extensions are loaded to conduct administrative tasks. The MMC presents a framework that hosts administrative tools and components to generate, save, and open sets of tools. Saved collections of these toolsets are called consoles.

Microsoft Security Service Provider Interface (SSPI)

The API for acquiring integrated security services for authentication, message integrity, message privacy, and secure quality of service (QOS) for a distributed application protocol.

migration

The method of transporting existing messaging systems to other systems by replicating the existing mailboxes, messages, and so on, and also importing the information into a new messaging system.

mirror set

A complete shadow copy of data that provides an identical twin for a selected disk. All the data that is written to the primary disk is also written to the shadow or mirror disk to allow administrators the leverage to instantly access another disk with a redundant copy of the information on a failed disk for fault tolerance.

mirrored volume

A single volume drive configuration duplicated on to another volume on a different hard drive. It provides fault tolerance.

mixed mode

The default operating mode of Exchange immediately after installation. This configuration allows legacy and Exchange 2000 the ability to coexist in an organization. Mixed mode facilitates interoperability between versions by limiting the functionality to features that both products share. Windows 2000 domain controllers and Windows NT 4 backup domain controllers can seamlessly coexist within a domain in mixed mode without serious issues.

moderated channel

A chat channel employed for small chat events. A chat user joining a moderated channel cannot post messages to the channel without permissions from a speaker who acts as a channel host.

mount point

Also known as a *mounted volume*, this drive access mechanism maps a volume (or partition) to an empty directory on an NTFS volume (or partition).

move mailbox upgrade

A technique of upgrading to Exchange 2000 Server where Exchange 2000 is installed on a new server. The users are then transported to the new server from a server running a legacy version of Exchange. Finally, the server running the earlier version of Exchange is removed.

multilink PPP

A function of RAS that can combine multiple data streams into one network connection so that more than one modem or ISDN channel can be used in a single connection.

Multiprocessing

The capability to distribute threads among multiple CPUs on the same system.

Multiprotocol Routing (MPR)

A protocol that allows routing over IP and IPX networks by connecting LANs or by connecting LANS to WANs.

Multipurpose Internet Mail Extensions (MIME)

A standard that makes binary data available over the Internet.

multitasking

The capability to run more than one program at the same time.

multithreading

The capability of an operating system and hardware to execute multiple pieces of code or threads simultaneously from a single program.

name resolution

The method of mapping a name to a matching address. DNS provides name resolution functionality.

Name Service Provider Interface (NSPI)

A part of the DSProxy process that can acknowledge Outlook client directory requests and pass them on to an address book provider.

namespace

A logical collection of resources that can be managed as a single unit. Also, a set of names associated with a domain or forest that identifies objects that belong to the domain or forest.

naming context

A self-contained portion of a directory tree that has its own properties. Active Directory includes the domain, configuration, and schema naming contexts. Exchange Server 5.5 also uses naming contexts that include Organization, Address Book Views, Site, Configuration, and Schema.

naming convention

A standardized method of generating names for objects, users, computers, groups, and so on.

native mode

An operating state of Exchange 2000 Server where it is running only Exchange 2000 Server. Switching to native-mode is irreversible. This enables a directory to scale up to millions of objects to overcome the restrictions of the legacy SAM. Native-mode demands that all domain controllers be upgraded to Windows 2000.

Network Access Server (NAS)

A component that offers access to a network. This is usually achieved by allowing users to dial in similar to the way a modem gives access to a computer.

network adapter (NIC)

A network interface card (placed within the client computer) that enables communication between a computer and network.

network bottleneck

A systemic log jam caused by disproportionate traffic on the network medium to which a computer is attached. Also, when a computer itself generates excessive traffic.

Network News Transfer Protocol (NNTP)

A standards-based protocol that includes basic commands to transfer Usenet newsgroup messages between clients and servers, and between servers. NNTP uses Transmission Control Protocol/Internet Protocol (TCP/IP) port 119.

news site

A collection of related newsgroups.

newsfeed

The flow of items from one USENET site to another.

newsgroup

An Internet discussion group that focuses on a particular category of interest.

NTFS file system

The file system designed for the Windows NT operating system that supports file system recovery and large storage media. NTFS also supports object-oriented programs by defining all files as objects with user-defined and system-defined attributes.

NT LAN Manager authentication (NTLM)

The authentication system used on Windows NT that is supported by Windows 2000 for backwards compatibility. NTLM is known as a challenge/response authentication protocol.

NWLink

Microsoft's implementation of Novell's IPX/SPX protocol used for Microsoft networking or for providing connectivity to Novell networks.

Object

Any block of data generated by a Windows-based application with Object Linking and Embedding (OLE), Security, and the Component Object Model. Also refers to the operating system process components as well as any single network entity like a file, folder, printer, application, or Registry entry. Also represents the basic unit of Active Directory—a distinct, named set of attributes that represents a concrete entity.

one-step migration

One of two migration processes available in the Migration Wizard. In a one-step migration, the Migration Wizard mines migration files from another messaging system server and imports them in one operation to Exchange 2000.

operations master

A domain controller assigned one or more special roles in an Active Directory domain. The domain controllers assigned these roles perform single-master operations; they are not allowed to occur at different places in the network at the same time. The ownership of the operations master role can be transferred to other domain controllers.

organization

A collection of computers that run Exchange Server and provide messaging and collaboration services within a business, an association, or a group.

organizational unit (OU)

An administrative partition container object of the Active Directory. OUs can contain users, groups, resources, as well as other OUs and delegate administration to distinct subtrees of the directory. Organizational units can be used to contain and assign specific permissions to groups of objects like users and printers. An OU cannot contain objects from other domains and is the smallest unit to which you can assign or delegate administrative authority.

orphan

A member of a mirror or a stripe set with parity that has failed catastrophically.

Outlook Web Access (OWA)

The Web browser interface for Exchange Server mailbox and Public Folder data. The OWA client in Exchange server 5.x uses Active Server Pages to deliver collaboration data into HTML, whereas the client in Exchange 2000 employs native access to the store.

page

A 4KB chunk of data—the smallest unit managed by the Virtual Memory Manager.

parity

Redundant data that is related to a block of information.

partition

A space set aside on a disk and assigned a drive letter. A partition can take up all or part of the space on a disk.

password

A unique string of characters that must be supplied before a logon or access is authorized. Passwords are a security measure used to restrict initial access to Windows 2000 resources.

password policy

A mechanism that determines the restrictions on the use of passwords within access control methods.

permission

The form of interaction that a user can have with a resource. It is the authorization for a user to perform an action.

Point-To-Point Protocol (PPP)

PPP is a protocol for communication between two computers on a serial interface, such as a public phone line.

Point-To-Point Tunneling Protocol (PPTP)

A networking technology that supports multi-protocol virtual private networks (VPNs). This protocol provides remote users with secure access to corporate networks on the Internet by dialing into an Internet Service Provider (ISP) or by connecting directly to the Internet.

policy

A set of configuration data that can be applied to objects of the same class in Active Directory. In Exchange 2000, this may include mailbox thresholds or deleted item retention. Policies can be used to simplify the administration of Exchange 2000.

port

Any physical communication channel to which a modem, direct cable, or other device can be connected to enable a link between two computers.

Post Office Protocol (POP)

The site of an access point to the Internet. A POP must have a unique IP address.

Post Office Protocol version 3 (POP3)

A standards-based protocol used for simple access to Inbox data. POP3 allows a client to download mail from an inbox on a server to the client computer where the messages are handled. All versions of Exchange Server except version 4 support POP3. POP3 uses TCP/IP port 110 for client-to-server access.

presence information

In Instant Messaging, the information visible to users that shows the online status of contacts (online, busy, away, and so on).

primary connection agreement

A connection agreement that matches objects that exist, and creates new objects that did not exist.

Primary Domain Controller (PDC)

A PDC is the Windows NT Server that manages the master copy of the account and security databases.

primary domain controller emulator master

The domain controller designated to perform as a Windows NT primary domain controller in order to service network clients that do not have Active Directory client software installed. It also replicates directory modifications to any Windows NT backup domain controllers (BDCs) in the domain.

Glossary

private key encryption
A method of encryption that uses a single key to encrypt and decrypt information.

privilege
A right granted to a user, program, or process.

process
A forceful runtime construct that is loosely tied to an entire application, the Windows 2000 kernel, or some other system component in Windows 2000. Every process has its own complete, private 2GB address space and a related virtual memory allocation.

profile
The personal configuration information for a particular user. A profile editor can be used to create profiles for single users or groups of users and as a result, manage the user changes to configuration data and other options.

protocol
A set of rules that define how a network device can communicate with other network devices. TCP/IP and IPX/SPX are protocols.

proxy
A host that listens to name query broadcasts and responds when a queried name is not on the local subnet. A proxy communicates with the name server to resolve names and then caches them for a specified time period.

Proxy ARP
A mechanism for a machine to answer an ARP request with its own physical address as a proxy for the host the ARP was addressed to. The Proxy ARP assumes responsibility for routing the message.

proxy server
A firewall component that manages Internet traffic to and from a LAN and can provide other features, such as document caching and access control.

public folder
A folder that co-workers can use to share a plethora of information. Access permissions decide who can view and use the folder. Public folders are stored on Exchange 2000 computers.

public folder hierarchy (tree)
A tree containing public folders with a single public folder store.

public folder replication
The process of keeping copies of public folders on other servers up to date and synchronized with each other.

public folder store
The portion of the Web Storage System that maintains information in public folders. A public folder store consists of a rich-text .edb file as well as a streaming native Internet content .stm file.

public key encryption
An encryption that uses two related keys. One is a private key and the other is a public key. A public key is known within a group of users, while a private key is known only to its owner.

public key infrastructure (PKI)
Represents the laws, policies, standards, and software that regulate certificates and public and private keys. It is a system of digital certificates, certification authorities, and other registration authorities that verify the validity of each party involved in an electronic transaction.

queue
A collection of documents waiting to be printed or threads waiting to be processed.

RAID 5 volume

A fault-tolerant drive configuration of 3 to 32 parts spread over one or more drives (up to 32). The data is written to all drives in equal amounts to spread the workload. The parity information is added to the written data to allow for drive-failure recovery. This is also known as *disk striping with parity*.

recipient

An Active Directory object that is mail-enabled, mailbox-enabled, or that can receive email. A recipient is an object within Active Directory that can take advantage of Exchange functionality.

recipient policy

Policies that are applied to mail-enabled objects to generate email addresses. They can be applied in a single action to thousands of users, groups, and contacts in Active Directory using a Lightweight Directory Access Protocol (LDAP) query interface.

Recipient Update Service

An Exchange 2000 service that updates the recipient objects within a domain with specific types of information.

Redundant Arrays of Independent Disks (RAID)

A mechanism for storing the identical data in different places (redundantly) on multiple hard disks. I/O operations can overlap in a balanced way, thus improving performance and mean time between failures. RAID appears to the operating system as a single logical drive.

Registry

The NT database that holds configuration, user, and security information for the system.

Remote Access Service (RAS)

The Windows 2000 service that allows users remotely log into the system over phone lines.

remote bridgehead server

A server that handles email flow to and from a routing group connector in a different routing group.

Remote login (RLOGIN)

Allows users to remotely log into systems and interact as if they were directly attached to the remote system.

Remote Procedure Calls (RPC)

A dependable synchronous protocol that moves data between clients and servers, and between servers. It's also a simple client/server routine that transfers functions and data among computers on a network. Programs can use RPC to request a service from a program located in another computer in a network without having to understand network details.

replica

A copy of a public folder that stores all of the folder's contents, permissions, and design elements. Replicas are handy for distributing user load on servers and, public folders geographically.

repudiation

When a sender denies that the message was ever sent. Also the denial of a receiver of a message that the message was ever received.

Request For Comments (RFCs)

A cataloged and numbered series of documents that cover topics and standards such as Internet protocols to proposals and observations.

resources

Any useful service or object on a network. Resources can include, but are not limited to, printers, shared directories, and software applications.

Glossary

reverse proxy server
A reverse proxy server is similar to a regular proxy server used for outbound network traffic except that it relays connection requests for inbound network traffic.

roaming profile
When a user with a roaming profile logs into any Windows 2000 system on a network, the user's profile is automatically downloaded and available throughout the organization.

router
A system responsible for selecting the path or paths upon which network traffic is transmitted.

routing group
A collection of Exchange 2000 Servers that can transfer messaging data to each another in a single-hop without going through a bridgehead server. Exchange Servers within a single routing group generally have full-time, reliable, high-bandwidth network connections between them. Similar to administrative groups, routing groups are optional and are not visible in System Manager unless they are enabled.

routing group bridgehead server
A server within a routing group that exchanges directory updates with a server in another routing group.

routing group connector
A connector that determines the connection of a local routing group to a server in a remote routing group. It also specifies the local bridgehead server, connection costs, schedules, as well as other configuration data.

Routing Information Protocol (RIP)
A widely distributed routing protocol used for managing routing information within a self-contained network such as a corporate LAN or an interconnected group of LANs.

routing service
A component in Exchange 2000 that builds link state tables.

RSA cryptographic algorithms
A widely used set of public key algorithms available from RSA Data Security, Inc. The Microsoft Base Cryptographic Service Provider and the Microsoft Enhanced Cryptographic Service Provider support these algorithms.

schema
The metadata that defines the type of objects within a given structure. In Active Directory, the schema determines the universe of objects that can exist and the mandatory and optional attributes of each object. Also, a logical model for data; an organizational framework. For each object class, the schema defines what attributes an instance of the class must have, what additional attributes it can have, and what object class can be a parent of the current object class.

schema master
The domain controller that performs write operations to the directory schema. Updates to the schema are replicated from the schema master to all other domain controllers in the forest, and only the schema master domain controller can perform this.

Secure Sockets Layer (SSL)
A protocol that was designed to institute a secure communications channel to prevent the interception of vital information.

Secure Sockets Layer (SSL) encryption
A method to encrypt information between hosts.

Secure Sockets Layer/Transport Layer Security (SSL/TLS)

A mechanism used mainly with HTTP communications to create an encrypted session link via the exchange of certificates and public encryption keys.

Security Accounts Manager (SAM)

The manager of all the security features in NT and NT Server.

security association

A collection of parameters that define the services and mechanisms needed to defend IPSec communications.

security descriptor

The Windows 2000 security descriptor is where the security settings for the object are stored. A security descriptor is made up of the security identifier (SID) of the object owner, a group SID used by the Portable Operating System Interface (POSIX) subsystem and Services for Macintosh, a discretionary access control list (DACL), and a system access control list (SACL).

security identifier (SID)

A data structure of variable length that uniquely identifies user, group, service, and computer accounts within a forest. Every account is issued a SID when first generated. Also, SID is a unique name that identifies a logged-on user to a security system. SIDs can identify one user or a group of users.

security options

Settings that define and control various security features, functions, and controls in the Windows 2000 environment.

security principal

In Active Directory, a user object is a security principal. Also, a user who can log on to a domain and access network resources.

Serial Line Internet Protocol (SNMP)

An implementation of the IP protocol over serial lines that has been made obsolete by PPP.

server

A networked computer that responds to client requests for network resources.

server cluster

A group of independent computers that work together to run a common set of applications. The computers are physically linked by cables and connected by cluster software. These links allow the computers to use problem-solving components while appearing to the user and applications as a single system.

Server Message Block (SMB)

A high-level protocol used when two Microsoft systems communicate over a network.

service

A programming structure used by an operating system to perform a function. Services can make resources available over a network, access resources over the network, and other tasks.

share

A resource that can be accessed over a network.

Simple Mail Transfer Protocol (SMTP)

An Internet standard protocol responsible for transporting mail over the Internet as well as between messaging servers. It is defined in RFC 821 and uses TCP/IP port 25. SMTP is the native transport protocol in Exchange 2000 Server.

Simple Network Management Protocol (SNMP)

One of the standard network-management protocols within the Internet.

Glossary

site

A collection of IP subnets. Computers in the same site have high-speed connectivity with each another. In Windows 2000, a site is one or more reliable and fast TCP/IP subnets. In earlier versions of Exchange, a site is a group of servers that share the same directory information and can communicate over high-bandwidth, permanent, and synchronous links.

Site Consistency Checker (SCC)

The updated iteration of the Exchange Server 5.5 KCC that works together with the Exchange Site Replication Service to guarantee that the knowledge consistency of sites and administration groups is preserved between Exchange 2000 and Exchange 5.5.

Site Replication Service (SRS)

A Directory Service akin to the Exchange Server 5.5 directory service. In Exchange 2000, it allows integration with downstream Exchange 5.X sites using both RPC and mail-based replication. The SRS works in concert with the Active Directory Connector to offer replication services from Active Directory to the Exchange 5.X Directory Service.

smart card

An access card that contains encoded information or even a microprocessor and a user interface. The encoded data or microprocessor is used to access a facility or secure system.

smart host

A designated server through which Exchange routes all outgoing messages. A smart host then makes the remote connection and is also known as a *relay host*.

snap-in

A component that adds control devices to a console for a precise service or object. It is also the software that makes up the smallest unit of a Microsoft Management Console (MMC) extension.

storage group

A set of up to six Exchange databases (mailbox stores and public folder stores) on an Exchange 2000 Server that share the same ESE instance and transaction log. Each Exchange 2000 Server can host up to 16 storage groups, one of which is reserved for data recovery.

store

The general name assigned to the storage subsystem on an Exchange Server. This term is also used to describe the Store.exe process and Exchange databases.

striped volume

A drive configuration of up to 32 parts on one or more drives or two or more entire drives (up to 32). The data is written to all drives in 64KB units to distribute the workload and improve performance. Striped volumes do not provide fault tolerance and cannot be mirrored or extended. If one partition or drive in the stripe set fails, all data is lost.

subnet mask

A bit mask used to identify the network and subnet bits of an Internet address from the host bits. Each bit used to represent the value is enabled as 1, with the host bits remaining 0.

System Attendant

An integral Exchange 2000 service that performs various tasks that are typically related to directory information.

System Monitor

A tool that tracks registered system or application objects. Each object provides one or more counters that can be followed to gather data relating to system behavior.

system partition

The active partition that stores the boot files required to display the boot menu and initiate the booting of Windows 2000.

system policies

Policies that apply to server-side objects, such as mailbox stores, public folder stores, and servers.

Systems Management Server (SMS)

Network-management software from Microsoft.

T.120

A standards-based protocol used with Exchange Data Conferencing. Microsoft NetMeeting is a T.120 compatible client application.

TAPI

Stands for telephony API and is used by applications to make data/fax/voice calls.

Transmission Control Protocol/Internet Protocol (TCP/IP)

A suite of protocols that evolved from the Department of Defense's ARPANET and is used for connectivity in LANs as well as the Internet.

TCP/IP filtering

A configuration option of Windows 2000 TCP/IP that allows you to designate precisely which types of incoming non-transit IP traffic are processed for each IP interface.

thread

The smallest unit of system execution which corresponds roughly to a task within an application, the Windows 2000 kernel, or within some other major system component. Any task that executes in the background is considered a thread.

token

A random character string given to users to enable advanced security for them.

traffic

The flow of information across a network.

transaction log file

A file that keeps a record of every message stored in a storage group. This file offers fault tolerance in case a database needs to be restored.

Transmission Control Protocol (TCP)

The reliable transport protocol of the Internet suite.

Transport Layer Security (TLS)

A generic encryption technology similar to Secure Sockets Layering (SSL). TLS encrypts data over the medium between a client and a server to prevent packet-sniffing and other security breaches. TLS is used by SMTP virtual servers in Exchange.

tree

Also known as a *directory hierarchy*, a tree is a hierarchical collection of one or more Windows 2000 domains that share a common naming structure. End points on the tree are more often than not objects. Nodes in the tree are containers that hold a group of objects or other containers.

Trivial File Transfer Protocol (TFTP)

A protocol that provides an unreliable, limited file-transfer capability.

trusted domain

A domain that is allowed to access resources on another domain.

Glossary

trust relationship

The relationship between two domains that makes it possible for a user in one domain to access resources in another domain.

two-step migration

One of two migration methods available in Migration Wizard. In a two-step migration, you first remove migration files from another messaging system server and then review or edit the migration files. Second, you import the migration files to Exchange.

Uniform Naming Convention (UNC)

A set of rules that define the naming format on a network to ensure consistent network connections to shared resources.

Uniform Resource Locator (URL)

A universal convention to identify a server's name and location on the Internet. For example, **www.microsoft.com.**

universal group

A Windows 2000 group available only in native mode that is valid anywhere in a forest. A universal group appears in the global catalog but contains primarily global groups from domains in a forest. This is the most basic form of group, and it can contain other universal groups, global groups, and users.

upgrade installation

The installation process where data and configuration settings from previous operating systems remain intact.

user

A security principal who can log onto the domain in Active Directory. A user can have an email address and/or an Exchange mailbox, making the object mail-enabled and/or mailbox-enabled, respectively. A user is the only Active Directory object that can have a mailbox associated with it. A user in Windows 2000 is the equivalent of a mailbox in previous versions of Exchange.

user account

An entity that stores the information that defines a user in the Windows 2000 environment.

User Datagram Protocol (UDP)

A protocol that works with IP to deliver unreliable, connectionless datagram-delivery service.

user mode

The locale where private user applications and their respective subsystems exist.

User Principal Name (UPN)

The multi-valued attribute of each user object that the system administrator can set.

user profile

A collection of user-specific settings that retain the state of the desktop, Start menu, color scheme, and more in a Windows operating system environment.

user rights policy

Determines which groups or users can perform specific privileged action.

virtual memory

In Windows 2000, it is a kernel service that stores memory pages not currently in use by the system. Virtual memory frees memory for other purposes as well as hides the memory swapping process from applications and higher-level services.

Virtual Private Network (VPN)

A remote LAN that can be accessed through the Internet using the PPTP.

virtual root

A shortcut pointer to a physical storage location that is typically defined to allow users and applications to connect with a short "friendly" path rather than navigating a complex hierarchy. With Hypertext Transfer Protocol (HTTP), a virtual root defines a mapping between a URL path and a physical storage location. For Network News Transfer Protocol (NNTP), a virtual root defines a mapping between a news group name and a physical storage location.

virtual server

An instance of any service type that appears to clients as a physical server that is normally implemented in IIS. An Exchange 2000 Server can host multiple virtual servers of similar type on each computer. Each virtual server can have separate configuration properties, such as bound IP addresses, port number, and authentication type.

volume

In basic storage, it is a collection from 2 through 32 partitions into a single logical structure. In dynamic storage, a volume is any division of a physical drive or collection of divisions into a drive configuration.

volume set

A collection of disk partitions that are treated as a logical drive. It can be expanded after being created. If you lose one drive in a volume set, you lose all the data in the entire set, because it offers no fault tolerance.

Web Distributed Authoring and Versioning (WebDAV)

An extension of Hypertext Transfer Protocol (HTTP) 1.1 that allows clients to conduct remote Web content authoring. The WebDAV content stored on a server can be accessed by a client through HTTP by using WebDAV extensions. Client applications can perform tasks provided by HTTP, including reading email and documents.

Web Storage System

A storage construct that offers a single repository for the administration of varied types of amorphous information within

one infrastructure. Web Storage System combines the features and functionality of a file system, the Web, and a collaboration server via a single, URL-addressable location for storing, accessing, and managing information, in addition to developing applications.

Web Store

The database architecture in Exchange 2000 that exposes all of its data through MAPI, HTTP, and Win 32 layers. As a result, an object stored in a Public Folder can be retrieved and manipulated through a Web browser or a standard client with a network redirector.

Wide area network (WAN)

A geographically dispersed network of networks, linked by routers and other communication associations. The Internet is the world's largest WAN.

Windows 2000 Advanced Server

The Microsoft network operating system (NOS) server designed to function as a high-end resource on a network.

Windows 2000 Professional

The Microsoft network operating system version designed to function as a client/ workstation on a network.

Windows 2000 Server

The Microsoft network operating system server designed to function as a resource host on a network.

Windows 3.x

An older, 16-bit version of Windows. Windows 2000 supports backward compatibility with most Windows 3.x applications.

Windows 95

The 32-bit version of Windows that can operate as a standalone system or in a networked environment.

Glossary

Windows 98
An updated version of Windows 95 with improved Internet and network connectivity.

Windows For Workgroups
A version of Windows 3.x that includes minimal network support to allow the software to act as a network client.

Windows Internetwork Naming Service (WINS)
A software component that maintains the name database for a Windows NT TCP/IP network.

Windows NT
The predecessor Microsoft network operating system to Windows 2000.

wizard
A graphical utility that has an interactive step-by-step interface to move the user through a detailed configuration process.

workstation
A client computer on a network.

X.25
A standard that defines packet-switching networks.

X.400 Connector
A Microsoft Exchange Server component combined with the message transfer agent (MTA). It can be configured to connect routing groups within Exchange, or to route messages to other X.400 systems.

zone
A contiguous portion of the DNS tree administered as a single separate entity by a DNS server in a DNS database. The zone contains resource records for all the names within the zone.

Index

M

P

U

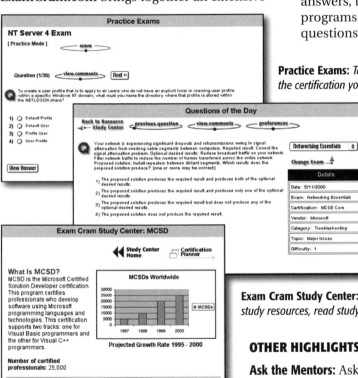

What's on the CD-ROM

The *MCSE Exchange 2000 Design Exam Prep's* companion CD-ROM contains elements specifically selected to enhance the usefulness of this book, including:

➤ The testing system for the book includes two options: You can choose between the Practice and Actual testing formats.

System Requirements

Software

➤ To successfully run this book's CD-ROM testing system, your minimum operating system must be Windows 98, NT 4, 2000, or ME.

➤ To successfully run this book's CD-ROM testing system, you also need Internet Explorer 5.x or later.

➤ To adequately prepare for the Exam and utilize all of the questions and Real-World Projects, your operating system must be Windows 2000 Server. (This software is not provided on this book's companion CD-ROM.)

➤ Exchange 2000 Server is also necessary. (This software is not provided on this CD-ROM.)

➤ Microsoft Visio 2000 is also recommended. (This software is not provided on this CD-ROM.)

Hardware

➤ At least an Intel (or equivalent) Pentium 133MHz processor is recommended.

➤ 128MB of RAM is the minimum requirement—256MB RAM is recommended to efficiently run the required software.

➤ 1GB of free hard disk space is recommended.

Software developed by Dreamtech Software India, Inc.